Luxemburger Juristische Studien –
Luxembourg Legal Studies

edited by

Faculty of Law, Economics and Finance
University of Luxembourg

Volume 22

Giorgia Bincoletto

# Data Protection by Design in the E-Health Care Sector

Theoretical and Applied Perspectives

Nomos

**The Deutsche Nationalbibliothek** lists this publication in the Deutsche Nationalbibliografie; detailed bibliographic data are available on the Internet at http://dnb.d-nb.de

ISBN 978-3-8487-8569-8 (Print)
978-3-7489-2989-5 (ePDF)

**British Library Cataloguing-in-Publication Data**
A catalogue record for this book is available from the British Library.

ISBN 978-3-8487-8569-8 (Print)
978-3-7489-2989-5 (ePDF)

**Library of Congress Cataloging-in-Publication Data**
Bincoletto, Giorgia
Data Protection by Design in the E-Health Care Sector
Theoretical and Applied Perspectives
Giorgia Bincoletto
532 pp.
Includes bibliographic references.

ISBN 978-3-8487-8569-8 (Print)
978-3-7489-2989-5 (ePDF)

Onlineversion
Nomos eLibrary

1st Edition 2021



Published by
Nomos Verlagsgesellschaft mbH & Co. KG
Waldseestraße 3–5 | 76530 Baden-Baden
www.nomos.de

Production of the printed version:
Nomos Verlagsgesellschaft mbH & Co. KG
Waldseestraße 3–5 | 76530 Baden-Baden

ISBN 978-3-8487-8569-8 (Print)
ISBN 978-3-7489-2989-5 (ePDF)
DOI https://doi.org/10.5771/9783748929895

*To my family*

# Preface

Health care for obvious reasons has become an even more relevant – or at least more publicly discussed – topic in the past two years in the wake of the Covid19-pandemic. Digitalisation and its consequences for all areas of society has been a very much debated topic over the last decade. The combination of health care and digital solutions in that sector has become one of *the* focal points of attention when discussing how to deal with a pandemic of the scale of Covid19. Even though one wished that it would not need such a type of proof for the relevance of finding adequate digital solutions in order to offer more effective services whilst respecting the legal framework and noteably fundamental rights such as the right to privacy, it can be seen as a confirmation of the relevance of the research topic for which you readers are holding the outcome in your hand – or viewing it on a screen respectively.

*Giorgia Bincoletto* explored in her Ph.D. thesis between the end of 2017 and 2021 a very specific aspect of EU data protection law and how it is relevant in "electronic health care" solutions: **"Data Protection by Design in the E-Health Care Sector: Theoretical and Applied Perspectives"**. We are very pleased that with the support of the Faculty of Law of the University of Trento and the "eHealth" Research Units within Fondazione Bruno Kessler and the Competence Center on Digital Health "TrentinoSalute4.0" we are able to bring the results of her thesis to a wider public attention by including this book, based on her thesis, in the **"Luxemburger Juristische Studien – Luxembourg Legal Studies"** with Nomos publisher as volume 22, also available as open access e-book. Digital solutions play a very important role in processing medical information and that in turn is a sensitive category of personal data concerning the patients which are at the same time data subjects. Therefore, it is of utmost importance that such solutions are especially considerate of the requirements to protect and secure the data involved. Not last with its inclusion as a core principle in the EU's General Data Protection Regulation, the concept of Privacy by Design is one of the answers to this challenge. Article 25 of the GDPR sets in its first paragraph the standards that are expected to be met in data processing in this regard, which include technical and organisational measures. *Giorgia Bincoletto* has attempted at analysing more in detail what these requirements mean in practice for solutions in the e-health care sector. She provides a thorough analysis of the principle and its evolution as well as a very comprehensible overview of data protection issues in the e-health sector. In view of existing standards in the United States of America, to the benefit of European readers, she includes a comparative analysis with those rules. In addition, being an interdisciplinary work, she also gives an overview of technological solutions and tools already in use or being developed, and measures these against the legal framework. With this basis her book can conclude with very concrete guidelines on how to implement data protection by design in e-health record systems, providing guidelines with a kind of checklist that can be used by software developers, data controllers but also any stakeholder involved in this sector. Focusing on e-health record systems allows a very specific answer to the research question which enriches the already very valuable theoretical analysis on which it is based.

The Ph.D. thesis of *Giorgia Bincoletto* was prepared in the framework of the joint international Ph.D. degree programme "Law, Science and Technology" (LAST-JD) of the University of Bologna and in a joint doctorate ("co-tutelle") with the University of Luxembourg. The programme offers an enriching atmosphere that brings together junior researchers on a broad range of topics related to digital matters and encourages an interdisciplinary approach to the research questions tackled. It is a challenging but inspiring task for the students enrolled to not only match this expectation but also conduct their research stays at the partner universities as part of their mobility within the programme. I was privileged to be *Giorgia Bincoletto*'s supervisor of this thesis and could witness how much she profited from the insight and different perspectives of the colleagues involved at the partner universities, both with the professors and research teams as well as with her colleagues in the programme. She was not only active researching her Ph.D. project topic and contributing to the work of my research team during her stay here in Luxembourg, but also published in and presented at international venues and has offered expert insight about Italian data protection authority decisions in the "European Data Protection Law Review". After completing her thesis with the defence on 26$^{th}$ March 2021 at which the jury expressed admiration for the excellent quality of the work, the manuscript was updated for this publication and reflects developments until October 2021. As mentioned in the first lines of this preface, recent events have accelerated the desire and push for e-solutions also in the health care sector. It is obvious that the research topic will move and further evolve in the coming years, but the work published here will remain of relevance as it offers guidelines that continue to be applicable even if new technological solutions will be developed.

I am convinced that anyone interested in data protection issues generally and even more so specifically in the current state of the e-health sector and specific solutions to creating electronic health record systems, will find this publication valuable and offering concrete solutions. I therefore hope that it will find many readers including potential future junior researchers that understand the value of interdisciplinary research such as the one offered in the LAST-JD-programme. I am also happy to see that *Giorgia Bincoletto* is continuing with the research for which she has laid the basis in her thesis as a post-doctoral researcher at the University of Trento.

*Dr. Mark D. Cole*
Professor for Media and Telecommunication Law
University of Luxembourg and
Director for Academic Affairs
Institute of European Media Law (EMR)

Luxemburger Juristische Studien –
Luxembourg Legal Studies

edited by

Faculty of Law, Economics and Finance
University of Luxembourg

Volume 22

# Acknowledgements

The publication of this work was supported by the Faculty of Law of the University of Trento, the "Health and Wellbeing Impact Area" within Fondazione Bruno Kessler and the Competence Center on Digital Health "TrentinoSalute4.0".

This book is based on the research I carried out during the Ph.D. which continued after the award of the title, and which is still ongoing. Designing technologies with data protection in mind is necessary not only to safeguard personal data, but also to ensure the exercise of other fundamental rights in the digital age.

I would like to acknowledge the professors that guided me along this journey. Prof. Roberto Caso, thank you for your constant support and constructive advice, and for welcoming me in the LawTech Group of the University of Trento, Faculty of Law. Prof. Monica Palmirani, thank you for mentoring me and making everything possible in the Law, Science and Technology Joint Doctorate of the University of Bologna. Prof. Mark David Cole, thank you for your guidance during the period at the University of Luxembourg and for helping me for this publication. My gratitude goes also to Ass. Prof. Paolo Guarda, for his stimulating thinking and advice since university.

I would like to thank all the colleagues and friends from the University of Bologna, the University of Luxembourg and the University of Trento.

Last but not least, I would like to dedicate this book to my family. Special thanks to Niccolò. You always and unconditionally encourage me: our two souls are one.

# Table of Contents

## List of tables

# List of figures

# Abbreviations and Acronyms

| | |
|---|---|
| **AMA** | American Medical Association |
| **CDR** | Clinical Data Repository |
| **C.F.R.** | Code of Federal Regulations |
| **CIS** | Clinical Information System |
| **CJEU** | Court of Justice of the European Union |
| **CNIL** | Commission Nationale de l'Informatique et des Libertés |
| **DPA** | Data Protection Authority |
| **DPIA** | Data Protection Impact Assessment |
| **DPbDf** | Data Protection by Default |
| **DPbD** | Data Protection by Design |
| **DPO** | Data Protection Officer |
| **eHDSI** | European e-Health Digital Services Infrastructure |
| **EC** | European Commission |
| **EDPB** | European Data Protection Board |
| **EDPS** | European Data Protection Supervisor |
| **EHR** | Electronic Health Record |
| **EMR** | Electronic Medical Record |
| **EHDS** | European Health Data Space |
| **ENISA** | European Union Agency for Network and Information Security |
| **EU** | European Union |
| **FIP** | Fair Information Practice |
| **FTC** | Federal Trade Commission |
| **FRA** | European Union Agency for Fundamental Rights |
| **GDPR** | General Data Protection Regulation |
| **IHE** | Integrating the Healthcare Enterprise |
| **HIE** | Health Information Exchange |
| **HIPAA** | Health Insurance Portability and Accountability Act |

| | |
|---|---|
| **HIS** | Hospital Information System |
| **HIE** | Health Information Exchange |
| **HIT** | Health Information Technology |
| **HITECH** | Health Information Technology for Economic and Clinical Health Act |
| **HL7** | Health Level Seven |
| **ICT** | Information and Communication Technologies |
| **IDMS** | Identity Management System |
| **IPC** | Information Privacy Commissioner |
| **ISO** | International Organisation for Standardisation |
| **NHS** | National Health Service |
| **OCR** | Health and Human Servives' Office for Civil Rights |
| **OECD** | Economic Cooperation and Development |
| **ONC** | Office of the National Coordinator for Health Information Technology |
| **PII** | Personally Identifiable Information |
| **PbD** | Privacy by Design |
| **PET** | Privacy Enhancing Technology |
| **PHR** | Personal Health Record |
| **SMEs** | Small and medium-sized enterprises |
| **TEU** | Treaty on European Union |
| **TFEU** | Treaty on the Functioning of the European Union |
| **US** | United States |
| **VSD** | Value Sensitive Design |
| **WHO** | World Health Organisation |

# Chapter 1 Introduction

## 1.1 *General introductory remarks*

The diffusion of digital technologies has a significant social and economic impact on societies[1]. Information technology provides great opportunities for individuals and communities in many domains[2].

In 2019, a qualitative study by the Organisation for Economic Cooperation and Development (OECD) examined how digital transformation affects human well-being[3]. Starting in the 1990s, the digital revolution has deeply transformed health, education, work-life balance, housing, social connections, governance, etc. The OECD's Report assesses these impacts by analysing pivotal and context-dependent opportunities and risks. One of the 11 specified "key dimensions" of people's well-being is *health*.

The digital age has especially revolutionised the healthcare delivery system and industry[4]. The term *e-health* identifies the use of information tech-

---

1 *See* the impact of the digital age on rights, freedoms and societies in Massimo Durante. *Potere computazionale. L'impatto delle ICT su diritto, società, sapere*. Meltemi Press, 2019. ISBN: 9788855190558; Stefano Rodotà. *Il diritto di avere diritti*. Gius. Laterza & Figli Spa, 2012. ISBN: 9788842096085; Stefano Rodotà and Paolo Conti. *Intervista su privacy e libertà*. GLF Editori Laterza, 2005. ISBN: 9788842076414; Stefano Rodotà. "Diritto, scienza, tecnologia: modelli e scelte di regolamentazione". In: *Rivista critica del diritto privato* 3 (2004), pp. 357–376. *See* also Giovanni Pascuzzi. *Il diritto dell'era digitale*. Il Mulino, Bologna, 2020. ISBN: 9788815290328; Fernanda Faini. *Data society. Governo dei dati e tutela dei diritti nell'era digitale*. Giuffrè Francis Lefebvre, 2019. ISBN: 9788828811947; Antonello Soro. *Persone in rete*. Fazi Editore, 2018. ISBN: 9788893254359; Tommaso Edoardo Frosini et al. *Diritti e libertà in Internet*. Le Monnier Università, 2017. ISBN: 9788800746502; Luciano Floridi. *The fourth revolution: How the infosphere is reshaping human reality*. Oxford: Oxford University Press, 2014. ISBN: 9780199606726.

2 *See* Giovanni Sartor. "Human rights and information technologies". In: *The Oxford handbook of law, regulation and technology*. Oxford University Press, 2017, pp. 424–450, p. 425. According to Sartor, information technology contributes to economic development, culture and education, art and science, public administration and communication, etc.

3 *See* OECD. *How's Life in the Digital Age? Opportunities and Risks of the Digital Transformation for People's Well-being*. 2019.

4 *See* Jelena Madir. *Healthtech. Law and Regulation*. Elgar Commercial Law and Practice, 2020. ISBN: 9781839104893.

nology for collecting and managing data related to health[5]. New digital technologies affect healthcare provision and improve the effectiveness and efficiency of health systems[6].

The positive impact of e-health technologies has been recognised at a national and international level[7]. On 26 May 2018 the World Health Assembly approved the Resolution on Digital Health, which highlights the potential of digital technologies to support health promotion and disease prevention by improving the accessibility, quality and affordability of health services[8]. However, it is difficult to gauge the concrete outcomes and multiple risks that arise with these opportunities.

Although digitisation has the potential to improve patient experiences and healthcare delivery, the increased production and advanced use of medical data open new scenarios that may expose people to high privacy risks[9]. Concerns about privacy, data protection and security of e-health technologies have been expressed by academic scholars[10], institutions, governments and public opinion[11]. Similarly, the WHO Assembly urges

---

5 *See* e.g. William W. Lowrance. *Privacy, confidentiality, and health research*. Vol. 20. Cambridge University Press, 2012. ISBN: 9781139107969.

6 *See* OECD, *How's Life in the Digital Age? Opportunities and Risks of the Digital Transformation for People's Well-being*. *See* further Chapter 3, Section 3.2.

7 *See* Walter Ricciardi. "Assessing the impact of digital transformation of health services: Opinion by the Expert Panel on Effective Ways of Investing in Health (EXPH)". In: *European Journal of Public Health* 29. Supplement 4 (2019), ckz185–769.

8 World Health Organisation (WHO), Resolution WHA71.7 on Digital Health of 26 May 2018. Retrieved from: <apps.who.int/gb/ebwha/pdf_files/WHA71/A71_R7-en.pdf?ua=1>. Last Accessed on 06/10/2021.

9 *See* OECD, *How's Life in the Digital Age? Opportunities and Risks of the Digital Transformation for People's Well-being*, pp. 22, 59–66. Potential discrimination of employees and insurances' speculations are other examples of risks.

10 *See* e.g. Lowrance, *Privacy, confidentiality, and health research*; Isabell Büschel et al. "Protecting human health and security in digital Europe: how to deal with the "privacy paradox"?" In: *Science and engineering ethics* 20.3 (2014), pp. 639–658; Samantha Adams, Nadezhda Purtova, and Ronald Leenes. *Under observation: The interplay between eHealth and surveillance*. Springer, 2017. ISBN: 9783319483429; Giuseppe Aceto, Valerio Persico, and Antonio Pescapé. "The role of Information and Communication Technologies in healthcare: taxonomies, perspectives, and challenges". In: *Journal of Network and Computer Applications* 107 (2018), pp. 125–154; Ziawasch Abedjan et al. "Data science in healthcare: Benefits, challenges and opportunities". In: *Data Science for Healthcare*. Springer, 2019, pp. 3–38. ISBN: 9783030052492.

11 *See ex multis* OECD. *OECD Recommendation on Health Data Governance*. 2017; Council of the European Union, EU Council. *Council conclusions on Health*

WHO Member States to develop more data protection policies for mitigating such risks[12].

The importance of ensuring the right to privacy and to data protection has grown in the digital age[13]. Technologies are often designed in a way that maximises the collection and the processing of personal data. The term "personal data" in the European Union is defined by Article 4 of the General Data Protection Regulation (GDPR)[14] as follows:

> "any information relating to an identified or identifiable natural person ('data subject'); an identifiable natural person is one who can be identified, directly or indirectly, in particular by reference to an

---

*in the Digital Society — making progress in data-driven innovation in the field of health*. Council conclusions 52017XG1221(01). Brussels, Belgium: Council of the European Union, Dec. 21, 2017; P. Arak and A. Wójcik. *Transforming eHealth into a political and economic advantage*. Polityka Insight, 2017; Francisco Lupiáñez-Villanueva et al. *Benchmarking Deployment of eHealth Among General Practitioners*. Luxembourg: Publications Office of the European Union. 2018.

12 *See* the Report by WHO, *supra* note 8, point n. 10, p. 3.

13 As regards the terminological difference, see Chapter 2, Section 2.2. On why privacy matters *see ex multis* the analysis by Daniel J. Solove. "The Myth of the Privacy Paradox". In: *Geo. Wash. L. Rev.* 89 (2021), pp. 1–51.

14 Regulation (EU) 2016/679 of the European Parliament and of the Council of 27 April 2016 on the protection of natural persons with regard to the processing of personal data and on the free movement of such data, and repealing Directive 95/46/EC (General Data Protection Regulation). O.J. L. 119, 4.5.2016. Generally, on the GDPR *see* Franco Pizzetti. *Privacy e il diritto europeo alla protezione dei dati personali: Dalla Direttiva 95/46 al nuovo Regolamento europeo*. G. Giappichelli Editore, 2016. ISBN: 9788892104501; Luca Bolognini, Enrico Pelino, and Camilla Bistolfi. *Il regolamento privacy europeo: commentario alla nuova disciplina europea sulla protezione dei dati, in vigore da maggio 2016*. Giuffrè Editore, 2016. ISBN: 9788814166594; Paul Voigt and Axel Von dem Bussche. *The EU General Data Protection Regulation (GDPR). A Practical Guide*. Cham: Springer International Publishing, 2017. ISBN: 9783319579580; Giusella Finocchiaro. *Il nuovo Regolamento europeo sulla privacy e sulla protezione dei dati personali*. Zanichelli, Torino, 2017. ISBN: 9788808521057; Vincenzo Cuffaro, Roberto D'Orazio, and Vincenzo Ricciuto. *I dati personali nel diritto europeo*. G. Giappichelli Editore, Torino, 2019. ISBN: 9788892112742; Rocco Panetta. *Circolazione e protezione dei dati personali, tra libertà e regole del mercato. Commentario al Regolamento UE n. 2016/679 (GDPR) e al novellato D.lgs. n. 196/2003 (Codice Privacy)*. Giuffrè Francis Lefebvre, 2019. ISBN: 9788828809692; Christopher Kuner et al. *The EU General Data Protection Regulation (GDPR): A Commentary*. Oxford University Press, 2020. ISBN: 9780198826491; Indra Spiecker gen. Döhmann et al. *The EU General Data Protection Regulation (GDPR): A Commentary*. Oxford University Press, 2020. ISBN: 9780198826491; Bart Van der Sloot. *The General Data Protection Regulation in Plain Language*. Amsterdam University Press, 2020. ISBN: 9789048553594.

identifier such as a name, an identification number, location data, an online identifier or to one or more factors specific to the physical, physiological, genetic, mental, economic, cultural or social identity of that natural person".

Instead, "personal information" is the predominant expression used in the US legal framework[15]. Decisions on the technological design affect individuals and their personal data or personal information in increasingly pervasive ways[16].

Generally, every design regulates its medium. In this study, the term *design* refers to the set of rules, procedures and activities that plan and define an Information and Communication Technology (hereinafter: ICT). From an engineering point of view, the International Standard ISO/IEC/IEEE 15288:2015(E) on "System and software engineering – System life cycle processes" defines "design" as the "process to define the architecture, systems elements, interfaces, and other characteristics of a system or system element"[17]. According to this standard, design is also the result of the process that includes all the information and specification of attributes and systems elements. However, in the present study the term is also used to indicate the organisational procedures and measures.

Design choices shape the interaction between users, as consumers or costumers, and the products and services they buy, or they have access to. Thus, how the technology is designed inevitably affects people. Hartzog investigated the impact of design choices on individual privacy in his book *Privacy's blueprint*[18]. As Hartzog noted, designers and engineers are choice

15 On this topic, *see* Christopher Anglim, Jane E. Kirtley, and Gretchen Nobahar. *Privacy Rights in the Digital Age*. Grey House Publishing, 2016. ISBN: 9781642650778. On the notion of "personal data" or information *see* Chiara Angiolini. *Lo statuto dei dati personali. Uno studio a partire dalla nozione di bene*. G. Giappichelli Editore, 2020. ISBN: 9788892134362; Lee A. Bygrave and Luca Tosoni. "Chapter I General principles (Articles 1–4). Article 4(1). Personal Data". In: *The EU General Data Protection Regulation (GDPR): A Commentary*. Oxford University Press, 2020, pp. 103–114. ISBN: 9780198826491.

16 *See* the prominent analysis by Woodrow Hartzog. *Privacy's blueprint: the battle to control the design of new technologies*. Harvard University Press, 2018. ISBN: 9780674976009.

17 *See* ISO. *ISO/IEC/IEEE International Standard-Systems and software engineering – System life cycle processes*. Tech. rep. ISO/IEC/IEEE 15288 First edition 2015-05-15, 2015.

18 Hartzog, *Privacy's blueprint: the battle to control the design of new technologies*. The author elaborated a blueprint for privacy defining a framework for law and policy.

architects[19]. When designing and developing ICTs, they determine how personal data are collected and processed in the hardware or software. According to the same scholar, technology shapes consumers' choices and behaviour for the following reasons[20]: privacy-relevant design is embedded in every action and operation (e.g. when creating an online account); design is power since it can impose an order and people are easily malleable; design is not neutral, but political.

Hence, design plays a central role and has a considerable impact on personal data. It can be argued that technical design represents a tool for enforcing a defined set of rules. Rules and constraints could be settled and imposed by the market, the law and the architecture of the code[21]. Legal rules can be prescribed by regulations, statutes, or principles. The regulatory framework on data protection and its principles define the rules for data processing. This set represents the protection *by regulation*. Conversely, the code regulates *by design*.

The present study attempts to show that the interaction between *law* and *design* could address some data protection issues in the existing legal framework of the European Union (EU) and in particular in the e-health sector. Fundamental for this purpose is the proactive approach called *privacy by design*, which aims to address data protection concerns by embedding legal requirements in the ICT's design.

Privacy by design (hereinafter also: PbD) is a major concept of interest within the field of privacy and data protection law[22]. Its main goal is to design a system, product or service in a way that "supports and applies" privacy principles and legal provisions[23]. It is important to note that technical and organisational strategies are both essential for PbD. Though so far high importance has been assigned to the technological aspects, admin-

---

19 Hartzog, *op. cit.*, p. 35.

20 Hartzog, *op. cit.*, pp. 21–55.

21 *See* the work of Lawrence Lessig. *Code and other Laws of Cyberspace*. 1999. ISBN: 9780465039128; Lawrence Lessig. *Code*. 2.0. New York: Basic Books, 2006. ISBN: 0465039146. *See* further Chapter 2, Section 2.2.

22 As will be presented later, PbD was first conceptualised by a Canadian Privacy Commissioner and was later recognised as an international principle for protecting privacy.

23 *See* the definition reported in Giorgia Bincoletto. "A Data Protection by Design Model for Privacy Management in Electronic Health Records". In: *Privacy Technologies and Policy, 7th Annual Privacy Forum, APF 2019, Rome, Italy, June 13–14, 2019*. Ed. by Maurizio Naldi et al. Lecture Notes in Computer Science. Springer International Publishing, 2019, pp. 161–181. ISBN: 9783030217525.

istrative and bureaucratic solutions are also fundamental for mitigating privacy and data protection risks.

Technical and organisational measures are combined in the General Data Protection Regulation. Article 25 establishes the binding obligations of *data protection by design* (from now on also: DPbD) and *data protection by default* (from now on also: DPbDf). As will be discussed in Chapter 2, privacy by design and data protection by design should be considered different concepts. Given this premise, the former will be the starting point of the discussion, while the latter will be central to the entire work.

Although extensive research has been carried out on PbD, there are few studies that have investigated in a systematic way the interactions between DPbD obligation and the healthcare context. Thus, this book examines how an e-health system in the EU could be developed and data processing carried out in a way that supports data protection principles, rules and requirements by design in order to better protect personal health data. This study investigates the significance of the data protection by design obligation in the e-health care sector by taking into account the legal framework of the EU.

As mentioned, the latest improvements in the e-health care field have led to new privacy and data protection issues. Personal health data represent sensitive information concerning a data subject and require a higher level of protection since they have been recognised in the particular category of personal data[24]. Therefore, enhancing data protection and security of e-health systems has become a primary interest in the EU[25].

E-health is an important component of the EU agenda. Although jurisdiction over health matters remains in the hands of Member States[26], health policies have been developed and promoted by EU institutions[27].

24 *See* further Chapter 3, Section 3.3.1.

25 *See* EC European Commission. "eHealth Action Plan 2012–2020. Innovative healthcare for the 21st century". In: *Communication from the commission to the European parliament, the council, the European economic and social committee and the committee of the regions. Brussels, 6.12. 2012* (2012). The EC stated that "effective data protection is vital for building trust in eHealth".

26 The EU shares the competence with Member states on "common safety concerns in public health matters" according to Article 4(k) of the Treaty on the Functioning of the European Union and supports and coordinates Member States' action according to Article 6(a) of the same Treaty. *See* Arak and Wójcik, *Transforming eHealth into a political and economic advantage*. *See* further Chapter 3, Section 3.3.

27 One of the main areas is free access to healthcare across countries, as will be described in Chapter 3, Section 3.3.

However, the issues related to data protection are considered barriers to the adoption of e-health technologies[28].

The European Commission's eHealth Action Plan 2012–2020 stated that in the e-health context ICTs should integrate the principle of privacy by design and by default[29]. In the Digital Single Market Strategy for Europe[30], the European Commission (EC) suggested that e-health infrastructures should be built in accordance with data protection rules[31]. Since the entry into force of the GDPR, the EU has a uniform framework for data protection law[32].

In this context, the role of DPbD in protecting personal health data is a relevant subject of investigation. The issue is how to comply with a principle, approach, or obligation that requires implementing technical and organisational strategies and measures by design for safeguarding the right to data protection.

Although the EU legal regime is the main focus of this research, an examination of a comparable legal system is indispensable for the topic[33]. Looking at the US system from a comparative perspective will be of great help in understanding how technical and administrative measures are

---

28 It has been highlighted that the concerns are voiced by both patients and health professionals. *See* Lupiáñez-Villanueva et al., *Benchmarking Deployment of eHealth Among General Practitioners*.

29 European Commission, "eHealth Action Plan 2012–2020. Innovative healthcare for the 21st century".

30 *See* the official website of the Digital Single Market Strategy at <https://ec.europa.eu/info/strategy/priorities-2019-2024/europe-fit-digital-age >. Last accessed 06/10/2021.

31 *See* EC European Commission. *Communication from the Commission to the European Parliament, the European Council, the Council, the European Economic and Social Committee and the Committee of the Regions on enabling the digital transformation of health and care in the Digital Single Market; empowering citizens and building a healthier society*. European Commission. Brussels, 25.4.2018 COM (2018) 233 final, 2018, p. 5. *See* also EC European Commission. *Communication from the Commission to the European Parliament, the European Council, the Council, the European Economic and Social Committee and the Committee of the Regions A European strategy for data*. European Commission. Brussels, 19.2.2020 COM (2020) 66 final, 2020.

32 In addition to the GDPR, the EU directive 2016/1148 on the security of network and information systems (NIS Directive) concerns "measures for a high common level of security of network and information systems across the Union" and it is transposed by Member States from national laws.

33 On the comparative methods used by different disciplines *see* Giorgio Resta, Alessandro Somma, and Vincenzo Zeno Zencovich. *Comparare. Una riflessione tra le discipline*. Mimesis Edizioni, 2020. ISBN: 9788857567310.

implemented in another legal framework that provides special rules for protecting health information[34].

Moreover, in light of the title of the present book "Data protection by design in the e-health care sector: theoretical and applied perspectives", the theoretical research on DPbD is a precursor to a more in-depth study on the healthcare context, including a case study on an e-health technology, the Electronic Health Record (EHR) system.

There is currently a lack of clarity and knowledge among developers, data controllers and stakeholders on how to comply with the DPbD provisions. The overall purpose is to contribute to the line of research that bridges the gap between the legal and technical disciplines on DPbD by providing a comprehensive set of guidelines for the implementation of the principle in the case study.

The book does not engage with ethical approaches, Big Data and Artificial Intelligence (AI) concerns[35]. Moreover, it is beyond the scope of this study to examine the interactions between Big Data and the e-health sector and the secondary use of personal health data. So, a discussion of AI and privacy or data protection lies beyond the scope of this research.

---

34 The comparative approach will be further explained in Section 1.2.

35 For the definition of Big Data *see* IBM. "The 5 Vs of big data". In: *IBM Watson Health Perspectives* (2016). As regards artificial intelligence and ethical issues *see* High-Level Expert Group on AI. *Ethics Guidelines for Trustworthy Artificial Intelligence, AI HLEG*. European Commission, 2019; Floridi, *The fourth revolution: How the infosphere is reshaping human reality*. On the opportunities and risks of AI in the legal domain *see* Alessandro Mantelero. "Regulating AI within the Human Rights Framework: A Roadmapping Methodology". In: *European Yearbook on Human Rights*. Intersentia Ltd., 2020, pp. 477–502. ISBN: 9781780689722; Amedeo Santosuosso. *Intelligenza artificiale e diritto. Perché le tecnologie di IA sono una grande opportunità per il diritto*. Mondadori Università, 2020. ISBN: 9788861848283, Barfield Woodrow, Ugo Pagallo. *Law and artificial intelligence*. Edward Elgar Publishing. 2020. ISBN: 9781789905144. In the data protection field *see* CoE Council of Europe. *Guidelines on artificial intelligence and data protection*. Council of Europe, 2019; Giovanni Comandé. "Unfolding the legal component of trustworthy AI: a must to avoid ethics washing". In: *Annuario di Diritto Comparato e di Studi Legislativi* XI (2020), pp. 39–62; Alessandro Mantelero. "AI and Big Data: A blueprint for a human rights, social and ethical impact assessment". In: *Computer Law & Security Review* 34.4 (2018), pp. 754–772; Ira S. Rubinstein. "Big data: the end of privacy or a new beginning?" In: *International Data Privacy Law* 3.2 (2013), pp. 74–87. On PbD and these trends *see* Laura Greco and Alessandro Mantelero. "Industria 4.0, robotica e privacy-by-design". In: *Dir. informazione e informatica* 6 (2018), pp. 875–900; Alessandro Mantelero. "La privacy all'epoca dei Big Data". In: *I dati personali nel diritto europeo*. G. Giappichelli Editore, Torino, 2019, pp. 1181–1212. ISBN: 9788892112742.

The reader should bear in mind that the study is based on the interactions between DPbD and the e-health sector for processing personal health data.

## *1.2 Research methodology and objectives*

In this subsection, a more detailed description of the research methodology and research questions are provided. The book draws on sources from law, social science, computer science and engineering.

The research can be divided between "theoretical perspective" and "applied perspective". Firstly, for the theoretical part of the research a legal and a comparative analysis is carried out. This examination is focused on PbD and DPbD by taking into account how these concepts have been elaborated by the literature, the institutions and EU data protection law. Then, a critical legal analysis on these principles is provided.

As mentioned, the research focuses on Article 25 of the GDPR. Therefore, the main perspective is EU law on data protection. However, the discussion is not always limited to that system in order to achieve an in-depth critical and comparative analysis with other perspectives. Case law is discussed where it has relevance for explaining legal concepts.

An entire chapter is dedicated to the e-health sector by investigating the data protection concerns of e-health technologies and the regulatory framework that applies. The case study of the EHR system will be analysed there by an interdisciplinary approach and by taking into account the state of the art of the technology, the applicable provisions in EU data protection law and the issues related to the data processing activities.

Moreover, a comparative law approach concentrates the study on the US framework because PbD has been recognised as an international principle in the field and there is a specific rule in the federal law of the US for e-health care, the Health Insurance Portability and Accountability Act of 1996 (HIPAA), which mandates the implementation of technical and organisational safeguards to protect health information. PbD is an international legal concept for the preventive protection of personal data, and it is based on the Fair Information Practices principles, which were first formulated in US law.

Comparative studies aim to establish similarities and differences between legal systems[36]. As scholars have highlighted, the primary purpose

36 On the methodology of comparative law *see ex multis* Rodolfo Sacco and Piercarlo Rossi. *Introduzione al diritto comparato*. Utet Giuridica, 2019. ISBN:

of comparative law as a science is to improve knowledge of each of the legal systems under scrutiny[37]. According to Zeno Zencovich, "comparing advances and deepens knowledge"[38]. The subject of investigation may be a legal rule or norm[39]. The scholar may uncover the rule by studying a "legal formant" or multiple "formants" in a legal system (i.e. statutory rule, formulation of scholars and decision of judges)[40]. It has been explained that legislative comparison aims to clearly present various solutions[41].

So, the research aims to compare Article 25 of the GDPR and the HIPAA Privacy and Security Rules that protect digital medical records.

---

9788859820826; Uwe Kischel. *Comparative Law*. Oxford University Press, 2019. ISBN: 9780198791355; Alessandro Somma. *Introduzione al diritto comparato*. Giappichelli, 2019. ISBN: 9788892130197; Ralf Michaels. "The Functional Method of Comparative Law". In: *The Oxford Handbook of Comparative Law*. Oxford University Press, 2019, pp. 340–382. ISBN: 9780198810230; Catherine Valcke. *Comparing law: comparative law as reconstruction of collective commitments*. Cambridge University Press, 2018. ISBN: 9781108555852; Devin Griffiths. "The comparative method and the history of the modern humanities". In: *History of Humanities* 2.2 (2017), pp. 473–505; Marieke Oderkerk. "The Need for a Methodological Framework for Comparative Legal Research: Sense and Nonsense of "Methodological Pluralism" in Comparative Law". In: *Rabels Zeitschrift für ausländisches und internationales Privatrecht/The Rabel Journal of Comparative and International Private Law* (2015), pp. 589–623; Geoffrey Samuel. *An Introduction to Comparative Law Theory and Method*. Hart Publishing, 2014. ISBN: 9781849466431; Pier Giuseppe Monateri. *Methods of Comparative Law*. Edward Elgar, 2014. ISBN: 9781781006535; Maurice Adams and Jacco Bomhoff. *Practice and Theory in Comparative Law*. Cambridge University Press, 2012. ISBN: 9780511863301; Konrad Zweigert and Hein Kötz. *Introduzione al diritto comparato*. Vol. 1. Giuffrè Editore, 2011. ISBN: 9788814155857; Pierre Legrand. *Le droit comparé*. Presses universitaires de France, 2011. ISBN: 9782130590767; Konrad Zweigert and Hein Kötz. *Introduction to comparative law*. Vol. 3. Clarendon Press Oxford, 1998.

37 *See* Sacco and Rossi, *Introduzione al diritto comparato*, p. 1; Zweigert and Kötz, *Introduzione al diritto comparato*, p. 17. A comparative legal research may also have an evaluative or regulatory objective, or it may aim to harmonise or standardise legislation in different states or nations. *See* Oderkerk, "The Need for a Methodological Framework for Comparative Legal Research: Sense and Nonsense of "Methodological Pluralism" in Comparative Law".

38 Vincenzo Zeno Zencovich. "Comparing comparative law". In: *Comparare. Una riflessione tra le discipline*. Mimesis Edizioni, 2020, pp. 227–240. ISBN: 9788857567310, p. 231.

39 Sacco and Rossi, *Introduzione al diritto comparato*, p. 11.

40 *See* Rodolfo Sacco. "Legal formants: a dynamic approach to comparative law (Installment I of II)". in: *The American Journal of Comparative Law* 39.1 (1991), pp. 1–34, p. 1.

41 *See* Zeno Zencovich, "Comparing comparative law", p. 235.

HIPAA is a sectorial regulation that protects identifiable health information by implementing organisational and technical measures. DPbD is a more general rule, but it is also applicable to personal health data and mandates the implementation of organisational and technical measures, as well. Both rules are obligations in their legal systems. The common problem is the need to better protect personal health data in a digital world by the use of safeguards. It is interesting to understand whether or not an e-health technology may be used in both the EU and the US systems. Particular attention will be given to the similarities and differences of privacy and data protection concepts and their principles (e.g. informational privacy vs. data protection, personal information vs. personal data, notice vs. privacy policy, etc.).

Secondly, in order to gain insights into e-health and to adopt an applied perspective, investigations are carried out on the existing technical solutions, engineering methodologies and approaches, and on a defined case study in the domain. Investigating for a data protection by design set of architectural and organisational guidelines for e-health systems demands an interdisciplinary approach. This method is needed in order to take into account both legal and technological concerns, identify the problems and try to find appropriate solutions[42].

Drawing on concepts and literature from law and information technology allows a wider perspective on the topic and related research issues.

Given the problems mentioned in the introductory remarks, the defined research goals and its methodologies, the research question addressed by the present book may be framed in the following way: How could an e-health system be designed, and the data processing be carried out in a way that supports and materialises data protection principles and legal requirements in order to protect personal health data?

In particular, the research work can be divided into the following sub-questions and related steps:

Theoretical perspective

- What does the privacy by design legal concept indicate historically and systematically? The research focuses on this principle of *regulation by design* and investigates the PbD principle by providing a critical

42 On the interdisciplinary method *see* Giovanni Pascuzzi. *La creatività del giurista. Tecniche e strategie dell'innovazione giuridica*. Zanichelli, 2013. ISBN: 9788808164162. On problem solving *see* Giovanni Pascuzzi. *Il problem solving nelle professioni legali*. Il Mulino, Bologna, 2017. ISBN: 9788815272997.

analysis to highlight advantages and challenges of its endorsement and implementation.

- According to Article 25 of the GDPR, what does the data protection by design obligation require? The research analyses the provision in detail and other related rules of the Regulation.
- Moving into the healthcare context, what are the applicable data protection principles and rules for the protection of personal health data in the EU and, in particular, for processing operated in EHR systems? The research examines the regulatory framework that applies to the processing of personal health data and uses a case study in the e-health care sector.
- What are the results of the comparative analysis between Article 25 GDPR and the HIPAA Privacy and Security Rules by looking at the US federal legal framework? The research compares the provisions by taking into account the differences and similarities between EU and US legal systems.

Applied perspective

- What are the existing technical tools and approaches for designing data protection? What are the suitable solutions and standards for developing EHR systems? The research deals with system and software design methods, and privacy engineering approaches. It also focuses on risk assessment, privacy enhancing technologies and standards applicable to the case study.
- What comprehensive set of technical and organisational guidelines may be provided for implementing DPbD in the e-health case study of an EHR system? Finally, the book provides a set of guidelines that includes measures and safeguards for DPbD implementation to explain how system and data processing could be designed so that they incorporate data protection principles and requirements.

## *1.3 Structure*

The book is structured as follows.

After these introductory remarks, Chapter 2 addresses the first and second points of the above mentioned sub-questions at a theoretical level. This part examines the concepts of privacy by design and data protection by design. Firstly, the Chapter presents the theoretical approach of *regulation by design* and summarises the history of privacy by design in a comparative way. Next, it conducts an extended critical analysis on the PbD concept with special attention to striking a balance between advantages and disadvantages that may result after a legal adoption of the rule. The Chapter then focuses on Article 25 of the GDPR, which provides the data protection by design obligation, and it also deals with the related legal requirements of the GDPR. Finally, it concludes by reflecting on a comparison between PbD and DPbD concepts and balancing the right to data protection against other rights and freedoms.

The third point of the theoretical perspective is addressed by Chapter 3, which provides a legal analysis of the e-health sector and presents the case study of an Electronic Health Record system. In particular, this Chapter firstly investigates the privacy and data protection concerns that emerge from the use of digital technologies for health purposes. Then, it critically reviews the data protection law for the processing of personal health data in the EU legal framework. After these theoretical considerations, the Chapter examines the case study, including the state of the art of the technology, the applicable rules in the EU, and its cross-border use across Member States that entails interoperability issues. At the end, Chapter 3 briefly concludes with other thoughts on balancing the right to data protection against other interests, and in particular against the public interest in the healthcare domain.

Chapter 4 deals with the comparative analysis of DPbD (EU) and the HIPAA Privacy Rule (US). The Chapter starts with a brief overview of informational privacy law in the US, and reviews the privacy principles in US federal law. The goal is to investigate the similarities and differences with the data protection principles of the GDPR in light of a PbD or DPbD implementation. Later, the Chapter summarises US health privacy law and presents HIPAA Privacy and Security Rules and their requirements. Finally, it compares DPbD and HIPAA under the different frameworks since looking at the US framework may be useful for understanding how technical and administrative measures for protecting personal data are implemented in the e-health context.

Chapters 5 and 6 refer to the applied perspective. On the one hand, Chapter 5 analyses the existing technical tools, approaches and methods for designing data protection; on the other hand, Chapter 6 presents the set of guidelines for implementing DPbD in the case study. In particular, Chapter 5 deals with some general notions of system and software engineering. Then, it analyses how the field of privacy engineering has proposed approaches for applying PbD or DPbD and for assessing privacy risks. Given the e-health care sector, and the case study on EHR, the

Chapter then investigates the privacy enhancing technologies and the recognised international standards used for EHR system development.

Chapter 6 provides the set of guidelines with technical and organisational strategies and measures to be implemented in the EHRs in the European Union legal framework. The foundations of the comprehensive set of guidelines are the GDPR and the current data protection law for data concerning health in the EU, the theoretical analysis and insights discussed in Chapter 2, 3 and 4 and the applied perspective on privacy engineering presented in Chapter 5. Finally, Chapter 6 investigates some potential liability scenarios in the event of inappropriate or ineffective DPbD implementation.

Conclusions are finally presented in Chapter 7.

# Chapter 2 Data protection by design: from privacy by design to Article 25 of the GDPR

## 2.1 *Introductory remarks*

This Chapter analyses the principles of privacy by design and data protection by design. The initial comparative introduction discusses the theoretical approach of regulation *by design* which has been specifically defined in the digital domain as *code is law* by Lawrence Lessig. This part briefly summarises the historical development of PbD in a comparative way by considering four significant steps of recognition in different legal frameworks.

Then, the Chapter provides an original and critical analysis of PbD by defining the advantages and disadvantages that may result from the adoption of a legal requirement for this principle. The results of this analysis have been classified in a table that compares the goals and challenges, which are further explained in detail with arguments from the legal, philosophical, economic, social, and technological domains.

The book is focused on data protection by design. Therefore, the following part of the Chapter deals with Article 25 of the GDPR by investigating and interpreting the requirement. It is important to define who shall comply with this rule, what the subject shall do, how and in which conditions. Some related provisions of the GDPR will be discussed.

Finally, the Chapter concludes by comparing PbD and DPbD concepts and by offering some notes on the need to balance the right to data protection, and DPbD, against other rights and freedoms.

## *2.2 A comparative introduction to privacy by design*

The interaction between law and technology for the protection of privacy has been an object of research since the 1960s[43]. In the digital age, law and technology interact in an even closer relationship[44].

According to Lessig, in the digital world law is not the only source of rules. The four existing modalities for regulation are law, social norms, market, and architecture[45]. In the real space law regulates through consti-

---

43 *See* Alan F. Westin. *Privacy and Freedom*. Atheneum, New York, 1967. In this prominent book the author discussed the legal problems arising in the use of technological control over individuals. According to Westin, US law should have responded to the conflicts between privacy and surveillance for protecting constitutional rights.

44 The "digital age" is characterised by specific elements defined by Pascuzzi in Pascuzzi, *Il diritto dell'era digitale*, pp. 21–24. First of all, objects can be represented through bit (0 and 1). Secondly, information (a set of bits) can be processed through computers. Thirdly, information can be transferred telematically. On law and technology *see* also Vittorio Frosini. *Informatica diritto e società*. Giuffrè Editore, 1992. ISBN: 9788814039294; Natalino Irti and Emanuele Severino. "Le domande del giurista e le risposte del filosofo (un dialogo su diritto e tecnica)". In: *Contratto e impresa* 16 (2 2000), pp. 665–679; Luigi Mengoni. "Diritto e tecnica". In: *Riv. trim. dir. proc. civ.* 2 (2001), pp. 1–10; Alessandro Mantelero. "Regole tecniche e regole giuridiche: iterazioni e sinergie nella disciplina di *internet*". In: *Contratto e impresa* (2 2005), pp. 658–686; Giancarlo Francesco Ruffo et al. *Privacy digitale. Giuristi e informatici a confronto*. G. Giappichelli Editore, 2005. ISBN: 9788834858059; Giorgio Spedicato. "Law as Code? *Divertissment* sulla *lex informatica*". In: *Ciberspazio e diritto* 2 (2009), pp. 233–259; Giusella Finocchiaro. "Riflessioni su diritto e tecnica". In: *Dir. dell'informazione e dell'informatica* (4–5 2012), pp. 831–840; Francesco Romeo. "Dalla Giuritecnica di Vittorio Frosini alla *Privacy by Design*". In: *Informatica e diritto* 2 (2016), pp. 9–23.

45 *See* the first edition of the book in Lessig, *Code and other Laws of Cyberspace*.

46 *See* Lessig, *Code*, p. 5. The author explains that "we must understand how a different "code" regulates — how the software and hardware (i.e., the "code" of cyberspace) that make cyberspace what it is also regulate cyberspace as it is". Lessig adopted a constitutional point of view (i.e. who regulates behaviour to achieve which values). According to his perspective, cyberspace is more than the Internet and is regulated through code. Therefore, design embeds the values of whatever entity does the coding. On this matter *see* further Giovanni Sartor. "Il diritto della rete globale". In: *Ciberspazio e diritto* 4 (2003), pp. 67–94. *See* also the criticism of Lessig's approach by David G. Post. "What Larry Doesn't Get: Code, Law and Liberty in Cyberspace". In: *Stanford Law Review* 52 (2000), pp. 1439–1459; and Chris Reed. *Making laws for cyberspace*. Oxford University Press, 2012. ISBN: 9780199657605, pp. 9, 208–211. According to these scholars, Lessig took a deterministic approach to the market that did not correspond to the way it worked in that historical moment. So, the market did not have the technological

tutions, statutes, and legal codes, but in the digital space, or cyberspace, the regulation also occurs with the *code*[46]. This approach has been called *code is law*[47].

In general, law as social control creates a rule backed by sanction that shapes actors' actions[48]. Another type of law confers and defines the matter of exercise of private or public powers[49]. A legal rule can be written in a legal text that is interpreted afterwards[50]. However, this rule can also be contained in a court's decision or be implicit as *cryptotype*[51]. Generally, a legal rule is settled by a State and enforced by a court. Law regulates in defined geographical limits[52]. By contrast, technical choices of architectural regulation create an embedded set of rules. This set has been defined *lex*

---

structure that Lessig used and the interactions between the four modalities of regulation are not linear. However, they recognised that law, market, social norms and code all regulated and influenced each other.

47 "Code" denotes both software and hardware in a broad sense.

48 According to Kelsen, law is the primary norm which stipulates the sanction. *See* Hans Kelsen. *General Theory of Law and State, the 20th Century Legal Philosophy*. Oxford University Press, 1949, p. 61. *See* also for the modern age, e.g., Lee Tien. "Architectural regulation and the evolution of social norms". In: *Yale JL & Tech.* 7 (2004), pp. 1–22, p. 6.

49 Hart explained the variety of laws in Herbert Lionel Adolphus Hart. *The concept of law*. Oxford University Press, 1997, pp. 26–49. The first edition of this book dates back to 1961. Legal rules are traditionally backed by sanctions commanded by a sovereign (rules of behaviour). This is Austin's theory of law. However, Hart observed that rules conferring legislative or judicial powers are not backed by a sanction. They are recognised as rules of the system (rules of recognition). The two minimum conditions that are necessary and sufficient for validating the existence of the legal system are: 1) rules of behaviour must be obeyed by the citizens; 2) rules of recognition must be effectively accepted as common public standards (*see* this book from p. 115).

50 Francesco De Vanna. "The Construction of a Normative Framework for Technology-Driven Innovations: A Legal Theory Perspective". In: *Use and Misuse of New Technologies*. Springer, 2019, pp. 185–208. ISBN: 9783030056483, p. 187; Spedicato, "Law as Code? *Divertissment* sulla *lex informatica*", pp. 248–249.

51 *See* Rodolfo Sacco. "Legal formants: a dynamic approach to comparative law (installment II of II)". in: *The American Journal of Comparative Law* 39.2 (1991), pp. 343–401, p. 385. Sacco asserted that in a legal system a specific rule could exist without being perceived. It has to be discovered because it is implicit and applied unintentionally. The cryptotype is the pattern that reveals the implicit rule, and is retrieved by the interpreter/scholar. To this end, comparative studies are fundamental because only by comparing the similarities and dissimilarities of systems is it possible to find the implicit and unrevealed rule.

52 This statement refers to the territorial sovereignty.

*informatica*[53]. The information flow in the network is regulated through a technical configuration whose jurisdiction is the network itself, and where the source of rule is not the State yet, but the rule embedded by a developer or producer[54]. In the Information Society a developer has the power to configure technical standards and to make them self-executed or automated, independently of any territory[55].

From an objective point of view, law regulates *ex post*, while architecture constraints *ex ante*[56]. People feel a norm constraint before any violation, but the rule works objectively *ex post*. Therefore, from a subjective perspective, it has been claimed that the technical rule is not perceived by people as in the case of law[57]. Architectural regulation directly influences the structure of the actions, and the deterrent effect does not guide actors' behaviour yet[58]. Thus, technology engages with what is possible straightaway[59].

Code regulates phenomena in parallel with the law. They are both a source of rules. Technical regulation does not substitute the traditional regulation. Who creates the technical rule, and who the code writer is, are

---

53 *See* Joel R. Reidenberg. "Lex informatica: The formulation of information policy rules through technology". In: *Tex. L. Rev.* 76 (1997), pp. 553–593.

54 *See* Reidenberg, *op. cit.*, p. 569. The author here compares legal regulation and *lex informatica* in a comparative and interesting table. On extraterritoriality of cyberspace *see* Reed, *Making laws for cyberspace*, pp. 29–47.

55 On the regulation by software *see* the critical approach in James Grimmelmann. "Regulation by software". In: *Yale LJ* 114 (2004), pp. 1719–1758. Information Society has been defined as a complex concept by Webster in the first chapter of Frank Webster. *Theories of the information society*. Routledge, 2006. ISBN: 9780415406338. According to this scholar, any definition should take into account technological and economic aspects.

56 *See* Maja Van der Velden. "Design as regulation". In: *International Conference on Culture, Technology, and Communication*. Springer. 2016, pp. 32–54, p. 37. Here the useful example is divided into objective and subjective perspectives. The former identifies how the constraint is observed when imposed, while the latter corresponds to when it is experienced. Firstly, architecture constrains up front like a locked door and law instead operates later on, like the rule on theft. Secondly, architecture and law constrain before the act from a subjective point of view. The author further elaborated Lessig's classification of objective and subjective perspectives. *See* the other edition of the work in Lessig, *Code*.

57 Here, law means the rule established in the community that has the power to influence and control actions. *See* Tien, "Architectural regulation and the evolution of social norms", pp. 15–16.

58 Tien, *op. cit.*, p. 7.

59 *See* Roger Brownsword. "Law, liberty and technology". In: *The Oxford handbook of law, regulation and technology*. Oxford University Press, 2017, pp. 41–68, p. 55.

questions that relate to the distribution of powers. On the one hand, design power belongs to private actors (e.g. developers, companies, Internet giants, etc.), which generally produce a product or offer a service. On the other hand, law can establish binding rules applicable to these products and services and their related technologies. It thus can be argued that law can interfere with the code and can change its regulation, just as it does with the market or with the architecture of buildings.

Furthermore, technology absorbs values and goals during the development process[60]. Developers may be unconscious of this reflection of values[61]. Nonetheless, design is never neutral and could embed social values[62]. Jurists assume that these values are embedded in constitutions, charters and legal provisions. Defining principles and values is strictly related to a specific society and its context. However, a change in perspective can help highlight that wherever technology is not neutral, and it is instead related to a set of values. Therefore, as Lessig suggests in his prominent book, in the digital age mankind can architect cyberspace in order to protect values that people recognise as fundamental[63].

Technological innovation could be considered an opportunity to embed political values in artefacts[64]. Thus, engineering and law should cooperate in shaping technology and taking advantage of the respective regulatory potential[65]. The wording "regulating code to regulate better"[66] suggests that technology, and its design, if regulated by law, could be used for

---

60 Technical choices are never neutral. *See* De Vanna, "The Construction of a Normative Framework for Technology-Driven Innovations: A Legal Theory Perspective", p. 197. The author wrote that the assumption of neutrality is illusory.

61 *See* Laurence Diver and Burkhard Schafer. "Opening the black box: Petri nets and Privacy by Design". In: *International Review of Law, Computers & Technology* 31.1 (2017), pp. 68–90, p. 74.

62 *See* Hartzog, *Privacy's blueprint: the battle to control the design of new technologies*, pp. 23, 43–51.

63 Lessig, *Code*.

64 *See* the sociological discussion in Bryan Pfaffenberger. "Technological dramas". In: *Science, Technology, & Human Values* 17.3 (1992), pp. 282–312. According to this scholar, political values are produced in society. In this work the term political assumes a higher meaning than the one related to factions and parties.

65 *See* De Vanna, "The Construction of a Normative Framework for Technology-Driven Innovations: A Legal Theory Perspective", p. 196. The author also added ethics in the relation between law and engineering creating a pluralistic perspective, which follows Lessig's suggestion on the *code is law* approach.

66 Lessig, *Code*, p. 114.

embedding legal principles and addressing legal problems in various contexts[67].

This might be the case of privacy and data protection concerns in cyberspace[68]. Indeed, the regulatory potential of law could be exploited for the protection of privacy- and data protection-related issues.

In brief, the right to privacy was first presented in a prominent American study as the principle that protects the "inviolate personality" of an

---

67 The technological regulation is frequently used for protecting intellectual property rights. The problem here is the growing number of infringements of copyrights that occur in the digital age. Protecting the digital expression of the intellectual work (DVD, CD, etc.) is the aim of the development of new tools and methods. The term Digital Rights Management (DRM) identifies the technologies that generally allow copyright owners to keep under control access to and use of digital content. For example, some DRM systems protect content against copying and are installed on consumers' devices. Different legal frameworks provided anti-circumvention provisions for defending DRM, such as in the US (Digital Millennium Copyright Act (DMCA) of 1998) and in the EU (Copyright Directive of 2001). As regards DRM systems, *see* Roberto (ed.) Caso. *Digital Rights Management. Problemi teorici e prospettive applicative. Atti del convegno tenuto presso la Facoltà di Giurisprudenza di Trento il 21 e 22 marzo 2007*. Quaderni del Dipartimento di Scienze Giuridiche, n. 70 dell'Università di Trento, 2008. ISBN: 9788884432193; Roberto Caso. *Digital Rights Management. Il commercio delle informazioni digitali tra contratto e diritto d'autore*. Privacy e innovazione. Trento: Digital Reprint. <eprints.biblio.unitn.it/4375/>, 2006; Stefan Bechtold. "Digital rights management in the United States and Europe". In: *The American Journal of Comparative Law* 52.2 (2004), pp. 323–382; Pamela Samuelson. "DRM {and, or, vs.} the law". In: *Communications of the ACM* 46.4 (2003), pp. 41–45; Dan L. Burk and Julie E. Cohen. "Fair use infrastructure for rights management systems". In: *Harv. JL Tech* 15 (2001), pp. 41–83. *See* also in relation to privacy issues Julie E. Cohen. "DRM and Privacy". In: *Berkeley Tech. LJ* 18 (2003), pp. 575–617; Lee A. Bygrave. "Privacy and data protection in an international perspective". In: *Scandinavian studies in law* 56.8 (2010), pp. 165–200; and Alessandro Palmieri. "DRM e disciplina europea della protezione dei dati personali". In: *Digital Rights Management. Problemi teorici e prospettive applicative. Atti del convegno tenuto presso la Facoltà di Giurisprudenza di Trento il 21 e 22 marzo 2007*. Quaderni del Dipartimento di Scienze Giuridiche, n. 70 dell'Università di Trento, 2008, pp. 197–212. ISBN: 9788884432193. DRM is an example of *code is law* in Alessandra Quarta and Guido Smorto. *Diritto privato dei mercati digitali*. Le Monnier università, 2020. ISBN: 9788800749756, pp. 62–65, which explained how intense the control is over digital contents within this phenomenon.

68 As will soon be explained, in the European Union, the right to privacy is considered a different right from data protection historically and systematically. Therefore, this work does not use the two terms as synonyms.

individual[69]. In the European literature the debate on privacy has been assigned to a civil law category ("diritti della personalità", "droits de la personalité", "derechos de la personalidad"), which groups the individual rights that are granted to a natural person for protecting intimate spheres, private life and personality in a physical dimension[70]. Since the definitions of privacy may often differ, conceptualising it is very complex and requires scholars to adopt different or pragmatic approaches[71]. For decades, legislators, authorities and courts around the globe have been creating a regulatory framework for the protection of privacy and personal data[72]. In recent

---

69 *See* Samuel D. Warren and Louis D. Brandeis. "Right to privacy". In: *Harv. L. Rev.* 4 (1890), pp. 193–220. On this paper *see* further Chapter 4, Section 4.2.

70 *See* Giorgio Resta. "Personnalité, Persönlichkeit, Personality: Comparative Perspectives on the Protection of Identity in Private Law". In: *European Journal of Comparative Law and Governance* 1.3 (2014), pp. 215- 243; Giorgio Resta. *Dignità, persone, mercati*. G. Giappichelli Editore, 2014. ISBN: 9788834849323, pp. 73–74. *See* also Guido Alpa and Giorgio Resta. *Le persone e la famiglia. Vol. 1: Le persone fisiche e i diritti della personalità*. Wolters Kluwer Italia s.r.l., 2019. ISBN: 9788859820871, pp. 145–163.

71 On this regard, *see* Daniel J. Solove. "Conceptualizing privacy". In: *Calif. L. Rev.* 90 (2002), pp. 1087- 1156. *See* also Dan Feldman and Eldar Haber. "Measuring and protecting privacy in the always-on era". In: *Berkeley Tech. LJ* 35 (2020), pp. 197–250.

72 The first data protection law is the Hessisches Datenschutzgesetz [1970] GVBl I 625 of the German State Hesse. For a useful synthesis of the historical development of privacy and data protection in the EU *see* Thomas Steinz. "The Evolution of European Data Law". In: *The Evolution of EU Law*. Oxford University Press, 2021. ISBN: 9780199592968; Christopher Kuner et al. *The EU General Data Protection Regulation (GDPR): A Commentary*, pp. 2–47; Hielke Hijmans et al. *The European Union as guardian of internet privacy*. Springer, 2016. ISBN: 9783319340906, pp. 39–58; Orla Lynskey. *The foundations of EU data protection law*. Oxford University Press, 2015. ISBN: 9780198718239; Pizzetti, *Privacy e il diritto europeo alla protezione dei dati personali: Dalla Direttiva 95/46 al nuovo Regolamento europeo*; Ronald Leenes et al. *Data protection and privacy: the age of intelligent machines*. Hart Publishing, 2017. ISBN: 9781509919345. As regards the US framework, *see* Daniel J. Solove and Paul M. Schwartz. *Information privacy law*. Wolters Kluwer Law & Business, 2018. ISBN: 9781454892755; the recent analysis in Neil M. Richards and Woodrow Hartzog. "Privacy's Constitutional Moment". In: *SSRN: <ssrn.com/ abstract=3441502>* (2019); Madeleine Schachter. *Informational and decisional privacy*. Carolina Academic Press, 2003. Internationally, *see* Lee A. Bygrave. *Data privacy law: an international perspective*. Vol. 63. Oxford University Press, 2014. ISBN: 9780199675555. At the international level, in 1948 the right to privacy was recognised as a fundamental right in the Universal Declaration of Human Rights (Article 12). In 1950, the right to respect for private life was affirmed in the European Convention on Human Rights (Article 8). With the advent of ICTs, the Convention for the Protection of Individuals

years, the advent of the digital age has linked the right to privacy with the concepts of "data" and "information". The digital environment has challenged the protection of the right to privacy conceived by scholars as "the right to be let alone"[73]. In 1967, the prominent US scholar Westin wrote that the increased collection and processing of information could lead to a "sweeping power of surveillance by government over individual lives and organisational activity"[74]. In the EU the right to data protection developed as a separated right[75]. The wording "data protection" derives from the German "datenschutz"[76]. This nomenclature better identifies the interest in protecting personal data as information out of a spatial dimension[77]. The Charter of Fundamental Rights of the European Union adopted this separate approach by recognising the respect for private and family life and the protection of personal data separately, and respectively, by Articles 7 and 8[78].

---

with regard to Automatic Processing of Personal Data became the only legally binding international instrument in the data protection field. On this regard, *see* Christos Giakoumopoulos, G. Buttarelli, and M. O'Flamerty. *Handbook on European data protection law*. European Union Agency for Fundamental Rights and Council of Europe, Luxembourg, 2018. ISBN: 9789294919014, pp. 24–27.

73 In the foundational text *The Right to Privacy* by Warren and Brandeis the tort of privacy aimed at protecting people against media and press (so-called yellow journalism). However, as Barbas pointed out in her investigation, this tort failed to address the new concerns of ICTs. *See* in Samantha Barbas. "Saving privacy from history". In: *DePaul L. Rev.* 61 (2011), pp. 973–1048. She describes the history of the right in the US from 1890 to the Modern Era. It is worth noting that after the analysis she concludes that privacy should be defined in holistic terms, having regard to technology, social norms and media practices. Privacy is not a rigid and static right.

74 Westin, *Privacy and Freedom*, p. 158.

75 *See* Hijmans et al., *The European Union as guardian of internet privacy*, p. 17.

76 *See* Bygrave, "Privacy and data protection in an international perspective", p. 168.

77 Bygrave, *op. cit.*

78 Article 7 "Respect for private and family life" states: "Everyone has the right to respect for his or her private and family life, home and communications". Article 8 on "Protection of personal data" reads as follows: "1. Everyone has the right to the protection of personal data concerning him or her. 2. Such data must be processed fairly for specified purposes and on the basis of the consent of the person concerned or some other legitimate basis laid down by law. Everyone has the right of access to data which has been collected concerning him or her, and the right to have it rectified. 3. Compliance with these rules shall be subject to control by an independent authority".

Under EU law, privacy and data protection are different fundamental rights, but they are closely connected[79]. As defined by Hijmans, the former right is a normative value, while the latter represents the legal structure that allows individuals to claim fair and lawful data processing[80]. In international contexts this distinction is not always appropriate because in some legal frameworks the term privacy could also be used for regulating the processing of personal data[81]. Regardless of any differences, both rights represent constitutional values that have to be guaranteed[82].

As mentioned in the introductory remarks, the huge collection of personal data and the multiple sources of invasions characterise the digital age. To date, several studies have investigated the relationship between

---

79 In Hijmans et al., *The European Union as guardian of internet privacy*, p. 62 the author explained why they are not identical concepts in the EU system. As mentioned, the Charter of Fundamental Rights of the European Union contains two different rights. In Bart Van der Sloot. "Legal Fundamentalism: Is Data Protection Really a Fundamental Right?" In: *Data protection and privacy: (In)visibilities and infrastructures*. Springer, 2017, pp. 3–30. ISBN: 9783319507965, Van der Sloot analysed these rights and explained that with GDPR the reference to the right to privacy has been deleted in the data protection texts (in the Data Protection Directive 95/46 there were lots of references, e.g. Article 1). This choice highlights the disconnection between privacy and data protection. So, the rights are nowadays treated by the literature as independent. On the distinction *see* also Juliane Kokott and Christoph Sobotta. "The distinction between privacy and data protection in the jurisprudence of the CJEU and the ECtHR". in: *International Data Privacy Law* 3.4

80 *See* Hijmans et al., *The European Union as guardian of internet privacy*, p. 6. Data protection is more specific than privacy because it is focused on data. The same author proposed the following solution: privacy is why protection is needed, whereas data protection is how protection is delivered. Bygrave agreed with this view in Bygrave, "Privacy and data protection in an international perspective".

81 As discussed in Chapter 4, in the US system the term is also associated with the protection of information related to an individual. Informational privacy is associated with the rules governing data collection. *See* e.g. Ronald Leenes and Bert-Jaap Koops. "'Code' and privacy-or how technology is slowly eroding privacy". In: *SSRN: <ssrn.com/abstract=661141>* (2005), p. 6.

82 Under EU law, according to Article 16 of the Treaty on the Functioning of the European Union, everyone has the right to the protection of personal data concerning them. This article represents the legal basis for the adoption of rules on data protection under EU law. As mentioned, in the EU system, privacy and data protection are also protected according to Articles 7 and 8 of the Charter of Fundamental Right, which has the same legal value as the constitutional treaties of the EU. *See* Giakoumopoulos, Buttarelli, and O'Flamerty, *Handbook on European data protection law*.

code and privacy[83]. The interaction between law and design could address some issues. Architectural regulation could be manipulated to protect privacy and data protection as functions of design, as door-closing does[84].

In this field, the concepts of *privacy by design* and *data protection by design* have been proposed by scholars and policy makers to mitigate concerns and achieve legal compliance, by taking into account how technology is designed. Moreover, even beyond the design implementation, policies and organisational strategies are still very important for these principles. PbD and DPbD are, indeed, global approaches. As will be explained later, the difference between PbD and DPbD is not merely related to the use of "privacy" or "data protection" in their expressions. It will be necessary to differentiate and compare the concepts accurately.

The expression *privacy by design* defines the approach that proposes to build privacy principles and provisions into the design and architecture of ICTs so as to improve legal compliance[85].

In the 1990s, Cavoukian pioneered the concept of PbD by creating a framework based on proactive and preventive solutions for protecting privacy[86]. In her words, PbD is "an engineering and strategic management

---

83 *See* e.g. three prominent studies that discussed this interaction from a legal theory perspective: Lessig, *Code and other Laws of Cyberspace*; Tien, "Architectural regulation and the evolution of social norms"; Leenes and Koops, "'Code' and privacy-or how technology is slowly eroding privacy".

84 Tien, "Architectural regulation and the evolution of social norms", p. 14.

85 According to Koops and Leenes, PbD can be defined as "the principle or concept according to which privacy should be built into systems from the design stage and should be promoted as a default setting of every ICT system". *See* Bert-Jaap Koops and Ronald Leenes. "Privacy regulation cannot be hardcoded. A critical comment on the 'privacy by design' provision in data-protection law". In: *International Review of Law, Computers & Technology* 28.2 (2014), pp. 159–171, p. 159.

86 *See* the presentation of the approach in Ann Cavoukian. "Privacy by design". In: *Information and privacy commissioner of Ontario, Canada* (2009). The PbD features should be embedded in the design specifications and implemented in the networked infrastructure and business practices. The former Privacy Commissioner of Ontario produced a number of studies on PbD from both theoretical and applied perspectives. *See* the research in Ann Cavoukian. "Privacy by design: the definitive workshop. A foreword by Ann Cavoukian, Ph.D". In: *Identity in the Information Society* 3.2 (2010), pp. 247–251; Ann Cavoukian. "Operationalizing privacy by design: A guide to implementing strong privacy practices". In: *Information and privacy commissioner of Ontario, Canada* (2012); Ann Cavoukian. "Privacy by design: leadership, methods, and results". In: *European Data Protection: Coming of Age*. Springer, 2013, pp. 175–202. ISBN: 9789400751705; Ann Cavoukian. "Evolving FIPPs: proactive approaches to privacy, not privacy paternalism". In: *Reforming European Data Protection Law*. Springer, 2015, pp. 293–309.

approach that commits to selectively and sustainably minimize information systems' privacy risks through technical and governance controls"[87].

Thus, this concept aims to achieve strong privacy protection before the invasion of the private sphere and the violation of the rule occur[88]. In an effort to share her approach, Cavoukian developed seven the Foundational Principles of Privacy by Design[89]. These are framed as follows, without hierarchy:

1. "Proactive not reactive, Preventative not remedial". The PbD approach aims to pre-empt privacy risks by identifying them in the design stage through a Privacy Impact Assessment. Technological measures should thus be combined with risk management and an organisational set-up. Privacy breaches should be prevented before they occurr. The leadership of a company has the responsibility to adopt this principle in its management by executing a privacy programme;
2. "Privacy as the Default Setting". The default rule means that data systems and business practices shall automatically protect data. The data subject has the option to do nothing and still be protected by default. To this end, minimising the collection of information is central;
3. "Privacy Embedded into design". Within PbD it is fundamental to embed privacy into the design as a component of the system without diminishing its functionality. Research by Cavoukian and the IPC's office shows that the incorporation is achievable;
4. "Full functionality – Positive-sum, Not zero-sum". The PbD approach aims to accommodate all stakeholders' interests in a win-win deal. Business interests are legitimate and should coexist with privacy. The

---

ISBN: 9789401793858. All the papers and books are collected at <www.ryerson.ca >. Last accessed 06/10/2021.

87 Cavoukian, "Operationalizing privacy by design: A guide to implementing strong privacy practices", p. 8.

88 Cavoukian often remarked that *privacy by Design comes before-the-fact, not after*. *See* e.g., Cavoukian, "Privacy by design: the definitive workshop. A foreword by Ann Cavoukian, Ph. D", p. 249.

89 *See ex multis* Ann Cavoukian. "Understanding How to Implement Privacy by Design, One Step at a Time". In: *IEEE Consumer Electronics Magazine* 9.2 (2020), pp. 78–82; Cavoukian, "Operationalizing privacy by design: A guide to implementing strong privacy practices", pp. 3–4; Ann Cavoukian et al. "Privacy by design: The 7 foundational principles". In: *Information and privacy commissioner of Ontario, Canada* 5 (2009), p. 1. On these principles *see* also the Guide by the Spanish DPA: AEPD Agencia Espanõla de Protección de Dados. *A Guide to Privacy by Design*. AEPD, 2019, pp. 7–10.

"privacy vs. security" dichotomy may be replaced by "privacy and security" because it is possible to maintain both;

5. "End-to-end security – full lifecycle protection". PbD is applied to the entire data life- cycle even before the collection of information and up to the erasure or the destruction of the assets where it is stored;
6. "Visibility and transparency – keep it Open". The data subject must be aware of the collection and of its purpose. The processing operations and business practices should be transparent and clear for the individual;
7. "Respect for User Privacy – keep it User-Centric". Within PbD, the data subject's interests shall be central even if they are not explicitly expressed. So, high importance should be given to privacy-friendly settings and privacy notices[90].

According to Cavoukian, PbD principles are adaptable and relevant for any of the PbD application areas[91]. The PbD framework has both an internal level (e.g. the design of ICTs) and an external one (the organisational steps of the business practices). For addressing privacy concerns, particular importance was attributed to security by default[92].

---

90 The term "notice" is usually used in common law systems, such as the Canadian framework. Under EU law, the information provided to the data subject is collected in the "privacy policy" in accordance with Articles 12, 13 and 14 of the GDPR. *See infra* Section 2.4.8.

91 In Cavoukian, "Operationalizing privacy by design: A guide to implementing strong privacy practices", p. 6, the areas are listed as: 1) CCTV/Surveillance Cameras in Mass Transit Systems; 2) Biometrics Used in Casinos and Gaming Facilities; 3) Smart Meters and the Smart Grid; 4) Mobile Devices and Communications; 5) Near Field Communications (NFC); 6) RFIDs and Sensor Technologies; 7) Redesigning IP Geolocation Data; 8) Remote Home Health Care; 9) Big Data and Data Analytics. Studies have been carried out in these contexts thanks to a fruitful collaboration with private stakeholders. *See* e.g Ann Cavoukian and Marilyn Prosch. *The roadmap for privacy by design in mobile communications: A practical tool for developers, service providers, and users*. Information and Privacy Commissioner of Ontario, 2011 and Ann Cavoukian et al. "Biometric encryption: creating a privacy-preserving 'Watch-List' facial recognition system". In: *Security and privacy in biometrics*. Springer, 2013, pp. 215–238. ISBN: 9781447152309; Cavoukian, "Understanding How to Implement Privacy by Design, One Step at a Time".

92 *See* Ann Cavoukian. *Global privacy and security, by design: Turning the "privacy vs. security" paradigm on its head*. 2017. The discussion here is focused on the public security issue. It is commonly perceived that more information is collected, more public safety and security are in place. However, this paradigm sacrifices a balance between privacy and security and the positive sum between them obtained

The framework is overtly based on the Principles of Fair Information Practices (hereinafter: FIPs)[93]. In 1973, the US Department of Health, Education & Welfare first defined the FIPs in the Report *Code of Fair Information Practice* with the aim of establishing safeguard requirements with a legal effect against automated personal data systems[94]. The authority distinguished the principles for two types of technologies – i.e. administrative automated personal data systems and systems used exclusively for statistical reporting and research – as minimum standards practices for protecting individuals[95]. Any violation would have been subject to sanctions[96].

FIPs were extended internationally in the OECD's Guidelines on the Protection of Privacy and Transborder Flows of Personal Data of 1980[97]. These Guidelines were revised in 2013 to create the OECD Privacy Framework[98]. The OECD's basic principles are listed as follows: "collection limitation principle, data quality principle, purpose specification principle,

---

with PbD approaches. According to Cavoukian, fostering technologies to this end is fundamental (and possible) even for policies against terrorism.

93 In Cavoukian, "Operationalizing privacy by design: A guide to implementing strong privacy practices",
p. 8, Cavoukian stressed that FIPs' perspectives inform her PbD principles (and, above all, the purpose specification and use limitation principles).

94 *See* Education & Welfare US Department of Health. *Report of the Secretary's Advisory Committee on Automated Personal Data Systems, Records Computers and the Rights of citizens*. United States, DHEW Publication NO. (OS)73–94. 1973. *See* at <www.justice.gov/opcl/docs/rec-com-rights.pdf>. Last accessed 06/10/2021.

95 *See* US Department of Health, *op. cit.*, p. 41. The five basic principles were defined as follows: 1) "There must be no personal-data record-keeping systems whose very existence is secret; 2) There must be a way for an individual to find out what information about him is in a record and how it is used; 3) There must be a way for an individual to prevent information about him obtained for one purpose from being used or made available for other purposes without his consent; 4) There must be a way for an individual to correct or amend a record of identifiable information about him; 5) Any organization creating, maintaining, using, or disseminating records of identifiable personal data must assure the reliability of the data for their intended use and must take reasonable precautions to prevent misuse of the data". Moreover, it was specified that deviations from the principles were allowed only exceptionally (*see* from p. 42).

96 The authority stressed that a violation would constitute an unfair practice backed by civil and criminal penalties.

97 OECD. *Guidelines on the Protection of Privacy and Transborder Flows of Personal Data, in the form of a Recommendation by the Council of the OECD*. 1980. On the FIPs *see* further Chapter 4, Section 4.2.

98 *See* OECD. *Guidelines on the Protection of Privacy and Transborder Flows of Personal Data, the OECD Privacy Framework*. 2013. *See* at <www.oecd.org/sti/ieconomy/oecd_privacy_framework.pdf>. Last accessed 06/10/2021.

use limitation principle, security safeguards principle, openness principle, individual participation principle, and accountability principle"[99]. These principles affirm the individual's right to self-determination[100].

Furthermore, the global foundational influence of the OECD's principles has been recognised by legal scholars[101]. It has been noted that these principles are highly influential internationally and serve as a bedrock foundation for privacy regulation policies[102]. It can thus be suggested that Cavoukian's principles are evidently based on the FIPs, especially as regards the visibility, transparency and user-friendly principles (PbD principles 5, 6, and 7).

Cavoukian's research as Ontario's Privacy Commissioner was quite successful internationally. Four notable examples and steps can be given before the introduction of a critical analysis on the concept of PbD.

Firstly, in 2009 the Article 29 Data Protection Working Party and Working Party on Police and Justice advocated for incorporating the principle of PbD into a new data protection framework of the EU[103]. According

---

99 *See* Part Two "Basic Principles of national application in the OECD's Privacy Framework". In this new version of the principles there are references to PbD as an innovative initiative. *See* the Report at the supplementary explanatory memorandum, pp. 103–105. Firstly, PbD is presented in connection with the Privacy Impact Assessment. Secondly, PbD could be an expression of the privacy management programme and the accountability principle, which is established in Part Three "Implementing Accountability" of the Guidelines.

100 Deirdre K. Mulligan and Jennifer King. "Bridging the gap between privacy and design". In: *U. Pa. J. Const. L.* 14 (2011), pp. 989–1034, p. 999.

101 *See* e.g. Marc Rotenberg. "Fair information practices and the architecture of privacy (What Larry doesn't get)". In: *Stan. Tech. L. Rev.* (2001), pp. 1–35, p. 16; Solove, "Conceptualizing privacy", p. 592; Mulligan and King, "Bridging the gap between privacy and design", p. 991; Ira S. Rubinstein and Nathaniel Good. "Privacy by Design: a Counterfactual Analysis of Google and Facebook Privacy Incidents'". In: *Berkeley Technology Law Journal* 28 (2013), pp. 1333–1409, p. 1344; Neil Richards and Woodrow Hartzog. "Taking trust seriously in privacy law". In: *Stan. Tech. L. Rev.* 19 (2015), pp. 431–472, p. 458.

102 *See* Hartzog, *Privacy's blueprint: the battle to control the design of new technologies*, p. 59.

103 *See* WP29 Article 29 Working Party, Working Party on Police, and Justice. *The Future of Privacy: Joint Contribution to the Consultation of the European Commission on the Legal Framework for the Fundamental Right to Protection of Personal Data*. 02356/09/EN, WP 168, 2009. The former Working Party (WP29) was institutionalised by article 29 of Directive 95/46 and had an advisory status acting independently from the other EU institutions. In accordance with Article 29, the WP was composed of one "representative of the supervisory authority or authorities designated by each Member State and of a representative of the

to the authorities, PbD represented a tool for innovating the framework and protecting against technological developments. ICTs should integrate privacy and data protection in their design settings by default. To this goal, a broad and consistent legal principle should be introduced in the law[104]. The requirement should be binding for data controllers, technology designers and producers at an early planning stage of ICTs, whose development should avoid or minimise the amount of personal data processed. Privacy-enhancing technologies (hereinafter: PETs) should be used in order to enhance security[105]. The principle of PbD should be framed in a flexible and technologically neutral way in order to be applied on a case-by-case basis and to be consistent regardless of time and context[106]. As will be explained in detail, the proposal of the GDPR and its final text contain a PbD requirement that assume some of the mentioned characteristics.

Secondly, with the Resolution on Privacy by design the concept gained global approval[107]. The 32nd International Conference of Data Protection Authorities and Privacy Commissioners emphasised PbD as a holistic concept and essential component of fundamental privacy protection. The Resolution recognised that a more robust approach is necessary for addressing the challenges to privacy and fully protecting individuals from the effects of the information life cycle in the ICTs. According to the Resolution, PbD principles should be promoted in the regulatory frameworks and beyond policies and rules (e.g. at organisational and research levels). Actually, the text listed Cavoukian's principles to encourage their legal adoption in countries[108]. Therefore, the Commissioners agreed that privacy should be embedded into design as a default protection. This Resolution was not legally binding. However, it can be argued that after its landmark adoption

---

authority or authorities established for the Community institutions and bodies, and of a representative of the Commission". The authority released several guidelines on data protection law contributing to the uniform application of the norms. It ceased to exist on 25 May 2018 and European Data Protection Board (EDPB) replaced it.

104 *See* Article 29 Working Party, Police, and Justice, *op. cit.*, p. 13.

105 For the notion of PETs *see infra* Section 2.3.

106 *See* Article 29 Working Party, Police, and Justice, *The Future of Privacy: Joint Contribution to the Consultation of the European Commission on the Legal Framework for the Fundamental Right to Protection of Personal Data*, p. 14.

107 32nd International Conference of Data Protection and Privacy Commissioners, Resolution on Privacy by Design, Jerusalem, Israel (27–29 Oct 2010).

108 It is worthy of note that the Former Commissioner personally encouraged the adoption of the PbD principles during the conference.

PbD was added to the agendas on data protection thanks to the promotion of data protection Authorities within their respective jurisdictions[109].

Thirdly, in 2011 in the US legal framework a Commercial Privacy Bill of Rights was proposed to protect consumer privacy[110]. This bill has set a provision concerning PbD, but it was never approved by Congress[111]. Under the proposed Section 103, the privacy by design requirement would have obligated a covered entity to implement a comprehensive information privacy programme proportionally to the size, type, and nature of the information collected. This programme should have been implemented by two categories of activities:

1. the incorporation of the "necessary development processes and practices throughout the product life cycle" for safeguarding personally identifiable information (PII)[112]. This information is based on "the reasonable expectations" of individuals on privacy and "the relevant threats that need to be guarded against in meeting those expectations";
2. the maintenance of "appropriate management processes and practices throughout the data life cycle" for complying with provisions, privacy policies and the privacy preferences of individuals.

The elements of these provisions that are consistent with Cavoukian's version of PbD are, on the one hand, the incorporation of practices throughout the product life-cycle and, on the other hand, the attention to a compliant organisational management. Both elements were based on the individual privacy preferences and expectations. This so-called relative approach is typical in US legislation[113]. As regards the differences, the provision was limited to covered entity and it aimed to protect only consumer privacy. A covered identity was defined as the person who processes information related to more than 5,000 individuals consecutively in a year or other specified subjects in Section 401 of the Bill. Therefore, the provision would have been applied only to medium-to-large commercial companies. According to Krebs, this Bill did not fulfil the PbD idea completely, but it

109 The same intuition has been expressed in Bincoletto, "A Data Protection by Design Model for Privacy Management in Electronic Health Records", p. 164.

110 *See* Commercial Privacy Bill of Rights Act of 2011, S. 799, 112th Congress (2011). The legislation was proposed by Senators John Kerry and John McCain.

111 The PbD provision was in the first Title "Right to security and accountability".

112 On the differences between PII and personal information *see*, e.g., Paul M. Schwartz and Daniel J. Solove. "Reconciling personal information in the United States and European Union". In: *Calif. L. Rev.* 102 (2014), pp. 877–916.

113 *See* Chapter 4, Section 4.2.

gave signals of its importance[114]. However, as mentioned, the text was only introduced in the Senate without any successful approval. Even Canadian scholars analysed the proposal, but despite the great contribution to the debate, a PbD requirement was never included in Canadian legislation, either[115].

Fourthly, PbD has been included by the Federal Trade Commission (FTC or the Commission) as a recommended business practice to promote the protection of consumer data in the US. In 2012, the FTC released the final Report "Protecting Consumer Privacy in an Era of Rapid Change, Recommendations for Businesses and Policymaker" encouraging a framework of best practises for consumer privacy[116]. The Commission noted that the Report aims to boost best practices without conflicting with other applicable statutory requirements[117]. The FTC called on Congress to extend privacy and security legislation and on companies to self-regulate their practices according to the recommendations. The FTC's framework applies to information that can be reasonably linked to a specific consumer, computer, or another device because it can identify an individual[118]. The companies that collect or use personally identifiable information are subject to the recommendations unless they only process non-sensitive data from fewer than 5,000 consumers per year and do not share data with third parties[119].

The FTC's best practices include privacy by design, simplified consumer choice for giving more control to consumer, and increased transparency. According to the Report, PbD is recommended for commercial practices in order to incorporate substantive privacy protection at every stage of the development of products and services[120]. PbD should be implemented

---

114 David Krebs. "Privacy by design: Nice-to-have or a necessary principle of data protection law". In: *J. Intell. Prop. Info. Tech. & Elec. Com. L.* 4 (2013), pp. 2–20, p. 10.

115 Krebs, *op. cit.*

116 FTC Federal Trade Commission. *Protecting Consumer Privacy in an Era of Rapid Change, Recommendations for Businesses and Policymaker*. FTC Report, 2012. The first report was issued in 2010; at the time, it received hundreds of public comments (also by European actors, such as the French DPA *Commission Nationale de l'Informatique et des Libertés*).

117 *See* Federal Trade Commission, *op. cit.*, p. 16.

118 *See* Federal Trade Commission, *op. cit.*, pp. 18–22.

119 *See* Federal Trade Commission, *op. cit.*, p. 22.

120 The baseline principle states that companies should promote consumer privacy throughout their organisations and at every stage of the development of their products and services.

systematically through substantive protections, such as data security, reasonable collection limits, sound retention practices and data accuracy[121]. While replying to the comments received in the report, the FTC explained that its framework embodies the OECD's Privacy Guidelines[122]. Moreover, the authority highlighted the importance of procedural protections for implementing the PbD principle: comprehensive data management should be maintained throughout the life-cycle of companies' products and services[123]. Thus, the FTC approach is focused on organisational measures leaving behind a more technical implementation. Nevertheless, the framework mentions PbD providing a basis for its adoption in the US[124]. In addition to the procedural program, the Commission advocated the use of privacy-enhancing technologies[125].

In sum, according to the FTC, PbD is a commercial best practice for every stage of product and service development established to protect consumer data. It can be argued that this notion is not a legally binding rule. However, it can be considered a softer kind of rule, that could be enforceable under Section 5 of the FTC Act[126]. Indeed, the FTC has a

---

121 *See* Federal Trade Commission, *Protecting Consumer Privacy in an Era of Rapid Change, Recommendations for Businesses and Policymaker*, p. 23. These four examples have been defined the FTC PbD principles by Stuart L. Pardau and Blake Edwards. "The FTC, the Unfairness Doctrine, and Privacy by Design: New Legal Frontiers in Cybersecurity". In: *J. Bus. & Tech. L.* 12 (2016), pp. 227–276, p. 231.

122 Federal Trade Commission, *Protecting Consumer Privacy in an Era of Rapid Change, Recommendations for Businesses and Policymaker*, p. 23.

123 *Ibid.*

124 Krebs, "Privacy by design: Nice-to-have or a necessary principle of data protection law", p. 11.

125 On the notion of privacy enhancing technologies *see* next Section 2.3.

126 Section 5 of the Federal Trade Commission Act (FTC Act), 15 USC. § 45. *See* <www.ftc.gov/ enforcement/statutes/federal-trade-commission-act>. Last accessed 06/10/2021. The FTC jurisdiction protects consumers against unfair and deceptive acts or practices by companies. This is a typical antitrust protection. However, in the same Section, the FTC expands the jurisdiction to protect consumer privacy issues. *See* Daniel J. Solove and Woodrow Hartzog. "The FTC and the new common law of privacy". In: *Colum. L. Rev.* 114 (2014), pp. 583–676, p. 598. In some instances, the authority requires adopting a comprehensive privacy programme with security measures. On the FTC's unfairness doctrine *see*, e.g. Pardau and Edwards, "The FTC, the Unfairness Doctrine, and Privacy by Design: New Legal Frontiers in Cybersecurity". According to Solove and Hartzog, the FTC's Reports help to understand its interpretation of Section 5. They are soft laws that may be enforced in the future. Under Section 5 the FTC has also the power to enforce the agreements between the EU and the US on data protection, e.g. the EU-US Privacy Shield Framework before the

prominent role of control on business practices towards US companies. According to Solove and Hartzog, the FTC jurisprudence is the most influential regulating force on privacy in the US because the statutory law is discordant, and the common law lacks rules[127]. In the US, the FTC is the closest body to a national data protection authority (hereinafter: DPA)[128].

After more than 20 years of efforts to develop and promote the concept, it finally obtained legal status in the EU where PbD has been articulated in Article 23 of the draft GDPR[129]. This Article has primarily established the obligation arising from the principle of data protection by design (and by default). The mentioned Article has been amended significantly, as will be explained in Section 2.4. Hence, the European Commission coined the wording *Data Protection by Design*.

According to the existing EU regulatory framework on data protection law, DPbD is a mandatory principle. Central is Article 25 of the GDPR. Before proceeding to examine this article, the following section will provide a critical analysis of the concept of privacy by design in order to deeply investigate the implications of the adoption and endorsement from legal, philosophical, technical, economic and societal points of view.

## 2.3 *A critical analysis of privacy by design*

According to Pagallo, without expecting that the technical tricks of design will ever tell us what the future of privacy will be, we can imagine that it is from design that we will be able to understand a lot about the privacy of the future[130].

---

Judgement of the European Court of Justice (Grand Chamber) of 16 July 2020 – Data Protection Commissioner v. Facebook Ireland Limited and Maximillian Schrems, C-311/18.

127 Solove and Hartzog, "The FTC and the new common law of privacy", p. 587.

128 Demetrius Klitou. *Privacy-invading technologies and privacy by design. Safeguarding Privacy, Liberty and Security in the 21st Century*. Vol. 25. Information Technology and Law Series. Springer, 2014. ISBN: 9789462650251, p. 41.

129 Proposal for a Regulation of the European Parliament and of the Council on the protection of individuals with regard to the processing of personal data and on the free movement of such data (General Data Protection Regulation). COM/2012/011 final – 2012/0011 (COD).

130 Own English translation of the words in Ugo Pagallo. "Privacy e design". In: *Informatica e diritto* 18.1 (2009), pp. 123–134.

Prior studies have noted the importance of values in design[131]. According to Friedman *et al.*, Value Sensitive Design (hereinafter: VSD) is a "theoretically grounded approach to the design of technology that accounts for human values in a principled and comprehensive manner throughout the design process"[132]. Thus, VSD aims to influence early on the design of technology in a proactive way[133]. In that study, privacy was considered a human value. Other scholars investigated the possibility of designing for the value of privacy[134]. By embedding values, VSD creates a so-called "normative technology"[135].

Essentially, PbD can be considered both a *code is law* and a VSD approach because it aims to design with the principles of privacy and the corresponding rules in mind[136]. PbD even goes beyond VSD because it is based on law[137].

In the privacy field, Privacy Enhancing Technologies (PETs) were invented in the 1990s to customise some information flow rules through technical design[138]. PETs identify technological mechanisms that intentionally aim to protect privacy[139]. In 1995 the first work that introduced PETs as a regulatory strategy was presented by the Information and Privacy

---

131 *See* e.g. Mulligan and King, "Bridging the gap between privacy and design", p. 1019; Jeroen Van den Hoven, Pieter E Vermaas, and Ibo Van de Poel. *Handbook of ethics, values, and technological design: Sources, theory, values and application domains*. Springer, 2015. ISBN: 9789400769700.

132 Batya Friedman, Peter H. Kahn, and Alan Borning. "Value sensitive design and information systems". In: *The handbook of information and computer ethics* (2008), pp. 69–101, p. 70.

133 *See* Friedman, Kahn, and Borning, *op. cit.*, p. 85. On VDS *see* also Janet Davis and Lisa P. Nathan. "Value sensitive design: Applications, adaptations, and critiques". In: *Handbook of Ethics, Values, and Technological Design: Sources, Theory, Values and Application Domains*. Springer, 2015, pp. 11–40. ISBN: 9789400769700.

134 *See* Martijn Warnier, Francien Dechesne, and Frances Brazier. "Design for the Value of Privacy". In: *Handbook of ethics, values, and technological design: Sources, theory, values and application domains*.
Springer, 2015, pp. 432–445. ISBN: 9789400769700.

135 *See* Klitou, *Privacy-invading technologies and privacy by design. Safeguarding Privacy, Liberty and Security in the 21st Century*, p. 261.

136 *See* Klitou, *op. cit.*, p. 262.

137 Klitou, *op. cit.*, p. 263.

138 *See* Reidenberg, "Lex informatica: The formulation of information policy rules through technology", p. 574.

139 *See* Lee A Bygrave. "Hardwiring privacy". In: *The Oxford Handbook of the Law and Regulation of Technology*. Ed. by Eloise Scotford and Karen Yeung. Oxford: Oxford University Press, 2017. Chap. 31, pp. 754–775. ISBN: 9780199680832, p.

Commissioner of Ontario and by the Dutch Data Protection Authority (the "Registratiekamer" or RGK). In their Joint Report the term "privacy technologies" refers to a variety of technologies that safeguard personal privacy by minimising or eliminating the collection of identifiable data[140]. PETs were often developed for the preservation of the values of confidentiality and anonymity. In 1997, Reidenberg described the classical PETs as technologies for securing the transmission of messages, transactions and Internet searches[141]. Then, these technologies started to achieve multiple functions, such as transparency and control. The broadening of focus reflected the expanding attention on systems' design[142]. Therefore, a prominent definition of PETs was summed up by Rubinstein as follows: these technologies are "applications or tools with discrete goals that address a single dimension of privacy, such as anonymity, confidentiality, or control over personal information"[143]. PETs can be classified according to their purposes[144]. Subject-oriented PETs limit the ability to recognise a specific subject (e.g. anonymiser), whereas other PETs are object-oriented since they protect data from identification. Transaction-oriented PETs protect the data used in a transaction (e.g. by deleting automatically) and system-oriented PETs create protected areas where the subject cannot be recognised, the object is not associated to anyone and the transaction data are deleted (e.g. secure socket layer, private communication technology or secure electronic transaction).

In a critical study on PbD, Koops and Leenes highlighted that in the last decades PETs have gained great support from policymakers and re-

---

756. In this study the author uses the term "hardwiring" to indicate the efforts of building privacy into information systems' architecture.

140 *See* H. Van Rossum, H. Gardeniers, et al. *Privacy-enhancing technologies: The path to anonymity*. Registratiekamer, Information, and Privacy Commissioner of Ontario, 1995.

141 According to the author, these are also examples of *lex informatica*. *See* Reidenberg, "Lex informatica: The formulation of information policy rules through technology", pp. 574–575.

142 *See* Bygrave, "Hardwiring privacy", p. 757.

143 *See* Ira S. Rubinstein. "Regulating privacy by design". In: *Berkeley Tech. LJ* 26 (2011), pp. 1409–1456, p. 1411. The author distinguished each category of PETs according to its purposes (e.g. preventing tracking and profiling, user control, etc.). On this topic *see* also the prominent work by Giuseppe D'Acquisto et al. *Privacy by design in big data: an overview of privacy enhancing technologies in the era of big data analytics*. European Union Agency for Network and Information Security, 2015, pp. 27–29.

144 *See* Pascuzzi, *Il diritto dell'era digitale*, p. 97.

searchers[145]. In 2007, the European Commission promoted the use and development of PETs to ensure that breaches of data protection rules and violations of individual's rights would be technically more difficult[146]. According to the authority, these technologies could boost a design of ICTs that minimises the processing of personal data and facilitates compliance with the law[147]. Technology has been recognised as a complementary tool to the existing legal framework and enforcement mechanisms[148]. As mentioned, in 2009 WP29 agreed on these aspects by promoting PETs along with PbD.

However, PETs are mere tools, mechanisms and instruments. By contrast, PbD is conceived as a comprehensive approach to fulfilling data protection rules. It should be pointed out that the idea of PbD first emerged with the concept of PETs, as a solution for the implementation of privacy principles[149]. Indeed, the concept of PbD is strictly related to the concept of PETs[150]. Operationally PbD could include PETs, but they are often not

145 Koops and Leenes, "Privacy regulation cannot be hardcoded. A critical comment on the 'privacy by design' provision in data-protection law", p. 159.

146 *See* EC European Commission. *Communication from the Commission to the European Parliament and the Council on Promoting Data Protection by Privacy Enhancing Technologies (PETs)*. European Commission. COM(2007) 228 final, 2007, p. 3. The definition of PETs adopted by the Commission (borrowed from the PISA project) is: "PET stands for a coherent system of ICT measures that protects privacy by eliminating or reducing personal data or by preventing unnecessary and/or undesired processing of personal data, all without losing the functionality of the information system". The Commission also described some examples of PETs: automatic anonymisation of data, encryption tools, cookie-cutters, the Platform for Privacy Preferences (P3P). In sum, the authority defined three objectives: 1) supporting the development of PETs by identifying their need and technological requirements and by sponsoring concrete projects; 2) supporting the use of available PETs by data controllers, through the promotion in the ICT industry and in the public sphere, and the creation of standards and a coordination of technical rules at the national level; 3) encouraging consumers to use PETs by raising awareness and facilitating informed choices.

147 *Ibid.*, p. 3.

148 *Ibid.*, p. 4. *See* also the first part of Section 2.2.

149 Pagona Tsormpatzoudi, Bettina Berendt, and Fanny Coudert. "Privacy by design: from research and policy to practice–the challenge of multi-disciplinarity". In: *Privacy Technologies and Policy, Third Annual Privacy Forum, APF 2015, Luxembourg, Luxembourg, October 7–8, 2015*. Lecture Notes in Computer Science. Springer, 2015, pp. 199–212, p. 200.

150 *See* e.g. Peter Hustinx. "Privacy by design: delivering the promises". In: *Identity in the Information Society* 3.2 (2010), pp. 253–255, p. 253; Inga Kroener and David Wright. "A strategy for operationalizing privacy by design". In: *The In-*

privacy-compliant *per se*. So, a PET can be considered a building block of PbD[151].

As mentioned, PbD shapes technologies at the service of the law[152]. Actually, PbD is an evolving framework that seeks to take privacy into account at many levels: not only the "forefront engineering life-cycle" but also "all levels of an organisation"[153]. At its core, PbD is a multifaceted concept[154].

From a legal perspective, PbD is defined broadly as regulation by design for building privacy into the design and architecture of technologies, systems and processes. Technologically, PbD is a list of measures and tools developed and implemented in a design process. Moreover, PbD involves various organisational components. Hence, it is conceivable that systems, devices and services could become "privacy-aware" and "privacy-friendly"[155]. Technology becomes more than a means; it is both a threat and a solution[156].

As noted by Bygrave, the multidimensional nature of PbD may detract from its utility[157]. The starting point for understanding PbD is the research by Cavoukian. As argued by Schartum, Cavoukian's principles are impor-

---

*formation Society* 30.5 (2014), pp. 355–365, p. 361; Simone Calzolaio. "*Privacy by design*. Principi, dinamiche, ambizioni del nuovo Reg. Ue 2016/679". In: *Federalismi.it* 24 (2017), pp. 1–21.

151 *See* Bygrave, "Hardwiring privacy", p. 759.

152 In Tsormpatzoudi, Berendt, and Coudert, "Privacy by design: from research and policy to practice–the challenge of multi-disciplinarity", p. 201 the authors observe that from a legal perspective PbD as an approach seeks technical solutions to address legal requirements.

153 Eric Everson. "Privacy by design: Taking ctrl of big data". In: *Clev. St. L. Rev.* 65 (2016), pp. 27–43, p. 28.

154 *See* for the expression: George Danezis et al. *Privacy and Data Protection by design – from policy to engineering*. European Union Agency for Network and Information Security, 2014, p. 3; D'Acquisto et al., *Privacy by design in big data: an overview of privacy enhancing technologies in the era of big data analytics*, p. 21; Bincoletto, "A Data Protection by Design Model for Privacy Management in Electronic Health Records", p. 164.

155 *See* Klitou, *Privacy-invading technologies and privacy by design. Safeguarding Privacy, Liberty and Security in the 21st Century*, p. 262; and Bincoletto, "A Data Protection by Design Model for Privacy Management in Electronic Health Records", p. 165.

156 Klitou, *Privacy-invading technologies and privacy by design. Safeguarding Privacy, Liberty and Security in the 21st Century*, p. 294.

157 Bygrave, "Hardwiring privacy", p. 758.

tant elements, but they are formulated as slogans[158]. So, despite the potential, the principle is not immune to criticism[159].

In order to provide a detailed investigation into the concept, the following theoretical and critical analysis allows a deeper insight into the idea of PbD by comparing and discussing the edges and disadvantages that could emerge with such a legal requirement.

The elements are classified in the following Table 2.1[160]. The first column list shows the advantages, and the second the respective disadvantages. The statements have been elaborated through a legal analysis, further based on remarks and arguments made by prominent scholars in the literature. This comparison attempts to show the effects of PbD on theories of law, rights and duties, on democracy, on the digital economy, and on technology and innovation.

The table is followed by a critical analysis of the lines. The order of discussion follows the horizontal line of the table. Every advantage is briefly elucidated just before the respective disadvantage with arguments from different disciplines. As regards the legal aspects, the investigation is not limited to a particular legal framework. If necessary, the discussion will specify the legal systems from time to time. The legal analysis assumes a primary role, but arguments from philosophy, economic theory, and social and technology studies are also presented. Moreover, the arguments are not related to the concept of PbD solely. Criticism and benefits of the *code is law* or of the *regulation by technology* approaches are discussed. Since some arguments raise complex and general debates at the theoretical level (e.g. on interpretation of the law), the examination of which are outside

158 *See* Dag Wiese Schartum. "Making privacy by design operative". In: *International Journal of Law and Information Technology* 24.2 (2016), pp. 151–175, p. 157. On the same opinion, *see* Rubinstein and Good, "Privacy by Design: a Counterfactual Analysis of Google and Facebook Privacy Incidents'", p. 1338. They wrote that the seven foundational principles are not of great assistance in applying the FIPs. These principles are more inspirational than practical.

159 Actually, according to Gürses *et al.* from the principles it is not clear what the term "privacy by design" means. *See* Seda Gürses, Carmela Troncoso, and Claudia Diaz. "Engineering privacy by design". In: *Computers, Privacy & Data Protection. International Conference on Privacy and Data Protection* 14.3 (2011), pp. 1–25, p. 3.

160 The table was first presented in Bincoletto, "A Data Protection by Design Model for Privacy Management in Electronic Health Records", p. 166. However, the discussion on the elements was not included in said work. Moreover, the content of the lines has been partly reformulated and ordered in a different and more coherent way in order to provide a more detailed and incisive explanation.

the scope of the present work, the analysis will limit the discussion to the connection with PbD, in order to highlight advantages and challenges of its endorsement and implementation.

*Table 2.1 Classification of the advantages and challenges of PbD*

| ADVANTAGES AND GOALS | DISADVANTAGES AND CHALLENGES |
|---|---|
| 1. PbD legal requirement is flexible and applicable to various contexts | A broad definition means difficult implementation |
| 2. PbD legal requirement is technologically neutral | Specific solutions must be provided for each technical context |
| 3. PbD improves the effectiveness of the law and empowers the rights of the data subject | Translating principles, values and rights into machine-readable language is a challenge |
| 4. PbD aims to implement rules, principles and values | Legal interpretation is flexible and dynamic. It is hard to define common principles in different legal frameworks. Conflicts between values are possible in the design stage |
| 5. PbD promotes proactive and preventive measures | The State delegates privacy regulation to companies. Private self-regulation may be incompatible with the democratic procedures of law making and law enforcement |
| 6. PbD prevents privacy breaches before they happen | Every embedded technical solution is rigid. Therefore, it is necessary to update measures frequently |
| 7. PbD is a global approach | Building privacy is critical for developers and not possible in every situation. Not all the provisions of data protection can be automated |
| 8. PbD requires concrete organisational measures | Companies sometimes lack knowledgeable organisation |
| 9. PbD requires effective measures and less bureaucratic solutions | PbD implementation demands investments and allocated resources |
| 10. PbD can increase privacy culture in society | There is a difficulty of comprehension of the topic for the layperson |

| ADVANTAGES AND GOALS | DISADVANTAGES AND CHALLENGES |
|---|---|
| 11. PbD can increase trust and confidence in products and services | In society there is an information asymmetry and a widespread lack of knowledge on design strategies |
| 12. PbD increases consumer satisfaction and could be an opportunity for business | Collecting and commercialising personal data are the core business of many companies |
| 13. There is a business opportunity for certifications and standards | Certification does not automatically mean compliance with the law |
| 14. PbD fosters the design of new privacy friendly technologies | Adapting the existing technologies is not easy |
| 15. There will be control over and ethics of the technology | There will be barriers to innovations |
| 16. PbD aims to implement user-centric technologies | There might be increasing costs for access to digital technologies |

Firstly, PbD can be included in a legal provision, and many privacy scholars have advocated for its explicit introduction in legislation[161]. According to Krebs, PbD as an organisational best practice is not sufficient, and has to be at the core of a legislative framework on privacy and data protection[162]. To this end, the provision on PbD shall be well drafted, clearly worded, and should avoid unnecessary ambiguity.

161 *See* e.g. Hustinx, "Privacy by design: delivering the promises"; Cavoukian, "Operationalizing privacy by design: A guide to implementing strong privacy practices"; Gürses, Troncoso, and Diaz, "Engineering privacy by design"; Mireille Hildebrandt. "Legal protection by design: objections and refutations". In: *Legisprudence* 5.2 (2011), pp. 223–248; Rubinstein, "Regulating privacy by design"; Krebs, "Privacy by design: Nice-to- have or a necessary principle of data protection law"; Klitou, *Privacy-invading technologies and privacy by design. Safeguarding Privacy, Liberty and Security in the 21st Century*; Tsormpatzoudi, Berendt, and Coudert, "Privacy by design: from research and policy to practice–the challenge of multi-disciplinarity"; Wiese Schartum, "Making privacy by design operative"; Giorgia Bincoletto. *La privacy by design. Un'analisi comparata nell'era digitale*. Privacy e innovazione. Roma: Aracne editrice, 2019. ISBN: 9788825524000.

162 Krebs insisted for Canadian systems particularly. *See* Krebs, "Privacy by design: Nice-to-have or a necessary principle of data protection law", p. 15.

So, such a legal requirement should mandate the approach and it could define some criteria for the design process[163]. If PbD is legally prescribed, liability and enforcement mechanisms should be in place[164]. Subjects should be accountable and liable[165]. It is worth noting that a legal provision should be established either for developers, who are the subjects that concretely arrange the design, or for data controllers[166]. The definition of data controller is not uniform in the legal frameworks. For the purpose of this section, data controller means "a party who, according to national law, is competent to decide about the contents and use of personal data regardless of whether or not such data are collected, stored, processed or disseminated by that party or by an agent on its behalf"[167]. Public institutions, organisations and agencies, and private companies should all embrace PbD.

Moreover, PbD requirements should be comprehensive, flexible and defined in a technologically neutral way in order to be applicable over time and in different contexts[168].

---

163 Bygrave, "Hardwiring privacy", p. 767, which also refers to standards.

164 As far as the present work is concerned, Privacy by design has been indirectly employed in some case law of the FTC and the Canadian Privacy Commissioner. As regards the cases, *see* Bincoletto, *La privacy by design. Un'analisi comparata nell'era digitale*, pp. 101–132. The most interesting cases in the US are *FTC v. FrostWire* and *FTC v. Google* of 2011, and *FTC v. Wyndham* of 2014. In Canada they are *Office of the Privacy Commissioner of Canada v. Google* of 2011 and *Office of the Privacy Commissioner of Canada v. WhatsApp* of 2012.

165 It may even be argued that subjects could be sanctioned for defective design of products and services. *See* Klitou, *Privacy-invading technologies and privacy by design. Safeguarding Privacy, Liberty and Security in the 21st Century*, p. 308. The scholar specified that liability should be subject to exemptions in the case of unlawful use or modification of the product/service and in the case of unlawful implementation by using a "state of the art" criterion of interpretation.

166 Klitou, *op. cit.*, pp. 268, 295. According to Klitou, directing requirements to data controllers only overesti- mates their capabilities and resources. Moreover, in a ubiquitous information society, where often there are cross-border data flows, the identity of the controllers is not easily determined. On the subjects of the law *see infra* Section 2.4.1.

167 This is the OECD's definition. *See* OECD, *Guidelines on the Protection of Privacy and Transborder Flows of Personal Data, the OECD Privacy Framework*, p. 13.

168 *See* Article 29 Working Party, Police, and Justice, *The Future of Privacy: Joint Contribution to the Consultation of the European Commission on the Legal Framework for the Fundamental Right to Protection of Personal Data*, p. 14. On technical neutrality *see infra*. *See* also EDPS European Data Protection Supervisor. *Opinion of the European Data Protection Supervisor on Promoting Trust in the Information Society by Fostering Data Protection and Privacy*. 2010, p. 8.

The principle should be applied on a case-by-case basis for it to be very concrete[169]. In fact, a rigid approach to PbD would be counter-productive because solutions cannot be "one-size-fits-all"[170]. They are normally tailored to a particular system or service (i.e. on an *ad-hoc basis*).

As regards the broad applicability, from a theoretical point of view jurisdiction does not seem critical for *lex informatica* because it may be applied on a transnational basis[171]. In this sense, *regulation by design* seems more flexible than *regulation by law* because it may be distributed at a global level. After the Resolution on Privacy by design, the concept is recognised as a transnational principle[172]. It has been argued that extra-territorial legal

---

169 *Ibid.*

170 Avner Levin. "Privacy by Design by Regulation: The Case Study of Ontario". In: *Can. J. Comp. & Contemp. L.* 4 (2018), pp. 115–159, p. 155.

171 Reidenberg, "Lex informatica: The formulation of information policy rules through technology", pp. 577- 578.

172 A summary of the legal history in three legal frameworks (US, Canada and EU) is provided here. On PbD history *see* also Calzolaio, "*Privacy by design*. Principi, dinamiche, ambizioni del nuovo Reg. Ue 2016/679". As previously mentioned, in the US the proposal in the Commercial Privacy Bill of Rights tried to include PbD in the US framework at the federal level. However, the Bill did not obtain the (hoped-for) approval of Congress, so the US framework does not have laws that explicitly and expressly includes PbD. US law on privacy is not uniform since there are both federal and national privacy-focused regulations. *See* e.g. Privacy Act of 1974, Children's Online Privacy Act of 1998, California Consumer Privacy Act of 2018. The US scholars recognised that in the context of law and technology this sector-based regulation is less efficient than a global and general approach to privacy. *See* e.g. Helen Nissenbaum. "From preemption to circumvention: if technology regulates, why do we need regulation (and vice versa)". In: *Berkeley Tech. LJ* 26 (2011), pp. 1367–1386. On US privacy *see* further Chapter 4. In spite of the work of the Privacy Commissioner in the 1900s, the Canadian legal system does not provide a legal requirement on PbD. The Canadian framework is divided into ten provinces where privacy is regulated at the federal level by the Personal Information Protection and Electronic Documents Act (SC 2000, c 5 "PIPEDA"). Some case studies in Ontario showed that PbD in Canada had limited engineering use, but great organisational potential. *See* the presentation and discussion on the studies in Levin, "Privacy by Design by Regulation: The Case Study of Ontario". On the Canadian law for privacy and data protection *see* Federica Giovanella. *Copyright and Information Privacy: Conflicting Rights in Balance*. Edward Elgar Publishing, 2017. ISBN: 9781785369353, Chapter 3. Finally, the EU included an obligation to implement technical and organisational measures by design in the draft of the GDPR, later emended and approved. The following section will explain in detail what is prescribed in the final Article 25 on data protection by design and will mention other legal rules on EU data protection law that include a similar provision.

effects and jurisdictional issues might be solved with PbD because protection of privacy may become a default mode in technology, wherever it is used[173]. Thus, embracing PbD might be useful for ensuring more global privacy and data protection[174]. PbD seeks to integrate either privacy or data protection requirements (or both), but each legal framework provides its rules. The jurisdiction where the implementation takes place therefore changes which rules the approach of PbD aims to incorporate. At the same time, technical configurations might be customised from one context to another by following a common approach[175]. The existence of different rules in separate legal frameworks represents a limit to an extended effect. Nevertheless, a common strategy on PbD may be "an outstanding lever for a constructive dialogue" on privacy issues "also at the international level"[176].

Although a legal requirement may be flexible and applicable to various contexts, a broad definition of designing privacy or data protection leads to difficult implementation. A vague design statute does not guide companies, and it might make enforcement arbitrary[177]. It has been argued that technology and law entail different systems of logic: the former operates by on-off rules, while the latter allows interpretative rules[178]. Thus, the translation into code is a challenge[179]. Bridging the gap between legal nat-

173 Ugo Pagallo. "On the principle of privacy by design and its limits: Technology, ethics and the rule of law". In: *European Data Protection: In Good Health?* Springer, 2012, pp. 331–346. ISBN: 9789400729032, p. 333.

174 Everson, "Privacy by design: Taking ctrl of big data", p. 40.

175 As an example, if the technology is implemented in the US, then customisations for the EU market should be made since the rules of information privacy and data protection are different. *See* further Chapter 4. It can also be argued that if the open source movement is accepted a wider social context, technological solutions would circulate easily and they could be customised easily. On the open source movement *see* the initial announcement of the GNU project by Richard Stallman in Richard Stallman. *The GNU project.* <www.gnu.org/gnu/initial-announcement.html>. 1998.

176 This is one of the ways forward for PbD identified by the EDPS in EDPS European Data Protection Supervisor. *Opinion 5/2018, Preliminary Opinion on privacy by design*. 2018, p. 18.

177 *See* Ari Ezra Waldman. "Privacy's Law of Design". In: *UC Irvine L. Rev.* 9 (2018), pp. 1239–1288, pp. 1257–1259.

178 *See* Deirdre K. Mulligan and Kenneth A Bamberger. "Saving governance-by-design". In: *Calif. L. Rev.* 106 (2018), p. 697, p. 710.

179 *See* Spedicato, "Law as Code? *Divertissment* sulla *lex informatica*", pp. 249–250. On the translation problem *see infra*.

ural language and computer language is definitely challenging[180]. Privacy legislation could be vague and ambiguous, while operational commands require precision[181]. Gürses *et al.* investigated the PbD from an engineering perspective. They found that the PbD principle could be too vague a concept for its concrete development[182]. The notions and concepts of privacy and data protection, and the definition of PbD are not uniform: there is a multitude of approaches[183]. A broad and vague definition of PbD hinders any common design methodology[184].

Therefore, *de iure condendo*, and in order to apply PbD, its provision should be framed in a detailed way by the legislator with some criteria for implementation, it should be well drafted and clearly worded, and a thorough legal analysis of applicable legal rules should be performed[185]. The PbD provision should be precise enough to ensure that what is required is sufficiently clear for stakeholders[186]. Theoretically, even the rules that PbD applies should be as specific as possible, but a will be further explained, law is often intentionally vague, and it is open to interpretation and to the balancing of competing interests.

Furthermore, PbD legal requirements should be technologically neutral, but specific solutions must be provided for every technical context. Cavoukian's definition of PbD does not refer to any specific digital technology. Technological neutrality has been defined as the attribute of the rule that does not impose nor discriminate in favour of a particular technology[187]. For the limited current purposes, a regulation is neutral when

---

180 *See* Klitou, *Privacy-invading technologies and privacy by design. Safeguarding Privacy, Liberty and Security in the 21st Century*, p. 283.

181 *See* Bygrave, "Hardwiring privacy", p. 767. According to Diciotti, a provision is ambiguous when the language leads to different meanings (e.g. in the case of polysemy), while it is vague when its meaning (i.e. the norm) is difficult to determine. *See* Enrico Diciotti. *Interpretazione della legge e discorso razionale*. G. Giappichelli Editore, 1999, pp. 360–381.

182 *See* Gürses, Troncoso, and Diaz, "Engineering privacy by design". Other engineering approaches will be discussed in Chapter 5.

183 Tsormpatzoudi, Berendt, and Coudert, "Privacy by design: from research and policy to practice–the challenge of multi-disciplinarity", p. 201.

184 Wiese Schartum, "Making privacy by design operative", p. 153.

185 On the need for details *see* Wiese Schartum, *op. cit.*, p. 159. The author pointed out that the detailed framing should be specified by legislators.

186 *See* Klitou, *Privacy-invading technologies and privacy by design. Safeguarding Privacy, Liberty and Security in the 21st Century*, pp. 284–285. The author mentions developers, manufactures and engineers.

187 Mireille Hildebrandt and Laura Tielemans. "Data protection by design and technology neutral law". In: *Computer Law & Security Review* 29.5 (2013), pp.

it is not associated with particular technology artefacts and practices[188]. As regards a general PbD requirement, technology specificity is not relevant. Specific technological solutions will be developed for each context. The legal requirement should be neutral in order to be effective in the future and not be obsolete and limited to a particular rationale. In fact, a principle should be stable and technologically neutral to be applicable for all new cases[189]. Thus, the aim of a neutral regulation is to prevent frequent and unnecessary amendments by legislators. This choice also avoids unjustified interference with the markets of technologies[190]. In some cases, targeted legislation is necessary; accordingly, the target will be the type of mechanism, instead of a specific technology in order to prevent continuous adaptation to new emerging solutions[191].

As a matter of fact, the approach of PbD does not provide fixed solutions and tools[192]. Specific solutions must be provided for each processing operation. As mentioned, technological neutrality is positive[193]. Nonethe-

509–521, p. 510. *See* also Reed, *Making laws for cyberspace*, pp. 189–193, which investigates the meaning of technological neutrality from a historical point of view and for different legal frameworks.

188 *See* Lyria Bennett Moses. "Regulating in the face of sociotechnical change". In: *The Oxford handbook of law, regulation and technology*. Oxford University Press, 2017, pp. 573–596, p. 586. The author discussed the regulatory potential of technology arguing that technology *per se* is irrelevant in justifying regulation (and its timing) because other societal implications influence the necessity to rule. Technology is a regulatory target, but technological specificity, level of regulation and timing are all aspect to be taken into account before framing a rule.

189 Bennett Moses, *op. cit.*, p. 589.

190 *See* Hildebrandt and Tielemans, "Data protection by design and technology neutral law", p. 510. The authors explain that if the rule refers to a particular technology, it will focus on that technology, thereby creating unjustified discrimination and a competitive disadvantage with other tools. It will result in unfair competition.

191 *See ibid.* The example analysed by the authors is the EU cookie legislation. It is worth noting that the authors concluded that the law is never perfectly neutral because it could interfere with the technological design instead of only addressing the use.

192 Tsormpatzoudi, Berendt, and Coudert, "Privacy by design: from research and policy to practice–the challenge of multi-disciplinarity", p. 205.

193 *See* also Aurelia Tamò-Larrieux. *Designing for privacy and its legal framework: data protection by design and default for the internet of things*. Law, Governance and Technology Series. Cham, Switzerland: Springer, 2018. ISBN: 9783319986241, pp. 194–195. The author defined regulation as an "enabler" that allows developers to design for privacy. Regulation should be drafted in a technologically

less, a neutral regulation might not guide the developer to the appropriate solution. To this end, the primary rule should remain neutral. As it may not be sufficient to ensure a PbD application in all cases, the legal framework could include specific regulations for distinct technological contexts where this rule should apply[194].

Moreover, privacy by design may improve the effectiveness of the law because design affects every user[195]. PbD seems more effective than other privacy approaches due to its timing: privacy protection is included as a component in the design[196]. PbD may be applicable even towards the emerging technologies that are not specifically regulated by the law yet. PbD may better ensure or almost fully guarantee compliance[197].

Such an approach attaches primary importance to principles and rights. It has been argued that PbD strengthens people's *habeas data*[198]. This principle can be defined as "individual protection against arbitrary action"[199]. PbD empowers individual protection, e.g. the exercise of the data subject's rights, that shall be considered from the beginning of the data processing.

---

neutral and goal-oriented way in order to enable the use of different tools and leave the concrete implementation to a lower level.

194 *See* Article 29 Working Party, Police, and Justice, *The Future of Privacy: Joint Contribution to the Consultation of the European Commission on the Legal Framework for the Fundamental Right to Protection of Personal Data*, p. 15. Article 29 Working Party argued that there could have been cases where a more concrete approach was necessary. Therefore, the legal framework should include more specific provisions for particular technological contexts.

195 *See* Hartzog, *Privacy's blueprint: the battle to control the design of new technologies*; and Klitou, *Privacy-invading technologies and privacy by design. Safeguarding Privacy, Liberty and Security in the 21st Century*, p. 263. According to Hart, efficiency of law means that the rule is obeyed more often than not. *See* Herbert Lionel Adolphus Hart and Joseph Raz. *The concept of law*. Oxford University Press, 2012. ISBN: 9780199644704, p. 103.

196 *See* Gaia Bernstein. "When new technologies are still new: windows of opportunity for privacy protection". In: *Vill. L. Rev.* 51 (2006), pp. 921–950, pp. 925–926. The author proposed to replace the term "legal intervention" with the term "social shaping". She explained that the early intervention on design shapes social values through technology from a social science point of view.

197 It has been claimed by Klitou, *Privacy-invading technologies and privacy by design. Safeguarding Privacy, Liberty and Security in the 21st Century*, p. 262.

198 *See* Pagallo, "On the principle of privacy by design and its limits: Technology, ethics and the rule of law", pp. 339–342.

199 *See* Pagallo, *op. cit.*, p. 339. The idea is the digital extension of the writ *habeas corpus*. On the traditional writ of English common law *see* William Blackstone. *Commentaries on the laws of England. Book 1: Of the rights of persons. 1765–1769*. Chicago, Ill.: University of Chicago Press, 1979. ISBN: 0226055361.

It should be stressed that the nature of the rights changes according to the legal frameworks[200].

This advantage may be opposed with the following disadvantage: translating principles, values and rights into machine-readable language is a challenge[201]. PbD requires the translation of rules into engineering and design requirements and business practices. Thus, incorporating PbD means including privacy or data protection considerations in the definition of software and hardware specifications[202]. Legislation is traditionally formulated with language that requires interpretation[203]. Since legal specifications may be inherently generic, the translation or the incorporation in the code is challenging[204]. According to Article 29 Working Party, technological standards could support in defining and specifying requirements[205]. Legal rules may be represented in machine readable forms. As will be reported in Chapter 5, Section 5.3, the Akoma-Ntoso standard – Architecture

200 As regards the EU *see* Section 2.4.8. In the US, rights are granted either by federal law and national law or by common law. For more details, *see* Chapter 4.

201 This challenge was immediately highlighted for the use of DRM in the intellectual property context and for the implementation of the *fair use* doctrine. *See* Roberto Caso. *Digital Rights Management. Il commercio delle informazioni digitali tra contratto e diritto d'autore*. Cedam, 2004. ISBN: 8813252536, pp. 188–191; Samuelson, "DRM {and, or, vs.} the law"; Cohen, "DRM and Privacy"; Timothy K Armstrong. "Digital rights management and the process of fair use". In: *Harv. JL & Tech.* 20 (2006), pp. 49–121; Dan L Burk. "Legal and technical standards in digital rights management technology". In: *Fordham L. Rev.* 74 (2005), pp. 537–573; Burk and Cohen, "Fair use infrastructure for rights management systems". According to this last article fair use allows "the use of otherwise protected material in criticism, comment, parody, news reporting, and similar uses in the public interest". It usually refers to works protected by copyright. Incorporating this rule is a principled approach for engineering privacy by design". In: *Privacy Technologies and Policy. 5th Annual Privacy Forum, 2017*. Springer, 2017, pp. 161–177.

202 *See* Rubinstein and Good, "Privacy by Design: a Counterfactual Analysis of Google and Facebook Privacy Incidents", p. 1353. On privacy engineering *see* Chapter 5, Section 5.3 of this book.

203 On the challenge of interpretation *see infra*.

204 *See* Woodrow Hartzog and Frederic Stutzman. "Obscurity by design". In: *Wash. L. Rev.* 88 (2013), pp. 385–418, p. 393. The authors proposed a new conceptualisation of PbD, namely *obscurity by design*. The concept of obscurity means that the information on the individual is not in the possession of an observer. The absence of visibility, unprotected access, identification and clarity enhances obscurity, especially in social technologies (*see* at p. 397).

205 *See* Article 29 Working Party, Police, and Justice, *The Future of Privacy: Joint Contribution to the Consultation of the European Commission on the Legal Framework for the Fundamental Right to Protection of Personal Data*, p. 14.

for Knowledge-Oriented Management of Any Normative Texts using Open Standards and Ontologies – provided the schema for the structure and semantic components of digital legislative documents in machine-readable form[206]. Legal ontologies can help to overcome the present challenge by proving methods for representing legal concepts[207].

Translating legal rules into software rules is complex because hard-coding law involves not only representing rules differently, and interpreting provisions or using norms, but also identifying and selecting the applicable and relevant requirements[208]. Courts rule on compliance *ex post* by balancing competing interests and positions and by finding the applicable rules for the concrete case in light of the rule of law, which includes the principles of consistency and legal certainty, and by way of a creative process[209]. According to Koops and Leenes, in the design stage the developer

---

206 *See* Monica Palmirani and Fabio Vitali. "Akoma-Ntoso for legal documents". In: *Legislative XML for the semantic Web*. Springer, 2011, pp. 75–100; Monica Palmirani. "Legislative change management with Akoma-Ntoso". In: *Legislative XML for the semantic Web*. Springer, 2011, pp. 101–130.

207 *See* Cesare Bartolini, Robert Muthuri, and Cristiana Santos. "Using ontologies to model data protection requirements in workflows". In: *JSAI International Symposium on Artificial Intelligence*. Springer, 2015, pp. 233–248. Generally, on legal ontologies for the privacy domain, see e.g. Valentina Leone, Luigi Di Caro, and Serena Villata. "Taking stock of legal ontologies: a feature-based comparative analysis". In: *Artificial Intelligence and Law* (2019), pp. 1–29; Cleyton Mário de Oliveira Rodrigues et al. "Legal ontologies over time: a systematic mapping study". In: *Expert Systems with Applications* 130 (2019), pp. 12–30. An important ontology that models legal concepts of the privacy domain (GDPR upfront) is PrOnto. *See* Monica Palmirani et al. "Legal Ontology for Modelling GDPR Concepts and Norms". In: *Legal Knowledge and Information Systems. JURIX 2018*. 2018, pp. 91–100; Monica Palmirani et al. "PrOnto Ontology Refinement Through Open Knowledge Extraction". In: *Legal Knowledge and Information Systems. JURIX 2019*. 2019, pp. 205–210; Monica Palmirani et al. "Hybrid Refining Approach of PrOnto Ontology". In: *Electronic Government and the Information Systems Perspective. EGOVIS 20*. Springer, 2020, pp. 3–17. *See* further Chapter 5, Section 5.3.

208 *See* Koops and Leenes, "Privacy regulation cannot be hardcoded. A critical comment on the 'privacy by design' provision in data-protection law", pp. 162–163; Majed Alshammari and Andrew Simpson. "Towards a principled approach for engineering privacy by design". In: *Privacy Technologies and Policy. 5th Annual Privacy Forum, 2017*. Springer, 2017, pp. 161–177.

209 A court interprets the law by way of a creative process. On the creativity of the judicial body with reference to the Italian framework, but which can be extended to a more general and wider debate on laws issued by judges, *see* Roberto Pardolesi and Giorgio Pino. "Post-diritto e giudice legislatore. Sulla creatività della giurisprudenza". In: *Foro it.* col. 113 (parte V 2017). The authors argued

should take into account applicable requirements, case law, legal history, and other relevant legal sources[210]. In a legal system there are general rules, but also domain-specific provisions that could affect data processing. Selecting all the applicable norms *ab initio* is a complex activity even for legal scholars and practitioners[211]. The choice of the sources will impact which norms are implemented, how the system or practice works, and by extension, what is available in the market and what is used for data processing.

The involvement of legal experts and stakeholders during the PbD implementation is essential for taking into account the relevant norms and existing interests. The team of designers must be interdisciplinary. As an example, Guarda and Zannone demonstrated that addressing the mentioned challenge is possible by following step-by-step and strict methods in the presence of legal experts as well as engineers[212]. In addition to this technological implementation, organisational strategies are an important part of the PbD approach that has to be added to the technical part to guarantee compliance with the law.

PbD aims to implement rules, principles and values established by policymakers[213]. The legal sources providing rules for a PbD implementation are firstly the applicable law on privacy and data protection, and secondly

---

that nowadays judicial creativity is inevitable, and is related to interpretation as an exercise of power. On the rule of law *see* e.g. the point of view of the European Court of Human Rights in Geranne Lautenbach. *The concept of the rule of law and the European Court of Human Rights*. Oxford University Press, 2013. ISBN: 9780199671199.

210 Koops and Leenes, "Privacy regulation cannot be hardcoded. A critical comment on the 'privacy by design' provision in data-protection law", p. 166.

211 Legal systems are complex by nature since there are several legal sources. *See* from a legal theory point of view the prominent words of Bobbio in Norberto Bobbio. *Teoria dell'ordinamento giuridico*. G. Giappichelli Editore, 1960, p. 25.

212 *See* the pioneering work of Paolo Guarda and Nicola Zannone. "Towards the development of privacy-aware systems". In: *Information and Software Technology* 51.2 (2009), pp. 337–350.

213 Paraphrasing Hildebrandt, it is arguable that "constitutional democracy entails that enacted law is seen as an instrument to achieve the goals of the democratic legislator". *See* Hildebrandt, "Legal protection by design: objections and refutations", p. 235, where the author proposes the concept of Ambient Law. According to her, this concept is built on privacy by design, value-sensitive design and values in design. Ambient law refers to smart environments and is described as "legal protection by design". It is not a law by technology, but a rule of law which aims to automatically implement legal norms in digital environments. So, PbD aims to achieve these goals.

the special legislation, and, if necessary, case law[214]. Principles could (and should) be used as supplements to the applicable legal requirements[215]. Legal principles could also be promoted for technical standards[216]. However, legal interpretation is flexible and dynamic. It seems difficult to define common principles in different legal frameworks. These are influential concerns from a legal theory point of view, and they will be briefly mentioned here in general terms.

A legal rule can be applied only if it is interpreted[217]. The interpretation has been described as an interaction between the legal source and the interpreter, who is influenced by multiple convictions[218]. As Hart has stressed, the open texture of the legal rule means that a balance between

---

214 *See* Wiese Schartum, "Making privacy by design operative", p. 163.

215 *See ibid.* Schartum specified that the implementation of the principles should be earlier checked with the applicable and specific law. Contracts could be an additional source of rules.

216 As indicated by Reidenberg, "Lex informatica: The formulation of information policy rules through technology", p. 589, the Canadian Standards Association Code worked with all the stakeholders – consumers, companies and governments – to define standards that respect principles defined by the law.

217 On legal interpretation *see ex multis* Fabrizio Politi. *Studi sull'interpretazione giuridica*. G. Giappichelli Editore, 2019. ISBN: 9788892120648, which discusses the history of interpretation and examines several approaches; Riccardo Guastini. *Saggi scettici sull'interpretazione*. G. Giappichelli Editore, 2017. ISBN: 9788892109629; Vittorio Villa. *Una teoria pragmaticamente orientata dell'interpretazione giuridica*. G. Giappichelli Editore, 2012; Giorgio Pino. *Diritti e interpretazione. Il ragionamento giuridico nello Stato costituzionale*. Il Mulino, 2010. ISBN: 9788815134271, which focuses on interpreting rights; Vincenzo Omaggio and Gaetano Carlizzi. *Ermeneutica e interpretazione giuridica*. G. Giappichelli Editore, 2010. ISBN: 9788834814239; Joseph Raz. *Between authority and interpretation: On the theory of law and practical reason*. Oxford University Press, 2009. ISBN: 9780199562688; Diciotti, *Interpretazione della legge e discorso razionale*; Robert Alexy and Aleksander Peczenik. "The concept of coherence and its significance for discursive rationality". In: *Ratio Juris* 3 (1990), pp. 130–147; Hans Kelsen. *General Theory of Norms*. Oxford University Press, 1991. ISBN: 9780198252177; Riccardo Guastini. *Problemi di teoria del diritto*. Il Mulino, 1980; Emilio Betti. *Interpretazione della legge e degli atti giuridici*. Giuffrè Editore, 1949. *See* also the point of view of other prominent scholars who focused on the approach called "analisi economica del diritto" in Guido Alpa et al. *Interpretazione giuridica e analisi economica*. Giuffrè Editore, 1982.

218 Sacco, "Legal formants: a dynamic approach to comparative law (installment II of II)", p. 344. On interpretation *see* also the words Raz, *Between authority and interpretation: On the theory of law and practical reason*.

competing interests should be struck case by case[219]. As an example, in the data protection context, legal rules allow flexible application in practice to facilitate the free flow of information and guarantee an adequate and proportionate level of protection[220]. The interpretation preserves the ductility of the legal text in a constantly variable society[221]. In this sense, law can be adaptive to a higher number of contexts[222].

Legal requirements are formulated in such a way to allow flexible application and make implementation challenging[223]. The creativity of the interpreter is related to a legal source, such as statutes and constitutions. Traditionally legal rule can be general or domain-specific, primary or secondary, descriptive or prescriptive, over-inclusive or under-inclusive[224]. The interpreter could also take into account other legal sources, such as case law. Legal interpretation could change over time[225]. The interpreter – i.e. scholars, judges or practitioners – use several categories of arguments and multiple schemes to attribute a meaning to a legal text[226].

---

219 *See* Hart and Raz, *The concept of law*, pp. 124–135. Hart dedicated some brilliant pages to the formalism of law.

220 Koops and Leenes, "Privacy regulation cannot be hardcoded. A critical comment on the 'privacy by design' provision in data-protection law", p. 166.

221 De Vanna, "The Construction of a Normative Framework for Technology-Driven Innovations: A Legal Theory Perspective", p. 189.

222 *See* the prominent theory of interpretation of Betti in Betti, *Interpretazione della legge e degli atti giuridici*, p. 4, which stresses: "(l'interpretazione) assolve il compito di mantenere sempre in vita, mediante l'intendere, le esigenze di un ordine dell'operare, e precipuamente assolve il compito di conservare in perenne efficienza nella vita di una società, norme, precetti e valutazioni normative, che sono destinati a regolarla o a servirle di orientamento".

223 Koops and Leenes, "Privacy regulation cannot be hardcoded. A critical comment on the 'privacy by design' provision in data-protection law", p. 166.

224 On characteristics of legal rules *see* the perspective on legal theory of Norberto Bobbio. *Studi per una teoria generale del diritto*. G. Giappichelli Editore, 1970.

225 For these last considerations and PbD *see* Koops and Leenes, "Privacy regulation cannot be hardcoded. A critical comment on the 'privacy by design' provision in data-protection law", p. 166; Klitou, *Privacy-invading technologies and privacy by design. Safeguarding Privacy, Liberty and Security in the 21st Century*, p. 284.

226 On schemes of legal interpretation *see* the research in the field of philosophy of law. *See ex multis* John R Searle. *Expression and meaning: Studies in the theory of speech acts*. Cambridge University Press, 1985. ISBN: 9780511609213; Kevin D Ashley. "Reasoning with cases and hypotheticals in HYPO". In: *International journal of man-machine studies* 34.6 (1991), pp. 753–796; Giovanni Sartor. "A formal model of legal argumentation". In: *Ratio Juris* 7.2 (1994), pp. 177–211; Neil MacCormick. "Argumentation and interpretation in law". In: *Argumentation* 9.3 (1995), pp. 467–480; Kent Greenawalt. "Constitutional and statutory

Some norms cannot be easily embedded by design. Where there is a consensus on the meaning of a rule, or the rule is framed in a detailed way it is less challenging than where there is not[227]. However, PbD does not aim to encode every legal rule and it promotes organisational measures, too.

In addition to this challenge, some conflicts between values are also possible in the design stage and during the interpretation of the requirements. First of all, it is worth noting that there might be concerns about the erosion of practical liberty by the use of technological design and management[228]. Following Brownsword, technological management could pre-

---

interpretation". In: *The Oxford Handbook of Jurisprudence and Philosophy of Law*. 2002. ISBN: 9780199270972; Riccardo Guastini. *Interpretare e argomentare*. Giuffrè Editore, 2011. ISBN: 9788814192951; Fabrizio Macagno et al. "Arguments of interpretation and argumentation schemes". In: *Studies on argumentation and legal philosophy. Further steps towards a pluralistic approach* (2015), pp. 51–80; Douglas Walton, Giovanni Sartor, and Fabrizio Macagno. "An argumentation framework for contested cases of statutory interpretation". In: *Artificial Intelligence and Law* 24.1 (2016), pp. 51–91; Eveline T. Feteris. *Fundamentals of legal argumentation*. Vol. 1. Springer, 2017. ISBN: 9789402411270; Giorgio Bongiovanni et al. *Handbook of legal reasoning and argumentation*. Springer, 2018. ISBN: 9789048194513. In the 1980s, Tarello classified 15 interpretative arguments or speech patterns used by any interpreter with the law. On interpretative arguments *see* Giovanni Tarello. "Argomenti interpretativi". In: *Digesto civ.* (1987), pp. 3–11, which intelligently explains and classifies these arguments. Tarello refers to practitioners who have to persuade a judge and scholars who propose a particular meaning of the law. The arguments are: 1) *argumentum a contrario*; 2) *argumentum a simili*, i.e. analogy; 3) *argumentum a fortiori*; 4) *argumentum a completitudine*; 5) argument of the consistency of legal discipline; 6) psychological argument; 7) historical argument; 8) apagogical argument, i.e. *argumentum ab absurdo* or *reductio ad absurdum*; 9) teleological argument; 10) economic argument; 11) *argumentum ab exemplo*; 12) systematic argument; 13) naturalistic argument; 14) the so-called argument "equitativo"; 15) *argumentum a coherentia* or *analogia iuris*. The same provision may assume different meanings in the arguments used. As an example, the law can be interpreted according to its strictest sense by excluding any extension of the meaning of the terms and any analogy (*ubi lex voluit dixit, ubi tacuit noluit*), or the interpreter can use an analogy or the *ratio legis* included in the preparatory works of the provision by a teleological argument. Tarello provides a specific description for each argument.

227 Klitou, *Privacy-invading technologies and privacy by design. Safeguarding Privacy, Liberty and Security in the 21st Century*, p. 284.

228 Brownsword, "Law, liberty and technology", p. 55. *See* also a similar discussion focused on filtering and the constitutional freedom of speech by Lessig in Lawrence Lessig. "What things regulate speech: CDA 2.0 vs. filtering". In: *Jurimetrics* 38.4 (1998), pp. 629–670.

vent or exclude actions in such a way that the agent is not free to do something, such as break the rules[229]. From a liberal perspective, this condition may diminish moral citizenship since it reduces practical options and, therefore, the autonomy of the agents. In this scenario, Hart's rules of behaviour are challenged. The individual does not have the choice to obey or disobey the rule. PbD thus might create a problem of general legitimacy of the rule because it might be necessary to justify this paternalistic use of technological regulation. Internalising privacy, as in the case of the PbD strategy, indisputably implicates a technological design. It may be supposed that a violation (a disobedience) impacting privacy interests is not practically possible. Brownsword argued that the moral virtue of respecting privacy might disappear, but, at the same level of argument, respecting privacy and data protection might be more urgent than this conceivable impingement on morality[230]. PbD implementation might prevent the possibility of negotiating the practical options[231]. Automation of privacy and data protection rules may impinge the rights to "self-determination" and "informational self-determination" of individuals[232]. Having a right to informational self-determination means that the individuals have the freedom of choice and the opportunity to make their own decisions on what happens with their personal data. It seems that with PbD individuals do not have the opportunity to make their own decisions on what happens with their intimacy or personal data. A response to this argument might be that discussing privacy practices is simply not feasible in the informational relationship performed in the digital market. Actually, the PbD settings take into account users' decisions, keeping them central. According to Cavoukian's seventh principle, the data subject's interests shall be central. If individuals want to give up their rights, they will change the protective default settings with less protective ones.

229 Brownsword, "Law, liberty and technology", p. 56. *See* also Roger Brownsword. *Law, Technology and Society: Reimagining the Regulatory Environment*. Routledge, 2019. ISBN: 9780815356462.

230 Brownsword concluded his chapter by highlighting that discussing the impact on liberty is still relevant in the present debate.

231 Again, Brownsword discussed this concern in Brownsword, "Law, liberty and technology", p. 65.

232 *See* Pagallo, "On the principle of privacy by design and its limits: Technology, ethics and the rule of law", p. 339. On the concept of self-determination *see* Theo Hooghiemstra. "Informational Self-Determination, Digital Health and New Features of Data Protection". In: *Eur. Data Prot. L. Rev.* 5 (2019), pp. 160–174, pp. 160–162, 171.

Moreover, design choices may create conflicts between values that influence other design choices[233]. The adoption of a particular theory of privacy or data protection configures different frameworks of values[234]. Privacy could acquire different features if conceived in terms of property rights, human dignity, total control, contextual integrity, restricted access or limited control over digital information[235]. Deciding which value should be privileged requires inquiries into the specific context[236]. In addition to privacy principles and values, legal systems establish other principles, inter-

233 Pagallo, "On the principle of privacy by design and its limits: Technology, ethics and the rule of law", p. 338.

234 According to Alpa, in the EU the protection of personal data and privacy involves three directions: the protection of human dignity and self-determination, the protection of the digital market, and the protection of the contracts for digital content that uses personal data. *See* Guido Alpa. "La "proprietà" dei dati personali". In: *Persona e mercato dei dati. Riflessioni sul GDPR*. Wolters Kluver, 2019, pp. 11–33. ISBN: 9788813370510. Therefore, legal rules embed different perspectives and values. In fact, according to Galgano, the GDPR protects both the right of the data subject to self-determination and control over personal data, and the right of the controller to process personal data in the free digital market. *See* Nadia Galgano Zorzi. "Le due anime del GDPR e la tutela del diritto alla *privacy*". In: *Persona e mercato dei dati. Riflessioni sul GDPR*. Wolters Kluwer, 2019, pp. 35–94. ISBN: 9788813370510. Despite the presence of this second soul of the GDPR, it does not conceive data protection in terms of property rights.

235 These are the examples provided by Pagallo in Pagallo, "On the principle of privacy by design and its limits: Technology, ethics and the rule of law", p. 338. One of the most influential privacy conceptions is Nissenbaum's theory of contextual integrity. *See* the prominent paper in Helen Nissenbaum. "Privacy as contextual integrity". In: *Wash. L. Rev.* 79 (2004), pp. 119–158. According to the philosopher, the right to informational privacy in terms of contextual integrity is related to the social phenomenon of distinct types of contexts, domains, spheres, institutions or fields (*see* at p. 137). Indeed, "contexts, or spheres, offer a platform for a normative account of privacy in terms of contextual integrity" (*see* at p. 138). Norms of appropriateness and distribution govern each context. Therefore, "whether a particular action is determined a violation of privacy is a function of several variables, including the nature of the situation, or context; the nature of the information in relation to that context; the roles of agents receiving information; their relationships to information subjects; on what terms the information is shared by the subject; and the terms of further dissemination" (*see* at p. 155). This theory highly influenced the US legal framework.

236 *See* Mulligan and King, "Bridging the gap between privacy and design", p. 1017. Mulligan *et al.* argued that Nissembaum's theory of privacy as contextual integrity should guide the design of privacy-protective platforms.

ests and rights that should be balanced in a conflict, such as intellectual property rights and freedom of information.

According to Hartzog, designers should have the freedom to balance values (and principles) case-by-case[237]. In general, the PbD approach does not aim to hinder the design process and its purposes, but seeks to find the right balance. Privacy and data protection are just two of the possible rights and values in place[238]. However, it should be highlighted that balancing rights and values is traditionally a task of the interpreter and judge. Therefore, once again, it should be stressed that a legal expert must be involved in the PbD implementation, which should be the result of interdisciplinary work.

PbD promotes proactive and preventive measures. This proactive approach for privacy represents a significant shift from the traditional one: policymakers directly call on private stakeholders[239]. Enforcing the law generally occurs after a violation (*ex post basis*)[240]. By contrast, technical constraints could prevent actions and auto-execute: the violation of the rule may not occur at all. This *ex ante* approach has efficient effects. For example, an information flow that violates a policy rule can be blocked by a self-executing filter[241]. Hence, *regulation by design* is "immediate": it prevents a forbidden behaviour from occurring with preventive measures[242]. If *regulation by design* is self-executing, the rule might be adjusted more quickly than in the case of law[243].

However, with a proactive approach it could be argued that the State delegates privacy regulation to companies. This private self-regulation may be incompatible with the democratic procedures of law making and law enforcement[244]. In architectural regulation the rule is set by a private party.

---

237 Hartzog, *Privacy's blueprint: the battle to control the design of new technologies*, p. 86.

238 On the need to balance data protection with other rights and liberties *see* further Section 2.7.

239 Levin, "Privacy by Design by Regulation: The Case Study of Ontario", p. 119.

240 *See* Reidenberg, "Lex informatica: The formulation of information policy rules through technology", p. 572.

241 Reidenberg, *op. cit.*, p. 581.

242 *See* Grimmelmann, "Regulation by software", p. 1723.

243 *See* the scenario presented by De Vanna, "The Construction of a Normative Framework for Technology- Driven Innovations: A Legal Theory Perspective", p. 191. Law is slow and requires a great democratic effort.

244 The term "self-regulation" implies several different phenomena. Generally, self-regulation is a creation of a norm by a private entity. *See* further Quarta and Smorto, *Diritto privato dei mercati digitali*, pp. 83–84.

As regards this concern, Tien identified the presence of a transparency problem[245]. The *code* hides the reasons, and the settings are invisible and defined by default[246]. In the *code as law* context, programmers might theoretically become the lawmakers who act at the disposal of the companies[247]. Law making operates in a different way that requires political decisions and is more than a regulation-oriented practice[248]. In addition, the enforcement activity normally requires public bodies, agencies or institutions. Nonetheless, it has been argued that the legislation activity is always public, but may not be "transparent" because of lobbying and influence peddling[249]. As regards *regulation by technology*, governments could participate in the creation process of standards for leading technological development with public goals[250]. As a result, these goals could be recognised as design objectives by the developers. Leenes and Koops suggest that if the government (i.e. the lawmaker) mandates an "enforcement code", such as PbD, there will always be a legitimate rule-making authority[251]. PbD shall be mandated by legislators and established in a specific provision.

PbD may prevent privacy breaches before they happen, but every embedded technical solution is rigid. Therefore, it is necessary to update measures frequently. The first statement is expressed in the Cavoukian's

---

245 *See* Tien, "Architectural regulation and the evolution of social norms", p. 3. On the lack of transparency *see* also Diver and Schafer, "Opening the black box: Petri nets and Privacy by Design", p. 74; Grimmelmann, "Regulation by software", pp. 1734–1738.

246 De Vanna, "The Construction of a Normative Framework for Technology-Driven Innovations: A Legal Theory Perspective", p. 200.

247 *See* Klitou, *Privacy-invading technologies and privacy by design. Safeguarding Privacy, Liberty and Security in the 21st Century*, p. 283.

248 *See* Serge Gutwirth, Paul De Hert, and Laurent De Sutter. "The trouble with technology regulation: why Lessig's 'Optimal Mix' will not work". In: *Regulating technologies: Legal futures, regulatory frames and technological fixes*. Oxford University Press, 2008, pp. 193–218. ISBN: 9781841137889, p. 196. According to these scholars, Lessig's approach demands the fixation of political ends in regulation. This is problematic for legal practitioners who construct the law in the interplay between their internal obligations and requirements, and the external mobilisations.

249 *See* Tien, "Architectural regulation and the evolution of social norms", p. 9; and Leenes and Koops, "'Code' and privacy-or how technology is slowly eroding privacy", p. 53.

250 Reidenberg, "Lex informatica: The formulation of information policy rules through technology", p. 591.

251 Leenes and Koops, "'Code' and privacy-or how technology is slowly eroding privacy", p. 51.

first principle: "proactive not reactive, preventative nor remedial". Identifying privacy risks at the initial stage with an assessment is typical for a PbD approach. In addition, according to the Cavoukian's fifth principle, the concept of security plays an important role for PbD. However, it is necessary to bear in mind that the approach *security by design* differs from PbD because designing in security does not entail that privacy has also been embedded[252]. As a matter of fact, addressing data security means that any collection is legitimate as long as data is safe[253]. PbD is a more holistic approach.

Privacy breaches are structural problems of ICTs and represent an opportunity for PbD[254]. Indeed, the increasing number of data breaches reinforces the need for privacy by design[255]. PbD, as previously with PETs, could prevent certain breaches from occurring because they are more difficult to carry out from a technical point of view[256]. The law could also impose liability for breaking technical rules, thereby creating an incentive to design properly[257]. It has been argued that proactivity of PbD both prevents incidents and has the potential to consider privacy opportunities well in advance[258]. A counterfactual analysis on Facebook's and Google's incidents demonstrates that these incidents could have been avoided by the application of accurate design practices[259].

---

252 Kroener and Wright, "A strategy for operationalizing privacy by design", p. 358.

253 Klitou, *Privacy-invading technologies and privacy by design. Safeguarding Privacy, Liberty and Security in the 21st Century*, p. 297.

254 Hustinx, "Privacy by design: delivering the promises", p. 254.

255 *See* the argument in European Data Protection Supervisor, *Opinion of the European Data Protection Supervisor on Promoting Trust in the Information Society by Fostering Data Protection and Privacy*, p. 6; EDPB European Data Protection Board. *Guidelines 1/2021 on Examples regarding Data Breach Notification*. 14 January 2021. Version for public consultation. European Data Protection Board, 2021.

256 As regards PETs, *see supra* note no. 146, p. 4. The EU Commission highlighted the importance of the use of PETs for preventing data breaches in a complementary way with the enforceable rules and obligation of the legal framework. European Commission, *Communication from the Commission to the European Parliament and the Council on Promoting Data Protection by Privacy Enhancing Technologies (PETs)*.

257 Reidenberg, "Lex informatica: The formulation of information policy rules through technology", p. 583.

258 *See* Wiese Schartum, "Making privacy by design operative", p. 155.

259 *See* the interesting analysis by Rubinstein and Good, "Privacy by Design: a Counterfactual Analysis of Google and Facebook Privacy Incidents'". In the

Despite this promising edge, *regulation by design* as much as any embedded technical solution tends to be rigid. By contrast, *regulation by law* and its interpretation changes over time. It has been highlighted that technical constraints are substantive inalienable rules[260]. They are costly and difficult to change once established, especially if they are deeper in the architecture[261]. Measures should be regularly updated to protect privacy. Privacy threats should be pre-empted, so that implemented solutions are future proof for a long time[262]. On the one hand, PbD is an approach that entails the regulation by code at its core; on the other hand, it is a dynamic approach that requires by default to be updated frequently and also takes into account organisational measures. On this concern, Klitou pointed out that PbD is an ongoing process that needs continuous advancement and re-assessment so as to not fall behind[263].

PbD is evidently a global perspective: it requires both "privacy-by-policy" and "privacy-by-architecture" approaches[264]. Companies usually prefer the former approach for easily complying with the law and shifting the responsibility to users[265]. An appropriate PbD adoption shall balance both approaches[266]. PbD is a full life-cycle approach that combines law and technology[267]. As a consequence, and once again, technical, legal and business stakeholders should collaborate and follow an interdisciplinary approach[268]. It could be difficult and time-consuming, but it is useful and valuable for workable solutions[269]. Clearly, building privacy is critical for developers and not possible in every situation. Although PbD adoption has been strongly encouraged, this approach is not meant to cover every

---

concluding remarks the authors suggested that PbD, when research is performed correctly, protects consumer privacy from breaches and other incidents.

260 Reidenberg, "Lex informatica: The formulation of information policy rules through technology", p. 572.

261 Reidenberg, *op. cit.*, pp. 582–583.

262 *See* Klitou, *Privacy-invading technologies and privacy by design. Safeguarding Privacy, Liberty and Security in the 21st Century*, p. 312.

263 *See* Klitou, *op. cit.*, p. 325.

264 On these approaches *see* further Chapter 5, Section 5.3.

265 Diver and Schafer, "Opening the black box: Petri nets and Privacy by Design", p. 73.

266 Diver and Schafer, *op. cit.*, p. 75.

267 Klitou, *Privacy-invading technologies and privacy by design. Safeguarding Privacy, Liberty and Security in the 21st Century*, pp. 265, 298.

268 Tsormpatzoudi, Berendt, and Coudert, "Privacy by design: from research and policy to practice–the challenge of multi-disciplinarity", p. 2020.

269 *Ibid.*

legal requirement. It is evident that making all data protection provisions automatic is out of reach[270].

PbD requires concrete organisational measures, but companies sometimes lack a knowledgeable organisation. PbD is further dedicated to business and policy levels across the entire organisation[271]. Management should identify tasks and define responsibilities for planning data processing and handling its operations. Concrete measures should be adopted in processes and projects touching every aspect[272]. As noted above, management has a pivotal role in defining data protection as one of the business priorities and objectives. Nevertheless, companies sometimes lack a knowledgeable organisation. In order to implement PbD both legal and technical experts should work together in every organisation[273]. Public authorities, institutions and agencies could lead by example in applying the rules and the PbD approach. According to the EDPS, public administration shall lead by example on data protection by design[274]. Indeed, public services should serve as a role model and be obliged to use only privacy-friendly technologies that are compliant with the law[275].

Furthermore, PbD requires effective measures and less bureaucratic solutions. PbD implementation aims to avoid the "privacy-as-bureaucracy" paradigm. PbD is a process that goes beyond a defined "to-do-list". Measures shall be effective and proportionate to the concrete risks for individuals that are posed by the data processing[276]. Privacy policies or notices should be consistent with the adopted measures and should not be simplistic forms. In order to adopt a PbD approach, investments and allocated resources are indispensable. The costs are often higher in management focus and organisational efforts than in money. Undoubtedly, PbD depends

---

270 *See* the words in Pagallo, "On the principle of privacy by design and its limits: Technology, ethics and the rule of law", p. 343.

271 *See* Ann Cavoukian. *Privacy by design: From rhetoric to reality*. Information and privacy commissioner of Ontario, Canada, 2014, p. 173.

272 *See ibid.*

273 *See* Wiese Schartum, "Making privacy by design operative", p. 162. This scholar claimes that both legal and software engineering expertise are required for privacy by design.

274 European Data Protection Supervisor, *Opinion 5/2018, Preliminary Opinion on privacy by design*, p. 18.

275 This is one of the recommendations in Danezis et al., *Privacy and Data Protection by design – from policy to engineering*, p. 50.

276 As further explained in Section 2.4, this is the approach of the EU.

on the means, resources and skills of the producers or developers[277]. Companies will invest in privacy programs, creating costs that they are usually reluctant to pay[278]. Small and medium enterprises (SMEs) may ignore a PbD requirement because of the implementation cost and the lower risk of being sanctioned[279].

However, these costs could be considered either as deferred costs to protect the company or insurance costs to safeguard against incidents and sanctions[280]. Companies that use a cost-benefit approach might realise that the expected costs represent a future saving, which is a positive investment in economic terms. Actually, a cost-benefit analysis requires reliable data to inform the decision. This data is scarce[281]. Therefore, investment decisions should be informed by other models. On the one hand, as will be explained later, privacy care has a positive impact on consumers' trust and satisfaction in products and services. On the other hand, public funding intervention could allocate some resources to supporting firms through economic incentives. Funding plays an important role in promoting PbD because the market forces are usually not in favour of it[282]. It is worth

277 *See* Klitou, *Privacy-invading technologies and privacy by design. Safeguarding Privacy, Liberty and Security in the 21st Century*, p. 285.

278 Rubinstein, "Regulating privacy by design", p. 1432. On privacy costs before the GDPR *see* the investigation by Alessandro Mantelero. *Il costo della privacy tra valore della persona e ragione d'impresa*. Vol. 24. Giuffrè Editore, 2007. ISBN: 9788814135682, which examines how privacy impacts companies' management from several points of view (e.g. organisation of employees, risk management, service outsourcing), and examines some concrete case studies.

279 *See* Diver and Schafer, "Opening the black box: Petri nets and Privacy by Design", p. 71. These scholars argue that the SMEs are at low risk of being caught. This concern is relevant because according to the European Union Agency for Network and Security (ENISA) SMEs dominate the business landscape of data processing. *See* Giuseppe D'Acquisto and Georgia Panagopoulou. *Guidelines for SMEs on the security of personal data processing*. European Union Agency for Network and Information Security, 2016.

280 A similar argument is used by the US Department of Health, Education & Welfare for supporting the application of the FIPs and their resulting privacy costs. *See* US Department of Health, *Report of the Secretary's Advisory Committee on Automated Personal Data Systems, Records Computers and the Rights of citizens*, p. 45.

281 *See* Rubinstein, "Regulating privacy by design", pp. 1437–1438. The author reported that there is neither reliable data on the benefits of privacy nor data on the costs.

282 *See* this argument in Danezis et al., *Privacy and Data Protection by design – from policy to engineering*, p. 51.

noting that PbD solutions are not necessarily sophisticated but have a range of degrees of sophistication[283]. Therefore, costs may also vary greatly.

PbD may also increase privacy culture in society, but it could be argued that there is a difficulty of comprehension for the layman on this topic. Cavoukian noted that with PbD privacy is not yet considered a compliance issue, but a business issue creating opportunities and a positive paradigm[284]. PbD introduces the opportunity to foster a privacy-first culture[285]. A particular culture of privacy grows within companies and enterprises[286]. Even in the present moment of increased attention on privacy and data protection problems, there is a difficulty of comprehension for the layman on the issues. The lack of technical knowledge and its normative implications have been explained by scholars[287]. People do not have the necessary information to contest a design decision and potentially condemn a wrong implementation. A consumer choice entails awareness and there is a considerable lack of it[288].

Moreover, PbD may contribute to increase trust and confidence in products and services, but in the Information Society there is an information asymmetry and a widespread lack of knowledge on design strategies. It has been claimed that PbD is about trust[289]. Ann Cavoukian usually presents PbD as a tool for restoring trust[290]. Since PbD translates principles into implementation of privacy-protective solutions, it has been argued that fostering trust in ICTs is possible[291]. Trust is an essential component of *healthy relationships and healthy societies*[292]. In the digital economy the

---

283 Klitou, *Privacy-invading technologies and privacy by design. Safeguarding Privacy, Liberty and Security in the 21st Century*, p. 264.

284 *See* e.g. Cavoukian, "Privacy by design: the definitive workshop. A foreword by Ann Cavoukian, Ph.D", p. 251.

285 Everson, "Privacy by design: Taking ctrl of big data", p. 30.

286 *See* Cavoukian, *Privacy by design: From rhetoric to reality*, p. 223.

287 *See* e.g. Tien, "Architectural regulation and the evolution of social norms".

288 *See* Leenes and Koops, "'Code' and privacy-or how technology is slowly eroding privacy", p. 51. The authors even reflect on the existence of a choice. More considerations on this concern are added to explain the next lines.

289 Everson, "Privacy by design: Taking ctrl of big data", p. 40. This author adds that the adoption of PbD is simply the right thing to do for Big Data.

290 *See* the sixth principle "visibility and transparency", in Section 2.2.

291 Cavoukian, "Operationalizing privacy by design: A guide to implementing strong privacy practices", p. 16.

292 *See* Richards and Hartzog, "Taking trust seriously in privacy law", p. 448; and Hartzog, *Privacy's blueprint: the battle to control the design of new technologies*, p. 98.

rhetoric of trust and privacy have been widely used internationally[293]. So much, that promoting consumer trust has become a goal for privacy and data protection regulation[294]. Ideally, a data protection framework aims to build trusting relationships between individuals and organisations[295]. Richards and Hartzog proposed a theory of privacy and trust: *privacy matters because it enables trust*[296]. From their perspective, trust is essential for privacy disputes especially in the information relationships[297]. From a digital perspective, where privacy pessimism arises, privacy rules serve constitutional values by creating trust and, therefore, the optimal conditions for intimacy and freedom of expression[298]. In their analysis the two scholars connected the concept of trust with the FIPs and they proposed adding "loyalty" as a foundational concept in privacy law in order to guide privacy discussions. In the EU data protection aims to create trust and boost growth and innovation[299]. As an example, the importance of creating trust due to digital development is highlighted in Recital 7 of the GDPR: trust is important for allowing the development of the digital economy across the EU market[300]. According to the European Commission, protective technology, such as PETs, could have a positive impact on consumers because people are more certain that data are managed in a proper way[301]. Since PbD is a particular approach to privacy, it can set foundation for trust over technology. According to the European Data

293 Kenneth A. Bamberger and Deirdre K. Mulligan. "Privacy on the Books and on the Ground". In: *Stan. L. Rev.* 63 (2010), pp. 247–315, pp. 280–281.

294 *See* Bamberger and Mulligan, *op. cit.*, p. 282. These authors observe that in the US privacy is associated with trust both for and against the creation of a regulation. However, the Federal Trade Commission's agenda was always dedicated to consumer protection in order to foster confidence and trust.

295 In this context the term organisation indicates both private parties (e.g. companies, firms) and public bodies (e.g. public administration, authorities).

296 Richards and Hartzog, "Taking trust seriously in privacy law", p. 447.

297 The two authors noted that trust is also essential for any commercial relationship in every context. *See* Richards and Hartzog, *op. cit.*, p. 452.

298 Richards and Hartzog, *op. cit.*, p. 456.

299 Hijmans et al., *The European Union as guardian of internet privacy*, p. 320.

300 Recitals set out the rationales of the creation of the uniform framework. In particular, the part mentioned states that (rapid technological) "developments require a strong and more coherent data protection framework in the Union, backed by strong enforcement, given the importance of creating the trust that will allow the digital economy to develop across the internal market".

301 *See supra* note no. 146. The EU Commission argued that greater respect for data protection rules has a trust impact on services based on the processing of personal data, such as e-health. European Commission, *Communication from*

Protection Supervisor (EDPS), PbD is a key tool for generating individual trust in ICTs[302]. Technologies should be reliable and secure for generating trust and PbD is a positive solution to achieve this goal. Thus, PbD could be seen as an example for enhancing trust in data protection law and for creating economic incentives in the EU[303].

Although it has been claimed that PbD could boost trust, it should be noted that in society there is an information asymmetry between different parties and a widespread lack of knowledge on design strategies. The information asymmetry exists between the digital environment and the user who acts without knowing, and controlling, the mechanisms in the background[304]. Scholars have argued that the information asymmetry is a kind of a "computational divide" where the user does not have any control on the digital environment[305]. This unprecedented asymmetry operates in knowledge and power[306]. Even in a "privacy as control" scenario, one risk is the creation of a "smoke screen" that misleads users' choices[307]. Consumers should have the opportunity to exercise an informed choice when purchasing products and using digital technology. More information and

---

*the Commission to the European Parliament and the Council on Promoting Data Protection by Privacy Enhancing Technologies (PETs).*

302 *See* European Data Protection Supervisor, *Opinion of the European Data Protection Supervisor on Promoting Trust in the Information Society by Fostering Data Protection and Privacy*, p. 4.

303 *See* Hijmans et al., *The European Union as guardian of internet privacy*, p. 320. The author suggests in his book that PbD should have been an instrument in economic policies of the EU. Moreover, it can create more trust in data protection law (*see* at p. 599).

304 *See* De Vanna, "The Construction of a Normative Framework for Technology-Driven Innovations: A Legal Theory Perspective", p. 187. Asymmetry is a market failure. *See* the useful explanation in Quarta and Smorto, *Diritto privato dei mercati digitali*, pp. 67–69.

305 De Vanna, "The Construction of a Normative Framework for Technology-Driven Innovations: A Legal Theory Perspective", p. 187. On the lack of consumer understanding *see* also Rubinstein, "Regulating privacy by design", p. 142. This information asymmetry even operates between the private and public sectors since authorities use ICTs, algorithms, data (and Big Data) to make decisions. *See* the interesting analysis by Maria Cristina Cavallaro and Guido Smorto. "Decisione pubblica e responsabilità dell'amministrazione nella società dell'algoritmo". In: *Federalismi.it* 16 (2019), pp. 2–22.

306 Shoshana Zuboff. *The age of surveillance capitalism: The fight for a human future at the new frontier of power*. Profile Books, 2019. ISBN: 9781610395694, p. 17.

307 *See* the criticism by Paul M. Schwartz. "Beyond Lessig's code for internet privacy: cyberspace filters, privacy control, and fair information practices". In: *Wis. L. Rev.* 2000.4 (2000), pp. 743–788, pp. 760–762.

transparency tools might overcome this disadvantage[308]. However, enhancing individuals' control might not be sufficient and, once again, a global approach is more advisable. PbD could increase consumers' satisfaction because it empowers them to control their privacy and personal data behind the screen[309].

Additionally, PbD has an impact on business because companies have the opportunity to use new technologies and adopt innovative internal processes and policies[310]. The quality of the design is thus a means for developing value for business[311]. A commitment to PbD could also be considered a competitive advantage that enhances business reputation[312]. However, collecting and commercialising personal data are the core business of many companies. The processed data has a substantial economic value, and is regarded as a business asset by firms[313]. Data is used to target or offer products and services, provide advertising in the online

---

308 *See* European Commission, *Communication from the Commission to the European Parliament and the Council on Promoting Data Protection by Privacy Enhancing Technologies (PETs)*, pp. 8–9. In the EU Commission's Communication on PETs the authority suggested that "simple and understandable information about possible technological tools to protect privacy must thus be provided to the user" and, therefore an "increased use of PETs and increased use of e-services which incorporate PETs will in turn mean economic reward to the industries using them, and may result in a snowball effect, encouraging other companies to pay greater attention to respecting the data protection rules".

309 Rubinstein, "Regulating privacy by design", p. 1422.

310 Anna Romanou. "The necessity of the implementation of Privacy by Design in sectors where data protection concerns arise". In: *Computer law & security review* 34.1 (2018), pp. 99–110, p. 102.

311 Klitou, *Privacy-invading technologies and privacy by design. Safeguarding Privacy, Liberty and Security in the 21st Century*, p. 281. According to the author, this statement is demonstrated in countless examples.

312 *See* European Data Protection Supervisor, *Opinion 5/2018, Preliminary Opinion on privacy by design*,
p. 19. *See* also Cavoukian, "Operationalizing privacy by design: A guide to implementing strong privacy practices"; Massimo Farina. *Il cloud computing in ambito sanitario tra security e privacy*. Giuffrè Francis Lefebvre, 2019. ISBN: 9788828817550, p. 21.

313 *See* the prominent analysis on the economics of privacy in Alessandro Acquisti, Curtis Taylor, and Liad Wagman. "The economics of privacy". In: *Journal of economic Literature* 54.2 (2016), pp. 442–492, p. 444; and the empirical study of Kenneth A. Bamberger et al. "Can you pay for privacy? consumer expectations and the behaviour of free and paid apps". In: *Berkeley Tech. LJ* 35 (2020), pp. 328–365.

ecosystem or is traded with other third parties[314]. So, it has been argued that the PbD approach may collide with the common logic of the digital economy, which incentivises the so-called "monetarization of monitoring" of end-users' data[315]. As an example, it is evident that the collection of personal data on social networks platforms is massive. A great amount of data is uploaded by users, and is also processed and inferred by companies and intermediaries, sometimes in an unsecured way[316].

Scholars classify some business models that represent approaches for monetising data. According to Elvy, the "pay-for-privacy" (PFP) approach requires the payment of a higher fee or price to avoid data collection and advertising[317]. Secondly, the "personal data economy" (PDE) approach attributes data ownership to individuals by empowering their control over information[318]. The former approach is less common than the latter, but

---

314 Acquisti, Taylor, and Wagman, "The economics of privacy", p. 444.

315 Bygrave, "Hardwiring privacy", p. 763.

316 A paradigmatic case on this issue is the Cambridge Analytica scandal of 2018. In this scandal the amount of data collected by a particular business model is crucial. Basically, this corporation developed a method to "micro-target" individual consumers or voters on Facebook with messages aimed at influencing their behaviour. *See* Jim Isaak and Mina J. Hanna. "User data privacy: Facebook, Cambridge Analytica, and privacy protection". In: *Computer* 51.8 (2018), pp. 56–59, p. 56. It is conceivable that this system influenced the US presidential elections of 2016. A data breach of 50 million profiles occurred and was revealed to *The Guardian* by whistleblower in 2018. *See* Carole Cadwalladr and Emma Graham-Harrison. "Revealed: 50 million Facebook profiles harvested for Cambridge Analytica in major data breach". In: *The Guardian* 17 (2018), p. 22. CEO Mark Zuckerberg was asked to testify before the European Parliament and the US Congress. The European Parliament adopted the Resolution of 25 October 2018 "on the use of Facebook users' data by Cambridge Analytica and the impact on data protection" (2018/2855(RSP)). The EDPS released an opinion "on online manipulation and personal data". *See* EDPS European Data Protection Supervisor. *Opinion 3/2018, EDPS Opinion on online manipulation and personal data*. 2018. On December 6, 2019 the FTC filed a complaint against Cambridge Analytica, LLC. Ten days later, the final approval of a settlement with the corporation was granted by the authority. On this file, *see* at <www.ftc.gov/enforcement/cases-proceedings/182-3107/cambridge-analytica-llc-matter>. Last accessed 06/10/2021.

317 *See* Stacy-Ann Elvy. "Paying for privacy and the personal data economy". In: *Colum. L. Rev.* 117 (2017), pp. 1369–1460, p. 1373. The author explain that companies usually provide discounts to consumers who give their consent to data collection and advertising.

318 Elvy, *op. cit.*, pp. 1374–1375. The author pointed out that this control can be illusory because of the lack of consumers' understanding of the privacy implications.

neither are widespread. The "data-as-payment" model, on the other hand, is very common. Consumers/users provide their data in exchange of a free product or service. This third model is used by big companies such as Google and Facebook to create an imperfect transaction where data has more value than the product or service provided[319]. Overall, these economic models raise concerns for privacy and, therefore, the PbD approach struggles against the logic of the digital market[320].

The market dynamics surrounding personal data have been defined as "surveillance capitalism" by prominent Harvard scholar Shoshana Zuboff[321]. Internet companies (e.g. Google) are surveillance capitalists that operate with the logic of information accumulation. The so-called "behavioural data" of users are extracted at large scale and then analysed. Only a small part of collected information is used for service improvement. The surplus is sold to other companies for advertising purposes and to create future market-based behavioural information[322]. The business model is described with an economic theory[323]. So, the different logic of minimisation and privacy protection seems inevitably at odds with the surveillance

319 Elvy, *op. cit.*, pp. 1384–1387.

320 It is interesting to note that sharing economy companies create the same privacy concerns. Even though they charge a price for their services, the narrative of manipulation remains the same. *See* e.g. Ryan Calo and Alex Rosenblat. "The taking economy: Uber, information, and power". In: *Colum. L. Rev.* 117 (2017), pp. 1623–1690, pp. 1648–1654. This article presents a case study on Uber. On law, sharing economy and digital markets *see* Quarta and Smorto, *Diritto privato dei mercati digitali*. This book explains the phenomena of the digital economy, and the effects on work and competition.

321 *See* the prominent book of Zuboff, *The age of surveillance capitalism: The fight for a human future at the new frontier of power*, p. 15. On this topic *see* also the analysis by Quarta and Smorto, *Diritto privato dei mercati digitali*, pp. 173–176. The authors point out that individuals are manipulated in surveillance capitalism. People are unaware of their choices.

322 *See* Zuboff, *The age of surveillance capitalism: The fight for a human future at the new frontier of power*. In particular, *see* Chapter 2. The author explains the history of the digital revolution in comparison with Ford's inventions. Zuboff describes in detail Google's history and business model. This company collects data from Internet searches.

323 In Zuboff's framing: "The summary of these developments is that the behavioural surplus upon which Google's fortune rests can be considered as surveillance assets. These assets are critical raw materials in the pursuit of surveillance revenues and their translation into surveillance capital. The entire logic of this capital accumulation is most accurately understood as surveillance capitalism, which is the foundational framework for a surveillance-based economic order: a surveillance economy" (*see* at p. 93).

model[324]. However, the same scholar mentions privacy by design in the vital and necessary accomplishment of a regulatory framework that might challenge this new capitalism. In fact, Zuboff argues that the EU legal framework might challenge the dynamics of surveillance capitalism with the rules on data protection[325].

The more people are aware of the processing activities, the more they will be protected, and the information asymmetry might be reduced within its power asymmetries. At the same time, it has been claimed that privacy regulation alone is insufficient to change this current capitalist model[326].

It may be also argued that with PbD there is a business opportunity for certifications and standards, but certification does not automatically mean compliance with the law. Certification is defined as a "conformity assessment activity"[327]. It is usually issued by an entity after a certification procedure. Certification might or might not be based on legislation. It is an opportunity because it has a voluntary basis. Certification can assist data controllers in demonstrating compliance with legal obligations. Moreover, certification can increase confidence in products and services[328]. Indeed, certification can play a significant role for PbD because the details of this complex approach can be defined by intermediaries between the regulator and the regulated, which may be appointed by data protection authorities[329]. An independent and standardised certification scheme on PbD could determine the validity and adequacy of solutions[330]. One example

---

324 As regards the relationship of surveillance capitalism to privacy, *see* Chapter 6 of the book, where the scholar perfectly describes the scenario of the mentioned disadvantage: internet companies are not interested in privacy protection because it is dangerous for their business model, which is at its core based on data (such as a new oil).

325 *Ibid.*, *see* Chapter 17 of the same book. According to the Harvard scholar, only timing and society will show if the economic model can change thanks to a new advanced regulatory framework such as the EU one.

326 Quarta and Smorto, *Diritto privato dei mercati digitali*, p. 176.

327 *See* ENISA European Union Agency for Network & Information Security. *Recommendations on European Data Protection Certification*. European Union Agency for Network and Information Security, 2017, p. 9.

328 *See* the argument used in Danezis et al., *Privacy and Data Protection by design – from policy to engineering*, p. 16.

329 *See* Levin, "Privacy by Design by Regulation: The Case Study of Ontario", p. 156. As will be explained in Section 2.5.3, this is the approach of the EU framework.

330 *See* Klitou, *Privacy-invading technologies and privacy by design. Safeguarding Privacy, Liberty and Security in the 21st Century*, p. 309.

of PbD certification is the one offered by the PbD Centre of Excellence at Ryerson University in Ontario[331]. This certification is based on FIPs[332].

Furthermore, standards are means for complying with the law. Technical standards can also be useful for data protection authorities because they represent a first point of reference for compliance-checking[333]. Standardisation is a form of regulation[334]. A standard is a self-regulation which is more flexible than a regulation subject to a democratic legislative process[335]. An international standard on PbD in currently under development by a technical committee of ISO[336]. Although certification and standards are widely useful, they do not automatically mean compliance with the law. Compliance is verified by the courts and by data protection authorities. In most cases certification does not reduce the liability of subjects[337]. Moreover, as with self-regulation, certification and standards are usually mar-

---

331 *See* Ann Cavoukian and Michelle Chibba. "Privacy seals in the USA, Europe, Japan, Canada, India and Australia". In: *Privacy and data protection seals*. Springer, 2018, pp. 59–82. ISBN: 9789462652286, p. 77. This certification programme is directed by Ann Cavoukian in collaboration with Deloitte.

332 *See* European Union Agency for Network & Information Security, *Recommendations on European Data Protection Certification*, p. 18. In this report the agency analyses certification, which does not signify compliance with a specific law, but uses Cavoukian's approach. Certification follows an important best practice: the entity that examines the product or service (i.e. Deloitte) is different from the entity that issue the certification (i.e. the Privacy by Design Centre of Excellence at Ryerson University).

333 Irene Kamara. "Co-regulation in EU personal data protection: the case of technical standards and the privacy by design standardisation 'mandate'". In: *European Journal of Law and Technology* 8.1 (2017), pp. 1–24, p. 2.

334 In the EU there is a specific regulation on European standards. *See* Regulation (EU) No 1025/2012 of the European Parliament and of the Council of 25 October 2012 on European standardisation, amending Council Directives 89/686/EEC and 93/15/EEC and Directives 94/9/EC, 94/25/EC, 95/16/EC, 97/23/EC, 98/34/EC, 2004/22/EC, 2007/23/EC, 2009/23/EC and 2009/105/EC of the European Parliament and of the Council and repealing Council Decision 87/95/EEC and Decision No 1673/2006/EC of the European Parliament and of the Council, O.J. L. 316, 14.11.2012.

335 *See* Tamó-Larrieux, *Designing for privacy and its legal framework: data protection by design and default for the internet of things*, p. 197.

336 *See* project ISO/PC 317 "consumer protection: privacy by design for consumer goods and services" at <www.iso.org/committee/6935430.html>. Last accessed 06/10/2021. Cavoukian mentions the importance of this standard in Cavoukian, "Understanding How to Implement Privacy by Design, One Step at a Time".

337 As will be explained in Section 2.5.3, certification does not avoid the liability of the data controller under the GDPR, but it will be taken into account by the DPA during the investigation and the proceedings.

ket-driven and, so, unsupervised by the authorities. Costs are high in the case of international certifications. Therefore, SMEs could be discouraged from paying such expensive costs to get certified. Copyrights on standards have transformed initial "public goods" into fragmented "club goods"[338]. However, it has been argued that both regulation and self-regulation are needed in a legal system[339].

PbD requirement incentivises the development of new privacy-friendly technologies from the beginning[340]. This is the aim of Cavoukian's seventh principle. In this sense, PbD has proven to be a useful innovation in the design community[341]. Since the approach is easily applicable to new technologies, adapting the existing solutions is not always feasible. As a result, strategies for the PbD implementation should be elaborated case-by-case after a balance between competing interests. Sometimes, the easier choice is to change technologies.

*Regulation by technology* is a form of control. It has been claimed that a new ethics of responsibility should revise some legal categories and inspire regulatory solutions[342]. Authorities might become involved in unusual types of activities, such as promoting technical standards[343]. The call for an ethical foundation in technology has a broad scope. PbD is arguably an unprecedented opportunity to boost respect for ethics in technology[344]. In this controlled scenario, there will be barriers to innovation. According to Quarta and Smorto, since the 1970s the word "innovation" has substituted the word "progress"[345]. An innovation is a technological novel creation

---

338 *See* this critique in Tamó-Larrieux, *Designing for privacy and its legal framework: data protection by design and default for the internet of things*, p. 197.

339 *Ibid.*

340 Hijmans et al., *The European Union as guardian of internet privacy*, p. 296.

341 Hartzog and Stutzman, "Obscurity by design", p. 391.

342 *See* De Vanna, "The Construction of a Normative Framework for Technology-Driven Innovations: A Legal Theory Perspective", p. 200. The author discusses design theory and argues for a regulation by law over technology.

343 In this sense, as mentioned above, an example is the collaboration between the Canadian Standard Association Group and the Government of Canada. *See* for lobbying information <lobbycanada.gc. ca/app/secure/ocl/lrs/do/clntAddr?cid=5290&sMdKy=1382894400185>; and for all the other information <www.csagroup.org/about-csa-group/>. Last accessed 06/10/2021.

344 *See* European Data Protection Supervisor, *Opinion 5/2018, Preliminary Opinion on privacy by design*, p. 21.

345 *See* Quarta and Smorto, *Diritto privato dei mercati digitali*, pp. 29–30.

that contributes to meeting society's recognised needs, i.e. it brings a better change by offering new and creative ways of responding to social needs[346].

The approach of privacy by design indirectly aims to control the development process of products and services in order to improve the protection of privacy and personal data. Studies reported by Lieshout show that privacy has potential negative consequences for innovation[347]. This scholar reports some empirical studies on the impact of privacy on business, concluding that the latter promotes innovation to the detriment of privacy. Interestingly, in this study PbD has been considered an innovative practice. On the one hand, proactive technological regulation, such as PbD, may stifle innovation because it requires anticipating any potential misuse and limits the developer[348]. On the other hand, new and creative solutions should be implemented in the market for applying PbD. Hence, the interpreter may evaluate PbD as an innovative approach for its own sake. Compromise is always necessary when designing with privacy in mind[349].

The last line of Table 2.1 indicates that PbD aims to implement user-centric technologies, but there might be increasing costs for access to digital technologies. PbD is pivotal for technological development, especially where specific data protection concerns arise[350]. Within PbD users should be considered upfront. They are supposed to have more control in the default settings. According to Cavoukian, user-centricity means designing for users and anticipating their privacy perceptions, needs, requirements, and default settings[351]. Generally, the design is user-centric when privacy settings are regulated towards users' needs. Engineering assigns a partially different meaning to the term user-centric. User-centred development (UCD) represents an engineering approach to software design. This is an

---

346 Quarta and Smorto, *op. cit.*, p. 30.

347 *See* Marc Van Lieshout. "Privacy and Innovation: From Disruption to Opportunities". In: *Data protection on the move*. Springer, 2016, pp. 195–212. ISBN: 9789401773768, pp. 204–206. The author uses the OECD's definition of innovation: something new to a firm, to the market and to the world.

348 *See* Hildebrandt and Tielemans, "Data protection by design and technology neutral law", p. 519. This study discusses the DPbD requirement in relation to the technological neutrality and its objectives (compensation, innovation and sustainability).

349 Everson, "Privacy by design: Taking ctrl of big data", p. 32.

350 *See* Romanou, "The necessity of the implementation of Privacy by Design in sectors where data protection concerns arise", pp. 104–109. The contexts analysed by the author are biometric technology, e-health and video surveillance.

351 Cavoukian, *Privacy by design: From rhetoric to reality*, p. 42.

interactive methodology that involves the user in the design process for giving input and feedback[352]. However, in the former sense, the interface and the default settings are of primary importance. In a prominent study, the French Data Protection Authority (CNIL) highlighted the need for regulation of design and architectures of choice for interfaces conceived in a broad sense[353]. According to the CNIL, interface design is crucial[354]. Indeed, interface design plays an important role in the effective enforcement of regulation[355]. User choices are directed through technological design and its interface. As a matter of fact, interfaces could use heuristics and biases to nudge users to act in certain ways[356]. A requirement for PbD can discourage companies from creating nudges. The legal concept of transparency is eminently user-centric, and is thus a central principle for achieving PbD[357]. User-centric default settings are also important because individuals usually stick with the existing default choice. This is the so-called "*status quo bias*"[358]. An appropriate default setting could improve this status. It is then arguable that in the future there might be increasing costs for access to digital technologies. Companies will invest in the development of compliant products and services and competition issues might impinge on the open sharing of solutions[359]. Therefore, goods and services may increase in price. However, policymakers could encourage companies

---

352 On this process *see* Michael DeBellis and Christine Haapala. "User-centric software engineering". In: *IEEE Expert* 10.1 (1995), pp. 34–41.

353 *See* CNIL Commission Nationale de l'Informatique et des Libertés. *La forme des choix. Données personnelles, design et frictions désirables. Cahier n. 6*. 2019, p. 39.

354 *See ibid.* The CNIL observes that "Le design des interfaces – entendu au sens large, depuis l'architecture du service jusqu'à la mise en forme des dispositifs d'information et de consentement – est bien un médium essentiel par lequel se joue la mise en application réelle du règlement et la conformité des services dans cet espace contraint".

355 According to CNIL, the regulation of architectures of choice will represent one of the most important areas of regulation in the next few years, even beyond mere data protection and privacy issues.

356 *See* Alessandro Acquisti et al. "Nudges for privacy and security: Understanding and assisting users' choices online". In: *ACM Computing Surveys (CSUR)* 50.3 (2017), pp. 1–41, p. 2. The authors explained in detail the phenomenon of nudge.

357 Commission Nationale de l'Informatique et des Libertés, *La forme des choix. Données personnelles, design et frictions désirables. Cahier n. 6*, p. 40.

358 *See* Hartzog and Stutzman, "Obscurity by design", p. 412.

359 *See* Wiese Schartum, "Making privacy by design operative", p. 173.

through public funding or other mechanisms to adopt appropriate measures and high standards, and effective policies[360].

The conflict between advantages and disadvantages shows that PbD is a promising principle with many significant concerns. It is challenging to find the right balance between edges and challenges. Despite all limitations, as Hartzog and Stutzman wrote, "it is clear that privacy by design is a useful way of addressing the privacy challenges that technology designers face"[361]. Stakeholders require tangible guidance on designing for privacy[362]. PbD could serve as a bridge between stakeholders – e.g. lawmakers, practitioners, engineers – and as a useful option for balancing competing interests[363].

To achieve these goals and move to implementation, it is necessary to internalise the approach and collaborate among disciplines. Regulation by design should be combined with procedural strategies. Hard and soft privacy should both be considered during implementation[364]. This is the approach of the European Union.

The EU legal framework tried to modernise the rules on data protection in 2016[365]. Indeed, a legal and enforceable obligation to adopt technical and organisational measures by design has been established with the new Regulation. The next section is dedicated to the analysis of this central legal requirement.

---

360 Reidenberg, "Lex informatica: The formulation of information policy rules through technology", p. 589.

361 These are the words of Hartzog and Stutzman, "Obscurity by design", p. 392.

362 Tamó-Larrieux, *Designing for privacy and its legal framework: data protection by design and default for the internet of things*, p. 197.

363 Klitou, *Privacy-invading technologies and privacy by design. Safeguarding Privacy, Liberty and Security in the 21st Century*, pp. 323, 328.

364 On the definition of hard privacy and soft privacy *see* Daniel Le Métayer. "Whom to Trust? Using Technology to Enforce Privacy". In: *Enforcing Privacy*. Springer, 2016, pp. 395–437. ISBN: 9783319250472, p. 397. The dissimilarity is related to a different trust assumption. The former identifies the strong approach which does not put trust in the data controller, while the latter trusts the data controller because it assumes that the data subject loses control over data and the controller deserves trust. *See* further Chapter 5, Section 5.3.

365 *See* Christopher Kuner et al. *The EU General Data Protection Regulation (GDPR): A Commentary*, pp. 5–43.

## 2.4 Deconstructing Article 25 of the GDPR

With its full applicability on 25 May 2018 the GDPR became the uniform and harmonised legal framework for regulating and protecting personal data in the EU. This section will analyse the legal basis for the principle of data protection by design.

The GDPR incorporates a general provision for data protection by design in the EU legal framework. This requirement and the provision on data protection by default are the most innovative and ambitious norms of the GDPR and they impose qualified duties on data controllers[366]. They represent an attempt to bring people and their rights back to the centre[367]. Basically, the Regulation states that in order to be able to demonstrate compliance with its norms the data controller shall adopt internal policies and implement measures which meet the principles of data protection by design and data protection by default[368].

Controllers, both private and public entities which process personal data, shall implement appropriate technical and organisational measures that achieve data protection principles in an effective manner and integrate the necessary safeguards into the processing at the time of the determination of the means for processing and at the time of the processing itself. They have to take into account some criteria, which are the state of the art, the cost of implementation and the nature, scope, context and purposes of processing, and the risks of varying likelihood and severity for rights and freedoms of natural persons posed by the same processing operations.

Therefore, technical and organisational measures are not defined by the law, but they must be appropriate and effective in relation to the data processing operations[369]. The controllers can demonstrate compliance

366 *See* Lee A Bygrave. "Data protection by design and by default: deciphering the EU's legislative requirements". In: *Oslo Law Review* 4.2 (2017), pp. 105–120, pp. 107, 114.

367 The expression is the translation of the words used by Panetta, *Circolazione e protezione dei dati personali, tra libertà e regole del mercato. Commentario al Regolamento UE n. 2016/679 (GDPR) e al novellato D.lgs. n. 196/2003 (Codice Privacy)*, p. 29.

368 *See* Recital 78 GDPR and Bincoletto, "A Data Protection by Design Model for Privacy Management in Electronic Health Records", p. 168.

369 *Ibid.*

through an approved certification mechanism. Article 25 is one of the best examples of the "accountability" approach[370].

Article 25(1), the legal basis for DPbD, reads as follows:

> "1. Taking into account the state of the art, the cost of implementation and the nature, scope, context and purposes of processing as well as the risks of varying likelihood and severity for rights and freedoms of natural persons posed by the processing, the controller shall, both at the time of the determination of the means for processing and at the time of the processing itself, implement appropriate technical and organisational measures, such as pseudonymisation, which are designed to implement data-protection principles, such as data minimisation, in an effective manner and to integrate the necessary safeguards into the processing in order to meet the requirements of this Regulation and protect the rights of data subjects".

Article 25(1) establishes the DPbD obligation that was initially defined in the Proposal of the GDPR in Article 23, later emended in the legislative process[371]. According to Bygrave, the differences between Article 25 and

370 *See* European Data Protection Supervisor, *Opinion 5/2018, Preliminary Opinion on privacy by design*. Previously, *see* also in European Data Protection Supervisor, *Opinion of the European Data Protection Supervisor on Promoting Trust in the Information Society by Fostering Data Protection and Privacy*, p. 19.

371 Art. 23, par. 1, Proposal *see* note no. 129, reads: "1. Having regard to the state of the art and the cost of implementation, the controller shall, both at the time of the determination of the means for processing and at the time of the processing itself, implement appropriate technical and organizational measures and procedures in such a way that the processing will meet the requirements of this Regulation and ensure the protection of the rights of the data subject. 2. The controller shall implement mechanisms for ensuring that, by default, only those personal data are processed which are necessary for each specific purpose of the processing and are especially not collected or retained beyond the minimum necessary for those purposes, both in terms of the amount of the data and the time of their storage. In particular, those mechanisms shall ensure that by default personal data are not made accessible to an indefinite number of individuals. 3. The Commission shall be empowered to adopt delegated acts in accordance with Article 86 for the purpose of specifying any further criteria and requirements for appropriate measures and mechanisms referred to in paragraph 1 and 2, in particular for data protection by design requirements applicable across sectors, products and services. 4. The Commission may lay down technical standards for the requirements laid down in paragraph 1 and 2. Those implementing acts shall be adopted in accordance with the examination procedure referred to in Article 87(2). According to Recital 130 of the Proposal, the European Commission should have the implementing power for defining

Article 23 of the Draft are the followings. Article 25 specifies two examples of measures and additional considerations to take into account, and includes the certification scheme[372]. As regards the factors, the increase in parameters completes the concrete evaluation of processing operations, but also complicates it by not explicitly providing for a hierarchy between them[373]. The additional important criteria are "the nature, scope, context and purposes of processing" and "the risks of varying likelihood and severity for rights and freedoms of natural persons posed by the processing". The timing is equal in both of the provisions, but Article 25 adds the reference to the data protection principles, which must be safeguarded in an "effective manner". Moreover, the European Parliament deleted the third and fourth paragraphs of Article 23 where the EU Commission would have been empowered to adopt: 1) delegated acts for specifying further criteria and requirements for appropriate measures and mechanisms, also applicable across sectors, products and services; 2) technical specifications for the requirements and standards form in relation to the responsibility of the controller. These delegated acts and standards would have been very useful for data controllers and practitioners in general[374]. Undoubtedly, these specifications would have been less binding, but they could have been modified frequently according to the technical state-of-the-art. This choice now leaves the floor to the market for standards and measures[375].

Article 25 has to be interpreted on a case-by-case basis because it contains a general provision with lots of criteria to be taken into account relating to specific data processing. The wording "taking into account" relates to a thought process that has to consider different elements and

---

standards forms in relation to the responsibility of the controller to data protection by design and by default".

372 *See* Bygrave, "Data protection by design and by default: deciphering the EU's legislative requirements", p. 114. This scholar also argued that Article 25 applies to processors, but the drafted version does not. As regards this aspect, *see* Section 2.4.1.

373 *See* Federico Sartore. "Privacy-by-design, l'introduzione del principio nel corpus del GDPR". in: *Circo- lazione e protezione dei dati personali, tra libertà e regole del mercato. Commentario al Regolamento UE n. 2016/679 (GDPR) e al novellato D.lgs. n. 196/2003 (Codice Privacy)*. Giuffrè Francis Lefebvre, 2019, pp. 295–307. ISBN: 9788828809692, p. 299.

374 *See* Bincoletto, *La privacy by design. Un'analisi comparata nell'era digitale*, p. 136.

375 *See ibid.*

multiple scenarios with specific risks[376]. The requirement does not provide a "one-size-fits-all" approach, but it leaves flexibility to data controllers[377]. Due to the generality and flexibility, this article constitutes the "architrave of the duties" of the data controller[378]. The provision contains an obligation to act, and in particular an obligation of results[379]. Actually, Article 25 follows Article 24, which is dedicated to the responsibility of the controller[380].

In general terms, it seems that the language of the text is vague and complex[381]. Commentators have argued that the provision offers little clarity and its legalese obscures the meaning[382]. However, this Article is a

---

376 *See* Lina Jasmontaite et al. "Data protection by design and by default: Framing guiding principles into legal obligations in the GDPR". In: *Eur. Data Prot. L. Rev.* 4 (2018), pp. 168–189, p. 177.

377 *See* Levin, "Privacy by Design by Regulation: The Case Study of Ontario", p. 152.

378 *See* Giuseppe D'Acquisto et al. *Intelligenza artificiale, protezione dei dati personali e regolazione*. Torino: G. Giappichelli Editore, 2018. ISBN: 9788892112575, p. 107.

379 *See* Jasmontaite et al., "Data protection by design and by default: Framing guiding principles into legal obligations in the GDPR", p. 173.

380 Article 24 GDPR: "1. Taking into account the nature, scope, context and purposes of processing as well as the risks of varying likelihood and severity for the rights and freedoms of natural persons, the controller shall implement appropriate technical and organisational measures to ensure and to be able to demonstrate that processing is performed in accordance with this Regulation. Those measures shall be reviewed and updated where necessary. 2. Where proportionate in relation to processing activities, the measures referred to in paragraph 1 shall include the implementation of appropriate data protection policies by the controller. 3. Adherence to approved codes of conduct as referred to in Article 40 or approved certification mechanisms as referred to in Article 42 may be used as an element by which to demonstrate compliance with the obligations of the controller". On Article 24 *see* Christopher Docksey. "Chapter IV Controller and Processor (Articles 24–43). Article 24. Responsibility of the controller". In: *The EU General Data Protection Regulation (GDPR): A Commentary*. Oxford University Press, 2020, pp. 555–570. ISBN: 9780198826491.

381 *See* Bygrave, "Data protection by design and by default: deciphering the EU's legislative requirements", p. 117.

382 *See* Ira S. Rubinstein and Nathaniel Good. "The trouble with Article 25 (and how to fix it): the future of data protection by design and default". In: *International Data Privacy Law* (2019), pp. 1–20, p. 2; Ari Ezra Waldman. "Data Protection by Design? A Critique of Article 25 of the GDPR". In: *Cornell Int'l L.J.* 53 (2020), pp. 147–167.

"conversation-starter" for all stakeholders because it seeks to increase the effectiveness of the protection set by the GDPR[383].

The requirement is technically neutral so as to prevent the risk of circumvention. In fact, Recital 15 GDPR explains that the protection of natural persons should be technologically neutral and should not depend on the techniques used in the processing[384]. The GDPR is neutral by design. A technologically neutral requirement avoids a circumventing case where a different technology is used than the one forbidden by the law[385]. Indeed, as noted above, the requirement will be applied "in the long term to various contexts independently from the technology progression"[386].

As far as this study is concerned, it is relevant to highlight that even Article 17 of Data Protection Directive 95/46/EC (DPD) referred to technical measures, but the emphasis was on security concerns[387]. The Directive did not contain an explicit requirement for privacy or data protection by

383 For the expression "conversation-starter" *see* Bygrave, "Data protection by design and by default: deciphering the EU's legislative requirements", p. 120. For the argument *see* European Data Protection Supervisor, *Opinion 5/2018, Preliminary Opinion on privacy by design*. This argument is pointed out in the executive summary of the Opinion.

384 *See* Recital 15 of the GDPR.

385 *See* Kamara, "Co-regulation in EU personal data protection: the case of technical standards and the privacy by design standardisation 'mandate'", p. 10.

386 Bincoletto, "A Data Protection by Design Model for Privacy Management in Electronic Health Records", p. 169.

387 *See* e.g. Bygrave, "Data protection by design and by default: deciphering the EU's legislative requirements", p. 108; and Tamò-Larrieux, *Designing for privacy and its legal framework: data protection by design and default for the internet of things*, p. 84. *See* Directive 95/46/EC of the European Parliament and of the Council of 24 October 1995 on the protection of individuals with regard to the processing of personal data and on the free movement of such data OJ L 281, 23.11.1995. This Directive is no longer in force because it has been repealed by the GDPR. The text of Article 17(1–2) DPD on "Security of processing" stated: "1. Member States shall provide that the controller must implement appropriate technical and organizational measures to protect personal data against accidental or unlawful destruction or accidental loss, alteration, unauthorized disclosure or access, in particular where the processing involves the transmission of data over a network, and against all other unlawful forms of processing. Having regard to the state of the art and the cost of their implementation, such measures shall ensure a level of security appropriate to the risks represented by the processing and the nature of the data to be protected. 2. The Member States shall provide that the controller must, where processing is carried out on his behalf, choose a processor providing sufficient guarantees in respect of the technical security measures and organizational measures governing the processing to be carried out, and must ensure compliance with those measures".

design, but the provision of Article 17 indirectly demands the implementation of measures that prevent unlawful data processing[388]. According to Recital 46 of DPD, the timing of these measures is the same as Article 25[389]. Nonetheless, this indirect provision did not attribute the powers of enforcing an implementation by design to the authorities[390]. Therefore, in 2010 the EDPS urged the Commission to propose a general provision on PbD and to promote this principle at the policy level[391].

It could be argued that Article 25 has other legal antecedents and that it is not the only provision in the EU framework on data protection by design[392].

---

388 *See* European Data Protection Supervisor, *Opinion of the European Data Protection Supervisor on Promoting Trust in the Information Society by Fostering Data Protection and Privacy*, p. 7; and Koops and Leenes, "Privacy regulation cannot be hardcoded. A critical comment on the 'privacy by design' provision in data-protection law", p. 164. According to Koops, Article 17 is a clear example of a system level requirement that aims to protect personal data against accidental or unlawful destruction or accidental loss.

389 Recital 46 DPD refers to "the time of the design of the processing system and the time of the processing itself".

390 *See* European Data Protection Supervisor, *Opinion of the European Data Protection Supervisor on Promoting Trust in the Information Society by Fostering Data Protection and Privacy*, p. 7.

391 *See* European Data Protection Supervisor, *op. cit.*, pp. 8, 21.

392 A long analysis on the legal antecedents is provided in Bincoletto, *La privacy by design. Un'analisi comparata nell'era digitale*, pp. 149–165. It is worth highlighting that the antecedents were mainly soft laws (e.g. recitals where the rationale of the norm is expressed), or communications of the EU Commission. As an example of a legal requirement, Regulation (EU) No 524/2013 of the European Parliament and of the Council of 21 May 2013 – on online dispute resolution for consumer disputes and amending Regulation (EC) No 2006/2004 and Directive 2009/22/EC (Regulation on consumer ODR) – establishes a privacy by design requirement for the EU Commission. Article 5(1) states that: "the Commission shall develop the ODR platform and be responsible for its operation, including all the translation functions necessary for the purpose of this Regulation, its maintenance, funding and data security. The ODR platform shall be user-friendly. The development, operation and maintenance of the ODR platform shall ensure that the privacy of its users is respected from the design stage ('privacy by design') and that the ODR platform is accessible and usable by all, including vulnerable users ('design for all'), as far as possible". This Regulation is in force. Moreover, as regards soft law, Regulation (EU) No 1024/2012 of the European Parliament and of the Council of 25 October 2012 – on administrative cooperation through the Internal Market Information System and repealing Commission Decision 2008/49/EC ('the IMI Regulation') – specifies at Recital 7 that the system follows the privacy-by-design principle of

As regards the other norms, it is first relevant to mention Directive 680/2016 and Regulation 2018/1745[393]. The former law was approved in the EU data protection reform package along with the GDPR[394]. The Data Protection Directive for Police and Criminal Justice Authorities sets the rules for "the processing of personal data by competent authorities for the purposes of the prevention, investigation, detection or prosecution of criminal offences or the execution of criminal penalties, and on the free movement of such data"[395]. According to Article 20, the Directive indicates that the Member States shall provide an obligation of DPbD for data controllers[396]. The latter represents the legislation applicable for data

---

offering a considerably higher level of protection and security. This Regulation is also in force.

393 All the EU-related provisions are also classified by Lee A. Bygrave. "Chapter IV Controller and Processor (Articles 24–43). Article 25. Data protection by design and by default". In: *The EU General Data Protection Regulation (GDPR): A Commentary*. Oxford University Press, 2020, pp. 571–581. ISBN: 9780198826491.

394 The Directive has applied since 5 May 2016 and the Member States had to incorporate it into their national law by 6 May 6 2018.

395 Directive (EU) 2016/680 of the European Parliament and of the Council of 27 April 2016 on the protection of natural persons with regard to the processing of personal data by competent authorities for the purposes of the prevention, investigation, detection or prosecution of criminal offences or the execution of criminal penalties, and on the free movement of such data, and repealing Council Framework Decision 2008/977/JHA, O.J. L. 119, 4.5.2016.

396 Article 20 Directive (EU) 2016/680: "Member States shall provide for the controller, taking into account the state of the art, the cost of implementation and the nature, scope, context and purposes of processing, as well as the risks of varying likelihood and severity for rights and freedoms of natural persons posed by the processing, both at the time of the determination of the means for processing and at the time of the processing itself, to implement appropriate technical and organisational measures, such as pseudonymisation, which are designed to implement data protection principles, such as data minimisation, in an effective manner and to integrate the necessary safeguards into the processing, in order to meet the requirements of this Directive and protect the rights of data subjects". Interestingly, this norm does not refer to the certification mechanism. The Eur-Lex portal lists the national transpositions that had to take into account Article 20 (*see* <eur-lex.europa.eu/>). As an example, the Italian act contains a specific provision on DPbD, borrowing the text of Article 25 GDPR almost entirely. *See* Article 16, D.Lgs. 18 maggio 2018, n. 51 Attuazione della direttiva (UE) 2016/680 del Parlamento europeo e del Consiglio, del 27 aprile 2016, relativa alla protezione delle persone fisiche con riguardo al trattamento dei dati personali da parte delle autorità competenti a fini di prevenzione, indagine, accertamento e perseguimento di reati o esecuzione di sanzioni penali, nonché alla libera circolazione di tali dati e che abroga la decisione quadro

processing carried out by EU institutions, bodies, offices and agencies[397]. Article 27 of Regulation 2018/1745 follows Article 25 GDPR entirely[398]. Moreover, according to the same Regulation, the processing of operational personal data in the area of freedom, security and justice applies the same DPbD rule[399].

In addition, Council Regulation 2017/1939 contains an article dedicated to DPbD. This Regulation implements enhanced cooperation on the establishment of the European Public Prosecutor's Office. The text of Article 67 is identical to the formulation of Article 25. Therefore, the office of EU Public Prosecutor shall implement appropriate technical and organisational measures designed to be compliant with the data protection principles and requirements by design[400].

Furthermore, in accordance with Regulation 2018/1240 establishing a European Travel Information and Authorisation System, the development of the EU central system shall follow the principle of data protection by design[401]. The need to build products, services, and processes in a

---

2008/977/GAI del Consiglio. 18G00080. G.U. Serie Generale n. 119 del 24–05–2018.

397 *See* Article 1(1), Regulation (EU) 2018/1725 of the European Parliament and of the Council of 23 October 2018 on the protection of natural persons with regard to the processing of personal data by the Union institutions, bodies, offices and agencies and on the free movement of such data, and repealing Regulation (EC) No 45/2001 and Decision No 1247/2002/EC. PE/31/2018/REV/1. O.J. L. 295, 21.11.2018.

398 Article 27 Regulation (EU) 2018/1725.

399 *See* Article 85 Regulation (EU) 2018/1725.

400 Article 67(1), Council Regulation (EU) 2017/1939 of 12 October 2017 implementing enhanced cooperation on the establishment of the European Public Prosecutor's Office ('the EPPO'). O.J. L. 283, 31.10.2017. *See* Hans-Holger Herrnfeld. "Article 67 Data protection by design and by default". In: *European Public Prosecutor's Office*. Nomos, 2021, pp. 513–514. ISBN: 9783848748846.

401 Article 73(3), Regulation (EU) 2018/1240 of the European Parliament and of the Council of 12 September 2018 establishing a European Travel Information and Authorisation System (ETIAS) and amending Regulations (EU) No 1077/2011, (EU) No 515/2014, (EU) 2016/399, (EU) 2016/1624 and (EU) 2017/2226. PE/21/2018/REV/1, O.J. L. 236, 19.9.2018: "(...) The development shall consist of the elaboration and implementation of the technical specifications, testing and overall project coordination. In this regard, the tasks of eu-LISA shall also be to: (a) perform a security risk assessment; (b) follow the principles of privacy by design and by default during the entire lifecycle of the development of ETIAS; and (c) conduct a security risk assessment regarding the interoperability of ETIAS with the EU information systems and Europol data referred to in Article 11".

way that follows the principles of security-by-design and privacy-by-design is stressed by the Cybersecurity Act[402]. This Regulation defines the objectives, tasks and organisational matters for ENISA and creates the framework for establishing and coordinating European cybersecurity certification schemes[403].

Finally, a provision of DPbD is expected in the future e-Privacy Regulation for cookies[404]. It is worth noting that the GDPR does not apply to processing of electronic communications services in public communication networks under Directive 2002/58/EC because this legislation is a *lex specialis*[405]. Therefore, if there is no obligation in the future regulation, Article 25 will not be applicable in this context[406].

All of these other provisions on DPbD have been established in order to create consistency within the EU legal system, where the GDPR is the main data protection law, and to modernise the framework[407].

---

402 Regulation (EU) 2019/881 of the European Parliament and of the Council of 17 April 2019 on ENISA (the European Union Agency for Cybersecurity) and on information and communications technology cybersecurity certification and repealing Regulation (EU) No 526/2013 (Cybersecurity Act). PE/86/2018/REV/1. O.J. L. 151, 7.6.2019. In particular, *see* Recitals 12 and 41.

403 *See* Article 1, Regulation 2019/881.

404 *See* Recital 23 of the Proposal for a Regulation of the European Parliament and of the Council concerning the respect for private life and the protection of personal data in electronic communications and repealing Directive 2002/58/EC (Regulation on Privacy and Electronic Communications), COM/2017/010 final – 2017/03 (COD). This Recital states: "the principles of data protection by design and by default were codified under Article 25 of Regulation (EU) 2016/679. Currently, the default settings for cookies are set in most current browsers to 'accept all cookies'. Therefore providers of software enabling the retrieval and presentation of information on the internet should have an obligation to configure the software so that it offers the option to prevent third parties from storing information on the terminal equipment; this is often presented as 'reject third party cookies' (...)". This text refers mostly to the default settings. However, the process for approval is pending and the act still in force is Directive 2002/58/EC of the European Parliament and of the Council of 12 July 2002 concerning the processing of personal data and the protection of privacy in the electronic communications sector (Directive on privacy and electronic communications), O.J. L. 201, 31.7.2002. On the e-privacy proposal *see* Elena Gil Gonzalez, Paul De Hert, and Vagelis Papakonstantinou. "The proposed ePrivacy Regulation: the Commission's drafts and the Parliament's drafts at a crossroads?" In: *Data Protection and Privacy. Data Protection and Democracy*. Hart Publishers, 2020, pp. 267–298. ISBN: 9781509932740.

405 *See* Article 95 GDPR on relationship with Directive 2002/58/EC.

406 Bincoletto, *La privacy by design. Un'analisi comparata nell'era digitale*, p. 169.

407 Bincoletto, *op. cit.*, pp. 172–173.

As previously mentioned, Article 25 GDPR contains an enforceable obligation. The GDPR sets a deterrence model providing administrative fines in case of infringement. It is possible, therefore, that a violation of this requirement is sanctioned[408]. In detail, a supervisory authority may impose fines pursuant to Article 82 and 83 GDPR[409]. According to paragraph 2(d) of Article 83, when deciding whether to impose an administrative fine and its amount, the DPA should take into account various criteria, including "the degree of responsibility of the controller or processor taking into account technical and organisational measures implemented by them pursuant to Articles 25" (and 32)[410]. Moreover, an infringement of the obligation of DPbD could be sanctioned with a fine of up to 10 million euro, or in the case of an undertaking, up to 2 % of the total worldwide annual turnover of the previous financial year, whichever is higher[411]. In 2018, the EDPS committed to supporting coordinated and effective enforcement of Article 25 in cooperation with the EDPB[412].

Apart from the risk of incurring in sanctions, there are no incentives for design per se[413]. However, the administrative fines could be very high for controllers, especially in the case of SMEs.

The concept of DPbD in the GDPR is based on the assumption that "the conditions for data processing are fundamentally being set by the software and hardware" used for the operations[414]. In order to understand how to

---

408 As an example, in 2020 the Italian DPA fined Vodafone Italia S.p.A. 12,251,601 euro for non-compliance with general data protection principles and some requirements of the GDPR, including Article 25. In particular, the company did not implement appropriate measures and mechanisms to control data processing operations and ensure the continuous compliance of the telemarketing activities carried out during the collection of personal data. *See* further on this decision Giorgia Bincoletto. "Italy – Italian DPA Against Vodafone: History of a € 12 million Fine". In: *Eur. Data Prot. L. Rev.* 6 (4 2020), pp. 554–559; and Chapter 6, Section 6.5.

409 *See* also Chapter 6, Section 6.5.

410 Article 83(2)(d) GDPR.

411 Article 83(4)(a) GDPR.

412 *See* European Data Protection Supervisor, *Opinion 5/2018, Preliminary Opinion on privacy by design*, p. 22. Additionally, the authority committed to providing guidance on the appropriate implementation of the principle.

413 *See* the criticism in Bygrave, "Hardwiring privacy", p. 771. On the enforcement of the proposal *see* Paul De Hert. "The EU data protection reform and the (forgotten) use of criminal sanctions". In: *International Data Privacy Law* 4.4 (2014), pp. 262–268.

414 *See* Voigt and Von dem Bussche, *The EU General Data Protection Regulation (GDPR). A Practical Guide*, p. 62.

apply and comply with this complex norm, it is necessary to investigate each part of the text in detail. For the explanation and investigation of the provision, the rule of the five *W-h* questions will be applied. The following subsection 2.4.1 provides the answer to the question "who?" identifying the subjects of the norm, while subsections from 2.4.2 to 2.4.6 deal with the complexity of the "what?". The answers to "when?" and "where?" are expressed in subsection 2.4.7. The remaining subsection 2.4.8 addresses the rationales and the "why?". In the end, the data protection by default requirement will be introduced in order to complete the investigation of Article 25 in section 2.4.9.

### 2.4.1 Identifying the subjects

Since Article 25 contains a legal and fully enforceable obligation, it is necessary to investigate whom shall comply with this rule. Following the GDPR definitions and requirements, the subjects involved are identified as follows.

Firstly, Article 25 explicitly refers solely to the controller. The term "data controller" refers to a "natural or legal person, public authority, agency or other body" which determines the purposes and means of the data processing[415]. This processing identifies "any operation or set of operations" that is performed on personal data[416]. When determining the purposes and means, the controller can act alone or jointly with others. If there are joint controllers, they will determine their respective responsibilities in a transparent manner through an arrangement, unless the law prescribes the conditions for them[417]. Moreover, the GDPR specifies that where the purposes and means of the data processing are determined by the EU or a Member State, the controller, or the specific criteria for its nomination,

415 *See* the definition in Article 4(7) GDPR. On the complexity of defining the data controller in practice and of distinguishing this subject from the processor, *see* Alessandro Mantelero. "Gli autori del trattamento dati: titolare e responsabile". In: *Giurispudenza Italiana* 171.12 (2019), pp. 2799–2805.

416 *See* the definition in Article 4(2) GDPR: "processing means any operation or set of operations which is performed on personal data or on sets of personal data, whether or not by automated means, such as collection, recording, organisation, structuring, storage, adaptation or alteration, retrieval, consultation, use, disclosure by transmission, dissemination or otherwise making available, alignment or combination, restriction, erasure or destruction".

417 *See* Article 26 GDPR.

may be provided for by Union or Member State law[418]. Each controller is fully liable for the processing under joint controllership[419].

It is worth mentioning the material and territorial scopes of the GDPR in order to restrict the data controllers that shall adopt DPbD rule.

According to the material scope of the GDPR, this regulation does not apply to data processing in the course of an activity which falls outside the scope of EU law (e.g. Member States' national security)[420]. Member States' activities on border checks, asylum and immigration are out of the scope of the regulation, too[421]. If a natural person processes data in the course of a purely personal or household activity, he or she is not considered a data controller subjected to the GDPR[422]. As noted above, Directive 2016/680 and its national implementations apply for law enforcement purposes. Finally, as previously mentioned, for data processing carried out by EU institution, bodies, offices and agencies, Regulation 2018/1745 applies. Since this Regulation contains an equal requirement, all the analysis of Article 25 is still pertinent for this material scope and the authorities, agencies and bodies included.

As regards the territorial scope, the GDPR applies to "the processing of personal data in the context of the activities of an establishment of a controller in the EU", regardless of whether the processing takes place there[423]. If the controller is not established in the EU, but the personal

---

418 *See* Article 4(7) GDPR.

419 *See* Article 82(4) GDPR.

420 *See* Article 2(a) GDPR. In order to understand the scope, it is necessary to read the Treaty on European Union and the Treaty on the Functioning of the European Union. *See* the Consolidated version, Official Journal C. 326, 26/10/2012, p. 1–390. There are no substantial differences with the Data Protection Directive.

421 *See* Article 2(b) GDPR.

422 *See* Article 2(c) GDPR. This rule represents the so-called "house-holder" exception.

423 *See* Article 3(1) GDPR. *See* Dan, Jerker B. Svantesson. "Chapter I General Provisions (Articles 1–4). Article 3. Territorial scope". In: *The EU General Data Protection Regulation (GDPR): A Commentary*. Oxford University Press, 2020, pp. 74–99. ISBN: 9780198826491; Christopher, Kuner. *Territorial Scope and Data Transfer Rules in the GDPR: Realising the EU's Ambition of Borderless Data Protection*. University of Cambridge Faculty of Law Research Paper No. 20/2021. On the notion of establishment *see* the Court of Justice case law. In particular, *see* the cases C-230/14 *Weltimmo s.r.o. v Nemzeti Adatvédelmi és Információszabadság Hatóság*, which ruled: "Article 4(1)(a) of Directive 95/46/EC of the European Parliament and of the Council of 24 October 1995 on the protection of individuals with regard to the processing of personal data and on the free movement

data relate to data subjects who are in the EU, the GDPR applies when the processing activities are related either to the offering of goods or services or to the monitoring of individuals' behaviour (e.g. targeting or profiling), as far as their actions takes place within the EU[424]. The last scenario where the GDPR applies is the processing carried out by a controller who is not established in the EU, but in a place where a Member State's law applies by virtue of public international law[425].

Data controllers that process personal data in accordance with the material and territorial scopes of the GDPR shall comply with the DPbD obligation and are accountable and liable for it. Despite the explicit text of Article 25, the data controller is not the only subject that has to be mentioned here. Another role that is central for data processing is the processor.

According to the GDPR's definitions, the processor is "a natural or legal person, public authority, agency or other body" which processes personal

---

of such data must be interpreted as permitting the application of the law on the protection of personal data of a Member State other than the Member State in which the controller with respect to the processing of those data is registered, in so far as that controller exercises, through stable arrangements in the territory of that Member State, a real and effective activity – even a minimal one – in the context of which that processing is carried out. In order to ascertain, in circumstances such as those at issue in the main proceedings, whether that is the case, the referring court may, in particular, take account of the fact (i) that the activity of the controller in respect of that processing, in the context of which that processing takes place, consists of the running of property dealing websites concerning properties situated in the territory of that Member State and written in that Member State's language and that it is, as a consequence, mainly or entirely directed at that Member State, and (ii) that that controller has a representative in that Member State, who is responsible for recovering the debts resulting from that activity and for representing the controller in the administrative and judicial proceedings relating to the processing of the data concerned"; and C-131/12 *Google Spain SL and Google Inc. v. Agencia Española de Protección de Datos and Mario Costeja González*, which ruled: "Article 4(1)(a) of Directive 95/46 is to be interpreted as meaning that processing of personal data is carried out in the context of the activities of an establishment of the controller on the territory of a Member State, within the meaning of that provision, when the operator of a search engine sets up in a Member State a branch or subsidiary which is intended to promote and sell advertising space offered by that engine and which orientates its activity towards the inhabitants of that Member State". *See* also EDPB European Data Protection Board. *Guidelines 3/2018 on the territorial scope of the GDPR (Article 3)*. European Data Protection Board, 2019.

424 *See* Article 3(2)(a) – (b) GDPR.

425 *See* Article 3(2)(a) – b) GDPR.

data “on behalf of the controller”[426]. The GDPR imposes constraints on the role of the processor. Data controllers must use trustworthy processors that provide sufficient guarantees to meet the requirement of the GDPR[427]. Therefore, processors (e.g. sub-contractors or service providers) shall implement appropriate technical and organisational measures in order to ensure that the controller complies with Article 25. Moreover, processors shall implement appropriate technical and organisational measures for securing processing in accordance with Article 32 GDPR[428].

A contract between controller and processor will govern the processing delegated by the former to the latter[429]. Even though the DPbD requirement does not refer to processors, they have to collaborate with the controllers and assist them in fulfilling the DPbD obligation in a transparent manner. The contract can take into account DPbD in one or more clauses so as to ensure that the processor considers the state of the art, the cost of implementation and the characteristics of the delegated processing, and to show that the measures have been implemented. Contractual liability protects the controller. Nonetheless, the controller will remain liable for violation of the legal requirement[430]. Despite calls to extend the obligation during the legislative process, it pertains only to data controller[431].

As regards the recipient and the third party, it seems that when they have access to personal data they do not have to fulfil the GDPR’s obligation because they do not define the conditions of the processing[432].

---

426 *See* Article 4(8) GDPR.

427 Indeed, Article 28(1) GDPR states: “Where processing is to be carried out on behalf of a controller, the controller shall use only processors providing sufficient guarantees to implement appropriate technical and organisational measures in such a manner that processing will meet the requirements of this Regulation and ensure the protection of the rights of the data subject”.

428 *See* Article 28(3)(c) and (f) GDPR.

429 Article 28(3) GDPR reads as follows: “Processing by a processor shall be governed by a contract or other legal act under Union or Member State law, that is binding on the processor with regard to the controller and that sets out the subject-matter and duration of the processing, the nature and purpose of the processing, the type of personal data and categories of data subjects and the obligations and rights of the controller (...)”.

430 On liability issues *see* further Chapter 6, Section 6.5.

431 *See* Jasmontaite et al., “Data protection by design and by default: Framing guiding principles into legal obligations in the GDPR”, p. 173.

432 *See* the definition of these subjects in Article 4(9) and (10) GDPR. The recipient is any person to whom personal data is disclosed, whether a third party or not. This last subject is a person other than the other subjects who is authorised to process personal data under the direct authority of the controller or processor.

Developers, programmers and engineers are not included in the legal provision. The disconnection between controllers and engineers questions the efficiency of the DPbD implementation strategy[433]. The EDPS wrote that the missed reference to developers is a serious limitation of the obligation[434].

Despite this obvious consideration, Recital 78 of the GDPR is a good tool for the interpreter because it connects Article 25 with the concept of accountability, expanding the concept of DPbD in the GDPR[435]. Recitals do not impose a legal obligation. However, Recital 78 explicitly refers to developers:

> "When developing, designing, selecting and using applications, services and products that are based on the processing of personal data or process personal data to fulfil their task, producers of the products, services and applications should be encouraged to take into account the right to data protection when developing and designing such products, services and applications and, with due regard to the state of the art, to make sure that controllers and processors are able to fulfil their data protection obligations".

Producers of products, services and applications do not have a direct obligation under GDPR, but they could help controllers comply with DPbD requirements[436]. So, during the development and design process developers are encouraged to keep DPbD in mind, especially as data minimisation[437]. Developers should consider the application of DPbD because "data

433 *See* the comment on the EU strategy in Bygrave, "Hardwiring privacy", p. 771.

434 *See* European Data Protection Supervisor, *Opinion 5/2018, Preliminary Opinion on privacy by design*, p. 8.

435 *See* e.g. Panetta, *Circolazione e protezione dei dati personali, tra libertà e regole del mercato. Commentario al Regolamento UE n. 2016/679 (GDPR) e al novellato D.lgs. n. 196/2003 (Codice Privacy)*, p. 29; Sartore, "Privacy-by-design, l'introduzione del principio nel corpus del GDPR", p. 301.

436 *See* Marit Hansen et al. *Recommendations on shaping technology according to GDPR provision. Exploring the notion of data protection by default.* European Union Agency for Network and Information Security, 2018, p. 5; Simone Calzolaio. "*Privacy by design*. Principi, dinamiche, ambizioni del nuovo Reg. Ue 2016/679". In: *Federalismi.it* 24 (2017), pp. 1–21. Bygrave argued that the encouragement set by Recital 78 is a "less stringent requirement". *See* Bygrave, "Chapter IV Controller and Processor (Articles 24–43). Article 25. Data protection by design and by default", p. 578.

437 Voigt and Von dem Bussche, *The EU General Data Protection Regulation (GDPR). A Practical Guide*, p. 62.

controllers might select products and services on the basis of the adopted design choices"[438]. Thus, the market might be shaped in a "privacy-friendly direction"[439].

In November 2019 the European Data Protection Board released "Guidelines 4/2019 on Article 25 Data Protection by Design and by Default" to provide further guidance on that specific obligation prescribed by the GDPR[440]. After public consultation, the EDPB adopted the final version of the Guidelines on 20 October 2020[441]. These Guidelines are addressed to data controllers, but "processors and producers" are indicated as potential addressees and "key enablers" for data protection by design and by default[442]. According to the authority, producers can cooperate with the controller to achieve the implementation of the measures since design choices are inevitably influenced by developers and their expertise[443]. As a result, they can obtain a competitive advantage in the market[444].

---

438 Bincoletto, "A Data Protection by Design Model for Privacy Management in Electronic Health Records", p. 169.

439 Bygrave, "Chapter IV Controller and Processor (Articles 24–43). Article 25. Data protection by design and by default", p. 578.

440 EDPB European Data Protection Board. *Guidelines 4/2019 on Article 25 Data Protection by Design and by Default.* 13 November 2019. Version for public consultation. European Data Protection Board, 2019.

441 EDPB European Data Protection Board. *Guidelines 4/2019 on Article 25 Data Protection by Design and by Default.* 20 October 2020. Version 2.0. European Data Protection Board, 2020. On this version *see* the report Giorgia Bincoletto. "European Union – EDPB Guidelines 4/2019 on Data Protection by Design and by Default". In: *Eur. Data Prot. L. Rev.* 6 (4 2020), pp. 574–579.

442 As regards this aspect of the EDPB's Guidelines 4/2019 version 1, the authority stated that "other actors, such as processors and technology providers, who are not directly addressed in Article 25, may also find these Guidelines useful in creating GDPR-compliant products and services that enable controllers to fulfil their data protection obligations". In the second version, the EDPB specified that: "The EDPB provides recommendations on how controllers, processors and producers can cooperate to achieve DPbDD. It encourages the controllers in industry, processors, and producers to use DPbDD as a means to achieve a competitive advantage when marketing their products towards controllers and data subjects".

443 European Data Protection Board, *Guidelines 4/2019 on Article 25 Data Protection by Design and by Default*, points 1, 94, 95 and 96. *See* also Bincoletto, "European Union – EDPB Guidelines 4/2019 on Data Protection by Design and by Default", p. 575.

444 European Data Protection Board, *Guidelines 4/2019 on Article 25 Data Protection by Design and by Default*, point 9.

The EDPB provided a step-by-step guidance for data controllers to comply with Article 25 GDPR. The authority interpreted the requirements of DPbD and DPbDf, investigated how data protection principles and rights could be implemented effectively, and listed key design and default elements with several concrete examples on data processing operations[445]. With this guidance, the text of Article 25 seems less vague than before. However, the EDPB included few notes on appropriate engineering methodologies or suitable technical approaches. In fact, despite the encouragement for processors and producers on cooperating for the implementation of Article 25, it can be argued that the language and the meaning of the document are more understandable by legal experts than by other practitioners[446].

The EDPB defines the core obligation of Article 25 as "the implementation of appropriate measures and necessary safeguards that provide effective implementation of the data protection principles and, consequentially, data subjects' rights and freedoms by design and by default"[447]. In order to effectively implement principles and rights, technical and organisational measures shall be implemented. In the next subsections the core of the provision will be analysed starting from the measures.

### 2.4.2 Defining technical and organisational measures

As noted above, the Data protection Directive already called for the implementation of measures[448]. The wording "technical and organisational measures" appears 18 times in the GDPR, in Chapter IV on controller and processor especially.

445 Bincoletto, "European Union – EDPB Guidelines 4/2019 on Data Protection by Design and by Default", p. 575.

446 Bincoletto, *op. cit.*, p. 579.

447 European Data Protection Board, *Guidelines 4/2019 on Article 25 Data Protection by Design and by Default*, p. 4. In the first version of the Guidelines the EDPB defined the core obligation as "the effective implementation of the data protection principles and data subjects' rights and freedoms by design and by default". *See* European Data Protection Board, *Guidelines 4/2019 on Article 25 Data Protection by Design and by Default*.

448 Recital 46, Article 17 Directive 95/46/EC. *See* Article 29 Working Party, Police, and Justice, *The Future of Privacy: Joint Contribution to the Consultation of the European Commission on the Legal Framework for the Fundamental Right to Protection of Personal Data*, p. 13.

According to Recital 78 GDPR, these measures are necessary for the protection of the rights and freedoms of natural persons with regard to the processing of personal data in order to ensure that the requirements of the GDPR are met[449]. The measures of DPbD are a sub-category of all the measures that the controller shall implement, and they particularly aim to demonstrate compliance with the Regulation[450].

The Recital mentioned above specifies that such measures could consist in[451]:

> "minimising the processing of personal data, pseudonymising personal data as soon as possible, transparency with regard to the functions and processing of personal data, enabling the data subject to monitor the data processing, enabling the controller to create and improve security features".

Therefore, the list of the possible measures is technologically neutral and open. The same strategy is used in the text of Article 25, where the "appropriate technical and organisational measures" are undefined. Commentators point out that the list remains very high-level and fails to give guidance[452].

As a matter of fact, the term "measure" should be understood broadly as any method or means that can be employed[453]. Actually, the legal requirement does not define a specific level of sophistication but indicates that the measures shall be appropriate for implementing data protection principles effectively[454]. Adopted and implemented measures should be documented and described in detail. It is not an explicit requirement.

---

449 Recital 78 GDPR.

450 *Ibid.*

451 *Ibid.*

452 *See* Rubinstein and Good, "The trouble with Article 25 (and how to fix it): the future of data protection by design and default", pp. 5–6.

453 *See* European Data Protection Board, *Guidelines 4/2019 on Article 25 Data Protection by Design and by Default*, point 8.

454 *See* European Data Protection Board, *op. cit.*, point 9. According to the authority, "examples that may be suitable, depending on the context and risks associated with the processing in question" include: "pseudonymization of personal data; storing personal data available in a structured, commonly machine readable format; enabling data subjects to intervene in the processing; providing information about the storage of personal data; having malware detection systems; training employees about basic "cyber hygiene"; establishing privacy and information security management systems, obligating processors contractually to implement specific data minimisation practices".

Nonetheless, in order to demonstrate compliance with the accountability principle the controller shall support the implementation with documents and reports.

Measures can be organisational or technical. These two categories and levels connect DPbD with the typical global PbD approach, which usually requires both policy strategies and technical solutions. Organisational measures are focused on policy and management levels, while technical measures are the manifestation of a technical design. It is worth mentioning that PETs, as specific technical solutions, can be used for assisting the DPbD implementation.

The explicit mention in Article 25 identifies pseudonymisation as an appropriate measure. However, it should be pointed out that the data controller always has to take into account all the various criteria expressed in the first part of the provision. If there is no need, pseudonymisation is not necessary. As mentioned, Recital 78 proposes minimisation, measures to enhance transparency and control, and measures to create and improve security during processing.

The example of pseudonymisation suggests a starting point for implementation that was not present in the draft of the Regulation. This specification does not preclude any other measure[455]. Pseudonymisation may just be a core strategy for DPbD[456]. It should be promoted as a DPbD measure by the authorities[457]. The GDPR uses this term to identify the processing of personal data where the personal data can "no longer be attributed to a specific data subject without the use of additional information", which is "kept separately" and is subject to technical and organisational measures in order to ensure that the personal data are not attributed to an identified or identifiable natural person[458]. So, pseudonymisation is strictly related to the identifiers of natural persons and pseudonymised data is still personal data. The identifier is the identifying information of

---

455 *See* Recital 28 GDPR.

456 *See* ENISA European Union Agency for Network & Information Security. *Recommendations on shaping technology according to GDPR provision. An overview on data pseudonymisation*. European Union Agency for Network and Information Security, 2018, p. 4.

457 *See ibid.* According to the agency, DPAs and EDPB should promote the strategy and provide guidance for controllers.

458 Article 4(5) GDPR. *See* also Luca Tosoni. "Chapter I General principles (Articles 1–4). Article 4(5). Pseudonymisation". In: *The EU General Data Protection Regulation (GDPR): A Commentary*. Oxford University Press, 2020, pp. 132–137. ISBN: 9780198826491.

the data subject. It can be a single piece of information or more complex data. The pseudonym is the information that substitutes that identifier after the pseudonymisation process. The additional information refers to the association between the mentioned identifier and the pseudonym. With the additional information, the pseudonym can be re-identified[459]. Pseudonymisation focuses on hiding the identifier[460].

ENISA defined pseudonymisation as follows[461]:

> "In broad terms, pseudonymisation refers to the process of de-associating a data subject's identity from the personal data being processed for that data subject. Typically, such a process may be performed by replacing one or more personal identifiers, i.e. pieces of information that can allow identification (such as e.g. name, email address, social security number, etc.), relating to a data subject with the so-called pseudonyms, such as a randomly generated values".

According to the Agency, the definition of the GDPR goes beyond a purely technical definition. In particular, the GDPR covers the protection of indirect identifiers relating to a data subject and additional information, too[462]. The main benefit of using pseudonymisation is hiding the identity of the data subject to any third party[463]. Moreover, if the data controller does not need the identifier for the processing, this subject can process only pseudonymised data, ensuring data protection by design[464]. The result of the application of this measure is the reduction of data-protection risks[465]. Indeed, pseudonymisation technically reduces the level of this risk[466].

---

459 For this explanation, *see* European Union Agency for Network & Information Security, *Recommendations on shaping technology according to GDPR provisions. An overview on data pseudonymisation*, p. 9.

460 *See* European Union Agency for Network & Information Security, *op. cit.*, p. 17. By contrast, encryption ensures that the whole dataset of identifiers is unintelligible.

461 *See* European Union Agency for Network & Information Security, *op. cit.*, p. 9.

462 *See ibid.*

463 *See* European Union Agency for Network & Information Security, *op. cit.*, p. 15.

464 *See ibid.*

465 *See* Recital 28 GDPR.

466 As regards the techniques for pseudonymisation and DPbD, *see* ENISA European Union Agency for Network & Information Security. *Recommendations on shaping technology according to GDPR provisions. Pseudonymisation techniques and best practices*. European Union Agency for Network and Information Security, 2019; Giuseppe D'Acquisto and Maurizio Naldi. *Big data e privacy by design. Anonimizzazione Pseudonimizzazione Sicurezza*. Torino: G. Giappichelli Editore, 2017. ISBN: 9788892106291, pp. 37–40. 117; another study that connects the

The next subsections investigate the established text on conditions of Article 25 that have to be taken into account when selecting and implementing technical and organisational measures. Balancing all the criteria is challenging. Therefore, the following subsections will provide some guidance on defining the criteria and explaining how they relate to one another.

### 2.4.3 Understanding the state of the art and balancing the costs of implementation

Article 25 defines the criteria that have to be balanced in applying the legal requirement. The first condition is the state of the art, while the second is the cost of implementation.

The expression *state of the art* is used in Article 25 and 32 of the GDPR[467]. However, the Regulation does not provide a definition of this criterion. In the legal domain the state of the art is frequently used in product liability and safety rules, environmental protection and IP and patent law, and their respective case law[468].

---

two concepts is D'Acquisto et al., *Intelligenza artificiale, protezione dei dati personali e regolazione*, pp. 116–119. Anonymisation guarantees more protection, but it is not always feasible, and scholars have proven that de-anonymisation is a concrete and high risk. The GDPR does not concern anonymous data in accordance with Recital 26. However, anonymised data differs from anonymous data because the former is personal data that has been anonymised after a process, while the latter is data that cannot be attributed to a natural person theoretically. Before the process of anonymisation, and until the end, the GDPR applies. On anonymisation techniques, *see* WP29 Article 29 Working Party. *Opinion 05/2014 on Anonymisation Techniques*. WP216 14/en, 2014. The Opinion refers to Directive 95/46/CE, but its general considerations are still applicable. *See* also Tamó-Larrieux, *Designing for privacy and its legal framework: data protection by design and default for the internet of things*, pp. 123–130; Stefano Torregiani. "Il dato non personale alla luce del Regolamento (UE) 2018/1807: tra anonimizzazione, *ownership* e *Data by Design*". In: *Federalismi.it* 18 (2020), pp. 317–341, pp. 322–326.

467 *See* also Recitals 78 and 83.

468 As an example, *see* some Court of Justice case law at <curia.europa.eu>: Case C-121/17 Teva UK and Case C-190/16 Werner Fries. In particular, in the Opinion of the Advocate General on case C-190/16 highlightes that the state of the art includes the "best practices, and scientific and technical progress in the field of (...)". In the legal domain the expression does not always have the same meaning. As regards patent law, according to paragraph 1 of Article 54 of the European Patent Convention "an invention shall be considered to be new if it

The first criterion is objective and dynamic. It refers to the existing scientific knowledge in a specific field. The state of the art includes both organisational and technical solutions.

In 2020 the German association TeleTrusT released the Guidelines "State of the Art" on IT security in cooperation with ENISA[469]. These Guidelines mention both Article 25 and 32 of the GDPR. This document specifies that the definition of state of the art shall be distinguished from the "generally accepted rules of technology" and the "existing scientific knowledge and research". The distinction is borrowed from the German case law[470]. In the middle of these two criteria there is the state of the art which can be described as "the procedures, equipment or operating methods available in the trade in goods and services for which the application thereof is most effective in achieving the respective legal protection objectives"[471]. A practical evaluation method can concretely determine the state of the art[472]. It can be suggested that this definition is useful for understanding what the state of the art in Article 25 is. Indeed, the EDPB quoted this approach in the Guidelines on DPbD[473].

In sum, the state of the art criterion requires taking into account what is currently available in the market for technical and organisational measures in order to achieve the effective implementation of the data protection principles. Data controllers should stay up to date on technological progress; and standards, codes of conduct and certification mechanisms could indicate the state of the art within a specific field[474]. To be com-

---

does not form part of the state of the art". The expression here refers to what generally exists earlier, including filed applications.

469 *See* TeleTrusT IT Security Association Germany. *Guidelines "State of the Art"*. TeleTrusT and ENISA, 2020.

470 TeleTrusT reported that the distinction follows the Federal Constitutional Court's Kalkar decision of 1978 (BVerfGE, 49, 89 – 135 f).

471 IT Security Association Germany, *Guidelines "State of the Art"*, p. 11. The short definition is: "a subject's best performance available on the market to achieve an object", where the "subject is the IT security measure" and "the object is the statutory IT security objective".

472 *See* IT Security Association Germany, *op. cit.*, p. 12. The mentioned Guidelines described the method for evaluating the state of the art. This method is based on average scores of two conditions. The x-axis shows the degree of proof in practice, while the y-axis shows the degree of recognition. They should both be measurable.

473 European Data Protection Board, *Guidelines 4/2019 on Article 25 Data Protection by Design and by Default*, p. 8.

474 European Data Protection Board, *op. cit.*, 8, point 19.

pliant with this dynamic requirement, the criterion should be evaluated continuously on the basis of technological advancements[475].

Secondly, the controller shall take into account the cost of implementation while estimating the alternative measures. Therefore, the cost of the measures existing in the state of the art is a subjective criterion. This criterion has been defined as economic feasibility: the legal requirement does not mandate unreasonably costly measures to the data controller[476]. So, the cost of DPbD should be feasible for the controller. The data controller can choose the measures available in the market at a reasonable price[477].

In general, costs are all the expenses that the controller has to bear from planning to implementation. It is arguable that these expenses are appropriate if suited to the level of protection required[478]. Therefore, during the selection of the measures what matters is if they adequately protect personal data. In the market there are several proprietary tools and solutions for protecting personal data. The costs are set by the private entities that have developed these tools. It is possible that unreasonably high costs are set. As a result, some controllers probably cannot afford such expense.

The EDPB explained that time, business costs and human resources should be taken into account when planning the cost of implementation. Cost is more than money[479]. Article 25 refers to the cost of implementing data protection principles during processing. Data controllers should plan and pay the costs that are necessary for this implementation[480]. The authority specified that inability to bear the costs does not excuse liability, but effective implementation must not necessarily lead to higher costs[481].

Both criteria are fundamental for planning DPbD measures. The condition of the state of the art encourages the controller to stay up-to-date, but the cost criterion allows a cost-benefit analysis for estimating the alternatives.

---

475 European Data Protection Board, *op. cit.*, 8, point 20. *See* also Bincoletto, "European Union – EDPB Guidelines 4/2019 on Data Protection by Design and by Default", p. 577.

476 Hildebrandt and Tielemans, "Data protection by design and technology neutral law", p. 517.

477 *See* Tamó-Larrieux, *Designing for privacy and its legal framework: data protection by design and default for the internet of things*, p. 184.

478 *See* Tamó-Larrieux, *op. cit.*

479 *See* European Data Protection Board, *Guidelines 4/2019 on Article 25 Data Protection by Design and by Default*, 9, point 23.

480 European Data Protection Board, *op. cit.*, p. 9.

481 *Ibid.*

Another important and explicit criterion of Article 25 that tailors the measures to the controller are the specifics of processing, i.e., its nature, scope, context and purposes. It will be analysed in the following subsection.

### 2.4.4 Evaluating the nature, scope, context and purposes of data processing

Article 25 requires evaluating and taking into account the "nature, scope, context and purposes" of processing. These contextual factors represent the characteristics of data processing operations[482]. They are subjective conditions. According to Bygrave, these factors may be largely determined by the controller during the DPIA[483].

Firstly, nature is actually the inherent characteristics of the processing[484]. It can be argued that the nature is the type of activity or operation of which the processing consists (e.g. collection, storage, disclosure)[485]. Moreover, the nature relates to the way the processing is carried out (e.g. automated means)[486]. Different operations need different safeguards. As an example, the controller should implement specific technical and organisational measures during the disclosure by transmission and others for the storage of personal data.

---

482 European Data Protection Board, *op. cit.*, 9, point 28.

483 Bygrave, "Chapter IV Controller and Processor (Articles 24–43). Article 25. Data protection by design and by default", p. 576.

484 European Data Protection Board, *Guidelines 4/2019 on Article 25 Data Protection by Design and by Default*, 9, point 28.

485 On the possible activities, *see* the open list in Article 4(2) GDPR reported *supra* note no.416.

486 *See* the interesting questions that the controller can raise in Jasmontaite et al., "Data protection by design and by default: Framing guiding principles into legal obligations in the GDPR", p. 179: "what means are used for the processing operation (e.g., automated)? Is the processing going to result in profiling of individuals that will allow evaluating the personal aspects relating to an individual whose data are being processed? Are there any third parties that are included in the processing? Is the processing carried out by a cloud-based infrastructure? Does the processing include aggregation of data sets? Is the processing activity performed outside the EU?".

Secondly, the scope of processing relates to its size and range[487]. Generally, the GDPR gives importance to the size and scale of processing[488]. The controller should choose the measures taking into account the range of personal data being handled, meaning how many data subjects are there and who are they, and which types of data are involved[489].

Thirdly, context refers to the circumstances of processing[490]. With this criterion the controller takes into account where processing takes place. This is also a metaphorical setting. The word refers to the situation and set of circumstances that constitute processing.

Lastly, purpose is one of the main concepts of data protection law. It refers to the aim of the processing operation[491]. According to Article 5(19)(b) GDPR, the purpose should be specified, explicit, legitimate and limited. When planning DPbD the purpose of each operation or set of operations shall be carefully considered.

In a report on security of processing ENISA identified seven questions that help companies define their processing operations and their contexts[492]. These questions represent the minimum to be asked for each processing operation and may be useful for DPbD planning. They are listed as follows:

- What is the personal data processing operation?
- What are the types of personal data processed?
- What is the purpose of the processing?
- What are the means used for the processing of personal data?[493]
- Where does the processing of personal data take place?

---

487 European Data Protection Board, *Guidelines 4/2019 on Article 25 Data Protection by Design and by*
*Default*, 9, point 28.

488 *See* Article 30(5) GDPR on the record and Article 35(3) GDPR on DPIA.

489 As will be explained in the following Chapters, personal health data should be processed with stronger safeguards.

490 European Data Protection Board, *Guidelines 4/2019 on Article 25 Data Protection by Design and by Default*, 9, point 28, which mentioned that the circumstances may influence the expectations of the data subject.

491 European Data Protection Board, *op. cit.*, 9, point 28.

492 *See* D'Acquisto and Panagopoulou, *Guidelines for SMEs on the security of personal data processing*, pp. 18–19. The same questions are reported in another report on security of personal data processing. *See* ENISA European Union Agency for Network & Information Security. *Handbook on Security of Personal Data Processing*. European Union Agency for Network and Information Security, 2017, p. 10.

493 As an example, the means could be automated or not.

- What are the categories of data subjects?[494]
- What are the recipients of the data?

After the state of the art, the cost of implementation and the characteristics of the processing, the last element to be taken into account is a specific risk analysis. Next subsection investigates this factor of Article 25.

### 2.4.5 Evaluating the risks posed by data processing

Generally, the GDPR requires taking into account a risk assessment. Risks are possible scenarios describing events and their consequences that are estimated in terms of severity and likelihood[495]. Risk management refers to the "coordinated activity to direct and control an organisation with regard to risk"[496].

After the GDPR, risk management has become a substantial part of corporate management activities. From an historical point of view, the concept of risk exists since the beginning of informational privacy and data protection law[497]. As will be explained in the following section on related requirements, the risk management approach has been further specified in Article 35 of the GDPR dedicated to the Data Protection Impact Assessment (hereinafter: DPIA).

Article 25 always requires taking into account any "risks of varying likelihood and severity for rights and freedom posed by the processing". Risks are criteria for determining the concrete measures to be implemented. Risk management is at the core of DPbD[498]. The approach is dynamic, and

494 Usually law prescribes particular rules for the processing of personal data related to children. The GDPR sets Article 8 for defining the conditions applicable to child's consent in relation to the offer of information society services.

495 WP29 Article 29 Working Party. *Guidelines on Data Protection Impact Assessment (DPIA) and determining whether processing is "likely to result in a high risk" for the purposes of Regulation 2016/679*. WP248 17/en, 2017, p. 6.

496 *Ibid.*

497 *See* Alessandro Mantelero. "Il nuovo approccio della valutazione del rischio nella sicurezza dei dati. Valutazione d'impatto e consultazione preventiva (Artt. 32–39)". In: *Il nuovo Regolamento europeo sulla privacy e protezione dei dati personali*. Zanichelli, Torino, 2017, pp. 287–330. ISBN: 9788808521057, p. 294; Alessandro Mantelero. "La gestione del rischio". In: *La protezione dei dati personali in Italia. Regolamento UE n. 2016/679 e d.lgs. 10 agosto 2018, n. 101*. Zanichelli, Torino, 2019, pp. 449–502. ISBN: 9788808820433, p. 452.

498 European Data Protection Supervisor, *Opinion 5/2018, Preliminary Opinion on privacy by design*, p. 8.

enables the identification and integration of the measures according to the concrete risks for individuals. Therefore, the measures are not the same under all operations. Once again, a "one-size-fits-all" approach does not comply with the legal requirement. The recommendation in the EDPB's Guidelines on Article 25 was to "always carry out a data protection risk assessment on a case by case basis for the processing activity at hand and verify the effectiveness of the appropriate measures and safeguards proposed", independently of the application of Article 35 GDPR[499].

The term "severity" indicates the magnitude of a risk, whereas "likelihood" expresses the possibility of a risk occurring[500]. The scale of severity could define the levels as low, medium, high and very high in relation to the consequences that the situation has on individuals. The evaluation of severity for right and freedoms is qualitative[501]. To assess the likelihood of risks, the evaluation is performed through probability rules and the levels could be estimated as negligible, limited, significant and maximum, all of which have different scores. To identify the risk as a whole, the controller should multiply the likelihood value by the impact value[502].

As regards the wording "rights and freedoms of natural persons", it should be pointed out that the GDPR frequently refers to fundamental rights and freedoms recognised in the Charter of Fundamental Rights of the European Union. In particular, the Regulation honours the right to respect for private and family life, home and communications (Art. 7), the protection of personal data (Art. 8), freedom of thought, conscience and religion (Art. 10), freedom of expression and information (Art. 11), freedom to conduct a business (Art. 16), the right to an effective remedy and to a fair trial (Art. 47), and cultural, religious and linguistic diversity (Art. 22)[503]. Other rights and freedoms are recognised by the same Charter. Therefore, the data controller shall assess the possible risks in relation to these rights and freedoms, and the subject shall evaluate their severity

---

499 European Data Protection Board, *Guidelines 4/2019 on Article 25 Data Protection by Design and by Default.*

500 CNIL Commission Nationale de l'Informatique et des Libertés. *Privacy Impact Assessment (PIA). Method- ology.* 2018, p. 6. For more details on the CNIL's approach, *see* Chapter 5, Section 5.4.

501 On this regard, *see* e.g. D'Acquisto and Panagopoulou, *Guidelines for SMEs on the security of personal data processing*, p. 20.

502 All the technical aspects on risk assessment will be presented in Chapter 5, Section 5.4.

503 *See* Recital 4 GDPR. On these rights and data protection law *see* Giakoumopoulos, Buttarelli, and O'Flamerty, *Handbook on European data protection law.*

and likelihood and then select the DPbD measures accordingly and proportionally[504].

### 2.4.6 Defining "appropriate" and "effective" criteria

Article 25 specifies that the measures shall be *appropriate* because they are designed to implement data protection principles in an *effective* manner. According to the EDPS, the two adjectives represent a special dimension of the DPbD obligation[505]. Effectiveness is at the heart of the concept of DPbD[506].

Firstly, it has been argued that "appropriate" entails a free discretion of the data controller[507]. This adjective implies the contextual and dynamic nature of the legal provision[508]. However, this discretion could always be scrutinised by the DPA or by a court. Measures are appropriate when they are designed to implement data protection principles (Art. 5 GDPR). As mentioned above, pseudonymisation has been explicitly indicated as appropriate.

Secondly, implementation shall be performed "in an effective manner". It is clear from the text that the goal is again the implementation of data protection principles. In order to address effectiveness, specific and dedicated measures shall be implemented for each processing operation and principle[509]. Generic measures are not sufficient nor effective. Chosen measures must be specific to the particular processing and robust[510].

Effectiveness relates to the proportionality principle which is used in the risk management approach[511]. As a result, this criterion can be a contextu-

504 On the risk management approach *see* also Section 2.5.2.

505 *See* European Data Protection Supervisor, *Opinion 5/2018, Preliminary Opinion on privacy by design*, p. 6.

506 European Data Protection Board, *Guidelines 4/2019 on Article 25 Data Protection by Design and by Default*, 7, point 13.

507 *See* Hildebrandt and Tielemans, "Data protection by design and technology neutral law", p. 517.

508 *See* Jasmontaite et al., "Data protection by design and by default: Framing guiding principles into legal obligations in the GDPR", p. 173.

509 *See* European Data Protection Board, *Guidelines 4/2019 on Article 25 Data Protection by Design and by Default.*

510 *See* European Data Protection Board, *op. cit.*, 7, point 14.

511 *See* Jasmontaite et al., "Data protection by design and by default: Framing guiding principles into legal obligations in the GDPR", p. 176.

al and measurable parameter that requires a professional judgement by experts[512].

It should be noted that Article 25 also requires the integration of necessary safeguards into the processing in order to meet the requirements of the GDPR and protect data subjects' rights. This expression follows the effective criteria but seeks consideration of all the provisions of the regulation. Appropriate measures shall be designed to integrate such safeguards.

The EDPB pointed out that "whether or not measures are DPbDD-compliant" depends on the "contexts of the particular processing in question and an assessment of the elements that must be taken into account when determining the means of processing"[513]. In order to demonstrate compliance and effectiveness (i.e. the measures are appropriate in an effective manner and safeguards are integrated), the controller can define and use subjective or objective metrics and "key performance indicators" (KPI), meaning measurable values that can demonstrate "how effectively the controller achieves their data protection objective"[514]. Alternatively, the subject may provide the rationale behind the chosen measures and safeguards.

However, there is no uniform or accredited approach in the literature. Documenting the implementation and explaining in detail the adopted solutions remain first reliable strategies. It can be argued that the vagueness and uncertainty of Article 25 come to light with the appropriate and effective conditions. Courts and DPAs will give some guidance when ruling on the future case law[515].

### 2.4.7 Identifying the time aspect of the requirement

Article 25 GDPR refers to "the time of the determination of the means for processing" and "the time of the processing itself". This phrasing refers to the design phase of the processing and its concrete operations and

---

512 *Ibid.*

513 *See* European Data Protection Board, *Guidelines 4/2019 on Article 25 Data Protection by Design and by Default*, 7, point 14.

514 *See* European Data Protection Board, *op. cit.*, 7, point 16. The EDPB suggested: "KPIs may be quantitative, such as the percentage of false positives or false negatives, reduction of complaints, reduction of response time when data subjects exercise their rights; or qualitative, such as evaluations of performance, use of grading scales, or expert assessments".

515 *See* some cases in Chapter 6, Section 6.5.

activities[516]. As a result, DPbD aims to provide safeguards for the whole project and data management life cycle[517].

Thus, the measures shall be implemented before and during the concrete operations of processing. The determination of the means refers to every detailed design element[518]. Therefore, in the time of the determination the controller has not yet defined the means to be incorporated and has the opportunity to take into account all the elements.

As noted in the critical analysis on PbD, the timing is crucial for efficiency and effectiveness. The sooner the measures are planned and implemented, the better the controller complies with DPbD. However, at the time of processing the controller shall maintain DPbD[519].

During the processing operations, the DPbD measures shall be re-evaluated regularly[520].

The purpose of DPbD is to be applied throughout the entire processing life cycle, including the life cycle of an IT system and of management practices.

So far, the study has deepened the answers to who, what, how, where and when. The next subsection deals with why and the rationales of Article 25 GDPR.

### 2.4.8 Towards the implementation of principles and rights

Article 25 establishes an obligation that seeks to:

1) "implement data-protection principles, such as data minimisation, in an effective manner";
2) "integrate the necessary safeguards into the processing in order to meet the requirements of this Regulation";
3) and "protect the rights of data subjects".

It has been argued that these objectives superimpose on one another because they all aim to comply with the data protection rules and, in partic-

516 *See* European Data Protection Supervisor, *Opinion 5/2018, Preliminary Opinion on privacy by design*, p. 5.

517 *See* European Data Protection Supervisor, *op. cit.*, p. 6.

518 *See* European Data Protection Board, *Guidelines 4/2019 on Article 25 Data Protection by Design and by Default*, 10, point 34. The EDPB uses as examples architecture, procedures, protocols, layout and appearance.

519 *See* European Data Protection Board, *op. cit.*, 10, point 35, and 11, point 37.

520 Bincoletto, "European Union – EDPB Guidelines 4/2019 on Data Protection by Design and by Default", p. 577.

ular, with the GDPR and the principles provided[521]. The entire GDPR contains 99 provisions. The appropriate measures shall be designed to ensure compliance with the entire Regulation[522]. However, distinct attention should be paid to principles and rights. DPbD aims to build principles for improving their traction[523].

As regards data protection principles, Article 5 GDPR has been mentioned frequently[524]. This provision sets out the principles relating to all processing of personal data. Scholars have argued that Article 25 is not clear about its scope because it mentions data minimisation only[525]. Another commentator criticised Article 25 by defining it a "catch-all provision with no specific requirements of its own"[526]. These claims might be persuasive, but they should be contested by a deeper analysis of the provision that aims to advocate for its concrete application.

For the present purposes, the principles will be analysed separately as presented in the following Table 2.2. The analysis presents the principles in connection with DPbD and provides brief implementation notes[527]. Detailed guidance for implementing the principles cannot be provided because concrete implementation is sector- and case-specific[528]. Nevertheless,

---

521 *See* Sartore, "Privacy-by-design, l'introduzione del principio nel corpus del GDPR", p. 300. The author stressed that the mention of the principle was only added in the final version of the text.

522 Jasmontaite et al., "Data protection by design and by default: Framing guiding principles into legal obligations in the GDPR", p. 175.

523 Bygrave, "Chapter IV Controller and Processor (Articles 24–43). Article 25. Data protection by design and by default", p. 573.

524 On all the principles *see* also Recital 39. Generally on all the principles of the GDPR *see* Cuffaro, D'Orazio, and Ricciuto, *I dati personali nel diritto europeo*, pp. 179–218; Giakoumopoulos, Buttarelli, and O'Flamerty, *Handbook on European data protection law*, pp. 115–135; Voigt and Von dem Bussche, *The EU General Data Protection Regulation (GDPR). A Practical Guide*, pp. 87–92; Bolognini, Pelino, and Bistolfi, *Il regolamento privacy europeo: commentario alla nuova disciplina europea sulla protezione dei dati, in vigore da maggio 2016*, pp. 92–118.

525 *See* Rubinstein and Good, "The trouble with Article 25 (and how to fix it): the future of data protection by design and default", p. 5.

526 Waldman, "Privacy's Law of Design". In Waldman, "Data Protection by Design? A Critique of Article 25 of the GDPR", p. 153, the author once again defines Article 25 a "catch-all provision" that is "repetitive of other sections of the GDPR and has no identity of its own".

527 Chapter 3 gives more technical considerations for the healthcare context.

528 Tamó-Larrieux, *Designing for privacy and its legal framework: data protection by design and default for the internet of things*, p. 167.

some organisational and technical measures to achieve each principle can be presented here[529].

*Table 2.2 Data protection principles*

| PRINCIPLE | DEFINITION |
|---|---|
| Lawfulness | Personal data shall be processed lawfully |
| Fairness | Personal data shall be processed fairly |
| Transparency | Personal data shall be processed in a transparent manner in relation to the data subject |
| Purpose limitation | Personal data shall be collected for specified, explicit and legitimate purposes |
| Data minimisation | Personal data shall be adequate, relevant and limited to what is necessary in relation to the purposes |
| Accuracy | Personal data shall be accurate and, where necessary, kept up-to-date |
| Storage limitation | Personal data shall be kept in a form which permits identification of data subjects for no longer than is necessary for the purposes |
| Integrity and Confidentiality (security) | Personal data shall be processed in a manner that ensures appropriate security of the personal data |
| Accountability | The controller shall be responsible for, and be able to demonstrate compliance with, principles |

529 As mentioned, the EDPB provided a list of key and guiding DPbD and DPbDf elements for each of the principles of Article 5. *See* European Data Protection Board, *Guidelines 4/2019 on Article 25 Data Protection by Design and by Default*, pp. 14–28.

The lawfulness principle essentially means that processing shall respect all applicable legal requirements[530]. In order for processing to be lawful, personal data shall be processed on a legitimate basis[531]. The legal grounds of processing are provided in Articles 6 and 9, and some specifications are set by Articles 7, 8 and 10 GDPR. For the processing of personal data, the lawful legal grounds are: a) data subject's consent; b) the performance of a contract; c) a legal obligation under Union or Member State law; d) the vital interest of the data subject or of another natural person; e) the performance of a task in the public interest set out by Union or Member State law; and f) a legitimate interest pursued by the data controller or a third party[532].

On the one hand, in order to implement the lawfulness principle at the time of the determination of the means the data controller shall define the legal basis for each processing operation or activity. On the other hand, during the processing life cycle the controller shall implement measures for ensuring that the processing operation or activity is in line with the legal basis[533]. Documents, such as consent forms and contractual clauses, should be prepared if consent or the contract is the legal ground. An assessment of the legitimate interest should be performed to understand whether such interest is overridden by interests or fundamental rights and freedoms of the data subject which require protection of personal data[534]. If and when the legal basis ceases to apply, measures should be

---

530 Cécile De Terwangne. "Chapter II Principles (Articles 5–11). Article 5. Principles relating to processing of personal data". In: *The EU General Data Protection Regulation (GDPR): A Commentary*. Oxford University Press, 2020, pp. 309–397. ISBN: 9780198826491, p. 314.

531 *See* Recitals 39 – 48 GDPR.

532 As regards the legal basis for special data (Art. 9), *see* Chapter 3. Each legal basis is further specified in Article 6. Article 7 sets some conditions for consent which generally has to be freely given, specific, informed and unambiguous (Art. 4(11)). Other conditions applicable to child consent are required by Article 8. On consent *see* also WP29 Article 29 Working Party. *Guidelines on consent under Regulation 2016/679*. WP259 17/en, 2017. Article 10 specifies that processing of personal data relating to criminal convictions and offences shall be carried out only under particular controls. On the legal basis of the GDPR *see* e.g. Fabio Bravo. "Il consenso e le altre condizioni di liceità". In: *Il nuovo Regolamento europeo sulla privacy e sulla protezione dei dati personali*. Zanichelli, Torino, 2017, pp. 101–177. ISBN: 9788808521057.

533 *See* European Data Protection Board, *Guidelines 4/2019 on Article 25 Data Protection by Design and by Default*, p. 16.

534 The Court of Justice elaborated the three-part test of legitimate interest under the Data Protection Directive in the case C-13/16 *Valsts policijas Rīgas regiona*

implemented to stop the processing (e.g. automatic alerts, technical configurations, internal policies). Examples are when the data subject withdraws the consent, or when the minor becomes an adult. Other grounds shall be defined.

In the GDPR the principle of fairness is always presented in connection with lawfulness and transparency[535]. Nonetheless, it represents a distinct and overarching principle of the Regulation. Indeed, the EDPB highlighted that fairness requires that "personal data shall not be processed in a way that is unjustifiably detrimental, unlawfully discriminatory, unexpected or misleading to the data subject"[536]. In a fair processing personal data have not been processed through unfair means or deceptions[537]. This definition may be too vague to support the controller in a concrete implementation. However, according to the fairness principle, processing does not have unforeseeable negative effects[538]. The concept of fairness is linked to the interests and expectations of the data subject[539].

Generally, measures against discrimination, nudges and power imbalances are implementing the principle of fairness. Only taking into account the nature, scope., context and purpose of the processing is it possible to

---

*pārvaldes Kārtības policijas pārvalde contro Rīgas pašvaldības SIA "Rīgas satiksme"*. The three steps are: 1) purpose test (whether there is a legitimate interest for processing); 2) necessity test (whether the processing is necessary for the purpose); 3) balancing test (whether an individual's interests, rights or freedoms override the legitimate interest). For further discussion of this test *see* Irene Kamara and Paul De Hert. "Understanding the balancing act behind the legitimate interest of the controller ground: A pragmatic approach". In: *Brussels Privacy Hub* 4.12 (2018), pp. 1–35.

535 In the GDPR, as regards "lawful and fair" *see* Recitals 39 and 45, and Article 6(2) – (3). For "fair and transparent" *see* Recitals 39, 60, 71, and Articles 13(2), 14(2), 40(2).

536 *See* European Data Protection Board, *Guidelines 4/2019 on Article 25 Data Protection by Design and by Default*, p. 17.

537 De Terwangne, "Chapter II Principles (Articles 5–11). Article 5. Principles relating to processing of personal data", p. 314.

538 Giakoumopoulos, Buttarelli, and O'Flamerty, *Handbook on European data protection law*, p. 117.

539 *See* Tamó-Larrieux, *Designing for privacy and its legal framework: data protection by design and default for the internet of things*, p. 88.

540 In order to clarify the concept, the EDPB used several key guiding elements in the Guidelines on Article 25. Some elements are: "Autonomy – data subjects should be granted the highest degree of autonomy possible to determine the use made of their personal data, as well as over the scope and conditions of that use or processing; interaction – data subjects must be able to communicate and exercise their rights in respect of the personal data processed by

define some concrete examples[540]. The principle of fairness goes beyond transparency obligations and seeks an ethical processing[541].

Data subjects should be informed of the existence, extent and purposes of the processing[542]. The principle of transparency is strictly connected to providing and receiving information, and enabling data subjects to understand their rights[543]. The processing shall be transparent, meaning that it shall be clear and open for data subjects. Specific articles of the GDPR embed this principle explicitly. Article 12 defines the extent and the modalities of transparency, which is strictly connected to information and the exercise of data subjects' rights. Articles 13 and 14 list the information to provide to the data subject, whether or not the personal data is collected from the individual[544]. Lastly, Article 34 sets the conditions for the communication of a personal data breach to the data subject. These provisions describe the content of communications that the controller shall provide to the data subject, including information on privacy policies.

Therefore, organisational strategies and privacy policies should be defined to ensure transparency and easy comprehension of what the processing entails. The language shall be clear, concise and plain and the information shall be provided in a concise, intelligible and easily accessible

the controller; expectation – processing should correspond with data subjects' reasonable expectations; non-discrimination – the controller shall not unfairly discriminate against data subjects; non-exploitation – the controller should not exploit the needs or vulnerabilities of data subjects; consumer choice – the controller should not "lock in" their users in an unfair manner. Whenever a service processing personal data is proprietary, it may create a lock-in to the service, which may not be fair, if it impairs the data subjects' possibility to exercise their right of data portability in accordance with Article 20; respect of rights – the controller must respect the fundamental rights of data subjects and implement appropriate measures and safeguards and not impinge on those rights unless expressly justified by law". Therefore, in the authority view, fairness can be related to a data subject's rights and freedoms. Other elements suggested by the EDPB refer to ethical aspects of the data processing (e.g. human intervention and fair algorithms). Actually, fairness is a typical ethical principle.

541 Giakoumopoulos, Buttarelli, and O'Flamerty, *Handbook on European data protection law*, p. 119.

542 *See* Recital 39 and 60 GDPR.

543 *See* Article 12 GDPR. *See* also European Data Protection Board, *Guidelines 4/2019 on Article 25 Data Protection by Design and by Default*, p. 15.

544 *See infra* on right to be informed.

(oral or written) form[545]. The communication of information could be targeted to the specific audience since the information should be relevant and applicable to the specific data subjects (e.g. children), and it could be layered or provided in a machine-readable form[546]. It should be noted that some information is related to technical aspects of the processing: the period of storage, the criteria for determining this period, and the existence of automated decision making with the logic that is involved[547]. As established by Article 12(2) GDPR, the exercise of the data subject's rights shall be facilitated. As a result, technical measures should be implemented in order to guarantee prompt answers to information requests, ensure the possibility of exercising the rights (e.g. by electronic means), and act upon requests referring to any right.

Moreover, the data controller can collect and process personal data only for specified, explicit and legitimate purposes. Further processing is lawful only if it is compatible with the purpose for which personal data was collected, with the exception of Article 89(1) GDPR on scientific research[548]. If the second purpose is incompatible, a new legal basis shall support the processing or personal data shall be anonymised. These statements sum-

545 For an explanation of these adjectives *see* WP29 Article 29 Working Party. *Guidelines on transparency under Regulation 2016/679*. WP260 17/en, 2018, pp. 7–10.

546 This is a key element of the EDPB's Guidelines. *See* European Data Protection Board, *Guidelines 4/2019 on Article 25 Data Protection by Design and by Default*, p. 15. Other interesting key elements of the transparency principle are: "universal design – information shall be accessible to all data subjects, include use of machine readable languages to facilitate and automate readability and clarity; comprehensible – data subjects should have a fair understanding of what they can expect with regards to the processing of their personal data, particularly when the data subjects are children or other vulnerable groups; multi-channel – information should be provided in different channels and media, not only the textual, to increase the probability for the information to effectively reach the data subject; layered – the information should be layered in a manner that resolves the tension between completeness and understanding, while accounting for data subjects' reasonable expectations".

547 *See* Article 22(1) and (4) GDPR. On the importance of transparent information about the algorithm *see* the report on an interesting case in Giorgia Bincoletto. "Italy – Supreme Court of Cassation on Automated Decision Making: Invalid Consent if an Algorithm is Not Trasparent". In Eur. Data Prot. L. Rev. 7 (2 2021), pp. 248–253.

548 The notion of "compatibile" should be interpreted on the basis of Article 6(4) of the GDPR. *See* further in De Terwangne, "Chapter II Principles (Articles 5–11). Article 5. Principles relating to processing of personal data", p. 316.

marise the rationale of the purpose limitation principle[549]. The purpose is a central concept for data protection law[550]. Any processing of personal data has a purpose. Each purpose shall be specifically defined prior to the collection of data from the very beginning[551]. A purpose shall be legitimate, and it shall not be ambiguous or kept hidden[552]. Implementing measures should limit the operations to the extent strictly necessary and proportionate to each defined purpose. Technical measures can limit the possibility of re-purposing personal data and organisational measures can control the reuse[553].

Data minimisation is the only principle explicitly mentioned in Article 25. This principle directly concerns the design of data processing systems[554]. It is connected to the principle of necessity. Measures shall ensure that personal data are adequate, relevant and limited in amount to what is necessary in relation to the purpose. As a matter of fact, data collection should be limited to what is necessary. Features and parameters of processing systems should be configured to achieve these goals, and when not possible deletion and anonymisation should occur[555]. Minimisation requires that identification of individuals should be possible only if needed for processing, meaning that pseudonymisation should be implemented, as previously explained, as well as other techniques, such as randomisation

549 *See* Article 5(1)(b), Article 6(4) and Recitals 49, 50 GDPR.

550 De Terwangne, "Chapter II Principles (Articles 5–11). Article 5. Principles relating to processing of personal data", p. 315, points out that this principle is a cornerstone of data protection law and a prerequisite for most other fundamental requirements.

551 *See* Tamó-Larrieux, *Designing for privacy and its legal framework: data protection by design and default for the internet of things*, p. 90.

552 De Terwangne, "Chapter II Principles (Articles 5–11). Article 5. Principles relating to processing of personal data", p. 315. A legitimate purpose does not create disproportionate interference with data subjects' rights and freedoms on the basis of the data controller's interests.

553 European Data Protection Board, *Guidelines 4/2019 on Article 25 Data Protection by Design and by Default*, p. 20.

554 *See* Tamó-Larrieux, *Designing for privacy and its legal framework: data protection by design and default for the internet of things*, p. 91. The author groups in the principle concerning design the principles of data minimisation, storage limitation, data security and accuracy.

555 *See* European Data Protection Board, *Guidelines 4/2019 on Article 25 Data Protection by Design and by Default*, p. 21.

and generalisation[556]. Actually, the EDPB suggested avoiding the processing altogether (e.g. data avoidance, limitation) when this is possible for the relevant purpose[557].

Furthermore, personal data shall be accurate and kept up-to-date. When inaccurate, data shall be erased or rectified without undue delay[558]. Accuracy is a mathematical concept that determines how close the result of an experimental measurement can be considered to the true value of the measured quantity. In the data protection domain personal data is accurate when it is true and complete. Organisational and technical measures should decrease inaccuracy in all the phases of data processing. An accuracy policy and guidelines could be prepared at the organisational level. Accuracy should be checked regularly because potential damage might be caused to the data subject[559].

Another principle of the GDPR is storage limitation. Processing shall keep personal data in a form which permits identification of data subjects for no longer than is necessary for the purpose. Further storage is permitted by implementing appropriate technical and organisational measures only in accordance with Article 89(1)[560]. Data controllers shall know what personal data are processed and for what amount of time they are stored for the purpose[561]. As mentioned, this information should be provided to data subjects. A retention policy and an inventory could be defined. After a certain period of time, measures should be implemented for anonymisation or erasure.

In addition, the integrity and confidentiality principles require that personal data shall be processed in a manner that ensures appropriate security. Protection against unauthorised access, unlawful processing, accidental

---

556 *See* e.g. Danezis et al., *Privacy and Data Protection by design – from policy to engineering*; D'Acquisto and Naldi, *Big data e privacy by design. Anonimizzazione Pseudonimizzazione Sicurezza*.

557 *See* European Data Protection Board, *Guidelines 4/2019 on Article 25 Data Protection by Design and by Default*, p. 21.

558 *See* Article 5(1)(d) GDPR.

559 *See* Giakoumopoulos, Buttarelli, and O'Flamerty, *Handbook on European data protection law*, p. 128. As an example, personal data related to banking information and creditworthiness shall be updated regularly in order to successfully obtain a loan from a bank.

560 *See* Article 5(1)(e) GDPR.

561 The EDPB noted that "it is vital that the controller knows exactly what personal data the company processes and why". The deciding factor is the purpose. *See* European Data Protection Board, *Guidelines 4/2019 on Article 25 Data Protection by Design and by Default*, p. 25.

loss, destruction or damage is included[562]. Integrity is the "property of accuracy and completeness" of personal data, while confidentiality refers to the "property that information is not made available or disclosed to unauthorized individuals, entities, or processes"[563]. Another typical security principle is availability, which is the "property of being accessible and usable on demand by an authorized entity" and it constitutes with the others the CIA triad. For these principles the measures are mainly designed in accordance with Article 32 on security of processing[564].

As previously noted for PbD, DPbD aims at proactively preventing data breaches from occurring. An information security policy should be defined at the organisational level and technical measures should be implemented in order to safeguard the security of the processing. Taking into account the specific circumstances of the processing, security measures could include pseudonymisation and encryption[565]. Moreover, secure transmission of data and authentication and authorisation tools prevent unauthorised access to personal data. Typical measures for security of processing are using "information security management system", "access control management", "intrusion detection and prevention system", performing a security risk assessment, keeping backups and logs, and defining incident response policies and notification procedures[566].

The last principle of Article 5 is accountability. This principle reminds the controller that the principles should be taken seriously because the subject is responsible for, and shall be able to demonstrate compliance, with them. Internal controls and allocation of responsibilities and duties should be defined, and documentation on measures, policies and procedures should be maintained as evidence[567]. Procedures for responding to DPA's or law enforcement's requests should be defined in advance.

562 *See* Article 5(1)(f) GDPR.

563 *See* these definitions in the recognised international standard ISO/IEC 27000:2018(en) Information technology — Security techniques — Information security management systems — Overview and vocabulary.

564 *See* Section 2.5.1.

565 Giakoumopoulos, Buttarelli, and O'Flamerty, *Handbook on European data protection law*, p. 131.

566 *See* European Data Protection Board, *Guidelines 4/2019 on Article 25 Data Protection by Design and by Default*, pp. 26–27. *See* further Chapter 5.

567 *See* Elisa Faccioli and Marco Cassaro. "Il "GDPR" e la normativa di armonizzazione nazionale alla luce dei principi: "accountability" e "privacy by design"". In: *Il Diritto industriale* 6 (2018), pp. 561–566. Generally, on designing for accountability *see* Joris Hulstijn and Brigitte Burgemeestre. "Design for the Values of Accountability and Transparency". In: *Handbook of Ethics, Values, and Techno-*

Designating a data protection officer (DPO) might facilitate compliance[568]. According to Docksey, accountability is one of the central pillars of the GDPR and one of its most significant innovations[569]. This principle is linked with Article 24 on responsibility of the controller that requires the controller to implement organisational and technical measures, including data protection policies, in order to ensure and be able to demonstrate that processing is performed in accordance with the GDPR[570]. However, accountability means more than responsibility, it is a "proactive and demonstrable responsibility", which also refers to transparency and liability, meaning that the controller should actively develop compliance and be able to demonstrate it[571]. The legal provision of Article 5(2) only mentions the controller, but it is arguable that the processor is accountable as well[572].

Stalla-Bourdillon *et al.* defined a DPbD workflow from the analysis of Article 5 by deriving eight nodes[573]. The first and second nodes are defying the purpose for data sharing and identifying the legal basis. Then, the controller should determine which data are necessary for that purpose (third node) and reduce a non-essential processing activity within the amount of data (fourth node). A data retention period should be set (fifth node) and the accuracy should be ensured (sixth node). The data controller should verify if the processing is fair in the DPbD workflow and if data

*logical Design: Sources, Theory, Values and Application Domains*. Springer, 2015, pp. 303–333. ISBN: 9789400769700. Auditing has a pivotal role for compliance.

568 *See* Giakoumopoulos, Buttarelli, and O'Flamerty, *Handbook on European data protection law*, p. 135.

569 Docksey, "Chapter IV Controller and Processor (Articles 24–43). Article 24. Responsibility of the controller", p. 557. This study investigates the precursors of accountability in EU legislation, in several international instruments, and even national developments.

570 Article 24 GDPR. For the text *see supra* note no. 380.

571 Docksey, "Chapter IV Controller and Processor (Articles 24–43). Article 24. Responsibility of the controller", p. 561. *See* also Panetta, *Circolazione e protezione dei dati personali, tra libertà e regole del mercato. Commentario al Regolamento UE n. 2016/679 (GDPR) e al novellato D.lgs. n. 196/2003 (Codice Privacy)*, p. 26, which refers to awareness and reliability; Giusella Finocchiaro. "Il principio di *accountability*". In: *Giurispudenza Italiana* 171.12 (2019), pp. 2778–2782, which investigates the meaning of the term in the GDPR.

572 *See* Giakoumopoulos, Buttarelli, and O'Flamerty, *Handbook on European data protection law*, p. 136.

573 *See* Sophie Stalla-Bourdillon et al. "Data protection by design: building the foundations of trustworthy data sharing". In: *Data & Policy* 2 (2020), e4, 1–10, e4–5.

are not altered or disclosed without permission to maintain confidentiality (seventh node). Finally, the controller should ensure a transparent and monitored processing (eighth node).

Article 25 also refers to the safeguards that shall be adopted for protecting rights. Chapter III of the GDPR is dedicated to the rights of the data subject, which are exercised based on a request[574]. These rights can be summarised as reported in the following Table 2.3[575].

*Table 2.3 Data subject's rights*

| RIGHT | DEFINITION |
|---|---|
| Right to be informed | Data subject has the right to obtain information |
| Right to access | Data subject has the right to access personal data and obtain certain related information |
| Right to rectification | Data subject has the right to obtain rectification of inaccurate or incomplete personal data |
| Right to erasure | Data subject has the right to obtain erasure of personal data in certain circumstances |
| Right to restriction | Data subject has the right to obtain temporarily restriction of processing |
| Right to data portability | Data subject has the right to receive personal data and have it ported to another controller under some circumstances |

574 *See* Articles 12–22 GDPR.

575 Generally on data subject's rights *see* Giakoumopoulos, Buttarelli, and O'Flamerty, *Handbook on European data protection law*, pp. 206–248; Cuffaro, D'Orazio, and Ricciuto, *I dati personali nel diritto europeo*, pp. 327-352; Voigt and Von dem Bussche, *The EU General Data Protection Regulation (GDPR). A Practical Guide*, pp. 141–185; Finocchiaro, *Il nuovo Regolamento europeo sulla privacy e sulla protezione dei dati personali*, pp. 179–250; Bolognini, Pelino, and Bistolfi, *Il regolamento privacy europeo: commentario alla nuova disciplina europea sulla protezione dei dati, in vigore da maggio 2016*, pp. 171–276.

| RIGHT | DEFINITION |
|---|---|
| Right to object | Data subject has the right to object to processing on some grounds |
| Right to have human intervention | Data subject has the right to not be subjected to a decision based solely on automated processing that has effects and the right to obtain human intervention and to contest that decision |

Generally, the controller should be aware of the existence of the different types of rights. The data controller should then define procedures and implement measures for handling the data subject's requests to exercise these rights, even by electronic means. Mechanisms to provide control to the data subject over personal data should be envisioned[576]. The requests shall be free of charge, unless they are manifestly unfounded or excessive[577].

Articles 12, 13 and 14 establish the right to be informed and the procedures for transparent and complete communication with the data subject[578]. Privacy policy shall be aligned with the legal requirements that list the specific information to be provided[579]. Machine-readable icons could

576 *See* Jasmontaite et al., "Data protection by design and by default: Framing guiding principles into legal obligations in the GDPR", p. 175.

577 *See* further Article 12(5) GDPR.

578 Actually, Article 12 aims to ensure the efficient exercise of information rights by providing for procedures, but it does not lay down a substantive right. The rights are defined in Articles 13 and 14. *See* Radim Polcˇák. "Chapter III Rights of the Data Subject (Articles 12–23). Article 12. Transparency information, communication and modalities for the exercise of the rights of the data subject". In: *The EU General Data Protection Regulation (GDPR): A Commentary*. Oxford University Press, 2020, pp. 398–412. ISBN: 9780198826491, pp. 401–402.

579 The elements that have to be provided are defined in Article 13 and 14 GDPR. The former lists the information required where personal data are collected from the data subject, while the latter where personal data have not been obtained from the data subject. The elements that they have in common are: the identity and the contact details of the controller and, where applicable, of the controller's representative; the contact details of the DPO, where applicable; the purposes of the processing for which the personal data are intended as well as the legal basis for the processing; the recipients and, if applicable, transfer to a third country; the data retention period or criteria for determining it; the existence of rights (15–20 GDPR) and of the possibility of withdrawing consent; the right to lodge a complaint to a DPA; the existence of automated

be used to give an overview of the processing in an easily visible, intelligible and clearly legible manner[580]. This right is related to the transparency principle described above. Completeness and accuracy of information in the processing activities are of paramount importance for exercising all the other rights of the data subject[581]. Consent forms, privacy policies, and

---

decision making, including profiling, and information about the logic involved. On Article 13 *see* Gabriela Zanfir-Fortuna. "Chapter III Rights of the Data Subject (Articles 12–23). Article 13. Information to be provided where personal data are collected from the data subject". In: *The EU General Data Protection Regulation (GDPR): A Commentary*. Oxford University Press, 2020, pp. 413–433. ISBN: 9780198826491. According to this chapter, it is important to stress that the obligation to provide information applies to all processing activities irrespective of the legal basis. On Article 14 *see* Gabriela Zanfir-Fortuna. "Chapter III Rights of the Data Subject (Articles 12–23). Article 14. Information to be provided where personal data have not been obtained from the data subject". In: *The EU General Data Protection Regulation (GDPR): A Commentary*. Oxford University Press, 2020, pp. 434–448. ISBN: 9780198826491. Providing the information when personal data are not obtained from the data subject is really important for notifying of the existence of the processing despite the absence of a direct contact between the subject and the data controller.

580 *See* Article 6(7) GDPR. On privacy icons *see* Arianna Rossi and Monica Palmirani. "What's in an Icon?" In: *Data Protection and Privacy: Data Protection and Democracy*. Hart Publishing, 2020, pp. 59–92. ISBN: 9781509932740. The authors explained that privacy policies are rarely read and poorly understood by data subjects. For this reason, this work proposed an icon set that follows the legal design methodology. On this methodology *see* the work of the Director of the Legal Design Lab based at Stanford Law School, Margaret Hagan. "Design Comes to the Law School". In: *Modernising Legal Education*. Cambridge University Press, 2020, pp. 109–125. ISBN: 9781108663311. On legal design *see* also Margaret Hagan. "Legal Design as a Thing: A Theory of Change and a Set of Methods to Craft a Human-Centered Legal System". In: *Design Issues* 36.3 (2020), pp. 3–15; Arianna Rossi et al. "Legal Design Patterns: Towards A New Language for Legal Information Design". In: *Internet of Things. Proceedings of the 22nd International Legal Informatics Symposium IRIS*. 2019, pp. 517–526; Arianna Rossi and Helena Haapio. "Proactive Legal Design: Embedding Values in the Design of Legal Artefacts". In: *Internet of Things. Proceedings of the 22nd International Legal Informatics Symposium IRIS*. 2019, pp. 537–544.

581 *See* Zanfir-Fortuna, "Chapter III Rights of the Data Subject (Articles 12–23). Article 13. Information to be provided where personal data are collected from the data subject", pp. 415–416, which reported that since the 1980s the right to information has been called a "chief" right. The importance of this right has also been highlighted by the Court of Justice in the case C-201/14 *Bara* under the DPD, where the court ruled: "As the Advocate General observed in point 74 of his Opinion, the requirement to inform the data subjects about the processing of their personal data is all the more important since it affects the

costumer information notices should be revised to achieve transparency. In particular, the privacy policies shall be specific to the processing activity, and the language shall be short, plain and direct[582].

Regarding the right to access, the data subject can obtain confirmation of whether and where personal data is being processed and have access to data. Article 15 GDPR also lists the information to be supplied after an access request. The right to access also entails the right to obtain a copy of personal data[583]. The request can be made by electronic means; thus, within one month of receipt of the request, personal data shall be provided by electronic means, unless otherwise requested[584]. This right enhances transparency and helps the data subject take control over their personal data since it provides a second more detailed layer of information and allows deeper knowledge of the processing that facilitates the exercise of other rights[585].

The right to rectification is addressed in Article 16 GDPR. The data subject has the right to obtain, without undue delay, rectification of inaccurate personal data or completion of incomplete data. This right is related to the accuracy principle. It has been pointed out that the notion of incompleteness shall be assessed with regard to the purpose of the processing activity since some missing personal data may need to be added[586]. Technical mechanisms could directly allow the data subject to update personal data.

---

exercise by the data subjects of their right of access to, and right to rectify, the data being processed, set out in Article 12 of Directive 95/46, and their right to object to the processing of those data, set out in Article 14 of that directive".

582 *See* Zanfir-Fortuna, *op. cit.*, pp. 426–427, which suggested avoiding legal constructions in the policies and the use of the words "may" and "could". The policies may even be layered for ease of reading.

583 *See* Articles 15(3) and (4) GDPR.

584 Article 12(3) GDPR.

585 Gabriela Zanfir-Fortuna. "Chapter III Rights of the Data Subject (Articles 12–23). Article 15. Right of access by the data subject". In: *The EU General Data Protection Regulation (GDPR): A Commentary*. Oxford University Press, 2020, pp. 449–468. ISBN: 9780198826491, p. 452. The modalities for the exercise of the right to access are provided by Article 12 GDPR.

586 Cécile De Terwangne. "Chapter III Rights of the Data Subject (Articles 12–23). Article 16. Right to rectification". In: *The EU General Data Protection Regulation (GDPR): A Commentary*. Oxford University Press, 2020, pp. 469–474. ISBN: 9780198826491, p. 473. This chapter even referred to this right as "the right to add missing elements instead of to correct existing data".

Moreover, the right to erasure or "to be forgotten" entails the erasure of personal data based on certain specified grounds[587]. The legal requirement lists five full-prevalence clauses where the right does not apply. However, where applicable, the controller that has made the personal data public shall take reasonable steps, including technical measures and taking into account available technology and the cost of implementation, in order to inform upon request the other controllers which are processing that personal data[588].

With the exercise of the right to restriction the data subject can obtain a temporary restriction of processing where one of the four defined conditions applies[589]. Some methods for restriction are "temporarily moving the

---

587 *See* Article 17 GDPR. On this right *see* also the CJEU case law. In particular, as a leading case *see* C-131/12 *Google Spain SL, Google Inc. v. Agencia Española de Protección de Datos (AEPD), Mario Costeja González*. In this famous case, the right to be forgotten is associated with the removal of a link provided by a search engine. This right has to be balanced with the general public's interest in access to information. In this regard *see* Herke Kranenborg. "Chapter III Rights of the Data Subject (Articles 12–23). Article 17. Right to erasure ('right to be forgotten')". In: *The EU General Data Protection Regulation (GDPR): A Commentary*. Oxford University Press, 2020, pp. 475–484. ISBN: 9780198826491. On the right to be forgotten *see* Thibault Douville. "Les variations du droit au déréférencement, note sous CJUE 24 sept. 2019 [2 arrêt]". In: *Recueil Dalloz* 7854 (9 2020), pp. 515–522; Oskar Josef Gstrein. "Right to be Forgotten: EU-ropean Data Imperialism, National Privilege, or Universal Human Right?" In: *Review of European Administrative Law* (1 2020), pp. 125–152; Alessandro Palmieri and Roberto Pardolesi. "Polarità estreme: oblio e archivi digitali. Nota a Corte di Cassazione, sez. I civile, ordinanza 27–03–2020, n. 7559". In: *Foro it.* 1570 (parte I 2020) and Alessandro Palmieri and Roberto Pardolesi. "Dal diritto all'oblio all'occultamento in rete: traversie dell'informazione ai tempi di Google". In: *Nuovi Quaderni del Foro italiano* 1 (2014), pp. 16–33 (which focused on the Italian framework but highlighted the different conceptions of the right to be forgotten in the digital and non-digital contexts); Silvia Martinelli. *Diritto all'oblio e motori di ricerca. Memoria e privacy nell'era digitale*. Vol. 5. Giuffrè Editore, 2017. ISBN: 9788814220661; Vincenzo Zeno Zencovich and Giorgio Resta. *Il diritto all'oblio su Internet dopo la sentenza Google Spain*. Roma TrEpress, 2015. ISBN: 9788897524274; and Franco Pizzetti. *Il caso del diritto all'oblio*. Vol. 2. G. Giappichelli Editore, 2013. ISBN: 9788834828168.

588 *See* Article 17(2) GDPR.

589 *See* Article 18. It should be noted that the legal requirement indirectly refers to some principles: accuracy, lawfulness and purpose limitation. On this right *see* Gloria González Fuster. "Chapter III Rights of the Data Subject (Articles 12–23). Article 18. Right to restriction of processing". In: *The EU General Data Protection Regulation (GDPR): A Commentary*. Oxford University Press, 2020, pp. 485–491. ISBN: 9780198826491.

selected data to another processing system, making the selected personal data unavailable to users, or temporarily removing published data from a website"[590]. The controller has a duty to communicate the exercise of these last three rights to recipients[591].

The right to data portability is a new right set by Article 20 GDPR[592]. The rationales of this right are enhancing informational self-determination, empowering data subjects and promoting competition[593]. The data subject has the right to receive personal data in a structured, commonly used and machine-readable format and transmit it to another controller when the legal basis is the consent, or the contract and the processing is carried out by automated means. Where technically feasible, the transmission could be directly performed by the first controller[594].

Portability requires specific technological implementation[595]. The crucial element is the format of data[596]. As noted by De Hert *et al.*, the efforts imposed upon data controllers are moderate because the GDPR does not establish a duty of developing interoperable formats[597]. The provision does not require a specific standard format. Therefore, if the format is chosen by the first controller, the second controller will have problems with the usability of the personal data. By contrast, if the second controller chooses

---

590 Recital 67 GDPR.

591 *See* Article 19 GDPR.

592 On this right *see* WP29 Article 29 Working Party. *Guidelines on the right to data portability*. WP242 16/en, 2017.

593 Orla Lynskey. "Chapter III Rights of the Data Subject (Articles 12–23). Article 20. Right to data portability". In: *The EU General Data Protection Regulation (GDPR): A Commentary*. Oxford University Press, 2020, pp. 497–507. ISBN: 9780198826491, pp. 499–500.

594 *See* also Recital 68 GDPR.

595 *See* the study by Janis Wong and Tristan Henderson. "The right to data portability in practice: exploring the implications of the technologically neutral GDPR". In: *International Data Privacy Law* 9.3 (2019), pp. 173–191. The authors created a program for making portability requests. They categorised the received file formats and evaluated compliance with the criteria. The results showed that compliance is difficult to achieve. Therefore, they proposed some technical definitions for structured, commonly used and machine readable formats. Only for the last criterion there are widely accepted standards in the market (e.g. XML).

596 *See* Paul De Hert et al. "The right to data portability in the GDPR: Towards user-centric interoperability of digital services". In: *Computer Law & Security Review* 34.2 (2018), pp. 193–203, p. 196.

597 *See* De Hert et al., *op. cit.*, p. 200. This interpretation is in accordance with Recital 68 GDPR.

the format, the first one will have an excessively onerous duty to transmit that format. This right should be seen as an opportunity to create interconnected user-centric platforms and to develop interoperable formats[598]. The data controller shall integrate in the processing the necessary safeguards to protect the right to portability at a technical level.

On some defined grounds the data subject has the right to object to processing[599] and the right to not be subject to a decision based solely on automated processing which produces legal or similarly significant effects[600]. When the processing is solely based on automated means and the legal basis is a contract or explicit consent, the data subject does not have the latter right; nonetheless, the data controller shall implement suitable measures to safeguard the other rights, freedoms and legitimate interests, and the data subject has the right to obtain human intervention for the decision, and to express their point of view on the decision[601].

---

598 *See* De Hert et al., *op. cit.*, p. 202. The authors argued that the right to portability encourages a real competition between providers and the creation of interoperable formats.

599 *See* Article 21 GDPR. *See* Gabriela Zanfir-Fortuna. "Chapter III Rights of the Data Subject (Articles 12–23). Article 21. Right to object and automated individual decision-making". In: *The EU General Data Protection Regulation (GDPR): A Commentary*. Oxford University Press, 2020, pp. 508–521. ISBN: 9780198826491.

600 *See* Article 22(1) GDPR. On automated decision-making and profiling *see* WP29 Article 29 Working Party. *Guidelines on Automated individual decision-making and Profiling for the purposes of Regulation 2016/679*. WP251 17/en, 2017; Robert R. Hoffman and Gary Klein. "Explaining explanation, part 1: theoretical foundations". In: *IEEE Intelligent Systems* 32.3 (2017), pp. 68–73; Sandra Wachter, Brent Mittelstadt, and Chris Russell. "Counterfactual Explanations without Opening the Black Box: Automated Decisions and the GPDR". In: *Harv. JL & Tech.* 31 (2017), p. 841; Bilyana Petkova and Franziska Boehm. "Profiling and the Essence of the Right to Data Protection". In: *The Cambridge Handbook of Consumer Privacy*. Cambridge University Press, 2018, pp. 285–300. ISBN: 9781316831960; Margot E Kaminski. "The right to explanation, explained". In: *Berkeley Tech. LJ* 34 (2019), p. 189; Elena Gil González and Paul de Hert. "Understanding the legal provisions that allow processing and profiling of personal data — an analysis of GDPR provisions and principles". In: *Era Forum*. Vol. 19. 4. Springer. 2019, pp. 597–621; Sandra Wachter, Brent Mittelstadt, and Luciano Floridi. "Why a right to explanation of automated decision-making does not exist in the general data protection regulation". In: *International Data Privacy Law* 7.2 (2017), pp. 76–99.

601 *See* Article 22(2) – (3) GDPR. On automated decision making *see* also Lee A. Bygrave. "Chapter III Rights of the Data Subject (Articles 12–23). Article 22. Right to automated individual decision-making, including profiling". In: *The EU General Data Protection Regulation (GDPR): A Commentary*. Oxford Univer-

While providing some guidance on Article 22, Article 29 Working Party created a list of measures that represent good practices when making solely automated decisions, including profiling[602].

This section has attempted to show the implications for implementing data protection principles and integrating safeguards for the rights. Each provision implies an implementation measure be it organisational or technical. More concrete suggestions will be provided in the next Chapters.

So far, this section has focused on the first paragraph of Article 25. The analysis has explained the factors and the core duties embedded in the DPbD principle. The following section will investigate the second part of the provision that provides the DPbDf requirement.

### 2.4.9 Data protection by default

Even though Cavoukian's formulation of the Seven Foundational Principles embeds a default principle in the PbD approach, the GDPR distinguishes between DPbD and DPbDf[603]. Article 25(2) on data protection by default establishes that:

> "2. The controller shall implement appropriate technical and organisational measures for ensuring that, by default, only personal data which are necessary for each specific purpose of the processing are processed. That obligation applies to the amount of personal data collected, the extent of their processing, the period of their storage and their accessibility. In particular, such measures shall ensure that by default personal data are not made accessible without the individual's intervention to an indefinite number of natural persons".

Data protection by default is a new obligation for the data controller. Article 25(2) mandates that the controller shall implement appropriate technical and organisational measures as default settings to ensure that

---

sity Press, 2020, pp. 522–542. ISBN: 9780198826491; Guido Noto La Diega. "Against the Dehumanisation of Decision-Making". In: *J. Intell. Prop. Info. Tech. & Elec. Com. L.* 9 (2018), pp. 3–33; Isak Mendoza and Lee A. Bygrave. "The right not to be subject to automated decisions based on profiling". In: *EU Internet Law*. Springer, 2017, pp. 77–98. ISBN: 9783319649559.

602 *See* Article 29 Working Party, *Guidelines on Automated individual decision-making and Profiling for the purposes of Regulation 2016/679*, p. 32.

603 *See* Calzolaio, "*Privacy by design*. Principi, dinamiche, ambizioni del nuovo Reg. Ue 2016/679".

the processing does not include personal data that are not necessary for the specific purpose. This is applicable to "the amount of personal data collected, the extent of their processing, the period of their storage and their accessibility" for each purpose of the processing.

In particular, the term "amount" relates both to the volume of personal data and the types, categories and level of details (i.e. granularity)[604]. The reference to the period of storage requires that if personal data is not needed after an operation for the primary purpose or the secondary and compatible purpose, it shall be deleted or anonymised by default[605].

The measures mentioned shall ensure that by default personal data are not accessible to an indefinite number of natural persons. Therefore, personal data cannot be made public or be disseminated by default. Access is limited to a finite number of natural persons. It has been argued that the wording "indefinite number" refers to a number "larger than the data subject intended or would have reasonably expected"[606].

The arguments presented earlier for identifying the subjects and on the appropriate criterion are valid for DPbDf, too. In this provision the principles and rights highlighted are: purpose specification, data minimisation, storage limitation and the right to access by the data subject[607]. The data controller should collect by default only necessary data that is adequate and relevant for the purpose, which should be specified, explicit

604 *See* European Data Protection Board, *Guidelines 4/2019 on Article 25 Data Protection by Design and by Default*, p. 12. Point 49 states: "Controllers should consider both the volume of personal data, as well as the types, categories and level of detail of personal data required for the processing purposes. Their design choices should take into account the increased risks to the principles of integrity and confidentiality, data minimisation and storage limitation when collecting large amounts of detailed personal data, and compare it to the reduction in risks when collecting smaller amounts and/or less detailed information about data subjects. In any case, the default setting shall not include collection of personal data that is not necessary for the specific processing purpose. In other words, if certain categories of personal data are unnecessary or if detailed data isn't needed because less granular data is sufficient, then any surplus personal data shall not be collected".

605 *See* European Data Protection Board, *op. cit.*, p. 13.

606 Jasmontaite et al., "Data protection by design and by default: Framing guiding principles into legal obligations in the GDPR", p. 186.

607 *See* the interesting analysis on data protection by default in D'Acquisto et al., *Intelligenza artificiale, protezione dei dati personali e regolazione*, p. 133.

608 *See* Jasmontaite et al., "Data protection by design and by default: Framing guiding principles into legal obligations in the GDPR", p. 186.

and legitimate[608]. Since DPbDf refers to accessibility, it is also linked to the principles of transparency, integrity and confidentiality[609].

The EDPS pointed out that the obligation of Article 25(2) seems to be implicit in the purpose limitation and minimisation principles. Despite this argument, the authority argued that the requirement has another rationale. The provision stresses the importance of the expectations of the data subjects in the sense that their personal data should not be processed "for other purposes than what the product or service is basically and strictly meant to do, leaving by default any further use turned off"[610].

Thus, the amount of personal data should correspond with the data strictly necessary to the basic functions of a product or service. Default settings should be friendly by default. With privacy-friendly default settings the user does not have "to change the settings of a service or product upon the first use" in order to be protected at a maximum level, meaning that the user avoids a difficult procedure and saves time[611].

According to ENISA, the default settings determine how the systems works if nothing is changed[612]. In order to comply with the obligation of the GDPR, the amount of personal data should be the minimum for the purpose, the processing activities should be minimised according to the same purpose, the timing of data storage should be limited as much as possible, as should the accessibility[613]. It is clear that the necessity principle

---

609 *See* Hansen et al., *Recommendations on shaping technology according to GDPR provision. Exploring the notion of data protection by default*, p. 12.

610 These are the words in European Data Protection Supervisor, *Opinion 5/2018, Preliminary Opinion on privacy by design*, p. 7.

611 *See* Voigt and Von dem Bussche, *The EU General Data Protection Regulation (GDPR). A Practical Guide*, p. 63.

612 *See* Hansen et al., *Recommendations on shaping technology according to GDPR provision. Exploring the notion of data protection by default*, p. 11.

613 *See ibid.* The Agency identified these four criteria that should be used by data controllers. The fist criterion refers to the minimum amount of data. The number of attributes, sensitive data and identifiable information items should be reduced. The second criterion indicates that the extent of the processing should be minimal in relation to each purpose. The controller should verify whether the operation is necessary for the purpose. The period of the storage should be minimum, too. This third criterion requires a defined storage, so as to limit copies, do no storage at all, or anonymise or erase as soon as possible. Finally, the fourth criterion limits the accessibility of personal data at the minimum level by organisational and technical strategies. Access should be limited by assigned access rights, or by encryption. The location of the storage and who are the recipients are important elements.

plays a central role[614]. In order to enhance transparency, the data subject should be informed of the properties of the default settings as well as the effects of changes[615].

The two requirements of Article 25 are different. DPbD is wider than the "by default" requirement, which is focused on data minimisation and confidentiality[616]. Furthermore, Article 25(2) is expressed in absolute terms without the conditions of the first paragraph[617]. It has thus been suggested that DPbDf presupposes DPbD[618].

Data protection by default is a methodology that applies before the beginning of any processing: the automatism required by the norm is feasible at the development stage especially[619]. In this sense, more importance to the "design stage" is given by paragraph 2 of Article 25 than by the first one. Also reading the norm alongside Recital 78, developers are indirectly forced to design properly by default[620]. This indirect effect should not be underestimated in the market[621]. DPbDf is especially relevant whenever the default settings can be changed by the user[622].

The measures for implementing DPbD and DPbDf could potentially overlap (e.g. in the case of minimisation and storage limitation)[623]. According to the EDPB, these two principles and obligations are "complementary

614 *See* Hansen et al., *op. cit.*, p. 34. The user should intervene for everything that is in addition to what is necessary for the specific purpose.

615 *See* Hansen et al., *op. cit.*, p. 19; and Tamó-Larrieux, *Designing for privacy and its legal framework: data protection by design and default for the internet of things*, p. 185.

616 Bygrave, "Data protection by design and by default: deciphering the EU's legislative requirements", p. 116; Bygrave, "Chapter IV Controller and Processor (Articles 24–43). Article 25. Data protection by design and by default", p. 577.

617 *See* Hansen et al., *Recommendations on shaping technology according to GDPR provision. Exploring the notion of data protection by default*, p. 14.

618 *See* Jasmontaite et al., "Data protection by design and by default: Framing guiding principles into legal obligations in the GDPR", p. 183.

619 *See* D'Acquisto et al., *Intelligenza artificiale, protezione dei dati personali e regolazione*, p. 112. The authors noted that DPbD requires a constant attention to the measures, while data protection by default applies before the processing automatically.

620 *See* D'Acquisto et al., *op. cit.*, pp. 114–115. According to this study, data protection by default could assume a prominent role in the future. It will have more importance than DPbD because it directly entails the design of the technologies and how they automatically process personal data.

621 *See* Hansen et al., *Recommendations on shaping technology according to GDPR provision. Exploring the notion of data protection by default*, p. 15.

622 Hansen et al., *op. cit.*, p. 13.

623 *See* Hansen et al., *op. cit.*, p. 22.

concepts, which mutually reinforce each other"[624]. The controller should bear in mind both distinct principles, and then follow them by adopting a holistic approach in the data processing. Indeed, the GDPR requires a "data protection first" approach, as will be shown in the next sections on the other requirements linked to Article 25.

### *2.5 The related provisions of the GDPR*

Under the GDPR several instruments promote compliance. The implementation of Article 25 should be coordinated with other rules that the GDPR sets out.

Primarily, it should be pointed out that the legal requirements on security of personal data facilitate and enhance compliance. Moreover, in certain situations, a DPO shall be appointed, a record of the processing shall be maintained, a DPIA shall be performed, codes of conduct could be adopted, and certification mechanisms, seals and marks could be established[625].

In some cases, the controller and the processor designate a DPO[626]. Among the tasks of this officer is monitoring compliance with the data protection law and with internal policies[627]. Therefore, where designated the DPO shall provide advice on and monitor the DPbD implementation[628]. According to Article 29 Working Party, the DPO plays a key role

---

624 *See* European Data Protection Board, *Guidelines 4/2019 on Article 25 Data Protection by Design and by Default*, point 5, which also noted: "Data subjects will benefit more from data protection by default if data protection by design is concurrently implemented – and vice versa".

625 *See* respectively Articles 37–39, 30, 35, 40–43 GDPR.

626 Article 37 GDPR mandates the appointment in any case where: "(a) the processing is carried out by a public authority or body, except for courts acting in their judicial capacity; (b) the core activities of the controller or the processor consist of processing operations which, by virtue of their nature, their scope and/or their purposes, require regular and systematic monitoring of data subjects on a large scale; or (c) the core activities of the controller or the processor consist of processing on a large scale of special categories of data pursuant to Article 9 and personal data relating to criminal convictions and offences referred to in Article 10". The Union or Member State law may require the designation in other cases.

627 *See* Article 39(1)(b) GDPR.

628 The DPO should have specific skills and expertise in the data protection field. *See* e.g. the standard UNI 11697:2017, which defines the professional profiles at the UNI web store.

in fostering a data protection culture within the organisation and promoting DPbD implementation[629].

The DPbD measures are not indicated in the list of necessary information that the controller shall record in accordance with Article 30 GDPR[630]. However, recording the processing activities is an organisational measure that may support DPbD.

Codes of conduct can contribute to the application of Article 25 GDPR by specifying some measures and procedures referred to in this provision[631]. As explained in the EDPB's guidelines, codes of conduct are "voluntary accountability tools which set out specific data protection rules for categories on controllers and processors", providing a "detailed description of what is appropriate, legal and ethical" in a sector[632]. According to Article 40, these codes are prepared "by associations and other bodies representing categories of controllers and processors". The compliance with such a code is monitored in accordance with Article 41[633]. In the following subsections the analysis will investigate in detail the rules that are more directly connected with Article 25: security measures, DPIA and certification mechanisms.

### 2.5.1 Security measures

The GDPR mandates the implementation of appropriate technical and organisational measures in order to ensure a secure processing of personal data, that protect against unauthorised or unlawful operations and against accidental loss, destruction or damage. The Second Section of Chapter IV of the GDPR is dedicated to the security of processing. Article 32 is the central provision[634]. In this part, the GDPR sets out the rules on

---

629 *See* WP29 Article 29 Working Party. *Guidelines on Data Protection Officers ('DPOs')*. WP243 17/en, 2017, p. 12.

630 *See* Article 30(1)(a) – (g).

631 Article 40(2)(h) GDPR.

632 EDPB European Data Protection Board. *Guidelines 1/2019 on Codes of Conduct and Monitoring Bodies under Regulation 2016/679*. European Data Protection Board, 2019, p. 7.

633 *See* the long Article 41. In particular, an independent and accredited body monitors compliance with a code.

634 On Article 32 *see* Cédric Burton. "Chapter IV Controller and Processor (Articles 24–43). Article 32. Security of processing". In: *The EU General Data Protection Regulation (GDPR): A Commentary*. Oxford University Press, 2020, pp. 630–639. ISBN: 9780198826491.

notification of a personal data breach to the DPA and on communication of the breach to the data subject[635].

The text of Article 32 on security of processing begins with the same words as Article 25[636]. Nonetheless, Article 32 refers to the principle of "integrity and confidentiality". Article 25 aims instead to implement all principles of Article 5.

For implementing appropriate security measures, the risk assessment is crucial[637]. After the description of the processing, the potential effects on the rights and freedoms can be identified through the following steps of the risk assessment[638]:

- Identifying the potential effects on the rights and freedoms of individuals in relation to illegitimate access to data, unwanted modification of data and temporary or definitive unavailability of data;

---

635 Articles 33 and 34 GDPR. As regards notification, *see* European Data Protection Board, *Guidelines 1/2021 on Examples regarding Data Breach Notification*; WP29 Article 29 Working Party. *Guidelines on Personal data breach notification under Regulation 2016/679*. WP250 18/en, 2018.

636 Article 32 (1) GDPR: "taking into account the state of the art, the costs of implementation and the nature, scope, context and purposes of processing as well as the risk of varying likelihood and severity for the rights and freedoms of natural persons, the controller and the processor shall implement appropriate technical and organisational measures to ensure a level of security appropriate to the risk, including inter alia as appropriate (...)."

637 *See* Recital 83 GDPR: "in order to maintain security and to prevent processing in infringement of this Regulation, the controller or processor should evaluate the risks inherent in the processing and implement measures to mitigate those risks, such as encryption. Those measures should ensure an appropriate level of security, including confidentiality, taking into account the state of the art and the costs of implementation in relation to the risks and the nature of the personal data to be protected. In assessing data security risk, consideration should be given to the risks that are presented by personal data processing, such as accidental or unlawful destruction, loss, alteration, unauthorised disclosure of, or access to, personal data transmitted, stored or otherwise processed which may in particular lead to physical, material or non-material damage". Article 32 (2) reads as follows: "2. In assessing the appropriate level of security account shall be taken in particular of the risks that are presented by processing, in particular from accidental or unlawful destruction, loss, alteration, unauthorised disclosure of, or access to personal data transmitted, stored or otherwise processed".

638 *See* CNIL. Commission Nationale de l'Informatique et des Libertés. *The CNIL's Guide on Security of personal data*. 2018, pp. 3–4; European Union Agency for Network & Information Security, *Handbook on Security of Personal Data Processing*.

- Identifying the human or non-human, internal or external sources of risks;
- Identifying the possible threats;
- Evaluating the severity and likelihood of the risks;
- Determining the measures to address the security risks.

When determining the measures, the state of the art shall be evaluated, as well as the cost of implementation and the specific characteristics of the processing activities[639]. Appropriate security measures should be implemented and documented, and periodical security audits should be carried out. Internal guidelines on notifications and procedures in case of data breach are secure organisational measures.

Article 32 explicitly adds the obligation for the processor, lists several examples of security measures, and refers to certification and codes of conduct as mechanisms to ensure compliance[640]. Within the list, pseudonymisation and encryption are methods to ensure security. The contract between the controller and the processor shows that the latter must take all measures pursuant to Article 32 in order to cooperate with the former[641].

The measures implemented according to Articles 25 and 32 are strictly connected and, therefore, it seems difficult to discriminate between technical DPbD measures and security measures[642]. Indeed, the texts of the provisions are similar and DPbD measures should aim at implementing data protection rules within the security principle (i.e. integrity and confidentiality).

However, DPbD obligation and the duty of security represent separate duties with different timing: the former shall be adopted both at the time of the determination of the means for processing and at the time of the

639 On the state of the art of security measures *see* IT Security Association Germany, *Guidelines "State of the Art"*, pp. 18–36.

640 Article 32(1) GDPR refers to these appropriate measures: "(a) the pseudonymisation and encryption of personal data; (b) the ability to ensure the ongoing confidentiality, integrity, availability and resilience of processing systems and services; (c) the ability to restore the availability and access to personal data in a timely manner in the event of a physical or technical incident; (d) a process for regularly testing, assessing and evaluating the effectiveness of technical and organisational measures for ensuring the security of the processing". Article 32(3) provides that "adherence to an approved code of conduct as referred to in Article 40 or an approved certification mechanism as referred to in Article 42 may be used as an element by which to demonstrate compliance".

641 Article 28(3)(c) GDPR.

642 *See* D'Acquisto et al., *Intelligenza artificiale, protezione dei dati personali e regolazione*, p. 109.

processing itself, while the latter at the time of the processing. Article 25 is inside Chapter IV, Section 1 on the general obligation of the controller and processor. It is explicitly a general and enforceable legal obligation. By contrast, Article 32 is in the next Section 2 on the security of processing, where the duty of security is not defined as an obligation. Despite the categorisation, compliance with Article 32 is backed by the same administrative fines provided for Article 25 in accordance with Article 83(4)(a) GDPR.

### 2.5.2 Data protection impact assessment

The DPIA is a specific assessment mandated by the GDPR. This process aims to identify and minimise the risks for data subject posed by processing. The operations on personal data present some inherent risks for individuals that depend on the nature and scope of processing[643]. It has been argued that data processing raises risks by default[644].

On some grounds conducting a DPIA is mandatory before the beginning of the processing, that is *ex ante*. In particular, Article 35 GDPR requires the controller to carry out an assessment of the impact of the envisaged processing operations or set of similar operations where, taking into account the nature, scope, context and purposes of the processing, its operation is likely to result in a high risk to the rights and freedoms of natural persons[645].

In addition to the general clause, the same legal requirement specifies three cases where the DPIA is particularly required[646]. After a consultation

---

643 Giakoumopoulos, Buttarelli, and O'Flamerty, *Handbook on European data protection law*, p. 179.

644 Katerina Demetzou. "Data Protection Impact Assessment: A tool for accountability and the unclarified concept of 'high risk' in the General Data Protection Regulation". In: *Computer Law & Security Review* 35.6 (2019), p. 105342.

645 Article 35(1) GDPR. *See* also Recitals 84, and 90 – 93 GDPR. On Article 35 *see* Eleni Kosta. "Chapter IV Controller and Processor (Articles 24–43). Article 35. Data protection impact assessment". In: *The EU General Data Protection Regulation (GDPR): A Commentary*. Oxford University Press, 2020, pp. 665–679. ISBN: 9780198826491.

646 Article 35(3) GDPR: "(a) a systematic and extensive evaluation of personal aspects relating to natural persons which is based on automated processing, including profiling, and on which decisions are based that produce legal effects concerning the natural person or similarly significantly affect the natural person; (b) processing on a large scale of special categories of data referred to in

with the EDPB, each DPA has established a list of the kind of processing operations that are, or are not, subject to the requirement[647].

When designated the DPO should collaborate on the assessment[648]. The involvement of the DPO is highly recommended from the beginning of the assessment since the officer can give constant adequate advice[649]. Even the data subjects or their representatives could advise the controller unless their involvement interferes with the protection of commercial or public interests or the security of processing operations[650].

The GDPR further establishes the minimum features of a DPIA. According to the legal requirement, it is necessary to systematically describe the operations, purposes and, where applicable, legitimate interest of the processing, including the explanation of the necessity and proportionality of these operations in relation to the mentioned purposes[651]. Moreover, it is clearly indispensable to include the assessment of the risks and all the measures envisaged by the controller to address the risks, including all the safeguards and mechanisms adopted to ensure the protection of personal data and to demonstrate compliance, taking into account the rights and legitimate interests of data subjects and other persons concerned[652].

---

Article 9 (1), or of personal data relating to criminal convictions and offences referred to in Article 10; or (c) a systematic monitoring of a publicly accessible area on a large scale". According to Article 29 Working Party, this list is non-exhaustive. *See* Article 29 Working Party, *Guidelines on Data Protection Impact Assessment (DPIA) and determining whether processing is "likely to result in a high risk" for the purposes of Regulation 2016/679*, p. 9.

647 *See* Article 35(4) and (5) GDPR. In 2019 the EDPB released the 28 opinions on the draft lists of the DPA of each Member State. *See* the website of EDPB at <edpb.europa.eu/our-work-tools/our-documents/topic/ data-protection-impact-assessment-dpia_en>. Last accessed 06/10/2021. For drafting the list, it is necessary to take into account the economic effects of such list for the free movement of personal data within the EU. *See* Article 35(6) GDPR on the consistency mechanism.

648 Article 35(2) GDPR. According to Article 39(1)(c), the DPO shall provide advice on DPIA when requested and monitor the analysis.

649 *See* Atanas Yordanov. "Nature and Ideal Steps of the Data Protection Impact Assessment under the General Data Protection Regulation". In: *Eur. Data Prot. L. Rev.* 3 (2017), pp. 486–495, p. 493.

650 Article 35(9) GDPR.

651 *See* Article 35(7)(a) and (b) GDPR.

652 *See* Article 35(7)(c) and (d) GDPR.

Since this assessment is complex, codes of conduct could be considered a useful tool for performing the analysis[653]. Even standards provide guidance on managing the process. Whenever the controller realises that there are high risks and fails to determine the measures, prior consultation with the DPA is required in accordance with Article 36.

After the initial analysis, the DPIA should be reviewed in order to monitor the consistency between the risk assessment and the operations of the processing and to perform new analysis in accordance with new risks[654].

The provision of Article 35 contains vague concepts, such as "large scale". The phrase "likely to result in high risk" is also unclear[655]. Hence, Article 29 Working Party specified nine criteria for identifying where the risk is high[656]. This attribute indicates high likelihood and/or high severity of the hypothetical event objectively assessed by the controller[657].

The decision on whether or not to perform an assessment should be made on a case-by-case basis[658]. Therefore, it should be pointed out that carrying out the DPIA is not mandatory for every processing operation. By contrast, DPbD measures and its internal risk evaluation shall always be implemented. The generic steps of a DPIA may be summarised as follows[659]:

---

653 *See* Article 35(8) GDPR, which states: "compliance with approved codes of conduct referred to in Article 40 by the relevant controllers or processors shall be taken into due account in assessing the impact of the processing operations performed by such controllers or processors, in particular for the purposes of a data protection impact assessment".

654 Article 35(11) GDPR.

655 *See* Yordanov, "Nature and Ideal Steps of the Data Protection Impact Assessment under the General Data Protection Regulation", p. 490. On the "large scale" criterion *see* further Chapter 3, Section 3.3.3.

656 *See* the criteria in Article 29 Working Party, *Guidelines on Data Protection Impact Assessment (DPIA) and determining whether processing is "likely to result in a high risk" for the purposes of Regulation 2016/679*, pp. 9–10. One of these criteria is the nature of data when it is sensitive or highly personal.

657 Demetzou, "Data Protection Impact Assessment: A tool for accountability and the unclarified concept of 'high risk' in the General Data Protection Regulation".

658 *See* Yordanov, "Nature and Ideal Steps of the Data Protection Impact Assessment under the General Data Protection Regulation", p. 491.

659 This framework has been elaborated on many sources. It is based on Article 35 GDPR, the WP29 Opinion on DPIA, a legal analysis of the GDPR and some sources on the subject that include: ISO/IEC 29134:2017(en) Information technology — Security techniques — Guidelines for privacy impact assessment; Commission Nationale de l'Informatique et des Libertés, *Privacy Impact Assessment (PIA). Methodology*; and Yordanov, "Nature and Ideal Steps of the Data

- Assessment of the necessity of the DPIA;
- Systematic description of the planned processing (nature, scope, context, purpose) for each operation or set of operations, and analysis of the personal data workflow and the assets on which they rely;
- Assessment of the necessity and proportionality of the processing operations in relation to the purposes by checking the compliance with data protection principles;
- Identification of the risks in relation to the rights and freedoms of individuals by evaluating their severity and likelihood;
- Identification of the measures and safeguards to address these risks;
- Where applicable, advice of the DPO, consultation with the data subjects, or prior consultation with the DPA;
- Documentation of the assessment and of the process;
- Periodic review of the assessment.

Several methodologies can assist the controller in carrying out the DPIA[660]. This scheme shows that DPbD planning and DPIA may be strictly connected because they take into account contextual factors and the risks for rights and freedoms. They are both iterative and proactive. Indeed, DPbD and DPIA processes require continuous improvement. Both concepts are aligned with the rationale of the accountability principle, which implies scalability, flexibility and technological neutrality. A correct application of DPbD and DPbDf may make a risk assessment unnecessary in many cases because the risk analysis is already integrated and mitigated[661].

---

Protection Impact Assessment under the General Data Protection Regulation", p. 490.

660 *See* Annex 1 of Article 29 Working Party, *Guidelines on Data Protection Impact Assessment (DPIA) and determining whether processing is "likely to result in a high risk" for the purposes of Regulation 2016/679*. Criteria for an acceptable DPIA are provided in Annex 2. *See* also the framework of CNIL provided in: CNIL Commission Nationale de l'Informatique et des Libertés. *Privacy Impact Assessment (PIA). Knowledge basis*. 2018; Commission Nationale de l'Informatique et des Libertés, *Privacy Impact Assessment (PIA). Methodology*; CNIL Commission Nationale de l'Informatique et des Libertés. *Privacy Impact Assessment (PIA). Templates*. 2018. This framework will be further analysed in Chapter 5, Section 5.4 of this book.

661 *See* e.g. Mantelero, "Il nuovo approccio della valutazione del rischio nella sicurezza dei dati. Valutazione d'impatto e consultazione preventiva (Artt. 32–39)", p. 308; Mantelero, "La gestione del rischio", p. 470; and Yordanov, "Nature and Ideal Steps of the Data Protection Impact Assessment under the General Data Protection Regulation", p. 490.

Since DPbD involves a trade-off of data subjects' rights, DPIA is a potential apt point in the compliance process for considering these trade-offs[662]. DPIA is an organisational strategy. Therefore, this assessment may be an important instrument to comply with the requirements of Article 25[663].

### 2.5.3 Certification mechanisms

The last related requirement to be addressed is the certification mechanism since the third part of Article 25 states:

> "3. An approved certification mechanism pursuant to Article 42 may be used as an element to demonstrate compliance with the requirements set out in paragraphs 1 and 2 of this Article".

Article 42 GDPR introduces certification mechanisms, data protection seals and marks as tools for demonstrating compliance of processing operations. In particular, the long legal requirement provides general rules for third-party certification[664]. This certification mechanism is audited by a third-party independent certification body and is supervised by a DPA[665]. The roles are divided as follows. On the one hand, the certification body assesses the conformity of the product or service with predefined requirements included in a technical standard or in the law and by way of a voluntary and transparent process, and where appropriate issues a certifi-

662 *See* Michael Veale, Reuben Binns, and Jef Ausloos. "When data protection by design and data subject rights clash". In: *International Data Privacy Law* 8.2 (2018), pp. 105–123, p. 117. In this study the authors analysed possible trade-offs (e.g. between control and confidentiality).

663 *See* Yordanov, "Nature and Ideal Steps of the Data Protection Impact Assessment under the General Data Protection Regulation", p. 490.

664 *See* for a discussion on Article 42 and 43 GDPR, Irene Kamara and Paul De Hert. "Data protection certification in the EU: Possibilities, actors and building blocks in a reformed landscape". In: *Privacy and data protection seals*. Springer, 2018, pp. 7–34. ISBN: 9789462652286; Ronald Leenes. "Chapter IV Controller and Processor (Articles 24–43). Article 42. Certification". In: *The EU General Data Protection Regulation (GDPR): A Commentary*. Oxford University Press, 2020, pp. 732–743. ISBN: 9780198826491; Ronald Leenes. "Chapter IV Controller and Processor (Articles 24–43). Article 43. Certification bodies". In: *The EU General Data Protection Regulation (GDPR): A Commentary*. Oxford University Press, 2020, pp. 744–754. ISBN: 9780198826491.

665 Kamara and De Hert, "Data protection certification in the EU: Possibilities, actors and building blocks in a reformed landscape", p. 14.

cate; on the other hand, the competent supervisory authority accredits the body in accordance with some criteria, and has the corrective powers to withdraw the certification, order the body to withdraw, and order it not to issue the certification where the requirements are not or no longer met[666]. The requirements depend on the aims of the certification, the type of product or system and its application area[667].

The typical phases of the assessment are: 1) submission of application by the controller or processor (i.e. interested party); 2) formal application review, evaluation, review, attestation, issuance of certification by the certification body; and 3) surveillance of the DPA[668]. ENISA suggested that the data protection authorities should adopt a common approach on the certification models, criteria and processes[669]. In 2019, the EDPB issued the Guidelines on certification under the GDPR in order to give advice to DPAs, certification bodies, national accreditation bodies, EC, to controllers and processors[670].

The certification mechanism of the GDPR is voluntary. Certification is both a means for demonstrating compliance and a tool for enhancing

666 *See* Article 42, 43 and 58(2)(h) GDPR, and Kamara and De Hert, *op. cit.*, p. 15. According to Article 58 GDPR, DPAs have the power to issue and withdraw certification and corrective power, too. Article 58(3)(f) states that the supervisory authority shall have the authorisation power "to issue certifications and approve criteria of certification in accordance with Article 42(5)". In Article 58(2)(h) it is specified that the authority has the corrective power "to withdraw a certification or to order the certification body to withdraw a certification issued pursuant to Articles 42 and 43, or to order the certification body not to issue certification if the requirements for the certification are not or are no longer met".

667 *Ibid.*

668 *See* EDPB European Data Protection Board. *Guidelines 1/2018 on certification and identifying certification criteria in accordance with Articles 42 and 43 of the Regulation*. European Data Protection Board. Version 3.0, 2019, p. 9. *See* also the scheme in Kamara and De Hert, "Data protection certification in the EU: Possibilities, actors and building blocks in a reformed landscape", p. 15. The author adapted the stages of an international standards to Article 42 GDPR.

669 *See* European Union Agency for Network & Information Security, *Recommendations on European Data Protection Certification*, p. 26.

670 European Data Protection Board, *Guidelines 1/2018 on certification and identifying certification criteria in accordance with Articles 42 and 43 of the Regulation*.

671 *See* Recital 100 GDPR that states: "in order to enhance transparency and compliance with this Regulation, the establishment of certification mechanisms and data protection seals and marks should be encouraged, allowing data subjects to quickly assess the level of data protection of relevant products and services".

transparency[671]. Therefore, certification is linked with the concept of accountability[672].

However, compliance with the GDPR cannot be certified. Article 42(4) explicitly specifies that a certification does not reduce the responsibility of the controller or the processor to comply with the Regulation, leaving intact the judgement of the supervisory authorities or the courts. Thus, certification is not a presumption of full conformity with the legal obligations stemming from the GDPR[673].

Nonetheless, it has been argued that certification is a means for "externalising in a concrete and objective way that technical and organisational measures (or a part of them depending on the scope of the certification) have been taken and implemented in a satisfactory manner"[674]. Moreover, according to Article 83 the DPA takes into account the adherence to an approved certification mechanism when imposing the fines[675].

In accordance with the third paragraphs of Article 25, DPbD may be translated into a certification requirement and its implementation may be certified by an accredited, independent and expert party. As previously noted for PbD, the certification could guide data subjects, it enhances their trust, and represents a competitive advantage in the market. In addition, the EDPB argued that "the ability to get a processing operation certified provides an added value to a controller when choosing between different processing software, hardware, services and/or systems from producers or processors", and that "certification seal may also guide data subjects in their choice between different goods and services"[676]. As a result, developers and providers may be indirectly encouraged to adopt a certification by implementing DPbD and DPbDf so as to obtain a competitive advantage in the market and enhance trust in the processing.

In summary, this section has investigated how the EU legal framework on data protection has established an obligation to regulate by design and by default data processing operations. It is now necessary to compare the concepts of PbD, as described in the critical analysis, and DPbD in order to explain why the wording cannot be used interchangeably.

---

672 *See* European Union Agency for Network & Information Security, *Recommendations on European Data Protection Certification*, p. 13.

673 Kamara and De Hert, "Data protection certification in the EU: Possibilities, actors and building blocks in a reformed landscape", p. 25.

674 *Ibid.*

675 Article 83(2)(j) GDPR.

676 *See* European Data Protection Board, *Guidelines 4/2019 on Article 25 Data Protection by Design and by Default*, p. 29.

## 2.6 *A comparison between privacy and data protection by design*

The concept pioneered by Ann Cavoukian differs from the GDPR's principle in many ways. This section explains the similarities and differences between PbD and DPbD.

PbD is usually connected with the FIPs, while DPbD is established in the EU data protection framework. Indeed, it has been argued that the concept of the GDPR is more comprehensive than PbD[677]. As noted above, the FTC pointed out that its framework incorporates the FIPs. DPbD is more ambitious because it goes beyond the FIPs and entails more rights and principles[678]. The EU principles are more wide-ranging than the FIPs, in the US conception especially[679]. For examples, the right to access in the GDPR (Art. 15) and the right to object automated decision making (Art. 22) are not in the FIPs. Thus, DPbD should integrate more safeguards in order to protect these specific rights of the data subject. The EU Charter of Fundamental Rights shall also be included because Article 25 refers to the rights and freedoms after mentioning the GDPR requirements.

Furthermore, both concepts represent broad proactive approaches. PbD is an international concept perceived as a principle and advocated by scholars and policymakers for the protection of privacy and personal data. It includes the protection of default settings. DPbD and DPbDf are separately defined in a legal requirement of a regulation focused on persona data. DPbD is a fully enforceable obligation, while PbD entails a visionary and ethical dimension[680].

The terms cannot be used interchangeably[681]. It has been pointed out that DPbD has been inspired by the concept of PbD[682]. Following the arguments and the lines of the critical analysis performed on PbD, some considerations on DPbD can be made.

It is arguable that Article 25 included a flexible and enforceable rule that is applicable to various contexts in the EU framework for the processing

---

677 Tsormpatzoudi, Berendt, and Coudert, "Privacy by design: from research and policy to practice–the challenge of multi-disciplinarity", p. 202.

678 Bygrave, "Hardwiring privacy", p. 761.

679 *See ibid.* On the comparison between EU and US principles *see* Chapter 4, Section 4.2.

680 *See* European Data Protection Supervisor, *Opinion 5/2018, Preliminary Opinion on privacy by design*, pp. 1, 5.

681 Bygrave, "Hardwiring privacy", p. 761.

682 *See* Luiz Costa and Yves Poullet. "Privacy and the regulation of 2012". In: *Computer Law & Security Review* 28.3 (2012), pp. 254–262, p. 260.

of personal data. However, the requirement has a broad definition that makes it difficult to implement, as previously noted. This provision does not seem clear enough for stakeholders. It does not define standards for the design process and misses the references to developers. Nevertheless, Article 25 is technologically neutral and dynamic and leaves room to specific customised solutions.

DPbD may improve the effectiveness of the GDPR by empowering data subjects. The translation and interpretation issues are still relevant, but several projects are underway to overcome the challenges. With DPbD and DPbDf the EU is promoting a proactive and preventive approach without completely delegating privacy regulation to companies.

DPbD is strictly connected to data security without confusing the approaches. It requires both "privacy-by-policy" and "privacy-by-architecture" strategies. Building data protection principles will not always be possible. However, the GDPR is a set of rules that has to be perceived as a whole. Article 25 is just a piece of the puzzle.

As explained, DPbD implementation demands organisational measures. The data controller in the material and territorial scope of the GDPR should adopt internal processes and bolster privacy management. Withing the GDPR, bureaucratic solutions for data protection are not sufficient for compliance.

Since 25 May 2018 large investments have been made in privacy programmes. It can be argued that DPbD and DPbDf can increase trust and confidence in products and services by creating opportunities for business. The relative concerns should not be forgotten, but the arguments adopted for balancing the disadvantages for PbD can be used here for DPbD.

Moreover, certification opportunity is directly mentioned by Article 25. EDPS explicitly presents DPbD as an opportunity for boosting the respect of ethics in technological development[683]. The GDPR does not aim to create barriers to innovation, but to provide a strong and more coherent data protection framework, backed by enforcement and given the importance of the digital internal market and the free movement of personal data within it[684]. It is hoped that DPbD will contribute to the creation of user-centric technologies and policies without excessively increasing the costs of access to them.

---

683 European Data Protection Supervisor, *Opinion 5/2018, Preliminary Opinion on privacy by design*, p. 21.

684 *See* Recitals 7 and 13 GDPR.

DPbD is a different version of Cavoukian's PbD. The following Table 2.4 summarises the main results of the comparison between the two concepts.

*Table 2.4 Summary of the comparison between PbD and DPbD*

| CRITERIA | PbD | DPbD |
|---|---|---|
| Legal system | International recognition at policy level | EU |
| Legal nature | Recommended practice | Principle and obligation |
| Theoretical framework | Privacy and data protection | Data protection |
| Embedded principles | FIPs | GDPR principles and EU Charter |
| Embedded rights | Non specified | Arts. 12–22 GDPR and Charter |
| Timing | Full life cycle | Full life cycle of processing |
| Flexibility | Yes | Yes |
| Technical neutrality | Yes | Yes |
| Subjects | All stakeholders | Data controller primarily |
| Privacy by Default | Included | Excluded |
| Security | Included | Separate duty |

Having defined what is meant by PbD, DPbDf and DPbD, and before proceeding to contextualise the latter principle in the healthcare context it is important to discuss the interplay between data protection and other fundamental rights.

## 2.7 *Balancing the right to data protection against other rights and freedoms*

The human rights discourse plays an increasing role in the debate on digital technologies[685]. The rights to privacy and data protection are not absolute rights. They may be limited, if necessary, to protect a general interest or other rights and freedoms[686]. A synergy between privacy and other legal values is possible, as are conflicts[687]. In society there are typically competing interests at play. In his pioneering book of 1967, Westin defined privacy as follows[688]:

> "Privacy is the claim of individuals, groups, or institutions to determine for themselves when, how, and to what extent information about them is communicated to others".

In Westin's view, privacy is never absolute, and it exists in the context of a relationship between the individual and society. The natural person has control over his or her data. The balances of privacy vary from society to society due to cultural differences[689].

This study focuses primarily on data protection in the EU. According to Recital 4 GDPR, the right to the protection of personal data shall be considered "in relation to its function in society and be balanced against other fundamental rights, in accordance with the principle of proportionality". As noted above, the GDPR refers to the Charter of Fundamental Rights of the European Union, and in particular to the respect for private and family life, for home and communications, the respect of freedom of thought, of conscience and religion, of freedom of expression and information, freedom to conduct a business, the right to an effective remedy and to a fair trial, and cultural, religious and linguistic diversity.

According to Article 52(1) of the Charter and the CJEU's case law, limitations to the right of data protection are admissible if all the following conditions are met[690]:

---

685 Sartor, "Human rights and information technologies", p. 434.

686 *See* Giakoumopoulos, Buttarelli, and O'Flamerty, *Handbook on European data protection law*, p. 35; Rodotà and Conti, *Intervista su privacy e libertà*.

687 Sartor, "Human rights and information technologies", p. 442.

688 Westin, *Privacy and Freedom*, p. 7.

689 Westin, *op. cit.*, p. 31.

690 *See* Article 52(1) of the Charter and Giakoumopoulos, Buttarelli, and O'Flamerty, *Handbook on European data protection law*, pp. 42–52. This Handbook also provides some examples of the case law where each condition is further explained by the CJEU.

1. Limitations are provided for by law with sufficient precision;
2. Limitations respect the essence of the right to data protection, meaning that they do not devoid a fundamental right of its basic content without any justification;
3. Limitations are necessary and proportionate. Limitations can apply only in so far as strictly necessary and the resulting advantages do not outweigh the disadvantages that arise for the fundamental rights at stake;
4. Limitations meet objectives of general interest recognised by the EU or the need to protect the rights and freedoms of others.

Moreover, Article 23 of the GDPR specifies that possible restrictions provided by law shall respect the essence of the fundamental rights and freedoms and they shall be necessary and proportionate measures in a democratic society in order to safeguard defined general interests, such as national security or the rights and freedoms of others[691]. This Article

691 *See* Article 23 GDPR. The interests to safeguard are: "(a) national security; (b) defence; (c) public security; (d) the prevention, investigation, detection or prosecution of criminal offences or the execution of criminal penalties, including the safeguarding against and the prevention of threats to public security; (e) other important objectives of general public interest of the Union or of a Member State, in particular an important economic or financial interest of the Union or of a Member State, including monetary, budgetary and taxation matters, public health and social security; (f) the protection of judicial independence and judicial proceedings; (g) the prevention, investigation, detection and prosecution of breaches of ethics for regulated professions; (h) a monitoring, inspection or regulatory function connected, even occasionally, to the exercise of official authority in the cases referred to in points (a) to (e) and (g); (i) the protection of the data subject or the rights and freedoms of others; (j) the enforcement of civil law claims". As regards the need to meet objectives of general interest, they are further defined in Article 3 of the Treaty of the EU and in other specific provisions. Article 3 of the Treaty states that: "1. The Union's aim is to promote peace, its values and the well-being of its peoples. (...) It shall combat social exclusion and discrimination, and shall promote social justice and protection, equality between women and men, solidarity between generations and protection of the rights of the child. (…) It shall respect its rich cultural and linguistic diversity, and shall ensure that Europe's cultural heritage is safeguarded and enhanced. (...) 5. In its relations with the wider world, the Union shall uphold and promote its values and interests and contribute to the protection of its citizens. It shall contribute to peace, security, the sustainable development of the Earth, solidarity and mutual respect among peoples, free and fair trade, eradication of poverty and the protection of human rights, in particular the rights of the child, as well as to the strict observance and the development of international law, including respect for the principles of the United Nations

recognises that the right to personal data shall be considered in relation to its function in society[692].

Thus, when striking the balance between the right to data protection and another interest, the solution shall be a prudent and fair balance at the legislative level, which is guided by the constitutional principles of necessity and proportionality[693]. These principles represent a dual requirement with which a legislative measure shall comply[694].

Proportionality and necessity are general principles of EU law that have been widely used in the Court of Justice's case law[695]. In order to assess

---

Charter (...)". *See* the implementation of Article 23 in Member States' legislation at Legal TIPIK. *Report on the implementation of specific provisions of Regulation (EU) 2016/679*. European Commission. Directorate – General for Justice and Consumers, Unit C.3 Data Protection, 2021, pp. 15–23.

692 *See* Dominique Moore. "Chapter III Rights of the Data Subject (Articles 12–23). Article 23. Restrictions". In: *The EU General Data Protection Regulation (GDPR): A Commentary*. Oxford University Press, 2020, pp. 543–554. ISBN: 9780198826491, p. 545.

693 On principles of European constitutional law *see* Armin von Bogdandy and Bast Jürgen. *Principles of European Constitutional law*. Hart Publishing, 2020. ISBN: 9781841138220. On striking the balance between constitutional rights *see* Robert Alexy. "Constitutional rights, balancing, and rationality". In: *Ratio Juris* (2003), pp. 131–140; Giorgio Pino. "Conflitto e bilanciamento tra diritti fondamentali. Una mappa dei problemi". In: *Ragion Pratica* 28 (2007), pp. 219–276; Pino, *Diritti e interpretazione. Il ragionamento giuridico nello Stato costituzionale*; Robert Alexy. *A theory of constitutional rights*. Oxford University Press, 2010. ISBN: 9780199584239; Riccardo Guastini. "Principi costituzionali: identificazione, interpretazione, ponderazione, concretizzazione". In: *Dialoghi con Guido Alpa. Un volume offerto in occasione del suo LXXI compleanno*. 2018, pp. 313–324. ISBN: 9788832136050.

694 *See* EDPS European Data Protection Supervisor. *EDPS Guidelines on assessing the proportionality of measures that limit the fundamental rights to privacy and to the protection of personal data*. European Data Protection Supervisor, 2019, p. 2.

695 *See* the analysis by Lynskey, *The foundations of EU data protection law*, which dedicates Chapter 5 to "Reconciling Data Protection with Other Rights and Interests". *See* also Bogdandy and Jürgen, *Principles of European Constitutional law*, pp. 505–512 Charlotte Bagger Tranberg. "Proportionality and data protection in the case law of the European Court of Justice". In: *International Data Privacy Law* 1.4 (2011), pp. 239–248; Marie-Pierre Granger, Kristina Irion, et al. "The Court of Justice and the Data Retention Directive in Digital Rights Ireland: telling off the EU legislator and teaching a lesson in privacy and data protection". In: *European Law Review* 39.4 (2014), pp. 835–850; Orla Lynskey. "The Data Retention Directive is incompatible with the rights to privacy and data protection and is invalid in its entirety: Digital Rights Ireland". In: *Common Market Law Review* 51.6 (2014), pp. 1789–1811; Jeanne Pia Mifsud Bonnici. "Exploring the non-absolute nature of the right to data protection". In:

the proportionality and necessity of a measure, the legislator may apply two step-by-step methodologies: the so-called "necessity test" and "proportionality test"[696]. In fact, the two principles imply two different tests, and the latter shall follow the former, since necessity is a pre-condition for proportionality[697].

The first analysis is the "necessity test", which describes whether the measure is effective for the objective to be pursued and whether it is less intrusive compared to other options for achieving the same goal[698]. The EDPS listed the four steps of this test as follows[699]:

1. Factually describing in detail the measure proposed;
2. Identifying whether this measure represents a limitation on the rights to privacy and data protection, and to other fundamental rights;
3. Considering the goal of the measure against which the necessity of a measure should be assessed (e.g. public security);
4. Choosing whether the measure is effective and the least intrusive.

Secondly, the "proportionality test" should be performed. According to the CJEU's case law and to the EDPS, the advantages resulting from the legislative and discretionary measure shall not be outweighed by the disadvantages the measure causes with respect to the exercise of fundamental rights[700]. So, the test shall assess what safeguards the measures shall pro-

---

*International Review of Law, Computers & Technology* 28.2 (2014), pp. 131–143; Raphaël Gellert. "Understanding data protection as risk regulation". In: *J. Int. Law* 18.11 (2015), pp. 3–16; Paul De Hert and Vagelis Papakonstantinou. "The new General Data Protection Regulation: Still a sound system for the protection of individuals?" In: *Computer law & security review* 32.2 (2016), pp. 179–194.

696 *See* respectively EDPS European Data Protection Supervisor. *Assessing the necessity of measures that limit the fundamental right to the protection of personal data: a Toolkit*. European Data Protection Supervisor, 2017; European Data Protection Supervisor, *EDPS Guidelines on assessing the proportionality of measures that limit the fundamental rights to privacy and to the protection of personal data*.

697 On the relationship between necessity and proportionality *see* European Data Protection Supervisor, *op. cit.*, p. 9.

698 European Data Protection Supervisor, *Assessing the necessity of measures that limit the fundamental right to the protection of personal data: a Toolkit*, p. 5.

699 *See* European Data Protection Supervisor, *op. cit.*, p. 9, which provides more guidance on each step with reference to the CJEU's case law.

700 European Data Protection Supervisor, *op. cit.* In particular, the authority highlights the ruling of the CJEU in the Digital Rights Ireland case. The reference is: Digital Rights Ireland Ltd v. Minister for Communications, Marine and Natural Resources and Others and Kärntner Landesregierung and Others. Judgement of the Court (Grand Chamber) of 8 April 2014. Joined Cases C-293/12 and C-594/12.

vide in a particular context in order to reduce the risks for the rights to a proportionate level. The four steps are[701]:

5. Assessing the legitimacy of the goal of the measure proposed and whether this measure genuinely meets this goal from an "advantage/benefit" point of view[702];
6. Assessing the scope, extent and intensity of the impact to the rights from a "disadvantage/cost" point of view;
7. Proceeding to a fair balance between the two previous points of view;
8. Taking a decision on the proposed measure[703]. If the measure is not proportionate, introducing safeguards is fundamental.

Looking at these tests, the "goal" of the measure is usually the protection of the competing right or interest. Actually, the right to data protection interacts with several rights. For example, a balance of free speech and data protection interests is the de-indexing information required by the right to be forgotten[704]. In Article 85, the GDPR explicitly refers to the rights to freedom of expression and to receive information stating that Member States shall reconcile the right to the protection of personal data with these other rights[705].

---

701 European Data Protection Supervisor, *EDPS Guidelines on assessing the proportionality of measures that limit the fundamental rights to privacy and to the protection of personal data*, p. 12.

702 This phase is called "suitability" and "in fact test" by Bogdandy and Jürgen, *Principles of European Constitutional law*, p. 506.

703 This is the so-called "proportionality in the narrow sense" phase in Bogdandy and Jürgen, *op. cit.*, p. 507. During the analysis the concept of margin of appreciation is used.

704 *See* Hartzog, *Privacy's blueprint: the battle to control the design of new technologies*, p. 80. *See* also the analysis by Oreste Pollicino. "L''autunno caldo' della Corte di giustizia in tema di tutela dei diritti fondamentali in rete e le sfide del costituzionalismo alle prese con i nuovi poteri privati in ambito digitale". In: *Federalismi.it* 19 (2019), pp. 2–15, which focuses on how the CJEU decided in its case law and how its decisions impacted the global digital market.

705 On the balance between privacy, data protection and freedom of expression *see* Christopher Docksey. "Four fundamental rights: finding the balance". In: *International Data Privacy Law* 6.3 (2016), pp. 195–209; Stefan Kulk and Frederik Zuiderveen Borgesius. "Privacy, Freedom of Expression, and the Right to Be Forgotten in Europe". In: *The Cambridge Handbook of Consumer Privacy*. Cambridge University Press, 2018, pp. 301–320. ISBN: 9781316831960; Giorgia Bincoletto. "Italy – Italian DPA Balancing Data Protection and Freedom of Expression: Essentiality and Fairness as key principles". In *Eur. Data Prot. L. Rev.* 7 (1 2021), pp. 115–119. On this right in the digital age *see* Giovanni Pitruzzella, Oreste Pollicino, and Stefano Quintarelli. *Parole e potere: libertà d'espressione, hate speech e fake news*. EGEA, 2017. ISBN: 9788823836419.

For the purposes of the present research, it is not necessary to discuss all the possible interactions of the right to data protection. Indeed, it is relevant to stress that when advocating the respect of DPbD and DPbDf, possible conditions may limit the right to data protection, and some balancing may be necessary[706]. This balancing results in an equilibrium between two rights or interests that avoids the sacrifice of one in favour of the other[707].

Generally, DPbD establishes a balance between competing interests by indicating the factors and criteria analysed above, such as the cost of implementation and the risks for rights and freedoms. As explained, a weighing process is already embedded in Article 25.

However, the obligation to implement DPbD could significantly affect the economic interests of the controller, which is recognised under freedom to conduct a business[708]. Whether the economic interests of private parties, or of the general public in the case of public tenders, could justify limiting the right to data protection is a general question[709]. According to some scholars, this interaction is a so-called "partial conflict" because a case-by-case approach is possible[710]. It is necessary to bear in mind that "data protection readjusts the balance of power between the data subject and those who process personal data", and it "reduces power asymmetry through the use of opt-in as a default setting"[711]. Within DPbD the law is responsive to the power of design by articulating boundaries, guidance, and goals to innovation[712]. As noted in the beginning of this book, design is powerful and political[713]. Striking the balance between the right to data protection and freedom to conduct a business may apply the general rules outlined above, but the concrete choice does not come from the

706 On balancing rights and the tasks of the courts and legislators *see* Giovanella, *Copyright and Information Privacy: Conflicting Rights in Balance*.

707 *See* Giovanella, *op. cit.*, p. 11. The author explains that she prefers the term "right", but the term "interest" is also frequently used by scholars.

708 Article 16 of the Charter of Fundamental Rights of the European Union states: "the freedom to conduct a business in accordance with Union law and national laws and practices is recognised".

709 Giakoumopoulos, Buttarelli, and O'Flamerty, *Handbook on European data protection law*, p. 78.

710 *See* further in Giovanella, *Copyright and Information Privacy: Conflicting Rights in Balance*, p. 8.

711 Lynskey, *The foundations of EU data protection law*, pp. 213, 214.

712 Hartzog, *Privacy's blueprint: the battle to control the design of new technologies*, p. 51.

713 *See* the Introductory Remarks.

legislator, but from the data controller, and (maybe) from the developer. The EU legislator introduced the "state of the art" and the "cost of implementation" criteria for providing concrete factors and some guidance for DPbD implementation. Nonetheless, courts and the DPAs while ruling on future case law will probably define more detailed steps for balancing these specific interests embedded in Article 25 GDPR.

In addition to the interests of the data controller, the implementation of DPbD in a specific context could create a conflict between the interests of the individual for the protection of his or her rights and freedoms, which are better guaranteed by design or by default, and of the public, which may want to use personal data for protecting substantial or general interests. A particular context where the protection of personal data under Article 25 may conflict with other public interests is the healthcare domain since personal health data may be used in the area of public health for protecting communities and societies against serious threats to health (e.g. pandemic), for conducting scientific research, or for ensuring high standards of health management. So, balances, necessary goals and exceptions, and proportionate safeguards may be needed in some situations. Also, for this reason, this work investigates the significance of DPbD in a specific field of the healthcare domain, which is e-health. More considerations on striking the balance between data protection and public health will be added at the end of the next Chapter.

Thus far, specific case law on the inner balance of Article 25 does not exist, but DPAs have started to sanction data controllers for non-compliance with its requirements[714]. It is arguable that future court rulings, and legislative measures will better specify how to balance the principle of DPbD and the right to data protection against other principles, rights and interests, especially. The fair balance will remain a necessary task of courts and legislators. In summary, this Chapter has attempted to provide a deep analysis of PbD and DPbD.

As pointed out by Tamó, the concrete implementation of these approaches depends on the actual technology at play, the sector where it is used and the context of the individual case[715]. The Chapter that follows moves on to consider the e-health field and the processing of personal health data, analysing the legal framework and presenting a case study of e-health technology: the Electronic Health Record system.

---

714 *See* Chapter 6, Section 6.5.

715 Tamó-Larrieux, *Designing for privacy and its legal framework: data protection by design and default for the internet of things*, p. 200.

# Chapter 3 Data protection and the e-health sector

## 3.1 *Introductory remarks*

This chapter is dedicated to the healthcare domain. Health is a critical part of people's well-being[716]. According to the WHO, health is a "state of complete physical, mental and social well-being and not merely the absence of disease or infirmity"[717]. Article 35 of the EU Charter of Fundamental Rights states that "everyone has the right of access to preventive health care and the right to benefit from medical treatment" and that "a high level of human health protection shall be ensured in the definition and implementation of all the Union's policies and activities"[718]. The right to access to healthcare is at the core of human well-being.

According to Abedjan *et al.*, public expenditure on healthcare will increase by one third by 2060 worldwide due to a rapidly ageing population[719]. In recent years, healthcare provision has been improved by the use of digital technologies[720]. Healthcare is one of the more data-intensive

716 *See* further on OECD, *How's Life in the Digital Age? Opportunities and Risks of the Digital Transformation for People's Well-being.*

717 *See* the comment on the definition in Daniel Callahan. "The WHO definition of 'health'". In: *Hastings Center Studies* (1973), pp. 77–87.

718 This last sentence is also used in Article 168 of the Consolidated versions of the Treaty on European Union and the Treaty on the Functioning of the European Union.

719 *See* Abedjan et al., "Data science in healthcare: Benefits, challenges and opportunities", p. 6. Other statistics are reported by Y. Quintana and C. Safran. "Global health informatics — an overview". In: *Global Health Informatics*. Elsevier, 2017, pp. 1–13. ISBN: 9780128045916.

720 *See* the evolution of the digitalisation of healthcare in D. Sigulem, M.P. Ramos, and R. de Holanda Albuquerque. "The New Medicine: From the Paper Medical Record to the Digitized Human Being". In: *Global Health Informatics*. Elsevier, 2017, pp. 152–167. ISBN: 9780128045916.

721 The World Health Organisation provides a portal on the Global Health Observatory with data and detailed indicators. *See* <www.who.int/data/gho>. Last accessed 06/10/2021.

sectors[721]. Even though ICTs have a great potential for supporting healthcare[722], some privacy and security concerns arise[723].

The first part of this chapter addresses some issues that have emerged from the use of technology for health purposes. Generally, the risk level for the processing of personal health data is high. Because of the sensitive nature of personal health data, special attention should be paid to privacy and data protection concerns of health and health-related data. Then, the Chapter focuses on the data protection law for the processing of personal health data in the EU legal framework. After these theoretical considerations, the Chapter presents the case study of the book, a specific e-health technology called Electronic Health Record system. The state of the art, the applicable rules, and cross-border use of this technology are examinated. Finally, the Chapter briefly concludes with other consideration on balancing the right to data protection against public interests in the healthcare context.

## 3.2 *Data protection concerns of e-health technologies*

Since the 1990s, ICTs have played an important role in improving access to and quality of healthcare, and the neologism *e-health* connects the use of digital technologies to this sector[724]. As mentioned in the first pages

---

722 *See* for some statistics OECD, *How's Life in the Digital Age? Opportunities and Risks of the Digital Transformation for People's Well-being.*

723 *See ex multis* EXPH Expert Panel on effective ways of investing in Health. *Assessing the impact of digital transformation of health services*. Luxembourg: Publications Office of the European Union. 2019; OECD, *OECD Recommendation on Health Data Governance*; Council of the European Union, EU Council, *Council conclusions on Health in the Digital Society — making progress in data-driven innovation in the field of health*; Hooghiemstra, "Informational Self-Determination, Digital Health and New Features of Data Protection"; Arak and Wójcik, *Transforming eHealth into a political and economic advantage*; Adams, Purtova, and Leenes, *Under observation: The interplay between eHealth and surveillance*; Paolo Guarda. "Telemedicine and Application Scenarios: Common Privacy and Security Requirements in the European Union Context". In: *Trento Law and Technology Research Group Research Paper n. 23* (2015); Lowrance, *Privacy, confidentiality, and health research*.

724 Aceto, Persico, and Pescapé, "The role of Information and Communication Technologies in healthcare: taxonomies, perspectives, and challenges", pp. 125, 128.

of this work, the digital processing of health data creates both enormous opportunities and critical challenges.

The digitisation should be considered as more than a technical process since it involves both ICTs and practices, services and healthcare-related processes[725]. For this reason, the definition of e-health provided by the European Commission is[726]:

> "The use of ICT in health products, services and processes combined with organisational change in healthcare systems and new skills, in order to improve health of citizens, efficiency and productivity in healthcare delivery, and the economic and social value of health".

In theory, the opportunities of the digital processing could be summarised as better clinical outcomes, more tailored therapeutic responses and more effective disease management[727]. E-health strengthens the quality and the effectiveness of the healthcare provision by improving service quality and health benefits, and by saving time[728]. Health Information Technologies (HITs) can respond to the needs of patients most effectively and efficiently[729]. E-health systems can also reduce costs and improve productivity of the health sector by reducing medical errors, improving billing and record-keeping, and decreasing unnecessary care[730]. It has been noted

---

725 For a description of the "digital transformation" of healthcare *see* Expert Panel on effective ways of investing in Health, *Assessing the impact of digital transformation of health services*, pp. 13–14.

726 European Commission, "eHealth Action Plan 2012–2020. Innovative healthcare for the 21st century", p. 3.

727 This summary is provided by Abedjan et al., "Data science in healthcare: Benefits, challenges and opportunities", p. 16. According to a study by Polityka Insight, the advantages are: "improved quality of care; better planning and resource allocation; cost efficiency; more efficient health landscape; enhancing the evidence base for health service delivery and policy making; real-time monitoring; providing better, tailored and personalized services; and preemptive measures". *See* Arak and Wójcik, *Transforming eHealth into a political and economic advantage*, p. 6.

728 Guarda, "Telemedicine and Application Scenarios: Common Privacy and Security Requirements in the European Union Context", pp. 1, 7. *See* also Paolo Guarda. "I dati sanitari". In: *I dati personali nel diritto europeo*. G. Giappichelli Editore, Torino, 2019, pp. 591–626. ISBN: 9788892112742, pp. 614–615.

729 Concetta Tania Di Iorio and Fabrizio Carinci. "Privacy and health care information systems: where is the balance?" In: *eHealth: Legal, Ethical and Governance Challenges*. Springer, 2013, pp. 77–105. ISBN: 9783642224744, p. 77.

730 *See* EC European Commission. *Communication from the Commission to the Council, the European Parliament, the European Economic and Social Committee and*

that "anytime" and "anywhere" monitoring, diagnosis and treatment are part of an "on-demand" culture which characterises the world of online commerce[731]. The traditional workplace has been completely redefined, the demand for health and social services increases, and new mobility phenomena, such as "hospital shopping", appear[732]. At the EU level, digital technologies have deeply changed the provision of healthcare by facilitating the sharing of data in more effective ways across countries and enabling new medical treatments[733]. E-health is a key e-strategy of the EU[734]. It represents a new industry of the digital age with great market potential.

---

*the Committee of the Regions on e-Health – making healthcare better for European citizens: An action Plan for a European e-Health Area*. European Commission. Brussels: COM (2004), 356 final. 2004, p. 6. The Commission made reference to the detailed study by Patricia Danzon and Michael Furukawa. "e-Health: effects of the Internet on competition and productivity in health care". In: *The economic payoff from the internet revolution*. Brookings Institution Press, 2001, pp. 209–244. ISBN: 9780815700654. This study has proven the major impact of the Internet on the health care sector by analysing the economic trends of the market.

731 *See* Ethan Katsh and Orna Rabinovich-Einy. "The Internet of On-Demand Healthcare". In: *Digital Justice: Technology and the Internet of Disputes*. Oxford University Press, 2017, pp. 82–107. ISBN: 9780190464585, p. 87.

732 *See* Paolo Guarda and Rossana Ducato. "From electronic health records to personal health records: emerging legal issues in the Italian regulation of e-health". In: *International Review of Law, Computers & Technology* 30.3 (2016), pp. 271–285, p. 272.

733 *See* Giorgia Bincoletto. "Data protection issues in cross-border interoperability of Electronic Health Record systems within the European Union". In: *Data & Policy* 2 (2020), pp. 1–11. DOI: 10.1017/dap.2020.2, p. 1, that reports the analysis of the EC European Commission. *Commission Staff Working document accompanying the document Communication from the Commission to the European Parliament, the Council, the European Economic and Social Committee and the Committee of the Regions on enabling the digital transformation of health and care in the Digital Single Market*. Brussels: SWD (2018) 126 final. 2018.

734 One of the first dedicated communications from the EC on this topic is European Commission, *Communication from the Commission to the Council, the European Parliament, the European Economic and Social Committee and the Committee of the Regions on e-Health – making healthcare better for European citizens: An action Plan for a European e-Health Area*. A detailed and recent report that assesses the impact of digital transformation in the EU is Expert Panel on effective ways of investing in Health, *Assessing the impact of digital transformation of health services*.

The EU Action Plans on e-health began in the early 2000s[735]. The innovative healthcare policy plans aim to foster the adoption of e-health throughout the EU and remove barriers to its deployment[736]. The "transformation of health and care" policy plays an important role in the Digital Single Market programme. In particular, three priorities have been identified by the European Commission in the "Communication on Digital Transformation of Health Care in the Digital Single Market"[737]. Firstly, the EC calls for enabling EU citizens to access and share their health data securely across the Member States. Secondly, improving data quality for research purposes, disease prevention and to enable personalised healthcare shall be areas of action. Finally, the Commission asserts that further action at the EU level is crucial for developing e-health tools for citizens' empowerment and person-centred care[738].

Key points of these plans are the legal and regulatory issues. Directive 2011/24/EU on the application of patients' rights in cross-border healthcare has set up the e-Health Network in order to support healthcare providers and centres of expertise in the Member States[739]. This Network is a voluntary platform which connects national authorities responsible for e-health designated by the Member States[740]. The main goals of the

---

735 The first plan was adopted in 2004 with the European Commission, *Communication from the Commission to the Council, the European Parliament, the European Economic and Social Committee and the Committee of the Regions on e-Health – making healthcare better for European citizens: An action Plan for a European e-Health Area.*

736 *See* European Commission, "eHealth Action Plan 2012–2020. Innovative healthcare for the 21st century".

737 EC European Commission. *Communication from the Commission to the European Parliament, the Council, the European Economic and Social Committee and the Committee of the Regions on enabling the digital transformation of health and care in the Digital Single Market; empowering citizens and building a healthier society.* European Commission. Brussels: COM (2018), 233 final. 2018.

738 These last three sentences appear in Bincoletto, "Data protection issues in cross-border interoperability of Electronic Health Record systems within the European Union".

739 Directive 2011/24/EU of the European Parliament and of the Council of 9 March 2011 on the application of patients' rights in cross-border healthcare. O.J. L. 88, 4.4.2011.

740 Article 14 Directive 2011/24/EU. The rules for the Network are established by the EC European Commission. *Commission Implementing Decision 2019/1765 of 22 October 2019 providing the rules for the establishment, the management and the functioning of the network of national authorities responsible for eHealth, and repealing Implementing Decision 2011/890/EU (notified under document C (2019) 7460).* European Commission. Brussels: COM (2019), 7460 O.J. L. 270, 24.10.2019.

Network are providing guidance to Member States on digital health at several levels and facilitating the interoperability of the national ICTs systems and cross-border transferability of electronic health data in cross-border healthcare[741].

E-health tools and solutions include multiple and heterogeneous technologies that can be divided into different fields[742]:

- Telemedicine and telecare (e.g remote patient monitoring)[743];
- Clinical information systems (e.g. the systems connected in electronic health record systems)[744];
- Integrated information networks, e-referrals and e-prescribing[745];

---

2019. *See* also at <ec.europa.eu/health/ehealth/key_documents_en#anchor0>. Last accessed 06/10/2021.

741 Article 4 of European Commission, *op. cit.*

742 The classification is provided by Martin R. Cowie et al. "e-Health: a position statement of the European Society of Cardiology". In: *European heart journal* 37.1 (2016), pp. 63–66, p. 63. A technical literature review on e-health technologies is provided by Isabel CP. Marques and João JM. Ferreira. "Digital transformation in the area of health: systematic review of 45 years of evolution". In: *Health and Technology* (2019), pp. 1–12.

743 On this sector *see* with specific reference to EU, Guarda, "Telemedicine and Application Scenarios: Common Privacy and Security Requirements in the European Union Context"; Carlo Botrugno. "Telemedicine in daily practice: Addressing legal challenges while waiting for an EU regulatory framework". In: *Health Policy and Technology* 7.2 (2018), pp. 131–136; Catalina Ionescu-Dima. "Legal challenges regarding telemedicine services in the European Union". In: *eHealth: Legal, Ethical and Governance Challenges*. Springer, 2013, pp. 107–133. ISBN: 9783642224744. *See* also CL Wen. "Telemedicine, eHealth and Remote Care Systems". In: *Global Health Informatics*. Elsevier, 2017, pp. 168–194. ISBN: 9780128045916; Silvia Melchionna and Francesca Cecamore. "Le nuove frontiere della sanità e della ricerca scientifica". In: *Circolazione e protezione dei dati personali, tra libertà e regole del mercato. Commentario al Regolamento UE n. 2016/679 (GDPR) e al novellato D.lgs. n. 196/2003 (Codice Privacy)*. Giuffrè Francis Lefebvre, 2019, pp. 579–620. ISBN: 9788828809692, pp. 601–608. Madir, *Healthtech*, pp. 3–6 and pp. 354–373. Telemedicine has been defined by Guarda as a complementary tool that enhances the delivery of health services at a distance with the transmission of medical data and information.

744 On this specific category of e-health technology *see* further Section 3.4.1. As mentioned, Electronic Health Record (EHR) is the case study for DPbD.

745 *See* e.g. Patrick Kierkegaard. "E-prescription across Europe". In: *Health and Technology* 3.3 (2013), pp. 205–219. Kierkegaard defines e-prescription as a simple tool for generating a prescription electronically and sending it directly to a pharmacy from the point-of-care. It is also used in hospitals for managing the supply of medicines.

- Disease registries and systems used for education, public health, patient and disease- related behaviour, and healthcare management[746];
- Mobile health (e.g. mobile apps)[747];

746 Population-based registries are run by several countries. As an example, Scandinavian countries have a sophisticated statistical infrastructure for public health with multiple registries. *See* Di Iorio and Carinci, "Privacy and health care information systems: where is the balance?", p. 80. On the Digital Youth Healthcare Registry in the Netherlands *see* Karolina La Fors-Owczynik. "Profiling 'Anomalies' and the Anomalies of Profiling: Digitalized Risk Assessments of Dutch Youth and the New European Data Protection Regime". In: *Under Observation: The Interplay Between eHealth and Surveillance*. Springer, 2017, pp. 107–138. ISBN: 9783319483429.

747 On mobile health from a legal perspective *see* e.g. Trix Mulder. "Health apps, their privacy policies and the GDPR". In: *European Journal of Law and Technology* 10 (1 2019); Madir, *Healthtech*, pp. 7–9; Eugenio Mantovani et al. "Towards a Code of Conduct on Privacy for mHealth to Foster Trust Amongst Users of Mobile Health Applications". In: *Data Protection and Privacy: (In)visibilities and Infrastructures*. Springer, 2017, pp. 81–106. ISBN: 9783319507965; EC European Commission. *Green paper on mobile Health*. European Commission. COM(2014) 219 final, 2014. The EC uses a WHO definition and states that mobile health covers "medical and public health practice supported by mobile devices, such as mobile phones, patient monitoring devices, personal digital assistants, and other wireless devices". From a technical perspective *see* e.g. Robert Istepanian, Swamy Laxminarayan, and Constantinos S Pattichis. *M-health*. Springer, 2006. ISBN: 9780387265599; Borja Martínez-Pérez, Isabel De La Torre-Díez, and Miguel López-Coronado. "Mobile health applications for the most prevalent conditions by the World Health Organization: review and analysis". In: *Journal of medical Internet research* 15.6 (2013), e120; Borja Martínez-Pérez, Isabel De La Torre-Díez, and Miguel López-Coronado. "Privacy and security in mobile health apps: a review and recommendations". In: *Journal of medical systems* 39.1 (2015), pp. 181–189; Waleed M Sweileh et al. "Bibliometric analysis of worldwide scientific literature in mobile-health: 2006–2016". In: *BMC medical informatics and decision making* 17.1 (2017), pp. 72–84; Achilleas Papageorgiou et al. "Security and privacy analysis of mobile health applications: the alarming state of practice". In: *IEEE Access* 6 (2018), pp. 9390–9403.

- Personalised health (e.g. wearable or implantable micro- and nano-technologies)[748];
- Big data (e.g. for predictive health), AI and Internet of Things[749].

E-health tools go beyond simply internet-based applications[750]. They can support, complement or substitute established health services, or they are

---

748 *See* e.g. from a legal perspective Bernd Blobel, DM. Lopez, and C. Gonzalez. "Patient privacy and security concerns on big data for personalized medicine". In: *Health and Technology* 6.1 (2016), pp. 75 – 81; and from a technical perspective Andrew G. Webb. "Mobile Health, Wearable Health Technology and Wireless Implanted Devices". In: *Principles of Biomedical Instrumentation*. Cambridge Texts in Biomedical Engineering. Cambridge University Press, 2018, pp. 235–270. ISBN: 9781316286210. For example, wireless implanted devices are pacemakers and cardiac re-synchronisation therapy devices. On biology-based personalised medicine *see* e.g. Lidia Becla et al. "Health technology assessment in the era of personalized health care". In: *International journal of technology assessment in health care* 27.2 (2011), pp. 118–126.

749 *See* e.g. from a legal perspective, Paolo Guarda. ""Ok Google, am I sick?": artificial intelligence, e-health, and data protection regulation". In: *BioLaw Journal-Rivista di BioDiritto* 15.1 (2019), pp. 359–375; Robin Pierce. "Machine learning for diagnosis and treatment: Gymnastics for the GDPR". In: *Eur. Data Prot. L. Rev.* 4 (2018), pp. 333–343; Agata Ferretti, Manuel Schneider, and Alessandro Blasimme. "Machine Learning in Medicine: Opening the New Data Protection Black Box". In: *Eur. Data Prot. L. Rev.* 4 (2018), pp. 320–332; Paolo Guarda and Livia Petrucci. "Quando l'intelligenza artificiale parla: assistenti vocali e sanità digitale alla luce del nuovo regolamento generale in materia di protezione dei dati". In: *BioLaw Journal-Rivista di BioDiritto* 2 (2020), pp. 425–446; Marta Arisi and Paolo Guarda. "Blockchain and eHealth: seeking compliance with the General Data Protection Regulation". In: *BioLaw Journal-Rivista di BioDiritto* 2 (2020), pp. 477–496; and from an interdisciplinary perspective, Chloé-Agathe Azencott. "Machine learning and genomics: precision medicine versus patient privacy". In: *Philosophical Transactions of the Royal Society A: Mathematical, Physical and Engineering Sciences* 376.2128 (2018), p. 20170350; Andreas Stylianou and Michael A. Talias. "Big data in healthcare: a discussion on the big challenges". In: *Health and Technology* 7.1 (2017), pp. 97–107. According to this last study, Big Data in health care is mainly produced by clinical data, pharmaceutical research, and patients' behaviour and sentiment data. The IoT has been added to the classification. On IoT for healthcare and e-consent *see* Yvonne O'Connor et al. "Privacy by design: informed consent and internet of things for smart health". In: *Procedia computer science* 113 (2017), pp. 653–658.

750 European Commission, *Communication from the Commission to the Council, the European Parliament, the European Economic and Social Committee and the Committee of the Regions on e-Health – making healthcare better for European citizens: An action Plan for a European e-Health Area*, p. 4.

completely new[751]. Solutions operate both on a patient-to-doctor basis (e.g. telecare) and on a doctor-to-doctor basis (e.g. e-prescribing).

These digital innovations bring better information sharing and processing in the healthcare system and mediate the relationship between the individual as a patient and the healthcare provider (e.g physician, hospital). Thus, it has been argued that a risk of dehumanisation of the patient-physician relationship may exist because of the mediation of digital tools in healthcare provision[752]. However, technology should be a means for improving healthcare without compromising the fiduciary relationship based on respect and trust[753]. Some e-health technologies, such as mobile apps, may even change the role of the patient from a passive to a more active role[754]. In the e-health context, people want to be more involved in decisions and the asymmetry in knowledge between patients and physicians decreases[755]. Indeed, the patient's empowerment is a valuable contribution of digital health services[756].

---

751 *See* the classification in Expert Panel on effective ways of investing in Health, *Assessing the impact of digital transformation of health services*, p. 30. Examples of supporting tools are personalised health systems. Telemedicine is complementary, whereas e-prescription is substituting. New tools are Big Data-based algorithms with treatment recommendations or medical chat-bots.

752 *See* Guarda, "Telemedicine and Application Scenarios: Common Privacy and Security Requirements in the European Union Context", pp. 10–11; Lupiáñez-Villanueva et al., *Benchmarking Deployment of Ehealth Among General Practitioners*, p. 46; Guarda, "I dati sanitari", p. 615.

753 *See* for further discussion on trust in e-health, Penny Duquenoy, Nermeen Magdi Mekawie, and Mark Springett. "Patients, trust and ethics in information privacy in eHealth". In: *eHealth: Legal, Ethical and Governance Challenges*. Springer, 2013, pp. 275–295. ISBN: 9783642224744.

754 *See* the arguments of the European Commission in European Commission, *Green paper on mobile Health*, p. 5. On patient engagement and e-health technologies *see* the analysis of H. de Fátima Marin and Connie Delaney. "Patient Engagement and Digital Health Communities". In: *Global Health Informatics*. Elsevier, 2017, pp. 218–231. ISBN: 9780128045916.

755 European Commission, *Communication from the Commission to the Council, the European Parliament, the European Economic and Social Committee and the Committee of the Regions on e-Health – making healthcare better for European citizens: An action Plan for a European e-Health Area*.

756 *See* Expert Panel on effective ways of investing in Health, *Assessing the impact of digital transformation of health services*, p. 78. On the notion of patient empowerment *see* Guarda, "I dati sanitari", p. 592; Giuseppe de Vergottini and Carlo Bottari. *La sanità elettronica*. Bononia University Press, 2018. ISBN: 9788869233234, p. 80; Carla Faralli, Raffaella Brighi, Michele Martoni, et al. *Strumenti, diritti, regole e nuove relazioni di cura: Il Paziente europeo protagonista nell'e-Health*. G.

After the advent of e-health technologies, the more crucial and widely discussed challenges are privacy, and data protection and security of health data[757]. These aspects concern each category of e-health technologies mentioned above. Privacy and data protection concerns are related to the specific intimacy of health status, to the sensitiveness of the category of personal health data, and the security risk level that processing operations with HITs entails[758]. Privacy, data protection and security might be seen both as issues of e-health technologies and rights or obligations established by the law for minimising the risks for rights and freedoms of individuals.

The first concern is the privacy of e-health technology, meaning the protection against the potential impingement on the right to respect for private and family life in accordance with Article 7 of the EU Charter on Fundamental Rights, and Article 8 of the European Convention on Human Rights[759].

---

Giappichelli Editore, Torino, 2015. ISBN: 9788892100671, pp. 61–63. This expression has been used since the 90s and scholars have extensively discussed its evolution in the digital world.

757 In Kierkegaard, "E-prescription across Europe", p. 215, the most challenging aspects of e-health are privacy, confidentiality, data protection and liability. *See* also Expert Panel on effective ways of investing in Health, *Assessing the impact of digital transformation of health services*, pp. 76, 81–83. The liability issue is a legal concern, and is related to the possible malfunctions of the systems and networks. According to the EC, the electronic commerce Directive applies to the provision of online health services. *See* further European Commission, *Communication from the Commission to the Council, the European Parliament, the European Economic and Social Committee and the Committee of the Regions on e-Health – making healthcare better for European citizens: An action Plan for a European e-Health Area*, p. 14. So, this regulatory framework applies. Moreover, within the use of e-health technologies the traditional medical error may be related to a technological error. The legal basis for the civil liability should be found in many sources (e.g. product and service liability). On liability and e-health *see* the legal analysis by Isabelle Andoulsi and Petra Wilson. "Understanding liability in eHealth: Towards greater clarity at European Union level". In: *eHealth: Legal, ethical and governance challenges*. Springer, 2013, pp. 165–180. ISBN: 9783642224744.

758 For a systematic classification of the concerns *see* Aceto, Persico, and Pescapé, "The role of Information and Communication Technologies in healthcare: taxonomies, perspectives, and challenges", p. 144.

759 Article 8 of the Convention states: "1. Everyone has the right to respect for his private and family life, his home and his correspondence. 2. There shall be no interference by a public authority with the exercise of this right except such as is in accordance with the law and is necessary in a democratic society in the interests of national security, public safety or the economic well-being of the

Generally, a patient's medical condition (i.e. health status) is strictly personal and related to the intimate sphere of a specific individual. The body and mind of a natural person are central to personal life and to the sense of personal identity[760]. Health status affects several aspects of individual life, such as the ability to find a job or to conduct one's own business, or to obtain loans or insurance, and one's personal condition impacts the social dimension of everyday life[761]. Healthcare preserves individual dignity[762]. So, the interplay between dignity and privacy protects the right to self-determination of an individual body[763]. In the healthcare domain the right to privacy protects the freedom of choice and the trust relationship between doctor and patient[764]. The maintenance of a trustworthy relationship is fundamental to effective individual care and treatment[765].

Thus, privacy in the e-health context is a complex and multifaceted concept because it protects a wide spectrum of interests[766]. Various dimensions of privacy are implicated, such as bodily privacy or physical privacy (i.e. the control over one's body, and intimacy), decisional privacy (i.e. the ability to make decisions on a treatment without undue influence), and privacy of private space (e.g. in one's home)[767].

---

country, for the prevention of disorder or crime, for the protection of health or morals, or for the protection of the rights and freedoms of others".

760 *See* Elizabeth Wicks. "Electronic health records and privacy interests: The English experience". In: *eHealth: Legal, ethical and governance challenges*. Springer, 2013, pp. 57–76. ISBN: 9783642224744, p. 58.

761 *See* Giacomo Di Federico. "Access to Healthcare in the European Union: Are EU Patients (Effectively) Protected Against Discriminatory Practices?" In: *The Principle of Equality in EU Law*. Springer, 2017, pp. 229–253. ISBN: 9783319661377, p. 249.

762 *See ibid.*

763 Ludovica Durst. "Il trattamento di categorie particolari di dati in ambito sanitario". In: *Circolazione e protezione dei dati personali, tra libertà e regole del mercato. Commentario al Regolamento UE n. 2016/679 (GDPR) e al novellato D.lgs. n. 196/2003 (Codice Privacy)*. Giuffrè Francis Lefebvre, 2019, pp. 65–79. ISBN: 9788828809692, p. 71.

764 *See* the explanation of the concept and its relationship with human dignity in Hooghiemstra, "Informational Self-Determination, Digital Health and New Features of Data Protection", p. 162.

765 OECD, *OECD Recommendation on Health Data Governance*, Annex, 12.

766 *See* Robin Pierce. "Medical Privacy: Where Deontology and Consequentialism Meet". In: *The Handbook of Privacy Studies: an Interdisciplinary Introduction*. Amsterdam University Press, 2019, pp. 327–331. ISBN: 9789462988095, p. 32.

767 *See* e.g. the discussion related to mobile health in Maartje GH Niezen. "Unobtrusiveness in mHealth design and use: A systematic literature study". In: *Under Observation: The Interplay Between eHealth and Surveillance*. Springer,

It has been highlighted that confidentiality of medical conditions is instantiated in the Hippocratic Oath taken by physicians where it requires them to keep secret whatever they see or hear during the practices[768]. This professional secrecy protects the confidentiality of a patient's treatments in the patient-physician relationship[769]. This oath set the foundation of medical ethics[770].

Actually, medical confidentiality is a general principle in the healthcare domain, and is usually recognised by law as duty of confidentiality[771]. Confidentiality refers to the moral duty of non-disclosure of information shared in the patient-physician relationship[772]. The maintenance of confidentiality is then supported on deontological grounds[773]. For example, in the Italian Code of Medical Ethics the duty of confidence is set by Article 10, and is related to all information learned, and even the death of the patient does not end this duty[774].

The legal basis of duty of confidentiality is not easy to find because there is not a single provision, but multiple requirements in contract law, tort law, criminal law, and statutory obligations[775]. Health care actors have the attributes of fiduciary status in their relationships with patients that results in more than a contract or other form of legal liability for healing the indi-

---

2017, pp. 9–29. ISBN: 9783319483429, p. 2. The author argued that the use of m-health applications creates a high risk of surveillance since m-health devices and services are unobtrusive for users.

768 Duquenoy, Mekawie, and Springett, "Patients, trust and ethics in information privacy in eHealth", p. 281. *See* also Tamara K. Hervey and Jean V. McHale. *Health law and the European Union*. Cambridge University Press, 2004. ISBN: 9780511617553, p. 161. This article stresses that privacy and confidentiality are distinct notions in the healthcare domain especially. The Hippocratic Oath is translated in English as follows: "Whatsoever things I see or hear concerning the life of men, in my attendance on the sick or even apart there from, which ought not to be noised abroad, I shall keep silence thereon, counting such things as sacred secrets".

769 *See* e.g. Mulder, "Health apps, their privacy policies and the GDPR".

770 Carissa Véliz. "Medical Privacy and Big Data". In: *Philosophical Foundations of Medical Law* (2019), p. 306, p. 308.

771 Wicks, "Electronic health records and privacy interests: The English experience", p. 58.

772 Véliz, "Medical Privacy and Big Data", p. 308.

773 *See* Hervey and McHale, *Health law and the European Union*, p. 162.

774 *See* Mario Tavani, Mario Picozzi, and Gabriella Salvati. *Manuale di deontologia medica*. Giuffrè Editore, 2007. ISBN: 9788814137297, p. 72.

775 Jonathan Herring. *Medical law and ethics*. Oxford University Press, 2016. ISBN: 9780198846956, p. 233.

vidual[776]. The duty of confidentiality arises from the mentioned attributes of fiduciary status and applies to professionals, hospitals and other health care providers[777]. Therefore, the breach of health confidentiality represents a cause of action in courts that is distinct from medical malpractice[778]. Moreover, the breach of confidentiality may be subject to professional disciplinary sanctions and criminal sanctions. It has been reported that breach of confidentiality is a criminal offence across many EU Member States[779].

In sum, confidentiality in healthcare is connected to the right to respect of private life[780]. It has been noted that privacy in the healthcare sector is necessary for guaranteeing an individual's dignity[781]. Since health is a central aspect of an individual's well-being, privacy and confidentiality are essential in a democratic society in order to protect people's private lives, their dignity, their right to not be discriminated against on the basis of their health status. The use of e-health technologies is challenging this guarantee since, now that medical information is collected in electronic form, more subjects may have access to health status, and may unlawfully share information with unauthorised third parties, or unauthorised parties may easily access to it illegally.

---

776 *See* Mark A. Hall. "Fiduciary Principles in Health Care". In: *The Oxford Handbook of Fiduciary Law*. Oxford University Press, 2019. ISBN: 9780190634100.

777 *See* Hall, *op. cit.*, p. 296.

778 *See ibid.* This statement is valuable for different legal frameworks.

779 *See* Hervey and McHale, *Health law and the European Union*, p. 16. As an example, the Italian Penal Code, Article 622 punishes anyone who, having knowledge for reasons of his or her profession reveals a secret without just cause, or uses it for his or her own or others' profit. The subject is punished if the act may result in harm with imprisonment of up to one year or a fine ranging from 30 to 516 euros. The offence is punishable on complaint by the injured person. In the Italian case law, the notion of profession is interpreted in a broad sense. *See* Laura Greco. "Il trattamento dei dati sanitari". In: *La protezione dei dati personali in Italia. Regolamento UE n. 2016/679 e d.lgs. 10 agosto 2018, n. 101*. Zanichelli, Torino, 2019, pp. 220–250. ISBN: 9788808820433, p. 232.

780 *See* Herring, *Medical law and ethics*, p. 277; Wouter Koelewijn. "Privacy from a Medical Perspective". In: *The Handbook of Privacy Studies: an Interdisciplinary Introduction*. Amsterdam University Press, 2019, p. 333. ISBN: 9789462988095.

781 *See* L. Palmieri. "Dai segreti alla riservatezza e poi al segreto". In: *Medicina Legale Quaderni Camerti* (XV 1993), p. 6; Licia Califano. "Fascicolo sanitario elettronico (Fse) e dossier sanitario. Il contributo del Garante privacy al bilanciamento tra diritto alla salute e diritto alla protezione dei dati personali". In: *Sanità Pubblica e Privata* (3 2015), pp. 141–159, p. 9.

Arguably, the individual ethical and legal obligation of confidentiality upon the physician is no longer sufficient in the digital world[782]. It has been noted that medical confidentiality has been put under pressure because of technological innovations[783]. Hence, a well-known case of the European Court on Human Rights shows a bridge between the need to protect the respect of private life and confidentiality of health information, and the necessity to look at data protection issues when the context is the digital processing of personal health data.

In the case *I v. Finland* of 2008, the European Court on Human Rights recognised that medical confidentiality of health data is protected by Article 8 on private and family life of the Convention for the Protection of Human Rights and Fundamental Freedoms[784]. The applicant was a nurse affected by HIV who instituted a civil proceeding against the district health authority where she worked for an alleged failure to keep her patient record confidential, in violation of her right to respect for her private life[785]. After the Finnish judicial proceedings, the nurse applied to the Strasbourg Court for alleged violation of Article 8 of the European Convention by arguing that the measures to safeguard her right to respect for her private life had not been sufficient. The Court later held that there had been a violation of that Article by founding it applicable in the case because information related to patients belongs to their private life. Article 8 then entails a positive obligation to adopt measures for securing the respect of private life in every individual's relations[786]. The hospital, as the data controller, failed to secure the data against unauthorised and unlawful access. Indeed, the Court ruled that[787]:

> "the protection of personal data, in particular medical data, is of fundamental importance to a person's enjoyment of his or her right to respect for private and family life as guaranteed by Article 8 of the Convention. Respecting the confidentiality of health data is a vital principle in the legal systems of all the Contracting Parties to the

---

782 Wicks, "Electronic health records and privacy interests: The English experience", p. 59.

783 Hooghiemstra, "Informational Self-Determination, Digital Health and New Features of Data Protection", p. 161.

784 The case of I v. Finland is Application no. 20511/03, Judgement of 17 July 2008.

785 The Judgement is available in the HUDOC database at <hudoc.echr.coe.int/eng>. Last accessed 06/10/2021.

786 *See* paragraph 36.

787 *See* paragraph 38.

> Convention. It is crucial not only to respect the sense of privacy of a patient but also to preserve his or her confidence in the medical profession and in the health services in general. The above considerations are especially valid as regards protection of the confidentiality of information about a person's HIV infection, given the sensitive issues surrounding this disease".

The Court linked the protection of the respect for private life to the protection of medical information, which is fundamental in a democratic society[788]. The importance of this case has been recognised by the literature and prominent scholars even referred to it as an indirect reference to DPbD that created a state's positive obligation to secure the respect of Article 8 ECHR in order to ensure confidentiality of health data[789].

Indeed, data protection and security of personal health data represent significant concerns of e-health technologies. This category of data is sensitive in nature and requires a high level of protection[790]. According to the European Commission, effective data protection is a key driver for building trust in e-health[791].

In the e-health context, data quality should be a high priority of e-health systems[792]. Personal health data should be accurate and kept up to date – as in paper-based healthcare provision – in order to ensure efficient and high-quality treatment. Using adequate data available in e-health technology is important since inadequate data may cause medication and medical errors. So, data protection rules may even be a means for preserving healthcare efficiency and guaranteeing the accuracy of data.

---

788 In another prior case of the European Court on Human Rights, *Z. v. Finland*, the importance of the protection of health information was considered necessary for a democratic society. *See* case no. 22009/93, Judgement of 25 February 1997.

789 *See* Waldman, "Data Protection by Design? A Critique of Article 25 of the GDPR", p. 160; Bygrave, "Data protection by design and by default: deciphering the EU's legislative requirements", p. 110.

790 OECD, *OECD Recommendation on Health Data Governance*.

791 *See* European Commission, "eHealth Action Plan 2012–2020. Innovative healthcare for the 21st century", p. 9.

792 *See* Katsh and Rabinovich-Einy, "The Internet of On-Demand Healthcare", p. 86.

Moreover, HIT security is a critical aspect[793]. The unauthorised access and misuse of health data are high risks in this sector[794]. In general, data breaches are typical security risks. Two of the main causes of data breach in the e-health care sector are hacking and maladministration[795]. In 2019, the EDPS reported that 90 % of the personal data breach security incidents in the EU were confidentiality breaches[796]. Actually, security is a huge problem in this context. Both technical and human factors are necessary for ensuring the confidentiality and integrity of health data[797].

It has been claimed that significant economic, psychological and social harms may be caused by unauthorised access or sharing of personal health data[798]. Actually, data about the health status can render the individual vulnerable in multiple ways[799]. As regards the economical level, the risk

---

793 *See* the security issue at European Commission, *Communication from the Commission to the Council, the European Parliament, the European Economic and Social Committee and the Committee of the Regions on e-Health – making healthcare better for European citizens: An action Plan for a European e-Health Area*, p. 14.

794 *See* Ferretti, Schneider, and Blasimme, "Machine Learning in Medicine: Opening the New Data Protection Black Box", p. 331; and Hooghiemstra, "Informational Self-Determination, Digital Health and New Features of Data Protection", p. 161.

795 *See* two following examples. In Kierkegaard, "E-prescription across Europe", p. 216, the author reported the Virginia Department of Health's data breach. 35 million prescription records were downloaded and encrypted by a hacker who asked for a ransom of $ 10 million. In Leslie Stevens et al. "Dangers from within? Looking inwards at the role of maladministration as the leading cause of health data breaches in the UK". in: *Data Protection and Privacy: (In)visibilities and Infrastructures*. Springer, 2017, pp. 205–239. ISBN: 9783319507965, the authors reported some statistical data on health data breaches in the UK showing an increasing trend. The main cause is maladministration of healthcare providers. In this article the scholars classified the concepts that maladministration entails (i.e. careless and negligent abuse of data).

796 *See* EDPS European Data Protection Supervisor. *Annual Report 2019*. 2019, Section 3.2.3. In the same year the U.S. Department of Health & Human Services reported a massive and increased number of healthcare breaches. *See* the report's statistics on the website of the authority at <www.hhs.gov/hipaa/for-professionals/breach-notification/breach-reporting/index.html>. In 2019 the number of breaches increased by 37.4 %.

797 Duquenoy, Mekawie, and Springett, "Patients, trust and ethics in information privacy in eHealth", p. 280.

798 Romanou, "The necessity of the implementation of Privacy by Design in sectors where data protection concerns arise", p. 106. *See* also Véliz, "Medical Privacy and Big Data", pp. 310–313.

799 Pierce, "Medical Privacy: Where Deontology and Consequentialism Meet", p. 328.

is related to the possible advantages that insurance companies or private companies may obtain on acquiring such information and imposing specific unethical clauses targeted to the specific individual illness[800]. In addition, the employment and social sectors may be influenced by illegal access to health data. An individual may suffer employment and social exclusion if unauthorised information spreads (e.g. on chronic illness). Stigma, embarrassment and various forms of discrimination may result from an inappropriate protection of personal health data (e.g. in the case of a genetic risk of a disease)[801]. So, the knowledge of medical information may impact family relationships, career and work[802]. Indiscriminate and unauthorised use of this data affects the human person and his or her dignity[803].

---

800 Romanou, "The necessity of the implementation of Privacy by Design in sectors where data protection concerns arise", p. 106.

801 *See* Pierce, "Medical Privacy: Where Deontology and Consequentialism Meet", p. 328.

802 Duquenoy, Mekawie, and Springett, "Patients, trust and ethics in information privacy in eHealth", p. 281. *See* also Job Rimmelzwaan. "Use of a Wearable Device to Promote Healthy Behaviors Among Employees of a Small-to-Medium Enterprise in the Netherlands". In: *Under Observation: The Interplay Between eHealth and Surveillance*. Springer, 2017, pp. 59–69. ISBN: 9783319483429. The author presented an interesting case study in the context of employment in the Netherlands. For the promotion of healthy conditions in a company, employees' data were collected by the employer through wearable devices. This article demonstrated that people were not aware of the amount of data and of the sharing even though they trust their employer. The author pointed out that these data reveal more information on employees than what is necessary for a workplace. A case study on US employer-sponsored wellness programmes has shown the impact on informational privacy of this processing in the employment and insurance context. *See* Anna Slomovic. "eHealth and privacy in US employer wellness programs". In: *Under Observation: The Interplay Between eHealth and Surveillance*. Springer, 2017, pp. 31–58. ISBN: 9783319483429. Wellness programmes create the possibility to charge different insurance prices in accordance with employees' health. This study is strictly related to the complexity of the healthcare system in the US where employer health plans guarantee healthcare provision to workers. However, it has also shown the problematic use of health data collected by e-health technologies, such as mobile and wearable devices, for employment and insurance purposes. This system leads to an unprecedented surveillance and abusive scenario. The programmes are voluntary, but employees feel they are required by their employers to use them. As a result, health data are used to manipulate individuals' health-related behaviours.

803 On personal health data and human dignity *see* the constitutional perspective in Vergottini and Bottari, *La sanità elettronica*.

Therefore, e-health technologies should be highly secure for protecting the processing of personal health data. Data protection law supplements the legal and ethical duty of medical confidentiality[804]. The EU legal framework on data protection may mitigate all mentioned concerns since patients are data subjects and healthcare providers are usually data controllers that shall comply with the GDPR[805].

The right to respect for private life, the duties of confidentiality, and data protection laws set a variety of obligations for protecting personal health data. The obligations should be seen as aspects of the fair and legal treatment of a patient[806]. Organising the processing on the basis of legal protection by design is necessary for preventing abuse in the e-health environment[807]. From the beginning of EU Action Plans on e-health, PbD and PETs have been considered of paramount importance[808].

This section has presented the critical aspects of e-health technologies by highlighting their potential, too. The section that follows investigates the regulatory framework for the protection of personal health data at the EU level.

## 3.3 *Regulatory framework for personal health data*

The current legal framework in the EU for assessing the data protection issues mentioned is primarily the GDPR. The processing of personal health data by private or public healthcare entities in providing healthcare is subject to the General Regulation. However, other relevant provisions apply to this sector. In this section some general considerations on the regulatory framework for the processing of health data at the EU level will be presented.

---

804 Wicks, "Electronic health records and privacy interests: The English experience", p. 67.

805 *See* Ferretti, Schneider, and Blasimme, "Machine Learning in Medicine: Opening the New Data Protection Black Box", p. 331. The authors explained the opacity of AI systems in the medical field in light of the GDPR.

806 Wicks, "Electronic health records and privacy interests: The English experience", p. 76.

807 *See* the interesting discussion which follows Nissenbaum's theory of contextual integrity in Hooghiemstra, "Informational Self-Determination, Digital Health and New Features of Data Protection", p. 166.

808 *See* European Commission, "eHealth Action Plan 2012–2020. Innovative healthcare for the 21st century", p. 9.

Personal data refers to all the information related to an identified or identifiable individual[809]. Personal data types can be divided into "common personal data", "personal data perceived as sensitive" by people and "sensitive data in the meaning of the GDPR"[810]. This last category is a subset of personal data that includes data revealing racial or ethnic origin, political opinions, religious or philosophical beliefs, trade union membership, genetic data, biometric data, data concerning health, data concerning a natural person's sex life and sexual orientation[811]. In the GDPR, the legal framework establishes a general prohibition of processing personal data that are particularly sensitive by their nature since the context of their processing could create significant risks in relation to fundamental rights and freedoms[812]. Therefore, the processing is allowed in specific cases only. This approach was adopted under the DPD, too. The rationale of the general prohibition is minimising the significant risks that the processing of particular categories of personal data creates. In fact, these categories of data allow conclusions on the data subjects "that are linked to their fundamental rights and freedoms, such as freedom of thought, conscience and religion" or non-discrimination[813].

Personal health data are included in the list of special categories of data because they reveal information on the health status of the data subject that is linked to other rights and freedoms, such as the right to respect private and family life, and non-discrimination, as discussed above. Following the GDPR wording, data concerning health merits heightened protection. It should be pointed out that the GDPR sets specific provisions for the processing of special categories of data but leaves space to Member States to adapt the application of the rules at a national level[814]. Actually, the protection and improvement of human health are a competence of the Member States where the EU has the power to carry out actions

---

809 Article 4 GDPR. *See* Chapter 1, Section 1.1.

810 *See* Commission Nationale de l'Informatique et des Libertés, *Privacy Impact Assessment (PIA). Knowledge basis*, p. 2. In the second category the CNIL inserts social security number, biometric data and banking data.

811 Article 9(1) GDPR.

812 These are the words of Recital 51 GDPR.

813 *See* for each data category the risks defined by Voigt and Von dem Bussche, *The EU General Data Protection Regulation (GDPR). A Practical Guide*, pp. 110–111.

814 *See* Article 9(4) GDPR: "Member States may maintain or introduce further conditions, including limitations, with regard to the processing of genetic data, biometric data or data concerning health".

to support, coordinate or supplement national actions[815]. Member States have the responsibility to define their health policies and organise and deliver health services and medical care, including the management of these services and the allocation of resources[816]. Nonetheless, protecting *health in all policies* is one of the transverse objectives of the EU[817]. In 2013, the EU even released a Decision on serious cross-border threats to health in order to coordinate the actions of Member States[818].

Under the DPD, many countries had sectoral legislation for the processing in the health care area[819]. Within the GDPR, the Member States can further define national rules on legal obligations related to personal health data, on tasks that should be carried out in the public interest, or on tasks that should be exercised under an official authority for private or public

---

815 Article 6(a) of the Consolidated versions of the Treaty on European Union and the Treaty on the Functioning of the European Union. On governance of health systems in the EU *see* Elias Mossialos et al. *Health systems governance in Europe: the role of European Union law and policy*. Cambridge University Press, 2010. ISBN: 9780511750496.

816 Article 168(7) of the Consolidated versions of the Treaty on European Union and the Treaty on the Functioning of the European Union.

817 On health and the limited competences of the Union *see* Giacomo Di Federico and Stefania Negri. *Unione Europea e Salute. Principi, azioni, diritti e sicurezza*. Cedam Wolters Kluwer, 2020. ISBN: 9788813370886; Vergottini and Bottari, *La sanità elettronica*, pp. 102–105. On *health in all policies see* Mark Flear. *Governing Public Health: EU Law, Regulation and Biopolitics*. Bloomsbury Publishing, 2015. ISBN: 9781849462204; Tamara K. Hervey and Jean V. McHale. *European Union health law*. Cambridge University Press, 2015. ISBN: 9781107010499; Scott L. Greer et al. *Everything you always wanted to know about European Union health policies but were afraid to ask*. World Health Organization. Regional Office for Europe, 2014. ISBN: 9789289050272. On medical law at the EU and Member States' levels *see* the extensive research of the International Encyclopaedia of Laws in Herman Nys. *IEL Medical Law*. Kluwer Law International, 2020. ISBN: 9789065449436.

818 *See* Decision No 1082/2013/EU of the European Parliament and of the Council of 22 October 2013 on serious cross-border threats to health and repealing Decision No 2119/98/EC. O.J. L. 293, 5.11.2013. Article 16 of this Decision is dedicated to the protection of personal data and refers to the DPD by stating that: "In the application of this Decision, personal data shall be processed in accordance with Directive 95/46/EC and Regulation (EC) No 45/2001. In particular, appropriate technical and organisational measures shall be taken to protect such personal data against accidental or illegal destruction, accidental loss, or unauthorised access and against any form of illegal processing. (...)".

819 *See* Bart Custers et al. "A comparison of data protection legislation and policies across the EU". In: *Computer Law & Security Review* 34.2 (2018), pp. 234–243, p. 240.

health[820]. Moreover, national laws can derogate the general prohibition on the processing of health data where legislative measures are subject to "appropriate" and "suitable safeguards" and aim to protect a public interest in accordance with the principles of necessity and proportionality[821]. According to a report commissioned by the European Commission, most of the Member States provided national conditions and limitations on the processing of data concerning health[822].

In the public healthcare context, legislative derogation from the general prohibition of processing personal health data is generally allowed for health security, for monitoring and alert purposes, for preventing or controlling diseases and for other serious threats to public health[823]. According to Recital 52 of the GDPR, the purposes of the derogation may be public health, the management of healthcare services, or archiving purposes in the public interest, scientific or historical research purposes or statistical purposes. The GDPR states that the expression of "public health", and

---

820 *See* further Section 3.3.2. In particular, Article 9(4) is the basis for the introduction of Member States' law on data concerning health.

821 Recital 52 GDPR.

822 *See* TIPIK, *Report on the implementation of specific provisions of Regulation (EU) 2016/679*, pp. 7–15: "Most of the Member States (BE, BG, CY, DE, EE, EL, ES, FI, FR, HR, HU, IE, IT, LT, LU, LV, MT, NL, PL, PT and RO) provide conditions/limitations on the processing of such data, while AT, CZ, DK, SE and SK do not provide any such specification clause". Moreover, "as regards data concerning health, the following conditions/limitations under Article 9(4) GDPR have been identified at national level: (i) listing the categories of persons who have access to such data (BE, BG, EL, ES, HU, LV, NL, PL); (ii) describing the function of those persons in processing such data (BE, LV); (iii) making the list of those persons available to the Data Protection Authority (BE); (iv) ensuring that those persons are subject to legal, statutory or other similar confidentiality obligations (BE, DE, ES, LT, PT); (v) allowing the processing only for specific purposes (EE, EL, FR, HR, HU, IE, LU, LV, NL, PL, PT, RO); (vi) requiring consent for processing to be in writing (EL, ES, FI, PT); (vii) requiring separate storage of data (ES) or limiting the time period (LV); (viii) requiring processing to be subject to compliance with specifications laid down by the national data protection authority (FR, IT) or to prior authorisation from the national data protection authority (FR, MT); and (ix) requiring anonymisation as a condition for access to data (PT). No Member States' legislation contained additional conditions or limitations with regard to the processing of genetic data, biometric data or data concerning health that could have the impact of restricting or prohibiting the free movement of personal data within the European Union".

823 *See* Recital 52 GDPR.

the underlying public interest, has been defined in Regulation (EC) No 1338/2008, whose Article 3 specifies that it means[824]:

> "All elements related to health, namely health status, including morbidity and disability, the determinants having an effect on that health status, health care needs, resources allocated to health care, the provision of, and universal access to, health care as well as health care expenditure and financing, and the causes of mortality".

So, the definition of this expression is broad and open to interpretation and shall be contextualised. Undoubtedly, the GDPR has given Member States freedom to restrict or extend the rules on personal health data processing[825]. In order to safeguard the interests of the natural person, the processing of personal data carried out for public health purposes shall be subject to suitable and specific measures and private third parties shall not process these data for other purposes[826]. Member States have this margin of manoeuvre for setting out specific processing situations without hampering the free and cross-border flow of personal health data[827]. Even though the wide margins of discretion of Member States could lead to a fragmentation of the EU legal framework and hinder the harmonisation of the GDPR, it is clear that the processing of data in the healthcare context involves cultural, social, ethical, political and economic factors, which undoubtedly differ from State to State[828]. It has been argued by

824 *See* Recital 54. Regulation (EC) No 1338/2008 of the European Parliament and of the Council of 16 December 2008 on Community statistics on public health and health and safety at work. O.J. L. 354, 31.12.2008.

825 The same approach was used in Data Protection Directive 95/46. *See* Di Iorio and Carinci, "Privacy and health care information systems: where is the balance?", p. 85. An interesting general comment on the EU health policy and its fragmentation is Scott L. Greer. "Resistance in European Union health care policy". In: *The Routledge Handbook of European Public Policy*. Taylor & Francis Group, 2017, pp. 357–363. ISBN: 9781317404026. Member States resist EU healthcare policy and tend not to respond to EU initiatives.

826 Recital 54 GDPR refers to employers or insurance and banking companies.

827 Recital 53 states that: "Member States should be allowed to maintain or introduce further conditions, including limitations, with regard to the processing of genetic data, biometric data or data concerning health. However, this should not hamper the free flow of personal data within the Union when those conditions apply to cross-border processing of such data".

828 Greco, "Il trattamento dei dati sanitari", p. 225. A brief comparative analysis post GDPR may be found in Amram Denise. "Ricerca e protezione dei dati personali concernenti la salute: il tentativo di armonizzazione al livello europeo post GDPR e le interpretazioni offerte dai sistemi irlandese, belga, spagnolo e

Lynskey that the choice of the EU legislator was "to respect the divergent constitutional and cultural traditions of the Member States by allowing them to legislate to protect national sensitivities"[829]. Hence, a different data protection implementation for health data may persist across the EU, but harmonising national laws is of utmost importance for the Digital Single Market Strategy[830]. According to the report on the implementation of Article 9(4) GDPR, in 2021 no Member States' legislation restricted or limited the free movement of personal data within the EU[831].

For decades high importance has been assigned to cross-border healthcare[832]. Directive 2011/24/EU cited above establishes patients' rights that shall be guaranteed in cross-border healthcare[833]. The rationales of this act are ensuring a high-quality level of human health protection and trust in cross-border healthcare and promoting cooperation among Member States on healthcare provision[834]. A healthcare provider is any entity that legally provides healthcare within the territory of a Member State[835]. So, Directive 2011/24/EU applies to individual patients (i.e. "insured" people)

---

italiano". In: *Rivista Italiana di Medicina Legale (e del Diritto in campo sanitario)* 1 (2019), pp. 211–223.

829 Lynskey, *The foundations of EU data protection law*, p. 73.

830 *See* Abedjan et al., "Data science in healthcare: Benefits, challenges and opportunities", p. 16; EDPS European Data Protection Supervisor. *Opinion 3/2020 on the European strategy for data*. European Data Protection Supervisor, 2020, p. 12. The EDPS pointed out "the need for further harmonization of data protection rules applicable to health data among the Member States".

831 *See* TIPIK, *Report on the implementation of specific provisions of Regulation (EU) 2016/679*, p. 9.

832 *See* from the European Commission, *Communication from the Commission to the Council, the European Parliament, the European Economic and Social Committee and the Committee of the Regions on e-Health – making healthcare better for European citizens: An action Plan for a European e-Health Area*; European Commission, *Communication from the Commission to the European Parliament, the Council, the European Economic and Social Committee and the Committee of the Regions on enabling the digital transformation of health and care in the Digital Single Market; empowering citizens and building a healthier society*.

833 On this Directive *see* Paul Quinn and Paul De Hert. "The Patients' Rights Directive (2011/24/EU) – Providing (some) rights to EU residents seeking healthcare in other Member States". In: *Computer Law & Security Review* 27.5 (2011), pp. 497–502; Miek Peeters. "Free movement of patients: Directive 2011/24 on the application of patients' rights in cross-border healthcare". In: *European Journal of Health Law* 19.1 (2012), pp. 29–60; Hervey and McHale, *European Union health law*.

834 *See* Recitals 2, 5 and Article 1 of the Directive.

835 Article 3(g) Directive 2011/24/EU.

who decide to seek healthcare from a healthcare provider in a Member State other than the Member State of affiliation[836]. The Member State of treatment provides healthcare to the insured person, despite not being the country of residence of the person or the country where this person has the right to sickness benefits. Each Member State designates one or more national organisational contact points for cross-border healthcare[837].

Thus, European patients have the right to access healthcare when they are abroad, and the costs of the service will be reimbursed. They also have the right to access their electronic medical records, and therefore the collected data[838]. Anyway, the Directive specified that its application should not prejudice the protection of personal data pursuant to the data protection law[839]. The free and cross-border flow of personal health data, and therefore the cross-border transfer, is recognised by the Directive, but it should comply with data protection rules for safeguarding the fundamental rights to privacy and to data protection[840]. Previously, the EDPS supported the initiative in its opinion on the proposal[841]. The authority highlighted that the cross-border exchange of electronic data would have increased the risk of inaccurate or illegitimate data processing in the context of ICT applications, especially[842]. So, the EDPS stressed the importance of a privacy by design implementation of e-health technologies[843]. In previous studies on healthcare, it has been suggested that Directive

836 *See* Recital 11. According to Article 3, the Member State of affiliation is the country which has the competence of granting a prior authorisation to the treatment outside the Member State of residence, or in another Member State.

837 Article 6 establishes the rules for the national contact points.

838 Article 4(2)(f) states that "in order to ensure continuity of care, patients who have received treatment are entitled to a written or electronic medical record of such treatment, and access to at least a copy of this record in conformity with and subject to national measures implementing Union provisions on the protection of personal data, in particular Directives 95/46/EC and 2002/58/EC". On this topic *see* further Section 3.4.3.

839 In Article 2 DPD is listed among other sources. Article 5 ensures the remote access to or a copy of patients' medical records "in conformity with, and subject to, national measures implementing Union provisions on the protection of personal data, in particular Directives 95/46/EC and 2002/58/EC".

840 In particular, *see* Recital 25.

841 Opinion of the European Data Protection Supervisor on the proposal for a directive of the European Parliament and of the Council on the application of patients' rights in cross-border healthcare. O.J. C. 128, 6.6.2009.

842 *See* paragraphs 20–23.

843 *See* paragraphs 27–34. Interestingly, the EDPS recommended the introduction of a specific Article on data protection and the incorporation of the notion of

2000/31/EC on electronic commerce may apply to e-health actors who act as information society services[844]. Following Recital 14 of this Directive, the EU data protection framework – i.e. DPD, and now the GDPR, and the e-privacy Directive – is fully applicable to information society services and the application of this Directive should be made in full compliance with the principles of data protection[845].

Another source of rule in the processing of health data at the EU level is Regulation 536/2014 on clinical trials of medicinal products for human use[846]. Generally, clinical studies and trials are investigations intended to verify the effects or reactions of medical products or therapeutic strategies. Data subjects' personal health data are processed to test the products in the course of a scientific research activity. According to Recital 161 of the GDPR, the relevant rules of Regulation 536/2014 shall apply[847]. Since clinical trials involve the intimate sphere of individuals, they should respect "the rights, safety, dignity and well-being of subjects", who have "priority over all other interests", and "the data generated should be reliable and robust"[848]. Thus, the GDPR applies within the framework of this Regulation[849].

The same healthcare providers defined by Directive 2011/24/EU, including hospitals and private clinics, shall also comply with the national implementations of Directive 2016/1148 on measures for networking and

---

privacy by design. However, the legislative process of the Directive did not take into account these two recommendations.

844 *See* Mossialos et al., *Health systems governance in Europe: the role of European Union law and policy*, p. 566; Botrugno, "Telemedicine in daily practice: Addressing legal challenges while waiting for an EU regulatory framework". *See* the definition of "information society service" in Directive 2000/31/EC of the European Parliament and of the Council of 8 June 2000 on certain legal aspects of information society services, in particular electronic commerce, in the Internal Market ('Directive on electronic commerce'). O.J. L. 178, 17.7.2000.

845 On this Directive *see* also Arno R. Lodder. "European Union E-Commerce Directive-Article by Article Comments". In: *Guide to European Union Law on E-Commerce*. Vol. 4. Elgar Commentaries series, 2017, pp. 15–58. ISBN: 9781785369339.

846 Regulation (EU) No 536/2014 of the European Parliament and of the Council of 16 April 2014 on clinical trials on medicinal products for human use, and repealing Directive 2001/20/EC. O.J. L. 158, 27.5.2014.

847 *See* Recital 161.

848 Recital 1 of the Regulation 536/2014.

849 Regulation 536/2014 still refers to the DPD at Recital 76 and Article 93, but the DPD has been repealed by the GDPR.

systems security[850]. The processing of personal data in this framework shall be carried out in accordance with the GDPR[851].

Moreover, it should be mentioned that in 2017 two Regulations on *in vitro* diagnostic medical devices and on medical devices provided the rules concerning these products and established the creation of the comprehensive electronic database "Eudamed"[852]. These acts follow the medical directives that aimed to harmonise the rules on the free circulation of medical devices in the EU[853]. Once again, the GDPR applies to the processing of personal health data carried out in Member States pursuant to these regulations[854].

---

850 Directive (EU) 2016/1148 of the European Parliament and of the Council of 6 July 2016 concerning measures for a high common level of security of network and information systems across the Union. O.J. L. 194, 19.7.2016. On this directive *see* Dimitra Markopoulou, Vagelis Papakonstantinou, and Paul de Hert. "The new EU cybersecurity framework: The NIS Directive, ENISA's role and the General Data Protection Regulation". In: *Computer Law & Security Review* 35.6 (2019), p. 105336.

851 Actually, Article 2 of this Directive refers to the DPD, which has been repealed by the GDPR.

852 The two Regulations are: Regulation (EU) 2017/746 of the European Parliament and of the Council of 5 April 2017 on *in vitro* diagnostic medical devices and repealing Directive 98/79/EC and Commission Decision 2010/227/EU. O.J. L. 117, 5.5.2017; and Regulation (EU) 2017/745 of the European Parliament and of the Council of 5 April 2017 on medical devices, amending Directive 2001/83/EC, Regulation (EC) No 178/2002 and Regulation (EC) No 1223/2009 and repealing Council Directives 90/385/EEC and 93/42/EEC. O.J. L. 117, 5.5.2017. Due to the COVID-19 emergency this Regulation has been amended by Regulation (EU) 2020/561 of the European Parliament and of the Council of 23 April 2020 amending Regulation (EU) 2017/745 on medical devices, as regards the dates of application of certain of its provisions. O.J. L. 130, 24.4.2020. According to the Regulation (EU) 2017/745, the expression "medical device" means "any instrument, apparatus, appliance, software, implant, reagent, material or other article intended by the manufacturer to be used, alone or in combination, for human beings for one or more of the following specific medical purposes: diagnosis, prevention, monitoring, prediction, prognosis, treatment or alleviation of disease; diagnosis, monitoring, treatment, alleviation of, or compensation for, an injury or disability; investigation, replacement or modification of the anatomy or of a physiological or pathological process or state, providing information by means of in vitro examination of specimens derived from the human body, including organ, blood and tissue donations".

853 *See* Mossialos et al., *Health systems governance in Europe: the role of European Union law and policy*, p. 568. Madir, *Healthtech*, pp. 25–28 and pp. 53–79.

854 *See* the reference made by the Regulations to the GDPR at Article 110 for Regulation 2017/745 and at Article 103 for Regulation 2017/746.

From a European perspective, a legal framework in this domain is the Council of Europe Convention for the Protection of Individuals with Regard to Automatic Processing of Personal Data (hereafter: "Convention 108") which is the "only legally binding multilateral agreement in the field of personal data protection"[855]. The Convention aims to protect Article 8 ECHR and act as a global information privacy standard[856]. EU data protection law has been influenced by the Council of Europe's Convention 108 and these two legal frameworks follow the same logic[857]. The Convention, which was amended in 2018, and then signed by all EU Member States mandates some principles, rules and safeguards to be implemented in domestic law[858]. It is worth mentioning that even the

855 This wording has been used by the European Commission in EC European Commission. *Proposal for a Council Decision authorising Member States to sign, in the interest of the European Union, the Protocol amending the Council of Europe Convention for the Protection of Individuals with regard to Automatic Processing of Personal Data (ETS No. 108)*. European Commission. Brussels: COM (2018), 449 final. 2018. On the relevance of the CoE Convention *see* Paul de Hert and Vagelis Papakonstantinou. "The Council of Europe Data Protection Convention reform: Analysis of the new text and critical comment on its global ambition". In: *Computer Law & Security Review* 30.6 (2014), pp. 633–642.

856 *See* the comment by Hert and Papakonstantinou, *op. cit.*, p. 641.

857 *See* Giakoumopoulos, Buttarelli, and O'Flamerty, *Handbook on European data protection law*; Mulder, "Health apps, their privacy policies and the GDPR". On the relevance of the Convention *see* e.g. Paul de Hert and Vagelis Papakonstantinou. "The Council of Europe Data Protection Convention reform: Analysis of the new text and critical comment on its global ambition". In: *Computer Law & Security Review* 30.6 (2014), pp. 633–642; European Commission, *Proposal for a Council Decision authorising Member States to sign, in the interest of the European Union, the Protocol amending the Council of Europe Convention for the Protection of Individuals with regard to Automatic Processing of Personal Data (ETS No. 108)*. On the territorial and functional scopes *see* Jorg Ukrow. "Data Protection without Frontiers: On the Relationship between EU GDPR and Amended CoE Convention 108". In: *Eur. Data Prot. L. Rev.* 4 (2018), pp. 239–247.

858 The authorisation to sign was provided by Council Decision (EU) 2019/682 of 9 April 2019 allowing Member States to ratify, in the interest of the European Union, the Protocol amending the Council of Europe Convention for the Protection of Individuals with regard to Automatic Processing of Personal Data. O.J. L. 115, 2.5.2019.

Modernised Convention 108 considers medical data a special category of data[859]. This Convention contains similar safeguards as the GDPR[860].

The Council also issued three specific and relevant documents on health data processing. Three recommendations are specifically devoted to medical data and how the processing should be carried out. The recommendations are legal instruments of the Council of Europe that are not binding for the Council of Europe's member states, but are aimed at providing policy frameworks and harmonising domestic law to ensure a higher level of protection of rights[861].

Firstly, Recommendation No. R(97) 5 on the protection of medical data of 13 February 1997 specifically applies to the collection and automatic processing of medical data – i.e. "all personal data concerning the health of an individual", including "data which have a clear and close link with health as well as to genetic data" – in the absence of a national law that provides other appropriate safeguards[862]. According to this Recommendation, the processing of medical data should be carried out only by healthcare professionals, or by subjects working on their behalf. Other controllers should be subject to equal rules of confidentiality or effective safeguards at the national level. As far as this study is concerned, this Recommendation sets the principles for the processing, the legitimate basis, the information that the data subject should receive, the rights of the data subject and the security safeguards that should be taken to protect medical data[863].

Secondly, Recommendation CM/Rec (2016) 8 of the Committee of Ministers to the member States on the processing of personal health-related data for insurance purposes, including data resulting from genetic tests, of 26 October 2016, is aimed at ensuring the respect for the fundamental

---

859 *See* Article 6 Convention 108. For the text of the Convention *see* <https://search.coe.int/cm/Pages/result_details.aspx?ObjectId=09000016807c65bf>. Last accessed 06/10/2021.

860 *See* the useful comparison by Ukrow, "Data Protection without Frontiers: On the Relationship between EU GDPR and Amended CoE Convention 108".

861 For the legal status of the Council's recommendations *see* Stefanie Schmahl and Marten Breuer. *The Council of Europe: its law and policies*. Oxford University Press, 2017. ISBN: 9780199672523, p. 763; Florence Benoît-Rohmer, Heinrich Klebes, et al. *Council of Europe law: towards a pan-European legal area*. Council of Europe Publishing, 2005. ISBN: 9789287155948, p. 107.

862 On a legal analysis of this Recommendation *see* Trix Mulder. "The Protection of Data Concerning Health in Europe". In: *Eur. Data Prot. L. Rev.* 5 (2019), p. 209, pp. 213–215.

863 *See* further the text of the Recommendation.

rights of individuals without discrimination in the context of insurance contracts[864]. This recommendation is relevant for the e-health sector since the processing of data for insurance purposes implies high risks for the rights of the data subject, as explained above[865].

Thirdly, Recommendation CM/Rec (2019) 2 of the Committee of Ministers to member States on the protection of health-related data of 27 March 2019 applies to the processing of personal health data in the public and private sectors. This document stresses the importance of taking steps to better protect health-related data. It is applicable to the exchange and sharing of health-related data carried out by e-health technologies. This Recommendation lists the principles concerning data processing, by including the same principles of the GDPR with some additions[866]. In addition to transparency, lawfulness, fairness, purpose limitation, data minimisation, accuracy, security, accountability, and storage limitation[867], the Committee specifies that personal health-related data "should, in principle and as far as possible, be collected from the data subject", unless the "data subject is not in a position to provide the data and such data are necessary for the purposes of the processing"[868]. The security principle requires the implementation of appropriate security measures by taking into account "the latest technological developments", "the sensitive nature of health-related data and the assessment of potential risks" in order to prevent security risks[869]. According to the Recommendation, the controller should take into account all the mentioned principles by default, incorporate the rights from the design of e-health technologies, and regularly carry out an impact assessment of the potential impact of the processing of data[870]. This is a direct reference to a DPbD implementation in the healthcare domain. Furthermore, whenever the controller is not a health professional, the processing is subject to rules of confidentiality and security that ensure a level of

864 *See* the General Provisions of the Recommendation.

865 *See* also Giakoumopoulos, Buttarelli, and O'Flamerty, *Handbook on European data protection law*, p. 337.

866 *See* Chapter II – Legal conditions for the processing of health-related data paragraph 4.

867 This principle has been established in paragraph 10.

868 *See* paragraph 4(d).

869 *See* paragraph 4(f). *See* also paragraph 13 on security. The Recommendation even refers to conditions for securing the e-health system's availability, integrity, and auditability, the storage and sharing of data, and the access mechanism. These are all aspects that a DPbD implementation should take into account. *See* further Chapter 6.

870 *See* paragraph 4.2.

protection equivalent to the one imposed on health professionals[871]. The document recommends the legitimate basis of processing[872], some specific safeguards for genetic data and for the sharing and communication of data[873]. The information to be provided and the rights and obligations are equivalent to the elements of the GDPR, but the Recommendation presents fewer details.

The focus of this research is on the GDPR, and its DPbD obligation. The next subsections will now focus on this framework by providing the definition of personal health data, the legal grounds for their processing and the other relevant legal requirements that are applicable in the context of e-health and useful for a DPbD implementation.

### 3.3.1 The definition of personal health data

The definition of personal health data and the delimitation of its scope have raised doubts of interpretation[874]. This section attempts to provide guidance on this definition.

According to Article 29 Working Party, the category of health-related data is one of the most complex of sensitive data since it is often associated with serious privacy infringements[875]. Following the WHO's definition of health, this concept refers to the complexity of individual well-being at physical, mental and social levels[876].

The DPD mentioned data concerning health in the category of sensitive data, without defining it. Scholars argued that the absence of a normative definition was justified by the intention to leave the practitioner free to

871 *See* paragraph 4.4.

872 *See* for a comparison with the GDPR Section 3.3.2.

873 *See* paragraphs 7–9.

874 *See* Guarda, "I dati sanitari", p. 595; Mulder, "The Protection of Data Concerning Health in Europe"; Koelewijn, "Privacy from a Medical Perspective", p. 336. Lee A. Bygrave and Luca Tosoni. "Chapter I General principles (Articles 1–4). Article 4(15). Data concerning health". In: *The EU General Data Protection Regulation (GDPR): A Commentary*. Oxford University Press, 2020, pp. 215–224. ISBN: 9780198826491.

875 WP29 Article 29 Working Party. *Advice paper on special categories of data ("sensitive data")*. Ref. Ares (2011) 444105, 20.04.2011. 2011, p. 10.

876 *See* the introductory remarks of this Chapter.

decide from time to time which information falls under the scope of the rules on health data[877].

In the judgement *Criminal proceedings v. Bodil Lindqvist* the Court of Justice argued that the notion of personal data concerning health should include a "reference to the fact that an individual has injured her foot and is on half-time on medical grounds"[878]. The judgement refers to a preliminary ruling of the Swedish Göta Court of Appeal. The criminal proceeding was opened against Mrs. Lindqvist, who was a volunteer in a parish of the Swedish Protestant Church and published on her website personal data of a number of people working with her. Mrs. Lindqvist was convicted for processing sensitive data without authorisation from the DPA. This case was issued under the DPD, but it is still relevant for the definition of data concerning health since the CJEU pointed out that a broad interpretation of this expression shall be given in order to include information concerning all aspects, both physical and mental, of the health status of an individual[879]. The ruling of the Court shows the difficulties surrounding the concept of health data since the concrete context defines more than a given list on information which is sensitive[880]. Interpreters should adopt a teleological approach.

Article 29 Working Party then analysed the notion under the DPD[881]. The term "health data" should be interpreted in a broad sense. The authority presented several examples of information concerning health in the

877 *See* Fausto Caggia. "Il trattamento dei dati sulla salute, con particolare riferimento all'ambito sanitario". In: *Il codice del trattamento dei dati personali. Giappichelli, Torino* 8 (2007), p. 405, p. 407.

878 Case C-101/01, Criminal proceedings against Bodil Lindqvist. Judgment of 6 November 2003. *See* also Giakoumopoulos, Buttarelli, and O'Flamerty, *Handbook on European data protection law*, p. 96.

879 *See* paragraph 50.

880 *See* the comment by Ian Lloyd. *Information technology law*. Oxford University Press, 2020. ISBN: 9780198830559, p. 42; and Peter Carey. *Data protection: a practical guide to UK and EU law*. Oxford University Press, 2018. ISBN: 9780198815419, p. 68, which specifies that personal data may be seen in context in order to determine whether or not they are actually special data. Other case law on sensitive data is reported by Ludmila Georgieva and Christopher Kuner. "Chapter II Principles (Articles 5–11). Article 9 Processing of special categories of personal data". In: *The EU General Data Protection Regulation (GDPR): A Commentary*. Oxford University Press, 2020, pp. 365–384. ISBN: 9780198826491, pp. 372–373.

881 *See* WP29 Article 29 Working Party. *Working Document on the processing of personal data relating to health in electronic health records (EHR)*. WP131 2007/en. 2007, p. 7.

legal sense, such as data on consumption of medicinal products, alcohol or drugs, genetic data, and any other data contained in the medical documentation of the treatment. In 2011 in order to clarify the scope of the notion in relation to lifestyle and well-being apps, WP29 pointed out that "medical data" are uniformly considered "health data", meaning "data about the physical or mental health status of a data subject that are generated in a professional medical context"[882]. All data relating to diagnosis, diseases, disabilities, medical history and clinical treatment should be included in this definition.

However, according to WP29, the expression "health data" is broader than the term "medical data" since it encompasses other related information, such as data about smoking and drinking habits, data on allergies, membership in a patient support group, information on illness in an employment context, data used in an administrative healthcare context, data about the purchase of medical products, devices and services when health status can be inferred from this information[883]. Merely lifestyle data, such as the number of steps during a daily walk, is "raw data" and is not "health data" in the legal sense. It should be noted that a grey area may remain since raw information can be often combined, and then conclusions on medical risk of the individual can be inferred, irrespective of whether they are accurate (e.g. using blood pressure and sex, age, etc.). According to WP29, these conclusions shall be considered "health data"[884].

Compared to the DPD, in Article 4 the GDPR clarifies the concept by expanding the definitions with health-related specifications on "genetic data" and "data concerning health"[885]. Commentators highlight that these

---

882 *See* WP29 Article 29 Working Party. *ANNEX – health data in apps and devices*. Annex to the letter of 5.2.2015, 2015.

883 Article 29 Working Party, *op. cit.*, p. 2.

884 Article 29 Working Party, *op. cit.*, p. 5. *See* also the commentary by Caterina Del Federico and Anna Rita Popoli. "Le definizioni". In: *La protezione dei dati personali in Italia. Regolamento UE n. 2016/679 e d.lgs. 10 agosto 2018, n. 101*. Zanichelli, Torino, 2019, pp. 63–88. ISBN: 9788808820433, p. 78.

885 For a brief comparison *see* Durst, "Il trattamento di categorie particolari di dati in ambito sanitario", pp. 66–67. The GDPR also adds the definition of "biometric data", which means any "personal data resulting from specific technical processing relating to the physical, physiological or behavioural characteristics of a natural person, which allow or confirm the unique identification of that natural person, such as facial images or dactyloscopic data". *See* Article 4 GDPR (14) GDPR. On biometric data *see* e.g. Els J. Kindt. *Privacy and Data Protection Issues of Biometric Applications. A Comparative Legal Analysis*. Springer Netherlands, 2013. ISBN: 97894007752.

specifications reflect the growing importance of e-health at the EU level in recent years[886]. So, it has been pointed out that now the data relating to health are defined and detached from the more general and generic interpretation previously adopted by authorities and legal practitioners[887].

The first term of "genetic data" is a special sub-category of data concerning health and refers to "personal data relating to the inherited or acquired genetic characteristics of a natural person which give unique information about the physiology or the health of that natural person and which result, in particular, from an analysis of a biological sample from the natural person in question"[888]; whereas the second term of "data concerning health" has been framed as follows[889]:

> "Personal data related to the physical or mental health of a natural person, including the provision of health care services, which reveal information about his or her health status".

Recital 35 further explains which data are related to health status by adding the timing dimension, extending the scope of the definition, and by stating that:

> "Personal data concerning health should include all data pertaining to the health status of a data subject which reveal information relating to the past, current or future physical or mental health status of the data subject".

---

886 *See* e.g. Durst, "Il trattamento di categorie particolari di dati in ambito sanitario", p. 72.

887 *See* Guarda, "I dati sanitari", p. 597.

888 Article 4(13) GDPR. Moreover Recital 35 also specifies that "genetic data should be defined as personal data relating to the inherited or acquired genetic characteristics of a natural person which result from the analysis of a biological sample from the natural person in question, in particular chromosomal, deoxyribonucleic acid (DNA) or ribonucleic acid (RNA) analysis, or from the analysis of another element enabling equivalent information to be obtained". On genetic data *see* e.g. Guarda, *op. cit.*, pp. 621–625; Mahsa Shabani and Pascal Borry. "Rules for processing genetic data for research purposes in view of the new EU General Data Protection Regulation". In: *European Journal of Human Genetics* 26.2 (2018), pp. 149–156; Kärt Pormeister. "The GDPR and Big Data: Leading the Way for Big Genetic Data?" In: *Annual Privacy Forum*. Springer. 2017, pp. 3–18; Mark Taylor. *Genetic data and the law: a critical perspective on privacy protection*. Vol. 16. Cambridge University Press, 2012. ISBN: 9780511910128; Laurie Graeme. *Genetic privacy: a challenge to medico-legal norms*. Cambridge University Press, 2002. ISBN: 0521660270.

889 Article 4(15) GDPR.

Not only information on the past, but also on the future health status should be considered personal data concerning health. The same Recital adds further interpretation and specifies some information which shall be included in the notion. It can be listed as follows:

- "information about the natural person collected in the course of the registration for, or the provision of, health care services as referred to in Directive 2011/24/EU of the European Parliament and of the Council to that natural person", which refers to the cross-border provision of healthcare described above;
- "a number, symbol or particular assigned to a natural person to uniquely identify the natural person for health purposes", which refers to administrative data used for healthcare purposes;
- "information derived from the testing or examination of a body part or bodily substance, including from genetic data and biological samples", which is the inferred data, or the laboratory data, or genetic data inferred from biological sample, such as chromosomal, DNA or RNA analysis;
- "any information on, for example, a disease, disability, disease risk, medical history, clinical treatment or the physiological or biomedical state of the data subject independent of its source, for example from a physician or other health professional, a hospital, a medical device or an in vitro diagnostic test", which is the traditional notion of "medical data".

In this definition the GDPR explicitly includes the data processed under the regulatory framework outlined above: Directive on the cross-border healthcare, and the two Regulations on *in vitro* diagnostic medical devices and on medical devices. As a result, the legal system on data protection is consistent. The GDPR applies to any personal data concerning health that is processed under the EU law. It refers to genetic information and biological samples, too. Moreover, as mentioned in the previous Chapter, it should be recalled that the Regulation 2018/1725 applies to the processing carried out by EU institutions, bodies and agencies. This Regulation uses the same definitions of genetic data, biometric data, and data concerning health[890].

Following the GDPR wording, it can be noted that the definition of data concerning health is broad[891]. It is now explicitly broader than simply

890 Article 3 lists all the definitions.

891 *See* e.g. Durst, "Il trattamento di categorie particolari di dati in ambito sanitario", p. 73; Koelewijn, "Privacy from a Medical Perspective", p. 337.

"medical data" and is applicable at the EU level. The explicit reference to administrative data related to health (i.e. the "number, symbol or particular assigned to a natural person to uniquely identify the natural person for health purposes") better specifies the concept by following the previous interpretations of WP29, DPAs and scholars[892]. The definition of personal data concerning health embeds both the strictly care level and the services that it includes. For the purpose of this book, the term "personal health data" means "data concerning health" in the meaning of the GDPR.

Recital 35 is more comprehensive than Article 4, but it does not define whether or not other types of "quasi-health" data (e.g. lifestyle and well-being data) are considered health data[893]. It may be argued that the future dimension of the definition embeds the data inferred with predictive analysis tools[894]. The legal notion surely includes the data related to any health status, the information collected in the cross-border exchange of health data, on clinical studies and trials, and all the information on any medical treatment or examination regardless of the sources. Hence, personal data which have a clear link with the description of the health status and the medical treatment of a person shall fall within the definition of Article 4 GDPR.

However, health apps or wearable devices can frequently generate inferences about health conditions or risk of illness[895]. Some prominent scholars tried to delimit the boundaries of health data using a computational approach based on the sensitivity of the data[896]. According to Malgieri and Comandé, raw data can be divided into "received data" (i.e. data provided by the data subject) and "observed data" (i.e. data collected through the system with sensors), whereas "complex data" consists of "inferred data" (i.e. descriptive data inferred by the controller containing different information, such as the health status) and "predicted data" (i.e.

---

892 In Melchionna and Cecamore, "Le nuove frontiere della sanità e della ricerca scientifica", p. 581, the author referred to several opinions of the Italian DPA. For the interpretation of the scholars *see* the discussion in Guarda, "I dati sanitari", pp. 593–597.

893 Mantovani et al., "Towards a Code of Conduct on Privacy for mHealth to Foster Trust Amongst Users of Mobile Health Applications", p. 90.

894 In Koelewijn, "Privacy from a Medical Perspective", the author mentions big data technologies generally.

895 *See* Gianclaudio Malgieri and Giovanni Comandé. "Sensitive-by-distance: quasi-health data in the algorithmic era". In: *Information & Communications Technology Law* 26.3 (2017), pp. 229–249, p. 230.

896 *See* Malgieri and Comandé, *op. cit.*

information on the future health status)[897]. It is necessary to determine whether or not data not directly related to the health status, but capable of revealing the future status (e.g. observed data on number of steps walked per year or inferred data on sexual habits), are health data. These scholars concluded that complex information should be considered "quasi-health" data since it is nearly as sensitive as health data, and it should be selected on a case-by-case basis in accordance with the two variables of "intrinsic sensitiveness" and "computational distance"[898]. The status of "quasi-health" data is comparable to sensitive data. Within this framework, it should be easily determined which information falls under the legal notion of health data following a case-by-case approach based on a strict methodology.

The notion resulting from the GDPR is consistent with the OECD's international definition of "personal health data", that is "any information relating to an identified or identifiable individual" (e.g. personal data) "that concerns their health, and includes any other associated personal data"[899]. The timing of health status indicated in the GDPR has also been used for the CoE definition in the Recommendation CM/Rec (2019) 2, where health-related data are "all personal data concerning the physical or mental health of an individual, including the provision of health-care services, which reveals information about this individual's past, current and future health"[900]. It has been argued that the use of the term "information" implies that the data itself is not protected, unless it is used to gain information on an individual's health status[901].

Finally, it should be noted that the literature and regulatory frameworks may use the notion of "particularly sensitive health data", which consists

897 The definitions are summarised from the description in Malgieri and Comandé, *op. cit.*, p. 232. *See* also Giovanni Comandé and Giulia Schneider. "Regulatory Challenges of Data Mining Practices: The Case of the Never-ending Lifecycles of 'Health Data'". In: *European Journal of Health Law* 25.3 (2018), pp. 284–307.

898 The proposed definition of "quasi-health" data is "information apparently not related to health conditions but which, if combined with biographical data (age, sex, etc.) and/or with statistical or biological studies, enables inference or prediction of individuals' health conditions with a certain degree of plausibility". The computational distance is related to the level of effort required to infer the information. Intrinsic sensitivity is a static variable, whereas computational distance is a dynamic variable, and they are inversely proportional. *See* Malgieri and Comandé, "Sensitive-by-distance: quasi-health data in the algorithmic era".

899 OECD, *OECD Recommendation on Health Data Governance*, p. 4.

900 *See* Chapter I – General Provision paragraph 2 and 3 of the Recommendation.

901 *See* Mulder, "The Protection of Data Concerning Health in Europe", p. 212.

in a sub-set of personal health data whose processing requires additional safeguards provided by national law[902].

Given the notion of personal health data and recalling the existence of a general prohibition on processing this data, in the next section the legitimate grounds for the processing of this category of data will be analysed in detail.

### 3.3.1 The legal grounds for processing

Generally, the legal grounds for the processing of sensitive data are narrower than the grounds for common personal data. The DPD established a general prohibition on processing sensitive data that has proven to be successful since it provided for few exceptions and several additional safeguards[903]. The advantages of this approach were summarised by Article 29 working Party as follows. The DPD gave a "strong political signal that the processing of sensitive data is generally prohibited" and it harmonised the categories of sensitive data providing legal certainty for data controllers on the limits[904]. At the same time, the complete harmonisation of the exceptions was not achieved in national implementing legislation[905].

Under the GDPR, the EU legal framework is better harmonised, but, as mentioned, Member States still have room to manoeuvre. Thus, it has been claimed that it is nearly impossible to carry out a real unification of the rules on the processing of health data at the EU level[906]. However, according to Recital 53 of the GDPR, the processing of personal data for health-related purposes should be allowed only in the context where it is "necessary to achieve those purposes for the benefit of natural persons and

---

902 *See* e.g. Califano, "Fascicolo sanitario elettronico (Fse) e dossier sanitario. Il contributo del Garante privacy al bilanciamento tra diritto alla salute e diritto alla protezione dei dati personali", which reports the notion existing in the Italian framework. Particularly sensitive data are HIV health status, abortion, sexual assault, drug abuse, and anonymous birth. *See* also Guarda, "I dati sanitari".

903 *See* the comments of Article 29 Working Party, *Advice paper on special categories of data ("sensitive data")*, p. 13.

904 *Ibid.*

905 *Ibid.*

906 Guarda, "I dati sanitari", p. 600.

society as a whole"[907]. So, the processing of personal health data may refer both to the individual interest and to public interests.

The enumeration of the legal grounds of processing, i.e. the exceptions to the general prohibition listed by Article 9 of the GDPR, is exhaustive. They largely overlap with the limits of the DPD[908]. However, as mentioned, Member States' laws "may maintain or introduce further conditions, including limitations, with regard to the processing of genetic data, biometric data or data concerning health"[909].

Firstly, article 9(2)(h) explicitly allows for processing personal health data when the purposes are preventative or occupational medicine, medical diagnosis, the provision of care or treatment, or the management of healthcare services on the basis of Union or Member State law or pursuant to a contract with a health professional[910]. In these cases, the processing shall be carried out by a healthcare professional who is subject to a duty of secrecy or confidentiality under Union or Member State law or other national provision[911]. The collected personal health data shall be necessary

---

907 Recital 53 GDPR. The Recital lists some contexts where this achievement is considered appropriate for society, which are: "the management of health or social care services and systems" that include several scenarios of "processing by the management and central national health authorities of such data for the purpose of quality control, management information" and of "the general national and local supervision of the health or social care system" and of "ensuring continuity of health or social care and cross-border healthcare or health security, monitoring and alert purposes"; "archiving purposes in the public interest, scientific or historical research purposes or statistical purposes", which are "based on Union or Member State law" and meet "an objective of public interest"; and "studies conducted in the public interest in the area of public health".

908 *See* further discussion at the end of this section.

909 Article 9(4) GDPR.

910 The grounds have been summarised in this way by Giakoumopoulos, Buttarelli, and O'Flamerty, *Handbook on European data protection law*, p. 336. The paragraph of the GDPR states: "(h) processing is necessary for the purposes of preventive or occupational medicine, for the assessment of the working capacity of the employee, medical diagnosis, the provision of health or social care or treatment or the management of health or social care systems and services on the basis of Union or Member State law or pursuant to contract with a health professional and subject to the conditions and safeguards referred to in paragraph 3".

911 *See* Article 9(3) GDPR: "3. Personal data referred to in paragraph 1 may be processed for the purposes referred to in point (h) of paragraph 2 when those data are processed by or under the responsibility of a professional subject to the obligation of professional secrecy under Union or Member State law or rules

for the treatment. As a result, it has been argued that healthcare providers should always check whether the collected personal health data is in reasonable proportion to the goal of one of the purposes listed above and whether less data could be sufficient to achieve it[912].

This legitimate ground may be called the "healthcare exception" and it is similar to a provision of the DPD[913]. Under the DPD, it has been claimed that this exception, restricted to a specific target of subjects, was difficult to apply in the healthcare sector since it was often not clear who belongs to the category of health professionals in practice or to the group of persons obliged to equivalent secrecy duties[914]. To interpret the notion of professional it is useful to look at other legislation applicable in the health sector. According to Article 3 of Directive 2011/24/EU the term "health professional" refers to a natural person who is "a doctor of medicine, a nurse responsible for general care, a dental practitioner, a midwife or a pharmacist within the meaning of Directive 2005/36/EC on the recognition of professional qualifications", or "another professional exercising activities in the healthcare sector which are restricted to a regulated profession" as defined by the same Directive, or "a person considered to be a health professional according to the legislation of the Member State of treatment"[915]. So, it can be argued that the exception of the GDPR refers to this category of subjects whose professional status is recognised by Union or Member State law, and to other categories subject to an equivalent secrecy under the law (i.e. non-medical professional).

---

established by national competent bodies or by another person also subject to an obligation of secrecy under Union or Member State law or rules established by national competent bodies".

912 *See* Koelewijn, "Privacy from a Medical Perspective", p. 339.

913 In this regard, the Directive at Article 8(3) stated that the prohibition on processing sensitive data "shall not apply where processing of the data is required for the purposes of preventive medicine, medical diagnosis, the provision of care or treatment or the management of health-care services, and where those data are processed by a health professional subject under national law or rules established by national competent bodies to the obligation of professional secrecy or by another person also subject to an equivalent obligation of secrecy".

914 Article 29 Working Party, *Advice paper on special categories of data ("sensitive data")*, p. 9. Article 29 Working Party called for a revision of the DPD for the broad term "health professional".

915 The definition refers to Directive 2005/36/EC of the European Parliament and of the Council of 7 September 2005 on the recognition of professional qualifications. O.J. L. 255, 30.9.2005. For example, in Chapter III, Section 2 is entirely dedicated to doctors of medicine.

The rationale underlined by this first exception is avoiding the compulsory collection of patient's consent in order to simplify and facilitate the performance of healthcare services[916]. In addition, any errors in the collection of consent does not affect the proper performance of activities of higher interest, such as those related to health protection since consent is not necessary[917]. As a result, when processing is instrumental to the provision of healthcare, the controllers do not need to collect consent and their operations are simplified. Undoubtedly, the general duty of confidentiality provided by law remains. As mentioned above, this duty is even covered by criminal law provisions in some countries[918]. So, the breach of this duty of confidentiality may be punished with criminal sanctions, and the duty of secrecy is usually provided by physicians' codes of medical ethics.

It should be pointed out that this "healthcare exception" never applies to the insurance sector. Insurance companies that are not healthcare providers process health data since this information is a necessary prerequisite for concluding and performing a health insurance contract. Therefore, the processing for insurance purposes collects personal health data, but it shall use another legitimate ground that is the consent of the data subject. It has been claimed that this consent does not often meet the legal requirements of explicit, informed and free consent due to the use of blanket declarations which cover numerous forms of data processing[919]. Anyway, another legal ground listed as an exception in Article 9 GDPR is the consent of the data subject to the specific processing and related purpose, where consent is explicit[920].

As regards explicit consent, it is not necessarily written since the requirement constrains the purpose of the consent, but the form of expression is free, and can even be oral or expressed though behaviour[921]. So, the

---

916 *See* Greco, "Il trattamento dei dati sanitari", p. 228.

917 *See ibid.*

918 *See* Hervey and McHale, *Health law and the European Union*, p. 162.

919 Article 29 Working Party, *Advice paper on special categories of data ("sensitive data")*, p. 9. Article 29 Working Party called for a revision of this aspect, too.

920 Article 9(2)(a) provides that the processing is allowed when "the data subject has given explicit consent to the processing of those personal data for one or more specified purposes, except where Union or Member State law provide that the prohibition referred to in paragraph 1 may not be lifted by the data subject".

921 Selvaggia F. Giovannangeli. "L'informativa agli interessati e il consenso al trattamento". In: *Circolazione e protezione dei dati personali, tra libertà e regole del mercato. Commentario al Regolamento UE n. 2016/679 (GDPR) e al novellato D.lgs. n. 196/2003 (Codice Privacy)*. Giuffrè Francis Lefebvre, 2019, pp. 100–141. ISBN: 9788828809692, p. 117.

individual shall explicitly and clearly express his or her will to grant permission for the processing and the controller has the burden of proof that the consent meets the GDPR requirements[922]. Although the form of consent is free, the controller is accountable for proving the receipt of the express statement of consent[923]. The consent shall respect the requirements of Article 7 and 8 GDPR – i.e. it shall be freely-given, specific, informed and unambiguous – and it shall explicitly refer to the personal health data concerned[924]. Union or Member State law could limit the applicability of this exception to specific categories of sensitive data. It has been pointed out that it is unlikely that such prohibition will be created by the EU since the EU has limited competence in this area[925]. Instead, the Member States can provide particular cases when the prohibition of processing health data may not be lifted by the consent of the data subject.

Explicit consent is required in circumstances where the data subjects are testing pharmaceutical products or medical devices and their personal genetic, health and related data are useful for the test phases and clinical trials[926]. The data collected in clinical trials can also be considered for secondary scientific research purposes. Regulation 536/2014 on clinical trials of medicinal products for human use requires the consent of the data subject for processing in the clinical study and trial, and also for the use of data outside the protocol of the clinical trial. The subject has the right to withdraw that consent at any time. As will be explained in the following paragraphs, Union or Member State law may establish a legitimate ground for processing which has scientific purposes. If this is the case, another exception following from Article 9 might apply to the processing of health data. Since Regulation 536/2014 refers to the applicable law on data protection[927], it should be established whether the basis for the processing of clinical data for scientific purposes remains consent under

---

922 Hooghiemstra, "Informational Self-Determination, Digital Health and New Features of Data Protection", p. 168.

923 On how this statement can be expressed *see* Article 29 Working Party, *Guidelines on consent under Regulation 2016/679*.

924 Voigt and Von dem Bussche, *The EU General Data Protection Regulation (GDPR). A Practical Guide*, p. 112. *See* also Koelewijn, "Privacy from a Medical Perspective", pp. 337–338.

925 Voigt and Von dem Bussche, *The EU General Data Protection Regulation (GDPR). A Practical Guide*, p. 112.

926 The example is provided by Massimiliano Granieri. "Il trattamento di categorie particolari di dati personali nel Reg. UE 2016/679". In: *Le Nuove leggi civili commentate* 1 (2017), pp. 165–190.

927 *See* Article 93 of the Regulation 536/2014.

Regulation 536/2014 or if it is a specific Union or Member State law without the consent of the data subject. According to Granieri, this scenario creates possible overlaps of the frameworks and legal uncertainty[928]. In the absence of a specific law, the consent of the subject will be required. Instead, in the presence of law, the rules will constitute the legitimate exception and ground, and they will provide the necessary safeguards and measures that protect the rights of the data subjects.

It is worth noting that consent to processing differs from consent to medical treatment. Both consents shall be informed and free. While the former is related to the specific data processing, the latter represents the free and informed expression of will of the patient who accepts the clinical or medical treatment[929]. The Convention on Human Rights and Biomedicine on the protection of human rights in the biomedical field establishes a general rule on consent by specifying that[930]:

> "An intervention in the health field may only be carried out after the person concerned has given free and informed consent to it. This person shall beforehand be given appropriate information as to the purpose and nature of the intervention as well as on its consequences and risks. The person concerned may freely withdraw consent at any time".

Moreover, under the EU Charter of Fundamental Rights in the fields of medicine and biology, the right to the integrity of the person encompasses the respect to free and informed consent of the person concerned[931]. The consent to treatment is a fundamental principle of medical law and it protects the principle of autonomy of the patient[932]. Even though the consent of processing is sometimes not necessary to legitimise the data processing, the healthcare provider shall always obtain consent for the treatment, and then the processing operations can begin.

---

928 *See* Granieri, "Il trattamento di categorie particolari di dati personali nel Reg. UE 2016/679".

929 On consent to treatment *see* Herring, *Medical law and ethics*, pp. 155–231.

930 Article 5 of the Convention for the protection of Human Rights and Dignity of the Human Being with regard to the Application of Biology and Medicine (ETS No.164). Oviedo, 04.04.1997. The text is available at <www.coe.int/en/web/conventions/full-list/-/conventions/rms/090000168007cf98>. Last accessed 06/10/2021.

931 Article 3 of the Charter.

932 Herring, *Medical law and ethics*, p. 155. According to Herring autonomy is the one fundamental ethical principle in the medical arena (p. 207).

Another situation where consent constitutes the legal basis is the processing carried out by commercial entities via mobile-health apps and wearable devices for health- and fitness-related purposes. In these contexts, the "healthcare exception" does not apply since medical professionals are not processing the data and the processing is not carried out under their responsibility, as required by Article 9(3) GDPR[933].

Legitimate grounds are also the obligations and rights in the field of employment and social security and social protection law[934]. The processing of personal health data is lawful when the processing is carried out in an employment, social security and social protection context whether the same processing is necessary for the purposes of carrying out the obligations of, and exercising specific rights of, the controller or of the data subject, and either Union or Member State law or a collective agreement authorises the processing and provides appropriate safeguards for the fundamental rights and the interests of the data subject. In the employment relationship employers normally process personal health data[935]. The main purpose is knowing if the employee is suitable for doing the job offered by the employer[936]. The assessment of working ability is covered by this exception for the employer and the exception of medical diagnosis for the healthcare professional. It has thus been argued that the GDPR made a preventive balance in favour of the employer since this subject can ascertain the work potential of their employee in terms of psycho-physical, attitudinal and technical-professional skills without asking for consent[937]. Another possible purpose is knowing the details of an employee's disability in order to properly adapt the workstation and the safety environment[938]. It seems that the employer has the legitimate interest of processing the employee's data *a priori*. However, the processing is carried out on the basis of Union or Member State law or pursuant to a collective agreement

933 *See* the legal analysis by Mulder, "Health apps, their privacy policies and the GDPR".

934 Article 9(2)(b) GDPR: "(b) processing is necessary for the purposes of carrying out the obligations and exercising specific rights of the controller or of the data subject in the field of employment and social security and social protection law in so far as it is authorised by Union or Member State law or a collective agreement pursuant to Member State law providing for appropriate safeguards for the fundamental rights and the interests of the data subject".

935 Voigt and Von dem Bussche, *The EU General Data Protection Regulation (GDPR). A Practical Guide*, p. 112.

936 *See* Greco, "Il trattamento dei dati sanitari", p. 229.

937 *See ibid.*

938 *See* Carey, *Data protection: a practical guide to UK and EU law*, p. 71.

that provides appropriate safeguards for the fundamental rights and the interests of the employee. These safeguards should protect the employee from unlawful discrimination during the job. So, the law should minimise the amount of health data to which the employer could have access.

Social security and social protection laws usually refer to occupational medicine which concerns the provision of healthcare assistance to employees and is aimed at preventing any damage caused to health by the conditions of the working environment, such as the risks arising from the presence of harmful objects[939]. The underlying purposes are prevention, diagnosis and therapy activities for the protection of the worker. So, this exception simplifies the processing as indicated for the "healthcare exception".

Furthermore, the individual may be physically or legally incapable of giving explicit consent, especially in healthcare scenarios. The natural person can be unconscious or absent, or he or she may not be reachable[940]. In those circumstances the GDPR then allows processing when it is necessary to protect the vital interests of the data subject or of another natural person[941]. Scholars specified that vital interests are all the existential needs and interests for the protection of life and physical integrity[942]. However, it has been argued that previous wishes of the data subject or the other person are always relevant: if it is known that the individual would not have consented to a processing under the emergency circumstances, the processing cannot be carried out lawfully under this "vital interest exception"[943]. So, an assessment of the data protection interests of the individual is required[944]. This exception instead operates when the processing does not meet the other legitimate grounds and it is necessary to save the life of a person. In the healthcare context, it might be an overlap between this "vital interest exception" and the "healthcare exception". Nevertheless,

---

939 *See* Greco, "Il trattamento dei dati sanitari", p. 230.

940 Giakoumopoulos, Buttarelli, and O'Flamerty, *Handbook on European data protection law*, p. 162.

941 Article 9(2)(c) states that when the "processing is necessary to protect the vital interests of the data subject or of another natural person where the data subject is physically or legally incapable of giving consent", the prohibition does not apply.

942 *See* Voigt and Von dem Bussche, *The EU General Data Protection Regulation (GDPR). A Practical Guide*, p. 112.

943 *See ibid.*

944 Georgieva and Kuner, "Chapter II Principles (Articles 5–11). Article 9 Processing of special categories of personal data", p. 377.

it has been argued that the former is not limited to the presence of a healthcare professional or a confidential scenario as the latter[945].

Foundations, associations or any non-profit bodies with a political, philosophical, religious or trade union aim can internally process the personal health data of their members, of their former members or of people who have regular contact with them in connection with their purposes when they do not communicate or share the data outside without the consent of the respective data subjects[946]. Some personal health data could be stored by these bodies if necessary for their purposes in light of the data minimisation principle.

Whether the individual makes personal health data public, the processing by a data controller is not prohibited[947]. Nevertheless, the data subject shall deliberately and manifestly make public these data. The publication of personal data shall be a free choice of the individual who makes the data freely available, for example in publicly accessible registers, websites, lists, forums or even public social network profiles[948]. Actually, nowadays there are several forums and websites dedicated to and used by people who suffer from the same disease, such as celiac disease, diabetes, clinical depression, and cancer.

Personal health data are frequently collected and disclosed by subjects for the establishment, exercise or defence of legal claims. This is another legitimate exception. Court cases involving traffic accidents, medical liability, and compensation from insurance companies are daily on the agenda of legal practitioners. Legal claims include court proceedings and administrative or out-of-court procedures[949]. Personal health data shall be related and limited to the specific legal claim for which the subject is

945 *See* Carey, *Data protection: a practical guide to UK and EU law*, p. 73.

946 This exception is provided by Article 9(2)(d): "processing is carried out in the course of its legitimate activities with appropriate safeguards by a foundation, association or any other not-for-profit body with a political, philosophical, religious or trade union aim and on condition that the processing relates solely to the members or to former members of the body or to persons who have regular contact with it in connection with its purposes and that the personal data are not disclosed outside that body without the consent of the data subjects". According to Recital 51 of the GDPR, these entities shall have the purpose of permitting the exercise of fundamental freedoms.

947 Article 9(2)(e) allows the processing that "relates to personal data which are manifestly made public by the data subject".

948 Voigt and Von dem Bussche, *The EU General Data Protection Regulation (GDPR). A Practical Guide*, p. 113.

949 *Ibid.*

acting. Even the court directly processes personal health data for its ruling, such as when an office technical consultation is arranged. Genetic data are processed in court cases for establishing parentage, or the health status is used as evidence which concerns details of an injury sustained by a victim of crime[950]. When a patient sues the hospital which has provided care, the hospital uses the recorded personal health data as proof in order to defend itself in the course of the legal proceedings[951]. Whenever processing is necessary for these legal claim purposes, the GDPR provides that the general prohibition does not apply[952].

Then, the GDPR establishes some exceptions for reasons of general public interest. In particular, the GDPR seeks to strike a balance between individual interest in the confidentiality of health data and collective interest in the use of these data[953]. So, the processing is lawful for reasons of substantial public interests pursuant to Union or Member State law when it is proportionate to the aim pursued, it respects the essence of the right to data protection and the law provides for suitable and specific measures in order to safeguard the fundamental rights and the interests of the data subjects[954]. Examples of activities carried out by public entities that entail a substantial public interest and that may process personal health data are: keeping public administrative records and registries and certificates of births, deaths and marriages; keeping registries of citizenship, immigration, asylum, and refugee status; carrying out administrative activities and issuance of certifications in connection with healthcare and welfare activities, including organ and tissue transplantation and human blood transfusions; management of public tasks related to occupational safety, population health and safety; granting social protection of motherhood, termination of pregnancy, assistance to the disabled; and providing edu-

950 Giakoumopoulos, Buttarelli, and O'Flamerty, *Handbook on European data protection law*, p. 162.

951 *See* Voigt and Von dem Bussche, *The EU General Data Protection Regulation (GDPR). A Practical Guide*, p. 114.

952 *See* Article 9(2)(f): "processing is necessary for the establishment, exercise or defence of legal claims or whenever courts are acting in their judicial capacity".

953 *See* Greco, "Il trattamento dei dati sanitari", p. 234.

954 Article 9(2)(g) GDPR. It can be noted that this formulation recalls the "necessity" and "proportionality" tests described in the end of the previous Chapter. Whether a national rule is intended to derogate from the general prohibition, this legislative measure shall pass the two tests and potentially provide safeguards.

cation and training at school[955]. In the e-health sector, some healthcare records may exist, and the data may be processed for substantial public interests on the basis of national statutory law which contains any necessary and proportionate safeguards for a digital processing of personal health data[956].

In addition to general public interest, other Union or Member States regulatory provisions can establish the possibility of processing personal health data for protecting interests in the area of public health[957]. As mentioned, this exception allows the protection of health security, the monitoring and control of diseases or of other serious threats to public health. The law shall define suitable and specific measures to still guarantee the rights and freedoms of individuals, and duties on professional secrecy shall be set. Under the DPD, examples of public health interests were protection against communicable diseases (e.g. HIV) or health promotion (e.g. against cancer and tobacco)[958]. Other examples of public interest in the area of public health are protection against serious cross-border threats to health (e.g. pandemic), and the necessity to ensure high standards of quality and safety of healthcare and of medicinal products or medical devices.

Finally, processing is allowed in accordance with Article 89 of the GDPR for archiving purposes in the public interest, scientific or historical research purposes or statistical purposes on the basis of proportionate and safeguarding Union or Member State law[959]. Once again, appropriate (i.e.

---

955 This list of examples has been borrowed from the list of processing activities that according to Article 2 *sextes* of the Italian Personal Data Protection Code entails a lawful substantial public interest. Article *sextes* provides the safeguards required by Article 9(2)(g) GDPR. Other examples were adopted before Brexit by the UK Government, which included in the 1998 Act e.g. "carrying on certain types of insurance (relating to disclosure of certain health data of relations of an insured)", "third party data processing for group insurance policies and insurance on the life of another", "identification or prevention of doping in sport". *See* the discussion in Carey, *Data protection: a practical guide to UK and EU law*, p. 76.

956 *See* Giakoumopoulos, Buttarelli, and O'Flamerty, *Handbook on European data protection law*, p. 163.

957 Article 9(2)(i) GDPR.

958 *See* Hervey and McHale, *Health law and the European Union*, pp. 330–385.

959 *See* Article 9(2)(j) that allows the processing that is "necessary for archiving purposes in the public interest, scientific or historical research purposes or statistical purposes in accordance with Article 89(1) based on Union or Member State law". The law "shall be proportionate to the aim pursued, respect the essence of the right to data protection and provide for suitable and specific

necessary and proportionate) safeguards shall be defined for protecting the individuals' rights and freedoms. In particular, technical and organisational measures shall be put in place for ensuring data protection principles, and data minimisation especially[960]. Whether the purposes can be achieved with the use of pseudonymised data, the measure of pseudonymisation shall be implemented. Personal health data may be used for improving scientific research, but specific safeguards should always protect the rights of the data subjects[961].

---

measures to safeguard the fundamental rights and the interests of the data subject". On this basis *see* further Giovanni Comandé. "Ricerca in sanità e data protection un puzzle... risolvibile". In: *Rivista Italiana di Medicina Legale (e del Diritto in campo sanitario)* 1 (2019), pp. 189–207. On the implementation of Article 89 in Member States' legislation *see* TIPIK, *Report on the implementation of specific provisions of Regulation (EU) 2016/679*, pp. 29–39; DG Health and Food Security. *Assessment of the EU Member States' rules on health data in the light of the GDPR*, pp. 60–81.

960 Article 89(1) GDPR. The following paragraphs of this provision provide the possibility for Union or Member State law to derogate from data subjects' rights by stating that: "2. Where personal data are processed for scientific or historical research purposes or statistical purposes, Union or Member State law may provide for derogations from the rights referred to in Articles 15, 16, 18 and 21 subject to the conditions and safeguards referred to in paragraph 1 of this Article in so far as such rights are likely to render impossible or seriously impair the achievement of the specific purposes, and such derogations are necessary for the fulfilment of those purposes. 3. Where personal data are processed for archiving purposes in the public interest, Union or Member State law may provide for derogations from the rights referred to in Articles 15, 16, 18, 19, 20 and 21 subject to the conditions and safeguards referred to in paragraph 1 of this Article in so far as such rights are likely to render impossible or seriously impair the achievement of the specific purposes, and such derogations are necessary for the fulfilment of those purposes. 4. Where processing referred to in paragraphs 2 and 3 serves at the same time another purpose, the derogations shall apply only to processing for the purposes referred to in those paragraphs".

961 On how the GDPR affected clinical research *see* the interesting study by Jacques Demotes-Mainard et al. "How the new European data protection regulation affects clinical research and recommendations?" In: *Therapie* 74.1 (2019), pp. 31–42. As mentioned in the first Chapter the interactions between Big Data and e-health data are beyond the scope of this book. However, for a synthesis on the possible uses and concerns of data analytics for healthcare *see* Menno Mostert et al. "From privacy to data protection in the EU: implications for big data health research". In: *European Journal of Health Law* 25.1 (2017), pp. 43–55, which provides the EU regulatory perspective; MIT Critical Data and M. Komorowski. *Secondary analysis of electronic health records*. Springer, 2016. ISBN: 9783319437422, which provides the technical perspective; I. Glenn Cohen and Harry S. Graver. "Cops, docs, and code: a dialogue between big data in health care and predictive

Regulation 2018/1725 is aligned with the GDPR, So, it provides similar legitimate grounds for the processing of sensitive data, but when referring to safeguards and other rules it mentions Union law only[962]. As regards a final comparison with the previous legal framework, the legal grounds for the processing of personal health data according to the GDPR and the Data Protection Directive are similar[963]. The GDPR uses several exceptions of the DPD and mainly adds the possibility of derogating from the prohibition for public interest in public health and archiving, research and statistics purposes[964]. In the exception related to the employment field, the GDPR also specifies social security and social protection law, which were never provided. The comparison of the legitimate exceptions is further described in the detailed Table 3.1.

*Table 3.1 Synthesis of the comparison between GDPR and DPD*

| LEGITIMATE BASIS | GDPR | DPD |
| --- | --- | --- |
| Explicit consent | Art. 9(2)(a) | Art. 8(2)(a), without the possibility of derogation |
| Obligation and rights in the field of employment, social security, social protection law | Art. 9(2)(b) | Art. 8(2)(b), but only employment law |
| Vital interest | Art. 9(2)(c) | Art. 8(2)(c) |

policing". In: *UCDL Rev.* 51 (2017), p. 437, which provides the US regulatory perspective. For a general commentary on healthcare scientific research and GDPR *see* Giulia Schneider. "Disentangling health data networks: a critical analysis of Articles 9 (2) and 89 GDPR". in: *International Data Privacy Law* (2019), pp. 253–271; Denise Amram. "Building up the "Accountable Ulysses" model. The impact of GDPR and national implementations, ethics, and health-data research: Comparative remarks". In: *Computer Law & Security Review* 37 (2020), p. 105413; Rossana Ducato. "Data protection, scientific research, and the role of information". In: *Computer Law & Security Review* 37 (2020), p. 105412.

962 *See* Article 10 Regulation 2018/1725.

963 For other comparisons with the DPD *see* Pormeister, "The GDPR and Big Data: Leading the Way for Big Genetic Data?", p. 7 and Georgieva and Kuner, "Chapter II Principles (Articles 5–11). Article 9 Processing of special categories of personal data", pp. 375–376.

964 With reference to a comparison *see* e.g. Greco, "Il trattamento dei dati sanitari".

| LEGITIMATE BASIS | GDPR | DPD |
|---|---|---|
| Data processed by non-profit entities | Art. 9(2)(d) | Art. 8(d), but limited |
| Data made public | Art. 9(2)(e) | Art. 8(2)(e) |
| Legal claim use | Art. 9(2)(f) | Art. 8(2)(3), but not the courts in the judicial capacity |
| Substantial public interest | Art. 9(2)(g) | Art. 8(2)(a) |
| Preventive or occupational medicine, assessment of the working capacity, medical diagnosis, medical treatment, management of health ser- vices and systems subject to conditions provided by law | Art. 9(2)(h) | Art. 8(3), but not occupational medicine, assessment of the working capacity, or social care system |
| Execution of a contract with healthcare professional | Art. 9(2)(h) | Not explicitly provided |
| Public interest in public health | Art. 9(2)(i) | Not provided, but Art. 8(4) referred to substantial public interest generally |
| Archiving in public interest, scientific, historical research, statistic | Art. 9(2)(j) | Not provided |

Moreover, the legal grounds for the processing of health data according to the GDPR and to the CoE's Recommendation CM/Rec (2019) 2 are essentially the same, as shown by Table 3.2[965]. After a comparison of the rules, it can be argued that where it is not further explained the lawful grounds coincide.

965 *See* Article 5 of the Recommendation CM/Rec (2019) 2.

*Table 3.2 Synthesis of the comparison between GDPR and CoE's Rec.*

| LEGITIMATE BASIS | GDPR | RECOMMENDATION |
|---|---|---|
| Explicit consent | Art. 9(2)(a) | Art. 5(b) |
| Obligation in the field of employment, social security, social protection law | Art. 9(2)(b) | Art. 5(a) employment and social protection |
| Vital interest | Art. 9(2)(c) | Art. 5(a) |
| Data processed by non-profit entities | Art. 9(2)(d) | Not provided |
| Data made public | Art. 9(2)(e) | Art. 5(d) |
| Legal claim use | Art. 9(2)(f) | Art. 5(a), not specifying the courts but also "reasons of public interest in the field of managing claims for social welfare and health insurance benefits and services, subject to the conditions provided for by law" |
| Substantial public interest | Art. 9(2)(g) | Art. 5(a) |
| Preventive or occupational medicine, assessment of the working capacity, medical diagnosis, medical treatment, management of health ser- vices and systems subject to conditions provided by law | Art. 9(2)(h) | Art. 5(a), but not occupational medicine or assessment of the working capacity |
| Execution of a contract with healthcare professional | Art. 9(2)(h) | Art. 5(c) |

| LEGITIMATE BASIS | GDPR | RECOMMENDATION |
|---|---|---|
| Public interest in public health | Art. 9(2)(i) | Art. 5(a), such as the protection against health hazards, humanitarian action or high standard of quality and safety for medical treatment, health products and medical devices, subject to the conditions provided for by law |
| Archiving in public interest, scientific, historical research, statistic | Art. 9(2)(j) | Art. 5(a), but further conditions in Chapter V |

Thus, at the EU level the legitimate grounds for processing of personal health data are overall consistent. Member State or Union law will provide the appropriate safeguard where derogation is set and they may establish further rules, but the main requirements are still laid down by the GDPR. So far, the notions and the exception which allow the processing of personal health data have been examined. The next section deals with the other data protection rules the data controller shall comply with in the context of e-health.

### 3.3.3 The relevant and applicable provisions of the GDPR

This section now summarises the other provisions of the GDPR that are relevant for the processing of personal health data. As much as in other fields, the application of the GDPR radically changed the protection of data by increasing the rights to be protected and the obligations to comply with[966]. In fact, in the context of personal health data some clarifications on the exercise of data subjects' rights and duties of the controller are indispensable. It is worth stressing that the concrete application of the

966 On the changes for the healthcare context after the GDPR *see* e.g. the Italian book Giuseppe Carro, Sarah Masato, and Massimiliano Domenico Parla. *La privacy nella sanità*. Giuffrè, Torino, 2018. ISBN: 9788814225215.

GDPR depends on a case-by-case basis, and the e-health technology being used. Nevertheless, the interpreter can make some general opinions on data protection in this specific field.

First of all, the patient has the right to be informed on the processing in the e-health technology in a separate way than the information received on the treatment (e.g. when seeking consent to the treatment). Whether the processing is based on the explicit consent of the data subject (e.g. the well-being app), the information on the existence of the right to withdraw this consent at any time shall be provided to the individual by specifying that his or her choice does not affect the lawfulness of processing based on prior consent[967].

Under the GDPR, the data subject has the right to receive more information than under the DPD, such as the contact details of the DPO, the data storage period or the criteria used to determine it, the existence of the right to lodge a complaint to a supervisory authority and of automated decision-making or profiling. So, the privacy policies shall be updated, and adequate in accordance with this new framework[968].

Generally, the right to access is highly important in the e-health field. According to Recital 63 of the GDPR data subjects have the right to access their personal health data in their medical records which contain different information such as "diagnoses, examination results, assessments by treating physicians and any treatment or interventions provided"[969]. This right may be exercised by electronic means. It has been claimed that the condition established by the GDPR for the right to access – which should not negatively affect the "rights or freedoms of others, including trade secrets or intellectual property" – might limit the right in the healthcare context[970]. However, this limitation might only apply in the cases where algorithms are used for generating the data, and the data controller may want to protect its IP rights. In the traditional e-health context, the patient has the right to access personal general and health data. The right to access implies also the right to obtain information on processing, such as important information on the recipients, and the right to obtain a copy

967 *See* Article 13(2)(c) and Article 14(2)(d) GDPR.

968 The importance of the use of user-friendly documents (e.g. icons), and the need to use an adequate, plain and clear language have been already highlighted in the previous Chapter, Section 2.4.8.

969 Recital 63 GDPR. *See* also Voigt and Von dem Bussche, *The EU General Data Protection Regulation (GDPR). A Practical Guide*, p. 151.

970 *See* Malgieri and Comandé, "Sensitive-by-distance: quasi-health data in the algorithmic era".

of the data being processed, that in the e-heath context may be provided in electronic form[971]. It is even possible for patients to request from the healthcare provider the log files to see who has accessed their data (e.g. medical staff)[972].

The right to rectification in the e-health field is particularly valuable since personal health data are often processed for medical diagnosis, assessment of the working capacity, or provision of social care. As mentioned, the accuracy and quality of data are essential for guaranteeing effective and efficient healthcare provision. Data subjects can easily ask for the rectification of common personal data by providing accurate data directly to the controller. However, patients may not be able to provide the accurate personal health data that should be processed in the e-health technology. Data subjects may instead ask the controller to rectify data which does not correspond to reality as far as they are aware. The controller will check the information, and if needed rectify inaccurate data[973].

The right to erasure is not easily applicable in the e-health context[974]. Whenever the data controller has a legal obligation to store and keep the data in accordance with a Union or Member State law (e.g. clinical information systems), or the subject is performing a task in the public interest or in the exercise of official authority (e.g. disease registries and systems for healthcare management), the data will not be erased in accordance with Article 17 GDPR[975]. Indeed, in the healthcare context the registries of the treatments are kept in accordance with the law not only for monitoring the patient, but also for proving the healthcare service performed by the professional. Public hospitals or healthcare entities are usually public administrations, which are not subject to the obligation of data erasure upon request. Moreover, Union or Member State law may prevent the erasure of data in the area of public health to protect the public interest involved, or for archiving, scientific, research, statistic or historical purposes, and the same law may potentially establish the appropriate safeguards (e.g. pseudonymisation)[976]. It has even been argued that the exceptions of

971 *See* Article 15 GDPR.

972 *See* Guarda, "I dati sanitari", p. 611.

973 *See* Article 16 GDPR.

974 As indicated in Chapter 2 Section 2.4.8, the right to erasure is established in Article 17.

975 Article 17(3)(b) GDPR.

976 Article 17(c) GDPR states that the right to erasure or to be forgotten does not apply if processing is necessary "for reasons of public interest in the area of public health in accordance with points (h) and (i) of Article 9(2) as well as Arti-

Article 17, which prevents erasure upon request by the data subject, imply not only protection against cross-border threats to health, and the need to ensure high standards of quality and safety of healthcare, medical products and devices, but also all the grounds of the "healthcare exception" of Article 9[977]. So, the data subjects of this processing may never obtain the erasure of data unless the timing of storage and the activities are lawfully finished. Another exception to the right to erasure is the need to keep data for the exercise or defence of legal claims, which here are usually related to medical malpractice, breach of confidentiality, or failure by healthcare providers to perform their duties[978].

Therefore, the right to be forgotten in the sense of the GDPR may apply in a few residual cases, such as the use of e-health apps. As indicated in the previous section, it is possible that the data subject has given the consent to processing with a purpose other than medical treatment (e.g. consent to clinical trial, or to an app) – this consent is the legal ground of the processing – but he or she decides to withdraw it. Whether no other ground applies, the data subject has the right to obtain the erasure of their data in accordance with Article 17(1)(b) GDPR. Another case where the erasure applies is the unlawful processing of personal health data[979]. If the controller has carried out the processing without a lawful legal ground, the data subject has the right to obtain erasure from the data controller.

Some Member States established a different right of concealment of specific personal health data[980]. In this case, data is not erased, but it is not intelligible to users of the e-health system without specific and exceptional permission. However, it can be argued that it is in the interest of the patient that the personal data are not erased in order to receive accurate and efficient care in the future. It might be the case that the patient asks for the erasure of common personal data, such as administrative data,

---

cle 9(3)". Moreover, Article 17(d) GDPR specifies that "for archiving purposes in the public interest, scientific or historical research purposes or statistical purposes in accordance with Article 89(1) in so far as the right referred to in paragraph 1 is likely to render impossible or seriously impair the achievement of the objectives of that processing", the data subject does not have the right to obtain erasure.

977 *See* Voigt and Von dem Bussche, *The EU General Data Protection Regulation (GDPR). A Practical Guide*, p. 160. Therefore, the exception may cover the grounds of Article 9(2)(h) and (i) GDPR.

978 Article 17(1)(e) GDPR.

979 Article 17(1)(d) GDPR.

980 For example, this right has been specified by the Italian and French legal frameworks for the EHR. *See* further for sources and explanation in Section 3.4.2.

address, or e-mail. The data controller shall determine whether these data are necessary for the main purpose. If so, the data will not be erased. If not, the controller will evaluate the exceptions mentioned above following a case-by-case approach.

Special considerations on the right to restriction for the processing of personal health data do not seem necessary. The controller can assess whether the four conditions of Article 18 GDPR apply. So, whether the data subject has contested the accuracy of the data, or the processing is unlawful, he or she may have the right to obtain a restriction. The same right may apply where the purposes of the processing are satisfied, but the data subject may need the data for the establishment, exercise or defence of legal claims, or where a request of objection is pending[981]. However, the right to object does not seem applicable in the e-health context as the provision of Article 21 refers to processing based on two grounds of Article 6, meaning the public task of an authority or the legitimate interest of the controller or a third party, and to marketing purposes. The common personal data processed in an e-health scenario are usually necessary or accessory for the processing of personal health data. Thus, the right to object might never apply in this field[982].

As regards the right to portability of Article 20 GDPR, it has been argued that it applies only insofar as the patient has provided their personal health data to the healthcare provider in a medical file or personalised health environment[983]. So, the portability can concern health data collected through the monitoring and recording of the subject's activities, such as heartbeat data recorded in a mobile health app[984]. However, the right to portability applies to data provided by the data subject and observed in the system, but it does not apply to inferred data and complex data which are generated by the controller[985]. It should be noted that whether the controller performs the healthcare task in the public interest or in the exercise of an official authority, the right to portability shall not apply. Therefore, once again, public hospitals may not apply this right. Nevertheless, the exercise and application of this right may foster access

981 *See* Article 18(1)(a) – (d) GDPR.

982 *See* Article 21(1) GDPR.

983 *See* Hooghiemstra, "Informational Self-Determination, Digital Health and New Features of Data Protection", p. 169.

984 Guarda, "I dati sanitari", p. 612.

985 *See* Malgieri and Comandé, "Sensitive-by-distance: quasi-health data in the algorithmic era", p. 247; Lynskey, "Chapter III Rights of the Data Subject (Articles 12–23). Article 20. Right to data portability", p. 503.

to healthcare in territories other than the one where the patient is treated, and cross-border access to healthcare, too[986]. The right to portability is also recommended by CoE Recommendation CM/REC (2019) 2, which stresses the importance of data transmission from one controller to another[987]. Indeed, portability may enhance continuity of care of a patient.

Moreover, profiling and automated decision-making are increasingly used in the healthcare context[988]. Under the GDPR the definition of profiling includes health as an aspect which is analysed or predicted by automated activities[989]. The health status can be inferred from raw data[990]. The application of Article 22 in the e-health context may be related to the use of AI for analysing aspects of a data subject's health or of the diagnosis[991]. The right to not be subject to automated processing applies almost always in the case of personal health data since they are sensitive data[992]. Nevertheless, Article 22(4) explicitly establishes that the right to not be subject to a decision based solely on automated processing is not applicable whether the data subject has given the explicit consent or the processing is necessary for reasons of a substantial public interest, and suitable safeguards are put in place[993]. The adopted safeguards and measures

986 A specific section of this book is dedicated to cross-border healthcare. *See infra* 3.4.3.

987 The right to portability is even recommended by Recommendation CM/REC (2019) 2 at Article 12.5, which specifies: "where the processing is performed by automatic means, the data subject should be able to obtain from the controller, subject to conditions prescribed by law the transmission – in a structured, interoperable and machine-readable format – of their personal data with a view to transmitting them to another controller (data portability). The data subject should also be able to require the controller to transmit the data directly to another controller".

988 *See* Article 29 Working Party, *Guidelines on Automated individual decision-making and Profiling for the purposes of Regulation 2016/679*.

989 *See* Article 4 (4) and Recital 71 GDPR.

990 As explained *infra* in Section 3.3.1, personal health data may be derived from common personal data which are combined through algorithms.

991 *See* Dimitra Kamarinou, Christopher Millard, and Jatinder Singh. "Machine Learning with Personal Data: Profiling, Decisions and the EU General Data Protection Regulation". In: *Journal of Machine Learning Research* (2017); Pierce, "Machine learning for diagnosis and treatment: Gymnastics for the GDPR".

992 *See* Gianclaudio Malgieri and Giovanni Comandé. "Why a right to legibility of automated decision-making exists in the general data protection regulation". In: *International Data Privacy Law* (2017), p. 246.

993 Article 9(4) states: "Decisions referred to in paragraph 2 shall not be based on special categories of personal data referred to in Article 9(1), unless point (a) or

shall correspond to the high sensitivity of data[994]. So, in these cases the data subjects have the right to obtain human intervention, express their individual point of view, and contest the automatic decision[995].

Finally, Union or Member State law may restrict the rights outlined above in accordance with Article 23 GDPR to protect other interests. As discussed above, the health sector is frequently subject to other national rules that derogate from or further specify the processing activities only insofar as the legislative measure is necessary and proportionate, and it respects the rights and freedoms of individuals in a democratic society. In sum, the considerations on the rights are indicated in the following Table 3.3.

*Table 3.3 Data subject's rights as a patient*

| RIGHT | APPLICATION IN E-HEALTH FIELD |
|---|---|
| Right to be informed | Obtaining information on processing in a separate form than information on the treatment |
| Right to access | Having access to medical records and obtaining related information and a copy of data |
| Right to rectification | Obtaining rectification of inaccurate or incomplete health data in the system |
| Right to erasure | Several exceptions from the application |
| Right to restriction | Obtaining temporary restriction of processing |

(g) of Article 9(2) applies and suitable measures to safeguard the data subject's rights and freedoms and legitimate interests are in place".

994 *See* Voigt and Von dem Bussche, *The EU General Data Protection Regulation (GDPR). A Practical Guide*, p. 183.

995 *See* Malgieri and Comandé, "Why a right to legibility of automated decision-making exists in the general data protection regulation", p. 246. According to the authors the right to explanation is not legally binding since it is specified in Recital 71 only.

| RIGHT | APPLICATION IN E-HEALTH FIELD |
| --- | --- |
| Right to data portability | Receive personal health data provided by the subject and having them ported to another con- troller under certain circumstances |
| Right to object | Not easily applicable |
| Right to human intervention | Exceptions from the application in case of explicit consent and substantial public interest, and safeguards apply |

In the accountability-based approach of the GDPR, some organisational requirements are established for processing sensitive data because this processing is "very risk-prone"[996]. Whether personal health data are processed on a large scale, the data controller shall[997]:

- maintain the record of processing;
- notify or communicate a data breach;
- carry out a DPIA;
- designate a DPO;
- implement appropriate technical and organisational measures based on the high risk potential.

In Chapter 2, Section 2.4.5, it has been claimed that the expression "on a large scale" is broad and open to interpretation[998]. It can be argued that processing is on a large scale when it involves considerable amounts of

996 Voigt and Von dem Bussche, *The EU General Data Protection Regulation (GDPR). A Practical Guide*, p. 116.

997 Even the CNIL listed the measures required in the healthcare context. The authority identified the measures as follows: "mettre en place un registre des traitements; mener des analyses d'impact pour les traitements considérés comme présentant un risque élevé pour les personnes; veiller à encadrer l'information des personnes concernées (patients, fournisseurs, étudiants, usagers, etc.) et s'assurer de l'effectivité de leurs droits (droit d'accès, de rectification, d'opposition, etc.); formaliser les rôles et responsabilités du responsable de traitement; lorsque cela est obligatoire, désigner un délégué à la protection des données (DPO); renseigner les actions menées pour garantir la sécurité des données". *See* the comment at <www.cnil.fr/fr/ quelles-formalites-pour-les-traitements-de-donnees-de-sante-caractere-personnel>. Last accessed 06/10/2021.

998 On the same opinion *see* Granieri, "Il trattamento di categorie particolari di dati personali nel Reg. UE 2016/679".

data at a regional, national or supranational level or when it potentially affects a large number of data subjects[999]. Article 29 Working Party defined some criteria to determine whether the processing is on a large scale, namely the number of data subjects, the volume of data and/or the range of different data items, the duration, or permanence, of the data processing activities, and the geographical extent of these activities[1000]. According to Article 30 GDPR, the data controller and processor who process sensitive data shall maintain a record of processing activities[1001]. The provision lists the information that the records should contain. For the e-health context, where the risk is high, describing the technical and organisational security measures is essential.

A data breach in the e-health context is likely to result in a high risk to the rights and freedoms of the data subjects[1002]. Therefore, the data controller shall notify the DPA of the personal data breach without undue delay, and if feasible no later than 72 hours after being made aware, by communicating details of the breach[1003]. At the same time, the personal data breach shall be communicated to the data subjects without undue delay unless the conditions indicated in Article 34(3) are met (e.g. the implementation of appropriate measures)[1004]. Typical and frequent examples of data breach in the e-health context are: sending the laboratory result to a person other than the recipient indicated in the instructions given to the patient, the publication of personal health data in open websites or forums, and the use of a personal pen-drive by the medical professional who then lost it[1005].

The designation of the data protection officer is binding for the processing of health data on a large scale and when this processing is a core activity of the controller or processor[1006]. Public administration shall designate a DPO, too[1007]. Therefore, hospitals, private clinics, and private

999 Voigt and Von dem Bussche, *The EU General Data Protection Regulation (GDPR). A Practical Guide*, p. 48.
1000 *See* Article 29 Working Party, *Guidelines on Data Protection Impact Assessment (DPIA) and determining whether processing is "likely to result in a high risk" for the purposes of Regulation 2016/679*, p. 10.
1001 Article 30(5) GDPR.
1002 *See* Guarda, "I dati sanitari", p. 611.
1003 *See* Article 33 GDPR.
1004 *See* Article 34 GDPR.
1005 *See* Carro, Masato, and Parla, *La privacy nella sanità*, pp. 77–78.
1006 Article 37(1)(c) GDPR.
1007 Article 37(1)(a) GDPR.

healthcare providers shall choose an independent DPO[1008]. Among the core activities of the hospital is the processing of health data since the provision of healthcare implies the collection the recording of health information[1009]. In addition to these cases, the processing of health data via wearable devices can be included in the notion of "regular and systematic monitoring" of Article 37(1)(b) GDPR[1010]. Therefore, the mandatory designation applies. There might be a single DPO for several healthcare facilities, unless they are hard to reach by the officer who has to efficiently and promptly support each data controller[1011].

Under the DPD, Member States required notification to the DPA of processing involving sensitive data[1012]. Under the GDPR, this notification is not required yet. However, the data controller that processes personal health data on a large scale shall carry out a DPIA in accordance with Article 35. The high risk in processing health data is *in re ipsa*[1013]. A DPIA is not mandatory for an individual physician or a healthcare professional, independently of the amount of data processed[1014]. A DPIA is instead mandatory for a hospital which processes patients' personal data in the hospital information system, since data are sensitive and processed on a large scale[1015]. The processing of personal health data in research projects and clinical trials is likely to require a DPIA as well, since they store a great amount of sensitive data[1016]. Actually, it has been pointed out that

1008 Guarda, "I dati sanitari", p. 611. On the role of the DPO in processing of personal health data *see* also Giorgio Pedrazzi. "Il ruolo del Responsabile della protezione dei dati (DPO) nel settore sanitario". In: *Rivista Italiana di Medicina Legale (e del Diritto in campo sanitario)* 1 (2019), pp. 181–186.

1009 Hospitals are examples in the investigation of core activities in Article 29 Working Party, *Guidelines on Data Protection Officers ('DPOs')*, p. 20.

1010 *See* Article 29 Working Party, *op. cit.*, p. 21.

1011 *See* Carro, Masato, and Parla, *La privacy nella sanità*, that recalls the WP opinion on DPO.

1012 *See* Article 18 of the DPD.

1013 Granieri, "Il trattamento di categorie particolari di dati personali nel Reg. UE 2016/679". *See* also Article 29 Working Party, *Guidelines on Data Protection Impact Assessment (DPIA) and determining whether processing is "likely to result in a high risk" for the purposes of Regulation 2016/679*, p. 9.

1014 *See* Recital 91 GDPR and Voigt and Von dem Bussche, *The EU General Data Protection Regulation (GDPR). A Practical Guide*, p. 51.

1015 This is an example where the DPIA is likely to be required by WP29. *See* Article 29 Working Party, *Guidelines on Data Protection Impact Assessment (DPIA) and determining whether processing is "likely to result in a high risk" for the purposes of Regulation 2016/679*, p. 11.

1016 *See ibid.*

the majority of medium-to-large healthcare facilities shall assess the risk through the DPIA, and even smaller ones, whether or not they have an agreement with the public national health service and are compared to this public entity[1017].

Moreover, Article 36 requires prior consultation of the controller with the DPA when the DPIA indicates that the processing has high risk, and the envisaged measures cannot mitigate this risk[1018]. Member States' law may establish a binding prior consultation for the processing carried out for reasons of public interest in the area of public health[1019].

Healthcare providers shall comply with the DPbD and DPbDf obligations, and the security principle. According to Article 83(2)(g) GDPR, the DPA will take into account the category of personal data subject to the violation. Indeed, the appropriate technical and organisational measures necessary to ensure the implementation of data protection principles apply even more for the special categories of data[1020]. The application of DPbD in the context of e-health implies the appropriate design of the technologies and services which process personal health data. E-health technologies shall be privacy- and data protection- compliant from the development stage[1021]. DPbD (and PbD) may reassign to the patient a crucial role within the care process, at the centre of the data flow[1022]. It has been argued that regulation by design for healthcare can facilitate the design of new health management infrastructure and helps achieve a good balance between care needs, individual protection of patients' fundamental rights and public health interests[1023]. DPbD is fundamental in the context of e-health, which requires an interdisciplinary approach "by default" and a

---

1017 *See* Carro, Masato, and Parla, *La privacy nella sanità*, p. 28.

1018 Article 36(1) GDPR.

1019 Article 36(5) GDPR. *See* also Article 29 Working Party, *Guidelines on Data Protection Impact Assessment (DPIA) and determining whether processing is "likely to result in a high risk" for the purposes of Regulation 2016/679*, p. 19.

1020 Durst, "Il trattamento di categorie particolari di dati in ambito sanitario", p. 67.

1021 *See* Melchionna and Cecamore, "Le nuove frontiere della sanità e della ricerca scientifica", p. 598.

1022 Raffaella Brighi and Maria Gabriella Virone. "Una tutela 'by design' del diritto alla salute. Prospettive di armonizzazione giuridica e tecnologica". In: *A Matter Of Design. Making Society Through Science And Technology* (2014), pp. 1211–1222, p. 1218.

1023 *Ibid.*

correct implementation of the principles from the beginning of the design stage[1024].

As the DPbD requires a case-by-case approach, a case study will be presented in the e-health domain. The selected technology is an Electronic Health Record system and it is further analysed in the next sections.

## *3.4 The case study of Electronic Health Record system*

EU policies on health and care stress the importance of the use and implementation of e-health systems, such as EHRs, since they allow more targeted, personalised, effective and efficient healthcare and reduce errors and length of hospitalisation[1025]. Electronic Health Record is a solution that can substitute the established, paper-based, health service[1026]. In this book this case study has been selected since it refers to a widely used technology which is considered a priority by EU policies and strategies. Actually, it is a key element for e-health policies at the EU level and is at

---

1024 *See* Guarda, "I dati sanitari", p. 609; Faralli, Brighi, Martoni, et al., *Strumenti, diritti, regole e nuove relazioni di cura: Il Paziente europeo protagonista nell'e-Health*, p. 304.

1025 *See* Bincoletto, "Data protection issues in cross-border interoperability of Electronic Health Record systems within the European Union".

1026 In the classification of the Expert Panel on effective ways of investing in Health, *Assessing the impact of digital transformation of health services*, EHR is an example of substituting an established health service. In general, on EHR *see* Paolo Guarda. *Fascicolo sanitario elettronico e protezione dei dati personali*. Vol. 94. Università degli Studi di Trento, Quaderni del Dipartimento di Scienze Giuridiche, 2011. ISBN: 9788884433671; Carolyn P. Hartley and Edward Douglass Jones. *EHR implementation: A step-by-step guide for the medical practice*. American Medical Association, 2012. ISBN: 9781603596305; Giovanni Comandé, Luca Nocco, and Violette Peigné. "Il fascicolo sanitario elettronico: uno studio interdisciplinare". In: *Rivista Italiana di Medicina Legale (e del Diritto in campo sanitario)* 1 (2012), pp. 106–121; Nicholas P. Terry and Leslie P. Francis. "Ensuring the privacy and confidentiality of electronic health records". In: *U. Ill. L. Rev.* (2007), pp. 681–736; Eric J. Bieber, Frank M. Richards, and James M. Walker. *Implementing an electronic health record system*. Springer, 2005. ISBN: 9781846281150; Carlisle George, Diane Whitehouse, and Penny Duquenoy. *eHealth: legal, ethical and governance challenges*. Springer Science & Business Media, 2012. ISBN: 9783642224744.

the heart of e-health practices[1027]. EHR represents a pivotal moment in the digitalisation of health data processing[1028].

The EHR aims to empower the patient, who becomes a crucial point in the information management system[1029]. This processing helps healthcare providers to better manage patients' treatment with accurate, up-to-date and complete data by enabling quick access to a digital record, which embeds diagnoses and prescriptions[1030]. As reported for the opportunities of e-health technologies, the EHR can reduce medical errors, allows a more effective treatment, and supports physicians' decision making[1031].

This technology is regularly used for the processing of personal health data in hospitals or clinics by general practitioners or specialist professionals[1032]. The EHR is an important digital tool for healthcare providers and hospitals since it archives all the personal health data of the patient and shares them among all the authorised operators who are entitled to the health treatment[1033]. For the sake of completeness, it is necessary to specify that in the literature the term Personal Health Record (PHR) is frequently used to indicate a digital record managed and controlled by the patient[1034]. This investigation mainly focuses on the EHR system, where

---

1027 *See* Arak and Wójcik, *Transforming eHealth into a political and economic advantage*, p. 14; Placide Poba-Nzaou and Sylvestre Uwizeyemungu. "Variation in electronic health record adoption in European public hospitals: a configurational analysis of key functionalities". In: *Health and Technology* 9.4 (2019), pp. 439–448, p. 440.

1028 *See* Paolo Guarda. "Biobanks and electronic health records: open issues". In: *Comparative Issues in the Governance of Research Biobanks*. Springer, 2013, pp. 131–141. ISBN: 9783642331169, p. 133.

1029 *Ibid.*

1030 Bincoletto, "A Data Protection by Design Model for Privacy Management in Electronic Health Records", p. 162.

1031 Ilias Iakovidis. "Towards personal health record: current situation, obstacles and trends in implementation of electronic healthcare record in Europe". In: *International journal of medical informatics* 52.1 – 3 (1998), pp. 105–115, p. 107. *See* also on the significance of the EHR Pradeep K. Sinha et al. *Electronic health record: standards, coding systems, frameworks, and infrastructures*. Wiley – IEEE Press, 2013. ISBN: 9781118281345, pp. 6–7.

1032 *See* the analysis on EU public hospitals in Poba-Nzaou and Uwizeyemungu, "Variation in electronic health record adoption in European public hospitals: a configurational analysis of key functionalities".

1033 Guarda, "I dati sanitari", p. 616.

1034 *See* e.g. Sinha et al., *Electronic health record: standards, coding systems, frameworks, and infrastructures*; Yakov Flaumenhaft and Ofir Ben-Assuli. "Personal health records, global policy and regulation review". In: *Health policy* 122.8 (2018), pp. 815–826. The PHR could be synchronised with the EHR on patient re-the contribution of the patient to the system is potentially available, but is not the primary source in terms of personal data, such as in the PHR system[1035].

In the past, all patients' information was collected on paper records, whereas in the e-health context it is often digitalised in an EHR system[1036]. The EHR goes beyond the paper-based record[1037]. Some authors defined this technology as the most important, and perhaps the most challenging, of the technological developments in the e-health context since it links and adds value to the other technologies[1038]. The EHR allows the data exchange between patients, healthcare providers, clinicians and pharmacies in order to support both individuals and physicians in accessing and providing care[1039]. EHR is designed to record and make accessible all data that are useful for the healthcare treatment[1040]. It is more than a tool because it is a complex system with several capabilities and functions[1041].

---

quest. *See* Rishi Saripalle, Christopher Runyan, and Mitchell Russell. "Using HL7 FHIR to achieve interoperability in patient health record". In: *Journal of biomedical informatics* 94 (2019), p. 103188. PHR is only one of the multiple models of digital repositories for healthcare. Guarda, *Fascicolo sanitario elettronico e protezione dei dati personali*, pp. 29–31, reportes that other systems are Electronic Medical Record (EMR) and Electronic Patient Record. On PHR *see* also Guarda and Ducato, "From electronic health records to personal health records: emerging legal issues in the Italian regulation of e-health"; Kim Wuyts et al. "What electronic health records don't know just yet. A privacy analysis for patient communities and health records interaction". In: *Health and Technology* 2.3 (2012), pp. 159–183, pp. 162–166.

1035 On the differences between the two tools *see* also Giovanni Comandé, Luca Nocco, and Violette Peigné. "An empirical study of healthcare providers and patients' perceptions of electronic health records". In: *Computers in Biology and Medicine* 59 (2015), pp. 194–201, p. 194.

1036 Bincoletto, "A Data Protection by Design Model for Privacy Management in Electronic Health Records", p. 162.

1037 The reason will be further explained in Section 3.4.1, where a brief comparison will be provided. On the main differences *see* e.g. G Hayes. "The requirements of an electronic medical record to suit all clinical disciplines". In: *Yearbook of medical informatics* 6.01 (1997), pp. 75–82.

1038 *See* Katsh and Rabinovich-Einy, "The Internet of On-Demand Healthcare", p. 89.

1039 *See* OECD, *How's Life in the Digital Age? Opportunities and Risks of the Digital Transformation for People's Well-being.*

1040 *See* Wicks, "Electronic health records and privacy interests: The English experience", p. 75.

1041 *See* Katsh and Rabinovich-Einy, "The Internet of On-Demand Healthcare", p. 91; Sinha et al., *Electronic health record: standards, coding systems, frameworks, and infrastructures*.

Therefore, EHRs provide the opportunity to access to personal health data ubiquitously, as the entire patient's medical history is potentially available online[1042].

In general terms, at its core an EHR is a system that healthcare providers use for documenting, monitoring, and managing healthcare delivery within their organisations[1043]. So, an EHR system seems clinician-focused, and the data processing seems limited to a single healthcare entity of the National Health Service (NHS). However, multiple providers may have access to the system, such as the general healthcare practitioner, pharmacists, professionals in a hospital or clinic, and other healthcare professionals of a Member State[1044]. Indeed, EHRs may contain information from all health care providers involved in the patient's care[1045]. Even a cross-border healthcare provision, and data processing, may be carried out in accordance with the EU interoperability policies on EHRs.

For these reasons, EHR systems raise data protection concerns that did not exist in the paper-based scenario. In the next sections, the investigation on this e-health solution deals with the state of the art of this technology, the issues of the applicable legal framework at the EU level, and the policies that enable cross-border processing within the problems that this processing entails.

### 3.4.1 The state of the art of EHR

The aim of this section is to briefly define the common core of data in an EHR and the common features and properties of this e-health technology. In general, the literature commonly defines an EHR as "a standard-based machine-processable information entity consisting of health data pertaining to an individual and resulting in an exhaustive aggregation of personal health data, which is longitudinal, cross-institutional and multi-

---

1042 Bincoletto, "A Data Protection by Design Model for Privacy Management in Electronic Health Records", p. 162.

1043 *See* Aceto, Persico, and Pescapé, "The role of Information and Communication Technologies in healthcare: taxonomies, perspectives, and challenges", p. 132.

1044 *See* Giakoumopoulos, Buttarelli, and O'Flamerty, *Handbook on European data protection law*, p. 338, which includes EHRs in the notion of e-health and mentions multiple actors.

1045 Bincoletto, "A Data Protection by Design Model for Privacy Management in Electronic Health Records", p. 162.

modal"[1046]. From the technical point of view, the personal health data in the EHR are collected by several entities as source systems (i.e. healthcare providers), which aggregate data in repositories in a given period of time (e.g. patient's life period), and use the whole resulting system of different ways of interaction. The EHR system consists in different connected elements. EHR then enables the provision of healthcare across organisations[1047]. It potentially streamlines the clinician's workflow[1048].

It has been pointed out that defining what is an EHR is very complex[1049]. The notion is an evolving concept[1050]. The ISO definitions related to EHR and Health Informatics have been framed after many attempts and several drafts since encapsulating the existing differences in the state of the art is not simple[1051]. Following ISO standard 20514:2005(en) on EHR, the useful definitions related to this technology can be textually reported in the following Table 3.4[1052]. ISO's definitions differentiate between EHR for integrated care and generic EHR because "there are still currently many variants of the EHR in health information systems which do not comply with the main EHR definition". Therefore, for the purpose of the present book the term EHR is identified by the generic ISO's definition outlined in the Table.

---

1046 Amnon Shabo. "Electronic Health Record". In: *Encyclopedia of Database Systems*. Springer, 2017, pp. 101–177. ISBN: 9781489979933.

1047 *See* Sinha et al., *Electronic health record: standards, coding systems, frameworks, and infrastructures*, p. 4.

1048 Quintana and Safran, "Global health informatics — an overview", p. 4.

1049 *See* e.g. Shabo, "Electronic Health Record"; Sinha et al., *Electronic health record: standards, coding systems, frameworks, and infrastructures*.

1050 Wuyts et al., "What electronic health records don't know just yet. A privacy analysis for patient communities and health records interaction".

1051 *See* Shabo, "Electronic Health Record", which summarises attempts to define EHR by commenting on the draft of ISO/TC 215 technical report. Electronic health record definition, scope, and context. Second draft of August 2003.

1052 The definitions are listed in the second Chapter of the standard in ISO. *Health informatics — Electronic health record — Definition, scope and context. 20514:2005(en)*. Tech. rep. ISO/TR, 2005.

*Table 3.4 Definitions of ISO/TR 20514:2005*

| OBJECT | DEFINITION |
|---|---|
| Electronic Health Record for Integrated Care (ICEHR) | "Repository of information regarding the health status of a subject of care, in computer processable form, stored and transmitted securely and accessible by multiple authorised users, having a standardised or commonly agreed logical information model that is independent of EHR systems and whose primary purpose is the support of continuing, efficient and quality integrated health care" |
| Electronic Health Record (EHR) | "Repository of information regarding the health status of a subject of care, in computer processable form" |
| Electronic Health Record Architecture (EHRA) | "Generic structural components from which all EHRs are built, defined in terms of an information model" |
| EHR extract | "Unit of communication of all or part of the EHR which is itself attestable and which consists of one or more EHR compositions" |
| EHR node | "Physical location where EHRs are stored and maintained" |
| EHR system | "Set of components that form the mechanism by which electronic health records are created, used, stored and retrieved including people, data, rules and procedures, processing and storage devices, and communication and support facilities" |
| Functional interoperability | "Ability of two or more systems to exchange information" |

| OBJECT | DEFINITION |
| --- | --- |
| Semantic interoperability | "Ability for information shared by systems to be understood at the level of formally defined domain concepts" |

So, while the EHR is a record – a data repository related to the health status of the data subject in electronically maintained form – the EHR system is a more complex concept, which includes several components that form the mechanism by which the EHR is used. In particular, it entails both an organisational level with "people, data, rules and procedures" and a technical level with "processing and storage devices, and communication and support facilities".

Moreover, the notions of functional and semantic interoperability are essential in this environment since the different sources of the record must be able to share and exchange information. Generally, interoperability means "the ability of a system or a product to work with other systems or products without special effort on the part of the customer"[1053]. Interoperability means not only that "information can be exchanged between many systems or services", but that "the receiving system is able to use the information to perform new actions"[1054]. The notion consists of many layers, namely technical, semantic, organisational and legal interoperability[1055]. Given two different systems, A and B, technical interoperability allows the exchange of data from A to B by neutralising the distance, while semantic interoperability ensures that A and B understand the data in the same way without ambiguity[1056]. It has been pointed out that, on the one hand, at a semantic level the formats by which the EHR is created should be reconciled; on the other hand, at a technical level the challenge is finding

1053 Standards University IEEE. *Standards Glossary*. IEEE, 2016.

1054 Bincoletto, "Data protection issues in cross-border interoperability of Electronic Health Record systems within the European Union", p. 2, which reports the definitions in Arak and Wójcik, *Transforming eHealth into a political and economic advantage*.

1055 Bincoletto, "Data protection issues in cross-border interoperability of Electronic Health Record systems within the European Union", p. 3.

1056 *See* A. Soceanu. "Managing the Interoperability and Privacy of e-Health Systems as an Interdisciplinary Challenge". In: *Systemics, Cybernetics and Informatics* 14.5 (2016), pp. 42–47; Bincoletto, "Data protection issues in cross-border interoperability of Electronic Health Record systems within the European Union", p. 3.

the appropriate approach for aggregating the data[1057]. Since "integration" is a core functionality of the EHR, the integration effort has always been a challenge from a technological viewpoint[1058]. In addition, organisational interoperability requires that separated business processes be aligned while using equivalent technology, and legal interoperability ensures that organisations that operate under different legal frameworks are able to work together, avoiding barriers on data processing[1059].

The EHR is primarily used for patient care delivery and patient care management, but it is useful for patient care support processes, financial and other administrative processes, and patient self-management, too[1060]. Previous research has established some requirements or attributes of the EHR, which may be listed as follows[1061]:

- "accessibility and availability", meaning the EHR allows continuous access to patient data or timely access to other information sources;
- "reliability", meaning the EHR ensures data integrity and the permanence of original information in an agreed format and for a given period of time;
- "usability and flexibility", meaning the EHR supports multiple user views and user- friendly interactions with the system;
- "integration", meaning the EHR enables the integration of different administrative and clinical information systems (CIS), e.g. from the pharmacy to the hospital;

1057 *See* Shabo, "Electronic Health Record".

1058 Iakovidis, "Towards personal health record: current situation, obstacles and trends in implementation of electronic healthcare record in Europe", p. 109.

1059 *See* EC European Commission. *New European Interoperability Framework, Promoting seamless services and data flows for European public administrations*. European Commission. Luxembourg: Publications Office of the European Union, 2017, pp. 25, 27.

1060 *See* Stephen P. Julien. "Electronic Health Records". In: *Public Health Informatics and Information Systems*. Springer, 2014, pp. 174–190. ISBN: 9780387227450. The author studied the technology in the US framework, but the uses concern the functionalities outlined above for the EU legal framework, too.

1061 Iakovidis, "Towards personal health record: current situation, obstacles and trends in implementation of electronic healthcare record in Europe", p. 107.

1062 On query and surveillance systems *see* James J. Cimino and Edward H. Shortliffe. *Biomedical Informatics: Computer Applications in Health Care and Biomedicine*. Springer-Verlag, 2006. ISBN: 9780387289861, p. 466.

- "performance", meaning the EHR ensures the provision of information normally within a few seconds, through query and surveillance systems[1062];
- "confidentiality and auditability", meaning the EHR normally provides an audit trail which documents the interactions with the system (i.e. user access), and uses authentication and authorisation systems for access control.

The concept of EHR is evidently connected with the clinical information system (CIS) of the healthcare provider. Since the first arrival of computers in the medical environment, hospitals developed hospital information systems (HIS) to use these technologies in all healthcare processes[1063]. In the 2000s, the use of networks allows the development of EHR solutions. The CIS is the subset of the HIS that is directly devoted to patient care[1064]. At the core of the CIS is the EHR, as the system for recording data collected in the hospital. A similar description can be provided for a private clinic. It has been highlighted that EHR is often used as synonym of CIS, but they are different systems since the EHR is a component of the CIS, which allows the integrated recording and access to patients' data[1065].

The literature classifies five functional components of an EHR that are typically implemented[1066].

1. Integrated view of a patient's data, e.g. medical history, or diagnoses, from different sources;
2. Clinical decision support system, which is a system for assisting the decision-making process of the user, e.g. a physician or a specialist[1067];

1063 *See* P. Degoulet, D. Luna, and F.G.B. de Quiros. "Clinical information systems". In: *Global Health Informatics*. Elsevier, 2017, pp. 129–151. ISBN: 9780128045916, p. 129.

1064 *Ibid.*

1065 *See* Degoulet, Luna, and Quiros, *op. cit.*, p. 132. This contribution provides a description of some CIS and EHR projects in Brazil and France.

1066 *See* Cimino and Shortliffe, *Biomedical Informatics: Computer Applications in Health Care and Biomedicine*, p. 452; Lupiáñez-Villanueva et al., *Benchmarking Deployment of Ehealth Among General Practitioners*. On the functional model *see* also Nicolas P. Terry. "Electronic health records: international, structural and legal perspectives". In: *Journal of Legal Medicine* 12.1 (2004), pp. 26–39.

1067 *See* Reed T Sutton et al. "An overview of clinical decision support systems: benefits, risks, and strategies for success". In: *NPJ Digital Medicine* 3.1 (2020), pp. 1–10, which provides a valuable definition: "clinical decision support system (CDSS) is intended to improve healthcare delivery by enhancing medical decisions with targeted clinical knowledge, patient information, and other health information. A traditional CDSS is comprised of software designed to be a direct aid to clinical decision making, in which the characteristics of

3. Clinician order entry, which helps the user in the order-entry process of information, e.g. of prescriptions or medications;
4. Access to multiple knowledge resources, such as images from laboratory results or radiology tests, which were previously isolated;
5. Integrated communication and reporting support, which allows the electronic integration of messages to a patient's record, and the notifications of medical results.

Source systems have a supporting infrastructure for their integration and data aggregation, and the clinical data repository (CDR) consolidates data from the sources, as a database[1068]. The interface of the EHR has a presentation layer that allows data entry and query for each patient. The EHR network allows the Health Information Exchange (HIE) between entities[1069]. Finally, the EHR storage system provides all the collected and integrated data.

The platforms may be distributed, and may be released by different vendors or developed independently[1070]. Usually, the EHR implementation is devoted to private companies, who sell or licence the product to healthcare providers. Clinical information systems often store data in proprietary formats[1071]. For these reasons, several standards have been developed for the EHR implementation, for clinical vocabulary, for data formats, for the communication of the record, for interoperability, and for the security features[1072]. As will be discussed in Chapter 5 Section 5.5, internationally recognised standards are widely used in the implementation of EHRs.

Compared to the paper-based record, the EHR is flexible and adaptable since the data are entered in some formats, and then displayed in other formats suitable for their interpretation; and data which were previously separated from the record, such as multimedia information, can now be

---

an individual patient are matched to a computerized clinical knowledge base and patient-specific assessments or recommendations are then presented to the clinician for a decision".

1068 *See* Guarda, *Fascicolo sanitario elettronico e protezione dei dati personali*, p. 35.

1069 *See* Guarda, *op. cit.*, p. 36.

1070 *See* Sinha et al., *Electronic health record: standards, coding systems, frameworks, and infrastructures*.

1071 *See* Aceto, Persico, and Pescapé, "The role of Information and Communication Technologies in healthcare: taxonomies, perspectives, and challenges", p. 132.

1072 *See* Iakovidis, "Towards personal health record: current situation, obstacles and trends in implementation of electronic healthcare record in Europe", p. 110; Sinha et al., *Electronic health record: standards, coding systems, frameworks, and infrastructures*, p. 8.

integrated with it[1073]. Data entry evidently may require more time than before, since the user should record the information through electronic interfaces in the system or scanning[1074]. The data are stored in a database and are accessible by remote access in the network. The same data are more legible and complete than the paper-based data since they are written in machine-readable form, there are multiple formats, and the system can even indicate the additional information to be added for the user[1075]. However, the EHR implies more costs than the paper-based record because it requires more technical, organisational and human factors. As the data are stored in digital form, the computer system might fail; therefore, systems should have disaster recovery plans[1076]. Users may be trained to use the system and the organisation should determine authorised users upfront. It has been highlighted that the implementation of the EHR may be slow and expensive and may bring about usability problems[1077]. At the same time, many projects over the years have focused on EHR technology, and provided good solutions[1078].

In 2018, a detailed study commissioned by the European Commission to DG Communications Networks, Content & Technology showed the common personal health data of EHR systems at the EU level. The data available in more than 90 % of cases or used in more than 80 % of them are listed as follows: "medication list; prescriptions and medications; basic medical parameters; problem list and diagnoses; immunisations; medical history; lab test results; symptoms reported by the patient; ordered tests; and clinical notes"[1079]. Other possible frequent data are: "treatment outcomes, administrative patient's data, patient's demographics, finances or billing data, and radiology test reports or images"[1080]. This information

---

1073 *See* Cimino and Shortliffe, *Biomedical Informatics: Computer Applications in Health Care and Biomedicine*, p. 448.

1074 *See* Cimino and Shortliffe, *op. cit.*, pp. 463–464.

1075 *See* Cimino and Shortliffe, *op. cit.*, pp. 449, 466.

1076 *See* Cimino and Shortliffe, *op. cit.*, p. 450.

1077 Quintana and Safran, "Global health informatics — an overview", p. 4.

1078 *See* e.g. the comparison by Terry, "Electronic health records: international, structural and legal perspectives". *See* also the work of the openEHR Foundation. An overview is provided by Dipak Kalra, Thomas Beale, and Sam Heard. "The openEHR foundation". In: *Studies in health technology and informatics* 115 (2005), pp. 153–173.

1079 *See* Lupiáñez-Villanueva et al., *Benchmarking Deployment of Ehealth Among General Practitioners*, p. 51.

1080 *See ibid.* Examples of documentation are also provided by the literature. According to Hartley, "information includes the chief complaint (or reason

represents the common core of data of the EHR. It is worth highlighting that the EHR typically collects both medical data and common personal data. Excluding financial and billing data, the other personal data can easily fall under the definition of data concerning health of the GDPR. So, the data have been combined by the eHealth Network with the functionalities available in the EHRs, as reported in the following Table 3.5[1081].

*Table 3.5 EHR overview: sub-dimensions and functionalities*

| SUB-DIMENSION | FUNCTIONALITIES |
|---|---|
| Integrated view of Health data | Symptoms, reason for appointment, clinical notes, vital signs, treatment outcomes, medical history, basic medical parameters (e.g. allergies), problem list/diagnoses |
| Clinical Decision Support System | Contraindications, drug-drug interactions, drug-lab interactions, drug-allergy alerts, clinical guidelines and best practices, being alerted to a critical laboratory value |

for visit) that the patient self-reports, the patient's past medical history, the patient's family and social history, and details of the physician's physical exam and findings (or problem list), assessment, and treatment plan. The treatment plan may include preventative measures, such as an annual exam or mammogram, and it may include treatment for an acute disease or life-long treatment for the management of a chronic disease. Also included are copies of faxes, signed permissions and consent forms, lab results, imaging reports, and other information provided by the patient. Unlike the paper chart, however, the EHR is a secure, real-time, interoperable point-of-care, patient-centric information resource for clinicians. Lab results can be posted into an electronic flow sheet, which is especially important for care managers tracking the patient's trends. The EHR also provides immediate access to the patient's current medications and closes loops in communication and response that result in delays or gaps in care, such as with billing, quality management, outcomes reporting, resource planning, and public health disease surveillance". *See* Hartley and Jones, *EHR implementation: A step-by-step guide for the medical practice*, p. 3.

1081 *See* Lupiáñez-Villanueva et al., *Benchmarking Deployment of Ehealth Among General Practitioners*, p. 59. The sub-dimensions have been aligned to the description provided above on the five typical functional components.

| SUB-DIMENSION | FUNCTIONALITIES |
|---|---|
| Clinical Order-Entry and Result Management | Medication list, prescriptions/medications, immunisations, lab test results, ordered tests |
| Access to Image | Radiology test images, radiology test reports |
| Integrated support with administrative data | Finances/billing, administrative patient data |

In sum, different components of source systems and clinical information systems store and archive valuable personal health and common data useful for the patient's care, and are connected in a network for supplying the same data in the EHR system[1082]. Three functions of the EHR may be grouped: the storage with the data at rest; the network where the data are transferred; and the computation area where the data are used[1083]. The access level of the users on the software application will be defined at the policy level through privacy access control. A typical EHR concept overview may be schematised as reported in Figure 3.1[1084].

1082 Cimino and Shortliffe, *Biomedical Informatics: Computer Applications in Health Care and Biomedicine*.

1083 For the typical ICT areas and the three data states *see* Matthijs Koot and Cees de Laat. "Privacy from an Informatics Perspective". In: *The Handbook of Privacy Studies: an Interdisciplinary Introduction*. Amsterdam University Press, 2019, pp. 213–255. ISBN: 9789462988095. According to the authors, "being aware of these three states helps grasp data and communications privacy from an informatics perspective, including potential threats to privacy and countermeasures to protect against such threats".

1084 Own graphic inspired by: Corporation MITRE. *Electronic Health Records Overview*. National Institutes of Health National, Center for Research Resources. 2006, p. 5; Bieber, Richards, and Walker, *Implementing an electronic health record system*, p. 90; Cimino and Shortliffe, *Biomedical Informatics: Computer Applications in Health Care and Biomedicine*, p. 453.

*Figure 3.1 EHR concept overview*

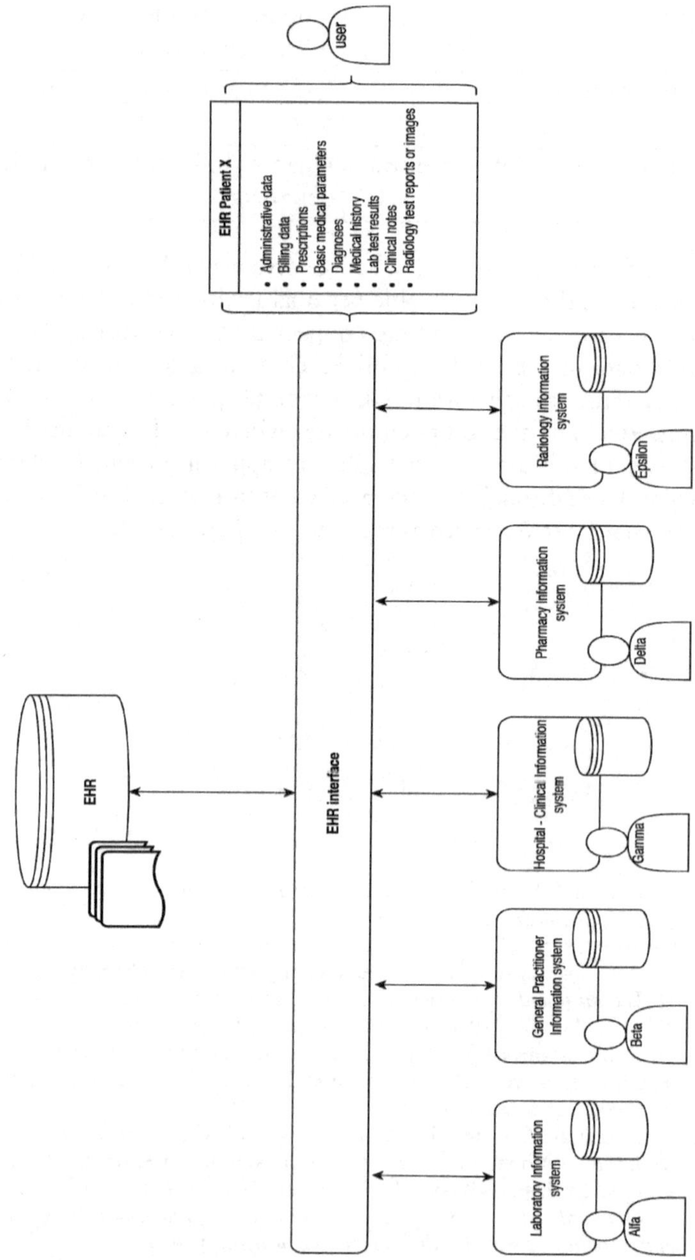

The privacy and confidentiality issues change when data are stored in electronic form[1085]. The EHR system must confront confidentiality, data protection and security principles and obligations. The next section discusses the EU legal framework applicable to the processing of data in the EHR systems.

### 3.4.2 The data protection framework for EHRs

The EHR is currently available and adopted in all Member States[1086]. At the EU level the data protection framework for EHRs is set out by Article 8 of the EU Charter of

Fundamental Rights, by the GDPR, and by Directive 2011/24/EU on patients' rights in cross-border healthcare[1087]. Regulation 910/2014 on electronic identification may also apply in the EHR context for guaranteeing secure electronic signatures, electronic identification and authentication of individuals in the system, while Directive 2016/1148 on security of network and information systems and its national transpositions establish other rules[1088]. The processing in the EHR should comply with the rules laid down in Article 8 of ECHR, the CoE Convention, CoE Recommendation No. R(97) 5, and CoE Recommendation CM/Rec (2019) 2[1089].

---

1085 *See* e.g. Terry, "Electronic health records: international, structural and legal perspectives"; Liesje De- muynck and Bart De Decker. "Privacy-preserving electronic health records". In: *IFIP International Conference on Communications and Multimedia Security*. Springer. 2005, pp. 150–159.

1086 *See* the detailed report by Lupiáñez-Villanueva et al., *Benchmarking Deployment of Ehealth Among General Practitioners*.

1087 Therefore, the framework outlined in Section 3.3 applies here. In this context Directive 2011/24/EU provides the rules for the cross-border use of EHRs, as will be further discussed in the next section.

1088 *See* EC European Commission. *Commission Recommendation (EU) 2019/243 of 6 February 2019 on a European Electronic Health Record exchange format*. European Commission. Brussels: COM (2019) 800 final, 2019, p. 3. *See* also the text of Regulation (EU) No 910/2014 of the European Parliament and of the Council of 23 July 2014 on electronic identification and trust services for electronic transactions in the internal market and repealing Directive 1999/93/EC. O.J. L. 257, 28.8.2014.

1089 All these rules are described in Section 3.3. In 2007 the WP29 listed the data protection framework applicable for EHR: Article 8 of ECHR; Article 8 of the EU Charter of Fundamental Rights; DPD; Directive 2002/58/EC on privacy and electronic communication; national laws of the Member States implementing these two Directives; rules laid down in the Council of Euro-

In addition to this general framework, every Member State can provide for specific rules on the EHR[1090]. It has been reported that health records have been regulated in the different Member States through healthcare laws, legislation on patients' rights and general legal rules and guidelines on privacy and protection of personal health data[1091].

As an example, in Italy Legislative Decree no. 179/2012 created the framework for the use of the EHR at the national level and defined this tool as "the set of data and digital documents relating to social and health information generated by present and past clinical events about the patient"[1092]. The Italian EHR may be populated by all subjects of the NHS at a regional level that are involved patient care, including the same patient in some cases[1093]. In 2009, the Italian DPA released some guidelines on

---

pe Convention for the Protection of Individuals with regard to Automatic Processing of Personal Data and the Additional protocol to Convention 108 regarding supervisory authorities and transborder data flows (ETS No. 181); Council of Europe Recommendation No. R(97) 5 on the protection of medical data (13 February 1997). *See* Article 29 Working Party, *Working Document on the processing of personal data relating to health in electronic health records (EHR)*, p. 6.

1090 For a legal analysis of the legal framework before the GDPR and under the DPD *see* Jos Dumortier and Griet Verhenneman. "Legal regulations on electronic health records: a prerequisite or an unavoidable by-product? – The legal aspects of electronic health records in Europe and the US analysed". In: *ICRI Research Paper, Interdisciplinary Centre for Law and ICT, K.U. Leuven* 5 (2011). *See* also the detailed report by Ltd. Milieu and Time.lex. *Overview of the national laws on electronic health records in the EU Member States and their interaction with the provision of cross-border eHealth services Report*. Brussels: 201/65. 2014. This study was mandated by the European Commission and it analysed the 28 Member States' legal framework in order to identify the rules on EHR and the existing legal barriers for cross-border access to records. The legal research used both legislation and guidelines and recommendations of the national DPAs.

1091 Jos Dumortier and Griet Verhenneman. "Legal regulation of electronic health records: a comparative analysis of Europe and the US". In: *eHealth: Legal, Ethical and Governance Challenges*. Springer, 2013, pp. 25–56. ISBN: 9783642224744, p. 50.

1092 Guarda and Ducato, "From electronic health records to personal health records: emerging legal issues in the Italian regulation of e-health", pp. 273–274.

1093 Guarda and Ducato, *op. cit.*, p. 274. The aim of the patient's contribution is the patient's empowerment. On the Italian EHR *see* also Guarda, *Fascicolo sanitario elettronico e protezione dei dati personali*; Faralli, Brighi, Martoni, et al., *Strumenti, diritti, regole e nuove relazioni di cura: Il Paziente europeo protagonista nell'e-Health*, pp. 193–202; Maria Gabriella Virone. *Il Fascicolo Sanitario*

EHR systems providing a list of safeguards to be implemented to protect the right to data protection of Italian patients[1094]. In this legal framework the EHR is instituted by the Regions and Autonomous Provinces for the purposes of care, scientific research in the medical, biomedical, and epidemiological fields, and for public healthcare planning, verification of care quality, and evaluation of health assistance at the governance level.

In France, the *dossier médical partagé* (DMP) stores the medical history of French patients and allows the collection of all other personal health data in specific areas in accordance with the *Code de la Santé publique*[1095]. The

---

*Elettronico. Sfide e bilanciamenti tra Semantic Web e diritto alla protezione dei dati personali*. Aracne Editrice, Roma, 2015. ISBN: 9788854883840, pp. 84–94; Rossana Ducato. "Database genetici, biobanche e "Health Information Technologies"". In: *Il diritto dell'era digitale*. Il Mulino, Bologna, 2016, pp. 305–320. ISBN: 9788815266170, pp. 315–320; Califano, "Fascicolo sanitario elettronico (Fse) e dossier sanitario. Il contributo del Garante privacy al bilanciamento tra diritto alla salute e diritto alla protezione dei dati personali"; Licia Califano. "The Electronic Health Record (EHR): Legal framework and issues about personal data protection". In: *Pharmaceuticals Policy and Law* 19.3 – 4 (2017), pp. 141–159; Vergottini and Bottari, *La sanità elettronica*; Carro, Masato, and Parla, *La privacy nella sanità*, pp. 179–194; Farina, *Il cloud computing in ambito sanitario tra security e privacy*, pp. 75–107.

1094 Italian Data Protection Authority, Guidelines on the Electronic Health Record and the Health File. Doc. web. 1672821. G.U. n. 178 of 3.08.2009. For comments on these guidelines *see* Califano, "The Electronic Health Record (EHR): Legal framework and issues about personal data protection".

1095 The rules are defined in the Code at Articles L.1111 – 14 – L.1111 – 21, R.1111 – 26 – R.1111 – 43 L.1110 – 4, R.1110 – 1. *See* the Code at <www.legifrance.gouv.fr/affichCode.do?cidTexte= LEGITEXT000006072665>; the DMP's official website at <www.dmp.fr>; and the CNIL portal at <www.cnil.fr/fr/dossier-medical-partage-dmp-questions-reponses>. Last accessed 06/10/2021. According to the official website, the DMP is organised into nine specific areas: a summary record, one for treatments, one for analyses, one for reports, one for imaging, one for certificates and one for prevention. On the *dossier see* e.g. Richard Pougnet and L. Pougnet. "Le dossier médical partagé: pour un usage centré sur la personne?" In: *Éthique & Santé* 16.2 (2019), pp. 64–70; Jacques Lucas. "Le partage des données personnelles de santé dans les usages du numérique en santé l'épreuve du consentement exprès de la personne". In: *Ethics, Medicine and Public Health* 3.1 (2017), pp. 10–18; Nathalie Devillier. "Les dispositions de la loi de modernisation de notre système de santé relatives aux données de santé". In: *Journal International de Bioéthique et d'Éthique des Sciences* 28.3 (2017), pp. 57–123; Valérie Siranyan. "La protection des données personnelles des patients face à la modernisation de notre système de santé". In: *Médecine & Droit* 158 (2019), pp. 112–117. Before 2016, the dossier was called *dossier médical personnel*. On this dossier *See* Guarda, *Fascicolo sanitario elettronico e protezione dei dati personali*, pp. 65–70.

dossier is populated by all professionals entitled to the patient's treatment. In Luxembourg, the EHR is called *Dossier de Soins Partagé* (DSP), and the services are grouped with the term eSanté[1096]. In 2019 the Luxembourgian DPA, the *Commission nationale pour la protection des données*, released a document on the protection of personal health data in the DSP and the applicable national law[1097]. So, these few examples show that a Member State usually establishes rules on EHR at a national level. Nevertheless, for the protection of personal data the general rules are still provided by the GDPR.

It has been argued that the legal definition of EHR should take into account two elements. On the one hand, the EHR may store in an electronic form all data previously stored on paper; on the other hand, the EHR may allow the sharing of data with all the entitled parties involved in the patient's treatment[1098]. At the EU level, the EHR has been defined by Article 29 Working Party as[1099]:

> "A comprehensive medical record or similar documentation of the past and present physical and mental state of health of an individual in electronic form and providing for ready availability of these data for medical treatment and other closely related purposes".

The legal definition has been framed by the "Working Document on the processing of personal data relating to health in electronic health records (EHR)" issued by WP29 in 2007. This document provided guidance on the applicable legal framework for EHR systems by establishing some general

---

1096 The rules are provided by Loi du 24 juillet 2014 "relative aux droits et obligations du patient, portant création d'un service national d'information et de médiation dans le domaine de la santé". The official portal is available at <www.esante.lu/portal/fr/espace-professionnel/my-dsp,140,196.html>. The EHR environment in Luxembourg has been schematised as reported at <www.esante.lu/portal/fr/agence-esante/la-plateforme-esante-et-ses-services/schema,397,428.html>. Last accessed 06/10/2021.

1097 *See* Avis complémentaire de la Commission nationale pour la protection des données relatif au projet de règlement grand-ducal précisant les modalités et conditions de mise en place du dossier de soins partagé, Délibération n° 51/2019 du 18.10.2019 at <cnpd.public.lu/dam-assets/fr/decisions-avis/2019/51-DSP.pdf>. Last accessed 06/10/2021. On this topic *see* also Délibération n 242/2018 du 5 avril 2018.

1098 Guarda, "Biobanks and electronic health records: open issues", p. 133.

1099 Article 29 Working Party, *Working Document on the processing of personal data relating to health in electronic health records (EHR)*.

principles and safeguards[1100]. It should be noted that the definition of EHR refers to the "medical treatment and other closely related purposes" for indicating the purposes of Article 8(3) of the DPD, meaning the purposes of preventive medicine, medical diagnosis, the provision of care or treatment or the management of health-care services, where the data are processed by a health professional or by an equivalent person[1101]. The GDPR adds the purposes listed in Article 9(2)(h), which include occupational medicine, and the assessment of the working capacity and processing of social care systems as explained above. So, even at a legal level the EHR is mainly a tool for supporting healthcare delivery and processes. Actually, the data in the EHRs may even be used for substantial public interest, public interest in the area of public health, or secondary research purposes in accordance with Article 89 of the GDPR, and so Union or Member State law provides the safeguards for rights and freedoms of data subjects[1102].

Generally, EHR systems can be centralised at a national level or decentralised at a local level[1103]. In 2021, it has been reported that 20 Member States have one national system, 11 Member States have several (national or local) systems and four states have no specific rules[1104]. The EHR system can be either used by one HIS, or by a group of hospitals and primary care systems in a regional or local network, while achieving the continuity of care in the NHS[1105]. Each subject has its own information structure in

---

1100 *See* the comment on this source by Guarda, "Telemedicine and Application Scenarios: Common Privacy and Security Requirements in the European Union Context", p. 13.

1101 *See* the footnote specification n. 3 of Article 29 Working Party, *Working Document on the processing of personal data relating to health in electronic health records (EHR)*, p. 4.

1102 In 2014, more than a half of the Member States had a specific law on secondary use of personal health data, which may also refer to data in the EHR. So, safeguards such as anonymisation were required. *See* further in Milieu and Time.lex, *Overview of the national laws on electronic health records in the EU Member States and their interaction with the provision of cross-border eHealth services Report*, pp. 46–48.

1103 In Dumortier and Verhenneman, "Legal regulation of electronic health records: a comparative analysis of Europe and the US", the author provides a comparative analysis on the solutions of the different Member States.

1104 *See* DG Health and Food Security. *Assessment of the EU Member States' rules on health data in the light of the GDPR*, p. 37.

1105 *See* Iakovidis, "Towards personal health record: current situation, obstacles and trends in implementation of electronic healthcare record in Europe", pp. 105–106.

which to process the data, but it is connected with the EHR. Potentially, multiple users can access the EHR system since different subjects interact in the data repository. The data processing entails activities with data in rest (e.g. recording, structuring, storage), data in use (e.g. collection, use, consultation), and data in transit (e.g. transmission, making available)[1106].

This structure makes "patient's data more readily available to a wider circle of recipients than before"[1107]. Therefore, data protection and confidentiality concerns are significant, and should be examined here[1108]. Indeed, the EHR goes beyond the fiduciary relationship between physician and patient, as described above. The analysis focuses on the roles in processing, the legitimate grounds, the necessary data protection safeguards for the national legal frameworks, and the rights and duties in the EHR environment.

Firstly, it is necessary to clarify the subjects and their roles in the processing of personal data. Each healthcare provider or pharmacist has its own purpose (i.e. provision of care or selling drugs) and usually determines its own means of processing (e.g. the system). Therefore, in the EHR environment there might be as many data controllers as there are actors involved[1109]. It is worth pointing out that the users of EHR systems (e.g. physicians, professionals, general practitioners) as access points may be delegated by the data controller (i.e. the healthcare entity, such as the hospital or the clinic) to process the data[1110]. The controller may use processors to carry out some processing operations. Whether the EHR implementation and functions are devoted to private companies, which sell or licence the product to healthcare providers, these entities may be designated as processor by a contract in accordance with Article 28 GDPR.

---

1106 The examples of activities recall the wording of Article 4 GDPR, whereas the distinction refers to the three types of data state.

1107 Article 29 Working Party, *Working Document on the processing of personal data relating to health in electronic health records (EHR)*, p. 5.

1108 *See* the discussion from an ethical point of view in Akhil Shenoy and Jacob M. Appel. "Safeguarding confidentiality in electronic health records". In: *Cambridge Quarterly of Healthcare Ethics* 26.2 (2017), pp. 337–341. This article also presents some potential safeguards in order to foster confidentiality.

1109 *See* e.g. Figure 3.1. That overview represents a decentralised environment because each provider stores the data-keeping record.

1110 It is arguable whether they may be considered recipients in accordance with Article 4(9) GDPR. Actually, they do not receive data by transmission, but directly perform processing activities. So, they concretely process the data in the EHR.

In an EHR environment the data controllers may be both the hospital, and the pharmacy, the clinic, or an individual private professional (a general practitioner), who collect the data – e.g. during a treatment, or a specific examination – process the data, and store them in the EHR storage system. Usually, they are not joint controllers because they do not fall under the definition of Article 26 GDPR: they do not determine the purposes and means jointly. However, they may jointly determine purposes and means in a more coordinated EHR environment[1111]. They all shall comply with the data protection principles of Article 5 GDPR.

Nevertheless, in an even more centralised EHR environment, one central institution controls the whole system and becomes the sole data controller that delegates the processing operations to different entities, i.e. processors[1112].

Secondly, some considerations on the legitimate ground of the processing should be made. As reported above, the definition of WP29 mentioned the "healthcare legitimate ground" of the DPD, which excluded the consent of the data subject. Actually, the authority explained that it is misleading to seek consent when the healthcare service is legitimised by an explicit derogation to the general prohibition on processing sensitive data[1113]. Nevertheless, it has been specified that for the creation of the patient's profile on the EHR system the explicit consent of this data subject may be necessary[1114]. The consent should also aim to indicate which personal health data can be collected and stored in the EHR, and who may have access to them[1115]. Remarkably, the patient can withdraw consent at any

---

1111 As an example, the Luxembourgian DPA specified that the data controller is not only the national central health authority, but also the entities involved in the treatment since different actors assume different responsibilities for the treatment and, therefore the processing. Thus, they are joint controllers. *See supra* Délibération n° 51/2019 du 18. 10.2019, p. 3. On the joint controllership in an EHR environment *see* also Guarda, *Fascicolo sanitario elettronico e protezione dei dati personali*, pp. 114–116.

1112 The description of centralised or decentralised storage is also provided by Article 29 Working Party, *Working Document on the processing of personal data relating to health in electronic health records (EHR)*, p. 17: "EHR as a system furnishing access to medical records kept by the health care professional, who has the obligation to keep records on the treatment of his patients – this is often called decentralised storage, or EHR as a uniform system of storage, to which medical professionals have to transfer their documentation; this is often called centralised storage".

1113 *See* the argument in Article 29 Working Party, *op. cit.*, p. 8.

1114 *See* Carro, Masato, and Parla, *La privacy nella sanità*, p. 189.

1115 *Ibid.*

time. If this happens, the patient's profile in the EHR shall be disabled, and the processing of personal health data will continue on a limited level outside the system.

However, it should be claimed that under the GDPR the processing of personal health data in the EHR may be carried out without consent in accordance with the "healthcare exception". It applies when the data are necessary for the purposes listed in that provision, and the processing is performed by a healthcare professional or a person subject to professional secrecy[1116]. It should also be noted that at the Member State level national law may specify the requirement establishing the consent provision or another legal basis for processing in the EHR[1117]. The Member State has this power in accordance with Article 9(4) GDPR, and the DPD provided for a similar derogation as well[1118]. It has been claimed that this discretion

---

1116 *See infra* Section 3.3.2.

1117 In 2014, Member States had different approaches, which could be divided into three groups: some states required consent for the creation of the EHR and the inclusion of data; others required consent for inclusion only; finally, no consent was required in the residual Member States. *See* Milieu and Time.lex, *Overview of the national laws on electronic health records in the EU Member States and their interaction with the provision of cross-border eHealth services Report*, pp. 32–33.

1118 In Italy, according to national law D.L. 18 Ottobre 2012 n. 179, art. 12 co. 5, the consent of data subject was necessary for the collection of the data in the EHR (i.e. the feeding of the EHR), the connections between providers and the access level of the professionals. In the COVID-19 crisis, D.L. 19 maggio 2020 n. 34 repealed Article 12, deleting the necessary consent. The Italian DPA has highlighted that for healthcare purposes consent is not necessary for the processing, but for the EHR processing the consent is still necessary under Italian law for the access level of the professionals in order to guarantee the right to self-determination of the patient. *See* the Doc-Web 9091942 of March 7 2019 at <www.garanteprivacy.it/ home/docweb/-/docweb-display/docweb/9091942>, and the Doc-Web 9351203 of May 25 2020 at <www. garanteprivacy.it/web/guest/home/docweb/-/docweb-display/docweb/9351203>. Last accessed 06/10/2021. A comment on this guidance is provided by Massimo Foglia. "Patients and Privacy: GDPR Compliance for Healthcare Organizations". In: *European Journal of Privacy Law & Technologies* (Special issue 2020), pp. 43–50. In France, in accordance with Décret n°2016–914 du 4 Juillet 2016 and the *Code de la Santé publique*, consent is necessary for the creation of the DMP and for the access level of the professionals. *See* at <www.dmp.fr/patient /faq>. Last accessed 06/10/2021. The *décret* is available at <www.legifrance.gou v.fr/affichTexte.do?cidTexte=JORFTEXT000032842901&dateTexte=20200530 >. Last accessed 06/10/2021. Other applicable rules are: Articles from L1111–14 to L1111–21, and from R1111–26 to R1111–43 of the *Code de la Santé publique*. According to the CNIL, the retention of medical information is based on a

reserved to Member States may create some obstacles for EHR that may impinge on access to safe and high-quality cross-border healthcare which is strongly promoted by the EU with Directive 2011/24[1119]. Where national law does not provide a specific rule, Article 9(2)(h) GDPR may be a lawful legal basis for the collection of data in the EHR system.

For non-medical staff in the EHR network national law may lay down binding rules to ensure an equivalent level of confidentiality, which allows the application of the "healthcare exception"[1120]. Whether or not the conditions of Article 9(2)(h) and 9(3) GDPR are applicable – e.g. the purpose goes beyond the medical treatment, there is not an obligation of confidentiality or secrecy – the processing shall seek another legitimate exception[1121]. Anyway, it is questionable whether the explicit consent

---

legal obligation. *See* CNIL. Commission Nationale de l'Informatique et des Libertés. *Référentiel relatif aux traitement de données personnelles pour les cabinets médicaux et paramédicaux*. 2020. On November 2020 Liechtenstein notified the proposal "Act of... on electronic health records (EGDG)" to the European Commission. Liechtenstein participates in the European Economic Area and so the GDPR applies there. The Act states that "the electronic health records fulfil a substantial public interest within the meaning of Article 9(2)(g) to (j) of Regulation (EU) 2016/679". So, this Act will be the Liechtenstein law pursuant to Article 9(2)(g), (h), (i), (j) GDPR. This Act establishes the applicable rules for the data processing, including subjects, content, principles and rights. It will enter into force "on 01 January 2022 if a referendum is not called within the statutory period, and otherwise on the day after its proclamation" (Article 21).

1119 *See* Califano, "The Electronic Health Record (EHR): Legal framework and issues about personal data protection", p. 148.

1120 This proposition was made in the Working Document by the WP29 under the DPD for allowing the application of this exception.

1121 In fact, in the Working Document on EHR the WP29 stated interestingly: "If the question were raised whether Article 8(3) of the Directive could serve as the sole legal basis for the processing of personal data in an EHR system, the Article 29 Working Party is of the opinion that Article 8(3) could only pertain to the processing of medical data for strictly those medical and health-care purposes mentioned therein, and strictly under the conditions that processing is "required" and done by a health professional or by another person subject to an obligation of professional or equivalent secrecy. Where the processing of personal data in an EHR goes in any way beyond these purposes or does not meet the said conditions, then Article 8(3) cannot serve as the sole legal basis for the processing of that personal data". And also: "The main and traditional safeguard in Art. 8(3) – apart from the purpose limitation and the strict necessity requirement – is the obligation of medical professionals to confidentiality concerning medical data about their patients. This may no longer be fully

of the data subject may provide more safeguards than other legitimate grounds[1122].

Consent may instead be an appropriate source of legitimisation of the access to data by health professionals. It expresses the informational self-determination of the patient. Applying the principle of control over personal health data, the patient needs to know with whom the data are shared[1123]. So, the EHR may be available without consent in order to simplify the processing activities related to the treatment, but consent may be necessary to establish which other category of professionals or which other entity in the network may access the repository[1124].

In an exceptional situation, where the other grounds do not apply, the protection of the vital interest of the data subject or another person may legitimate the processing in the context of the EHR[1125]. Additionally,

---

applicable in an EHR environment, as one of the purposes of EHR is to grant access to medical documentation".

1122 As an example, consent will be necessary for automated processing which is not strictly related to a healthcare purpose, or in the AI and Big Data environment where the EHR may be used for predictions and inferences beyond the traditional healthcare treatment.

1123 *See* Koelewijn, "Privacy from a Medical Perspective". The author reported three principles for informational medical privacy: control over data, subsidiary principle, and purpose limitation principle.

1124 This is the approach presented by the Italian DPA in the Doc-Web 9351203 of May 25 2020 (*see supra* note no. 1118): "In particolare, è stata ritenuta opportuna – e dall'Autorità condivisa – l'eliminazione del consenso all'alimentazione del Fascicolo, confermando invece quello (autenticamente espressivo di autodeterminazione informativa) relativo alla consultazione da parte dei professionisti sanitari. Tale modifica contribuisce a semplificare notevolmente il processo di costituzione dell'fse rendendolo quindi automaticamente disponibile a prescindere da manifestazioni di volontà individuali, ma confermando il consenso del paziente quale fonte di legittimazione dell'accesso ai dati, da parte del professionista sanitario. Lo spettro del fascicolo è ampliato, sino a comprendere tutti i documenti, sanitari e socio-sanitari, riferiti alle prestazioni erogate, a carico o meno del SSN, includendo dunque tra i soggetti abilitati all'alimentazione la generalità degli esercenti le professioni sanitarie che seguano il paziente".

1125 WP 29 reported this scenario: "by way of example: assume a data subject has lost consciousness after an accident and cannot give his consent to the necessary disclosure of known allergies. In the context of EHR systems this provision would allow access to information stored in the EHR to a health professional in order to retrieve details on known allergies of the data subject as they might prove decisive for the chosen course of treatment". This example of the authority may be misleading since the processing seems justified by the "healthcare exception" once again.

Member State law may provide the use of EHR in the area of public health, or for a substantial public interest, or for research purposes by providing the appropriate safeguards.

As explained above, the definition of personal health data should include the administrative data processed in the e-health context, such as the number or symbol used to identify the patient. So, following the classification of functionalities of the EHR carried out by the EC (and classified in Table 3.5)[1126], processing with the EHR involves data concerning health in a broad sense, administrative data related to health status, and common personal data and billing data. Only the last category is beyond the scope of the "healthcare exception". Name, surname, contact details, and billing data are common personal data, and the lawfulness of their processing is laid down by Article 6 of the GDPR. Thus, it seems that the lawful grounds may be either performance of the contract between the patient and the healthcare provider, or compliance with a legal obligation to which the provider is subject, or a legitimate interest.

Thirdly, the data protection concerns and necessary safeguards for the EHR are related to the particular structure of the data processing. Under the DPD, WP29 reflected on the suitable legal safeguards necessary to guarantee data protection within an EHR, and indicated 11 recommendations for the creation of rules in the national legal frameworks[1127]. So, the recommendations may be grouped and further elaborated as follows[1128]:

1. The processing in the EHR shall respect the right to self-determination of the patient on when and how data are used in light of Article 8 of the EU Charter and Article 8 of the ECHR. So, processing in the EHR

1126 *See infra* in Section 3.4.1 the description of the study conducted by Lupiáñez-Villanueva et al., *Benchmarking Deployment of Ehealth Among General Practitioners*.

1127 *See* Article 29 Working Party, *Working Document on the processing of personal data relating to health in electronic health records (EHR)*, pp. 13–21.

1128 This list is based on the safeguards reported by the WP29, but has been updated and further integrated with an independent legal analysis based on the considerations of the previous sections. Even the order has been changed. The topics of the recommendation of WP29 were listed as follows: "1) Respecting self determination; 2) Identification and authentication of patients and health care professionals; 3) Authorization for accessing EHR in order to read and write in EHR; 4) Use of EHR for other purposes; 5) Organisational structure of an EHR system; 6) Categories of data stored in EHR and modes of their presentation; 7) International transfer of medical records; 8) Data security; 9) Transparency; 10) Liability issues; 11) Control mechanisms for processing data in EHR".

may require both opt-in and opt-out solutions, or rights to refuse[1129]. A national law establishing the use of the EHR should provide both opt-in requirements for choosing whether particularly sensitive personal health data (e.g. abortion, abuse) may be collected in the EHR, and also opt-out requirements for the data subjects. These opt-out requirements should allow the patient to prevent the disclosure to particular healthcare professionals of a category of data or specific data. As a result, the choice of the data subject will be central for processing in the EHR. The right to self-determination may allow the patient to limit the data to be stored and the operations to be performed in the EHR[1130]. However, the data subject should be well-informed on the risks since any choice of limitation may impact the healthcare treatment. In fact, it has been claimed that comprehensive and complete EHRs provide a better overview of a patient's health than incomplete records[1131];

2. The national law could even define the categories of personal data stored in an EHR and how they are presented in the interface[1132]. Only relevant data should be stored in the EHR, and the access points may have different access requirements, especially in the case of particularly sensitive personal health data. National rules may provide exceptions and particular modules with special safeguards[1133];
3. The EHR system should be set with reliable mechanisms and limits for the identification and authentication of healthcare professionals, staff

---

1129 WP29 stated that agreeing to the EHR is different from simply consenting.

1130 This is one fundamental conclusion in Guarda, *Fascicolo sanitario elettronico e protezione dei dati personali*, p. 220.

1131 *See* Milieu and Time.lex, *Overview of the national laws on electronic health records in the EU Member States and their interaction with the provision of cross-border eHealth services Report*.

1132 As an example, Liechtenstein's "Act of... on electronic health records (EGDG)" (*see* note no.1118) includes: "a) administrative data collected by the Office of Health for each insured person; this includes in particular: 1. name and address of the insured person; 2. personal identification number (IDN); 3. other insurance information; b) health data and genetic data of the participant, which are collected in accordance with Articles 5 to 7. 2) The government shall regulate detailed rules for data referred to in paragraph 1(a) by way of regulation" (Article 3). Data that must be stored are "a) letters of referral and medical reports; b) letters of transfer and discharge reports; c) laboratory findings; d) diagnostic imaging findings; and e) medications" (Article 5).

1133 The protection of "particularly sensitive health data" defined above in Section 3.3.1 may be an example.

and patients[1134]. It has been pointed out that in the EHR "data should not only be protected against outsiders, but also against insiders"[1135]. A national law may give guidance on these fundamental aspects[1136]. Internal policies and guidelines should define the methods for identification and authentication in the organisations or institutions since different approaches could be set (e.g. e- signature or smart cards)[1137]. So, any access should be temporary and traceable[1138];

4. Therefore, the EHR system should require authorisation for professionals involved to access the EHR in order to read and elaborate data. Access to the EHR could vary according to the roles of professionals in the patient's treatment, and the patient may have the right to prevent access to the record and to have autonomous access to it. The categories of professionals could be established previously by Member State law[1139]. As an example, a specialist may have access to more data than a general practitioner, and this subject more than a nurse[1140]. As regards this principle, Recommendation CM/Rec (2019) 2 of CoE suggests that whether an electronic medical file is used, "the exchange and sharing of data between health professionals should be limited to the information strictly necessary for the coordination or continuity of care, prevention or medico-social and social monitoring of the indi-

---

1134 As will be discussed in Chapter 6, these aspects are crucial for a DPbD implementation of the EHR.

1135 Demuynck and De Decker, "Privacy-preserving electronic health records", p. 150.

1136 Once again it is interesting to mention Liechtenstein's solution. The Act of 2020 refers to the provisions of the E-Government Act, limits authorisation to healthcare providers and subjects involved in the medical treatment, and specifies that "government shall regulate the detailed rules for the principles of data processing by way of regulation, in particular with regard to access authorisation" (Article 4).

1137 As for other contexts, an overview of Member States' approaches is provided by Milieu and Time.lex, *Overview of the national laws on electronic health records in the EU Member States and their interaction with the provision of cross-border eHealth services Report*, pp. 36–37.

1138 These two principles are highlighted by Guarda, *Fascicolo sanitario elettronico e protezione dei dati personali*, pp. 222–223.

1139 This is one of the recommendations at the national level by Milieu and Time.lex, *Overview of the national laws on electronic health records in the EU Member States and their interaction with the provision of cross-border eHealth services Report*, p. 10. At the EU level the report explained that an agreement was very difficult to achieve.

1140 *See* Milieu and Time.lex, *op. cit.*, p. 36.

vidual". Access by professionals should be adjusted in accordance with their tasks and authorisations, and measures should be taken to protect the security of the record[1141];

5. The EHR must be set with strict requirements and measures for data security (e.g. PETs). National law may indicate some specific and neutral measures[1142]. It was reported that almost all Member States required encryption of data in the EHR and few countries even established a legal obligation for encryption[1143];
6. National law or internal guidelines should describe the organisational structure of the EHR system, which may be centralised or decentralised at the local, regional (e.g. Italy, Spain) or national (e.g. France) level[1144]. Actually, the structure of the network and storage are fundamental for determining the roles in the processing activity, as discussed above;
7. National law should also provide requirements for transparency at the organisational level of the healthcare service (e.g. notification requirements, or information to the patient);
8. National legal framework should establish the general prohibition from using the EHR for purposes other than the provision of care, such as insurance purposes[1145]. Nevertheless, exceptions and safeguards

1141 *See* Article 8.3 and 8.4 of the CoE Recommendation CM/Rec (2019) 2.

1142 As will be discussed in Chapter 6, security aspects are pivotal for the implementation of the EHR.

1143 In 2014 the Member States that required this obligation were Austria, Italy, and Poland. *See* Milieu and Time.lex, *Overview of the national laws on electronic health records in the EU Member States and their interaction with the provision of cross-border eHealth services Report*, p. 29. In Liechtenstein's Act encryption is indicated as a security measure, but further requirements must be laid down through government regulation (Article 9 on data security). *See* note no. 1118.

1144 *See* Milieu and Time.lex, *op. cit.*, which describes the situation of the Member States in 2014 and DG Health and Food Security. *Assessment of the EU Member States' rules on health data in the light of the GDPR* for 2021.

1145 As discussed in Section 3.3.2, the insurance purposes are outside the scope of the "healthcare exception". Insurance companies will process personal health data for their contracts outside the EHR environment by seeking the explicit consent of the data subjects. Insurance companies should not be recipients of the EHR processing since they cannot guarantee neither the respect of the duty of confidentiality of physicians or the principles related to a healthcare purpose. In Greece, pursuant to Article 23 of Law 4624/2019, data stored in a personal electronic health care record cannot be processed for other purposes, including employment and insurance purposes. *See* also TIPIK, *Report on the implementation of specific provisions of Regulation (EU) 2016/679*, p. 10.

may be laid down by national law for other uses, or a secondary use of personal health data in the EHR for scientific medical research purposes, or other purposes related to a public interest[1146];

9. It is of paramount importance that national law establishes that international transfer out of the EU of EHRs may be performed only in aggregated anonymised or pseudonymised form since this scenario is problematic for the high data protection risks[1147];
10. The legal frameworks should lay down rules for liability where a violation occurs in the EHR environment[1148];
11. Finally, national law should establish control mechanisms for evaluating the safeguards set down for processing in the EHR. WP29 suggested special arbitration procedures, the definition of rules on liability of one entity among the others in the EHR network, and regular internal and external data protection auditing. Independent auditing requirements may attest to the implementation of data protection principles and security policies[1149].

Compliance with these principles may enhance the protection of personal data in the EHR system.

In addition to these aspects, it is worth mentioning the data minimisation principle, which limits processing to the data necessary for the treatment purpose, DPbD and DPbDf obligations, and the accountability principle. According to the data minimisation principle, the data in the EHR should be limited to what is necessary for the healthcare purpose, be adequate and relevant; to this end, pseudonymisation techniques may be

1146 CoE Recommendation CM/Rec(2019) 2 specifies that "insurance companies cannot be regarded as recipients authorised to have access to the health-related data of individuals unless law provides for this with appropriate safeguards and in accordance with principle 5" (Article 9.2). Moreover, a specific section of the Recommendation is dedicated to research purposes (Article 15).

1147 In this book the data transfer out of the EU has never been mentioned. The GDPR sets out the rules for transfer in Articles 44–50 by providing specific mechanisms and safeguards. *See* Christopher Kuner. "Chapter V Transfers of Personal Data to Third Countries or International Organisations (Articles 44–50)". In: *The EU General Data Protection Regulation (GDPR): A Commentary*. Oxford University Press, 2020, pp. 755–862. ISBN: 9780198826491.

1148 It might even be possible that rules on medical liability (e.g. on negligence) are set for EHRs, but national law should provide for it. *See* the recommendation by Milieu and Time.lex, *Overview of the national laws on electronic health records in the EU Member States and their interaction with the provision of cross-border eHealth services Report*, p. 62.

1149 In some Member States this auditing was even binding. *See* Milieu and Time.lex, *op. cit.*, pp. 29–30.

useful[1150]. The DPbD and DPbDf obligations shall be central in the EHR implementation.

Fourthly, following the considerations in Section 3.3.3 on the relevant provision to comply with in the e-health context, it is worth examining here some aspects on data protection rights and duties in the EHR environment under the GDPR.

As regards the right to be informed, the privacy policy will comply with Articles 13 and 14 GDPR and the information will be provided in a concise, transparent, intelligible and easily accessible form, using clear and plain language[1151]. In particular, the information on the timing of data storage is fundamental in the EHR context. Storage of the patient's data in the EHR may last a lifetime for healthcare purposes, but may also last for longer in accordance with specific national law, which requires storage for administrative purposes (i.e. general public interest) or even scientific research purposes[1152]. It has been suggested that initial information on the

---

1150 *See* Abedjan et al., "Data science in healthcare: Benefits, challenges and opportunities". In the Guidelines on Article 25, and in particular in the section dedicated to the implementation of the minimisation principle, the EDPB used the following example of EHR: "A hospital is collecting data about its patients in a hospital information system (electronic health record). Hospital staff needs to access patient files to inform their decisions regarding care for and treatment of the patients, and for the documentation of all diagnostic, care and treatment actions taken. By default, access is granted to only those members of the medical staff who are assigned to the treatment of the respective patient in the speciality department she or he is assigned to. The group of people with access to a patient's file is enlarged if other departments or diagnostic units are involved in the treatment. After the patient is discharged, and billing is completed, access is reduced to a small group of employees per speciality department who answer requests for medical information or a consultation made or asked for by other medical service providers upon authorization by the respective patient".

1151 The expressions are borrowed from Article 12 GDPR.

1152 Generally, in this last scenario, data will be pseudonymised or anonymised. As an example of the timing of the storage of personal health data, in Italy the radiology results shall be stored for at least for 10 years (art. 4, D.M. of 14 February 1997). The same timing is established by Act of 24 July 2014 on patients' rights and obligations in Luxembourg. Milieu and Time.lex, *Overview of the national laws on electronic health records in the EU Member States and their interaction with the provision of cross-border eHealth services Report*, pp. 48–49, reports that usually countries rely on general rules on archiving duration, so the timing is frequently set to ten years. In France, the *dossier médical* shall be retained for 20 years on the basis of Article R. 1112–7 of the *Code de la Santé Publique*. *See* Commission Nationale de l'Informatique et des Libertés,

EHR collection and ordinary operations could be provided immediately, then additional information on other specific processing activities could be provided progressively[1153]. As a result, the data subject may pay more attention to the fundamental information and be made aware of the additional information one later.

The right to access and the right to rectification fully apply to the EHR environment[1154]. As described above, the GDPR mentions medical records in Recital 63 so as to specify that the data subject has the right to access these records in order to be aware of all the information on health treatment. When possible, this access can be executed through remote access to the system[1155]. The data controller should ensure that the EHR can be consulted by the data subject, and that copies of the record can be easily obtained[1156]. The data subject could also have the possibility of knowing who accessed the EHR, even directly online[1157]. It has been claimed that access to the data of the EHR might be mediated by a healthcare professional in order to explain to the patient the significance of the specific

---

*Référentiel relatif aux traitement de données personnelles pour les cabinets médicaux et paramédicaux*, p. 7 and CNIL. Commission Nationale de l'Informatique et des Libertés. *Référentiel des durées de conservation dans le domaine de la santé hors recherche*. 2020.

1153 *See* Califano, "Fascicolo sanitario elettronico (Fse) e dossier sanitario. Il contributo del Garante privacy al bilanciamento tra diritto alla salute e diritto alla protezione dei dati personali", p. 21.

1154 Article 29 Working Party, *Working Document on the processing of personal data relating to health in electronic health records (EHR)*, p. 7.

1155 The study by Milieu and Time.lex, *Overview of the national laws on electronic health records in the EU Member States and their interaction with the provision of cross-border eHealth services Report*, p. 42, specifies that in 2014 more than one third of the Member States allowed the data subject/patient to download the data in the EHR. However, all Member States granted access to the EHRs. In 2021, 20 Member States have an ICT system through which data subjects can access their personal health data. *See* DG Health and Food Security. *Assessment of the EU Member States' rules on health data in the light of the GDPR*, p. 88.

1156 *See* Carro, Masato, and Parla, *La privacy nella sanità*, p. 191.

1157 This possibility is usually set by Member State law. *See* Milieu and Time.lex, *Overview of the national laws on electronic health records in the EU Member States and their interaction with the provision of cross-border eHealth services Report*, pp. 10, 42–43. As an example, in Liechtenstein's Act of 2020 mentioned above the data subject has the right "to read all of the data contained in the electronic health records", even "by electronic access via the access portal of the eHealth platform or by written notification to the Office of Health" (Article 7).

personal health data[1158]. So, the rationales may be protecting the patient and giving information on the data, but in a concrete digital scenario this mediation is difficult to achieve since the EHR may be accessed by the patient autonomously and by electronic means. Therefore, the personal health data in the record could be associated with a brief explanation by the healthcare professional or could be signalled in a way that suggests seeking medical advice on the same data[1159]. According to the EC, having access to EHR has been shown to improve quality of care and patient safety. If interoperable, given patient mobility, EHRs will also improve conditions for treatment in other Member States, following the rules of Directive 2011/24/EC[1160].

The right to rectification is obviously applicable, but the EHR should contain the versioning of the record for accountability and proofing purposes. Actually, the ability to rectify personal health data with data provided by the patient is questionable. Given the healthcare purposes, the EHR shall contain accurate and high-quality data. So, it has been claimed that, on the one hand, the ability to directly modify personal health data shall be prohibited for the EHR being trustworthy[1161]; and on the other hand, the need to update data in the EHR is based on general rules on data protection, health data and medical ethics[1162]. Whether the data subject

---

1158 *See* Guarda, *Fascicolo sanitario elettronico e protezione dei dati personali*, pp. 128–129. While commenting on the Italian rules (now repealed by the GDPR), the author explains that mediation is useful for facilitating the comprehensibility of medical data by the patient and for filtering the information in a way that respects the fiduciary relationship between physician and patient. This solution has been criticised by the literature. However, as reported by this source, even the DPD suggested that Member State law could have specified that access to medical data could be obtained only through a health professional (Recital 42). As an example, in France, according to Article L1111–7 of the *Code de la santé publique*, the patient has the option to choose mediation of the healthcare professional or access by himself or herself.

1159 *See* Guarda, *op. cit.*, pp. 131–135.

1160 *See* for these last sentences European Commission, *Communication from the Commission to the Council, the European Parliament, the European Economic and Social Committee and the Committee of the Regions on e-Health – making healthcare better for European citizens: An action Plan for a European e-Health Area*.

1161 *See* the recommendation by Milieu and Time.lex, *Overview of the national laws on electronic health records in the EU Member States and their interaction with the provision of cross-border eHealth services Report*, p. 10.

1162 *See* Milieu and Time.lex, *op. cit.*, p. 40, which also provides the list of countries where the task of updating EHRs is specifically mandated by law.

has directly inputted some data, the system may allow for him or her to modify this specific data.

Furthermore, as mentioned in Section 3.3.3, the right to erasure has some limits in the healthcare context. In the EHR environment, the law usually requires keeping the data, or the data controller performs public tasks including storing personal data. As a result, personal health data are never erased unless they are processed unlawfully, or a specific provision allows their erasure[1163]. For this reason, and in order to empower the patient, a right of concealment has been established in some legal frameworks to give the patient the power not to reveal to users some data contained in the EHR[1164]. The patient can ask to conceal a data entry in the EHR, and the choice is revocable over time. This personal health data is therefore accessible only to the professional who originally generated it or collected it, or to the patient, and the occurred option of concealment should not be intelligible to other users (so-called "concealment of the concealment")[1165]. Actually, this right has been criticised by healthcare

1163 In this regard, CoE Recommendation CM/Rec (2019) 2 stated that the data subject has the right to erasure of data processed in violation of the provisions of CoE Convention 108 (Article 12.2). It has been reported that few countries allow patients to erase data (Austria and France). *See* Milieu and Time.lex, *op. cit.*, p. 43 and DG Health and Food Security. *Assessment of the EU Member States' rules on health data in the light of the GDPR*, p. 91. In Liechtenstein, data in the EHR are deleted ten years after the expiration of compulsory national insurance (Article 10 of the Act of 2020 on EHR).

1164 In France the patient has the right to "masquage", that is the option to request to hide documents from some health professionals. Nevertheless, the document remains visible to the physician who created it, to the general practitioner and the patient. The choice is revocable anytime. The "masking is masked" since the choice shall not be visible to other professionals. *See* Lucas, "Le partage des données personnelles de santé dans les usages du numérique en santé l'épreuve du consentement exprès de la personne", p. 13. *See* also at <www.dmp.fr/ps/faq>. Last accessed 06/10/2021. In Liechtenstein, the data subject will have the right "to hide or delete health data and genetic data relating to him or her" pursuant to Article 7 of the proposal of Act on EHR of 2020. *See* note no. 1118. In Italy there are comparable rights of "oscuramento" and "oscuramento dell'oscuramento". *See* further the next footnote.

1165 As regards Italy, *see* Califano, "The Electronic Health Record (EHR): Legal framework and issues about personal data protection", p. 156; Guarda and Ducato, "From electronic health records to personal health records: emerging legal issues in the Italian regulation of e-health"; Ducato, "Database genetici, biobanche e "Health Information Technologies"", p. 317; Carro, Masato, and Parla, *La privacy nella sanità*, pp. 190–191; Farina, *Il cloud computing in ambito sanitario tra security e privacy*, p. 84. As reported by the literature, the right of

providers since it limits the EHR potentiality. However, a right of concealment guarantees the right to make free and informed decisions on which data the subject wants to communicate to the physician, and it implies the desire to request the opinion of another specialist without the latter being influenced by the former professional[1166].

Data portability may be useful for guaranteeing treatment in a different EHR environment. However, semantic and technical interoperability limits this right, and it applies only to data provided by the patient and not processed by a public authority[1167].

All the organisational requirements outlined above for the e-health context are necessary in the EHR environment for the same reasons explained there. It is evident that in this context both the likelihood and the gravity can be evaluated as high-level and that personal health data are processed on a large scale. Thus, the record of the processing, the notification and communication of data breaches, the risk assessment with a DPIA, the designation of the DPO and the implementation of organisational and technical measures are usually binding requirements for the EHR[1168]. The present case study then will provide the DPbD set of guidelines with technical and organisational measures for complying with this legal framework in Chapter 6.

As mentioned, EHRs are associated with increased risk of security and data protection. Hence, it is particularly interesting that the first fine for violation of the GDPR was charged to a hospital by the Portuguese Data

---

concealment was firstly proposed by the Italian DPA in its Guidelines of 16 July 2009 (*see supra* note no. 1094). The DPA argued that "without diminishing the definite utility of a complete EHR" it should "be possible to prevent the entry in it of some data concerning health related to individual clinical events (e.g., with reference to the outcome of a specific specialist examination or the prescription of a drug). This is similar to the patient-physician relationship, in which the former can make an informed decision not to inform the latter of certain events". Then, the right to concealment has been established by the first regulatory act approved in accordance with Article 12(7) of D.L. 179/2012.

1166 *See* Califano, "The Electronic Health Record (EHR): Legal framework and issues about personal data protection", p. 156; Claudio Filippi and Melchionna Silvia. "I trattamenti di dati in ambito sanitario". In: *Le nuove frontiere della privacy nelle tecnologie digitali*. Aracne Editrice, 2016, pp. 469–533. ISBN: 9788825507942, p. 493.

1167 On interoperability *see infra* the following section.

1168 Indeed, the EHR system is associated with data protection concerns related to how and by whom the record will be used. Following the WP29 list of principles, specific safeguards should be established.

Protection Authority (CNPD) in December 2018[1169]. The fine amounted to 400,000 euros. The Portuguese DPA sanctioned the hospital for the violation of Article 5(1)(c) and (f) of the GDPR on data minimisation and security. In particular, after an inspection the authority found that the system for patient management was not compliant with these two principles because access to patients' personal data was not limited[1170]. Specifically, the hospital did not implement technical and organisational measures for limiting the identification and authentication of the users in accordance with their profiles and the different levels of access that corresponded to each category of workers[1171]. The security of the personal data was not guaranteed because there was not enough security and an audit system for the access mechanisms was not set[1172]. According to CNPD, the hospital acted freely and voluntarily, and knowing that the conduct was prohibited and punished by the law[1173]. In arguing the decision, the authority described the circumstances in which the information access systems operated and the specific conditions of access with their relative weaknesses[1174]. The system counted 985 users with doctor-level access, but the hospital had only 296 doctors. Access was granted to too many profiles.

Therefore, the hospital violated the principle of data minimisation by allowing indiscriminate access to an excessive set of professionals who should have only accessed in occasional and previously justified cases[1175]. Moreover, the hospital violated the principles of integrity and confidentiality, and Article 32 GDPR on security, by not implementing the technical and organisational measures that should prevent unlawful access to personal data[1176]. When deciding on the amount of the administrative fine the authority gave regard to Articles 25 and 32 of the GDPR by stating that the defendant's responsibility regarding the violation of the restrictions of

1169 *See* the website of the Comissão Nacional de Protecção de Dados at <www.cnpd.pt/english/index_en.htm>. Last accessed 06/10/2021.

1170 The decision is Deliberação n. 984/2018. The decision has not been translated into English, but is available in Portuguese at <www.cnpd.pt/home/decisoes/Delib/20_984_2018.pdf>. Last accessed 06/10/2021.

1171 *See* paragraph 26. In paragraphs 8 – 13, the authority specified that the categories were administrative worker, technician, doctor, computer technician, assistant, surgeon, anaesthetist, nutritionist, physical therapist, psychologist, welfare worker.

1172 *Ibid.*

1173 *Ibid.*

1174 *See* Part IV "Motivação da decisão de facto", pp. 7 and 7v.

1175 *See* p. 7v.

1176 *Ibid.*

the levels of access was high, since it consciously allowed the association of the functional group of "doctors" to whom only a "technician profile" should be granted. It was the responsibility of the hospital to ensure the control of the need or the deletion of the profiles, including through appropriate audit procedures[1177]. The measures were not appropriate for the risks[1178]. It thus can be argued that the risk assessment was not adequate, and that the patient management system was not designed properly.

The case shows that a DPbD approach is not only binding, but also pivotal for a medical record. Following the words of the Italian DPA, in the context of e-health the measures of DPbD and DPbDf are a decisive example of how technology, if supported by a forward-looking "vision" in social as well as legal terms, can represent the solution, instead of the problem, and strengthen citizens' confidence in the health system[1179].

So far, this Chapter has presented the legal framework for personal health data and the case study on the EHR with the state of the art of this technology and the applicable data protection rules. The next section deals with cross-border processing of data in the EHR environment, where it applies primarily Directive 2011/24/CE.

### 3.4.3 Cross-border interoperability issues

This section presents the EU interoperability policy and investigates the use of EHRs across Member States for providing healthcare. Cross-border interoperability and secure access to EHR systems abroad raise several data protection issues. So, this part identifies the rules and obligations established by the GDPR that should be taken into account in the context of EHR interoperability across Member States[1180].

As mentioned above, in the "transformation of health and care" policy of the EU agenda access to healthcare and sharing of personal health data are priorities. In recent years EU institutions and Member States

1177 *See* p. 8v.
1178 *See* p. 10.
1179 *See* the text of the Doc-Web 9351203 of 25 May 2020 (*see supra* note no. 1118).
1180 A paper has been published on the main issues of this section, Bincoletto, "Data protection issues in cross-border interoperability of Electronic Health Record systems within the European Union". This section then further elaborates the topic.

have launched projects, initiatives and studies[1181], and made significant investments[1182].

In the past, the EU Council urged Member States to conceive initiatives and strategies enabling interoperability of digital health technologies across the EU[1183]. In this scenario, the EHR has always played an important role. EU institutions have claimed many times the urgent need to make progress on standardisation and interoperability of e-health systems to foster a greater use of these digital tools[1184], and to enable the free flow of patients, products and services in the EU market[1185]. In 2020, the European Commission presented the project on the creation of a common space in the area of health named "European Health Data Space ('EHDS')" within its European strategy for data[1186]. According to the EC, this space will be "essential for advances in preventing, detecting and curing diseases as well as for informed, evidence-based decisions to improve the accessibili-

1181 P. Van Langenhove et al. "eHealth European Interoperability Framework". In: *Vision on eHealth EIF, a study prepared for the European Commission by the Deloitte team* 1 (2013).

1182 See the Health policies in the EU budget (2021–2027) at <ec.europa.eu/health/funding/future_health_budget_en>. Last accessed 06/10/2021. *See* Arak and Wójcik, *Transforming eHealth into a political and economic advantage*.

1183 *See* EU Council, Council of the European Union. *Council Conclusions on Safe and efficient healthcare through eHealth. 2980th Employment, Social Policy, Health and Consumer Affairs Council meeting*. Council of the European Union. Brussels: 1.12.2009, 2009.

1184 *See* European Commission, *Commission Staff Working document accompanying the document Communication from the Commission to the European Parliament, the Council, the European Economic and Social Committee and the Committee of the Regions on enabling the digital transformation of health and care in the Digital Single Market*.

1185 *See* European Commission, *Communication from the Commission to the Council, the European Parliament, the European Economic and Social Committee and the Committee of the Regions on e-Health – making healthcare better for European citizens: An action Plan for a European e-Health Area*.

1186 *See* European Commission, *Communication from the Commission to the European Parliament, the Euro- pean Council, the Council, the European Economic and Social Committee and the Committee of the Regions A European strategy for data*. The EDPS released a specific opinion on the EHDS: EDPS European Data Protection Supervisor. *Preliminary Opinion 8/2020 on the European Health Data Space*. 2020. According to the EDPS, Article 9(2)(i) and 8j) may be the possible legal grounds for processing operations in the EHDS.

ty, effectiveness and sustainability of the healthcare systems"[1187]. EHRs are included in this vision as fundamental digital tools that improve access to citizens' health data[1188].

In addition, Directive 2011/24/EU on patients' rights in cross-border healthcare fosters the right to access healthcare, and personal health data, in any EU Member State[1189]. In particular, it has been highlighted that this Directive establishes a right to have a medical record and have it accessible across borders for the first time in an act of the EU[1190]. The European Health Insurance Card (EHIC) entitles the patient to obtain the healthcare services by a doctor or a public or NHS-affiliated health facility in another Member State. The Directive also stresses the importance of safeguarding the right to data protection during cross-border healthcare services and the transfer of data[1191].

EHR systems might be interoperable at the EU level for fostering cross-border access to healthcare, but the lack of interoperability between them is still a great barrier to access to personal health data in another Member State[1192]. In the healthcare context, the concept of interoperability has rapidly evolved[1193]. A generic definition of the concept within the context of European public service delivery, is[1194]:

---

1187 European Commission, *Communication from the Commission to the European Parliament, the European Council, the Council, the European Economic and Social Committee and the Committee of the Regions A European strategy for data*.

1188 *See* point 4.

1189 A report on the progresses of the Member States is usually provided by the EC. *See* EC European Commission. *Report from the Commission to the European Parliament and the Council on the operation of Directive 2011/24/EU on the application of patients' rights in cross-border healthcare*. European Commission. COM/2018/651 final, 2018, where "e-health" has a specific section.

1190 *See* the analysis by Vergottini and Bottari, *La sanità elettronica*, p. 112, which makes reference to Article 4(2)(f) and Article 5(b) of the Directive. According to these authors, the individual also has the right to file an action before an administrative court.

1191 *See* Recital 25 of Directive 2011/24/EU.

1192 EC European Commission and College of Europe. *Synopsis Report. Consultation: Transformation Health and Care in the Digital Single Market*. Publications Office of the European Union. 2018; European Commission, *Communication from the Commission to the European Parliament, the European Council, the Council, the European Economic and Social Committee and the Committee of the Regions A European strategy for data*, point 4.

1193 *See* Bernd Blobel. "Interoperable EHR Systems–Challenges, Standards and Solutions". In: *European Journal for Biomedical Informatics* 14.2 (2018), pp. 10–19.

1194 *See* the useful and official glossary at <ec.europa.eu/cefdigital/wiki/display/EHOPERATIONS/eHDSI+ Glossary>. Last accessed 06/10/2021.

"The ability of disparate and diverse organisations to interact towards mutually beneficial and agreed common goals, involving the sharing of information and knowledge between the organisations, through the business processes they support, by means of the exchange of data between their respective ICT systems".

So, as mentioned in Section 3.4.1, interoperability implies a variety of layers. The European Interoperability Framework (EIF) for public services made considerable efforts to promote each level[1195]. The first EC Recommendation on this topic was released in 2008, and was aimed at allowing the exchange and use of data collected in the national EHR between neighbouring and non-neighbouring Member States[1196]. The EC urged interoperability of EHRs at technical, semantic, organisational and legal levels, adding a political layer, which was leveraging investments and adapting policies[1197].

A possible cross-border and interoperable environment of EHR systems can be described as follows. Given a Member State of origin *Alpha* and a Member State of treatment *Beta*, the patient originally from *Alpha* seeks healthcare treatment in *Beta* when she is there on holiday[1198]. The patient summary of her EHR in *Alpha* – i.e. a structured part of the EHR – may be accessed by the healthcare professional in *Beta* to provide better clinical treatment. Other examples of data that interoperability may cover are prescriptions for medications or investigations, examination reports, clinic appointments, which are originally collected in the different national or regional records, but could be interoperable cross-border as well[1199]. In *Beta* the healthcare professional may use the local EHR to generate and collect the diagnosis. The two countries have contact points for the data

1195 *See* the projects and studies funded by the EU at <ec.europa.eu/digital-single-market/en/news/ ehealth-studies-overview>. Last accessed on 06/10/2021.

1196 *See* EC European Commission. *Recommendation of 2 July 2008 on cross-border interoperability of electronic health record systems*. European Commission. Brussels: COM (2008) 3282 final, 2008.

1197 *See* European Commission, *op. cit.*; Bincoletto, "Data protection issues in cross-border interoperability of Electronic Health Record systems within the European Union", p. 3.

1198 As mentioned in Section 3.3, Directive 2011/24/CE defines country of origin – country of residence or country that originally lawfully provides healthcare – and country of treatment.

1199 *See* Soceanu, "Managing the Interoperability and Privacy of e-Health Systems as an Interdisciplinary Challenge".

exchange with their respective data repositories[1200]. These points represent the national organisational nodes providing functionalities for the proper and bidirectional working of the network[1201] The following Figure 3.2 is a visualisation of the connections of the network[1202].

1200 As indicated in Section 3.3, Article 6 of the Directive 2011/24/CE allows the designation of one or more national contact points.

1201 The list of contact points is provided at <ec.europa.eu/health/sites/health/files/ cross_border_care/docs/ cbhc_ncp_en.pdf>. Last accessed 06/10/2021. For example, in Spain the contact point is the Ministry of Health and in the Netherlands it is the Netherlands NCP Cross-border Healthcare.

1202 Own graphic inspired by the case study by Network eHealth. *Guidelines on minimum/non-exhaustive patient summary dataset for electronic exchange in accordance with the cross-border Directive 2011/24/EU*. eHealth Network, 2013, p. 7.

*Figure 3.2 EHR interoperability concept overview*

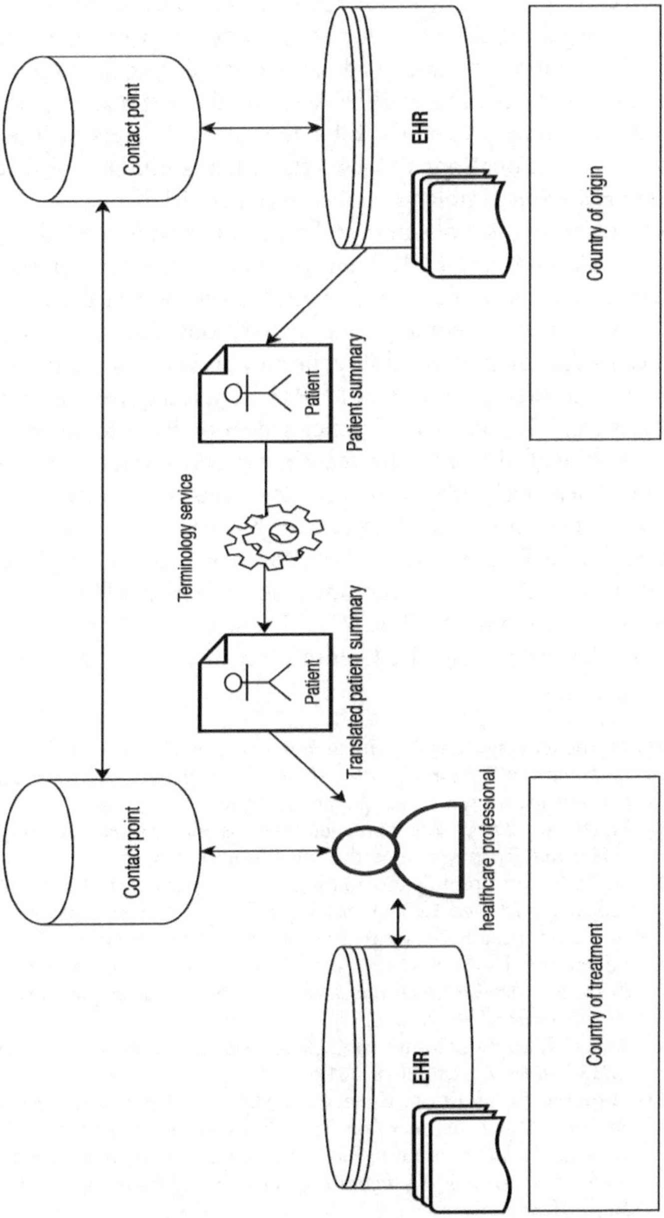

As explained in the previous section, Member States may have different specific rules for regulating EHRs. The legal framework is fragmented, but the general rules for data protection are provided by the GDPR. In 2014, before the GDPR, it was reported that only six Member States had provided legal requirements for cross-border exchange and that less than half of the Member States had implemented specific technical rules or standards to achieve this end[1203]. Actually, the vast majority of these countries did not have a framework for the different layers of interoperability and neither national nor EU law established a binding legal requirement in the EHR system implementation to achieve it[1204].

An online public consultation by the EC highlighted the very important need to support EHR interoperability with harmonised standards. In particular, the results of this consultation showed the need for "open exchange formats, common data aggregations and robust EU standards for health data quality, reliability, privacy and cybersecurity"[1205]. It should be clear that interoperability of EHRs does not require uniformity of technologies, and EU rules and policies do not have to impose it[1206], but the existence of different data repositories and several data formats across countries negatively affects cross-border access to personal health data and increases the costs of providing care for NHS[1207].

Actually, EHRs were mostly based on closed proprietary solutions; as a result, in the EU market interoperable and open EHR system solutions were not commonly delivered[1208]. Then, the EU Council called upon the Member States and the Commission to promote the use of interna-

---

1203 *See* the lengthy study by Milieu and Time.lex, *Overview of the national laws on electronic health records in the EU Member States and their interaction with the provision of cross-border eHealth services Report.*

1204 Bincoletto, "Data protection issues in cross-border interoperability of Electronic Health Record systems within the European Union", p. 3.

1205 *See* European Commission and Europe, *Synopsis Report. Consultation: Transformation Health and Care in the Digital Single Market.* The participants even agreed on the need for future EU legislation on these issues.

1206 Milieu and Time.lex, *Overview of the national laws on electronic health records in the EU Member States and their interaction with the provision of cross-border eHealth services Report.*

1207 *See* EC European Commission. *Road-map*. European Commission. Ref. Ares (2018) 5986687, 22.11.2018, 2018.

1208 European Commission, *Commission Staff Working document accompanying the document Communication from the Commission to the European Parliament, the Council, the European Economic and Social Committee and the Committee of the Regions on enabling the digital transformation of health and care in the Digital Single Market.*

tional and open standards and stressed the need to create common data structures, coding systems and terminologies to improve EHR interoperability[1209]. In order to achieve the different interoperability layers, some conditions may be put in place[1210]:

- a "thorough understanding of the operational environment" of the EHR;
- the identification of "interrelationships and needs" of all the stakeholders;
- the presence of recommendations for concretely "redesigning services and processes";
- supporting "policies for the implementation" of interoperable solutions;
- promoting incentives and availability of adequate resources, including finances and time.

Then, the European e-Health Digital Services Infrastructure (eHDSI) was created by the EC and by the eHealth Network for the cross-border exchange of patient summary and e-prescription tools[1211]. The eHDSI is pivotal for connecting the different EHR environments, and the national contact points[1212].

The EC's Recommendation 2019/243 of 6 February 2019 on a European Electronic Health Record exchange format represented a significant step towards EHR interoperability. In 2018, the European Commission proposed to define recommendations on how EHR systems could be accessed and shared more easily across Member States[1213]. The EC opened a public

---

1209 *See* Bincoletto, "Data protection issues in cross-border interoperability of Electronic Health Record systems within the European Union", p. 3 on Council of the European Union. *Council conclusions on Health in the Digital Society; making progress in data-driven innovation in the field of health*. Council of the European Union. 2017/C 440/05, 2017.

1210 *See* A. Kouroubalia and D. G. Katehakis. "The new European interoperability framework as a facilitator of digital transformation for citizen empowerment". In: *Journal of Biomedical Informatics* 94 (2019), p. 103166.

1211 As reported by the official website "eHealth Digital Service Infrastructure (eHDSI or eHealth DSI) is the initial deployment and operation of services for cross-border health data exchange under the Connecting Europe Facility". *See* <ec.europa.eu/cefdigital/wiki/display/EHOPERATIONS/eHealth+DSI+Operations+Home>. See also the description of the eHDSI Mission at <ec.europa.eu/cefdigital/wiki/display/EHOPERATIONS/ eHDSI+Mission>. Last accessed 06/10/2021.

1212 *See* also the commentary by Vergottini and Bottari, *La sanità elettronica*, p. 128.

1213 *See* European Commission, *Road-map*.

consultation which showed that EU standard formats for EHR systems would have made access to health data easier for patients, health professionals and other authorised parties using different records across the EU. After the feedback period, the EC released the final version of the Recommendation on EHRs[1214]. Recommendation 2019/243 is aimed at creating a European Electronic Health Record Format by defining the principles that the system should comply with for cross-border interoperability[1215]. The EC framework explicitly includes[1216]:

- the "principles that should govern the access and the exchange" of EHRs across borders;
- a set of "common technical specifications" in certain health information domains (i.e. the baseline for the Exchange Format);
- an organisational process to take forward the further elaboration of the Format.

In detail, this Recommendation establishes wide-ranging technical specifications for secure access to EHRs and their interoperability, and promotes best practices for ensuring data protection and integrity of personal health data. Various technical specifications are indicated as a baseline for future development[1217]. Following the EC words, Member States should ensure high standards in EHR systems for protecting personal health data, and should also secure EHR networks so as to avoid data breaches and minimise security risks[1218]. To this end, Regulation 910/2014 may provide the rules on the secure electronic identification means.

Moreover, Member States should use the digital tools provided by the eHDSI and take appropriate measures to support the use of interoperable EHR systems at policy and legal levels. It should be remembered that the e-Health Network collaborates with Member States to support their e-health policies[1219]. Therefore, the Network is involved in the governance

---

1214 *See* European Commission, *Commission Recommendation (EU) 2019/243 of 6 February 2019 on a European Electronic Health Record exchange format.*

1215 Bincoletto, "Data protection issues in cross-border interoperability of Electronic Health Record systems within the European Union", p. 3 on European Commission, *Commission Recommendation (EU) 2019/243 of 6 February 2019 on a European Electronic Health Record exchange format*.

1216 European Commission, *op. cit.*, p. 5.

1217 Bincoletto, "Data protection issues in cross-border interoperability of Electronic Health Record systems within the European Union", p. 4.

1218 *See* European Commission, *Commission Recommendation (EU) 2019/243 of 6 February 2019 on a European Electronic Health Record exchange format*, p. 5.

1219 *See* also all the relevant framework in Section 3.3.

processes outlined by the EC, which consist of so-called "national digital health networks". These networks should be set up by Member States by "involving representatives of the relevant competent national authorities and, where appropriate, regional authorities dealing with digital health matters and the interoperability of electronic health records, and security of networks and information systems, and the protection of personal data", including national DPAs[1220]. The rationale is fostering organisational and legal interoperability by governance solutions.

Additionally, the baseline for the European Electronic Health Record Exchange Format provides some interoperability specifications to represent and exchange personal health data in patient summaries, e-prescription and e-dispensation tools, laboratory results, medical imaging and reports and hospital discharge reports[1221]. It is worth noting that these systems collect data which are at the core of EHR systems[1222]. The Commission's Exchange Format will be further improved in the future through a joint coordination process, which will take into account the latest technological and methodological innovations, and will be jointly monitored by the EC and the e-Health Network[1223].

As regards the principles for data processing and data exchange across borders, they are set out in the Annex of the Recommendation[1224]. These principles focus on EHR technical and organisational aspects. It has been argued that "EU citizens should be able to access and securely share their electronic health data across borders, to choose to whom they provide

1220 The EC further specifies that "national digital health networks should involve the following: (a) the national representative of the eHealth Network; (b) national, or regional, authorities with clinical and technical competence for digital health matters; (c) supervisory authorities established under Article 51 of Regulation (EU) 2016/679; (d) competent authorities designated pursuant to Directive (EU) 2016/1148".

1221 *See* European Commission, *Commission Recommendation (EU) 2019/243 of 6 February 2019 on a European Electronic Health Record exchange format*, p. 6. The technical specifications will be indicated in Chapter 5 Section 5.5 on EHR standards.

1222 The Recommendation includes even e-prescription and e-dispensation, which are usually separate from the EHR, but can be connected to it in the same local or national network.

1223 *See* European Commission, *Commission Recommendation (EU) 2019/243 of 6 February 2019 on a European Electronic Health Record exchange format*, pp. 7–8.

1224 *See* EC European Commission. *Annex to the Commission Recommendation on a European Electronic Health Record exchange format.* European Commission. Brussels: COM (2019) 800 final, 2019, pp. 1–2.

access and the level of detail of the shared health information"[1225]. A high level of data protection shall be guaranteed. The principles can be listed as follows:

- "Citizen-centric by design", meaning that EHR systems should be implemented with DPbD and DPbDf principles so as to place the individual at the centre and comply with the GDPR;
- "Comprehensiveness and machine-readability", meaning that EHRs should be as comprehensive as possible to support an efficient healthcare service, and the data should be stored in machine-readable formats in order to enhance their reuse. Health data should be integrated in interoperable formats;
- "Data protection and confidentiality", meaning that EHRs should be implemented in full compliance with confidentiality rules and data protection law from design stage onward. Particular attention should be paid to transparency, the right to access, and the data subject's other rights;
- "Consent or other lawful basis", meaning that the presence of a legitimate legal basis for the data processing (e.g. a lawful exception) should be always verified;
- "Auditability", meaning that the EHR systems should implement auditing and logging mechanisms for registering and verifying any processing operation;
- "Security", meaning that appropriate technical and organisational measures should be implemented in order to secure EHR systems from security risk, such as "unauthorised or unlawful processing of health data" and "accidental loss, destruction or damage". The users of EHRs should be trained properly so as to be aware of the risks;
- "Identification and authentication", meaning that EHRs should use strong and secure access mechanisms (i.e. identification and authentication). The EC mentions national electronic identification schemes as defined in Regulation 910/2014 for ensuring secure access of citizens;
- "Continuity of service", meaning that the EHR exchange service is necessary to ensure the continuity and availability of care across borders.

Hence, it can be noted that these principles are consistent with the list of principles provided by the WP29 for a national or local EHR. The cross-border processing of data in EHRs requires similar safeguards, which should be adjusted to an even more connected scenario.

---

1225 Bincoletto, "Data protection issues in cross-border interoperability of Electronic Health Record systems within the European Union", p. 4.

Even though the Recommendation represents an important step for EHRs, some challenges should be noted here[1226]. In the present legal framework, it will be necessary to remove the residual legal and organisational barriers that exist at Member States' level and to efficiently sustain cooperation across countries[1227]. As indicated above, the EC will monitor the implementation of technical specifications. The responsibility of achieving technical progress remains upon the EHR environment at Member States' level, and therefore upon the market of EHR solutions. Looking at the concrete benefits of the detailed Recommendation, it may be suggested that an EU legislation will better harmonise the standards than the present soft-law approach. However, privacy and data protection concerns are significant.

The cross-border interoperability context increases data protection and security risks because systems are more interconnected than at a national or local level and the amount of personal health data rises, as well as the number of actors involved. Therefore, it is interesting to investigate this context in light of the GDPR by relating the concerns to the respective interoperability layer.

Firstly, legal interoperability requires consistency that avoids the creation and persistence of barriers between legislation of different legal frameworks[1228]. As discussed in this Chapter, the GDPR sets general and consistent requirements for processing of personal health data across the EU. Nonetheless, specific rules for data processing may be established by Member States with possible different regulatory approaches[1229]. Since EHR systems are managed by national or local healthcare providers, the fragmentation of the existing national frameworks may impinge on the legal interoperability layer. Thus, to ensure a "consistent and higher level of data protection"[1230], Member States should define clear interoperability

---

1226 The challenges were also reported *ibid.*

1227 The first electronic cross-border health service was provided by Luxembourg in 2019. *See* <www. esante.lu/portal/fr/espace-patient/questions-reponses,142,579.html?>. The other 22 countries are reported at <ec.europa.eu/health/ehealth/electronic_crossborder_healthservices_en>. Last accessed 06/10/2021.

1228 *See* European Commission, *New European Interoperability Framework, Promoting seamless services and data flows for European public administrations*.

1229 Bincoletto, "Data protection issues in cross-border interoperability of Electronic Health Record systems within the European Union", p. 5.

1230 *See* Recital 10 GDPR, which suggests an equivalent level of protection through a consistent and high level of protection and the removal of obstacles across Member States.

policies. Legal interoperability could be eased "by ensuring an aligned interpretation of the GDPR provisions and homogeneous applications of data protection principles in all Member States"[1231].

As explained above in Section 3.4.1, organisational interoperability concerns policies, business practices and procedures that should be coordinated to avoid barriers. In the cross-border interoperability context, a patient's data is first processed in a EHR system in a Member State *Alpha*, then it is exchanged and used in another Member State *Beta* for a new treatment or medical consultation. Where personal health data is merely disclosed by transmission from state *Alpha* to *Beta*, the provider in state *Beta* is merely a recipient[1232]. Instead, where in *Beta* the subject accesses the data, uses them, collects medical data of a treatment, and exchanges data in the EHR interoperability network, this subject is an independent data controller which performs processing operations. As a result, two or more data controllers and processors will process the patient's data. It may be argued that they are joint controllers. These controllers may not fall under the definition in Article 26 of the GDPR, since they are independent in the most common scenarios unless a more coordinated environment can be defined (e.g. joint teams for a medical treatment). It could be hypothesised that different Member States will provide rules on the arrangements of joint controllership.

So, all the subjects shall comply with the GDPR and are accountable separately, but as shown by the EC's list above, the implementation of data

---

1231 For this paragraph and the following one, *see* Bincoletto, "Data protection issues in cross-border interoperability of Electronic Health Record systems within the European Union", p. 5.

1232 As an example, in June 2020 in Malta the cross-border service for patient summary is available for Maltese citizens or residents who travel to Luxembourg, Portugal and Croatia. The privacy policy states that: "who processes and has access to this data? (recipients of personal data) Your Patient Summary data will be accessible only by authorised and identifiable health professionals involved in your treatment, under professional secrecy, in the country of treatment. Each country of treatment participating in the eHDSI system has undertaken to ensure that the participating health professionals and healthcare providers on their territory have adequate information and training about their duties. Details of the participating countries will be published on the eHDSI website. The Patient Summary data will be transferred through a secure technical gateway provided by the eHealth National Contact Point designated by each country. Malta's technical gateway is operated by the Government's IT agency and a private software services company, both of which are bound by strict data protection clauses in their contracts". *See* the privacy policy at <deputyprimeminister.gov.mt/en/imu/cbeh/Pages/Home.aspx>. Last accessed 06/10/2021.

protection principles respects the same safeguards. Thus, the stakeholders could share documentation on cross-border processing to demonstrate compliance. Actually, the contact points of Member States may use the tools of the eHealth Digital Service Infrastructure, as recommended by the EC. The same EC is directly involved in the eHDSI as an EU Institution since it maintains the network for the data exchange. When interoperability is enhanced with the eHDSI, the security of the transmission of personal health data is maintained by the private network that is developed by the EC[1233]. As a consequence, the GDPR applies to Member States, contact points and healthcare providers, whereas Regulation 2018/1725 applies to the EC. In Joint Opinion 1/2019 "on the processing of patients' data and the role of the European Commission within the eHealth Digital Service Infrastructure (eHDSI)", the EDPB and the EDPS jointly argued that the EC is the processor of eHDSI processing operations since it is involved in the development of technical measures[1234].

Beyond the allocation of responsibilities and roles, the presence of the legal basis for cross-border exchange should be investigated. The patient summary in the EHR system is created in one Member State at the local, regional or national level, then it is exchanged in the network thorough the contact points. So, a first legal basis can be identified in *Alpha* in accordance with the rules and conditions described in the previous section. The further processing abroad in *Beta* should be lawful, and so the legal ground should be legitimate as well. Cross-border exchange, access and use of the EHR (and its patient summary) should be possible only if the legal basis of the first Member State is still applicable or another ground applies in the concrete case. In 2014, no Member State required patient consent for cross-border access[1235]. The last EC Recommendation mentions the explicit consent of the citizen concerned or any other lawful

1233 Bincoletto, "Data protection issues in cross-border interoperability of Electronic Health Record systems within the European Union", p. 5

1234 *See* EDPB European Data Protection Board and EDPS European Data Protection Supervisor. *EDPB-EDPS Joint Opinion 1/2019 on the processing of patients' data and the role of the European Commission within the eHealth Digital Service Infrastructure (eHDSI)*. EDPB and EDPS Joint Opinion 1/2019, 2019. Indeed, the EC does not determine the purposes and means of processing, but implements technical measures as processor. Therefore, the EC shall specify its duties in a future "Implementing Act".

1235 *See* Milieu and Time.lex, *Overview of the national laws on electronic health records in the EU Member States and their interaction with the provision of cross-border eHealth services Report*.

basis pursuant to Articles 6 and 9 of the GDPR[1236], and some privacy policies now mention consent[1237]. Although it may not be possible to foresee the legitimate ground, it may be suggested that each Member State may provide a legislative basis for the data exchange in accordance with the "healthcare exception" of Article 9(2)(h) or, if necessary, with additional room to manoeuvre of Article 9(4) GDPR.

Moreover, the purpose limitation principle may be circumvented at the organisational level[1238]. Generally, where data in the EHR is collected for healthcare purposes only, no different use is lawful. The secondary use of personal health data for research or scientific purposes will be lawful in accordance with Article 89 of the GDPR. Therefore, a Member State law should provide explicit derogation. The first purpose in the state *Alpha* could even envisage EHR interoperability for medical treatments in the privacy policy. Even so, where the provider in the *Gamma* state is a mere recipient, meaning that personal health data is merely disclosed by transmission from state *Alpha* to *Gamma*, the further processing (i.e. consultation) should be restricted to the limits of the main treatment purpose or should be compatible with it[1239]. Instead, where in *Beta* the subject accesses the data, uses them, collects medical data of a treatment, and exchanges data in the EHR interoperability network, this subject is an independent data controller which performs processing operations. Then, the new controller in *Beta* will organise its own processing activities by determining the purposes, thus finding the specific legal ground and providing the information as prescribed by the GDPR. It has been claimed that the patient should have the opportunity to "opt-out of the data sharing and exchange"[1240].

Since the EC indicated that particular attention should be paid to transparency, data exchange processing should be performed in a transparent

---

1236 *See* European Commission, *Annex to the Commission Recommendation on a European Electronic Health Record exchange format*.

1237 The reference is made to Malta's policy. *See supra* note no.123, where it is specified that interoperability access is available with explicit consent only.

1238 *See* Bincoletto, "Data protection issues in cross-border interoperability of Electronic Health Record systems within the European Union", p. 6.

1239 The argument follows the definition of the purpose limitation principle of the GDPR.

1240 European Commission, *Communication from the Commission to the European Parliament, the Council, the European Economic and Social Committee and the Committee of the Regions on enabling the digital transformation of health and care in the Digital Single Market; empowering citizens and building a healthier society*.

manner. The data controllers in both *Alpha* and *Beta* should provide the patient with the relevant and complete information. Thus, it may be recommended that in *Beta* the information should be translated into the native language of the subject or be provided in another language which is well-known to him or her[1241].

Moreover, as discussed for the national EHR environment, it is arguable that a complete DPIA shall be carried out since the risk level is high, a record of the activities should be maintained, a DPO should be designated, and this subject should have knowledge of the data protection concerns on all the different interoperability layers. Thus, joint methodologies on DPIA and records at the EU level could support the stakeholders, who should cooperate with the national DPAs, which are all coordinated in the EDPB[1242]. The assessments may also be made publicly available.

In addition to the legal and organisational layers of cross-border processing, it is now necessary to focus on the data protection issues of the technical aspects emerging in this context[1243]. Cross-border exchange should follow and comply with the principles set out in the GDPR and in the Annex of the EC. Some of these principles are related to the technical development of the EHR, and others to necessary technical and organisational measures to be implemented in processing. Both sources mention storage limitation, confidentiality, security, DPbD and DPbDf. The EC adds comprehensiveness, machine-readability, identification and authentication, and auditability[1244].

As regards the storage of the EHR systems, personal health data collected and stored should be limited to what is "significant for the healthcare purpose" and for the comprehensiveness of the records during cross-border access and use. Even though minimising the amount of data might be complex and interfere with the management of care, it is unavoidable for preventing any misuse in the interoperability context. The data collected should be integrated in interoperable formats, but they should also be accurate and kept up-to-date in all EHR systems in order to support the efficiency of the healthcare service. These systems should be operative for "no longer than what is necessary", meaning that the time limitation on

1241 *See* Bincoletto, "Data protection issues in cross-border interoperability of Electronic Health Record systems within the European Union", p. 6.

1242 On these last considerations *see* also Bincoletto, *op. cit.*, p. 7.

1243 For the following considerations *see* Bincoletto, *op. cit.*

1244 *See* once again the European Commission, *Annex to the Commission Recommendation on a European Electronic Health Record exchange format*.

the repositories could be agreed among stakeholders, and it should be defined in the privacy policies[1245].

Another aspect in this context relates to access and confidentiality of the record. Firstly, the patient has the right to access the medical record in both *Alpha* and *Beta* in accordance with Directive 2011/24/CE and Article 15 of the GDPR. Actually, access is the main goal of the interoperability policy. As explained for the national EHR environment, the data subject also has the right to know who has accessed the EHR, the right to rectification, and to data portability[1246]. In some Member States, the patient may have the right to concealment, meaning that in *Beta* some data collected in *Alpha* may not be available to the next healthcare provider, and vice-versa. Thus, EHRs' interoperable systems should have the technical functions to execute all the patient's requests for the exercise of data protection rights[1247]. Secondly, in the interoperability context the access mechanisms of healthcare providers – meaning both the professionals and the administrative staff in the state of treatment – should be considered priorities, as shown in the list of principles of WP29. Hence, the access and exchange of data in EHRs should be secure and implemented in full compliance through access control strategies and policies, secure communication chan-

1245 Bincoletto, "Data protection issues in cross-border interoperability of Electronic Health Record systems within the European Union" has highlighted that the duration of EHRs archiving is strictly related to the relevance of the collected data and so, it depends on the circumstances. Following the previous example of Malta, the privacy policy states that "in the case of persons domiciled in Malta, the storage period of medical records in Malta is currently for the lifetime of the patient and ten years thereafter, while in the case of other patients, such as persons visiting from other countries, the storage period is ten years". *See supra* note no. 1232. Milieu and Time.lex, *Overview of the national laws on electronic health records in the EU Member States and their interaction with the provision of cross-border eHealth services Report*, p. 64, recommended that the timing should be identical across the EU.

1246 In some contexts where the tasks are carried out as a public interest by way of legislative measure, the right to data portability may not apply. It is interesting to report that in the Preliminary Opinion on the European Health Data Space the EDPS highlighted this limit of application. Despite that, the authority invited the Commission to specify the application of this right in the legislative proposal on EHDS. *See* European Data Protection Supervisor, *Preliminary Opinion 8/2020 on the European Health Data Space*, pp. 13–14.

1247 Bincoletto, "Data protection issues in cross-border interoperability of Electronic Health Record systems within the European Union", p. 6.

nels and high security standards in order to prevent any unauthorised access[1248].

Interoperable EHRs should then protect the data confidentiality and security of personal health data. Appropriate security measures should be implemented in both contact points, and their EHRs, to prevent data breaches and incidents[1249]. In addition to the security safeguards of the GDPR, as mentioned in Section 3.3, Directive 2016/1148 on security of network and information systems and its national transpositions apply. In particular, in Annex II of this Directive healthcare providers of the interoperability context are listed as operators of essential services which are subject to the requirements of the same Directive and to its national transpositions.

Other common security measures for an interoperable EHR system are auditing, logging of accesses, and back-up mechanisms[1250]. Using harmonised standards for the implementation may ease the compliance of this environment[1251]. Some technical specifications, standards and protocols based on the European Electronic Health Record Format have also been reported by the eHealth Network after the EC Recommendation[1252].

Finally, DPbD obligation must play a major role in the development of interoperable EHRs[1253]. It has been argued that cross-border data exchange should be "designed with data protection in mind too", meaning that "appropriate measures should be embedded in the network infrastructure

---

1248 *See ibid.*, which follows European Commission, *Annex to the Commission Recommendation on a European Electronic Health Record exchange format*.

1249 *See* e.g. Ed Conley and Matthias Pocs. "GDPR Compliance Challenges for Interoperable Health Information Exchanges (HIEs) and Trustworthy Research Environments (TREs)". In: *European Journal of Biomedical Informatics* 14.3 (2018), pp. 48–61.

1250 *See* Bincoletto, "Data protection issues in cross-border interoperability of Electronic Health Record systems within the European Union", p. 7.

1251 *See* Conley and Pocs, "GDPR Compliance Challenges for Interoperable Health Information Exchanges (HIEs) and Trustworthy Research Environments (TREs)"; Adeel Anjum et al. "An efficient privacy mechanism for electronic health records". In: *Computers & Security* 72 (2018), pp. 196–211.

1252 *See* Network eHealth. *eHealth Network Guidelines to EU Member States and the European Commission on an interoperable eco-system for digital health and investment programmes for a new/updated generation of digital infrastructure in Europe*. eHealth Network, 2019. The standards will be presented in Chapter 5 Section 5.5.

1253 *See* Conley and Pocs, "GDPR Compliance Challenges for Interoperable Health Information Exchanges (HIEs) and Trustworthy Research Environments (TREs)".

to secure the access and the data sharing"[1254]. Both the EHR systems and the EU standard formats in the country of origin and in the country of treatment should be designed to "effectively implement the various data protection principles, to guarantee the compliance with the law and to protect the rights of data subjects"[1255]. Open and extendable architecture with DPbD modelling and embedded risk analysis tools provides systematic protection for storage and for the interoperable exchange of personal health data[1256]. As argued in Chapter 2 Section 2.5.3, certification may be used to demonstrate compliance with DPbD and DPbDf obligations, and a one-size-fits-all solution is not available. However, the European EHR Exchange Format of the EC represents a baseline for any EHR implementation.

The implementation of the EC's Recommendation and of the measures outlined above may finally foster the interoperability of EHRs to empower cross-border access to healthcare. Within the EU legal framework, the absence of a uniform and specific legislation on EHRs, and their interoperability, may remain an obstacle for each interoperability layer since progress is the task of the Member States and, as a matter of fact, depends on an update of the state of the art of EHRs. Nonetheless, the EC highly recommended improving cross-border interoperability of EHRs in order to comply with data protection provisions. The GDPR lays down the main requirements that healthcare providers must comply with when using EHRs. Personal health data in EHR systems must also be protected *ex ante* by design and by default. EU policies, methodologies and standards could be a starting point towards productive interoperability.

Then, since the GDPR and its DPbD requirements are applicable in all Member States, a common EU strategy on DPbD for EHRs systems could enhance the "fair and compliant flow of personal health data across EU and therefore, of patients and products"[1257]. This strategy could also lead developers of EHRs to find "clearer and well-defined rules to be followed during systems design"[1258]. Hence, in Chapter 6 a set of guidelines will be presented. Before that, Chapter 5 deals with the technical aspects –

---

1254 Bincoletto, "Data protection issues in cross-border interoperability of Electronic Health Record systems within the European Union", p. 7.

1255 *Ibid.*

1256 *See* Abedjan et al., "Data science in healthcare: Benefits, challenges and opportunities".

1257 Bincoletto, "Data protection issues in cross-border interoperability of Electronic Health Record systems within the European Union", p. 7.

1258 *See* for these conclusive considerations *ibid.*

which defines DPbD methodologies, technologies, and standards to be used – and Chapter 4 will provide a comparative analysis with the US legal framework since it sets a specific privacy rule for the healthcare context and EHR systems that requires the implementation of security measures. Before concluding this Chapter on e-health and the case study, the next section follows the final considerations of the previous Chapter on the need to balance the right to data protection with other rights since in this context specific brief considerations may be added to that analysis.

### *3.5 Balancing the right to data protection against public health*

Privacy and data protection are relevant concerns, but at the same time there may be other competing interests at stake. They are not absolute rights. In the context of e-health, the two typical competing interests are on the one hand the right to privacy and data protection of a natural person, and on the other hand, the interest in public health and security. The right to data protection is reconcilable with public health, but safeguards shall be implemented. So, where the data protection right may be restricted to protect the general interest in public health, the least intrusive solutions shall always be preferred in accordance with the requirements of necessity and proportionality. It can be noted that collective health is not an absolute goal capable of legitimising any compression of the individual's rights and freedoms, but it is the "sum" of the protection of each individual's health[1259].

As mentioned, the EU has shared competence with the Member States in specific fields of common safety concerns in public health matters, but the Member State can define its own national health policy and organise healthcare provision, management of health services and allocation of resources[1260]. So, the way to obtain the right balance between competing

1259 *See* ISS Bioethics COVID-19 Working Group. *Data protection in COVID-19 emergency*. Rapporto ISS COVID-19 n. 42/2020, 2020, p. 6.

1260 *See* further on Ionescu-Dima, "Legal challenges regarding telemedicine services in the European Union", p. 109; Di Federico, "Access to Healthcare in the European Union: Are EU Patients (Effectively) Protected Against Discriminatory Practices?"; Kai P. Purnhagen et al. "More Competences than You Knew? The Web of Health Competence for European Union Action in Response to the COVID-19 Outbreak". In: *European Journal of Risk Regulation* (2020), pp. 1–10. Article 168(7) of the TFEU recognises these competences. According to Di Federico, the differences among Member States may create discrimination

interests relies on a concrete case-by-case analysis at the national level[1261]. Member States can set national laws as legal grounds for processing personal health data for substantial public interest, public health interests or medical research interests in accordance with Article 9(2)(g), (i), (j) GDPR, but appropriate and specific safeguards shall always be provided in order to protect the rights and freedoms of the data subjects.

The recent pandemic emergency of COVID-19[1262] has required prompt answers to Member States on how to strike the balance between the rights to privacy and data protection and the public interests of protecting individual or collective health[1263]. Digital technologies were developed to trace individuals, monitor their symptoms or record the contacts of infected people in order to control the movement of population or to enforce confinement measures[1264]. These activities fall under the definition of "processing" of personal data, and the technologies developed during

---

across the EU and impinge on patients' rights. It is of paramount importance to promote equality in healthcare.

1261 This consideration was made even before the GDPR with reference to the DPD, in Di Iorio and Carinci, "Privacy and health care information systems: where is the balance?", p. 87.

1262 The technical name of the infection is SARS-CoV-2. *See* Kristian G. Andersen et al. "The proximal origin of SARS-CoV-2". In: *Nature medicine* 26.4 (2020), pp. 450–452.

1263 *See* CoE Council of Europe. *Digital solutions to fight COVID-19. 2020 Data Protection Report*. Council of Europe. October 2020, 2020; Hannah van Kolfschooten and Anniek de Ruijter. "COVID-19 and privacy in the European Union: A legal perspective on contact tracing". In: *Contemporary Security Policy* (2020), pp. 1–14; Giovanni Comandé, Denise Amram, and Gianclaudio Malgieri. "The democracy of emergency at the time of the coronavirus: the virtues of privacy". In: *Opinio Juris in comparatione. preprint* 1 (2020), pp. 106–121; Oreste Pollicino. "Fighting Covid-19 and Protecting Privacy Under EU Law – A Proposal Looking at the Roots of European Constitutionalism". In: *blog-iacl-aidc.org* (2020). At a comparative level from different perspectives *see* also the Special issue of the journal Diritto Pubblico Comparato ed Europeo – online on "Covid-19 and its constitutional implications" at <www.dpceonline.it/index.php/dpceonline/issue/view/43>. Last accessed 06/10/2021.

1264 *See* the contact tracing solutions collected by the Data Protection Law & Covid-19 Observatory at <lsts.research.vub.be/en/contact-tracing-apps>. Last accessed 06/10/2021. Data Protection Law & Covid-19 Observatory is a collaborative monitoring platform which documented data protection law resources related to the emergency, including soft law and DPA opinions. *See* also the extraordinary measures at the international level described by Joseph A. Cannataci. *Preliminary evaluation of the privacy dimensions of the coronavirus disease (COVID-19) pandemic*. A/75/147. Special Rapporteur of the Human Rights Council on the right to privacy, 2020.

the emergency impact the right to privacy, the right to data protection of personal data, including personal health data, and other fundamental rights and freedoms, such as dignity, self-determination, democracy, non-discrimination, and freedom of movement.

However, this is not the first time in history. In the past, other serious threats to health required measures for tracing individuals[1265]. In 2020, within the GDPR's framework, Member States' measures were adopted on the basis of Article 9(2)(i) – (j), and Article 23[1266].

Health Threats Decision No 1082/2013/EU provided some definitions which can be still used during the COVID-19 outbreak[1267]. The term "contact tracing" referred to "measures implemented in order to trace persons who have been exposed to a source of a serious cross- border threat to health, and who are in danger of developing or have developed a disease". "Epidemiological surveillance" is processing which implies "the systematic collection, recording, analysis, interpretation and dissemination of data and analysis on communicable diseases and related special health issues". To prevent or control a serious threat to health, a "public health measure" mitigates its impact on public health by collecting a large quantity of personal health data. Any processing of personal data has its purpose,

---

1265 *See* Patrycja Dąbrowska-Kłosińska. "Tracing individuals under the EU regime on serious, cross-border health threats: An appraisal of the system of personal data protection". In: *European Journal of Risk Regulation* 8.4 (2017), pp. 700–722; Hannah van Kolfschooten. "EU Coordination of Serious Cross-Border Threats to Health: The Implications for Protection of Informed Consent in National Pandemic Policies". In: *European Journal of Risk Regulation* 10.4 (2019), pp. 635–651, which refers to Ebola; Greer et al., *Everything you always wanted to know about European Union health policies but were afraid to ask*.

1266 *See* the comparative analysis by Giorgio Resta. "La protezione dei dati personali nel diritto dell'emergenza Covid-19". In: *Giustiziacivile.com* (2020). *See* e.g. Dianora Poletti. "Il trattamento dei dati inerenti alla salute nell'epoca della pandemia: cronaca dell'emergenza". In: *Persona e Mercato* (2 2020), pp. 66–76, which focuses on the Italian situation. Some scholars in the UK even proposed a Bill on Corona-virus safeguards on the basis of the GDPR. *See* Lilian Edwards et al. "The Coronavirus (Safeguards) Bill 2020: Proposed protections for digital interventions and in relation to immunity certificates". In: *LawArXiv, pre-print* (2020). It is worth noting the Data Protection Law & Covid-19 Observatory's classification of law resources. DPAs' opinions are also collected by the IAPP portal at <iapp.org/resources/article/dpa-guidance-on-covid-19/>. It is also worth mentioning the research done by Privacy International organisation at <privacyinternational.org/examples/ tracking-global-response-covid-19>. Last accessed 06/10/2021.

1267 *See* Article 3 of the Decision No 1082/2013/EU.

which can be justified in an emergency health crisis, but it should always be designed to serve humankind[1268].

Therefore, the Joint Statement on Digital Contact Tracing issued by the Chair of the Committee of Convention 108 and the Data Protection Commissioner of the Council of Europe claimed that necessary data protection safeguards should be implemented when adopting extraordinary measures to protect public health[1269]. Indeed, several authorities and institutions described appropriate safeguards by creating lists of principles to comply with in the COVID-19 crisis[1270]. On this matter, the previous case law of the ECtHR and the CJEU in the proportionality and security field can also be applied[1271]. The ECtHR indicated that exceptional measures that limit fundamental rights shall be limited in time, be issued according to

---

1268 Recital 4 GDPR.

1269 *See* Alessandra Pierucci and Jean-Philippe Walter. *Joint Statement on Digital Contact Tracing*. Chair of the Committee of Convention 108 and Data Protection Commissioner of the Council of Europe. Strasbourg, 28 April 2020, 2020.

1270 *See* EDPB European Data Protection Board. *Guidelines 03/2020 on the processing of data concerning health for the purpose of scientific research in the context of the COVID-19 outbreak*. European Data Protection Board, 2020; EDPB European Data Protection Board. *Guidelines 04/2020 on the use of location data and contact tracing tools in the context of the COVID-19 outbreak*. EDPB. 21 April 2020, 2020; EC European Commission. *Communication for the Commission Guidance on Apps supporting the fight against COVID 19 pandemic in relation to data protection*. 2020/C 124 I/01), 2020; EC European Commission. *Commission Recommendation (EU) 2020/518 of 8 April 2020 on a common Union toolbox for the use of technology and data to combat and exit from the COVID-19 crisis, in particular concerning mobile applications and the use of anonymised mobility data*. L 114/7. 14 April 2020, 2020; Network eHealth. *Interoperability guidelines for approved contact tracing mobile applications in the EU*. eHealth Network. Brussels, Belgium, 13 May 2020, 2020; CNIL Commission Nationale de l'Informatique et des Libertés. *Deliberation N°. 2020–046 of April 24, 2020 delivering an opinion on a proposed mobile application called "StopCovid"*. CNIL, 2020; Committee on Bioethics (DH-BIO). *DH-BIO Statement on human rights considerations relevant to the COVID-19 pandemic*. DH-BIO/INF (2020) 2. 14 April 2020, 2020; Group, *Data protection in COVID-19 emergency*; Pierucci and Walter, *Joint Statement on Digital Contact Tracing*.

1271 *See* the interesting analysis by Kolfschooten and Ruijter, "COVID-19 and privacy in the European Union: A legal perspective on contact tracing", which studies the case law on proportionality and security threats to be applied to the Corona-virus outbreak.

1272 Carlo Casonato. "Health at the time of covid-19: tyrannical, denied, unequal health". In: *paper presented at the Conference Biolaw, Globalization and Pandemic. Challenges in the context of COVID-19* (2020), pp. 1–7, p. 2.

the rule of law with a democratic decision-making process, and respect the principle of proportionality after passing a rationality test[1272].

The following legal analysis will use the technical neutrality principle, by avoiding reference to a specific contact-tracing technology or warning method. It will refer to the necessary safeguards for processing personal health data in the emergency health situation that processes a large scale of data in order to protect public and individual health[1273].

First of all, data protection principles of Article 5 of the GDPR shall be guaranteed, but rights and duties can be carefully limited. So, the legal basis should be set by national law in accordance with the GDPR (i.e. lawfulness), and processing should be fair and transparent (i.e. fairness and transparency). The EC has specified that "relying on the law as the legal basis would contribute to legal certainty" since it provides the lawful details of the allowed processing, including the identity of the data controller (i.e. national public health authority)[1274], the processor, the recipients, the specific purpose, and all the safeguards[1275]. The processing settings and privacy policies shall be clear and transparent to data subjects. However, the policies should take into account any limitation to the rights and obligations[1276].

It has also been recommended that open source and open data concepts shall be applied in emergency processing, and the language of the policies

---

1273 According to Plutino, the EU has failed to have a unified approach, but has provided guidelines aimed at inspiring national policies. *See* Marco Plutino. "'Immuni'. Un'*exposure notification* app alla prova del bilanciamento tra tutela dei diritti e degli interessi pubblici". In: *MediaLaws Rivista di Diritto dei Media* 2 (2020), pp. 172–193, p. 176, which also focuses on the Italian tracking *Immuni*.

1274 The EDPB suggested that national public health authorities could be the data controllers, but other subjects and roles could be identified by law. *See* European Data Protection Board, *Guidelines 04/2020 on the use of location data and contact tracing tools in the context of the COVID-19 outbreak*, p. 7.

1275 *See* European Commission, *Communication for the Commission Guidance on Apps supporting the fight against COVID 19 pandemic in relation to data protection*. A pan-European approach coordinated at the EU level was recommended by the EC, but the Member States followed different lines of action. So, the present discussion will not refer to a specific legal framework.

1276 Since Article 23 allows a limitation to the rights and obligations established in Articles 12 to 22 and Article 34, some information usually contained in the policies may not be provided. Nevertheless, all the authorities recommended the need to ensure fair and transparent processing to respect the essence of the right to data protection and privacy.

shall be plain to enhance transparency[1277]. Transparency is also a frequent argument for the proportionality test in CJEU case law[1278]. The principle of fairness protects against unforeseeable negative effects, discrimination, and power imbalance[1279]. Thus, the safeguards should prevent stigmatisation while respecting confidentiality, and the measures should be "the least intrusive yet effective"[1280]. In fact, processing should be trustworthy, and the data subjects may choose whether or not to participate in the monitoring programmes voluntarily[1281].

Moreover, the processing of personal health data is allowed insofar as it only serves the purpose of controlling the pandemic crisis (i.e. purpose

1277 *See* point XI of Pierucci and Walter, *Joint Statement on Digital Contact Tracing*, p. 6; European Data Protection Board, *Guidelines 04/2020 on the use of location data and contact tracing tools in the context of the COVID-19 outbreak*, pp. 13–14.

1278 *See* e.g. *Digital Rights Ireland* of 2014: Judgement of the Court (Grand Chamber) of 8 April 2014. Digital Rights Ireland Ltd v. Minister for Communications, Marine and Natural Resources and Others and Kärntner Landesregierung and Others. Requests for a preliminary ruling from the High Court (Ireland) and the Verfassungsgerichtshof. Joined Cases C-293/12 and C-594/12. On this case *see* Kolfschooten and Ruijter, "COVID-19 and privacy in the European Union: A legal perspective on contact tracing", p. 9.

1279 *See* Chapter 2, Section 2.4.8.

1280 These sentences represent the first and second principles recommended in European Commission, *Commission Recommendation (EU) 2020/518 of 8 April 2020 on a common Union toolbox for the use of technology and data to combat and exit from the COVID-19 crisis, in particular concerning mobile applications and the use of anonymised mobility data*.

1281 *See* point II of Pierucci and Walter, *Joint Statement on Digital Contact Tracing*, p. 4. The voluntary basis has been frequently recommended for avoiding the creation of a widespread and problematic surveillance scenario. On health surveillance, and Orwell's risk *see* the special issue of Rivista n. 158 Formiche. *Orwell 2020. Il virus della sorveglianza*. Rubettino, 2020. ISBN: 9788849863314.

1282 The purpose limitation principle has been stressed by all the authorities. The EDPS pointed out that it is "an essential safeguard to provide individuals with the confidence that the data they provide will not be used against them in an unexpected manner". *See* European Data Protection Supervisor, *Opinion 3/2020 on the European strategy for data*, p. 5. The CoE specified that the purpose shall exclude further processing for commercial or law enforcement purposes. *See* Pierucci and Walter, *Joint Statement on Digital Contact Tracing*, pp. 4–5. On the same opinion *see* European Data Protection Board, *Guidelines 04/2020 on the use of location data and contact tracing tools in the context of the COVID-19 outbreak*, p. 7.

limitation)[1282], and is extraordinary and temporary[1283]. The temporary character is actually an argument to be used in the proportionality test in light of the goal of the measure. As a result, the timing of the data storage should be proactively pre-defined taking into account the medical relevance, so personal health data should be kept for no longer than is necessary (i.e. storage limitation)[1284]. Then, they shall be deleted, erased or anonymised when there is no longer a threat to public health[1285].

Data minimisation should govern all processing activities. Personal health data shall be reduced to the strictest minimum[1286]. As explained in the previous Chapter in Section 2.7, the assessment in the "necessity test" will take into account the extent of what is strictly necessary for pursuing the goal of the measure. Personal health data should be limited and, if need, pseudonymised, and then the requirements of DPbD and DPbDf, and the preventive risk assessment (i.e. DPIA) are pivotal and shall be central[1287]. The EC recommended that a list of the personal health data to

---

1283 *See* Kolfschooten and Ruijter, "COVID-19 and privacy in the European Union: A legal perspective on contact tracing", p. 6; Pierucci and Walter, *Joint Statement on Digital Contact Tracing*, p. 7.

1284 *See* European Commission, *Communication for the Commission Guidance on Apps supporting the fight against COVID 19 pandemic in relation to data protection*. In particular, *see* point 3.7. *See* also European Data Protection Board, *Guidelines 04/2020 on the use of location data and contact tracing tools in the context of the COVID-19 outbreak*, p. 8.

1285 It should be specified that the data will probably be anonymised for secondary medical research purposes since authorities have the rare opportunity to use a large amount of medical data on a disease. However, it is not clear whether the anonymised health data will be as useful as personal health data. Member States can provide the ground under Article 9(2)(j) GDPR and Article 89 GDPR. On the research field *see* European Data Protection Board, *Guidelines 03/2020 on the processing of data concerning health for the purpose of scientific research in the context of the COVID-19 outbreak*; Gianclaudio Malgieri. "Data Protection and Research: A vital challenge in the era of Covid-19 Pandemic". In: *Computer Law & Security Review* (2020); Amram, "Building up the "Accountable Ulysses" model. The impact of GDPR and national implementations, ethics, and health-data research: Comparative remarks"; Stuart McLennan, Leo Anthony Celi, and Alena Buyx. "COVID-19: Putting the General Data Protection Regulation to the Test". In: *JMIR Public Health and Surveillance* 6.2 (2020), e19279.

1286 *See* point V of Pierucci and Walter, *Joint Statement on Digital Contact Tracing*, p. 5.

1287 *See* European Data Protection Board, *Guidelines 04/2020 on the use of location data and contact tracing tools in the context of the COVID-19 outbreak*, p. 9. The authority highlighted the importance for the DPIA to be publicly available.

be collected should be defined in the legal basis[1288]. The risk to rights and freedoms shall be minimised *ex ante*[1289].

During the processing activities, personal health data should be kept up-to-date and processing should respect the accuracy principle[1290]. Personal health data shall be used adequately, and shall not be disseminated, but shared among involved actors while implementing organisational and technical measures[1291]. Thus, it has been claimed that processing should receive the approval of a national DPA[1292], use appropriate security measures (e.g. encryption, cryptographic techniques), and follow cybersecurity requirements in order to protect availability, integrity, and confidentiality of personal data[1293]. The authorities have drawn attention to the use of a completely automated decision that can affect individuals since data subjects have the right not to be subject to a decision based solely on that kind of processing activity[1294].

---

Joseph A. Cannataci, Special Rapporteur on the right to privacy for the United Nations, also stressed in his report the importance of the privacy by design approach. *See* Cannataci, *Preliminary evaluation of the privacy dimensions of the coronavirus disease (COVID-19) pandemic*, p. 15.

1288 *See* European Commission, *Communication for the Commission Guidance on Apps supporting the fight against COVID 19 pandemic in relation to data protection*.

1289 *See* point III of Pierucci and Walter, *Joint Statement on Digital Contact Tracing*, p. 4.

1290 According to the CoE, "as the implications may be serious (self-isolation, testing) for the individuals identified as potential contacts of someone infected, ensuring the quality and accuracy of data is crucial". *See* Pierucci and Walter, *op. cit.*, p. 5.

1291 *See* European Commission, *Communication for the Commission Guidance on Apps supporting the fight against COVID 19 pandemic in relation to data protection*. In particular, *see* point 3.5.

1292 In European Commission, *op. cit.*, the EC recommended the involvement of the DPA, but not a formal notification. However, the EC suggested a consultation.

1293 *See* European Commission, *Commission Recommendation (EU) 2020/518 of 8 April 2020 on a common Union toolbox for the use of technology and data to combat and exit from the COVID-19 crisis, in particular concerning mobile applications and the use of anonymised mobility data*; Pierucci and Walter, *Joint Statement on Digital Contact Tracing*; European Data Protection Board, *Guidelines 04/2020 on the use of location data and contact tracing tools in the context of the COVID-19 outbreak*.

1294 As anticipated *infra* in Section 3.3.3, this right usually applies in the healthcare context. *See* European Commission, *Communication for the Commission Guidance on Apps supporting the fight against COVID 19 pandemic in relation to data protection*; Pierucci and Walter, *Joint Statement on Digital Contact Tracing*, p. 5.

It should be noted that the final principle of accountability guarantees overall compliance with data protection rules[1295]. Oversight and audits may ensure the respect of these rules. Technologies may be interoperable, so safeguards shall be implemented even in the interoperability scenario[1296]. A more coordinated solution at the EU level would have been a great way of ensuring widespread protection and for better safeguarding democracy and freedoms.

Looking now to the use of EHRs in the COVID-19 situation, some brief considerations can be made. The use of EHRs is useful during a pandemic for connecting organisations and public entities and healthcare providers to check symptoms, monitor treatment outcomes, signal the diagnosis, and collect laboratory results on the tests. Hence, during the pandemic more data may be added to the personal health data collected in the individual's EHR before the health emergency.

Even telemedicine and telecare tools can be very useful in the health emergency since they support authorities "anytime" and "anywhere" during the healthcare provision while preserving safe distances among individuals. The benefit is more effective and widespread disease management than before[1297]. It is clear that this benefit is related both to people infected by Corona-virus and people with other pre-existing diseases who cannot go to hospital for multiple reasons (e.g. during general confinement measures).

Nevertheless, it can also be argued that the use of EHR systems or other e-health technologies in an exceptional processing for public health purposes must be carefully evaluated. EHRs potentially contain all the medical history of the data subject. Therefore, other processing operations that connect the EHR with different e-health technologies or ICTs should

---

The EDPB suggested that the algorithm should be auditable. It pointed out that false positives may occur to a certain degree, but where technically feasible a transparent explanation should be given. *See* European Data Protection Board, *Guidelines 04/2020 on the use of location data and contact tracing tools in the context of the COVID-19 outbreak*, p. 8.

1295 *See* point XIII of Pierucci and Walter, *Joint Statement on Digital Contact Tracing*, p. 4.

1296 *See* eHealth, *Interoperability guidelines for approved contact tracing mobile applications in the EU*.

1297 *See* e.g. Francesco Girardi et al. "Improving the Healthcare Effectiveness: The Possible Role of EHR, IoMT and Blockchain". In: *Electronics* 9.6 (2020), pp. 884–900, which analysed the importance of using digital instruments like the EHR or PHR in a health emergency, which can also be bolstered by the use of blockchain or IoT tools.

be prohibited or allowed insofar as restrictive and preventive technical and organisational measures are concretely implemented. The recipients of the personal health data should not be entitled to access all the data in the EHR[1298]. The stigmatisation and discrimination risk level is very high since the Corona-virus is inevitably bound with social exclusion of infected or potentially infected individuals. Even the interoperability policies on EHRs at the EU level should not be used as means for avoiding either the provision of safeguards or the general prohibition on the processing of personal health data[1299].

National laws should provide detailed rules for the use of an EHR in an exceptional processing whose purpose is not solely the provision of individual healthcare, but also the control of a threat to public health. These rules should take into account the DPbD and DPbDf principles, which embed the risk management approach and the need to balance concrete processing characteristics against rights and freedoms.

Protection and regulation by design were discussed in the Second Chapter, where PbD and DPbD were discussed in detail. The present Chapter investigated the e-health care sector and the specific case study for a DPbD implementation. PbD has been recognised as an international principle, and in US federal law there is a specific rule for the implementation of measures in the e-health care context and for EHRs. The protection of personal health data is a global issue, and the technologies are often implemented independently of the physical borders. Therefore, the following Chapter will conduct a comparative analysis between the US HIPAA Privacy Rule in the US legal framework and the DPbD obligation of the GDPR.

---

1298 A problematic scenario is for example access by the employer to the EHR for work purposes.

1299 On the cross-border exchange of data during the pandemic *see* the Commission Implementing Decision (EU) 2020/1023 of 15 July 2020 amending Implementing Decision (EU) 2019/1765 as regards the cross-border exchange of data between national contact tracing and warning mobile applications with regard to combatting the COVID-19 pandemic. C/2020/4934. O.J. L. 227I, 16.7.2020.

# Chapter 4 A comparative analysis with the US legal framework

## 4.1 *Introductory remarks*

This Chapter is dedicated to the comparative analysis with the US legal framework. Looking at this framework is of great help in understanding how technical and administrative measures for protecting personal data are implemented in the e-health context. The US system has specific rules in this sector on measures for protecting the informational privacy of patients. Since PbD has been recognised as an international legal concept for the proactive protection of personal data, and it is based on the principles of Fair Information Practices – which were first defined in the US – this investigation aims to compare Article 25 of the GDPR and the HIPAA Privacy and Security Rules, which establish the specific US requirements for healthcare, including the implementation of safeguards to digital medical records.

This comparative analysis is a "micro comparison" since it compares individual legal rules[1300]. This methodology of comparative research requires the definition of a problem and a general hypothesis, and the rules can be compared if they have the same functions[1301]. The comparison aims to re-

1300 *See* Zweigert and Kötz, *Introduzione al diritto comparato*.

1301 *See* Zweigert and Kötz, *op. cit.* On functionalism, including critical aspects, *see* Michaels, "The Functional Method of Comparative Law"; Kischel, *Comparative Law*, pp. 88–101; Valcke, *Comparing law: comparative law as reconstruction of collective commitments*, pp. 194–205; Francesca Bignami. "Formal versus Functional Method in Comparative Constitutional Law". In: *Osgoode Hall Law Journal* 53 (2 2016), pp. 442–471; Samuel, *An Introduction to Comparative Law Theory and Method*, pp. 65–78; Jaakko Husa. "Functional Method in Comparative Law–Much Ado About Nothing?" In: *European Property Law Journal* 2.1 (2013), pp. 4–21; Antonios E. Platsas. "The functional and the dysfunctional in the comparative method of law: some critical remarks". In: *Electronic Journal of Comparative Law* 12.3 (2008); Michele Graziadei. "The functionalist heritage". In: *Comparative Legal Studies: Traditions & Transitions*. Oxford University Press, 2019, pp. 100–127. ISBN: 9780511522260; Jaakko Husa. "Farewell to functionalism or methodological tolerance?" In: *Rabels Zeitschrift für ausländisches und internationales Privatrecht/The Rabel Journal of Comparative and International Private Law* H. 3 (2003), pp. 419–447.

search the similarities and differences and frame the different solutions in common perspectives[1302]. As pointed out by Michaels, "functional equivalence is similarity in difference; it is finding that institutions are similar in one regard (namely in one of the functions they fulfil) while they are (or at least may be) different in all other regards"[1303]. HIPAA is devoted to the protection of identifiable health information by the implementation of organisational and technical measures. DPbD is a more general rule, but it is applicable to personal health data and mandates the implementation of organisational and technical measures, too. Both rules are obligations for the subject who shall comply. The common problem is the need to better protect personal health data in a digital world through safeguards. It is also interesting to understand whether or not an EHR may be used in both EU and US legal frameworks. The preliminary answer is no.

The Chapter begins with a brief overview of information privacy law in the US and privacy principles in US federal law. The goal is to investigate the similarities and differences with the data protection principles of the GDPR in the light of a PbD or DPbD implementation. Then, the Chapter focuses on US health privacy law and the central HIPAA Privacy and Security Rules. Finally, a comparison between DPbD and HIPAA is provided.

### 4.2 *Overview of informational privacy in the US and the FIPS*

As noted above, in the US the term "privacy" refers both to the protection of private and family life, i.e. privacy in the EU sense, and the protection of personally identifiable information (PII).

Actually, in US the right to privacy entails different conceptions[1304]: the *right to be let alone*, which was first defined by Warren and Brandeis[1305];

1302 *See* Zweigert and Kötz, *Introduzione al diritto comparato*, p. 49. On the history of legal comparison *see* Pier Giuseppe Monateri. "Il diritto comparato tra disciplina critica, scienza normale e ingegneria politica". In: *Comparare. Una riflessione tra le discipline*. Mimesis Edizioni, 2020, pp. 205–224. ISBN: 9788857567310.

1303 Michaels, "The Functional Method of Comparative Law", p. 371.

1304 *See* the prominent classification by Solove, "Conceptualizing privacy".

1305 In 1890, Warren and Brandeis adopted the expression "right to be let alone" that was firstly used by Judge Cooley in the book *Law of torts*. *See* Thomas M. Cooley. *Law of Torts*. Callaghan & Company, 1888. They interpreted the common law principle of an "inviolate personality" which protected personal writings and productions against publication in any form by invoking the protection of the privacy of an individual from any invasion carried out by

*limited access to the self*, i.e. the ability to shield oneself from unwanted access by others[1306]; *secrecy*, i.e. the concealment of certain matters from others[1307]; *control over personal information*, i.e. informational privacy[1308]; *person-hood*, i.e. the protection of one's personality, individuality, and dignity[1309]; and *intimacy*, i.e. the control over, or limited access to, one's intimate relationships or aspects of life[1310].

Historically, four US "invasion of privacy" torts protect the right to privacy in US common law: intrusion, disclosure of private facts, false light, and appropriation of name or likeness[1311]. Four different kinds of invasion correspond to four distinct privacy interests of a plaintiff[1312]:

---

the press during the new technological development (e.g. yellow journalism and the Kodak camera), unless one of the legitimate exceptions applied (i.e. consent to the publication, the presence of a public or general interest, and in the case of privileged communication under law of slander and libel). The limitations are described in Warren and Brandeis, "Right to privacy", pp. 214–218. *See* also Chapter 2, Section 2.2.

1306 As Solove pointed out in Solove, "Conceptualizing privacy", pp. 1102–1105, the conception of "limited access" is advanced by several theorists. Among them, Gavison defined limited access as the interaction between secrecy, anonymity, and solitude.

1307 This conception has been developed by the case law on the constitutional right to privacy. *See amplius infra*.

1308 *See infra* the analysis of US informational law.

1309 This conception of privacy has been used by the US Supreme Court. In *Union Pacific Railway Co. v. Botsford*, 141 U.S. 250 (1891), the US Supreme Court ruled that "no right is held more sacred, or is more carefully guarded by the common law, than the right of every individual to the possession and control of his own person, free from all restraint or interference of others, unless by clear and unquestionable authority of law". In *Planned Parenthood v. Casey*, 505 U.S. 833 (1992), the Supreme Court held that "because abortion involves the purposeful termination of potential life, the abortion decision must be recognized as sui generis, different in kind from the rights protected in the earlier cases under the rubric of personal or family privacy and autonomy".

1310 The conception of intimacy goes beyond autonomy and refers to the dimension of a private and close relationship among individuals. *See* Solove, "Conceptualizing privacy", pp. 1121–1124.

1311 The first categorisation of the four torts was provided by William Prosser. "Privacy". In: *Cal. L. Rev.* (48 1960), p. 383. *See* also Daniel J. Solove and Paul M. Schwartz. *Privacy, information, and technology*. Wolters Kluwer Law & Business, 2009. ISBN: 9780735579101, p. 26; Daniel J. Solove and Paul M. Schwartz. *Privacy Law Fundamentals*. International Association of Privacy Professionals, 2019. ISBN: 9781948771252, pp. 17–22, 28–29.

1312 *See* Restatement (Second) of Torts § 652B, 652D, 652E, 652C (1977). *See* also Schachter, *Informational and decisional privacy*, pp. 58–76.

1. Intrusion upon seclusion or solitude, or into the plaintiff's private affairs, meaning someone has intentionally transgressed the plaintiff's right to seclusion by physical trespass or otherwise and this intrusion is highly offensive to a reasonable person. As an example, in *Hamberger v. Eastman* 206 A. 2d 239 (1964) the court applied tort of intrusion for the installation of a secret recording device by the landlord/defendant in the bedroom of a couple/plaintiff;
2. Public disclosure of embarrassing private facts, meaning someone has published or made available facts that are not newsworthy or legitimate matters of public interest and this disclosure is highly offensive to a reasonable person. As an example, in *Barber v. Time, Inc.*, 159 S.W.2d 291 (Mo. 1942) the court held that publishing an article with a picture of a woman, who was in hospital for a particular physical ailment and was not a public figure, was a violation of her right to privacy;
3. Publicity which places the plaintiff in a false light in the public eye, meaning someone has given publicity to the plaintiff's matters that is highly offensive to a reasonable person and in disregard of the falsity of this matter. For instance, when a photograph is published out of context, the person portrayed can give rise to a false light action. In *Wood v. Hustler Magazine, Inc.*, 736 F.2d 1084 (1984) a stolen nude photograph of the plaintiff was published in a pornographic magazine without checking that the consent form was valid;
4. Appropriation of the plaintiff's name or likeliness for personal advantage, meaning someone has appropriated the plaintiff's name or likeness for their own use or benefits. As an example, the violation of the right of publicity was found in *Carson v. Here's Johnny Portable Toilets, Inc.*, 698 F.2d 831 (6th Cir. 1983) where a corporation used the famous catchphrase "here's Johnny" of the star of "The Tonight Show" on portable toilets without consent.

The US Constitution does not mention the right to privacy. Thus, privacy does not appear as a constitutional and fundamental right[1313]. Nonetheless, courts protect this individual right against coercion, violence or threats by their judicial interpretation of certain provisions of the Bill of Rights. In particular, US privacy has evolved from the interpretation

1313 *See* for a comparison with the EU Richards and Hartzog, "Privacy's Constitutional Moment", pp. 45–46.

of the First, Fourth, Fifth, Ninth and Fourteenth Amendments of the Constitution[1314].

---

1314 Amendment I: "Congress shall make no law respecting an establishment of religion, or prohibiting the free exercise thereof; or abridging the freedom of speech, or of the press; or the right of the people peaceably to assemble, and to petition the Government for a redress of grievances". Amendment IV: "The right of the people to be secure in their persons, houses, papers, and effects, against unreasonable searches and seizures, shall not be violated, and no Warrants shall issue, but upon probable cause, supported by Oath or affirmation, and particularly describing the place to be searched, and the persons or things to be seized". Amendment V: "No person shall be held to answer for a capital, or otherwise infamous crime, unless on a presentment or indictment of a Grand Jury, except in cases arising in the land or naval forces, or in the Militia, when in actual service in time of War or public danger; nor shall any person be subject for the same offence to be twice put in jeopardy of life or limb; nor shall be compelled in any criminal case to be a witness against himself, nor be deprived of life, liberty, or property, without due process of law; nor shall private property be taken for public use, without just compensation". Amendment IX: "The enumeration in the Constitution, of certain rights, shall not be construed to deny or disparage others retained by the people". Amendment XIV: "Section 1. All persons born or naturalized in the United States, and subject to the jurisdiction thereof, are citizens of the United States and of the State wherein they reside. No State shall make or enforce any law which shall abridge the privileges or immunities of citizens of the United States; nor shall any State deprive any person of life, liberty, or property, without due process of law; nor deny to any person within its jurisdiction the equal protection of the laws. Section 2. Representatives shall be apportioned among the several States according to their respective numbers, counting the whole number of persons in each State, excluding Indians not taxed. But when the right to vote at any election for the choice of electors for President and Vice President of the United States, Representatives in Congress, the Executive and Judicial officers of a State, or the members of the Legislature thereof, is denied to any of the male inhabitants of such State, being twenty-one years of age, and citizens of the United States, or in any way abridged, except for participation in rebellion, or other crime, the basis of representation therein shall be reduced in the proportion which the number of such male citizens shall bear to the whole number of male citizens twenty-one years of age in such State. Section 3. No person shall be a Senator or Representative in Congress, or elector of President and Vice President, or hold any office, civil or military, under the United States, or under any State, who, having previously taken an oath, as a member of Congress, or as an officer of the United States, or as a member of any State legislature, or as an executive or judicial officer of any State, to support the Constitution of the United States, shall have engaged in insurrection or rebellion against the same, or given aid or comfort to the enemies thereof. But Congress may by a vote of two-thirds of each House, remove such disability. Section 4. The validity of the public debt of the United

So, despite the absence of an explicit reference in the Constitution, in the US there is a judicial recognition of a constitutional right to privacy in personal affairs[1315]. In the leading case *Grisworls v. Connecticut* 381 U.S. 479 (1965), the Court held that the Bill of Rights has "penumbras" where the right to privacy can be guaranteed[1316]. As an example, the constitutionally based interest in avoiding disclosure of private facts was held in *Whalen v. Roe* 429 U.S. 589 (1977), where the Supreme Court recognised a "threat to

States, authorized by law, including debts incurred for payment of pensions and bounties for services in suppressing insurrection or rebellion, shall not be questioned. But neither the United States nor any State shall assume or pay any debt or obligation incurred in aid of insurrection or rebellion against the United States, or any claim for the loss or emancipation of any slave; but all such debts, obligations and claims shall be held illegal and void. Section 5. The Congress shall have power to enforce, by appropriate legislation, the provisions of this article". For all the Amendments *see* the website of the US Senate at <senate.org>.

1315 *See* Daniel J. Solove and Paul M. Schwartz. *Information privacy law*. Wolters Kluwer Law & Business, 2011. ISBN: 9780735510401, pp. 247–313.

1316 The "constitutional penumbral theory" was explicitly set by *Grisworls v. Connecticut*, but in Justice Holmes' dissenting opinion of *Olmstead v. United States* 277 U.S. 438 (1928) the judge anticipated that "I am not prepared to say that the penumbra of the Fourth and Fifth Amendments covers the defendant". The prominent dissenting opinion of Judge Brandeis states: "The protection guaranteed by the Amendments is much broader in scope. The makers of our Constitution undertook to secure conditions favorable to the pursuit of happiness. They recognized the significance of man's spiritual nature, of his feelings, and of his intellect. They knew that only a part of the pain, pleasure and satisfactions of life are to be found in material things. They sought to protect Americans in their beliefs, their thoughts, their emotions and their sensations. They conferred, as against the Government, the right to be let alone – the most comprehensive of rights, and the right most valued by civilized men. To protect that right, every unjustifiable intrusion by the Government upon the privacy of the individual, whatever the means employed, must be deemed a violation of the Fourth Amendment. And the use, as evidence in a criminal proceeding, of facts ascertained by such intrusion must be deemed a violation of the Fifth. Applying to the Fourth and Fifth Amendments the established rule of construction, the defendants' objections to the evidence obtained by wiretapping must, in my opinion, be sustained. It is, of course, immaterial where the physical connection with the telephone wires leading into the defendants' premises was made. And it is also immaterial that the intrusion was in aid of law enforcement. Experience should teach us to be most on our guard to protect liberty when the Government's purposes are beneficent. Men born to freedom are naturally alert to repel invasion of their liberty by evil-minded rulers. The greatest dangers to liberty lurk in insidious encroachment by men of zeal, well meaning but without understanding".

privacy implicit in the accumulation of vast amounts of personal information in computerized data banks or other massive government files" and ruled a duty to avoid disclosure which "has its roots in the Constitution". *Whalen v. Roe* is a leading case since the Court recognised both decisional privacy and informational privacy while evaluating the validity of the New York State statute on computerisation of schedules of prescription drugs.

Additionally, courts employ a flexible test by balancing the invasion of an individual's privacy against government or public interest (e.g. in searching and punishing crimes), and applying the concept of "reasonable expectation of privacy"[1317]. This concept is based on the Fourth Amendment, which protects against government searches and seizures. In the concurring opinion of *Katz v. United States* 389 U.S. 347 (1967) Justice Harlan analysed the case law and the Fourth Amendment, and stated:

> "My understanding of the rule that has emerged from prior decisions is that there is a twofold requirement, first that a person have exhibited an actual (subjective) expectation of privacy and, second, that the expectation be one that society is prepared to recognize as 'reasonable'. Thus a man's home is, for most purposes, a place where he expects privacy, but objects, activities, or statements that he exposes to the 'plain view' of outsiders are not 'protected' because no intention to keep them to himself has been exhibited".

The "reasonable expectation of privacy" test is adopted by courts to solve privacy issues and balance competing interests[1318].

Informational or information privacy law in the US involves the rules that protect personal information[1319]. The concept of "personally identi-

---

1317 On this test *see* the leading cases of *Olmstead v. United States* 277 U.S. 438 (1928) (with Brandeis' dissenting opinion); *Katz v. United States* 389 U.S. 347 (1967) (interpreting the Fourth Amendment against unreasonable searches and seizures by the police); *California v. Greenwood* 486 U.S. 35 (1988); *Kyllo v. United States* 533 U.S. 27 (2001) (interpreting the Fourth Amendment against the use of a thermal-imaging device at a private home).

1318 *See ex multis* Daniel J. Solove. "Fourth amendment pragmatism". In: *BCL Rev.* 51 (2010), pp. 1511–1538; Richard A Epstein. "Privacy and the Third Hand: Lessons from the Common Law of Reasonable Expectations". In: *Berkeley Tech. LJ* 24 (2009), pp. 1199–1227; Peter Winn. "Katz and the origins of the reasonable expectation of privacy test". In: *McGeorge L. Rev.* 40 (2009), pp. 1–12; Richard A. Posner. "The uncertain protection of privacy by the Supreme Court". In: *The Supreme Court Review* 1979 (1979), pp. 173–216.

1319 On US informational privacy *see* Westin, *Privacy and Freedom*; Richard A. Posner. "The right of privacy". In: *Ga. L. Rev.* 12 (1977), pp. 393–422; Anita

fiable information" (PII) is not uniformly defined in this legal system, whereas personal data in the EU has a single definition which refers to any information relating to an identified or identifiable person[1320]. It has been pointed out that PII is largely limited to identified information, which is narrower than the EU concept[1321]. Therefore, when the term "information" is used in this book, it will refer to information that directly identifies the individual. However, as will be explained, the notion of identifiable health information is more similar to the EU definition of personal health data than to the concept of PII since it also may embed indirectly identifying information on health.

Informational privacy law is fragmented, and it is a "hodgepodge of various constitutional protections, federal and state statutes, torts, regulatory rules, and treaties"[1322]. Data controllers frequently rely on self-regulations on specific subject matters in defined commercial fields, and they are

---

L Allen. "Coercing privacy". In: *Wm. & Mary L. Rev.* 40 (1998), pp. 723–757; Julie E Cohen. "Examined lives: Informational privacy and the subject as object". In: *Stan. L. Rev.* 52 (1999), pp. 1373–1437; Paul M Schwartz. "Privacy and democracy in cyberspace". In: *Vand. L. Rev.* 52 (1999), pp. 1607–1701; Rotenberg, "Fair information practices and the architecture of privacy (What Larry doesn't get)"; Solove, "Conceptualizing privacy"; Richard C. Turkington and Anita L. Allen. *Privacy Law: cases and materials*. West Group, 2002; Schachter, *Informational and decisional privacy*; Will Thomas DeVries. "Protecting privacy in the digital age". In: *Berkeley Tech. LJ* 18 (2003), pp. 283–311; Daniel J. Solove. "A taxonomy of privacy". In: *U. Pa. L. Rev.* 154 (2005), pp. 477–560; Bamberger and Mulligan, "Privacy on the Books and on the Ground"; Richards and Hartzog, "Taking trust seriously in privacy law"; Anglim, Kirtley, and Nobahar, *Privacy Rights in the Digital Age*; Giovanella, *Copyright and Information Privacy: Conflicting Rights in Balance*, pp. 153–165; Solove and Schwartz, *Information privacy law*; Stephen P. Mulligan, Wilson C. Freeman, and Linebaugh Chris D. *Data Protection Law: An Overview*. Congressional Research Service R45631, 2019; Richards and Hartzog, "Privacy's Constitutional Moment"; Solove and Schwartz, *Privacy Law Fundamentals*.

1320 *See* Schwartz and Solove, "Reconciling personal information in the United States and European Union"; Mark Burdon. *Digital Data Collection and Information Privacy Law*. Cambridge Intellectual Property and Information Law. Cambridge University Press, 2020. ISBN: 9781108283717, pp. 155–170.

1321 *See* Schwartz and Solove, "Reconciling personal information in the United States and European Union", p. 891. The authors claimed that the US definition is too reductionist, whereas the European one is too broad. Therefore, they proposed the new concept of PII 2.0 by differentiating the protection of identifiable and identified information on a harm-based approach.

1322 Solove and Hartzog, "The FTC and the new common law of privacy", p. 587.

self-responsible for complying with them[1323]. Thus, in the US the rules for protecting PII are diffuse and there is not a uniform and omnibus act like the GDPR[1324]. The US approach is mainly sectoral[1325]. The legislator intervenes only on a narrowly targeted basis, when it is necessary[1326]. Even the so-called Privacy Act of 1974 was limited to a specific subject matter, i.e. the information used and disseminated by the federal agencies[1327]. The rationale of this legislative technique is the need to respond promptly to both scandals and regulatory vacuums caused by technological progress and evolution[1328]. So, the statutes are more granular and tailored to a specific field than in a one-size-fits-all regulation[1329].

Additionally, as previously mentioned, the US does not have a national data protection authority, but the FTC case plays a prominent and influential role, since the authority has a mandate on consumer protection under Section 5 of the FTC Act against unfair and deceptive commer-

1323 *See* Klitou, *Privacy-invading technologies and privacy by design. Safeguarding Privacy, Liberty and Security in the 21st Century*, p. 42.

1324 *See* Klitou, *op. cit.*, p. 41.

1325 *See* Kerstin N. Vokinger, Daniel J. Stekhoven, and Michael Krauthammer. "Lost in Anonymization – A Data Anonymization Reference Classification Merging Legal and Technical Considerations". In: *The Journal of Law, Medicine & Ethics* 48.1 (2020), pp. 142–148, pp. 143–144; Feldman and Haber, "Measuring and protecting privacy in the always-on era", p. 201. Conversely, the EU approach is omnibus.

1326 *See* Klitou, *Privacy-invading technologies and privacy by design. Safeguarding Privacy, Liberty and Security in the 21st Century*, p. 40.

1327 Privacy Act of 1974, 88 Stat. 1896. On the Privacy Act *see* Solove and Schwartz, *Information privacy law*, pp. 701–727.

1328 *See* Ugo Pagallo. *La tutela della privacy negli Stati Uniti d'America e in Europa: modelli giuridici a confronto*. Giuffrè Editore, 2008. ISBN: 8814142696, p. 61, which provides several examples of acts responding to scandals (e.g. Watergate and Privacy Act) and progress (e.g. Electronic Communications Privacy Act of 1986).

1329 *See* Michael L. Rustad and Thomas H. Koenig. "Towards a global data privacy standard". In: *Fla. L. Rev.* 71 (2019), pp. 365–453, p. 381.

1330 On the authority of the FTC *see* Solove and Hartzog, "The FTC and the new common law of privacy", p. 587; Kenneth A. Bamberger and Deirdre K. Mulligan. *Privacy on the ground: driving corporate behavior in the United States and Europe*. MIT Press, 2015. ISBN: 9780262029988, p. 48; Rustad and Koenig, "Towards a global data privacy standard", pp. 383–384; Vokinger, Stekhoven, and Krauthammer, "Lost in Anonymization – A Data Anonymization Reference Classification Merging Legal and Technical Considerations", pp. 144–145. *See* also Evan Selinger, Jules Polonetsky, and Omer Tene. *The Cambridge Handbook of Consumer Privacy*. Cambridge University Press, 2018. ISBN: 9781316831960.

cial practices[1330]. This authority recommends the PbD approach[1331] and promotes respect of the FIPs in business practices[1332]. As a result, the protection of the right to privacy has been connected to the promotion of consumer trust, and its regulatory development became consumer-oriented[1333]. In fact, the California Consumer Privacy Act (CCPA) of 2018 protects California consumers' privacy[1334].

In order to apply the PbD principle in the US system, it is necessary to investigate the informational privacy principles which apply there. Given the fragmented framework, there is not a single list of general principles for the processing of information.

Generally, in the US the processing of PII does not require a legal ground since this legal concept is neither used in the legislation nor developed by the literature. The free flow of information is highly promoted by the courts and the law regulates activities when they may cause harm to individuals[1335]. This is a crucial difference with the EU legal framework, where the grounds are defined in a closed list and lawfulness is the first data protection principle. In the US, the system focuses instead on a procedural notification mechanism called "notice-and-consent" or "notice-and-choice", where consent may be either an opt-in tool for allowing the use or disclosure of information or an opt-out one and the notice provides

---

1331 *See* Chapter 2, Section 2.2.

1332 An annual report of the FTC collects its enforcement activity on privacy. *See* the document from 2019 at <www.ftc.gov/system/files/documents/reports/privacy-data-security-update-2019/2019-privacy-data-security-report-508.pdf>. Last accessed 06/10/2021.

1333 *See* the interesting analysis connected to the timing of privacy institutionalisation in Bamberger and Mulligan, *Privacy on the ground: driving corporate behavior in the United States and Europe*, pp. 185–186. *See* also Jules Polonetsky, Omer Tene, and Evan Selinger. "Consumer Privacy and the Future of Society". In: *The Cambridge Handbook of Consumer Privacy*. Cambridge University Press, 2018, pp. 1–21. ISBN: 9781316831960.

1334 The Act is included in California Civil Code sections 1798.100 *et seq.* It took effect in 2020. *See* <oag.ca.gov/privacy/ccpa>. Last accessed 06/10/2021. On CCPA *see* Eric Goldman. "An Introduction to the California Consumer Privacy Act (CCPA)". In: *Santa Clara Univ. Legal Studies Research Paper* (2020). *SSRN*: *<papers.ssrn.com/sol3/papers.cfm?abstract_id=3211013&download=yes>*; Nicholas F. Palmieri III. "Who Should Regulate Data: An Analysis of the California Consumer Privacy Act and Its Effects on Nationwide Data Protection Laws". In: *Hastings Sci. & Tech. LJ* 11 (2020), pp. 37–60.

1335 *See* Daniel J. Solove and Paul M. Schwartz. "ALI Data Privacy: Overview and Black Letter Text". In: *UCLA Law Review* 68 (2020), p. 21.

the information on the processing[1336]. The notice element is the common feature of this legal system. In addition, the system usually provides for exceptions to the authorisation/choice requirement.

Traditionally, informational privacy does not specify either the minimisation principle or the purpose specification requirement[1337]. However, in the healthcare context the data minimisation and purpose limitation principles have more importance[1338]. In summary, informational privacy requires not engaging in unfair or deceptive practices, not causing harm to consumers, and following the "notice-and-choice" paradigm[1339].

In this context, the Code of Fair Information Practice provided the principles for the processing of information in automated data systems at the federal level in 1973[1340]. FIPs are the practises which address how personal information should be collected, used, retained, managed, and deleted[1341]. The basic information privacy principles played and continue to play a significant role[1342]. The FIPs provide a starting point for different legal frameworks: they embed "a common language of privacy across countries"[1343]. Several sets of principles can be reconnected under the same term of FIPs, since this common ground is highly flexible.

Following the FIPs of 1973[1344] and using the current legal terms, processing of personal information should not be secret, and the individual should be able to know what information is collected and used by the controller (i.e. notice principle). The same individual should have the right to prevent the use of the information for a different purpose from the one

1336 *See* Burdon, *Digital Data Collection and Information Privacy Law*, p. 142.

1337 *See* Burdon, *op. cit.*, p. 174.

1338 *See* the following Section 4.3.

1339 Richards and Hartzog, "Privacy's Constitutional Moment", p. 19.

1340 On the FIPs *see supra* Chapter 2 Section 2.2.

1341 Anglim, Kirtley, and Nobahar, *Privacy Rights in the Digital Age*, p. 196.

1342 *See* Solove and Schwartz, *Information privacy law*, p. 37; Rotenberg, "Fair information practices and the architecture of privacy (What Larry doesn't get)"; Rubinstein and Good, "Privacy by Design: a Counterfactual Analysis of Google and Facebook Privacy Incidents'"; Richards and Hartzog, "Privacy's Constitutional Moment", pp. 14–20.

1343 Woodrow Hartzog. "The Inadequate, Invaluable Fair Information Practices". In: *Md. L. Rev.* 76 (2016), pp. 952–982, p. 960. In Richards and Hartzog, "Privacy's Constitutional Moment", p. 17, it is argued that "it is fair to say that the FIP model of privacy regulation has been adopted by virtually every country in the world that has decided to take data protection seriously".

1344 The list is provided in Chapter 2, Section 2.2, note no. 95. *See* US Department of Health, *Report of the Secretary's Advisory Committee on Automated Personal Data Systems Records Computers and the Rights of citizens*.

of the collection, unless consent is given (i.e. choice or consent principle). Moreover, the individual should have the right to correct or amend the information (i.e. participation principle). The controller should assure the reliability of information for its intended use and prevent any misuse (i.e. security principle). It has been pointed out that these principles in contemporary terms can be summarised as: transparency, use limitation, access and correction, data quality, and security[1345]. These FIPs were adopted in the Privacy Act of 1974[1346]. The FIPs of 1973 may also be evaluated as a narrower and limited set of principles similar to the GDPR's: fairness, lawfulness, purpose limitation, accuracy, and security.

The US literature frequently refers to the OECD's principles in discussing an evolution of the FIPs to be applied to PII[1347]. In fact, in the US there is no more recent set of comprehensive principles than the Code of the US Department of Health, Education and Welfare. The OECD's Guidelines of 1980 – which were revised in 2013, although the core principles were not emended – are not legally binding, but they have been highly influential in several countries, are broader than CoE's Convention 108, and contain eight basic internationally recognised principles[1348]. Despite the fact that only FIPs of 1973 have been explicitly referred to in the US framework, the OECD principles may be used there by practitioners as a baseline of the PbD approach.

The OECD's Guidelines have been considered the most influential form of FIPs; even though they do not use the term, they rely on the US version of 1973[1349]. The Guidelines are considered a "second generation of

1345 *See* Fred Cate. "The Failure of Fair Information Practice Principles". In: *Consumer Protection in the Age of the Information Economy*. 2006, pp. 343–379. ISBN: 9780754680468, p. 346. The author highlighted that the FIPs were the basis of the Privacy Act of 1974.

1346 *See* e.g. DeVries, "Protecting privacy in the digital age", p. 289.

1347 *See* e.g. Rotenberg, "Fair information practices and the architecture of privacy (What Larry doesn't get)"; Solove, "A taxonomy of privacy", p. 547; Schwartz and Solove, "Reconciling personal information in the United States and European Union", p. 909; Frederik Zuiderveen Borgesius, Jonathan Gray, and Mireille van Eechoud. "Open data, privacy, and fair information principles: Towards a balancing framework". In: *Berkeley Technology Law Journal* 30.3 (2015), pp. 2073–2131, pp. 2102–2107.

1348 A detailed investigation on the Guidelines is provided by Bygrave, *Data privacy law: an international perspective*, pp. 43–51.

1349 Anglim, Kirtley, and Nobahar, *Privacy Rights in the Digital Age*, p. 196. *See* also Hartzog, "The Inadequate, Invaluable Fair Information Practices", p. 958.

FIPs"[1350]. So, a summary of the principles as revised in 2013 is provided in the following Table 4.1[1351].

*Table 4.1 OECD privacy principles*

| PRINCIPLE | DEFINITION |
|---|---|
| Collection Limitation | The collection of personal data should be limited and data should be obtained by lawful and fair means and, where appropriate, with knowledge or consent |
| Data Quality | Personal data should be relevant to the purposes, and, to the extent necessary for those purposes, they should be accurate, complete and up-to-date |
| Purpose Specification | The purposes should be specified no later than at the time of the collection and the subsequent use limited to that purpose or compatible with it |
| Use Limitation | Personal data should not be disclosed, made available or otherwise used for purposes other than those specified except with the consent of the data subject or by the authority of law |
| Security Safeguards | Personal data should be protected by reasonable security safeguards against security risks |
| Openness | There should be a general policy of openness about personal data |

1350 Hartzog, *op. cit.*, p. 965.

1351 The definitions of the principles have been condensed from the OECD's Guidelines of 2013.

| PRINCIPLE | DEFINITION |
|---|---|
| Individual Participation | Individuals should have the right to obtain information, erasure, and rectification |
| Accountability | The data controller should be accountable for complying with measures which give effect to the other principles |

Comparing the OECD's principles with the GDPR, it can be argued that some principles are similar[1352]. The OECD's framework does not provide either the legal grounds of processing of the GDPR or other conditions for a lawful processing. It refers to consent only, and does not contain additional safeguards for particular categories of data[1353]. However, the collection limitation principle has a similar rationale as the lawfulness and fairness principles: setting limits to collection activities in the absence of legal conditions[1354]. At the same time, it may be argued that the principle of collection limitation relies too heavily on the notion of consent[1355]. The data quality, purpose specification, use limitation and security safeguard principles are similar to purpose limitation, accuracy and integrity and confidentiality principles, but they are less detailed. The OECD principles do not contain either data minimisation or storage limitation principles. The accountability principle is consistent with the definition of Article 5(2) GDPR. In the OECD's framework there are completely new principles, i.e. openness and individual participation, but they entail safeguards that the GDPR establishes in Chapter III on the rights of the data subject. As a result, other very detailed rules reflect those principles.

1352 In Bygrave, *Data privacy law: an international perspective*, p. 45, the author argued that the OECD Guidelines are even similar to the former version of the CoE principles since the bodies collaborated extensively during the drafting. *See* also the analysis by Paul De Hert. "Data protection as bundles of principles, general rights, concrete subjective rights and rules: piercing the veil of stability surrounding the principles of data protection". In: *Eur. Data Prot. L. Rev.* 3 (2017), pp. 160–179, which comments on the principles and their roles in the legal systems.

1353 This choice is consistent with US law.

1354 On the rationale of fair and lawful processing *see* Bygrave, *Data privacy law: an international perspective*, pp. 146–147.

1355 *See* Anglim, Kirtley, and Nobahar, *Privacy Rights in the Digital Age*, p. 197.

The GDPR provides broader guarantees since it is a specific framework on data protection, whereas the OECD's framework aims to generally provide general internationally recognised principles. So, the application of a PbD or a DPbD approach might differ since the implementation may follow partially different principles. Nonetheless, the core data protection or informational privacy principles may be similar.

Cavoukian often referred to the OECD's version of the FIPs for a PbD approach[1356]. Despite the multiple versions of the FIPs, Cavoukian classified five core principles: purpose specification and use limitation – i.e. reasons for the processing of PII should be identified at or before the time of collection and the use or disclosure should be limited to them – user participation and transparency – i.e. individuals should be empowered – and strong security (confidentiality, integrity, availability)[1357]. These principles may be the starting point for business and management practices.

It should be noted that in the Report of 2012 on PbD the FTC used the notion of FIPs of 1973[1358]. The same authority previously defined five core principles for the protection of online consumers' privacy after reviewing the FIPs, the OECD's of 1980, the DPD's principles, and the Canadian framework: notice or awareness of consumers, choice or consent, access or participation, integrity or security, and enforcement or redress[1359]. The definitions are reported in the following Table 4.2[1360].

---

1356 *See* e.g. Cavoukian, *Privacy by design: From rhetoric to reality*, p. 12.

1357 *See* Cavoukian, *op. cit.*, pp. 165–166.

1358 *See* Chapter 2 Section 2.2. The authority also made reference to the proposal by Congress on a "Consumer Privacy Bill of Rights" based on the FIPs, which was never approved. The privacy principles in this proposal were: transparency, individual control, respect for context, security, access, accuracy, focused collection, and accountability. *See* the Report by the White House during the Obama administration, *Consumer Data Privacy in a Networked World: A Framework for Protecting Privacy and Promoting Innovation in the Global Digital Economy* of February 2012 at <obamawhitehouse.archives.gov/sites/default/files/privacy-final. pdf>. Last accessed 06/10/2021.

1359 *See* FTC Federal Trade Commission. *Privacy Online: A Report to Congress*. FTC Report, 1998.

1360 The definitions of the principles have been condensed from the FTC's Report of 1998 and Cate, "The Failure of Fair Information Practice Principles", p. 352.

*Table 4.2 FTC privacy principles*

| PRINCIPLE | DEFINITION |
|---|---|
| Notice/Awareness | Consumers should receive notice of an entity's policy before the collection of PII in order to make informed decisions |
| Choice/Consent | Consumers should have the opportunity to choose how PII may be used, for secondary use also |
| Access/Participation | Consumers should have the opportunity to access PII and contest accuracy and completeness |
| Integrity/Security | PII should be accurate and secure through reasonable steps |
| Enforcement/Redress | There should be a mechanism in place to enforce the core principles of privacy protection |

It has been pointed out that this list is a "remarkable landmark along the evolution of modern FIPS" since the FTC cited the full range of FIP documents, including Directive 95/46, and identified the five principles that those documents have in common[1361]. However, the FTC's principles missed the fundamental collection or use limitation principle, the fairness and the data quality or accuracy principles, and reduced the entire framework to the notion of notice. In particular, the FTC's approach is focused on the concepts of "privacy as control" and "notice-and-choice", where the notice, and the following opt-out or opt-in individual's authorisation, are central.

Hence, the FTC's set of principles guarantees the fewest substantive protections, whereas the OECD Guidelines may be considered to be somewhere in the middle, and the EU's principles entail the widespread protective framework[1362].

While discussing the application of PbD in the US legal framework, two US scholars, Rubinstein and Good, proposed a new formulation of the FIPs which encapsulated other interpretations of the principles so that it

1361 Cate, *op. cit.*, p. 353. Later, the FTC abandoned the enforcement principle.
1362 *See* the comment of *ibid.*

could be used as a set of design principles[1363]. They argued that the FIPs could be considered the foundation of international privacy law and, as they are open-ended principles, could be flexible and with a wide range of application[1364]. The principles are reported here *verbatim*[1365]:

1. "Defined limits for controllers and processors of personal information on the collection, processing, and use of personal data (often referred to as data minimization);
2. Data quality (accurate, complete, and timely information);
3. Limits on data retention;
4. Notice to individual users;
5. Individual choice or consent regarding the collection and subsequent use of personal information;
6. Reasonable security for stored data;
7. Transparent processing systems that affected users can readily understand and act on;
8. Access to one's personal data;
9. Enforcement of privacy rights and standards (including industry self-regulation, organizational measures implemented by individual firms, regulatory oversight and/or enforcement, and civil litigation)".

This formulation of the FIPs takes into account the previous interpretations of the OECD Guidelines and the FTC, by specifying the data quality principle, the importance of the notice and choice, the openness and enforcement principles. Additionally, it is more similar to the GDPR than the OECD's framework since this list of principles includes data minimisation, data retention and transparency. Thus, a PbD implementation with these nine principles in the US system may be more consistent with a DPbD approach whether or not these principles are used in the design stage of technologies and business practices.

The US alignment with the GDPR principles – which is part of the so-called "Brussels Effect"[1366] – is indirectly promoted by the American

1363 *See* Rubinstein and Good, "Privacy by Design: a Counterfactual Analysis of Google and Facebook Privacy Incidents'", p. 1343.

1364 *See* Rubinstein and Good, *op. cit.*, p. 1344.

1365 *See ibid.*

1366 The so-called "Brussels Effect" was coined by Anu Bradford in 2012. *See* lastly Anu Bradford. *The Brussels effect: How the European Union rules the world*. Oxford University Press, 2020. ISBN: 9780190088583. According to Bradford, the EU influenced and influences policies and norms around the world, including legislative initiatives and business behaviours. As reported by Bygrave, the data protection domain is the example *par excellence* of this effect. *See* Lee

Law Institute (ALI), which proposed the following data privacy principles in a law reform project in 2019: transparency, individual notice, consent, confidentiality, use limitation, access and correction rights, data retention and disposal duties, data portability, data security, onward transfer, and accountability and enforcement[1367]. These principles aimed to be consistent with US privacy law and advance it boldly by revitalising the FIPs and by using EU legal categories, like data controller or processor[1368]. The project has been promoted by the two prominent US professors Paul M. Schwartz and Daniel J. Solove[1369].

First of all, the transparency principle follows the traditional "notice-and-choice" US approach by requiring a transparency statement to be used by regulators so that "the data controllers and data processors clearly, conspicuously, and accurately explain the current personal data activities". Then, the individual notice principle entails the need to "inform individuals about how their personal data is being collected, used, and shared" in a privacy notice, and the provision of a heightened notice "for any data activity that is significantly unexpected or that poses a significant risk of causing material harm to data subjects"[1370]. This double notice enhances the individual side of the "notice-and-choice" approach since the subject may be more conscious of what the processing entails and may give a more informed consent. The US system traditionally relies on consent more than the EU system, so the existence of the notice and the following clear consent are necessary, especially where a heightened notice is provided[1371].

---

A. Bygrave. "The 'Strasbourg Effect' in Data Protection: Its Logic, Mechanics and Prospects in Light of the 'Brussels Effect'". In: *University of Oslo Faculty of Law Research Paper No. 2020–14* (2020). Both the DPD and the GDPR influenced norms worldwide. The *de facto* "Europeanisation" creates a global standard of protection. So, the GDPR had the effect of turning European-style privacy laws at a global level. *See* Richards and Hartzog, "Privacy's Constitutional Moment", p. 4. A paradigmatic example of this effect in the US is the California Consumer Protection Act, which is important since tech and key companies of the digital age are the headquartered in Silicon Valley's State. The CCPA has many similarities with the GDPR, but is more limited in scope. On non-convergence between EU and US data protection laws *see* Fernanda G. Nicola and Oreste Pollicino, "The Balkanization of Data Privacy Regulation". In: *W. Va. L. Rev.* 61 (2020), pp. 60–105.

1367 *See* Rustad and Koenig, "Towards a global data privacy standard", p. 386.

1368 Solove, "Conceptualizing privacy", p. 7.

1369 *See* Solove and Schwartz, "ALI Data Privacy: Overview and Black Letter Text".

1370 Solove, "Conceptualizing privacy", pp. 16–17.

1371 Solove, *op. cit.*, p. 18.

The confidentiality principle is a novelty for the US system that closes a gap in the framework since the concept uses the US notion of the "reasonable expectation of privacy" to protect information "when there is an express or implied promise of confidentiality or a legal obligation of confidentiality"[1372]. As previously noted for the EU legal framework, the duty of confidentiality is particularly important in the e-health sector. So, the introduction of this principle in the FIPs for a PbD approach may be highly recommended.

The use limitation principle refers to the secondary use of PII: the collection does not require a specific legal ground, but the secondary use should seek consent or an exception to allow the processing. So, a lawfulness principle is not included, but the secondary use of information shall be justified. This secondary use is exceptionally allowed for the "fulfilment of a contract to which the data subject is a party", for "the significant advancement of the protection of health or safety of the data subject or other people", and "as in the GDPR, a catch-all for serving a significant legitimate interest without posing a significant risk of material harm to the data subject or others and without being significantly unexpected"[1373]. These scenarios are similar to some legal grounds of the GDPR in Articles 6 and 9.

Moreover, the principles of access and correction include the right to access to PII and the right to request correction of any error in the information to protect its accuracy. The data portability principle has also been included since it is an emerging concept used both in the GDPR and in the California Consumer Privacy Act[1374].

Then, the data destruction principle states that PII "that no longer serves the uses identified in the notice that was provided or other legitimate interests shall be destroyed using reasonable procedures to ensure that it is unreadable or otherwise indecipherable"[1375]. Other limits shall be set to the retention of information, which shall be stored "only for legitimate purposes that are consistent with the scope and purposes of notice provid-

1372 Solove, *op. cit.*, p. 20.
1373 Solove, *op. cit.*, p. 21.
1374 *See* Solove, *op. cit.*, p. 22.
1375 Solove, *op. cit.*, p. 23.

ed to the data subject"[1376]. Nonetheless, a right to erasure is not included in the ALI's principles in spite of the specific provision in the CCPA[1377].

The data security principle has been framed as one of "the most common requirements of data privacy statutes and regulations", which provides reasonable safeguards for protecting information, and the accountability principle requires the development of reasonable and comprehensive privacy programmes[1378]. It should be noted that a PbD principle is not included by the ALI for "not pushing US law too far", but it is specified in the accountability principle description that[1379]:

> "A data controller or data processor shall analyze the privacy and security implications early on in the development of any new product, service, or process. This analysis shall be conducted in a reasonable manner, at a reasonable time, and with a reasonable thoroughness. This analysis shall be documented. A data controller or data processor shall examine how the product, service, or process should be designed to address the privacy or security issues identified in the analysis. The outcome of this examination shall be reflected in the final design of the product, service, or process. Reasonable design choices shall be made. Design choices and the reasoning that supports them shall be documented".

So, the general accountability approach refers to design choices, but it is more organisational than technical in accordance with the vision of the FTC's Report on PbD. At the same time, the risk management, security, contextualised and flexible approach proposed by the ALI project are similar to the considerations previously exposed on Article 25 of the GDPR.

Finally, the ALI's enforcement principle mandates effective, proportionate and dissuasive remedies[1380]. This ALI's project is a prominent effort to reform the FIPs by including OECD's and GDPR's concepts in light of a modern path forward of informational privacy. However, FIPs alone are not sufficient in affecting the design of technologies and business

1376 *Ibid.*

1377 CCPA, Cal. Civ. Code § 1798.105. The ALI project does not include a right to erasure or to be forgotten because there is no agreement in the ALI's membership. *See ibid.*

1378 Solove, *op. cit.*, pp. 24–27.

1379 Solove, *op. cit.*, p. 44.

1380 Solove, *op. cit.*, p. 28. All the principles described above are summarised in the Black Letter at Solove and Schwartz, "ALI Data Privacy: Overview and Black Letter Text", pp. 32–46.

practices. As argued by Hartzog, FIPs do not address the structural problems and risks of data processing[1381]. Since they are centred around the concepts of "control over information" and consent ("notice-and-choice"), they are not enough in the digital age where the way in which technologies and practices are designed is crucial. Thus, privacy law should address the design of technologies, and FIPs should be supported and enforced with design-based protection[1382]. Including a PbD principle is pushing US law far towards a more protective and realistic privacy approach.

Having discussed the US legal framework for PII and the principles that can be applied, the next section deals with US rules for the protection of personal health information and for processing electronic health information in the EHRs.

## *4.3 The US legal framework for health informational privacy and for EHRs*

The healthcare domain demands a "deep, culturally significant, and relationship-based" level of protection because of the nature of information involved and of the exceptional possible threats[1383]. In the US several rules regulate health informational privacy or "medical privacy" at both the state and federal level[1384]. The US Constitution does not explicitly grant the

1381 *See* the criticism in Hartzog, "The Inadequate, Invaluable Fair Information Practices". In sum, "FIPs are inadequate because: (1) they have important blind spots regarding the collection, use, and disclosure of personal information that cannot be resolved through more specificity or better implementation; and (2) they fail to address the user bandwidth problem that would persist even if users were given every bit of control imaginable over their data" (at p. 966).

1382 *See* Hartzog, *op. cit.*, pp. 981–982.

1383 Nicolas P. Terry. "Regulatory disruption and arbitrage in health-care data protection". In: *Yale J. Health Pol'y L. & Ethics* 17 (2017), pp. 143–208, p. 197.

1384 *See* Solove and Schwartz, *Information privacy law*, pp. 429–559. On US privacy of health care information *see* Paul M Schwartz. "Privacy and the economics of personal health care information". In: *Tex. L. Rev.* 76 (1997), p. 1; Joy Pritts. *The state of health privacy: an uneven terrain (a comprehensive survey of state health privacy statutes)*. Health Privacy Project, Institute for Health Care Research and Policy, 1999; Turkington and Allen, *Privacy Law: cases and materials*, pp. 221–293; Frank Pasquale and Tara Adams Ragone. "Protecting health privacy in an era of big data processing and cloud computing". In: *Stan. Tech. L. Rev.* 17 (2013), pp. 595–654; Yann Joly and Bartha Maria Knoppers. *Routledge handbook of medical law and ethics*. Routledge, 2016. ISBN: 9781138204126; Sharona Hoffman. "Medical Privacy and Security". In: *The Oxford Handbook of U.S. Health Law*. 2017, pp. 267–288. ISBN: 9780199366521; Frank Pasquale.

federal government authority over health, but a federal system and state systems coexist[1385]. Public health is managed both by the federal system and by the 50 separate states legal systems, where local systems operate under stakeholders' agreements[1386].

Thus, in the US there is a lack of a unified and coordinated healthcare system: the provision of healthcare is managed by "a patchwork of public and private insurance plans", "federal, state, and local governments", and "institutions and individual providers who are often unconnected to one other"[1387]. US citizens usually obtain healthcare coverage through employer health plans or private health insurance plans[1388]. So, contracts are signed between employer, employee, and insurance companies, or between the individual and a private fund or company. It has even been pointed out that since most people receive health benefits at their workplace, employers have a great incentive to weed out employees with expensive healthcare needs so as to pay less for the provision of medical services[1389]. As a result, employers frequently require information about medical history of employees' families or genetic information[1390]. The Genetic Information Nondiscrimination Act (GINA) of 2008 protects against

---

"Health Information Law". In: *The Oxford Handbook of U.S. Health Law*. 2017, pp. 193–212. ISBN: 9780199366521; Christina Munns and Subhajit Basu. *Privacy and healthcare data: 'choice of control' to 'choice' and 'control'*. Taylor & Francis, 2016. ISBN: 9781472426864, pp. 81–98; Daniel J. Solove and Paul M. Schwartz. "Health privacy". In: *Information privacy law*. Wolters Kluwer Law & Business, 2018, pp. 475–602. ISBN: 9781454892755; Vokinger, Stekhoven, and Krauthammer, "Lost in Anonymization – A Data Anonymization Reference Classification Merging Legal and Technical Considerations"; Matthew DeNoncour. *Healthcare technology regulation in the US*. In: *Healthtech, Law and Regulation*. Elgar Commercial Law and Practice, 2020 pp. 80–113. ISBN: 9781839104893.

1385 Margo Edmunds. "Governmental and legislative context of informatics". In: *Public health informatics and information systems*. Springer, 2014, pp. 47–66. ISBN: 9780387227450, p. 50.

1386 *Ibid.* This article defines the US public health system as a three-tiered network of state and local agencies that work in partnership with the federal government.

1387 *See* Sara E. Wilensky and Joel B. Teitelbaum. *Essentials of Health Policy and Law*. Jones & Bartlett Learning, 2019. ISBN: 9781284151619, p. 49.

1388 *See* Joly and Knoppers, *Routledge handbook of medical law and ethics*, p. 56.

1389 Schwartz, "Privacy and the economics of personal health care information", p. 26.

1390 *See* Solove and Schwartz, *Information privacy law*, pp. 540–541.

employers' and insurance companies' discrimination based on genetic tests[1391].

Medical information is collected and used through these insurance plans, during the traditional healthcare provision, and in e-health processing (e.g. apps, Big Data). So, in this legal framework health information may be processed by: employers, who wish to hire an employee in good health; business entities, which manage medical financial funds; drug companies or advertisers and marketers; and healthcare providers and health insurers[1392].

Even in the US system, medical confidentiality is frequently connected to an individual's right to privacy[1393]. The right to privacy limits data collection, whereas confidentiality limits the disclosure of information[1394]. US physicians take the Hippocratic Oath, and must not reveal information and communications under the ethical duty of confidentiality and the physician-patient fiduciary relationship. The American Medical Association's Code of ethics (AMA's Code) explicitly mentions this duty by specifying that physicians shall respect patients' confidences to safeguard their autonomy and trust[1395].

---

1391 Genetic Information Nondiscrimination Act, Public Law 110–233, 122 STAT. 881. GINA prohibits the collection of information. *See* for a legal critical analysis Bradley A. Areheart and Jessica L. Roberts. "GINA, Big Data, and the Future of Employee Privacy". In: *Yale L.J.* 128 (2018), pp. 710–790.

1392 *See* Sharona Hoffman and Andy Podgurski. "In sickness, health, and cyberspace: protecting the security of electronic private health information". In: *BCL. Rev.* 48 (2007), pp. 331–386, p. 334.

1393 *See* Anglim, Kirtley, and Nobahar, *Privacy Rights in the Digital Age*, pp. 352–354. This article reports that all 50 American States have enacted legislation on medical confidentiality, and the breach of the fiduciary relationship between the physician or medical professionals and the patient. The duty is actually and usually an obligation.

1394 Nicolas P. Terry. "Privacy and the health information domain: properties, models and unintended results". In: *European Journal of Health Law* 10.3 (2003), pp. 223–237, p. 224.

1395 The duty is currently framed as: "A physician shall respect the rights of patients, colleagues, and other health professionals, and shall safeguard patient confidences and privacy within the constraints of the law". *See* AMA website at <www.ama-assn.org/about/publications-newsletters/ama-principles-medical-ethics>. Last accessed 06/10/2021. The Code of Medical Ethics Opinion 3.1.1 AMA specifies that respecting patient privacy means respecting patient autonomy and trust. Patient privacy includes the respect of personal space (i.e. physical privacy), personal data (i.e. informational privacy), personal choices (i.e. decisional privacy), and personal relationships with family members and other intimates (i.e. associational privacy). In the Code of Medical Ethics Opin-

In this context, the primary source of rule is the statutory level, but privacy torts and tort law (i.e. common law) protect medical confidentiality, too. In *McCormick v. England* 494 S.E.2d 431 (S.C. Ct. App. 1997), the holding first states: "breach of confidentiality is a distinct tort from the tort of public disclosure of private facts" (i.e. a privacy tort)[1396]. The duty of confidentiality is based on the existence of a fiduciary relationship between the patient and the physician. As pointed out in *Doe v. Roe* 93 Misc. 2d 201 (1977), "the very needs of the profession itself require that confidentiality exist and be enforced". The same duty persists in the information society where health records are kept in electronic form. In *Doe v. Mills*, 536 N.W.2d 824 (Mic. App. 1995), the court found disclosure of medical information to be a violation of a privacy tort. Breach of confidentiality is recognised as the tort which provides remedy when a professional divulges confidential information unlawfully[1397]. In *Susan S. v. Israels*, 55 Cal.App.4th 1290 (1997) the court recognised a public disclosure of private facts tort for the disclosure of mental health records.

When the Supreme Court held the constitutionally based interest in avoiding disclosure of private facts in *Whalen v. Roe*, the Court recognised the protection of health records and drug records which could be disclosed for state public interest. The Court ruling has been interpreted as the

---

ion 3.2.1, the Association further elaborated on confidentiality of personal information. It pointed out that patients could decide whether and to whom their personal health information is disclosed, but patient's consent might not be required. The disclosure should be restricted to the minimum amount of necessary information, and the patient should receive a notification whenever feasible. Allowed exceptions to the consent should be the disclosure to other healthcare professionals for providing care, to public authorities under explicit law, and to other third parties for a third and independent medical judgement (for patient's safe).

1396 On tort liability for disclosure of patient information *see* Solove and Schwartz, *Information privacy law*, pp. 437–446; Solove and Schwartz, "Health privacy", pp. 483–492.

1397 Solove and Schwartz, *Privacy, information, and technology*, p. 31. It has been pointed out that most states establish a lawful disclosure without individual consent to protect third parties from identifiable harm, to report information for public health purposes under law, and to report a medical emergency. *See* Lawrence O. Gostin, James G. Hodge Jr., and Lauren Marks. "The Nationalization of Health Information Privacy Protections". In: *Tort & Insurance Law Journal* (2002), pp. 1113–1138, p. 1120. On liability concerns of electronic medical record *see* Sharona Hoffman and Andy Podgurski. "E-Health hazards: provider liability and electronic health record systems". In: *Berkeley Tech. LJ* 24 (2009), pp. 1523–1582, which focuses on EHRs and PHRs.

judicial recognition of a right to health informational privacy[1398]. In *Doe v. Southeastern Pennsylvania Transp. Authority* 886 F. Supp. 1186 (E.D. Pa. 1994), the court observed that confidentiality of medical records may fall under the protection of the Fourth Amendment of the Constitution. Disclosure of medical information is not a constitutional privacy violation in itself since disclosure may be reasonably necessary or permissible[1399]. However, courts can protect patients' right to privacy under the Constitution and under certain circumstances. As an example, in *Peninsula Counseling Center v. Rahm* 105 Wn.2d 929 (1986), judge Pearson's dissenting opinion stated that medical information is "of the type which, if disseminated, would tend to cause a reasonable person substantial concern, anxiety, or embarrassment"; therefore, this information should be protected "from compelled disclosure". Once again, a balancing act between public interests and an individual's privacy interest is performed by courts.

A number of states protect medical information in medical confidentiality laws, patient access law, and comprehensive health privacy laws[1400]. In particular, it has been pointed out that state law requirements grant patients access to their medical records, restrict use and disclosure of personal health information, establish privileges for specific categories, institute requirements relating to specific medical conditions, such as alcohol or sexually transmitted disease, and require breach notification in particular circumstances[1401]. Thus, medical confidentiality shall be maintained under statutory, common law and ethical duties[1402].

An important basis for protecting confidentiality in the health context can also be found in the FIPs of 1973 since they were drafted by the US Department of Health with reference to the computerised processing

---

1398 Healthcare providers could store the information of patients who received prescriptions for drugs that could be illegally abused on the basis of a state procedure and public interest despite the privacy rights of the patients. On this case *see* also the Annotation on the Supreme Court's website at <supreme.justia.com/cases/ federal/us/429/589/>. Last accessed 06/10/2021.

1399 *See* Schachter, *Informational and decisional privacy*, p. 350.

1400 *See* Solove and Schwartz, *Information privacy law*, p. 462; Solove and Schwartz, "Health privacy", p. 506.

1401 Hoffman, "Medical Privacy and Security", p. 274.

1402 *See* e.g. the interesting case of a surgeon with AIDS. In *Estate of Behringer v. Medical Center at Princeton*, 249 N.J. Super. 597 (1991), the holding established a standard of confidentiality on HIV tests and illustrated how to balance privacy against public interest on disclosure.

of medical data by public health agencies[1403]. The Department of Health and Human Services (hereinafter: HHS) is the major operating agency for protecting health and health information of US citizens[1404].

In 1996 the US Congress enacted a federal health regulation: the Health Insurance Portability and Accountability Act of 1996 (hereinafter: HIPAA)[1405]. This Act is a "landmark legislative event" for healthcare in the US[1406]. The primary purpose of this regulation was to permit employees to change jobs without losing the existing conditions in their health plans, and then allow more flexible insurance claims at the federal level[1407]. So, the HIPAA protected the continuity of health insurance when employees changed jobs and sought to avoid discrimination against individual participants in and beneficiaries of group health insurance plans[1408]. It has been pointed out that the HIPAA even envisaged the need to standardise health data to enhance its electronic exchange and improve national healthcare delivery[1409]. The first version of the text did not provide any rules mandating privacy protection for medical data, but the public debate and several privacy advocates claimed a need for it[1410]. Therefore, the Department of Health and Human Services promoted several regulations on privacy and security to be integrated into the HIPAA. Only in 2002, during the Bush administration, was the HIPAA Privacy Rule approved and in 2003 it became effective[1411]. In the same year the Security Rule was published, and it became effective in 2005.

---

1403 William A. Yasnoff. "Privacy, Confidentiality, and Security of Public Health Information". In: *Public Health Informatics and Information Systems*. Springer, 2014, pp. 155–172. ISBN: 9780387227450, p. 158.

1404 *See* Edmunds, "Governmental and legislative context of informatics", p. 53.

1405 Health Insurance Portability and Accountability Act of 1996 (HIPAA), 110 Stat. 1936 (1996); 45 USC § 1320d-2(b).

1406 Edmunds, "Governmental and legislative context of informatics", p. 56.

1407 *See* Solove and Schwartz, *Information privacy law*, p. 463; Solove and Schwartz, "Health privacy", p. 509.

1408 Schwartz, "Privacy and the economics of personal health care information", p. 40.

1409 Edmunds, "Governmental and legislative context of informatics", p. 56.

1410 On the first version of HIPAA *see* e.g. Francoise Gilbert. "Privacy of Medical Records – The Health Insurance Portability and Accountability Act of 1996 Creates a Framework for the Establishment of Security Standards and the Protection of Individually Identifiable Health Information". In: *N.D.L. Rev.* 73 (1997), pp. 93–108. The author concluded that the Act did not sufficiently address confidentiality issues.

1411 For a comment before the application *see* Peter D Jacobson. "Medical records and HIPAA: is it too late to protect privacy?". In: *Minn. L. Rev.* 86 (2001), pp.

So, the HIPAA requirements for protecting medical information are the Privacy and Security Rules, which are published at 45 Code of Federal Regulations (C.F.R.) parts 160 through 164[1412]. While these provisions are not explicit, they identify personal health information as a category of sensitive information deserving higher protection than common PII[1413].

The HIPAA pre-empts statutory national law unless the latter is more stringent than the former. The more stringent requirement refers to the "ability of the patient to withhold permission and to effectively block disclosure" of personal health information[1414]. So, the law is more stringent when it gives more control to the patient over information. As an example, a more stringent rule is California's Confidentiality of Medical Information Act, which is more comprehensive than the HIPAA[1415]. Other examples may be provided by the case law. In *Creely v. Genesis Health Ventures, Inc.*, 2004 U.S. Dist. LEXIS 25489 (ED Pa Dec. 17, 2004), a

---

1497–1514. The author argued that privacy protection is as necessary as the disclosure and use of PHI for public health purposes. *See* also Joy L. Pritts. "Altered states: state health privacy laws and the impact of the Federal Health Privacy Rule". In: *Yale J. Health Pol'y L. & Ethics* 2 (2001), pp. 327–364, which gave great importance to the right to access and amend health records, and Nathan J Wills. "A tripartite threat to medical records privacy: Technology, HIPAA's privacy rule and the USA Patriot Act". In: *JL & Health* 17 (2002), pp. 271–296, which summarises the requirements by highlighting their rationales and criticising several aspects.

1412 Generally on HIPAA Privacy and Security Rules *see* Burdon, *Digital Data Collection and Information Privacy Law*, p. 175; Hoffman, "Medical Privacy and Security"; Yasnoff, "Privacy, Confidentiality, and Security of Public Health Information"; Edmunds, "Governmental and legislative context of informatics"; Di Iorio and Carinci, "Privacy and health care information systems: where is the balance?"; Janine Hiller et al. "Privacy and security in the implementation of health information technology (electronic health records): US and EU compared". In: *BUJ Sci. & Tech. L.* 17 (2011), pp. 1–39; Dumortier and Verhenneman, "Legal regulations on electronic health records: a prerequisite or an unavoidable by-product? – The legal aspects of electronic health records in Europe and the US analysed"; Gostin, Hodge Jr., and Marks, "The Nationalization of Health Information Privacy Protections"; Tamela J. White and Charlotte A. Hoffman. "The Privacy Standards Under the Health Insurance Portability and Accountability Act: A Practical Guide to Promote Order and Avoid Potential Chaos". In: *W. Va. L. Rev.* 106 (2004), pp. 709–780.

1413 On the same opinion *see* Dumortier and Verhenneman, "Legal regulation of electronic health records: a comparative analysis of Europe and the US", p. 33.

1414 *See* Solove and Schwartz, *Information privacy law*, p. 479.

1415 *See* California Civil Code 56.10 – 56.16. *See* also Anglim, Kirtley, and Nobahar, *Privacy Rights in the Digital Age*, p. 426.

state privacy law was considered more stringent than the HIPAA since it prohibited use or disclosure in circumstances under which such use or disclosure otherwise would have been permitted under the HIPAA. In *United States Ex Rel. Pogue v. Diabetes Treatment Ctrs. of Am.*, 2004 U.S. Dist. LEXIS 21830 (DDC May 17, 2004), Florida law was not pre-empted as more stringent than HIPAA. Moreover, a state law may be more protective than the HIPAA on specific types of health information (e.g. genetic or mental health)[1416].

Where the state law is more stringent than the HIPAA, it shall apply. However, it is difficult to determine whether the state law is more stringent than the HIPAA, as argued by Tomes[1417]. In *Arons v. Jutkowitz*, 9 N.Y.3d 393, 850 N.Y.S. 2d 345, 880 N.E.2d 831, 2007 N.Y. LEXIS 3355 (NY Nov. 27, 2007), the Court ruled that where a state provision has no comparable or analogous federal provision in the HIPAA, or the opposite is the case, there is no possibility of pre-emption because there is nothing to compare and no contrary requirement. As a result, the state provision is effective. Given that the HIPAA does not pre-empt stricter state or local statutory law, it can be argued that the HIPAA represents a minimum set of rules for medical information in the US[1418]. In fact, before the HIPAA state laws were very limited[1419]. The Privacy Rule sets the first national standards for protecting the privacy of health information in the US, by providing a minimum of basic protections[1420].

In summary, the HIPAA Privacy Rule and the Security Rule establish federal standards for protecting personal health information, require appropriate safeguards and set limits and conditions on use and disclosure[1421]. The HIPAA Privacy Rule is based on the FIPs[1422]. It has been claimed that it does not elevate medical privacy to a constitutional right,

---

1416 *See* on the effects of pre-emption Gostin, Hodge Jr., and Marks, "The Nationalization of Health Information Privacy Protections", pp. 1130–1131.

1417 Jonathan P. Tomes. "20 Plus Years of HIPAA and What Have We Got". In: *Quinnipiac Health L.J.* 22 (2018), pp. 39–106, p. 96.

1418 Yasnoff, "Privacy, Confidentiality, and Security of Public Health Information", p. 160.

1419 *See* Hiller et al., "Privacy and security in the implementation of health information technology (electronic health records): US and EU compared", p. 9; and Pritts, "Altered states: state health privacy laws and the impact of the Federal Health Privacy Rule".

1420 Di Iorio and Carinci, "Privacy and health care information systems: where is the balance?", p. 98.

1421 *See infra* Sections 4.4.1, 4.4.2, 4.4.3.

1422 *See* Richards and Hartzog, "Privacy's Constitutional Moment", p. 19.

but it identifies privacy as the legitimate interest which guarantees protection against unauthorised disclosure of medical information[1423]. The HIPAA is limited in scope. In particular, the scope of HIPAA requirements is limited to covered entities, which is a limited range of health-related entities, healthcare providers and recipients. Covered entities shall apply the rules, and an office of the US Department of Health and Human Services is responsible for checking their compliance. A covered entity may use and disclose personal health information only by respecting the Privacy Rule. The Security Rule mandates administrative, physical and technical safeguards. It even lists technical policies and procedures which are related to access, audit, and integrity controls and it defines standards. Moreover, when a covered entity is implementing the security measures it shall take into account its capabilities, its infrastructure and the cost of implementation. The HIPAA requires a risk analysis, and puts emphasis on organisational measures.

The definition of "personal health information" in the US refers to "individually identifiable health information", meaning a subset of health data that can be referred to an individual and is transmitted or maintained in any form or medium[1424]. As pointed out in *Holman v. Rasak*, 486 Mich. 429, 785 N.W.2d 98, 2010 Mich. LEXIS 1446 (Mich July 13, 2010), the notion can include information orally transmitted to the physician by the patient. Under the HIPAA the definition refers to a particular form of health information, that is "protected health information" (PHI) and is framed as follows[1425].

> "Individually identifiable health information is information that is a subset of health information, including demographic information collected from an individual, and:

1423 White and Hoffman, "The Privacy Standards Under the Health Insurance Portability and Accountability Act: A Practical Guide to Promote Order and Avoid Potential Chaos", p. 712.

1424 In Lauren Newman. "Keep Your Friends Close and Your Medical Records Closer: Defining the Extent to Which a Constitutional Right to Informational Privacy Protects Medical Records". In: *J.L. & Health* 32 (2019), pp. 1–26, the author argues that the Supreme Court's interpretation of what medical information is constitutionally protected is not uniform. Therefore, this article points out that all medical information should be protected by the Constitution to protect individuals against identity theft and data breaches (of medical records, especially).

1425 *See* 45 C.F.R. § 160.103.

1. is created or received by a health care provider, health plan, employer, or health care clearinghouse; and
2. relates to the past, present, or future physical or mental health or condition of an individual; the provision of health care to an individual; or the past, present, or future payment for the provision of health care to an individual;
and (i) that identifies the individual;
or (ii) with respect to which there is a reasonable basis to believe the information can be used to identify the individual".

The US notion of PHI is coherent with the OECD's definition of personal health data[1426]. PHI protects both directly and indirectly identifiable health information[1427]. For example, it covers information collected in a medical record, conversations and clinicians' notes, information about the patient in a health insurer's computer system; and billing information about the patient[1428]. PHI refers both to the present and future health status. So, the notion might not be detailed and comprehensive as in the GDPR, but it is broad (e.g. both physical and mental state) and it is open to interpretation as well. It even refers to genetic information, and to the provision of healthcare[1429]. There is neither a reference to the number used for identifying the individual during the healthcare provision nor a mention of information on laboratory tests (or of inferred data[1430]). However, these specifications of the GDPR are established in its Recitals and not in the general definition of the type of data, and the HIPAA includes the identification number in the list of identifiers that can be removed to de-

---

1426 For the GDPR's and OECD's concepts *see* Chapter 3, Section 3.3.1.

1427 *See* Di Iorio and Carinci, "Privacy and health care information systems: where is the balance?", p. 98.

1428 *See* Anglim, Kirtley, and Nobahar, *Privacy Rights in the Digital Age*, p. 268.

1429 On genetic information in the US *see* Solove and Schwartz, *Information privacy law*, pp. 526–559. An interesting case on this topic is *Moore v. Regents of the University of California* 793 P.2d 479 (Cal. 1990), where the Court affirms the patient's autonomy over the body but rejects a property-based approach. Genetic information is strictly related to an individual's identity, and it embeds a high discrimination risk.

1430 In Hoffman and Klein, "Explaining explanation, part 1: theoretical foundations", p. 277, "medically inflected data" is considered out of the HIPAA's definition despite the growing ability of prediction of social networks and social media interactions. On the same opinion *see* Terry, "Regulatory disruption and arbitrage in health-care data protection", p. 188.

identify PHI[1431]. Commentators mention the medical record number, the biometric identifiers and the account number among the HIPAA's identifiers[1432]. Thus, legal interpretation may consider a piece of information as PHI or equally "personal health data" despite the differences between the legal frameworks.

Even in the US, personal health information may be collected in HIT and EHR systems to ensure the continuity of patients' care while supporting the diagnosis, managing the treatment, and storing their medical histories[1433]. It has been pointed out that PHI is frequently collected in a record under a unique personal identifier which is associated with the individual and shared among a health network of different entities[1434]. The United States Code defines an EHR as "an electronic record of health-related information on an individual that is created, gathered, managed, and consulted by authorized health care clinicians and staff"[1435].

The general description of the state of the art of the EHR system is valid for the US legal framework since it uses internationally recognised concepts and standards[1436]. In US EHR systems have the functionalities to support clinical decisions, order entry, and administrative processes, to manage health information and data, and to exchange and integrate PHI from different sources[1437]. Both private medical providers and government agencies store electronic medical records in health information systems that collect demographic, financial, medical, and genetic information, per-

---

1431 *See* 45 C.F.R. § 160.514(b)(2)(i)(l)(C) and Gostin, Hodge Jr., and Marks, "The Nationalization of Health Information Privacy Protections", p. 1124.

1432 *See* Alexis Guadarrama. "Mind the Gap: Addressing Gaps in HIPAA Coverage in the Mobile Health Apps Industry". In: *Hous. L. Rev.* 55 (2018), pp. 999–1025, p. 1007; White and Hoffman, "The Privacy Standards Under the Health Insurance Portability and Accountability Act: A Practical Guide to Promote Order and Avoid Potential Chaos", p. 717.

1433 *See* e.g. Lauren Bair Jacques. "Electronic health records and respect for patient privacy: A prescription for compatibility". In: *Vand. J. Ent. & Tech. L.* 13 (2011), pp. 441–462; Julien, "Electronic Health Records"; Nicolas P. Terry. "Meaningful adoption: What we know or think we know about the financing, effectiveness, quality, and safety of electronic medical records". In: *Journal of Legal Medicine* 34.1 (2013), pp. 7–42.

1434 *See* Anglim, Kirtley, and Nobahar, *Privacy Rights in the Digital Age*, p. 268.

1435 *See* 42 U.S.C. § 17921 (2006).

1436 *See* Chapter 3, Section 3.4.1, where the state of the art has been explained with internationally recognised concepts, from a legal framework perspective.

1437 *See* Julien, "Electronic Health Records".

sonal identifiers (e.g. social security number) and circumstantial elements (e.g. being the victim of a violent crime)[1438].

EHRs are used for care purposes, but they also play an important role for US data-based health research[1439]. Even employers may obtain and use EHRs, but they frequently manage or build PHR systems for their employees[1440]. After the GINA of 2008 employers cannot access the genetic information of employees and their families in the EHR, unless specific authorisation is provided by the individual[1441].

As in the EU, achieving EHR interoperability has been an important goal of US government and stakeholders[1442]. However, the absence of a coordinated national healthcare system may impinge on the creation of a comprehensive network of healthcare providers, pharmacies, and private physicians. In the US a fragmentation of EHRs, and also of the individual's medical history, seems inevitable due to the multilevel and complex healthcare system.

Therefore, the concept of EHR may be frequently mislabelled in the US. When analysing processing in the EHR environment, it will be necessary to evaluate on a case-by-case basis whether "EHR" is used in place of an electronic medical record (EMR) managed only by one provider, i.e. one data controller, or it is used for indicating the record shared among multi-

---

1438 Gostin, Hodge Jr., and Marks, "The Nationalization of Health Information Privacy Protections", pp. 1117- 1118.

1439 *See* Fred Cate. "Protecting privacy in health research: the limits of individual choice". In: *Calif. L. Rev.* 98 (2010), pp. 1765–1804, p. 1781; Sharona Hoffman and Andy Podgurski. "Balancing privacy, autonomy, and scientific needs in electronic health records research". In: *SMUL Rev.* 65 (2012), pp. 85–144; David M. Parker, Steven G. Pine, and Zachary W. Ernst. "Privacy and Informed Consent for Research in the Age of Big Data". In: *Penn St. L. Rev.* 123.3 (2019), pp. 703–733. Secondary research uses of health data should comply with the HIPAA Privacy Rule.

1440 *See* the prominent analysis by Sharona Hoffman. "Employing e-health: the impact of electronic health records on the workplace". In: *Kan. JL & Pub. Pol'y* 19 (2009), pp. 409–432. Walmart, Intel and BP developed their own PHR systems. Employers may obtain medical information under several statues, such as the Americans with Disabilities Act of 1990 or ADA 42 U.S.C. § 12101.

1441 *See* Hoffman, *op. cit.*, p. 418.

1442 *See* Hoffman, *op. cit.*, pp. 413–414; Julien, "Electronic Health Records", pp. 179–180; Terry, "Regulatory disruption and arbitrage in health-care data protection", pp. 184–186.

ple providers[1443]. Hospitals, physicians, insurers and pharmacies frequently keep their own and separate EMRs[1444].

Anyway, the reasonable expectation of privacy of electronic PHI in EHRs and patient's confidentiality should be protected to safeguard individuals against discrimination, social stigma and misuse[1445]. In particular, it has been pointed out that accessibility, security, accuracy, and interoperability should be considered central issues of EHRs[1446]. Hence, in 2008 the Office of the National Coordinator for Health Information Technology (ONC) released a pivotal document on electronic medical privacy, listing eight principles for establishing a uniform national approach intended to address privacy and security issues of medical informational privacy in the public and private sector[1447]. The ONC's framework was aimed at complementing and working with existing federal, state, and local laws. To come up with the list of principles, the ONC reviewed several other sets of principles, including OECD's and FTC's principles, HIPAA rules and even principles of other legal frameworks (e.g. DPD, PIPEDA). The ONC's principles should apply to "all health care-related persons and entities that participate in a network for the purpose of electronic exchange of

---

1443 As an example, the Veterans Health Administration developed a portal which allows access to medical information collected in physicians' EHRs. *See* Leslie P Francis. "When patients interact with EHRs: problems of privacy and confidentiality". In: *Hous. J. Health L. & Pol'y* 12 (2011), pp. 171–199, pp. 174–176. So, this is not a typical EHR environment because there is no other provider.

1444 *See* on the fragmentation William Nicholson Price II. "Risk and Resilience in Health Data Infrastructure". In: *Colo. Tech. L.J.* 16 (2017), pp. 65–86, pp. 69–70. *See* also Terry and Francis, "Ensuring the privacy and confidentiality of electronic health records", p. 683. This article clearly differentiates between electronic medical records of individual providers and electronic health records of multiple providers.

1445 *See* Gostin, Hodge Jr., and Marks, "The Nationalization of Health Information Privacy Protections", p. 1118.

1446 On the privacy and confidentiality concerns of EHRs *see* Terry and Francis, "Ensuring the privacy and confidentiality of electronic health records", which suggests an opt-in solution for using the EHR and describes the multiple issues.

1447 ONC Office of the National Coordinator for Health Information Technology. *Nationwide Privacy and Security Framework for Electronic Exchange of Individually Identifiable Health Information*. Office of the National Coordinator for Health Information Technology, U.S. Department of Health and Human Services, 2008. *See* the comment by Jacques, "Electronic health records and respect for patient privacy: A prescription for compatibility", p. 460.

individually identifiable health information". Thus, the processing of PHI in EHRs should follow certain principles[1448]:

1. individual access, meaning that the individual should have the timely means of access to PHI and obtain it in a readable form and format;
2. correction, meaning that the individual should have the timely means to contest the accuracy or integrity of PHI, have it amended or dispute a denied request in a documented format;
3. openness and transparency, meaning that policies, procedures, and technologies that directly affect the individual should be open and transparent;
4. individual choice, meaning that the individual should have the opportunity to make an informed decision about the collection, use, and disclosure of PHI;
5. collection, use and disclosure limitation, meaning that PHI should be limited to the extent necessary to fulfil the specified purpose, and not used to discriminate inappropriately;
6. data quality and integrity, meaning that PHI should be complete, accurate and up-to-date to the extent necessary to fulfil the specified purpose, and PHI should not be modified or deleted in an unauthorised manner;
7. safeguards, meaning that PHI should be secured and protected with reasonable administrative, technical, and physical safeguards;
8. accountability, meaning that "these principles should be implemented, and adherence assured, through appropriate monitoring and other means and methods should be in place to report and mitigate non-adherence and breaches".

Overall, these principles may build trust in the electronic exchange of PHI. They are not legally binding, but are used to write policies and interpret the HIPAA[1449]. The ONC's principles established a "a uniform, consistent approach intended to address the privacy and security challenges related to EHRs, independent of any specific institution or legal paradigm"[1450]. Looking at the previous discussion on the FIPs, the ONC's framework

---

1448 Office of the National Coordinator for Health Information Technology, *Nationwide Privacy and Security Framework for Electronic Exchange of Individually Identifiable Health Information*.

1449 *See* Dumortier and Verhenneman, "Legal regulations on electronic health records: a prerequisite or an unavoidable by-product? – The legal aspects of electronic health records in Europe and the US analysed".

1450 Jacques, "Electronic health records and respect for patient privacy: A prescription for compatibility", p. 460.

clearly followed the FIPs of 1973 and the OECD's Guidelines of 1980. It is worth noting that not only should the use and disclosure of PHI be limited in the EHR, but also the collection of information, as argued in Chapter 3 for the EU legal framework[1451].

The Health Information Technology for Economic and Clinical Health Act (hereinafter: HITECH) of 2009 represented a significant privacy law and federal legal regulation for promoting the use of EHRs[1452]. HITECH was included in the American Recovery and Reinvestment Act (ARRA) which sought to encourage the adoption of e-health systems in the US by allocating billions of resources to eligible hospitals and professionals[1453]. In particular, HITECH encouraged the use of EHRs, EMRs and electronic prescriptions to aggregate and distribute PHI. Healthcare providers registered in a subsidy process to receive funds while making a "meaningful use of certified EHR technology"[1454]. HITECH enabled more coordination and alignment within and among states on EHRs to create an interconnected system of healthcare delivery[1455].

In sum, this Act mandated some changes in the HIPAA: it increased penalties, extended the scope of the HIPAA to business associates of covered entities, and required a data security breach notification and a three-year audit trial[1456]. The introduction of the audit trial was an important novelty since it mandated the record of disclosures, which should be

1451 In particular, *see* Chapter 3, Section 3.4.2.

1452 Health Information Technology (HITECH) Provisions of American Recovery and Reinvestment Act of 2009, Title XIII, Subtitle D (Pub. L. 111–5, 123 Stat. 115, significantly codified at 42 U.S.C. § 17937 and 17954).

1453 *See* Dumortier and Verhenneman, "Legal regulation of electronic health records: a comparative analysis of Europe and the US", p. 42; J.A. Magnuson and Patrick W. O'Carroll. "Introduction to public health informatics". In: *Public health informatics and information systems*. Springer, 2014, pp. 3–18. ISBN: 9780387227450, p. 12; Yasnoff, "Privacy, Confidentiality, and Security of Public Health Information", p. 160; Pasquale, "Health Information Law", pp. 203–205.

1454 Terry, "Meaningful adoption: What we know or think we know about the financing, effectiveness, quality, and safety of electronic medical records", p. 15.

1455 Hartley and Jones, *EHR implementation: A step-by-step guide for the medical practice*, p. 6.

1456 *See* Solove and Schwartz, *Information privacy law*, p. 468; Yasnoff, "Privacy, Confidentiality, and Security of Public Health Information", p. 160; Hiller et al., "Privacy and security in the implementation of health information technology (electronic health records): US and EU compared", p. 11.

available to the individual upon request on the basis of a specific right[1457]. The obligation of data breach notification was established both for covered entities and their business associates. Business associates are the third-party vendors with which the covered entities contract. After the HITECH, they are bound to the Privacy Rule by statute of law[1458]. Independent online PHR vendors are still not bound to the rules. However, it has been pointed out that these entities are subject to the FTC Act for their practices[1459].

In 2013, the Department of Health and Human Services released the "Omnibus Final Rule", which implemented the changes of the HITECH Act in the HIPAA's Privacy and Security Rules, as well as in 45 C.F.R.[1460].

HITECH tried to regulate EHR and PHI exchange within this environment by focusing on its standardisation[1461]. It has been reported that healthcare providers were encouraged by the HITECH Act to use certified EHR: this technology was supposed to collect complete and accurate information so that patient care could be improved, providers could better access to medical information, and patients could have been empowered by increased access to their medical records[1462]. Three pillars have been identified for the use of certified EHRs: using this technology in a "meaningful" manner; using the systems for the electronic exchange of health information to improve national quality of healthcare; and using the technology to submit clinical quality and other measures for health[1463].

The HITECH Act conditioned public funding on the "meaningful use" of EHRs: a beneficiary could be funded insofar as the EHR was implemented with defined functional requirements (i.e. basic information, clini-

---

1457 *See* Yasnoff, "Privacy, Confidentiality, and Security of Public Health Information", p. 160.

1458 *See* Dumortier and Verhenneman, "Legal regulation of electronic health records: a comparative analysis of Europe and the US", p. 48. The author highlights that business associates are bound by statute of law. Therefore, covered entities need to ensure the implementation of the rules by their business associates.

1459 *See ibid.*

1460 Solove and Schwartz, "Health privacy", p. 510. On the Omnibus Rule *See* Hartley and Jones, *EHR implementation: A step-by-step guide for the medical practice*, pp. 88–89.

1461 Dumortier and Verhenneman, "Legal regulations on electronic health records: a prerequisite or an unavoidable by-product? – The legal aspects of electronic health records in Europe and the US analysed".

1462 Magnuson and O'Carroll, "Introduction to public health informatics", p. 13.

1463 Hartley and Jones, *EHR implementation: A step-by-step guide for the medical practice*, p. 6.

cal health information, and medical history)[1464]. In addition to functional requirements, EHRs should follow basic standards on data entry and portability, and the standards defined by "Authorized Testing and Certification Bodies" with reference to the ISO's standards[1465]. The Office of the National Coordinator for Health Information Technology reported that in 2017 nearly 86 % of office-based physicians adopted any EHR, and nearly 80 % adopted a certified record[1466]. However, it is always necessary to concretely evaluate whether the record in use is an EMR or an EHR[1467]. In the US the potential of the EHR is great for enhancing healthcare, but the level of frustration of stakeholders is still high due to the uncoordinated environment[1468].

So, the applicable framework for EHRs and EMRs are primarily the HIPAA, consumer protection guidelines and self-regulatory instruments (e.g. standards, contracts, codes of conduct, and privacy seals)[1469]. In fact, HIPAA Privacy and Security Rules apply to typical healthcare providers (physicians, doctors and pharmacies).

Common law and tort law (public disclosure and intrusion, especially) protect health information in US EHRs too, but this protection is circumscribed[1470]. As previously mentioned, statutory law also regulates medical

1464 *See* Pasquale, "Health Information Law", p. 204.

1465 *See* Pasquale, *op. cit.*, p. 205.

1466 *See* ONC Office of the National Coordinator for Health Information Technology. *Office-based Physician Electronic Health Record Adoption*. 2019.

1467 After the initial phase of ARRA, Terry claimed that there were far more EMRs than EHRs in use. *See* Terry, "Meaningful adoption: What we know or think we know about the financing, effectiveness, quality, and safety of electronic medical records", p. 27.

1468 Katsh and Rabinovich-Einy, "The Internet of On-Demand Healthcare", p. 85.

1469 *See* Dumortier and Verhenneman, "Legal regulation of electronic health records: a comparative analysis of Europe and the US", p. 50. The authors argue that the US the legal framework is less extensive than in Europe, but equally complicated. The right to privacy and the right to avoid disclosure of personal matters have been recognised by courts, but the legal framework protecting them is "a complex patchwork of laws different from state to state and often narrowly targeting a particular population, health condition, data collection effort or specific type of health care organizations". *See* also Jacques, "Electronic health records and respect for patient privacy: A prescription for compatibility".

1470 *See* the reference to case law on electronic health information in Solove and Schwartz, "Health privacy", and Terry and Francis, "Ensuring the privacy and confidentiality of electronic health records", p. 708.

records and medical confidentiality, and it can pre-empt HIPAA requirements where more stringent[1471].

Moreover, 45 C.F.R. § 170 provides the standards, implementation specifications, and certification criteria for EHRs and HITs[1472]. An EHR "edition base" shall include patients' demographics and clinical health information, such as medical history and problem lists[1473]. The main functions are those previously explained in Chapter 3: the integrated view of and access to a patient's information, the clinical decision support system, the clinician order entry, and the health information and communication exchange[1474]. Certification criteria establish whether EHRs meet applicable standards and implementation specifications[1475]. It should be noted that the certification criteria on EHRs provided by the Code are extremely useful for understanding how privacy and security requirements may be framed by a legislator in great detail[1476]. The criteria are divided in required and "optional"[1477]. The privacy and security criteria are specifically defined in 45 C.F.R. § 170.315(d)[1478].

Health information in medical records is also protected by the Privacy Act of 1974, as amended in 2010 at 5 U.S.C. § 552a, and which applies to federal agencies. Under the Privacy Act, individuals have the right to access, and request correction of, medical records maintained by an agency[1479]. The same Act indicates several general requirements for the agen-

1471 *See ibid.*

1472 This section has been revised at 85 FR. 25642, 25639, May 1, 2020, and has been effective since June 30, 2020.

1473 45 C.F.R. § 170.102.

1474 *See* Chapter 3, 3.4.1 in line with 45 C.F.R. § 170.102(2).

1475 The central requirements are 45 C.F.R. § 170.299, which incorporates by reference certain standards, and § 170.315 2015 on edition health IT certification criteria.

1476 *See* e.g. 45 C.F.R. § 170.315, which was amended in 2020.

1477 As an example, in the "computerized provider order entry – medications" criterion at 45 C.F.R. § 170.315(a), it is mandatory to "enable a user to record, change, and access medication orders", whereas it is optional to "include a "reason for order" field".

1478 Chapter 5 will take into account the criteria, safeguards and standards for EHRs that have been adopted by the Code of Federal Regulations.

1479 *See* § 552a of the Privacy Act: "the term "record" means any item, collection, or grouping of information about an individual that is maintained by an agency, including, but not limited to, his education, financial transactions, medical history, and criminal or employment history and that contains his name, or the identifying number, symbol, or other identifying particular assigned to the individual, such as a finger or voice print or a photograph". On the access, it is

cies, which shall respect a form of data minimisation principle, guarantee transparency by informing the individuals, preserving accuracy, and implementing policies and administrative, technical and physical safeguards to ensure security and confidentiality of the records[1480]. However, this

---

established that "each agency that maintains a system of records shall (1) upon request by any individual to gain access to his record or to any information pertaining to him which is contained in the system, permit him and upon his request, a person of his own choosing to accompany him, to review the record and have a copy made of all or any portion thereof in a form comprehensible to him, except that the agency may require the individual to furnish a written statement authorizing discussion of that individual's record in the accompanying person's presence; (2) permit the individual to request amendment of a record pertaining to him and (A) not later than 10 days (excluding Saturdays, Sundays, and legal public holidays) after the date of receipt of such request, acknowledge in writing such receipt; and (B) promptly, either (i) make any correction of any portion thereof which the individual believes is not accurate, relevant, timely, or complete; or (ii) inform the individual of its refusal to amend the record in accordance with his request, the reason for the refusal, the procedures established by the agency for the individual to request a review of that refusal by the head of the agency or an officer designated by the head of the agency, and the name and business address of that official".

1480 *See* § 552a(e): "each agency that maintains a system of records shall (1) maintain in its records only such information about an individual as is relevant and necessary to accomplish a purpose of the agency required to be accomplished by statute or by executive order of the President; (2) collect information to the greatest extent practicable directly from the subject individual when the information may result in adverse determinations about an individual's rights, benefits, and privileges under Federal programs; (3) inform each individual whom it asks to supply information, on the form which it uses to collect the information or on a separate form that can be retained by the individual (...); (5) maintain all records which are used by the agency in making any determination about any individual with such accuracy, relevance, timeliness, and completeness as is reasonably necessary to assure fairness to the individual in the determination; (6) prior to disseminating any record about an individual to any person other than an agency, unless the dissemination is made pursuant to subsection (b)(2) of this section, make reasonable efforts to assure that such records are accurate, complete, timely, and relevant for agency purposes; (7) maintain no record describing how any individual exercises rights guaranteed by the First Amendment unless expressly authorized by statute or by the individual about whom the record is maintained or unless pertinent to and within the scope of an authorized law enforcement activity; (8) make reasonable efforts to serve notice on an individual when any record on such individual is made available to any person under compulsory legal process when such process becomes a matter of public record; (9) establish rules of conduct for persons involved in the design, development, operation, or maintenance of any system of records, or in maintaining any record, and instruct each

Act applies to government agencies only, and not to private healthcare providers[1481].

Furthermore, the FTC's consumer protection applies to companies which process PHI, even in EHRs[1482]. As an example, in 2014 the FTC filed a complaint against the corporation Accretive Health, which offered services to hospital systems, for failing to provide reasonable and appropriate security for consumers' personal information against unauthorised access[1483]. In 2020, the FTC found that the seller of emergency travel

---

such person with respect to such rules and the requirements of this section, including any other rules and procedures adopted pursuant to this section and the penalties for noncompliance; (10) establish appropriate administrative, technical, and physical safeguards to insure the security and confidentiality of records and to protect against any anticipated threats or hazards to their security or integrity which could result in substantial harm, embarrassment, inconvenience, or unfairness to any individual on whom information is maintained; (...)".

1481 Gostin, Hodge Jr., and Marks, "The Nationalization of Health Information Privacy Protections", p. 1122, which points out the weaknesses of a specific privacy statutory and regulative strategy: "Although existing federal and state privacy statutes and regulations are meaningful and serve valuable ends, they share several weaknesses: (1) like constitutional privacy protections, most statutes apply primarily to government collections, uses, or disclosures of health information, and thus often do not confer protections to health information in the private sector; (2) they fail to address the new challenges to individual privacy arising from the automation of medical records; (3) they collectively represent a patchwork effort to address the privacy and security of specific health information; (4) some kinds of data are treated as superconfidential (e.g., H1V/AIDS), while other data are virtually unprotected, leading to inconsistencies and unfairness; (5) they do not effectively balance competing individual interests in privacy with the need to use the data for the common good; and (6) some state laws prohibit disclosures without informed consent, but make so many exceptions as to negate the prohibition". Then the authors claim the need for a comprehensive approach to health privacy protection.

1482 *See* Dumortier and Verhenneman, "Legal regulations on electronic health records: a prerequisite or an unavoidable by-product? – The legal aspects of electronic health records in Europe and the US analysed", which also refers to PHRs.

1483 Accretive Health, F.T.C. No. C-4432 (2014), available at <www.ftc.gov/enforcement/cases-proceedings/ 122–3077/accretive-health-inc-matter>. Last accessed 06/10/2021. According to the FTC, "Accretive Health created unnecessary risks of unauthorized access or theft of personal information by: a. Transporting laptops containing personal information in a manner that made them vulnerable to theft or other misappropriation; b. Failing to adequately restrict access to, or copying of, personal information based on an employee's need for information; c. Failing to ensure that employees removed information

membership plans SkyMed International Inc. failed to provide reasonable security for the collected health information of members' records[1484]. The FTC's framework is an important baseline for protection against the entities that are not subject to the HIPAA since they are not covered entities[1485]. The FTC Act protects against entities engaged in a commercial activity, and not non-profit and governmental entities; nonetheless, it has been highlighted that the FTC can generally settle larger fines than the HIPAA[1486]. The FTC's scope covers unfair and deceptive practices. It may be argued that the PbD approach may be a recommended practice in this field on the basis of the FTC's actions. In fact, in the Report of 2012 the FTC referred to the healthcare sector by pointing out that its framework on consumer protection did not overlap with the HIPAA, but it is meant to encourage best practices among healthcare companies[1487].

---

from their computers for which they no longer had a business need; and d. Using consumers' personal information in training sessions with employees and failing to ensure that the information was removed from employees' computers following the training". Moreover, in 2011 a data breach involving the information of 23,000 patients occurred.

1484 SkyMed International Inc., F.T.C. No. C-1923140 (2020), available at <www.ftc.gov/enforcement/ cases-proceedings/1923140/skymed-international-inc-matter>. Last accessed 06/10/2021. In particular, SkyMed: "a. failed to develop, implement, or maintain written organizational information security standards, policies, procedures, or practices; b. failed to provide adequate guidance or training for employees or third-party contractors regarding information security and safeguarding consumers' personal information; c. stored consumers' personal information on Respondent's network and databases in plain text, without reasonable data access controls or authentication protections; d. failed to assess the risks to the personal information stored on its network and databases, such as by conducting periodic risk assessments or performing vulnerability and penetration testing of the network and databases; e. failed to have a policy, procedure, or practice for inventorying and deleting consumers' personal information stored on Respondent's network that is no longer necessary; and f. failed to use data loss prevention tools to regularly monitor for unauthorized attempts to transfer or exfiltrate consumers' personal information outside of Respondent's network boundaries". The investigation showed that 130,000 cloud records were publicly available online for at least five months.

1485 *See* Guadarrama, "Mind the Gap: Addressing Gaps in HIPAA Coverage in the Mobile Health Apps Industry", p. 1011, which refers to mobile health application industry.

1486 Solove and Schwartz, "Health privacy", p. 533.

1487 *See* the Report at p. 16–17. *See* Chapter 2, note no. 116.

EHR privacy is also explicitly protected by ethical confidentiality rules. According to AMA's Code of Medical Ethics Opinion 3.3.1, US physicians have an ethical obligation of confidentiality to manage medical records appropriately[1488]. Appropriate management entails a "clear policy prohibiting access to patients' medical records by unauthorised staff", and an information retention which respects patients' future health care needs. Medical records should be made available to patients on request, to subsequent physicians or other authorised person where necessary, and on the basis of law. The record may be transferred on request, and the physician should not refuse, but a reasonable fee may be asked. This is a sort of right to data portability. During the processing, the storage of the records should be safe, and when they have to be discarded, they should be destroyed completely. A notification on how to access the medical record and for how long it will be available should be received by the patient (i.e. information retention).

Opinion 3.3.2 of the AMA explicitly refers to electronic records by recommending that physicians choose an electronic system "that conforms to acceptable industry practices and standards". The system should be able to restrict data entry and access only to authorised users, routinely provide monitoring and auditing tools, implement security measures to ensure data security and integrity, as well as policies and practices "to address record retrieval, data sharing, third-party access and release of information, and disposition of records"[1489]. The patient could request a notice on how

1488 *See* this opinion and the following one at <www.ama-assn.org/delivering-care/ethics/ management-medical-records>. Last accessed 06/10/2021. *See* also Francis, "When patients interact with EHRs: problems of privacy and confidentiality", which reports the valuable concepts of the AMA's Opinions on EHRs.

1489 The other "Breach of Security in Electronic Medical Records" Opinion 3.3.3 further elaborates on the concept of security. In particular, it specifies: "when used with appropriate attention to security, electronic medical records (EMRs) promise numerous benefits for quality clinical care and health-related research. However, when a security breach occurs, patients may face physical, emotional, and dignitary harms. Dedication to upholding trust in the patient-physician relationship, to preventing harms to patients, and to respecting patients' privacy and autonomy create responsibilities for individual physicians, medical practices, and health care institutions when patient information is inappropriately disclosed. The degree to which an individual physician has an ethical responsibility to address inappropriate disclosure depends in part on his or her awareness of the breach, relationship to the patient(s) affected, administrative authority with respect to the records, and authority to act on behalf of the practice or institution. When there is reason to believe that patients'

confidentiality and integrity of information are protected. So, as in the EU, the access and security of electronic medical records are central issues to be addressed with both administrative and technical safeguards. The AMA's opinions are consistent with HIPAA requirements.

Overall, it can be argued that the protection of health information privacy and EHRs remains fragmented since the US healthcare system is managed by different entities, whose e-health technologies are often mutually incompatible and not interoperable[1490]. However, the HIPAA Privacy and Security Rules are specific health information requirements, which are dedicated to the protection of the e-health sector and whose implementation seeks organisational and technical safeguards. In order to investigate the similarities and differences between US and EU approaches to protecting identifiable health information, the next Section focuses on HIPAA Privacy and Security Rules in detail.

## *4.4 Analysing the HIPAA Privacy and Security Rules*

The analysis of the HIPAA Rules will be divided into three sections. The first section deals with the general requirements on applicability, while the

---

confidentiality has been compromised by a breach of the electronic medical record, physicians should: (a) Ensure that patients are promptly informed about the breach and potential for harm, either by disclosing directly (when the physician has administrative responsibility for the EMR), participating in efforts by the practice or health care institution to disclose, or ensuring that the practice or institution takes appropriate action to disclose. (b) Follow all applicable state and federal laws regarding disclosure. Physicians have a responsibility to follow ethically appropriate procedures for disclosure, which should at minimum include: (c) Carrying out the disclosure confidentially and within a time frame that provides patients ample opportunity to take steps to minimize potential adverse consequences. (d) Describing what information was breached; how the breach happened; what the consequences may be; what corrective actions have been taken by the physician, practice, or institution; and what steps patients themselves might take to minimize adverse consequences. (e) Supporting responses to security breaches that place the interests of patients above those of the physician, medical practice, or institution. (f) Providing information to patients to enable them to mitigate potential adverse consequences of inappropriate disclosure of their personal health information to the extent possible".

1490 Nicholson Price II, "Risk and Resilience in Health Data Infrastructure". The author concludes the analysis on the healthcare system by suggesting the creation of a centralised data-driven infrastructure of medical technologies.

second and third sections are dedicated to the Privacy Rule and Security Rule respectively.

### 4.4.1 General requirements

The HIPAA seeks to guarantee medical privacy by "data type" and "by custodian type"[1491]. The Privacy Rule protects individually identifiable health information, defined as "protected health information" (PHI), regardless of the form in which the information is stored, whereas the Security Rule protects the sub-set of this category of information which is in electronic form (e-PHI)[1492]. These rules are based on the principle of technological neutrality and follow the FIPs. De-identified health information does not fall under the HIPAA, if the anonymisation respects some standards and other implementation specifications[1493].

---

1491 Terry, "Regulatory disruption and arbitrage in health-care data protection", p. 205.

1492 *See* 45 C.F.R. § 160.501 and Solove and Schwartz, *Information privacy law*, p. 465.

1493 On de-identified health information and HIPAA Privacy Rule, and a comparison of anonymisation with the GDPR *see* Elizabeth A. Brasher. "Addressing the Failure of Anonymization: Guidance from the European Union's General Data Protection Regulation". In: *Colum. Bus. L. Rev.* (2018), pp. 209–253, pp. 220–223. *See* also Hoffman and Podgurski, "Balancing privacy, autonomy, and scientific needs in electronic health records research", pp. 95–97. PHI is fully de-identified when 18 items are removed (45 C.F.R. § 164.514(b)(2)(i)): "(A) Names; (B) All geographic subdivisions smaller than a State, including street address, city, county, precinct, zip code, and their equivalent geocodes, except for the initial three digits of a zip code if, according to the current publicly available data from the Bureau of the Census: (1) The geographic unit formed by combining all zip codes with the same three initial digits contains more than 20,000 people; and (2) The initial three digits of a zip code for all such geographic units containing 20,000 or fewer people is changed to 000. (C) All elements of dates (except year) for dates directly related to an individual, including birth date, admission date, discharge date, date of death; and all ages over 89 and all elements of dates (including year) indicative of such age, except that such ages and elements may be aggregated into a single category of age 90 or older; (D) Telephone numbers; (E) Fax numbers; (F) Electronic mail addresses; (G) Social security numbers; (H) Medical record numbers; (I) Health plan beneficiary numbers; (J) Account numbers; (K) Certificate/license numbers; (L) Vehicle identifiers and serial numbers, including license plate numbers; (M) Device identifiers and serial numbers; (N) Web Universal Resource Locators (URLs); (O) Internet Protocol (IP) address num-

The HIPAA applies to "covered entities", namely health plans, health care clearinghouses and healthcare providers that transmit any health information in electronic form in connection with a transaction format defined by the Act, and their business associates[1494]. The definitions of covered entities are the following[1495]:

> "Health care clearinghouse means a public or private entity, including a billing service, repricing company, community health management information system or community health information system, and "value-added" networks and switches, that does either of the following functions:
> 1. Processes or facilitates the processing of health information received from another entity in a nonstandard format or containing nonstandard data content into standard data elements or a standard transaction;
> 2. Receives a standard transaction from another entity and processes or facilitates the processing of health information into nonstandard format or nonstandard data content for the receiving entity".
> "Health care provider means a provider of services (as defined in section 1861(u) of the Act, 42 U.S.C. 1395x(u)), a provider of medical or health services (as defined in section 1861(s) of the Act, 42 U.S.C. 1395x(s)), and any other person or organization who furnishes, bills, or is paid for health care in the normal course of business".
> "Health plan means an individual or group plan that provides, or pays the cost of, medical care (as defined in section 2791(a)(2) of the PHS Act, 42 U.S.C. 300gg-91(a)(2))".

A healthcare clearinghouse is a recipient of PHI that processes and aggregates medical information[1496]. Examples of clearinghouses include billing services, repricing companies, value-added networks, and banks[1497]. A

---

bers; (P) Biometric identifiers, including finger and voice prints; (Q) Full face photographic images and any comparable images; and (R) Any other unique identifying number, characteristic, or code...".

1494 *See* 45 C.F.R. § 160.102 on applicability.

1495 *See* 45 C.F.R. § 160.103. There are also "hybrid entities" which are less regulated than covered entities since their purpose is not the provision of care or only components of an entity process health information.

1496 White and Hoffman, "The Privacy Standards Under the Health Insurance Portability and Accountability Act: A Practical Guide to Promote Order and Avoid Potential Chaos", p. 718.

1497 *See* Rebecca Herold and Kevin Beaver. *The practical guide to HIPAA privacy and security compliance*. CRC Press, 2015. ISBN: 9781439855591, p. 12.

healthcare provider is the typical healthcare entity, such as physician, hospital, nurse, pharmacist, or medical technician[1498]. So, a healthcare provider may be either an individual or an organisation that provides personal care, including related billing service[1499]. Both private entities (e.g. health insurance company) and government organisations (e.g. Medicaid[1500]) that provide for the cost of medical care fall under the definition of health plans[1501]. So, health insurance insurers and government- and state-funded programmes are health plans subject to the HIPAA.

Since HITECH, the HIPAA applies to business associates of covered entities, which process information on their behalf[1502]. So, business associates can include a health information organisation that provides transmission services of PHI, and offers PHR on behalf of a covered entity, and a

---

1498 White and Hoffman, "The Privacy Standards Under the Health Insurance Portability and Accountability Act: A Practical Guide to Promote Order and Avoid Potential Chaos", p. 718, which includes "doctors, nurses, therapists, hospitals, medical technicians, nursing homes, rehabilitations centers, psychologists, pharmacists, and therapists".

1499 Herold and Beaver, *The practical guide to HIPAA privacy and security compliance*, p. 12.

1500 On this initiative *see* Wilensky and Teitelbaum, *Essentials of Health Policy and Law*, pp. 233–248. Medicaid is the federal public health insurance programme for indigent people. *See* also the official website at <www. medicaid.gov/>. Last accessed 06/10/2021.

1501 *See* Gostin, Hodge Jr., and Marks, "The Nationalization of Health Information Privacy Protections", p. 1126.

1502 *See* 45 C.F.R. § 160.102(b). According to 45 C.F.R. § 160.103 business associate of a covered entity means "a person who: (i) on behalf of such covered entity or of an organized health care arrangement (as defined in this section) in which the covered entity participates, but other than in the capacity of a member of the workforce of such covered entity or arrangement, creates, receives, maintains, or transmits protected health information for a function or activity regulated by this subchapter, including claims processing or administration, data analysis, processing or administration, utilization review, quality assurance, patient safety activities listed at 42 CFR 3.20, billing, benefit management, practice management, and repricing; or (ii) provides, other than in the capacity of a member of the workforce of such covered entity, legal, actuarial, accounting, consulting, data aggregation (as defined in § 164.501 of this subchapter), management, administrative, accreditation, or financial services to or for such covered entity, or to or for an organized health care arrangement in which the covered entity participates, where the provision of the service involves the disclosure of protected health information from such covered entity or arrangement, or from another business associate of such covered entity or arrangement, to the person".

subcontractor that creates, receives, maintains, or transmits PHI[1503]. Even EHR system vendors may be included in this definition if they are third parties that offer the EHR systems under a contract with the healthcare providers. As another example, lawyers, accountants and billing companies are usually contractors of covered entities whose work involves the use and disclosure of PHI[1504]. Business associate agreements and contracts between the covered entity and its business associates will define the safeguards that the latter shall provide for information disclosed by the former[1505].

The HIPAA has come under criticism by commentators who have pointed out that significant health-related activities do not fall under the definition of covered entity[1506]. In fact, the definition of covered entity has been criticised as too narrow[1507]: many subjects that process health information operate outside the HIPAA's conditions, leaving a large gap[1508]. EHR and EMR providers are subject to HIPAA Privacy and Security Rules. Nonetheless, it has been pointed out that employers utilising employer health plans and PHRs or EHRs are not covered entities while administering the plans, but the HIPAA's requirements may apply to health plans that disclose

1503 *See* 45 C.F.R. § 160.103(3).

1504 *See* Gostin, Hodge Jr., and Marks, "The Nationalization of Health Information Privacy Protections", p. 1126, which was published before the HITECH but referred to examples of business associates. *See* also White and Hoffman, "The Privacy Standards Under the Health Insurance Portability and Accountability Act: A Practical Guide to Promote Order and Avoid Potential Chaos", p. 719, which includes "malpractice insurers, accountants, certain vendors, lawyers, and collection agencies". Herold and Beaver, *The practical guide to HIPAA privacy and security compliance*, p. 13 points to these sectors: "legal, actuarial, accounting, consulting, data aggregation, management, administrative, accreditation, or financial services".

1505 *See* Tomes, "20 Plus Years of HIPAA and What Have We Got", p. 78, which discusses the cost of the drafting activity.

1506 *See* Solove and Schwartz, *Information privacy law*, p. 473; Dumortier and Verhenneman, "Legal regulation of electronic health records: a comparative analysis of Europe and the US"; Hoffman and Klein, "Explaining explanation, part 1: theoretical foundations", pp. 275–276; Hoffman, "Medical Privacy and Security", p. 275; Terry, "Regulatory disruption and arbitrage in health-care data protection"; Guadarrama, "Mind the Gap: Addressing Gaps in HIPAA Coverage in the Mobile Health Apps Industry".

1507 *See* also Hoffman and Podgurski, "In sickness, health, and cyberspace: protecting the security of electronic private health information", p. 334.

1508 Anglim, Kirtley, and Nobahar, *Privacy Rights in the Digital Age*, p. 270; Guadarrama, "Mind the Gap: Addressing Gaps in HIPAA Coverage in the Mobile Health Apps Industry"; Solove and Schwartz, "Health privacy", p. 514.

PHI to employers pursuant to a confidential agreement[1509]. So, employers are bound by the HIPAA Privacy Rule only to the extent that they act as insurers, i.e. they provide the plans as health plans[1510]. Online health services (e.g. apps, m-health, Google Health) are frequently excluded[1511]. Websites, mobile apps, and other e-health services shall not comply with HIPAA requirements[1512]. Future regulation may extend the definition to the emerging subjects of the e-health domain, or it may cover protected health information regardless of the entity that processes it[1513].

---

1509 *See* Gostin, Hodge Jr., and Marks, "The Nationalization of Health Information Privacy Protections", p. 1126, which refers to 45 C.F.R. § 164.504(f)(l)(1), (2).

1510 Hoffman, "Employing e-health: the impact of electronic health records on the workplace", p. 424. In the case *Beard v. City of Chicago*, 2005 U.S. Dist. LEXIS 374 (ND Ill Jan. 10, 2005), it is ruled that under the HIPAA the definition of PHI excludes PHI in employment records held by a covered entity in its role as employer.

1511 Dumortier and Verhenneman, "Legal regulation of electronic health records: a comparative analysis of Europe and the US", pp. 34–35; Terry, "Regulatory disruption and arbitrage in health-care data protection", pp. 181–184. Google Health is building an EHR tool to connect different healthcare providers. The tool will store EMRs, connect providers, organise PHI, aggregate health information and use AI. *See* the first presentation at <www.youtube.com/watch?v=P3SYqcPXqNk>. Last accessed 06/10/2021. Other services in the G Suite are related to healthcare. Cloud Healthcare API allows "easy and standardized data exchange between healthcare applications and solutions built on Google Cloud". *See* the information on the product at <cloud.google.com/healthcare>. Even this tool uses analytics and AI applications.

1512 On the concerns of online health networking *see* Patricia Sanchez Abril and Anita Cava. "Health privacy in a techno-social world: a cyber-patient's bill of rights". In: *Nw. J. Tech. & Intell. Prop.* 6 (2007), pp. 244–277. From 2007 to 2019, Microsoft HealthVault collected PHI as web-based portals. This tool was more similar to a PHR than an EHR.

1513 *See* the analysis in Guadarrama, "Mind the Gap: Addressing Gaps in HIPAA Coverage in the Mobile Health Apps Industry", p. 1019. The HIPAA should be extended by federal legislative action. Moreover, other self-regulative initiatives should start from the developers of health applications. In Hoffman and Klein, "Explaining explanation, part 1: theoretical foundations", p. 285, it is suggested that Texas's definition of covered entity may be used since it is more inclusive. *See* TEX. HEALTH & SAFETY CODE ANN. 181.001(b)(2) (West): "Covered entity means any person who: (A) for commercial, financial, or professional gain, monetary fees, or dues, or on a cooperative, nonprofit, or pro bono basis, engages, in whole or in part, and with real or constructive knowledge, in the practice of assembling, collecting, analyzing, using, evaluating, storing, or transmitting protected health information. The term includes a business associate, health care payer, governmental unit, information or computer management entity, school, health researcher, health care facility,

### 4.4.2 The HIPAA Privacy Rule

Generally, it has been argued that the HIPAA Privacy Rule requires covered entities to give patients notice of privacy practices and protects EHRs from illegal use or disclosure of PHI[1514]. The term "use" may include the employment, application, utilisation and examination of PHI[1515]. A disclosure is a release, transfer, or provision of access in any manner outside the covered entity[1516]. The HIPAA mandates some duties at the organisational and technical level for uses and disclosures. The implementation of the safeguards is an obligation subject to civil and criminal sanctions.

As previously mentioned, the legal ground for processing is not a traditional legal category in the US. Data processing is generally permitted, and the approach of "notice-and-control" usually applies (at least) on the basis of the consent of the individual. Nonetheless, the HIPAA provides a general rule on use and disclosure of PHI, that prohibits processing, except when it is explicitly permitted by the rules[1517]. So, despite the absence of explicit grounds and of the lawfulness principle, the HIPAA indirectly provides the conditions for a "lawful processing". Where the purpose is treatment, payment and healthcare operations, consent is not necessary. However, the individual's authorisation is necessary for other specified purposes and secondary uses, but some exceptions may apply. The HIPAA's exceptions are comparable with the grounds of Article 9 GDPR, and they can be summarised here[1518].

---

clinic, health care provider, or person who maintains an Internet site; (B) comes into possession of protected health information; (C) obtains or stores protected health information under this chapter; or (D) is an employee, agent, or contractor of a person described by Paragraph (A), (B), or (C) insofar as the employee, agent, or contractor creates, receives, obtains, maintains, uses, or transmits protected health information". As a result, the definition of covered entity may be related to the nature of information, instead of a closed list of categories of the subject.

1514 Terry and Francis, "Ensuring the privacy and confidentiality of electronic health records", p. 714.

1515 Herold and Beaver, *The practical guide to HIPAA privacy and security compliance*, p. 72.

1516 Herold and Beaver, *op. cit.*, p. 73.

1517 *See* 45 C.F.R. § 160.502.

1518 The HIPAA defines the exceptions in great detail. The following paragraphs will summarise the exceptions by defining the contexts of processing where consent is not required, and without listing every condition established in 45 C.F.R. § 164.512. The comparison with the EU law is not new. Before the GDPR Dumortier and Verhenneman, "Legal regulation of electronic health

The HIPAA frequently refers to disclosure of PHI to other subjects that can be considered recipients. The potential disclosures are categorised by the literature as "required" and "permissive". The former category includes the disclosure to the patient or his/her representative, and the disclosure for audit or other enforcement purposes, while the latter refers to all other disclosures (e.g. for treatment or on the basis of statutory law). Permissive disclosure may or may not require patient's consent. As a result, it has been claimed that the healthcare provider has more control than the individual over what PHI will be disclosed to recipients or what PHI will remain confidential[1519].

First of all, HIPAA provisions allow processing when information is disclosed directly to the individual, or when the purpose of the use or disclosure is treatment, payment or a healthcare operation. Under the HIPAA "treatment" means "the provision, coordination, or management of health care and related services by one or more health care providers, including the coordination or management of health care by a health care provider with a third party", the "consultation between health care providers relating to a patient", "or the referral of a patient for health care from one health care provider to another"[1520]. In particular, the treatment, payment and healthcare operation purpose embes the following five scenarios[1521]:

1. "A covered entity may use or disclose protected health information for its own treatment, payment, or health care operations;
2. A covered entity may disclose protected health information for treatment activities of a health care provider;
3. A covered entity may disclose protected health information to another covered entity or a health care provider for the payment activities of the entity that receives the information;

records: a comparative analysis of Europe and the US", p. 49, highlighted that the exceptions for research or for treatment are comparable to the exemptions for the prohibition on the processing of personal health data in the EU. *See* also Dumortier and Verhenneman, "Legal regulations on electronic health records: a prerequisite or an unavoidable by-product? – The legal aspects of electronic health records in Europe and the US analysed".

1519 *See* Hiller et al., "Privacy and security in the implementation of health information technology (electronic health records): US and EU compared", p. 15; Munns and Basu, *Privacy and healthcare data: 'choice of control' to 'choice' and 'control'*, p. 93.

1520 *See* 45 C.F.R. § 164.501.

1521 45 C.F.R. § 160.506(c).

4. A covered entity may disclose protected health information to another covered entity for health care operations activities of the entity that receives the information, if each entity either has or had a relationship with the individual who is the subject of the protected health information being requested, the protected health information pertains to such relationship, and the disclosure is: (i) for a purpose listed in paragraph (1) or (2) of the definition of health care operations; or (ii) for the purpose of health care fraud and abuse detection or compliance;
5. A covered entity that participates in an organized health care arrangement may disclose protected health information about an individual to other participants in the organized health care arrangement for any health care operations activities of the organized health care arrangement".

So, the first hypothesis may be compared with Art. 9(2)(h) GDPR (the "healthcare exception") since both rules allow for processing where the covered entity/data controller has the provision of care or treatment as a purpose. The covered entity is directly the healthcare provider, but the HIPAA's rules do not refer to a contract with a professional or to a statutory law, as the GDPR does. The covered entity may use and disclose PHI on the basis of the HIPAA directly. The duty of confidentiality specified by Article 9(3) GDPR for this exception is not included in the HIPAA, but in US medical confidentiality may be granted by ethical codes and by statutory laws[1522].

The other scenarios reported above refer to disclosures to subjects that are related to the provision of care or to the payment of services. Applying these rules to the EHR environment, it seems that the processing is permitted without any consent or authorisation by the individual, if the transmission of e-PHI among healthcare providers in the network is necessary for treatment purpose.

It should also be noted that the HIPAA includes the insurance sector in these exceptions since health insurers and health plans can be covered entities. This is an important difference with the GDPR, where processing for insurance purposes is not allowed under the "healthcare exception" since it shall seek the explicit consent of the data subject[1523].

For other purposes, uses and disclosures, the covered entities shall seek the patient's valid authorisation, i.e. the patient's consent, or the authorisation of a personal representative, unless one of the explicit exceptions

1522 *See infra* Section 4.3.
1523 *See* the argument in Chapter 3, Section 3.3.2.

applies[1524]. In the HIPAA individual consent is an opt-in authorisation, and the use, disclosure, and secondary use shall be consistent with this authorisation[1525]. A valid authorisation shall be written in plain language and limited in time, and shall identify certain core elements, such as the type of PHI, the purpose of the use and disclosure, and the name of the entities involved (e.g. the various recipients)[1526]. The authorisation shall be signed by the individual who shall be informed of the "the right to revoke the authorization in writing", unless some exceptions apply[1527]. The covered entity shall also provide the individual with a copy of the authorisation. Where the authorisation is not valid, the covered entity may be sanctioned[1528].

It has been pointed out that the concept of authorisation under the HIPAA Privacy Rule is similar to consent under the GDPR[1529]. In particular, similarities may include: "the expression of concern relating to clarity" and the need to separate authorisation and consent from other documentation; the prohibition of conditioning services on the basis of authorisation/consent; the existence of the right to revoke an authorisation in the US and the right to withdraw consent in the EU; and the particular attention to marketing purposes[1530]. Both the HIPAA and the GDPR require a free expression of will explicitly dedicated to health information and separated from consent to the medical treatment. Unlike the GDPR, the HIPAA establishes a specific written form for the authorisation, and is more detailed and directive than the GDPR on content of this authorisation[1531].

---

1524 *See* 45 C.F.R. § 160.508.

1525 *See* Burdon, *Digital Data Collection and Information Privacy Law*, p. 175. The consistency is specified in 45 C.F.R. § 164.508(a).

1526 Solove and Schwartz, "Health privacy", p. 515. The elements are listed in 45 C.F.R. § 164.508(c).

1527 *See* 45 C.F.R. § 164.508(c)(i)(2).

1528 *See* e.g. *Martin v. Rolling Hills Hosp., Llc*, 2020 Tenn. LEXIS 154 (Tenn Apr. 29, 2020), where the court specified that "under federal law, a medical authorization is not HIPAA compliant if the authorization has not been filled out completely, with respect to a core element". In this case, the defendants demonstrated that the authorisation of the hospital lacked three core elements required by the HIPAA.

1529 Stacey A Tovino. "The HIPAA Privacy Rule and the EU GDPR: illustrative comparisons". In: *Seton Hall L. Rev.* 47 (2017), pp. 973–994, p. 992.

1530 *Ibid.*

1531 *Ibid.*

According to the HIPAA, consent is necessary for any use or disclosure of psychotherapy notes (except in some authorised cases), for marketing purposes, and for the sale of PHI. Whether the purpose of the processing activities is marketing or commercial, the patient's authorisation is always required. The HIPAA defines marketing by listing activities of the covered entities or third parties that fall under this categorisation[1532]. It is interesting that HIPAA classifies these three binding consent requests. The GDPR simply requires explicit consent without defining concrete contexts. Here the rationale seems to be on the one hand the need to better protect psychotherapy notes, which are highly sensitive, and on the other hand, the opportunity to better safeguard PHI where the purpose of the use and disclosure becomes merely commercial. Clearly, the binding authorisation is problematic if the individual is not sufficiently informed of the risks of the use and disclosure of medical information[1533].

Several exceptions allow primary and secondary uses of PHI without a patient's authorisation. Firstly, use and disclosure may directly be required by law[1534]. Secondly, under the "public health exception" public health authorities and agents can process PHI without the consent of the individual for public health purposes, including preventing and controlling diseases, reporting information to defined authorities, and workplace surveillance[1535]. The public health exemption is established on the basis of the experience of public health agencies, which have to accomplish mandated activities, such as disease surveillance, outbreak investigation, and other public health purposes[1536]. It has been reported that healthcare providers have been reluctant to share information with public health authorities so as not be sanctioned under the HIPAA; however, this compliance concern is caused by a general lack of understanding of the rules, since public agen-

1532 *See* 45 C.F.R. § 164.501.

1533 For considerations on informational asymmetry and nudging, *see* Chapter 2, Section 2.3.

1534 As an example, the publication of death records sought by historical societies were considered permissible under Nebraska's public records statute in the case *State Ex Rel. Adams County Historical Soc'y v. Kinyoun*, 277 Neb. 749, 765 N.W.2d 212, 2009 Neb. LEXIS 80 (Neb May 15, 2009).

1535 *See* Yasnoff, "Privacy, Confidentiality, and Security of Public Health Information", p. 160; Gostin, Hodge Jr., and Marks, "The Nationalization of Health Information Privacy Protections", p. 1115. *See* for more details, 45 C.F.R. § 164.512(a) – (b).

1536 Edmunds, "Governmental and legislative context of informatics", p. 57.

cies may even be considered covered or hybrid entities[1537]. This exception is similar to the "public health" ground of the GDPR, but the HIPAA establishes more detailed conditions for its applicability[1538].

In the employment sector, the covered healthcare provider may disclose PHI to the employer in some circumstances, i.e. to conduct an evaluation on medical surveillance of the workplace, or to evaluate a work-related illness or injury[1539]. The entity may also disclose information to comply with laws on workers' compensation programmes or other similar benefit programmes for work-related injuries or illness[1540]. These exceptions demonstrate the need to use PHI in the context of employment, but they are different from the GDPR's employment basis because in the HIPAA's provision the controller/covered entity and the employer are different subjects. As explained, employers are usually out of the HIPAA's scope of application. Thus, the GDPR's ground of Art. 9(2)(b) is very different since it is based on the assessment of the working capacity from the employer to its employee and the on the basis of social security and social protection law. Conversely, the HIPAA refers to the disclosures operated by a covered entity to an employer for defined purposes.

Another permitted exception is the disclosure on victims of abuse, neglect or domestic violence, where PHI is communicated to a government authority, including a social service or protective services agency, which is authorised by law to receive this category of information[1541]. This particular exception is not provided by the GDPR, but it may be established by Member States under Article 9(4) GDPR.

The "judiciary and administrative proceedings exception" allows the use of PHI by a covered entity in a legal proceeding, and the "law enforcement exception" allows the disclosure of PHI to law enforcement officials pursuant to a court order, subpoena or other legal order[1542]. The HIPAA defines the particular information that can be disclosed in these contexts, such as demographic data, the type of injury and the description of medical conditions.

---

1537 *See* Yasnoff, "Privacy, Confidentiality, and Security of Public Health Information", p. 1.

1538 *See* 45 C.F.R. § 164.512(a).

1539 *See* 45 C.F.R. § 160.512(b)(v).

1540 *See* 45 C.F.R. § 164.512(l).

1541 *See* 45 C.F.R. § 164.512(c).

1542 Gostin, Hodge Jr., and Marks, "The Nationalization of Health Information Privacy Protections", p. 1115. *See* 45 C.F.R. § 164.512(e) – (f).

The provisions for these exceptions are actually very detailed. From a comparison of these requirements with Art. 9(2)(f) of the GDPR it is clear that the GDPR is more limited than the HIPAA. In fact, the HIPAA permits disclosure for law enforcement purpose in cases where EU Directive (EU) 2016/680 applies (and not the GDPR).

PHI can be used for "health research" purposes where one of the three following conditions apply: when an Institutional Review Board (IRB) or a privacy board provides explicit authorisation in this sense after a specific procedure, when PHI is de-identified, or when the individual provides explicit and written authorisation[1543]. The HIPAA does not specify whether use and disclosure may be permitted for archiving purposes in the public interest, or for scientific, historical or statistical purposes as in the GDPR, nor does it require a law as a legal basis. Looking at this exception, the procedure of the institutional or privacy board or the de-identification process may provide some guarantees for individual rights.

The emergency treatment exception (i.e. vital interest ground) is not provided by the HIPAA, but disclosure of PHI is permitted if the covered entity believes in good faith that it is necessary "to prevent or lessen a serious and imminent threat to the health or safety of a person or the public", and the recipient is "reasonably able to prevent or lessen the threat"[1544]. Moreover, specialised government functions often need the disclosure of PHI, such as in the case of military and veterans' activities. So, the HIPAA permits processing where some defined functions should be performed by public entities[1545]. This exception may be considered similar to the public interest ground where a specific statute defines the purpose of the processing and the disclosure.

The following table summarises the comparison between the HIPAA's exceptions detailed above and the legal grounds for processing of the GDPR described in Chapter 3, Section 3.3.2. As shown in this Table 4.3, many legal bases have similar conditions as the HIPAA, but none are identical.

---

1543 *See* 45 C.F.R. § 164.512(i), § 164.514(a) and § 164.508(a)(1). *See* Cate, "Protecting privacy in health research: the limits of individual choice", p. 1788, which contests the concept of a patient's authorisation because of potential abuse.

1544 *See* 45 C.F.R. § 164.512(j). Notably, the rules on privacy notice specify that in an emergency treatment situation the notice shall be delivered as soon as reasonably possible, implying that this situation occurs in the treatment, payment and healthcare context.

1545 *See* 45 C.F.R. § 164.512(k).

*Table 4.3 Summary of the comparison between GDPR grounds and HIPAA rules*

| LEGITIMATE BASIS (EU), RULE/ EXCEPTION (US) | GDPR | HIPAA |
|---|---|---|
| Consent | Explicit consent, Art. 9(2)(a) (e.g. apps) | Valid authorisation, explicitly for marketing and psychotherapy notes § 164.508 |
| Employment use | Obligation and rights in the field of employment, social security, social protection law, Art. 9(2)(b) | Work-related illness or injury or work-related surveillance by the employer, and workers compensation § 164.512(b)(v)- (l) |
| Vital interest | Vital interest, Art. 9(2)(c) | Uses and disclosures to avert a serious threat to health or safety § 164.512(j) |
| Data made public | Art. 9(2)(e) | Not provided |
| Data on abuse | Not provided | Information on abuse, neglect, domestic violence, § 164.512(c) |
| Legal use | Legal claim use, Art. 9(2)(f) | Judicial and administrative proceedings, law enforcement purpose, § 164.512(f) |
| Public interest | Substantial public interest, Art. 9(2)(g) | Specialised government functions, § 164.512(k) |

| LEGITIMATE BASIS (EU), RULE/ EXCEPTION (US) | GDPR | HIPAA |
|---|---|---|
| Healthcare exception | Preventive or occupational medicine, assessment of the working capacity, medical diagnosis, medical treatment, management of health services and systems subject to conditions provides by law, Art. 9(2)(h) | Treatment, payment, healthcare provision |
| Contract with healthcare professional | Execution of a contract with healthcare professional, Art. 9(2)(h) | Not provided |
| Public health | Public interest in public health, Art. 9(2)(i) | Public health activities, health oversight activities, serious threats to health or safety, § 164.512(b)(1) |
| Research | Archiving in public interest, scientific, historical research, statistic, Art. 9(2)(j) | After a privacy board's decision § 164.512(i) |

Under the previous circumstances, the covered entity shall implement policies and procedures to limit the amount of information to be disclosed. The "minimum necessary rule" is a sort of minimisation principle that has been introduced in the HIPAA where it is specified that covered entities shall make reasonable efforts to limit PHI to "the amount reasonably necessary to achieve the purpose of the disclosure"[1546]. Hence, a covered entity shall use and disclose the minimum amount of PHI to the extent it is necessary to fulfil the intended purpose or carry out any function[1547]. To this end, the covered entity should evaluate its practices and

1546 *See* 45 C.F.R. § 164.514(d).

1547 *See* Dumortier and Verhenneman, "Legal regulation of electronic health records: a comparative analysis of Europe and the US", p. 49, which point

limit unnecessary or inappropriate access to, and disclosure of, protected health information[1548]. Implementing policies and procedures for routine disclosures may limit the PHI disclosed to the amount reasonably necessary to achieve the purpose[1549]. It can be argued that the HIPAA provides a form of information minimisation related to medical confidentiality[1550]. This rule is flexible, like the data minimisation principle. It may even enhance patient autonomy and promote trust in the healthcare system[1551]. However, this requirement does not apply to treatment purposes and to a few other exceptions, such as disclosure with the individual's authorisation or disclosure required by law[1552].

As regards an individual's rights, the HIPAA Privacy Rule includes: the right to receive a privacy notice; where applicable, the right to request restriction and to receive confidential communications; the right to access (i.e. right to inspect and obtain a copy) and the right to rectification of PHI (i.e. right to amend); the right to obtain a record of when and why PHI has been shared with others for certain purposes (i.e. right to receive an accounting of disclosures); and the right to file a complaint to the Health and Human Services' Office of Civil Rights[1553]. Commentators define these rights as fair information practices for health consumers[1554].

---

out that this rule was introduced after the ARRA in 2009. *See* also Terry, "Regulatory disruption and arbitrage in health-care data protection", p. 99.

1548 Terry, *op. cit.*

1549 Hartley and Jones, *EHR implementation: A step-by-step guide for the medical practice*, p. 103.

1550 *See* Burdon, *Digital Data Collection and Information Privacy Law*, p. 175.

1551 Gostin, Hodge Jr., and Marks, "The Nationalization of Health Information Privacy Protections", p. 1131.

1552 *See* Solove and Schwartz, *Information privacy law*, p. 467, which reports § 164.502(b)(1). As regards EHRs and medical records, it is further specified that for all uses, disclosures, or requests to which the "minimum necessary rule" applies, a covered entity "may not use, disclose or request an entire medical record, except when the entire medical record is specifically justified as the amount that is reasonably necessary to accomplish the purpose of the use, disclosure, or request". *See* 45 C.F.R. § 164.514(d)(5). *See* also Herold and Beaver, *The practical guide to HIPAA privacy and security compliance*, pp. 95–98.

1553 Hiller et al., "Privacy and security in the implementation of health information technology (electronic health records): US and EU compared", pp. 13–14.

1554 *See* e.g. Gostin, Hodge Jr., and Marks, "The Nationalization of Health Information Privacy Protections", p. 1128.

Unlike the GDPR, the patient's rights to erasure, to portability, and to not be subject solely to an automated decision are not granted[1555].

Firstly, the individuals have the right to receive a notice of privacy practice which shall contain certain information and be written in plain language[1556]. As previously mentioned, the individual shall be informed of the right to revoke the authorisation while providing consent[1557]. After that, the notice shall be given to the individual and also be available on request later[1558]. The HIPAA even mandates the statement that shall be used as the header of the notice: "this notice describes how medical information about you may be used and disclosed and how you can get access to this information. Please review it carefully"[1559]. Moreover, the content of the notice shall include several details, including a description of the uses and disclosures and of each purpose, a statement on the individual's rights and how they can be exercised, references to covered entities' duties (e.g. on notifying a breach), and contact details[1560]. The notice can be provided electronically.

Secondly, individuals have the right to request restriction to the use and disclosure of information[1561]. However, this option is significantly limited[1562]. The right to request restriction applies in few conditions because, despite the ability to request limitation of the use of PHI during a treatment, payment or healthcare operation, the covered entity may or may not agree to the restrictions[1563]. This entity shall restrict the use

---

1555 Some comparative considerations on the existing rights will be provided in the next section.

1556 *See* 45 C.F.R. § 164.520. *See* also the list of binding statements in Herold and Beaver, *The practical guide to HIPAA privacy and security compliance*, pp. 102–103.

1557 Solove and Schwartz, "Health privacy", p. 515, which emphasises this right.

1558 Hartley and Jones, *EHR implementation: A step-by-step guide for the medical practice*, p. 94, suggests seeking professional advice from a counsel to write the notice and then providing the notice at the first visit to the healthcare facility.

1559 *See* 45 C.F.R. § 164.520(b)(1)(i). An example of compliant structure of an HIPAA privacy notice is provided in Herold and Beaver, *The practical guide to HIPAA privacy and security compliance*, pp. 153–158.

1560 *See* the binding elements in 45 C.F.R. § 164.520(b)(1)(ii). In 45 C.F.R. § 164.520(b)(2), HIPAA lists the optional elements.

1561 *See* 45 C.F.R. § 164.502, § 164.522.

1562 *See* the discussion in Hiller et al., "Privacy and security in the implementation of health information technology (electronic health records): US and EU compared", p. 15; Munns and Basu, *Privacy and healthcare data: 'choice of control' to 'choice' and 'control'*, p. 92.

1563 45 C.F.R. § 164.522(a).

and disclosure for payment purposes only. Interestingly, the individual also has the right to request confidential communication of PHI (i.e. an accommodation of communication preferences) from the covered entity by alternative means where it is reasonable[1564].

The right to access to health information also applies in the US. In particular, individuals have the "right to inspect" (i.e. access) their medical record and obtain a copy of it "in a designed record set"[1565]. However, this right has several limitations, and is not absolute[1566]. It does not apply to psychotherapy notes or to "information compiled in reasonable anticipation of, or for use in, a civil, criminal, or administrative action or proceeding". In other cases, the covered entity may deny the access request on the basis of "nonrenewable grounds for denial": if the covered entity is a correctional institution and the information may jeopardise the health, safety, security, custody, or rehabilitation of the individual or of others; while the information is used in the course of a research; if the information is collected in a record subject to the Privacy Act; and if the information is obtained from another entity under the duty of confidentiality[1567]. The HIPAA also lists renewable grounds for denial by including the following cases: if a licensed healthcare professional evaluates that access is "reasonably likely to endanger the life or physical safety of the individual or another person"; and if the PHI makes reference to another person or the request for access is made by the individual's personal representative, and a licensed health care professional evaluates that access may cause harm as reported in the first cases[1568]. As a result, the discretion of the covered entity is combined with a professional judgement.

Where the right of access is applicable, the form and format of access are requested directly by the individual, even electronically, and the request shall be satisfied in a timely manner[1569]. So, in an EHR environment the

---

1564 45 C.F.R. § 164.522(b).

1565 *See* 45 C.F.R. § 164.524(a)(1).

1566 On this right *see* e.g. Hartley and Jones, *EHR implementation: A step-by-step guide for the medical practice*, pp. 124–127.

1567 *See* 45 C.F.R. § 164.524(a)(2).

1568 *See* 45 C.F.R. § 164.524(a)(3). The individual has the right to have the denial reviewed by another licensed healthcare professional designated by the covered entity. The covered entity shall give access to the other accessible information and write the denial in plain language by explaining the basis for the denial and by describing how the individual may complain to the entity pursuant to a procedure.

1569 *See* 45 C.F.R. § 164.524(c). The covered entity has 30 days to satisfy the request. The individual may agree to a summary of PHI in place of the entire designed

individual may request to receive the data electronically. Notably, the individual has the right to "transmit the copy of protected health information directly to another person designated": this is a sort of right to portability[1570]. The HIPAA Privacy Rule allows patients access to their PHI, but this right does not include a right to establish the provenance of the data and the purpose for which it is used, as in the EU. A right to concealment is not explicitly provided[1571]. However, commentators suggested the possibility of establishing a right to flag particularly sensitive information as "confidential" to keep it secret from the healthcare network[1572].

Moreover, the individual has the right to correct inaccurate or missing PHI maintained in a record set[1573]. After the request, the covered entity has 60 days to identify the record, provide the amendment and inform the individual[1574]. The covered entity may deny its applicability in whole or in part, but may explain the basis for denial in written form[1575].

As regards the right to receive "an accounting of disclosures", it is a particular right of the HIPAA that applies to the information disclosed in the six years prior to the request[1576]. However, disclosures for carrying out treatment, payment and healthcare operations are excluded, as well as other eight circumstances[1577]. As a result, the right is again highly

---

record set. The covered entity may charge the individual for the request. The fee shall be reasonable, and cost based.

1570 *See* 45 C.F.R. § 164.524(c)(3)(ii).

1571 *See* this right in the EU system at Chapter 3, Section 3.4.2.

1572 *See* Jacques, "Electronic health records and respect for patient privacy: A prescription for compatibility", p. 461.

1573 *See* 45 C.F.R. § 164.526(a).

1574 *See* 45 C.F.R. § 164.526(b) and (c).

1575 *See* 45 C.F.R. § 164.526(d).

1576 *See* 45 C.F.R. § 164.528(a).

1577 The cases are listed by 45 C.F.R. § 164.528(a)(1): "An individual has a right to receive an accounting of disclosures of protected health information made by a covered entity in the six years prior to the date on which the accounting is requested, except for disclosures: (i) To carry out treatment, payment and health care operations as provided in § 164.506; (ii) To individuals of protected health information about them as provided in § 164.502; (iii) Incident to a use or disclosure otherwise permitted or required by this subpart, as provided in § 164.502; (iv) Pursuant to an authorization as provided in § 164.508; (v) For the facility's directory or to persons involved in the individual's care or other notification purposes as provided in § 164.510; (vi) For national security or intelligence purposes as provided in § 164.512(k)(2); (vii) To correctional institutions or law enforcement officials as provided in § 164.512(k)(5); (viii) As part of a limited data set in accordance with § 164.514(e); or (ix) That occurred prior to the compliance date for the covered entity".

limited. Anyway, the written accounting of disclosures shall contain specific elements established by the HIPAA, including the date, the contact details of the recipients, a brief description of the PHI and the basis for disclosure[1578].

The HIPAA Privacy Rule protects confidentiality of PHI and grants these individual rights. In addition to the Privacy Rule, the Security Rule adds protection to a subset of PHI, that is electronic protected health information.

### 4.4.3 The HIPAA Security Rule

The Security Rule covers e-PHI protection by providing administrative, physical and technical safeguards[1579]. The Rule mandates effective procedures to avoid improper disclosure of PHI and regular risk assessments to plan remedial actions[1580]. It has been pointed out that the goals of the Security Rule revolve around the confidentiality, integrity, and availability of electronic PHI, i.e. the central concepts of security or CIA triad[1581]. In particular, the rationale of the Security Rule is protecting the confidentiality, integrity and availability of e-PHI at a reasonable and appropriate level[1582].

The Security Rule is also designed to be technologically neutral[1583]. The approach is highly scalable and flexible, but it also mandates the implementation of specific standards[1584]. The legislative technique of providing a list of specific standards has the virtue of giving guidance and specificity,

---

1578 *See* 45 C.F.R. § 164.528(b).

1579 *See* Solove and Schwartz, *Information privacy law*, p. 468.

1580 Yasnoff, "Privacy, Confidentiality, and Security of Public Health Information", p. 160; Ryan M. Krisby. "Health care held ransom: modifications to data breach security & the future of health care privacy protection". In: *Health Matrix* 28 (2018), pp. 365–401.

1581 Herold and Beaver, *The practical guide to HIPAA privacy and security compliance*, p. 206. On confidentiality, integrity, and availability *see* Chapter 1, Section 2.5.1.

1582 *See* Hoffman and Podgurski, "In sickness, health, and cyberspace: protecting the security of electronic private health information", p. 336.

1583 *See* Hartley and Jones, *EHR implementation: A step-by-step guide for the medical practice*, p. 149.

1584 The standards for all e-PHI are defined in 45 C.F.R. § 162.308, § 164.310, § 164.312, § 164.314 and § 164.316.

but important safeguards may be omitted, or they may not be updated over time[1585].

The HIPAA provides a comprehensive security approach that covers both the technical and organisation levels. The general rules on security are divided into four general requirements[1586]:

1. implementing administrative, technical and physical safeguards to ensure confidentiality, integrity and availability of processed e-PHI (i.e. created, received, maintained or transmitted e-PHI);
2. implementing technical and physical safeguards to protect e-PHI against reasonably anticipated threats to its security or integrity;
3. safeguarding e-PHI against unauthorised use or disclosure;
4. ensuring that not only the covered entity, but also its employees and workforce, comply with the Rule.

The three categories of safeguards – administrative, physical, and technical – should work together to limit privacy and security risks[1587]. As mentioned above, the approach is flexible. In fact, it is specified that "covered entities and business associates may use any security measures that allow the covered entity or business associate to reasonably and appropriately implement the standards and implementation specifications" defined in the rules[1588]. The implementation of reasonable and appropriate measures is highly contextual since the covered entity shall take into account its size, complexity, and capabilities, technical infrastructure, hardware and software security capabilities, the costs of implementation of the security measures, and the probability of risks of security breaches[1589].

Hence, no one-fits-all approach is provided by the Security Rule. Actually, the requirement of reasonable and appropriate measures can be

1585 *See* the comment by Solove and Schwartz, "ALI Data Privacy: Overview and Black Letter Text", p. 24. An example of requirement with the list of standards is 45 C.F.R. § 162.1302. This requirement defines the standards for referral certification and authorisation transaction. Interestingly, the standards are divided according to time period and are frequently updated.

1586 *See* 45 C.F.R. § 164.306. *See* also Hoffman and Podgurski, "In sickness, health, and cyberspace: protecting the security of electronic private health information", p. 339; Klitou, *Privacy-invading technologies and privacy by design. Safeguarding Privacy, Liberty and Security in the 21st Century*, p. 272; Dumortier and Verhenneman, "Legal regulation of electronic health records: a comparative analysis of Europe and the US", p. 34.

1587 *See* Krisby, "Health care held ransom: modifications to data breach security & the future of health care privacy protection", p. 372.

1588 45 C.F.R. § 164.306(b)(1).

1589 45 C.F.R. § 164.306(b)(2). *See* also § 164.530(i)(1).

considered a "tacit acknowledgement that perfection is not achievable and that the goal of protecting the privacy of patient health information, while important, justifiably may be balanced against other constraints and imperatives", as ruled in *Bereston v. Uhs of Del., Inc.*, 2018 D.C. App. LEXIS 83 (DC Mar. 8, 2018).

The Security Rule establishes administrative, physical, technical and organisational safeguards within their implementation specifications, which can be "required" or "addressable"[1590]. The safeguards or "standards" and the "required" implementation specifications shall always be implemented as binding tools, whereas the "addressable" implementation specifications leave covered entities some discretion[1591]. The "addressable" specification is not optional, but the entity can assess whether it is reasonable and appropriate, and where not, a more reasonable and appropriate specification may be implemented in its place as an equivalent alternative[1592]. The decision shall be the outcome of a risk analysis[1593]. The measures shall be maintained, reviewed and modified continuously since the measures shall always ensure reasonable and appropriate protection of e-PHI[1594].

Administrative safeguards include organisational and management measures, meaning policies and procedures[1595]. This category of safeguards covers nearly two-thirds of implementation requirements under the Security Rule[1596]. The security management process is central in preventing, detecting and containing security breaches[1597]. In fact, the Security Rule requires both a risk analysis and several risk managements practices[1598]. In particular, the covered entity shall conduct a risk analysis by assessing the

1590 45 C.F.R. § 164.306(d).

1591 *See* Krisby, "Health care held ransom: modifications to data breach security & the future of health care privacy protection", p. 372.

1592 45 C.F.R. § 164.306(d).

1593 *See* Hartley and Jones, *EHR implementation: A step-by-step guide for the medical practice*, p. 151.

1594 45 C.F.R. § 164.306(e).

1595 45 C.F.R. § 164.304: "Administrative safeguards are administrative actions, and policies and procedures, to manage the selection, development, implementation, and maintenance of security measures to protect electronic protected health information and to manage the conduct of the covered entity's or business associate's workforce in relation to the protection of that information".

1596 Eric C. Thompson. *Building a HIPAA-Compliant Cybersecurity Program*. Apress, 2017. ISBN: 9781484230602, p. 47.

1597 45 C.F.R. § 164.308(a)(1)(i).

1598 A table on the administrative requirements is provided by Herold and Beaver, *The practical guide to HIPAA privacy and security compliance*, pp. 214–225.

potential threats and it shall then implement sufficient security measures to reduce the risks to a "reasonable and appropriate level"[1599].

The Office of the National Coordinator for Health Information Technology (ONC) and the Health and Human Services' Office for Civil Rights (OCR) developed a useful downloadable Security Risk Assessment (SRA) Tool to conduct a compliancy assessment[1600]. Other "required" administrative measures are the so-called "sanction policy" and the "information system activity review". The former mandates appropriate sanction policies against workforce members who fail to comply with the administrative procedures, while the latter requires the implementation of procedures for regularly reviewing the records of the information system activity, such as audit logs, access reports, and security incident reports[1601].

Access and authorisation mechanisms for limiting the access of the workforce to e-PHI are provided under the category of "addressable" administrative specifications[1602]. Access to and sharing of e-PHI should be limited through reasonable and appropriate precautions, such as authorisation policies and procedures. In particular, the suggested implementation specifications are: security reminders, procedures for protection from malicious software, log-in monitoring, and password management. Therefore, hospital employees who are not responsible for treatment shall not have access to health information[1603]. Employees should be trained in security policies and procedures, and shall be sanctioned for any violation[1604]. These considerations apply to e-PHI in the EHRs. So, it has been argued that the workforce should also be trained to use EHRs correctly by following "good practices that respect patient privacy"[1605]. In fact, another "addressable" administrative specification is "security awareness and training"[1606].

1599 45 C.F.R. § 164.308(a)(1)(ii)(A) and (B).

1600 *See* the official website and the tool at <www.healthit.gov/topic/privacy-security-and-hipaa/ security-risk-assessment-tool>. Last accessed 06/10/2021.

1601 45 C.F.R. § 164.308(a)(1)(ii)(C) and (D).

1602 45 C.F.R. § 164.308(a)(3) and (4).

1603 *See* Dumortier and Verhenneman, "Legal regulation of electronic health records: a comparative analysis of Europe and the US", p. 34, which argues that this aspect of the Privacy Rule is comparable with the EU proportionality principle.

1604 Yasnoff, "Privacy, Confidentiality, and Security of Public Health Information", p. 160.

1605 Jacques, "Electronic health records and respect for patient privacy: A prescription for compatibility", p. 461.

1606 45 C.F.R. § 164.308(a)(5)(i) – (ii).

Furthermore, the HIPAA Security Rule establishes that the covered entity shall implement policies and procedures to address security incidents, report the breaches, and then mitigate the effects of an occurred incident[1607]. Contingency plans are necessary to respond promptly to emergencies. To ensure protection during an emergency situation, a data backup plan, a disaster recovery plan, and an emergency mode operation plan are explicitly "required" in advance[1608]. Instead, testing and revision procedures of the plans and an assessment on specific characteristics are just "addressable" measures. However, a periodical evaluation of the plans is always binding[1609].

The administrative safeguards that are defined as "organisational" specifications refer to business associate contracts and to other arrangements[1610]. Business associates that create, receive, maintain, or transmit e-PHI on the covered entity's behalf shall ensure satisfactory safeguards of compliance. To this end, the contract or agreement shall specify the implementation specifications of the business associates and indicate the permitted use and disclosure of PHI[1611]. Some organisational requirements even establish a regime for the mentioned contract or agreements between the covered entity and its business associate (or another sub-contractor), and for groups of health plans[1612].

Other administrative requirements are defined in the Privacy Rule[1613]. Covered entities shall designate a privacy official, who is responsible for privacy policies and procedures, and a contact person, who receives privacy complaints. This contact person can be the same official, or not[1614]. The privacy official reports directly to management and this subject is responsible for the implementation of the HIPAA compliance programme[1615]. The workforce members shall be trained on policies and procedures to protect PHI and to limit unlawful uses and disclosures.

---

1607 45 C.F.R. § 164.308(a)(6). Examples of security policies are provided by Herold and Beaver, *The practical guide to HIPAA privacy and security compliance*, pp. 239–248.

1608 45 C.F.R. § 164.308(a)(7).

1609 45 C.F.R. § 164.308(a)(8).

1610 45 C.F.R. § 164.308(b).

1611 On business associate contracts and use and disclosure of PHI *see* 45 C.F.R. § 164.505(e), which describes the elements of the contracts in details.

1612 45 C.F.R. § 164.314.

1613 45 C.F.R. § 164.530.

1614 *See* Solove and Schwartz, "Health privacy", p. 514.

1615 *See* Hartley and Jones, *EHR implementation: A step-by-step guide for the medical practice*, pp. 91–92, which reports several of the official's activities.

Training all workforce members on privacy and security is an ongoing formal and informal process[1616]. So, physicians are included, and they should be trained on patients' privacy rights, policies, procedures and administrative, physical and technical safeguards[1617]. The covered entity shall have and apply sanctions to employees who do not comply with the rules[1618].

Any harmful effect in violation of administrative requirements shall be mitigated to the extent practicable. The mitigation requirement does not specify what actions should be taken to resolve harm, but the covered entity shall seek a solution in the first phase of a complaint (e.g. on a privacy breach). Documenting and retaining information for six years on safeguards, policies, and procedures are important administrative requirements[1619]. It has been suggested that HIPAA documentation should include: privacy policies and procedures, privacy notices, authorisations, patient requests (e.g. on rights), dispositions of complaints and documentation of other actions, and documentation of activities and designations[1620].

Physical safeguards refer to measures necessary for securing the buildings and the equipment, for protecting against the risks posed by natural and environmental causes and unauthorised intrusion[1621]. Storage back-up, secure planning, access control and validation mechanisms, and privacy records are provided under the category of "addressable" physical specifications[1622]. The workstations of the workforce should be secured to perform their functions in a safe environment, including the hardware and the software employed. The only "required" physical safeguards are a

---

1616 *See* Hartley and Jones, *op. cit.*, p. 95. An example of external training is provided by Professor Daniel Solove in his blog at <teachprivacy.com/hipaa-training/>. Last accessed 06/10/2021. Covered entities may choose in the catalogue different types of training and may receive a final certification.

1617 *See* Hartley and Jones, *op. cit.*, p. 96.

1618 45 C.F.R. § 164.530(e). In Hartley and Jones, *op. cit.*, p. 97, there are some examples of sanctions: verbal reminder, privacy retraining, reminder in the employee's personnel file, suspension, and termination.

1619 45 C.F.R. § 164.530(j).

1620 *See* further in Hartley and Jones, *EHR implementation: A step-by-step guide for the medical practice*, p. 96.

1621 45 C.F.R. § 164.304: "Physical safeguards are physical measures, policies, and procedures to protect a covered entity's or business associate's electronic information systems and related buildings and equipment, from natural and environmental hazards, and unauthorized intrusion". *See* also Krisby, "Health care held ransom: modifications to data breach security & the future of health care privacy protection", p. 373.

1622 45 C.F.R. § 164.310(a) – (d).

"disposal" – which mandates "policies and procedures to address the final disposition of electronic protected health information, and/or the hardware or electronic media on which it is stored" – and a "media re-use" – which refers to the "procedures for removal of electronic protected health information from electronic media before the media are made available for re-use"[1623].

The concept of technical safeguards includes "the technology and the policy and procedures for its use that protect electronic protected health information and control access to it"[1624]. The HIPAA requires the use of unique user identification names or numbers, and emergency access procedures[1625]. Automatic log-off after a specific period of inactivity of the system, encryption and decryption mechanisms, audit log controls, authentication mechanisms, and secure communications channels are all "addressable" measures. So, encryption is explicitly included as a reasonable and appropriate measure by the Security Rule.

Given these three categories of safeguards, the implementation specifications shall always be documented in written form[1626]. This documentation shall be retained for six years, made available to the workforce that should implement the measures, and updated periodically.

Then, the ARRA included the breach notification rule in the Security Rule. In particular, the breach notification rule mandates the notification of the breach to every individual affected by the data breach in a specific written form[1627]. The notification shall be made without unreasonable delay and no later than 60 days after the discovery of the occurred breach. The HIPAA enumerates the elements of the notification in extensive de-

1623 45 C.F.R. § 164.310(d)(2).

1624 45 C.F.R. § 164.304.

1625 45 C.F.R. § 164.312.

1626 45 C.F.R. § 164.316.

1627 For the definition of the breach *see* 45 C.F.R. § 164.402; for the rules on the notification *see* 45 C.F.R. § 164.404.

1628 The required elements in 45 C.F.R. § 164.404 are: "(A) a brief description of what happened, including the date of the breach and the date of the discovery of the breach, if known; (B) a description of the types of unsecured protected health information that were involved in the breach (such as whether full name, social security number, date of birth, home address, account number, diagnosis, disability code, or other types of information were involved); (C) any steps individuals should take to protect themselves from potential harm resulting from the breach; (D) a brief description of what the covered entity involved is doing to investigate the breach, to mitigate harm to individuals, and to protect against any further breaches; and (E) contact procedures for intail[1628] Even the media (e.g. television or websites), the OCR, and the business associate can receive a notification under specific circumstances[1629].

HIPAA Privacy and Security Rules contain obligations for the covered entities. The Health and Human Services' Office of Civil Rights enforces these Rules if a covered entity is not complaint with them. Actually, the individual does not have the right to sue covered entities for violations, but the option to file a complaint with the Office[1630]. As pointed out in the case law – *Rigaud v. Garofalo*, 2005 U.S. Dist. LEXIS 7791 (ED Pa May 2, 2005), *Orr v. Carrington*, 2019 U.S. Dist. LEXIS 5407 (2019), *Paris v. Herring*, 2019 U.S. Dist. LEXIS 205964 (2019) – courts can dismiss patients' claims for lack of subject matter. In *Montgomery v. Cuomo*, 291 F. Supp. 3d 303, 317 n.42 (W.D.N.Y. 2018) the court held that "only the Secretary of Health and Human Services or other government authorities may bring a HIPAA enforcement action. There is no private right to sue for a HIPAA violation". So, only the OCR may investigate and impose civil penalties if a covered entity fails to comply with the HIPAA[1631].

---

dividuals to ask questions or learn additional information, which shall include a tollfree telephone number, an e-mail address, Web site, or postal address. (2) plain language requirement. The notification required by paragraph (a) of this section shall be written in plain language".

1629 *See* 45 C.F.R. § 164.406, § 164.408, § 164.410.

1630 *See* 45 C.F.R. § 164.306, which provides the right to file a complaint and the specific conditions: "(a) Right to file a complaint. A person who believes a covered entity or business associate is not complying with the administrative simplification provisions may file a complaint with the Secretary. (b) Requirements for filing complaints. Complaints under this section must meet the following requirements: (1) A complaint must be filed in writing, either on paper or electronically. (2) A complaint must name the person that is the subject of the complaint and describe the acts or omissions believed to be in violation of the applicable administrative simplification provision(s). (3) A complaint must be filed within 180 days of when the complainant knew or should have known that the act or omission complained of occurred, unless this time limit is waived by the Secretary for good cause shown. (4) The Secretary may prescribe additional procedures for the filing of complaints, as well as the place and manner of filing, by notice in the Federal Register". On the OCR's enforcement activities *see* e.g. Roger Hsieh. "Improving HIPAA Enforcement and Protecting Patient Privacy in a Digital Healthcare Environment". In: *Loy. U. Chi. LJ* 46 (2014), pp. 175–223.

1631 *See* 45 C.F.R. § 164.306 on the compliance review of the Office, § 164.310 on the cooperation duties of the covered entity and business associates, § 160.402, § 160.404, § 160.408 on civil penalties, and the following paragraphs for the procedure and subpoena.

As reported by the OCR, individuals most often complain about impermissible uses and disclosures of protected health information, lack of safeguards, lack of patient access to PHI, lack of administrative safeguards of e-PHI, and use or disclosure of more than the minimum necessary PHI[1632]. The Office also reported that the most common types of covered entities to be sanctioned are general hospitals, private practices and physicians, outpatient facilities, pharmacies and health plans. The OCR often concludes resolution agreement with covered entities that have violated the HIPAA. As explicitly stated in every agreement, this kind of settlement is not an admission, concession, or evidence of liability, but a way to resolve a "potential violation" of HIPAA requirements. As an example, in *Parkview Health System, Inc. Resolution Agreement and Corrective Action Plan* the entity agreed to pay a resolution amount and comply with a Corrective Action Plan for having left "71 cardboard boxes of medical records unattended and accessible to unauthorised persons on the driveway"[1633]. In 2020, the health insurance plan Premera Blue Cross paid over 6 million dollars to settle a data breach that affected 10 million individuals had been caused by a cyberattack[1634]. The entity did not conduct an "accurate and thorough assessment of the potential risks and vulnerabilities to the confidentiality, integrity, and availability of ePHI", and it did not implement "security measures sufficient to reduce risks and vulnerabilities to a reasonable appropriate level", meaning the plan potentially violated 45 C.F.R. § 164.308(a)(1)(ii)(A) and 164.308(a)(1)(ii)(B)[1635].

The literature has considered the absence of a private cause of action a great limitation of legal protection of PHI[1636]. It has been argued that the HIPAA has several deficiencies. In sum, the HIPAA does not apply to the new emerging private sector on e-health, individuals do not have a right

---

1632 *See* Office for Civil Rights (OCR) at <www.hhs.gov/hipaa/for-professionals/compliance-enforcement/data/enforcement-highlights/index.html>. Content last reviewed on 15 December 2020. Last accessed 06/10/2021.

1633 *See* Solove and Schwartz, "Health privacy", pp. 526–531, which also provides the New York Presbyterian Hospital Resolution Agreement and Corrective Action Plan.

1634 The Premera Blue Cross (PBC) Resolution Agreement and Corrective Action Plan is available at <www.hhs.gov/hipaa/for-professionals/compliance-enforcement/agreements/premera/index.html>. Last accessed 06/10/2021.

1635 *See* p. 2 of the mentioned agreement.

1636 *See* Hoffman and Klein, "Explaining explanation, part 1: theoretical foundations", p. 278, which reports that a private cause of action was provided by California's Confidentiality of Medical Information Act. *See* also Terry, "Regulatory disruption and arbitrage in health-care data protection".

to verify in detail how the information has been used under the rules, the HIPAA gives little guidance on the concrete implementation and on how to achieve compliance, and finally it has an insufficient enforcement mechanism[1637].

It may at first be recommended that the regulatory scope of the protection of medical information be extended beyond the "custodian-type" paradigm and to all health information. As regards the limited guidance on implementation, the HIPAA's flexible approach seems broad as it omits reference to clear guidelines on technical protection[1638]. However, it should be noted that the rules are very detailed. This level of detail goes beyond the protection of informational privacy in the US. At the same time, encryption and other technical safeguards are simply "addressable" during the transmission of e-PHI. Neither a state-of-the-art criterion nor broader reference to other processing activities (e.g. storage, aggregation) are included. It has been pointed out that the HIPAA needs more efficient and stringent storage and backup requirements[1639]. Nonetheless, many specific standards and implementation requirements have been specified in the Security Rule and the level of administrative and organisational safeguards seems very high. Finally, the enforcement mechanism might be amended to provide a private cause of action, as in the EU legal framework. At the same time, the OCR guarantees independent enforcement at the administrative level, which might be considered similar to the enforcement of a DPA in a Member State.

After this analysis of the HIPAA Privacy and Security Rules, the upcoming final section will provide a comparison with the EU legal framework, with particular reference to the data protection by design obligation.

### *4.5 A comparison between HIPAA and DPbD in the e-health context*

This section presents a comparison between HIPAA Privacy and Security Rules and the DPbD requirement of the GDPR applied to the e-health

1637 *See* Hoffman and Podgurski, "In sickness, health, and cyberspace: protecting the security of electronic private health information", p. 337.

1638 *See* Krisby, "Health care held ransom: modifications to data breach security & the future of health care privacy protection", pp. 383–384. *See* also Hoffman and Podgurski, "In sickness, health, and cyberspace: protecting the security of electronic private health information", p. 353.

1639 *See* Krisby, "Health care held ransom: modifications to data breach security & the future of health care privacy protection", pp. 384–385.

care sector, and to EHRs especially. In particular, the elements of the comparative analysis are presented in the following order: the scope of application and the rationale of the norms, the object and the recommended measures, and the underlying principles and rights.

The HIPAA is devoted to the protection of PHI, e-PHI, PHRs, EMRs and EHRs by the implementation of defined policies, procedures, and technical specifications. DPbD is a more general rule, but it is applicable to personal health data and to EHRs, and it mandates the implementation of organisational and technical measures, as well, without defining them. Both rules contain obligations subject to sanctions. Despite some similarities this analysis will show that an EHR may not be used in both EU and US legal frameworks since the DPbD principle goes beyond a set of measures to be implemented. An explicit legal recognition of PbD in the US law may bring these frameworks closer together[1640]. However, HIPAA requirements may still be considered useful examples of measures for DPbD guidelines for EHRs.

First of all, it has been specified above that the concept of PHI and personal health data are not equal. Nonetheless, the GDPR's definition of "data concerning health" and the HIPAA's definition of e-PHI both protect the "medical data" of the past, current and future health status, and other data related to health, such as genetic information, and the identifiers or the numbers assigned to healthcare services[1641]. A prominent US scholar suggested using the GDPR's definition of "data concerning health" for a new federal law on health informational privacy[1642]. Terry claimed the need to include any identifiable health information under the HIPAA to broaden its scope[1643].

Both the HIPAA and DPbD do not apply to anonymous and anonymised data, where the process of anonymisation is effective. In fact, the HIPAA dedicates several requirements to de-identification of PHI in order to allow its use and disclosure (e.g. for research purposes). Article 25 of the GDPR does not mention anonymisation since this activity takes personal data out of the scope of the GDPR, where its rules do not apply[1644]. In addition, neither rule applies to raw data. Actually, the discussion on

1640 On the FTC's Report on PbD and the proposal for a Consumer Bill of Rights *see* Chapter 2, Section 2.2.

1641 *See* respectively Article 4(15) GDPR and 45 C.F.R. § 160.103.

1642 *See* Terry, "Regulatory disruption and arbitrage in health-care data protection", p. 205.

1643 *See ibid.*

1644 *See* Recital 26 of the GDPR.

"quasi-health data" is not feasible in the HIPAA context since health apps and wearable devices are out of its scope[1645]. In the US the protection of observed, complex, and predicted health information might be guaranteed by other rules, including the FTC Act, which may apply to HIT companies where that information identifies the individual.

The HIPAA is domain-limited since only defined health entities, as well as their uses and disclosures of PHI, fall under its application[1646]. The HIPAA does not apply to all the data controllers that process identifiable health information. In fact, the focus is the entity rather than the information; as a result, this framework is fragmented "by custodian type" and it defines sector-specific duties[1647]. Instead, DPbD obligation is generally applicable to data controllers that process personal data according to the material and territorial scope of the GDPR[1648].

Despite the fact that the HIPAA always refers to "use and disclosure" and not to "processing", it may be argued that they are examples of data processing activities by looking at Article 4(2) GDPR. The term "use" of the HIPAA Privacy Rule may subsume "recording, organisation, structuring, storage, adaptation or alteration, retrieval, consultation, use" of the GDPR. The term "disclosure" may instead subsume "disclosure by transmission, dissemination or otherwise making available" of information to recipients[1649]. The HIPAA might not include "alignment or combination, restriction, erasure or destruction" and "collection"[1650]. The GDPR definition of data processing is evidently broader than the activities specified in the HIPAA, where the scope is focused on the disclosure of information in particular. Indeed, in the EHR context it has been claimed that "HIPAA can be interpreted as based on the assumption that health information will be collected from the individual; its focus is on the subsequent protection, use, and sharing of that information", whereas "the EU framework begins with detailed considerations about whether the information may be col-

1645 On the definition of "personal health data" *see* Chapter 3, Section 3.3.1.

1646 45 C.F.R. § 160.102.

1647 *See* Terry, "Regulatory disruption and arbitrage in health-care data protection", p. 164.

1648 *See* Chapter 2, Section 2.4.1.

1649 *See infra* the definitions of use and disclosure reported in Section 4.4.2.

1650 Terry in Terry, "Regulatory disruption and arbitrage in health-care data protection", p. 162 argues that the HIPAA leaves a narrow set of requirements to data collection.

lected and how to protect patients in the original collection process"[1651]. This is a significant difference between the two frameworks since only the GDPR concerns the full life cycle of processing activities.

Moreover, the GDPR provides some rules on personal health data, but it remains a uniform and general regulation, which is sector-neutral. The different sectorial approach of the HIPAA is consistent with the nature of the US legal system and the US informational privacy regulatory framework, where the sectorial regulation is typical. In the US the legal framework is less comprehensive and harmonised than in the EU. At the same time, the HIPAA is more detailed than other statutory laws at the national and federal level by providing "relatively robust protections against unauthorized uses of health information", which are more consistent when compared to other sectors[1652].

This federal law on health information pre-empts less stringent local and statutory law, but it can be pre-empted by other more stringent national statutes[1653]. As outlined in Chapter 3, Member State law may provide more detailed rules for the e-health care sector and EHRs in light of their competence on public health[1654]. So, even in the EU there might be more stringent rules on health data protection. In the US framework many resources have been allocated to e-health improvement in recent decades, and the HIPAA is guiding healthcare providers in the slow adoption of EHRs[1655]. As pointed out above, the US health environment is highly fragmented. Thus, a more uniform and coordinated environment like in the Member States (and in the EU) may ease the use of EHRs in this legal system.

In the US the relationship of a covered entity with its business associate is regulated through a contract or an agreement for ensuring compliance with the rules when the information is used by the business associate on behalf of the entity. The need for a contractual agreement is similar to the contract between the data controller and the processor[1656]. The business associate shall directly implement the HIPAA requirements, including the

---

1651 Hiller et al., "Privacy and security in the implementation of health information technology (electronic health records): US and EU compared", p. 31.

1652 *See* Terry, "Regulatory disruption and arbitrage in health-care data protection", p. 162.

1653 45 C.F.R. § 160.202.

1654 In particular, *see* Sections 3.3 and 3.4.2.

1655 *See* HITECH at note no. 1452.

1656 The respective requirements are Article 28 of the GDPR and 45 C.F.R. § 164.505(e).

Security Rule. By contrast, as explained above, the DPbD requirement is not specifically addressed to processors or technological developers[1657]. Third parties shall not comply with Article 25 of the GDPR. This represents a limitation of the DPbD principle. Even so, the obligation to implement measures on the data controller may have an indirect impact on the processor according to Recital 78 of the GDPR.

As regards the rationale of the rules, the goal of the HIPAA Privacy Rule is "to balance the interest of individuals in maintaining the confidentiality of their health information with the interests of society in obtaining, using, and disclosing health information to carry out a variety of public and private activities"[1658]. DPbD is a general obligation of the controller that seeks the implementation of technical and organisational measures for protecting principles and rights of the data subjects by design. Even DPbD requires balancing controller's interests with the necessity to protect data subjects by defining some criteria. Both the HIPAA Security Rule and DPbD aim at protecting information/data through a set of measures ensuring accountability with the law. Despite the absence of a PbD requirement in the US legal frameworks, the HIPAA has been included in the examples of rules that give an important role to technical means for protecting privacy[1659].

However, DPbD goes beyond a set of standards or implementation specifications. It is an example of *regulation by design*. The GDPR covers the design phase of the data processing and its concrete activities. Notably, the timing of the HIPAA provisions never refers to the phase before the use or disclosure of PHI or e-PHI. It may be argued that the HIPAA compliance programme and safeguards should be projected in advance, but it does not explicitly refer to the design of practices and technologies.

Article 25 of the GDPR is open. By contrast, the HIPAA defines, enumerates and lists the categories of safeguards in a detailed and complex way[1660]. Nonetheless, the language of the rules requires interpretation in both cases. The HIPAA, like DPbD, does not mandate a one-size-fits all ap-

---

1657 *See* Chapter 2, 2.4.1.

1658 Tovino, "The HIPAA Privacy Rule and the EU GDPR: illustrative comparisons", p. 979.

1659 *See* Klitou, *Privacy-invading technologies and privacy by design. Safeguarding Privacy, Liberty and Security in the 21st Century*, p. 272.

1660 On the complexity of the HIPAA's rules *see* Guarda, *Fascicolo sanitario elettronico e protezione dei dati personali*, pp. 86–90.

proach, but a case-by-case approach[1661]. As a matter of fact, the implementation of measures is a never-ending approach in both legal frameworks. Overall, in both frameworks the measures shall be maintained during the activities and be revised periodically. As a result, the cost of implementation of these rules has a significant impact both on controllers and on covered entities[1662].

It may be pointed out that the physical, administrative and technical safeguards of the HIPAA embed specifications that can be considered "technical and organisational measures" under the GDPR. The adjective "appropriate" is used in Article 25 of the GDPR and in the HIPAA in a partially different way. In the EU, "appropriate" entails a discretion on choosing any measure that can implement data protection principles, whereas in the US the adjective is used to evaluate and potentially adopt the "addressable" specified safeguards, while the "required" safeguards shall always be implemented[1663]. Both the HIPAA and DPbD mention the context of the activities, the concrete characteristics of the data controller/covered entity, the costs of implementation and the risk level in the criteria to be taken into account while defining the measures[1664]. Thus, the approaches of the rules are scalable, flexible, and even technically neutral.

Despite the absence of the state of the art criterion in the Security Rule, the HIPAA explicitly provides standards to be adopted in some specific areas, for EHRs especially[1665]. As a result, the state of the art is often directly defined by the legislator[1666]. Where not defined, it should be claimed that HIPAA does not include an "effective criterion" for the measures, but only the "appropriate" one. So, it may be argued that the HIPAA does not require an implementation of rules and principles in "an effective manner".

Comparing the organisational requirements set by the GDPR for processing a large amount of sensitive data with the HIPAA requirements, it can be noted that under both regulations the subjects shall maintain a record on the activities, notify or communicate a data breach, carry out a

1661 *See* Tomes, "20 Plus Years of HIPAA and What Have We Got", p. 91 for HIPAA, and Chapter 2, Section 2.4.2 for DPbD.

1662 *See* on the costs of HIPAA the detailed investigation by Tomes, *op. cit.*, which suggests a reform of the HIPAA to find "a more cost-effective way to protect privacy". On the cost of DPbD, *see* Chapter 2, Section 2.4.3.

1663 On the GDPR's criteria *see* Chapter 2, Section 2.4.6.

1664 *See* on DPbD Chapter 2, Section 2.4.4 and 2.4.3.

1665 On EHR standards *see* also 45 C.F.R. § 170 amended in 2020.

1666 On defining the state of the art of DPbD *see* Chapter 2, Section 2.4.3.

risk assessment, and designate a DPO/privacy official[1667]. Indeed, the risk assessment is considered a required organisational measure for protecting personal health data/PHI both in the EU and in the US. While Article 25 mandates taking into account the risks during the implementation of the measures and Article 32 of the GDPR establishes a separate duty on security, the HIPAA uses the risk assessments as an "administrative safeguard" and embeds security measures. The HIPAA enumerates several policies and procedures that are crucial in the e-health context[1668].

Despite some similarities at the organisational level, the HIPAA does not require an appropriate design of the technologies and of the business practices from the development stage of the technology processing e-PHI. The HIPAA is more detailed than the EU rules on security and measures for the system[1669]. Actually, the HIPAA includes technical specifications that may be subsumed as DPbD measures if they are implemented before the processing in a designed stage of the EHR. Some HIPAA Security Rule requirements may be considered examples of measures for a DPbD implementation in the EHR since they are targeted towards the e-health context and include several detailed safeguards suggested by Article 29 Working Party and by the EC[1670]: mechanisms and limits for identification and authentication, access control, audit control, secure network communication, and encryption[1671]. Nevertheless, the HIPAA Security Rule focuses on the use or disclosure phase only and classifies these measures as "addressable safeguards".

Furthermore, the GDPR refers to certification as a tool for complying with DPbD and DPbDf obligations. In the HIPAA certification is a means for ensuring the "meaningful use" of EHRs. As regards the enforcement of the rules, an entity that violates the HIPAA may face civil and criminal

1667 For the GDPR *see* Chapter 3, Section 3.3.3.

1668 *See infra* in Section 4.4.3 the references to the organisational safeguards.

1669 Hiller et al., "Privacy and security in the implementation of health information technology (electronic health records): US and EU compared", p. 35.

1670 *See* Article 29 Working Party, *Working Document on the processing of personal data relating to health in electronic health records (EHR)*, European Commission, *Commission Recommendation (EU) 2019/243 of 6 February 2019 on a European Electronic Health Record exchange format*, and Chapter 3, Sections 3.4.2 and 3.4.3.

1671 Interestingly, in the technical safeguards HIPAA explicitly mentions encryption, while the GDPR used only the neutral term of pseudonymisation. *See* Chapter 2, Section 2.4.2.

penalties[1672], whereas DPbD may be enforced through the GDPR's administrative fine process, and judicial and non-judicial remedies. Anyway, the absence of a private cause of action is evidently a great limitation of the HIPAA.

This comparison takes into account the principles and rights involved in Article 25 GDPR and HIPAA Rules. As discussed in Chapter 2, DPbD obligation refers to principles and rights of the GDPR and the EU Charter[1673]. Generally, the HIPAA does not refer to informational principles or FIPs. From the text, it is clear that it applies a sector-based confidentiality and disclosure-centred model[1674]. US scholars have pointed out that the HIPAA is based on FIPs[1675]. Other principles have been defined by the ONC on EHRs[1676].

The previous Section has discussed and compared the different grounds for the use and disclosure of PHI and the possible similarities with GDPR. Both the HIPAA and GDPR establish multiples grounds or exceptions which go beyond the authorisation/consent of the individual/data subject. It should be remembered that the principle of lawfulness, except for the choice or consent, and other "GDPR-lite" principles (e.g. fairness) are not included in the FIPs[1677].

Looking at the HIPAA requirements, it may be argued that the detailed rules on privacy notice and the right to receive an accounting of disclosures may enhance transparency between the covered entity and the individual. Notably, the ONC's principles for processing PHI in EHRs include openness and transparency as crucial principles for processing medical information and the individual choice principle states that the individual should have the opportunity to make informed decisions about the use and disclosure of PHI. Only in a transparent context, a decision may be informed. As explained for the DPbD obligation, the language is important for easing comprehension and transparency[1678]. Even the HIPAA in-

1672 *See* the practical table on HIPAA violation and penalties in Tomes, "20 Plus Years of HIPAA and What Have We Got", p. 98.

1673 Chapter 2, Section 2.4.8.

1674 Nicolas P. Terry. "Protecting patient privacy in the age of big data". In: *UMKC L. Rev.* 81 (2012), pp. 385–415, p. 406.

1675 *See* Richards and Hartzog, "Privacy's Constitutional Moment", p. 19.

1676 *See infra* note no. 1448.

1677 *See infra* Section 4.2.

1678 *See* Chapter 2, Section 2.4.8.

troduces a "plain language" requirement for notification and information to the individual and for the individual's authorisation[1679].

According to the ONC's principles, PHI should be limited to the extent necessary to fulfil the specified purpose, and not used to discriminate inappropriately. The purpose limitation principle is not directly provided in the HIPAA. However, the HIPAA indirectly restricts the purposes by listing the possible disclosures. The "minimum necessary rule" of the HIPAA limits how much PHI can be used or disclosed. Hence, PHI should be limited to the minimum necessary to accomplish the envisaged purpose. The rationale of this rule is similar to the data minimisation principle, which is embedded in the concept of DPbD and DPbDf[1680]. The HIPAA derogates the minimum rule where it establishes that it does not apply to the disclosures related to treatment purposes, individual's consent, or disclosure required by law[1681]. It seems that the data minimisation principle does not have any derogation in the GDPR. However, as previously explained[1682], the data minimisation principle in the e-health environment means that the system should collect all the data necessary for treatment purposes. In particular, EHRs should be as comprehensive as possible to support healthcare provision[1683]. The same concept is included in the derogation for treatment purpose of the HIPAA.

The right to amend of the HIPAA is an expression of the accuracy principle. This GDPR concept has been recognised by the ONC in two different principles. The ONC's principle of "correction" states that the individual should have the timely means to contest the accuracy or integrity of PHI, have it amended or dispute a denied request in a documented format. "Data quality and integrity" recommends that PHI be complete, accurate and up-to-date to the extent necessary to fulfil the specified purpose, and that PHI should not be modified or deleted in an unauthorised manner.

Both DPbD and HIPAA give great importance to security and its principles of integrity, confidentiality and availability. In most cases the reasonable HIPAA administrative, technical, and physical safeguards require security measures and policies since the Security Rule obviously aims to

1679 *See* 45 C.F.R. § 164.404(c)(2), § 164.508(i)(3), § 164.512(e)(1)(ii), § 164.520(b)(1).

1680 *See* Chapter 1, Section 2.4.8.

1681 *See* Tomes, "20 Plus Years of HIPAA and What Have We Got", p. 99 on 45 C.F.R. § 164.502(b), § 164.514(d).

1682 *See* Chapter 3, Section 3.4.2.

1683 *See* Chapter 2, Section 3.4.3.

enhance security of e-PHI. It may be claimed that this Rule is dedicated to electronic information only. However, it surely applies to the EHR environment.

The last principle of accountability is included in the ONC's principles and it may be argued that it is implied in the HIPAA requirements on documentation, on the privacy officer, on mitigation and civil and criminal penalties. Nonetheless, the lack of a private action and the limits of the enforcement exposed above, and the absence of a data protection authority, force an effective accountability on the covered entity.

Under the HIPAA, an individual's rights are more limited than under GDPR. The following Table 4.4 summarises the rights provided by the two frameworks.

*Table 4.4 GDPR vs. HIPAA rights*

| GDPR RIGHTS | HIPAA RIGHTS |
|---|---|
| Right to be informed | Right to receive a notice |
| Right to access | Right to inspect and obtain copy of PHI |
| Right to rectification | Right to amend |
| Right to erasure | Not provided |
| Right to restriction | Right to request restriction |
| Right to data portability | Right to transmit a copy of PHI |
| Right to object | Not provided |
| Right to have human intervention | Not provided |
| Not provided | Right to request confidential communication |
| Not provided | Right to receive an accounting of disclosures |

The right to be informed and the right to receive a notice of privacy practice guarantee that the data subject or the individual obtains the information on processing in plain language. HIPAA requirements on notice are very detailed. The elements of a privacy policy in the EU and a privacy notice in the US are different[1684]. It is worth noting that the

1684 *See* Articles 13 and 14 of the GDPR and 45 C.F.R. § 164.520.

HIPAA contains more (required and optional) elements than the GDPR. However, a long and complex privacy notice seems difficult to read and be understood by individuals.

The right to access is granted by both legal frameworks[1685]. The HIPAA Privacy Rule and Article 15 of the GDPR entail the right to obtain a copy of PHI/personal data and to make the request electronically. It should be noted that in the HIPAA several circumstances limit this right[1686]. Nonetheless, where applicable, the right to inspect even allows the transmission of PHI to a third party which is a limited version of the right to data portability[1687]. The possibility of knowing who accessed the EHR – that has been suggested for EHR in the EU[1688] – may be guaranteed by the HIPAA under the right to receive an accounting of disclosures[1689].

The HIPAA provides the right of revocation of the individual's authorisation and the right to amend information which are almost identical to the right to withdraw consent and right to rectification of GDPR[1690]. Nonetheless, it should be specified that the covered entity is not required to implement the changes[1691]. In the HIPAA there are not rights equal to the rights to object and to have human intervention. As mentioned, in the e-health context the right to object of GDPR is not easily applicable and the right to have human intervention applies in automated processing activities[1692]. Despite the absence of a right to erasure in the HIPAA, it is important to remember that in the e-health context and EHRs this right

1685 Article 15 of the GDPR and 45 C.F.R. § 164.524(a).

1686 Terry argued that all data should be accessible upon request. *See* Terry, "Regulatory disruption and arbitrage in health-care data protection", p. 205.

1687 45 C.F.R. § 164.524(c). Lynskey reported the HIPAA requirement as an example of an international instrument of the right to data portability in Lynskey, "Chapter III Rights of the Data Subject (Articles 12–23). Article 20. Right to data portability", p. 501.

1688 *See* Chapter 3, Section 3.4.2.

1689 The individual may receive information of the disclosure of PHI in the network. However, this information does not refer to the professional who accessed the EHR as an employee of the covered entity.

1690 *See* the comparison in Tovino, "The HIPAA Privacy Rule and the EU GDPR: illustrative comparisons", p. 990.

1691 Hiller et al., "Privacy and security in the implementation of health information technology (electronic health records): US and EU compared", p. 32. The covered entity may provide a denial.

1692 *See* Chapter 3, Section 3.3.3.

is difficult to apply[1693]. Health information shall be retained for clinical reasons, billing records, and other public purposes[1694].

In summary, the next Table 4.5. compares the two rules as discussed here.

*Table 4.5 Synthesis of the comparison between DPbD and HIPAA*

| CRITERIA | DPbD – GDPR | HIPAA – US |
|---|---|---|
| Legal system | EU | US |
| Legal nature | Principle and obligation | Multiple obligations and duties |
| Theoretical framework | Data protection | Informational privacy |
| Embedded principles | GDPR principles and EU Charter | Not explicitly provided |
| Embedded rights | Arts. 12–22 GDPR and Charter | 45 C.F.R. § 164 |
| Timing | Full life cycle of processing | Use and disclosure |
| Flexibility | Yes | Yes |
| Technical neutrality | Yes | Yes |
| Subjects | Data controller primarily | Covered entities and business associates |

1693 *See* the arguments in Chapter 2, Section 3.4.2.

1694 *See* Tovino, "The HIPAA Privacy Rule and the EU GDPR: illustrative comparisons", pp. 992–993, which provides some concrete examples: "Health insurers, too, need to maintain billing and payment records for purposes of determining whether patients have satisfied their annual deductibles, have met their annual out-of- pocket maximums and, if President Trump repeals the Affordable Care Act, whether insureds or applicants for insurance have preexisting health conditions that could make them ineligible for insurance coverage of a future illness. Health oversight agencies, including the Centers for Medicare and Medicaid Services, the Office for Civil Rights, and the Drug Enforcement Agency, also need billing and other administrative records to identify health care fraud and abuse, to detect privacy violations, and to become aware of problematic prescription patterns. In summary, the obligation to maintain and the ability to produce health-related records upon request is critical to the smooth functioning of the health care delivery system as well as the health care financing system, helping to explain some of the key differences between the GDPR and the Privacy Rule, especially with respect to erasure".

| CRITERIA | DPbD – GDPR | HIPAA – US |
|---|---|---|
| Security | Separate duty | Included |

The US framework has more detailed technical and organisational specifications than GDPR and is focused on health information. Both EU and US laws protect identifiable personal health information, but in the US the regulation is binding only for covered entities. The European data protection framework applies to all kinds of processing of personal data and to the full life cycle of processing activities of the data controllers. In comparison to the EU, rights and principles in the US appear more limited. Despite the level of detail, it has been argued that US healthcare protection should move beyond the HIPAA and provide an additional framework for protecting medical informational privacy, including the collection of information[1695]. To this end, healthcare entities should apply the FIPs[1696].

Adopting the FTC's approach of privacy by design will improve the patient's medical privacy[1697]. A new federal law on health information might integrate the FIPs as general protective principles and might also give the FTC the enforcement power to act as a data protection authority even beyond the scrutiny of unfair practices[1698]. An effective and appropriate application of PbD or DPbD solutions may strengthen the dialogue between these legal frameworks.

Notwithstanding the different structures of legal protection in the EU and in the US, the applicable rules for the health information domain of these legal systems share the need to enhance the safeguards and control over the design of EHRs and medical records. Regulators on both sides of the Atlantic mandate organisational and technical measures to be implemented in a case-by-case approach. So, after the theoretical investigation of these four Chapters on data protection by design, the legal framework and the e-health care sector, and the comparison with the US, the next Chapter will discuss the technical tools for designing data protection in order to provide the instruments for the elaboration of the guidelines.

1695 *See* Terry, "Regulatory disruption and arbitrage in health-care data protection".
1696 *See* Terry, *op. cit.*, p. 169.
1697 *See* Terry, "Protecting patient privacy in the age of big data", p. 405.
1698 This opinion is pointed out by Terry, "Regulatory disruption and arbitrage in health-care data protection", p. 201.

# Chapter 5 Technical tools for designing data protection

## *5.1 Introductory remarks*

This Chapter is dedicated to a more applied perspective in the technological domain. As explained above, one of the main challenges faced by PbD, and now by DPbD, is finding a proactive approach that combines the legal and technical perspectives to design privacy or data protection. The task of identifying technologies that protect rights (and principles) must not be limited to legislators[1699]. Anyone who develops or uses information technology to process data should take legal rules into account by adopting organisational and technological solutions that promote those rules[1700].

Thus, the present Chapter investigates the existing technical tools and methods for designing data protection. It first introduces some general systems and software engineering concepts. Then it focuses on privacy engineering approaches, by looking at some significant contributions for PbD and DPbD, and at the risk assessment framework, which is crucial for Article 25 of the GDPR.

Given the e-health care sector, and the case study on EHR, the Chapter then presents some suitable PETs and recognised international standards that are useful for EHR implementation. These insights are tools for defining the DPbD guidelines to be applied in the EHR environment.

## *5.2 System and software development design*

The EHR system is complex, and has a set of components that includes both hardware and software: database management systems and their hardware, EHR software with its architecture and interface, and the net-

---

1699 Giovanni Sartor. *L'informatica giuridica e le tecnologie dell'informazione: Corso di informatica giuridica*. Vol. 2. G. Giappichelli Editore, 2016. ISBN: 9788892105935, p. 41.

1700 *See ibid.*, which refers to "values" instead of rules from a legal informatics perspective.

work[1701]. This section deals briefly with systems engineering aspects and secondly with software development issues.

Generally, a system is built through the interdisciplinary approach of systems engineering[1702]. System development mainly involves three different implementations: infrastructure, platform design and software design[1703]. So, systems engineering is not merely software development.

System requirements (i.e. its properties) are defined in the early development stage in order to select the specific architectures and technologies solutions to be built. In particular, functional requirements determine how the system behaves and interacts, what capabilities it provides and what information it processes[1704]. The non-functional requirements refer to the criteria required to understand how well the functions of the system are achieved, such as effectiveness, quality and cost. The definition of system requirements follows the identification of stakeholders' requirements, which are statements of what experts, users, customers, and personnel need from the specific system to be implemented[1705]. While system requirements are defined in formal or semi-formal language, component requirements can be expressed as textual and problem-oriented requirements, and through use cases.

So, privacy or data protection needs may be identified by the stakeholders who then provide the requirements to the developers to take them into account while defining the system requirements. Actually, PbD and DPbD demands the translation of rules into design requirements both in hardware and in software[1706].

The integration of privacy rules may raise terminological problems since some terms are used in the legal field with different meanings than the

---

1701 *See* as an example the openEHR technical specifications available at <specifications.openehr.org/>. Last accessed 06/10/2021. In particular, Figure 7 describes the health service environment with multiple layers and components.

1702 For an introduction to system engineering *see* the first chapter of Bruce Powel Douglass. *Agile Systems Engineering*. Online version. Morgan Kaufmann, 2016. ISBN: 9780128023495. In this book, systems engineering is defined as "an interdisciplinary approach to building complex and technologically diverse systems".

1703 *See* e.g. the life cycle in Douglass, *op. cit.*, p. 22.

1704 Douglass, *op. cit.*, p. 5.

1705 On whom may be the stakeholders *see* Douglass, *op. cit.*, p. 68.

1706 For PbD *see* Ann Cavoukian, Stuart Shapiro, and R. Jason Cronk. "Privacy engineering: Proactively embedding privacy, by design". In: *Office of the Information and Privacy Commissioner* (2014).

same terms have in the technological domain[1707]. As discussed above, privacy and data protection principles are expressed in broader terms than engineering requirements are, and are subject to interpretation[1708]. Technology operates by on-off rules, whereas law by interpretative rules[1709].

Therefore, legal rules should be analysed, requirements or use cases may be identified, and then they may be translated into concrete functional or non-functional system requirements by following a methodology[1710]. Some rules may affect the entire architecture of an information system, while others may regulate its run-time level[1711].

Moreover, as previously noted, the adoption of a particular concept of privacy or data protection configures different frameworks of values and dimensions[1712]. Incorporating values requires the competence of a system designer, but also comprehensive knowledge of the legal field or the support of other legal experts[1713]. Taking into account data protection needs

---

1707 *See* Stefan Schiffner et al. "Towards a roadmap for privacy technologies and the General Data Protection Regulation: A transatlantic initiative". In: *Privacy Technologies and Policy. 6th Annual Privacy Forum, APF 2018*. Springer. 2018, pp. 24–42, p. 35.

1708 *See* Chapter 2, Section 2.3. *See* also Alshammari and Simpson, "Towards a principled approach for engineering privacy by design", pp. 163–164.

1709 *See* Waldman, "Privacy's Law of Design", p. 1257.

1710 *See* N. Van Dijk et al. "Right engineering? The redesign of privacy and personal data protection". In: *International Review of Law, Computers & Technology* 32.2 – 3 (2018), pp. 230–256, pp. 239–241, which reports the opinions of representatives from the engineering community. Some experts are critical of the ability to translate legal principles, whereas others are more optimistic. Following a methodology really contributes to the effort.

1711 *See* Koops and Leenes, "Privacy regulation cannot be hardcoded. A critical comment on the 'privacy by design' provision in data-protection law", p. 164. The authors classify Article 17 of the DPD as a system level requirement, and the time for data retention as a run-time requirement. They even classify language requirements as "requirements for the policy language that derive from legal provisions".

1712 A summary of the different frameworks and rationales is provided by Tamò-Larrieux, *Designing for privacy and its legal framework: data protection by design and default for the internet of things*, pp. 27–39.

1713 On the complexity of achieving technical design that incorporates values *see* Mary Flanagan, Daniel C. Howe, and Helen Nissenbaum. "Embodying values in technology: Theory and practice". In: *Information technology and moral philosophy*. Cambridge University Press, 2008, pp. 322–353. ISBN: 9780511498725. *See* also Chapter 2, Section 2.3.

is not a trivial problem. A privacy system engineering methodology should be adopted[1714].

An EHR system also embeds a software system. Software development is a well-structured activity, which includes multiple phases and interactions[1715]. Software development can follow different methodologies.

Methodologies can be divided into two main categories: structured methodologies, which collect models with detailed planning, management and documentation, and agile methodologies, which are characterised by iterative processes and less planning[1716].

To explain software development in relation to PbD, ENISA uses the waterfall model, which can be considered a structured methodology that includes the seven following phases: concept development, analysis, design, implementation, testing, evaluation, and maintenance[1717]. The waterfall model is a traditional development model that relies on documentation and detailed planning and management[1718]. Each phase may rely on a privacy engineering approach[1719]. The various stages and their implementation are sequential, meaning that one phase must not be started before the previous has ended and has been documented[1720]. The advantage of the waterfall model seems to be the great attention to the first phase on concept development and identifying requirements. Since it is not easy to go back to a previous phase, each one should be carefully carried out.

---

1714 Privacy engineering approaches will be presented in the next Section 5.3.

1715 *See* Sartor, *L'informatica giuridica e le tecnologie dell'informazione: Corso di informatica giuridica*, pp. 114–117.

1716 Hans-Christian Estler et al. "Agile vs. structured distributed software development: A case study". In: *Empirical Software Engineering* 19.5 (2014), pp. 1197–1224, which tries to compare the models in a case study.

1717 *See* Danezis et al., *Privacy and Data Protection by design – from policy to engineering*, p. 18.

1718 *See* Seda Gürses and Joris Van Hoboken. "Privacy after the agile turn". In: *The Cambridge Handbook of Consumer Privacy*. Cambridge University Press, 2018, pp. 579–601. ISBN: 9781316831960, p. 582.

1719 Danezis et al., *Privacy and Data Protection by design – from policy to engineering*, p. 17: "To support privacy by design throughout the software development each of these phases rely on different concepts. In the concept development and analysis phases so called privacy design strategies (defined further on) are necessary. The known concept of a design pattern is useful during the design phase, whereas concrete (privacy-enhancing) technologies can only be applied during the implementation phase".

1720 *See* Olga Filipova and Rui Vilão. *Software Development From A to Z*. Springer, 2018. ISBN: 9781484239445, p. 27, which reports as phases: requirements, analysis, design, coding, testing, and maintenance.

As a result, data protection requirements may be cautiously taken into account with the waterfall model. At the same time, the disadvantage seems to be that this methodology is not very flexible and takes a long time to carry out, and if a data protection requirement is not considered in the first phase, it will be difficult and expensive to change the final version of the project later on[1721]. It has been pointed out that the waterfall cycle is lacking the creative process that is needed for PbD[1722]. So, this methodology may be used for DPbD implementation, but presents some challenges.

In addition to the waterfall model, over the last few decades the agile software model has been increasingly adopted[1723]. It has been reported that it seems to be the mainstream software development method worldwide[1724]. The agile model is "based on iterative development, frequent inspection and adaptation, and incremental deliveries in which requirements and solutions evolve through collaboration in cross-functional teams and through continuous stakeholder feedback"[1725]. Hence, this model is characterised by short development cycles, continuous testing, simplicity and user centricity[1726]. The development usually follows the modularity principle, which allows independent implementation of modules in the system to manage its complexity[1727]. Developers can continuously add new features or modify existing ones in a never-ending development phase which is called *perpetual beta*[1728]. A large number of approaches can be identified as agile methods[1729].

---

1721 *See* the comment in Filipova and Vilão, *op. cit.*, p. 28.

1722 *See* Schiffner et al., "Towards a roadmap for privacy technologies and the General Data Protection Regulation: A transatlantic initiative", p. 39.

1723 *See* Gürses and Van Hoboken, "Privacy after the agile turn", pp. 582–583.

1724 Rashina Hoda, Norsaremah Salleh, and John Grundy. "The rise and evolution of agile software development". In: *IEEE software* 35.5 (2018), pp. 58–63.

1725 ISO/IEC/IEEE. *ISO/IEC/IEEE 26515:2018 Systems and software engineering — Developing information for users in an agile environment*. Tech. rep. ISO/IEC/IEEE Second edition 2018–12, 2018.

1726 *See* Gürses and Van Hoboken, "Privacy after the agile turn", p. 582.

1727 *See* Gürses and Van Hoboken, *op. cit.*, p. 586.

1728 *See* Gürses and Van Hoboken, *op. cit.*, p. 593.

1729 *See* David Parsons. "Agile software development methodology, an ontological analysis". In: <www. researchgate.net/> (2011), which refers to Agile Microsoft Solutions Framework, Agile UP, Crystal Clear, DSDM, eXtreme Programming (XP), Feature Driven Development, Scrum. This article contains a useful ontology of agile methods which tries to show the common elements.

Despite the potential risk of infringements in a continuous process, it is possible to quickly redesign features on demand. Changing requirements even late in development is one of the 12 principles of the "Manifesto for Agile Software Development" of 2001[1730]. This Manifesto has been criticised for being too vague for a scientific work, but it started the discussion on how to use an iterative development method[1731]. The methodology focuses on solving problems, rather than following fixed planning[1732]. Agile planning is dynamic and employs continuous verification and incremental progress. In fact, agile often involves planning only for the short term and the implementation of processes goes in parallel[1733]. The iterative development cycle is still based on requirements and feedback.

The advantage of agile methods seems to be the ability to quickly change the requirements at any phase with an interdisciplinary team. As a result, DPbD technical implementation remains an ongoing process as

---

1730 *See* Kent Beck et al. *Manifesto for agile software development.* <agilemanifesto.org/>. 2001. The principles are: "1) Our highest priority is to satisfy the customer through early and continuous delivery of valuable software; 2) Welcome changing requirements, even late in development. Agile processes harness change for the customer's competitive advantage; 3) Deliver working software frequently, from a couple of weeks to a couple of months, with a preference to the shorter timescale; 4) Business people and developers must work together daily throughout the project; 5) Build projects around motivated individuals. Give them the environment and support they need, and trust them to get the job done; 6) The most efficient and effective method of conveying information to and within a development team is face-to-face conversation; 7) Working software is the primary measure of progress; 8) Agile processes promote sustainable development. The sponsors, developers, and users should be able to maintain a constant pace indefinitely; 9) Continuous attention to technical excellence and good design enhances agility; 10) Simplicity -the art of maximizing the amount of work not done- is essential; 11) The best architectures, requirements, and designs emerge from self-organizing teams; 12) At regular intervals, the team reflects on how to become more effective, then tunes and adjusts its behaviour accordingly". It is worth noting that these principles pay great attention to good design and teamwork, even promoting a sort of interdisciplinarity in principle 4.

1731 *See* Maarit Laanti, Jouni Similä, and Pekka Abrahamsson. "Definitions of agile software development and agility". In: *European Conference on Software Process Improvement.* Springer. 2013, pp. 247–258, which reports criticism and provides a table on agile principles and what they emphasise.

1732 Douglass, *Agile Systems Engineering*, p. 44. The book summarises the benefits at p. 83.

1733 ISO/IEC/IEEE, *ISO/IEC/IEEE 26515:2018 Systems and software engineering — Developing information for users in an agile environment.*

required by law. At the same time, the disadvantage seems to be that this methodology does not take into account the need to carefully plan the requirements before the first delivery of the project, with all the potential risks for data protection[1734]. It has been argued that while agility requires sprints, privacy analysis needs time and patience[1735]. So, once again this methodology may be used for DPbD implementation, but it also presents some challenges. The requirement and planning phase should remain a relevant stage for DPbD, within the possibility of changing the *status quo* pursuant to a new rule or a new aspect of the data processing.

In 2017, the Norwegian Data Protection Authority released some guidelines on "software development with Data Protection by Design and by Default"[1736]. The Authority declared that it had used as starting points the Microsoft Security Development Lifecycle (SDL), the Secure Software Development Life Cycle (S-SDLC) and the ENISA report *Privacy and Data Protection By design – from policy to engineering*[1737]. The guidelines contained a circular diagram with seven key activities in the software development process as pieces of a ring puzzle. This circularity represents the ongoing process needed to apply data protection by design and aims to show a general methodology for its development.

The authority described seven activities or steps: training, requirements, design, coding, testing, release, and maintenance. Within an organisation, the description of these activities may be summarised as follows:

- Training: the management and employees of an organisation should have knowledge of which data protection requirements are applicable, which information security tools are usable and which methodology

1734 *See* the comment in Filipova and Vilão, *Software Development From A to Z*, p. 28.

1735 *See* Schiffner et al., "Towards a roadmap for privacy technologies and the General Data Protection Regulation: A transatlantic initiative", p. 36.

1736 *See* Datatilsynet Norwegian Data Protection Authority. *Guidelines on software development with Data protection by Design and by Default*. 2017. According to Bygrave, these guidelines are useful for the application of Article 25 of the GDPR. *See* Bygrave, "Chapter IV Controller and Processor (Articles 24–43). Article 25. Data protection by design and by default", p. 577. This document was also quoted by the EDPB in European Data Protection Board, *Guidelines 4/2019 on Article 25 Data Protection by Design and by Default*. As argued in Bincoletto, "European Union – EDPB Guidelines 4/2019 on Data Protection by Design and by Default", p. 578, the guidelines of the Norwegian DPA are a valuable knowledge base for engineering data protection and building-in the requirements of the GDPR.

1737 Danezis et al., *Privacy and Data Protection by design – from policy to engineering*.

should be applied. To achieve this know-how, a training plan should be prepared by the organisation;

- Requirements: data protection and information security product and operational requirements should be established in advance for the development team in order to mitigate the possible risks. These requirements are strictly related to the concrete context and the applicable legal framework. Moreover, they could be expressed as a checklist and follow international standards. In this step, a risk assessment and, if required, a DPIA should be performed;
- Design: all previous specifications should be reflected in the design step, when the organisation should set the design requirements describing software characteristics and functionality. Two categories could be identified. Firstly, the so-called "data oriented design requirements" are: minimising the amount of personal data; hiding and protecting the collected data; separating the processing or the storage; aggregating the data as much as possible; and configuring data protection by default settings. Secondly, the "process oriented design requirements" are: providing information on how the software works and data are processed; giving control to the data subject; documenting all the adopted technical safeguards and demonstrating compliance with the rules[1738];
- Coding: the aim of this activity is "to write secure code", which is regularly subject to code analysis and code reviews. Developers should use recognised and up-to-date tools for software development from a list approved by the organisation and should document every adopted choice. All of the code functions and modules should be safe, even if they are developed by third parties;
- Testing: in this activity the implementation is compared with the planned data protection and security requirements by testers. In particular, security, dynamic, fuzz, and penetration testing should be performed;
- Release: an incident response plan should be prepared in the release phase;
- Maintenance: handling incidents and data breaches as planned is important, as well as maintaining a management system for data protection and information security.

The approach recommended by the Norwegian authority is particularly interesting for DPbD since it includes a strong analysis of the applicable

1738 These requirements follow the "privacy design strategies" that will be presented *infra* in Section 5.3.2.

legal framework and risk assessment before the design stage, it considers the difference between "data-oriented design requirements" and "process-oriented design requirements", which respectively refer to technical and organisational requirements, and it is convincing on the need to adopt an interdisciplinary approach[1739].

Any approach should take into account the personal data life cycle since data are processed both in the system and in the software. Tamó-Larrieux groups the possible life cycle phases into four main steps: data collection, data analysis, the use of data, data erasure or deletion[1740]. This author classifies the planning process and accessing and retrieving activities during the collection phase. The analysis step refers to storing, mining and managing databases, while the use step includes making predictions and decisions. The last phase identifies the moment when data is erased or recycled for further use.

Personal data life cycle may be re-classified as "data collection", "data use" *in latu sensu* and "data erasure". The phases are relevant for the data protection domain since different rules, and then measures, apply in each of them[1741]. Another valuable distinction is considering data at rest, data in use, and data in transit. While defining the requirements for the design stage, all these distinctions should be taken into account[1742].

After these brief considerations on system and software development, the following section will investigate the privacy engineering approaches.

## *5.3 Overview of privacy engineering approaches*

In 1967 privacy appeared for the first time as research topic in a computer science conference[1743]. In the 1980s, David Chaum proposed cryptographic protocols to control and monitor data exchange that combined system

1739 This categorisation will be taken into account in the next Chapter for the set of guidelines.

1740 *See* the life cycle of data framework in Tamó-Larrieux, *Designing for privacy and its legal framework: data protection by design and default for the internet of things*, pp. 149–151.

1741 Tamó-Larrieux argued that legislators have the data life cycle in mind while establishing the data protection framework. *See* Tamó-Larrieux, *op. cit.*, p. 151.

1742 Even these distinctions will be used in the next Chapter for the set of guidelines.

1743 Tamó-Larrieux, *Designing for privacy and its legal framework: data protection by design and default for the internet of things*, p. 104.

requirements with privacy[1744]. Over the 1990s a privacy technology community grew rapidly[1745]. At that time privacy conversations were mainly focused on preserving internet anonymity[1746].

As mentioned in Chapter 2, in the 1990s engineers started developing privacy-enhancing technologies to customise some information flow rules through technical design, while protecting privacy[1747]. PETs are ICT measures, applications or tools, that address a single dimension of privacy, such as anonymity or confidentiality, by eliminating or minimising personal data or by preventing unlawful uses without losing the functionality of an information system[1748]. So, PETs were progressively developed for the preservation of multiple values, including confidentiality, anonymity, transparency and control[1749]. As an example, confidentiality may be en-

1744 *See* David Chaum. "Untraceable electronic mail, return addresses, and digital pseudonyms". In: *Communications of the ACM* 24.2 (1981), pp. 84–90 and David Chaum. "Showing credentials without identification". In: *Workshop on the Theory and Application of Cryptographic Techniques*. Springer. 1985, pp. 241–244, which briefly describes the basic credential system.

1745 *See* George Danezis and Seda Gürses. "A critical review of 10 years of privacy technology". In: *Proceed- ings of surveillance cultures: a global surveillance society* (2010), pp. 1–16, p. 1, which reports the history. Some valuable studies from that period are: Victoria Bellotti and Abigail Sellen. "Design for privacy in ubiquitous computing environments". In: *Proceedings of the Third European Conference on Computer-Supported Cooperative Work 13–17 September 1993, Milan, Italy ECSCW'93*. Springer. 1993, pp. 77–92; Simon G Davies. "Re-engineering the right to privacy: how privacy has been transformed from a right to a commodity". In: *Technology and privacy: The new landscape* 143 (1997), pp. 143–166 Philip E. Agre and Marc Rotenberg. *Technology and privacy: The new landscape*. Mit Press, 1998. ISBN: 9780262011624.

1746 In 1993 the New Yorker published a famous cartoon by Peter Steiner where a dog sitting on a chair at a desk in front of a computer says to another dog sitting on the floor: "On the Internet, nobody knows you're a dog".

1747 *See* Chapter 2, Section 2.3. *See* also Reidenberg, "Lex informatica: The formulation of information policy rules through technology"; Bygrave, "Hardwiring privacy"; Van Rossum, Gardeniers, et al., *Privacy-enhancing technologies: The path to anonymity*.

1748 *See* Rubinstein, "Regulating privacy by design", p. 1411; Danezis and Gürses, "A critical review of 10 years of privacy technology"; European Commission, *Communication from the Commission to the European Parliament and the Council on Promoting Data Protection by Privacy Enhancing Technologies (PETs)*. For examples of technologies and techniques for enhancing trust *see* Le Métayer, "Whom to Trust? Using Technology to Enforce Privacy".

1749 *See* Bygrave, "Hardwiring privacy", p. 757.

forced with encryption, and security with an identity management system (IDMS)[1750].

The technologies for enforcing privacy have been classified into two main categories: "technologies for avoiding or reducing as much as possible the disclosure of personal data, hence enforcing the data minimisation principle" that avoid giving trust to data controllers (i.e. hard privacy), and "technologies for enforcing the rights of the subject if personal data is disclosed or processed", hence placing a certain amount of trust over controllers (i.e. soft privacy)[1751]. Thus, hard privacy is mostly about data minimisation seeking to avoid any disclosure, whereas soft privacy is mostly about data management seeking to share data in a way that protects and enforces rights[1752]. In the second category data management and users' choices play an important role.

The concept of PbD emerged with PET development and is strictly related to them since the approach of implementation can include these tools as building blocks[1753]. The same statement may refer to DPbD. PETs and standards may be components of a PbD or DPbD approach, but this concept is more comprehensive than a set of tools[1754]. Protecting personal data *by design* demands a proactive privacy engineering approach.

1750 *See* on encryption Le Métayer, "Whom to Trust? Using Technology to Enforce Privacy", p. 400; Whitfield Diffie and Susan Landau. *Privacy on the line: The politics of wiretapping and encryption*. Updated and expanded edition. The MIT Press, 2007. ISBN: 9780262042406; and on IDMS Danezis and Gürses, "A critical review of 10 years of privacy technology", p. 3.

1751 *See* Le Métayer, "Whom to Trust? Using Technology to Enforce Privacy", p. 397. According to the author, the use of these technologies is not sufficient, since a more proactive and comprehensive approach is necessary.

1752 *See* Rubinstein and Good, "The trouble with Article 25 (and how to fix it): the future of data protection by design and default", p. 9. As an example, hard privacy includes anonymous communication channels, selective disclosure credentials, private information retrieval, and homomorphic encryption. Soft privacy includes cookie management tools, privacy dashboards, and auditable secure logs.

1753 *See* once again Hustinx, "Privacy by design: delivering the promises"; Kroener and Wright, "A strategy for operationalizing privacy by design"; D'Acquisto et al., *Privacy by design in big data: an overview of privacy enhancing technologies in the era of big data analytics*; Tsormpatzoudi, Berendt, and Coudert, "Privacy by design: from research and policy to practice–the challenge of multi-disciplinarity"; Bygrave, "Hardwiring privacy".

1754 *See* Cavoukian, Shapiro, and Cronk, "Privacy engineering: Proactively embedding privacy, by design".

According to Gürses *et al.*, privacy engineering is "an emerging field of research that focuses on designing, implementing, adapting and evaluating theories, methods, techniques and tools to systematically capture and address privacy issues in the development of sociotechnical systems"[1755]. Privacy engineering mainly derives from the software engineering field, but it also embeds other computer science fields, including information security, human-computer interaction and machine learning[1756].

Privacy engineering means using engineering principles and processes to embed privacy and data protection features and measures in technical design on a case-by-case basis and for the data life-cycle[1757]. Actually, this computer science field may be used for all the following goals[1758]:

- "Designing and constructing processes, products, and systems with privacy in mind that appropriately collect or use personal information;
- Supporting the development, implementation, and measurement of privacy policies, standards, guidelines, and rules;
- Analysing software and hardware designs and implementation from a privacy and user experience perspective;
- Supporting privacy audits;
- Working with other stakeholders to ensure privacy requirements are met outside as well as inside the engineering space".

*Regulation by design* is aimed at the first goal primarily. Privacy or data protection requirements may turn into either functional components of the

1755 Gürses and Van Hoboken, "Privacy after the agile turn", p. 581.

1756 Van Dijk et al., "Right engineering? The redesign of privacy and personal data protection", p. 235.

1757 *See* Tamó-Larrieux, *Designing for privacy and its legal framework: data protection by design and default for the internet of things*, p. 232. *See* also the definition of Michelle Dennedy, Jonathan Fox, and Tom Finneran. *The privacy engineer's manifesto: getting from policy to code to QA to value*. Apress, 2014. ISBN: 9781430263562, p. 29: "Privacy engineering as a discrete discipline or field of inquiry and innovation may be defined as using engineering principles and processes to build controls and measures into processes, systems, components, and products that enable the authorized, fair, and legitimate processing of personal information". Interestingly, this book also specifies that "privacy engineering is not merely a call for mindful engineering where personal information is involved. The call for privacy engineering use and study is a call for leadership, innovation, and even a good measure of courage to change the status quo for design and information management". So, this discipline is even useful for technological innovation.

1758 Dennedy, Fox, and Finneran, *op. cit.*, p. 30.

system or non-functional ones[1759]. So, systematic methods should provide the means for representing, eliciting and analysing the requirements[1760].

In the literature, several approaches of privacy engineering can be distinguished[1761]. The approaches may define strategies and goals that developers should take into account when working on a concrete project or they may establish priorities and development methods.

First of all, the taxonomy of "privacy-by-policy" and "privacy-by-architecture" is frequently used for explaining privacy engineering approaches[1762]. The former concept refers to strategies that implement the "notice-and-choice" principle, while the latter refers to strategies that minimise the collection of information by using pseudonymisation or anonymisation techniques[1763]. However, it seems that this categorisation is mainly focused on US concepts. It may be argued that both HIPAA Privacy and Security Rules in the US and DPbD in the EU require more comprehensive and hybrid strategies.

Some approaches focus on modelling privacy requirements from an organisational point of view for adopting privacy by design. PbD is actually an approach that requires both technical and organisational measures. Lentzsch *et al.* observed a lack of adoption of PbD approaches focused on process-driven strategies and socio-technical design[1764]. So, they proposed a socio-technical design (STD) approach that brought together users, privacy experts and developers through workshops and used a modelling annota-

1759 Cavoukian stated that privacy is usually ancillary to the primary purposes of a system. Then, it is frequently a non-functional requirement. *See* Cavoukian, Shapiro, and Cronk, "Privacy engineering: Proactively embedding privacy, by design".

1760 *See* Guarda and Zannone, "Towards the development of privacy-aware systems", p. 19.

1761 *See* the overviews by Seda Gürses and Jose M. Del Alamo. "Privacy engineering: Shaping an emerging field of research and practice". In: *IEEE Security & Privacy* 14.2 (2016), pp. 40–46; Sarah Spiekermann and Lorrie Faith Cranor. "Engineering privacy". In: *IEEE Transactions on software engineering* 35.1 (2008), pp. 67–82; Guarda and Zannone, "Towards the development of privacy-aware systems".

1762 *See* e.g. Spiekermann and Cranor, "Engineering privacy", p. 73; Cavoukian, Shapiro, and Cronk, "Privacy engineering: Proactively embedding privacy, by design", pp. 12–13; Gürses and Del Alamo, "Privacy engineering: Shaping an emerging field of research and practice".

1763 Spiekermann and Cranor, "Engineering privacy", p. 79.

1764 Christopher Lentzsch et al. "Integrating a Practice Perspective to Privacy by Design". In: *International Conference on Human Aspects of Information Security, Privacy, and Trust*. Springer. 2017, pp. 691–702.

tion called SeeMe. Their modelling is guided by questions addressed to the participants and further aspects should be added according to the discussion[1765].

The PriS method is a requirement engineering methodology, but it proposes to incorporate privacy requirements as organisational goals to be achieved in the early development stage[1766]. PriS uses eight privacy goals, namely "identification, authentication, authorisation, data protection, anonymity, pseudonymity, unlinkability and unobservability". The method first requires eliciting the goals that are relevant for the concrete project. Then, it is necessary to analyse the impact of the selected goals on business processes and their support systems and to model the privacy-related processes with the Enterprise Knowledge Development (EKD) framework[1767]. After that, the developer can identify the techniques that support these privacy-related processes with privacy-process patterns. The PriS approach is also based on a formal representation of the phases[1768]. Despite the complexity and comprehensiveness of this approach, it does not specifically take into account privacy or data protection principles as defined by the law. However, new approaches use the PriS methodology to create new privacy process patterns that are useful for engineers[1769].

In a prominent study investigating how "engineering privacy by design" could be addressed, Gürses *et al.* defined five steps that have to be re-iterated many times when developing a system with privacy and data minimisation embedded at the core[1770]:

1. Clearly describing system functionality (i.e. functional requirements analysis);
2. Minimising data (e.g. using advanced cryptography techniques);
3. Modelling attackers, threats and risks, including a typical risk analysis;

---

1765 Lentzsch et al., *op. cit.*

1766 Christos Kalloniatis, Evangelia Kavakli, and Stefanos Gritzalis. "Addressing privacy requirements in system design: the PriS method". In: *Requirements Engineering* 13.3 (2008), pp. 241–255; Christos Kalloniatis, Petros Belsis, and Stefanos Gritzalis. "A soft computing approach for privacy requirements engineering: The PriS framework". In: *Applied Soft Computing* 11.7 (2011), pp. 4341–4348.

1767 *See* Kalloniatis, Kavakli, and Gritzalis, "Addressing privacy requirements in system design: the PriS method", p. 245.

1768 *See* Kalloniatis, Kavakli, and Gritzalis, *op. cit.*, pp. 247–249.

1769 *See* Vasiliki Diamantopoulou et al. "Supporting privacy by design using privacy process patterns". In: *IFIP International Conference on ICT Systems Security and Privacy Protection*. Springer. 2017, pp. 491–505.

1770 *See* Gürses, Troncoso, and Diaz, "Engineering privacy by design", pp. 18–19.

4. Analysing multilateral security requirements since privacy measures should not be detrimental to other important security objectives of a system;
5. Implementing and testing the design to understand whether it embeds the solution "that fulfils the integrity requirements revealing the minimal amount of private data".

According to this study, data minimisation has a central role in the PbD approach, and it shall be considered its guiding principle. Article 25 of the GDPR highlights the importance of this principle by using it as an example of the data protection principle. At the same time, Gürses' approach included security and risk assessment as fundamental steps from a privacy engineering point of view.

A group of researchers proposed a methodology for enabling PbD in medical record sharing[1771]. As a methodology, the CHINO project proposed starting with the extraction of compliance and business requirements from the legal provisions and the involved stakeholders, respectively, by following five steps with different actors[1772]:

1. Identification of business requirements, which is performed by a chief information officer;
2. Identification of compliance requirements, which is performed by a chief compliance officer;
3. Definition of compliance-aware data management scenarios, which is performed by a business analyst;
4. Definition of executable processes and policies, which is performed by a business analyst and by developers;
5. Deployment and execution inside run-time environment, which are performed by developers.

This approach used both European and HIPAA rules for extracting requirements that are applicable to a specific use case in the healthcare domain. The requirements have been identified as "privacy policies", and they take into account different roles. The benefit of this study is showing how requirements and data management operations can be modelled by using the Business Process Model and Notation (BPMN)[1773].

---

1771 Jovan Stevovic et al. "Enabling privacy by design in medical records sharing". In: *Reforming European Data Protection Law*. Springer, 2015, pp. 385–406. ISBN: 9789401793858.

1772 Stevovic et al., *op. cit.*

1773 *See* the current BPMN specifications at <www.bpmn.org>. Last accessed 06/10/2021.

In the *Preliminary Opinion on privacy by design* the EDPS quoted the framework of so-called "Six protection goals for privacy engineering" as an example of existing useful methodologies[1774]. This framework was proposed by Hansen *et al.* in 2015 and it defined six goals that can be used by engineers for deriving requirements, choosing techniques and technologies, and evaluating the privacy impacts and conditions of systems[1775]. Three goals are the CIAD triad, i.e. confidentiality, integrity and availability. These traditional security principles are fundamental for any development of ICT system[1776].

Beyond these goals, according to this framework, engineers should consider another triad: unlinkability, transparency and intervenability[1777]. The goal of unlinkability entails that "processes have to be operated in such a way that the privacy-relevant data are not linkable to any privacy-relevant information outside of the domain"[1778]. This goal embeds the principles of data minimisation and purpose limitation, and it can be achieved through pseudonymisation or anonymisation. In this study transparency refers to openness and accountability and it means that "all privacy-relevant data processing – including the legal, technical, and organizational setting – can be understood and reconstructed at any time"[1779]. Logging, detailed documentation, and information delivery mechanisms are common techniques for achieving transparency. Finally, the research defines intervenability as the "property that intervention is possible concerning all ongoing or planned privacy-relevant data processing", including the execution of data

1774 European Data Protection Supervisor, *Opinion 5/2018, Preliminary Opinion on privacy by design*, p. 13.

1775 Marit Hansen, Meiko Jensen, and Martin Rost. "Protection goals for privacy engineering". In: *2015 IEEE Security and Privacy Workshops*. IEEE. 2015, pp. 159–166.

1776 Engineers may use encryption, access control mechanisms, and other techniques like redundancy and virtualisation.

1777 This triad has also been endorsed by the Spanish DPA in the Guide on privacy by design. The authority created a table where the triad is associated with the GDPR's principles: unlinkability embeds data minimisation, storage limitation, and integrity and confidentiality; transparency embeds lawfulness, fairness and transparency, and purpose limitation; intervenability/control embeds purpose limitation, accuracy, integrity and confidentiality, and accountability. *See* Agencia Espanõla de Protección de Datos, *A Guide to Privacy by Design*, pp. 13–14.

1778 Hansen, Jensen, and Rost, "Protection goals for privacy engineering", p. 160.

1779 *Ibid.*

subject's rights[1780]. Overall, the six goals may conflict with one another and then the developer may mitigate such a conflict by deciding on concrete priorities[1781]. This approach is an abstract model that is useful for guiding the developer by using strategies, but these strategies are still quite broad, and they do not define explicit requirements.

Another approach quoted by the EDPS is the "privacy design patterns" framework. In general, design patterns are tools used for making decisions about the organisation of a software system since they describe its commonly recurring structure and components[1782]. It has been highlighted that the work on privacy patterns is recommended in the field of PbD[1783]. In fact, detailed privacy patterns could be used for deciding how system architecture should be implemented in specific parts. These patterns have been classified by the literature, and they include several PETs[1784]. Thanks to an international and institutional collaboration, the portal *privacypatterns.eu* collects and discusses the published privacy patterns[1785]. As an example, the "Pseudonymous Messaging" pattern establishes that "a messaging service is enhanced by using a trusted third party to exchange the identifiers of the communication partners by pseudonyms"[1786]. A standardisation process may enhance the use of design patterns. As such, the approach is not comprehensive, and it is very abstract. So, privacy design

---

1780 *Ibid.* As regards this last goal, the authors states that few techniques could have been implemented.

1781 Hansen, Jensen, and Rost, *op. cit.*, p. 161.

1782 Danezis et al., *Privacy and Data Protection by design – from policy to engineering*, p. 17; Jaap-Henk Hoepman. "Privacy design strategies". In: *IFIP International Information Security Conference*. Springer, 2014, pp. 446–459, p. 448.

1783 Koot and Laat, "Privacy from an Informatics Perspective", p. 246; Agencia Espanõla de Protección de Dados, *A Guide to Privacy by Design*.

1784 *See* Munawar Hafiz. "A collection of privacy design patterns". In: *Proceedings of the 2006 conference on Pattern languages of programs*. 2006, pp. 1–13; Munawar Hafiz. "A pattern language for developing privacy enhancing technologies". In: *Software: Practice and Experience* 43.7 (2013), pp. 769–787; Jörg Lenhard, Lothar Fritsch, and Sebastian Herold. "A literature study on privacy patterns research". In: *2017 43rd Euromicro Conference on Software Engineering and Advanced Applications (SEAA)*. IEEE. 2017, pp. 194–201. A long selection on patterns is also provided by Agencia Espanõla de Protección de Dados, *A Guide to Privacy by Design*, pp. 32–43.

1785 *See* the official website at <privacypatterns.eu>. Last accessed 06/10/2021.

1786 *See* the pattern at <privacypatterns.eu/#/patterns/pseudonymous-messaging>. Last accessed 06/10/2021.

patterns should be used with other design strategies and architectural tactics[1787].

Privacy is considered both a functional and a non-functional requirement in the "Privacy- Enhancing ARchitectures" (PEARs) methodology. The PEARs framework is based on the analysis of quality attributes of a system and it proposes four tactics for achieving privacy protection through requirements[1788]. The developer first analyses and identifies the scenarios, selects architecture techniques that influence the scenarios (i.e. tactics) and verifies the impact of the techniques on response measures[1789]. The four tactics for privacy by design that influence the non-functional requirements of a system are classified as minimisation tactics (e.g. anonymisation), enforcement tactics (e.g. access rights), accountability tactics (e.g. logging), and modifiability tactics (e.g. change policies)[1790]. These tactics are described with patterns, and they use PETs. So, the approach proposes a methodology that includes both the use of patterns or PETs and the description of non-functional requirements.

In 2017, Guarda *et al.* proposed a methodology based on three building blocks for applying privacy and data protection at the beginning of the design process, for solving the problem of the natural language of the legal requirements, and for providing evidence on the compliance checking[1791]. Firstly, they elaborated "a declarative framework to specify the processing of data for certain purposes together with legal requirements and security policies at design-time"[1792]. Secondly, they introduced an interdisciplinary approach for deriving formal specifications from legal rules. Thirdly, they suggested automated techniques to solve security analysis and compliance checking problems. This interdisciplinary research was based on data protection requirements of the DPD.

1787 *See* Hoepman, "Privacy design strategies".

1788 *See* Antonio Kung. "PEARs: privacy enhancing architectures". In: *Proceedings of the Annual Privacy Forum of 2014*. Springer. 2014, pp. 18–29.

1789 *See* Kung, *op. cit.*, p. 21.

1790 *See* Kung, *op. cit.*, pp. 23–24.

1791 *See* Paolo Guarda, Silvio Ranise, and Hari Siswantoro. "Security analysis and legal compliance checking for the design of privacy-friendly information systems". In: *Proceedings of the 22nd ACM on Symposium on Access Control Models and Technologies*. 2017, pp. 247–254.

1792 Guarda, Ranise, and Siswantoro, *op. cit.*, p. 248.

As regards the formal representation of legal norms, the great contribution of the legal informatics field should be mentioned[1793]. It does not propose engineering approaches, but it provides valuable instruments to be taken into account. In particular, to represent legal resources the so-called LegalRuleML, a robust and expressive XML annotation, created a framework for modelling normative rules that satisfies the legal domain requirements[1794]. LegalRuleML provided an integrated and self-contained representation of legal resources available on the Web that is useful for a legal reasoning level combined with an ontological layer. As previously mentioned, the Akoma-Ntoso standard also provided the schema for the structure and the semantic components of digital legislative documents in machine readable form[1795]. It has been pointed out that LegalRuleML can represent and store the logical content of the legal provisions, while Akoma-Ntoso can be used to tag the original textual content of the legal documents[1796]. The DAPRECO (DAta Protection REgulation COmpliance) research project used these instruments and the legal ontology PrOnto[1797],

---

1793 On legal informatics *see* Giovanni Sartor, Maria Angela Biasiotti, and Fabrizio Turchi. *Tecnologie e abilità informatiche per il diritto*. G. Giappichelli Editore, 2018. ISBN: 9788834839409; Sartor, *L'informatica giuridica e le tecnologie dell'informazione: Corso di informatica giuridica*; Giovanni Sartor. "Il diritto nell'informatica giuridica". In: *Rivista di filosofia del diritto* 4 Speciale (2015), pp. 71–92; Massimo Durante and Ugo Pagallo. *Manuale di informatica giuridica e diritto delle nuove tecnologie*. Utet Giuridica, 2012. ISBN: 9788859807773; Giovanni Sartor. "Legislative information and the web". In: *Legislative XML for the Semantic Web*. Springer, 2011, pp. 11–20; Mariangela Biasiotti et al. "Legal informatics and management of legislative documents". In: *Global Center for ICT in Parliament Working Paper* 2 (2008); Vittorio Frosini and Donato Antonio Limone. *L'insegnamento dell'informatica giuridica*. Liguori, 1990. ISBN: 8820719169.

1794 *See* Monica Palmirani et al. "LegalRuleML: XML-based rules and norms". In: *International Workshop on Rules and Rule Markup Languages for the Semantic Web*. Springer. 2011, pp. 298–312; Tara Athan et al. "LegalRuleML: Design principles and foundations". In: *Reasoning Web International Summer School*. Springer. 2015, pp. 151–188.

1795 *See* Palmirani and Vitali, "Akoma-Ntoso for legal documents"; Palmirani, "Legislative change management with Akoma-Ntoso".

1796 Livio Robaldo et al. "Formalizing GDPR provisions in Reified I/O logic: the DAPRECO knowledge base". In: *Journal of Logic, Language and Information* (2019), pp. 1–49.

1797 Monica Palmirani et al. "PrOnto: Privacy ontology for legal reasoning". In: *International Conference on Electronic Government and the Information Systems Perspective*. Springer. 2018, pp. 139–152; Palmirani et al., "Legal Ontology for Modelling GDPR Concepts and Norms"; Palmirani et al., "PrOnto Ontology

to create a knowledge base on the GDPR that is useful for legal reasoning and automated compliance checking[1798].

Overall, engineering approaches have attempted to provide more guidance to developers on privacy by design. The research to date has tended to focus on PbD and privacy strategies trying to combine system engineering methods and modelling with broad concepts and principles. Three other relevant approaches for engineering privacy are the "PRIPARE project", "privacy design strategies" and the "LIDDUN methodology", which will be analysed separately in the following subsections.

### 5.3.1 The PRIPARE project

The PEARs project was connected to another EU-funded project called "Preparing Industry to PbD by supporting its Application in Research" (PRIPARE)[1799]. At the time of this project the GDPR was under discussion, so the legislation used by the team was its draft version of 2015.

PRIPARE's methodology included the typical system engineering phases – namely analysis, design, implementation, verification, release, maintenance and decommission – and it added the central phase "environment & infrastructure", which required the implementation of an appropriate organisational structure during the application of all the other steps[1800]. In spite of the indication of these phases, the PRIPARE methodology is iterative and non-linear[1801]. Several roles should be involved in the

---

Refinement Through Open Knowledge Extraction". On other privacy legal ontologies *see* Leone, Di Caro, and Villata, "Taking stock of legal ontologies: a feature-based comparative analysis"; Oliveira Rodrigues et al., "Legal ontologies over time: a systematic mapping study". *See* also Chapter 2, Section 2.3.

1798 Robaldo et al., "Formalizing GDPR provisions in Reified I/O logic: the DAPRECO knowledge base".

1799 *See* Nicolás Notario et al. "PRIPARE: a new vision on engineering privacy and security by design". In: *Cyber Security and Privacy Forum*. Springer. 2014, pp. 65–76; Nicolás Notario et al. "PRIPARE: integrating privacy best practices into a privacy engineering methodology". In: *2015 IEEE Security and Privacy Workshops*. IEEE. 2015, pp. 151–158; Nicolás Notario et al. *PRIPARE. Privacy-and Security-by design Methodology Handbook. 2016*. 2017.

1800 Notario et al., *op. cit.*, p. 14.

1801 The report specified that the PRIPARE methodology is compatible with most agile methodologies since the seven phases can be reiterated many times. *See* Notario et al., *op. cit.*, pp. 103–104.

development process: systems engineers, privacy and security officers, data subjects, DPAs, end users and project managers.

During the analysis phase, given a set of privacy and security principles obtained with a legal assessment, the requirements gathering of PRIPARE should be performed with the involvement of all stakeholders and an initial risk assessment. The principles used by PRIPARE were: "consent and choice; purpose legitimacy and specification; collection limitation; data minimization; use retention and disclosure limitation; accuracy and quality; openness, transparency and notice; individual participation and access; accountability; information security; privacy compliance"[1802]. These principles refer both to FIPs, OECD Guidelines and GDPR principles. For each principle a fixed list of goal-oriented guidelines should be mapped and then techniques to fulfil these guidelines should be identified.

As a result, operational requirements are obtained from privacy principles. For example, guidelines of the data minimisation principles are: "avoid and minimise the use of personal data along its whole life-cycle"; "limit the ability of external parties from inferring personal data from sources coming from different controllers"; "minimize the traces left by transactions and interactions with a system or service"[1803].

Having defined the operational requirements, the design phase should concretely build the system through privacy and security patterns, tactics, PEARs, strategies and PETs. So, this approach took into account different architecture approaches during the effective implementation. This project also showed that the implementation of privacy by design should follow the high-level analysis of the legal principles and the operationalisation of these principles in guidelines and strategies. For this reason, privacy experts should be given a seat at the table.

The PRIPARE project then described several formal approaches for architecture design and classified existing techniques from the literature[1804]. In order to check whether the implementation respects legal requirements, the system developer and the project manager should express the implementation with formal semantics and use a verification tool or a theorem prover to verify the implementation with the properties and the scenarios[1805]. Prior to the release, even a dynamic analysis on the code should be

1802 Notario et al., *op. cit.*, p. 40.
1803 *See* Notario et al., *op. cit.*, p. 43.
1804 *See* Notario et al., *op. cit.*, pp. 56–62.
1805 *See* Notario et al., *op. cit.*, pp. 67–68.

performed through testing tools, instrumentation techniques, and dynamic flow analysis[1806].

After the release of the system, an incident response plan should be created, and the privacy impact assessment should be published. Examination and re-examination should be iterative phases during the use of the system, including periodical risk assessment, and every analysis should be reported and documented in detail to ensure accountability.

This project provided a list of guidelines and applied criteria that are associated with privacy principles[1807]. These guidelines and the PRIPARE method may be considered a useful starting point for a DPbD approach. It should be noted, however, that a DPbD implementation should now take into account the data protection principles and requirements of the approved text of the GDPR.

An interesting project that is using GDPR concepts and lexicon is the "Architectural View for Data Protection by Design" of KU Leuven University[1808]. This research provides a meta-model for the data protection architectural viewpoint with UML class diagrams[1809]. The model identifies GDPR actors, their roles in the processing activities, and provides data flow diagrams (DFDs) and some requirements expressed as criteria (e.g. the documentation criterion). Interestingly, the research has been validated with a case study on the e-health domain[1810].

### 5.3.2 Privacy design strategies

Privacy design strategies are general strategies that are aimed at achieving privacy protection by limiting how the system structure is realised during the first phases of the development cycle[1811]. The strategies should guide the software development cycle in the concept and analysis phase in choosing quality attributes. So, in this approach privacy influences non-functional requirements. Later, in the design phase design patterns

---

1806 *See* Notario et al., *op. cit.*, p. 69.

1807 *See* Notario et al., *op. cit.*, pp. 120–132.

1808 *See* Laurens Sion et al. "An architectural view for data protection by design". In: *2019 IEEE International Conference on Software Architecture (ICSA)*. IEEE. 2019, pp. 11–20.

1809 *See* Sion et al., *op. cit.*, p. 14.

1810 The research in Sion et al., *op. cit.* refers to a patient monitoring system.

1811 Danezis et al., *Privacy and Data Protection by design – from policy to engineering*, p. 18.

remain useful, as do PETs during the implementation phase. These strategies usually suggest a waterfall methodology, but they simply refer to the requirement phase that is useful in agile methods, too[1812].

A key study on privacy design strategies was carried out by Hoepman in 2014[1813]. In particular, eight privacy design strategies were proposed with their respective design patterns. The data protection rules used by this framework were the OECD Guidelines, Article 8 of the European Convention of Human Rights, and the DPD[1814]. So, the selected principles were: "purpose limitation (comprising both specification of the purpose and limiting the use to that stated purpose); data minimisation; data quality; transparency (openness in OECD terms); data subject rights (in terms of consent, and the right to view, erase, and rectify personal data); the right to be forgotten; adequate protection (security safeguards in OECD terms); data portability; data breach notifications; accountability and (provable) compliance"[1815]. It may be noted that these principles follow both the OECD Guidelines, the FIPs and European principles (e.g. right to be forgotten and data portability).

The first four strategies were data-oriented, while the other four were process-oriented. The strategies can be summarised as follows[1816]:

1. Minimise. The first strategy states that the amount of personal data should be limited to the minimum. Minimising the amount of data means selecting data before collection, or anonymising (and pseudonymising) data after collection. Thus, this strategy corresponds to the data minimisation principle under the GDPR or the "minimum necessary rule" of the HIPAA, and to purpose limitation;
2. Hide. This strategy requires hiding personal data from anybody or from unauthorised entities preserving data confidentiality. Typical examples of hide design patterns are encryption and anonymisation that achieve data minimisation;
3. Separate. The third strategy is aimed at processing personal data in a distributed way whenever possible by separating the performed activities or the data storage related to a single individual. Decentralised

1812 Jaap-Henk Hoepman. "Privacy Design Strategies (The Little Blue Book)". In: *Radboud University Repository* (2018), p. 22.

1813 *See* Hoepman, "Privacy design strategies".

1814 Hoepman, *op. cit.*, pp. 449–450.

1815 Hoepman, *op. cit.*, p. 451.

1816 *See* Hoepman, *op. cit.*; Danezis et al., *Privacy and Data Protection by design – from policy to engineering*; Agencia Espanõla de Protección de Datos, *A Guide to Privacy by Design*, pp. 16–24.

services or separation of databases are useful for this strategy to respect the purpose limitation principle;
4. Aggregate, later defined as Abstract. The last data-oriented strategy requires processing personal data at the highest level of aggregation that corresponds to the least level of detail that is useful to the controller. Again, anonymisation techniques may be appropriate;
5. Inform. As the first process-oriented strategy, informing data subjects on the existence and context of the processing is highly important for protecting transparency and data subject's rights. The information should refer to the purpose and means of the processing, including the security of the used system and documentation on design. The data subject should be informed of the recipients and existing rights. Design patterns of this strategy are: platforms for privacy preferences, data breach notification, and transparency-enhancing techniques;
6. Control. According to this strategy the data subject should have the means to control the processing of personal data. As an example, user-centric identity management helps the individual control the processed data. The principles for this strategy are data quality and data portability;
7. Enforce. This strategy states that a privacy policy should be in place. Actually, the strategy refers to practices and measures compatible with the legal requirements, instead of referring to the concrete document where the information is provided. So, this strategy is strictly related to the accountability principle;
8. Demonstrate. Even this last strategy is connected to accountability. The controller should demonstrate compliance with the applicable legal requirements. Logging and auditing are typical examples of techniques for this strategy.

This framework later took into account the GDPR requirements and assigned applicable architectural tactics to the privacy strategies[1817]. This resulted in a more concrete approach. At the same time, Hoepman *et al.* used the FTC's version of the FIPs to include the US market and the concept of PII. As an example, the tactics for the "minimize strategy" are: "exclude", meaning refraining from processing partly or entirely with opt-out solutions; "select", meaning deciding on the full or partial use of personal data with opt-in-solutions; "strip", meaning removing unnecessary

1817 *See* Michael Colesky, Jaap-Henk Hoepman, and Christiaan Hillen. "A critical analysis of privacy design strategies". In: *2016 IEEE Security and Privacy Workshops (SPW)*. IEEE. 2016, pp. 33–40.

personal data categories in the system; and "destroy", meaning deleting personal data after the retention period[1818].

In addition to strategies and tactics, several examples of state of the art techniques and technologies were classified in Hoepman's Little Blue Book in 2018. This collection should address organisations, designers, and engineers that need to build privacy by design systems[1819]. Privacy design strategies are useful for defining requirements, but they should be combined with the applicable privacy and data protection principles. Besides, anonymisation is not always feasible.

### 5.3.3 LIDDUN methodology

The last methodology of this overview is the LIDDUN methodology, which is based on the creation and analysis of the system data flows and of privacy threat patterns[1820]. In particular, LIDDUN is based on diagrams for mapping entities, processes and flows, and stresses the importance of risk analysis[1821].

The LIDDUN methodology has been recognised by the literature as a modelling framework that supports the elicitation of privacy requirements and mitigation of privacy threats[1822]. The acronym LIDDUN actually embeds the following privacy threat categories: "linkability, identifiability, non-repudiation, detectability, disclosure of information, unawareness,

---

1818 *See* Colesky, Hoepman, and Hillen, *op. cit.*, p. 35.

1819 *See* Hoepman, "Privacy Design Strategies (The Little Blue Book)".

1820 Danezis et al., *Privacy and Data Protection by design – from policy to engineering*, p. 13.

1821 *See* the comment of the EDPS in European Data Protection Supervisor, *Opinion 5/2018, Preliminary Opinion on privacy by design*, p. 14.

1822 *See* Mina Deng et al. "A privacy threat analysis framework: supporting the elicitation and fulfilment of privacy requirements". In: *Requirements Engineering* 16.1 (2011), pp. 3–32; Kim Wuyts, Riccardo Scandariato, and Wouter Joosen. "LIND(D)UN privacy threat tree catalog". In: *CW Reports 675* (2014); Kim Wuyts, Riccardo Scandariato, and Wouter Joosen. "Empirical evaluation of a privacy-focused threat modeling methodology". In: *Journal of Systems and Software* 96 (2014), pp. 122–138; Sion et al., "An architectural view for data protection by design", p. 12; Notario et al., *PRIPARE. Privacy-and Security-by design Methodology Handbook. 2016*; Laurens Sion et al. "Interaction-based privacy threat elicitation". In: *2018 IEEE European Symposium on Security and Privacy Workshops (EuroS&PW)*. IEEE. 2018, pp. 79–86.

non-compliance"[1823]. These threats may be posed by an external entity during a data flow where a user is performing a process.

The LIDDUN framework models the data flow, and provides threat tree catalogues for describing the envisaged scenarios of the same threats. The mapping of the privacy threats is combined with software-based system components and a formal modelling[1824]. This modelling may help the developer elicit concrete privacy requirements and select technical solutions that are able to fulfil these requirements.

Hence, unlike the PRIPARE methodology and privacy strategies that start with the analysis of principles or goals, and after that perform a risk analysis, LIDDUN begins with risk modelling and then includes the requirements. LIDDUN does not explain how to select the PETs that correspond to a privacy requirement, but it provides mitigation strategies and state of the art techniques based on the envisaged threats. It does not even use a specific set of privacy principles[1825]. The benefit of this approach is using semantics and abstract modelling to guide developers while recognising the risks. This approach is not comprehensive, but it may be used during a privacy impact assessment as a technical component[1826].

So far, this Chapter has presented several privacy engineering approaches. Overall, these frameworks should not be seen as self-excluding. During a risk assessment, data flow mapping and threat analysis and modelling like LIDDUN may help the developer identify risks and find solutions to mitigate these risks. During the system and software development, after choosing a development method (e.g. waterfall or agile), privacy design strategies or goals, design patterns, architectural tactics and PETs help the developer to define the functional and non-functional system requirements with privacy protection. A comprehensive methodology like PRIPARE provides guidelines for all the phases of the development life cycle and includes stakeholders' organisational and management level.

1823 The description of the threats is provided in Sion et al., *op. cit.*

1824 *See* Kristian Beckers. "Comparing privacy requirements engineering approaches". In: *2012 Seventh International Conference on Availability, Reliability and Security*. IEEE. 2012, pp. 574–581, p. 577.

1825 For this criticism of LIDDUN *see* Alshammari and Simpson, "Towards a principled approach for engineering privacy by design", pp. 165–166; and Maria Grazia Porcedda. "'Privacy by Design' in EU Law". In: *Privacy Technologies and Policy. 6th Annual Privacy Forum, APF 2018*. Springer. 2018, pp. 183–204, p. 189.

1826 Sion et al., "Interaction-based privacy threat elicitation", p. 85.

Risk analysis and assessment are pivotal components of all the methodologies. In fact, a privacy engineering framework should always be combined with a privacy risk analysis. The next section deals with this aspect, by investigating general concepts and discussing some applicable methodologies for the data protection impact assessment.

### *5.4 Guidance on the risk assessment framework*

Privacy engineering and DPbD require an efficient approach to risk assessment. As mentioned in Chapter 2, risk is the product of likelihood of an event and its severity: *risk = likelihood × severity.*

Where risk may be defined as the "effect of uncertainty on objectives", likelihood is "the chance of something happening" – that is the event or "occurrence or change of a particular set of circumstances"[1827] – and severity is the measure of the possible consequences of the source of this event, i.e. its potential harm. So, the event or threat identifies a circumstance or set of circumstances that causes harm to personal data. The likelihood – i.e. the probability that this event will happen[1828] – is frequently scaled from 0 to 1, whereas the severity – i.e. the impact – is scaled with qualitative terms.

In the data protection domain, likelihood and severity are both usually scaled from "low", "medium", "high" to even "very high"[1829]. At the same time, scores 1, 2, 3 may be assigned to the three first levels. As regards the likelihood, if the event or threat is unlikely to happen, the level is low; if it is possible or likely to materialise, the level is respectively medium or high[1830]. Severity refers to the consequences of the event on the individual.

---

1827 ISO. *ISO/Guide 73:2009(en) Risk management — Vocabulary*. Tech. rep. ISO/TMBG, 2009.

1828 ISO, *op. cit.*, specifies that likelihood may refer to either probability or frequency. Actually, the word probability usually refers to the mathematical term. Therefore, ISO points out that "in risk management terminology, "likelihood" is used with the intent that it should have the same broad interpretation as the term "probability" has in many languages other than English".

1829 European Union Agency for Network & Information Security, *Handbook on Security of Personal Data Processing*; Fabio Guasconi et al. *Reinforcing trust and security in the area of electronic communications and online services. Sketching the notion of "state-of-the-art" for SMEs in security of personal data processing.* European Union Agency for Network and Information Security, 2018, p. 18.

1830 D'Acquisto and Panagopoulou, *Guidelines for SMEs on the security of personal data processing*, p. 29.

Where the individual may encounter few inconveniences, the level is low, whereas where the inconveniences are significant and serious, the level is high[1831]. This evaluation performed by the data controller is a qualitative process.

While discussing the security risk assessment of data processing, ENISA suggested considering separately the risks related to the network and the technical resources of the data controller, to processes and procedures of the data processing operations, to different parties and people involved in the data processing, and to the business sector and specific scale of the processing (e.g. large scale)[1832]. More specifically, the data controller should use as parameters for the processes and procedures of the data processing the category of personal data, the criticality of the processing operations (e.g. profiling), the volume of data, special characteristics of the data controller (e.g. public entity), and special characteristics of the data subjects (e.g. minors)[1833]. So, the data controller could assign to each mentioned area a level and a score to added up with the others[1834]. The security risk assessment may be carried out in parallel with a privacy or data protection risk assessment.

In sum, the data controller should evaluate likelihood and severity as "low, medium or high" and combine the levels to obtain the risk level.

---

1831 *See* all the descriptions of the levels in European Union Agency for Network & Information Security, *Handbook on Security of Personal Data Processing*, p. 11: "Low, individuals may encounter a few minor inconveniences, which they will overcome without any problem (time spent re-entering information, annoyances, irritations, etc.). Medium, individuals may encounter significant inconveniences, which they will be able to overcome despite a few difficulties (extra costs, denial of access to business services, fear, lack of understanding, stress, minor physical ailments, etc.). High, individuals may encounter significant consequences, which they should be able to overcome albeit with serious difficulties (misappropriation of funds, blacklisting by financial institutions, property damage, loss of employment, subpoena, worsening of health, etc.). Very high, individuals may encounter significant, or even irreversible consequences, which they may not overcome (inability to work, long-term psychological or physical ailments, death, etc.)".

1832 *See* European Union Agency for Network & Information Security, *op. cit.*, pp. 12–15; D'Acquisto and Panagopoulou, *Guidelines for SMEs on the security of personal data processing*, pp. 24–25.

1833 *See* D'Acquisto and Panagopoulou, *op. cit.*, p. 21.

1834 ENISA also provides an example of final range of 4–5 for low, 6–8 for medium and 9–12 for high. *See* the table in D'Acquisto and Panagopoulou, *op. cit.*, p. 31.

Thus, the level of risk may be visualised as reported in the following Table 5.1[1835].

*Table 5.1 Risk level*

| Likelihood | Severity | Low | Medium | High |
|---|---|---|---|---|
| | Low | Low risk | Medium risk | High risk |
| | Medium | Low risk | Medium risk | High risk |
| | High | Medium risk | High risk | High risk |

Having defined these fundamental concepts applicable to an assessment, it is worth examining how to conduct a data protection risk assessment, i.e. the DPIA. This task is complex since it requires several categories of skills, including risk management, business expertise and knowledge of security[1836].

As mentioned in Chapter 2, Section 2.5.2, Article 29 Working Party released some guidelines on DPIA and the GDPR[1837]. Valuable DPIA guidelines have also been provided by the European project PRIAM and the French DPA, the CNIL[1838].

1835 Own graphic inspired by: European Union Agency for Network & Information Security, *Handbook on Security of Personal Data Processing*; Guasconi et al., *Reinforcing trust and security in the area of electronic communications and online services. Sketching the notion of "state-of-the-art" for SMEs in security of personal data processing*, p. 14.

1836 Jules Sarrat and Raphael Brun. "DPIA: how to carry out one of the key principles of accountability". In: *Privacy Technologies and Policy. 6th Annual Privacy Forum, APF 2018*. Springer. 2018, pp. 172–182.

1837 Article 29 Working Party, *Guidelines on Data Protection Impact Assessment (DPIA) and determining whether processing is "likely to result in a high risk" for the purposes of Regulation 2016/679.*

1838 Other useful guidelines that are applicable outside the EU can be derived from the NIST risk management framework of the US government and from ISO/IEC standards. NIST publishes several guidelines on computer security and risk assessment. *See* the official website at <csrc.nist.gov/publications/>. Last accessed 06/10/2021. Noteworthy among them is the NIST Privacy Framework National Institute of Standards and NIST Technology. *NIST Privacy Framework: A Tool for Improving Privacy Through Enterprise Risk Management,*

The PRIAM framework combines the legal and technical fields to create a privacy risk assessment that is based on the specific attributes and components of a system[1839]. In fact, this approach starts with information gathering that collects information on the functional components of the system, the interface, the data flows, the supporting assets and the actors and roles (i.e. stakeholders). Even the technical and organisational measures already implemented should be analysed and collected as information. According to Le Métayer *et al.*, the assessment should involve the entire life cycle of the processing performed through a system[1840]. The identification of actors and roles is fundamental for defining data flows. PRIAM defines a risk source as "any entity (individual or organization) which may process (legally or illegally) data belonging to a data subject and whose actions may directly or indirectly, intentionally or unintentionally lead to privacy harms". Each risk source should be described through accurate attributes and be evaluated using a scale. The controller should also identify feared events and privacy harms. After this first phase, the risk assessment can be carried out following a methodology based on harm trees[1841]. As a result, the risk assessment is a systematic, traceable and computational activity[1842].

The CNIL approach has been recommended by the PRIPARE project[1843]. The methodology is divided into four steps[1844]:

1. Defining and describing the characteristics of data processing. During this phase the controller should identify the other subjects and the recipients of personal data, and this subject should also describe the operations and the supporting assets[1845]. Even the standards applicable to processing should be identified;

---

*Version 1.0*. National Institute of Standards and Technology, 2020. On risk analysis and HIPAA *see* Thompson, *Building a HIPAA-Compliant Cybersecurity Program*. The ISO standards will be quoted in the next Section.

1839 *See* Daniel Le Métayer and Sourya Joyee De. *PRIAM: a Privacy Risk Analysis Methodology*. Research Report RR-8876, Inria, Research Centre Grenoble, 2016.

1840 *See* Le Métayer and De, *op. cit.*, p. 9.

1841 *See* Le Métayer and De, *op. cit.*, pp. 32–38.

1842 Le Métayer and De, *op. cit.*, p. 40.

1843 *See* Notario et al., *PRIPARE. Privacy-and Security-by design Methodology Handbook. 2016*, p. 116.

1844 *See* Commission Nationale de l'Informatique et des Libertés, *Privacy Impact Assessment (PIA). Methodology*; Commission Nationale de l'Informatique et des Libertés, *Privacy Impact Assessment (PIA). Templates*.

1845 Comparing this phase with the steps of the DPIA illustrated in Chapter 2, Section 2.5.2, it should be noted that it embeds both the assessment of the

2. Analysing the proportionality and the necessity of data processing, and whether it protects data subjects' rights. The CNIL suggests explaining and justifying the choices related to all the data protection principles of Article 5 GDPR. These choices should be the best possible solutions. The assessment on the rights refers to the need to explain how the controller is expected to comply with Articles 12–22 and 28 of the GDPR. The CNIL provided a detailed template for assessing the protection of principles and rights[1846];
3. Assessing data protection risks that are associated with data security and ensuring they are properly addressed. This is the phase where the controller should identify threats, estimate and evaluate likelihood and severity, and find "planned controls", meaning safeguards related to the data being processed, at security and governance levels. The three main threats are illegitimate access to personal data, unwanted change and disappearance. In the first category of controls the authority includes: encryption, anonymisation, data partitioning, logical access control, logging, integrity monitoring, archiving, and paper document security. These may be considered examples of technical measures. Among the controls for ensuring security, the CNIL mentions workstation security, backups, network security, monitoring, hardware security, and protection against non-human sources of risk. At organisational levels the possible controls are management of rules, risk management, project and incident management, personnel management and supervision, and relations with third parties. These may be considered examples of organisational measures;
4. Documenting the process to monitor and re-iterate on it in a continuous improvement process. The CNIL's template divides the controls for checking the "unsatisfactory, planned improvement or acceptable" levels of compliance. The CNIL interestingly suggests preparing a visual representation of the planned controls and the risks through graphs. Any formal advice of the DPO should be documented.

Within the methodology and template, the CNIL released an extended and comprehensive knowledge base for conducting the DPIA[1847]. In this

need for the instruments and the systematic description of the processing envisaged for each processing operation and asset.

1846 Comparing this phase with the steps of the DPIA illustrated in Chapter 2, Section 2.5.2, it may be noted that analysis on need and proportionality should be performed in relation to the purpose of the processing.

1847 Commission Nationale de l'Informatique et des Libertés, *Privacy Impact Assessment (PIA). Knowledge basis*.

study the authority maps examples of types of risks and of outcomes of feared events, and proposes a method for estimating severity and likelihood, which are scaled from "negligible", "limited", "significant" to "maximum" levels.

After the classification of threats, the CNIL described the proposed "planned controls" mentioned above. As an example, encryption means making personal data unintelligible to anyone without access authorisation on the basis of symmetric or asymmetric techniques, and it shall follow specific measures[1848]. Encryption may be used for: equipment, databases, standalone files, email, and communication channels. Data partitioning is another control that reduces risks[1849]. The CNIL suggested separating the personal data necessary for each processing operation and creating different access rights to reduce the occurrence of data breaches. The large contribution of the CNIL is particularly valuable since it combines a methodology with know-how and state of the art measures, as ENISA usually does for security and data protection topics.

In 2019, the CNIL published open-source software for carrying out the DPIA called "PIA"[1850]. This tool is available for Windows, Linux and Mac OS operating systems, supports several languages, and has a user-friendly interface. PIA can be used as a legal and technical knowledge base for a data protection impact assessment on the basis of the GDPR and the CNIL framework. Since it provides a modular assessment, the data controller can easily customise this tool.

It should be underlined that despite the existence of methodologies and tools, every data controller should always specify and contextualise the assessment based on their context and business[1851].

Having defined a framework for the risk assessment, the following section describes techniques and standards to be taken into account during a DPbD approach.

---

1848 Commission Nationale de l'Informatique et des Libertés, *op. cit.*, pp. 14–17.
1849 Commission Nationale de l'Informatique et des Libertés, *op. cit.*, p. 18.
1850 *See* the official website at <www.cnil.fr/en>. Last accessed 06/10/2021.
1851 *See* the arguments in Sarrat and Brun, "DPIA: how to carry out one of the key principles of accountability".

## *5.5 Existing standards and PETs for EHR systems*

This section summarises some existing standards and PETs that may be useful for the EHR implementation. It is out of the scope of this section to provide a taxonomy of the tools. The section presents recommended standards and a few PETs mentioned in the literature[1852].

As Hartzog noted, standards are crucial for implementing privacy and security since they guide compliance activities by providing useful and widely adopted specifications and solutions[1853]. Despite the fact that standards are usually not binding, they provide so-called best practices, and

---

1852 *See* J.A. Magnuson and Brian E. Dixon. *Public health informatics and information systems*. Springer, 2020. ISBN: 9783030412159; Josep Domingo-Ferrer and Alberto Blanco-Justicia. "Privacy-Preserving Technologies". In: *The Ethics of Cybersecurity*. Springer, Cham, 2020, pp. 279–297; AGID Agenzia per l'Italia Digitale. *Linee Guida per l'adozione di un ciclo di sviluppo di software sicuro*. Linee guida per lo sviluppo del software sicuro. Allegato 1, 2020; AGID Agenzia per l'Italia Digitale. *Linee Guida per la modellazione delle minacce e individuazione delle azioni di mitigazione conformi ai principi del Secure/Privacy by Design*. Linee guida per lo sviluppo del software sicuro. Allegato 4, 2020; Stefan Schulz, Robert Stegwee, and Catherine Chronaki. "Standards in healthcare data". In: *Fundamentals of Clinical Data Science*. Springer, Cham, 2019, pp. 19–36; Farina, *Il cloud computing in ambito sanitario tra security e privacy*; ENISA European Union Agency for Network & Information Security. *ICT security certification opportunities in the healthcare sector*. European Union Agency for Network and Information Security, 2018; Tamó-Larrieux, *Designing for privacy and its legal framework: data protection by design and default for the internet of things*; W. Ed Hammond. "Standards for Global health information systems". In: *Global Health Informatics*. Elsevier, 2017, pp. 94–108; European Union Agency for Network & Information Security, *Handbook on Security of Personal Data Processing*; Danezis et al., *Privacy and Data Protection by design – from policy to engineering*; J.A. Magnuson, Riki Merrick, and James T. Case. "Public Health Information Standards". In: *Public health informatics and information systems*. Springer, 2014, pp. 133–155. ISBN: 9780387227450; Sinha et al., *Electronic health record: standards, coding systems, frameworks, and infrastructures*; Hartley and Jones, *EHR implementation: A step-by-step guide for the medical practice*; Pierluigi Perri. *Privacy, diritto e sicurezza informatica*. Giuffrè Editore, 2007. ISBN: 8814137021, pp. 143–163; Cimino and Shortliffe, *Biomedical Informatics: Computer Applications in Health Care and Biomedicine*, pp. 265–311.

1853 Hartzog, *Privacy's blueprint: the battle to control the design of new technologies*, p. 164.

are useful for PbD, and DPbD[1854]. Nonetheless, it should be noted that standards are not free of charge[1855].

As regards ISO international standards on security and privacy, the following list identifies the key tools that provide guidance to data controllers and processors:

- ISO/Guide 73:2009(en) on risk management vocabulary, which was mentioned above, with the other ISO standards on this topic, which are ISO 31000:2018 and IEC 31010:2019 on risk management guidelines and risk assessment techniques respectively[1856];
- ISO/IEC 29100:2011 and ISO/IEC 29101:2018, which create a high-level privacy framework for processing in ICTs[1857]. ISO/IEC 29100 defines 11 privacy principles: "consent and choice; purpose legitimacy and specification; collection limitation; data minimisation; use, retention and disclosure limitation; accuracy and quality; openness, transparency and notice; individual participation and access; accountability; information security; and privacy compliance"[1858]. According to the standard, these principles should guide the design and development of ICTs;
- ISO/IEC 27001:2013, on information security management, which provides requirements at the organisational level, and ISO/IEC 27002:2013 on information security controls[1859]. ISO/IEC 27001 recommends creating an information security policy, organising roles and responsibili-

1854 *See* Kroener and Wright, "A strategy for operationalizing privacy by design", p. 362, which refers to PbD.

1855 *See* the comment in Tamó-Larrieux, *Designing for privacy and its legal framework: data protection by design and default for the internet of things*, p. 174; Magnuson, Merrick, and Case, "Public Health Information Standards", pp. 136–138.

1856 ISO, *ISO/Guide 73:2009(en) Risk management — Vocabulary*; ISO. *ISO 31000:2018 Risk management — Guidelines*. Tech. rep. ISO/TC 262, 2018; ISO. *IEC 31010:2019 Risk management — Risk assessment techniques*. Tech. rep. ISO/TC 262, 2019.

1857 ISO. *ISO/IEC 29100:2011 Information technology — Security techniques — Privacy framework*. Tech. rep. ISO/IEC, 2011; ISO. *ISO/IEC 29101:2018 Information technology — Security techniques — Privacy architecture framework*. Tech. rep. ISO/IEC, 2018. The amendment AMD 1:2018 was added to the first standard.

1858 Looking at these principles it may be argued that they followed the OECD Guidelines, the FIPs and the DPD's principles. *See* a discussion on the principles in Chapter 4, Section 4.2.

1859 ISO. *ISO/IEC 27001:2013(en) Information technology — Security techniques — Information security management systems — Requirements*. Tech. rep. ISO/IEC, 2013; ISO. *ISO/IEC 27002:2013 Information technology — Security techniques — Code of practice for information security controls*. Tech. rep. ISO/IEC, 2013.

ties, identifying security risks and planning actions for addressing these risks, and providing the resources for the security management system. The organisation should document the assessment, monitor security performance, and conduct internal audits;

- ISO/IEC 27035–1:2016 and ISO/IEC 27035–2:2016 on information security incident management, which present concepts for detecting, reporting, assessing, and responding to security incidents[1860];
- ISO/IEC 29134:2017, which provides guidance for privacy impact assessment[1861];
- ISO/IEC 27000:2018, on information security management systems and techniques, which explains the preservation of confidentiality, integrity, and availability[1862];
- ISO/IEC 27005:2018, on information security risk management, which is based on a recognised risk assessment approach[1863];
- ISO/IEC TS 19608:2018, which provides guidance for developing security and privacy functional requirements which are based on ISO/IEC 15408, an evaluation standard on IT security[1864];
- ISO/IEC 24760–1:2019 on identity management and privacy protection[1865]. This standard defined an identity management system as "mechanism comprising of policies, procedures, technology and other resources for maintaining identity information including associated metadata";

---

1860 ISO. *ISO/IEC 27035–1:2016 Information technology — Security techniques — Information security incident management — Part 1: Principles of incident management*. Tech. rep. ISO/IEC, 2016; ISO. *ISO/IEC 27035–2:2016 Information technology — Security techniques — Information security incident management — Part 2: Guidelines to plan and prepare for incident response*. Tech. rep. ISO/IEC, 2016. These standards are under review and will be replaced by ISO/IEC WD 27035–1.3 and ISO/IEC WD 27035–2.3.

1861 ISO. *ISO/IEC 29134:2017 Information technology — Security techniques — Guidelines for privacy impact assessment*. Tech. rep. ISO/IEC, 2017.

1862 ISO, *ISO/IEC 27001:2013(en) Information technology — Security techniques — Information security management systems — Requirements*.

1863 ISO. *ISO/IEC 27005:2018(en) Information technology — Security techniques — Information security risk management*. Tech. rep. ISO/IEC, 2018.

1864 ISO. *ISO/IEC TS 19608:2018 Guidance for developing security and privacy functional requirements based on ISO/IEC 15408*. Tech. rep. ISO/IEC, 2018; ISO. *ISO/IEC 15408–1:2009 Information technology — Security techniques — Evaluation criteria for IT security — Part 1: Introduction and general model*. Tech. rep. ISO/IEC, 2009.

1865 ISO. *ISO/IEC 24760–1:2019 IT Security and Privacy — A framework for identity management — Part 1: Terminology and concepts*. Tech. rep. ISO/IEC, 2019.

- ISO/IEC TR 27550:2019 on privacy engineering and system life cycle processes[1866];
- ISO/IEC 27701:2019, which extends ISO/IEC 27001 and ISO/IEC 27002 on privacy information management[1867];
- ISO/IEC 27007:2020 on information security management systems and auditing;
- ETSI TR 103 456, which is a European standard providing guidance on the NIS Directive on security of network and information systems[1868].

Additionally, as mentioned in Chapter 2, ISO/PC 317 is currently under development to provide the first international standard on privacy by design that will be applicable to any data processing involving consumer goods and services[1869].

During the implementation of the EHR system and its source systems two main areas of standards and PETs should at least be taken into account: interoperability and accessibility. Several ISO standards are specifically available for health informatics and EHR:

- As mentioned above, ISO standard 20514:2005(en) on the definition of EHR and EHR system[1870];
- ISO 18308:2011, which provides the requirements for an EHR architecture[1871]. This standard defines the structure of an EHR, which should store both clinical and administrative information, and should support authentication, data integrity, confidentiality, non-repudiation, and audit of accessed information[1872];

1866 ISO. *ISO/IEC TR 27550:2019 Information technology — Security techniques — Privacy engineering for system life cycle processes*. Tech. rep. ISO/IEC, 2019.

1867 ISO. *ISO/IEC 27701:2019 Security techniques — Extension to ISO/IEC 27001 and ISO/IEC 27002 for privacy information management — Requirements and guidelines*. Tech. rep. ISO/IEC, 2019. On this standard and the GDPR *see* Eric Lachaud. "ISO/IEC 27701 Standard: Threats and Opportunities for GDPR Certification". In: *Eur. Data Prot. L. Rev.* 6 (2 2020), pp. 194–210.

1868 ETSI. *ETSI TR 103 456 V1.1.1 (2017–10) Implementation of the Network and Information Security (NIS) Directive*. Tech. rep. ETSI/CYBER, 2017.

1869 *See* Chapter 2, Section 2.3, comment on line 13.

1870 *See* Chapter 3, Section 3.4.1 on ISO, *Health informatics — Electronic health record — Definition, scope and context. 20514:2005(en)*.

1871 ISO. *ISO 18308:2011 Health informatics — Requirements for an electronic health record architecture*. Tech. rep. ISO/TC 215, 2011.

1872 *See* the analysis by Sinha et al., *Electronic health record: standards, coding systems, frameworks, and infrastructures*, pp. 16–21. This article argues that the standard did not provide any details on these requirements.

- ISO 17090–1:2013 on digital certificate services, which will be replaced by ISO/DIS 17090–1[1873];
- ISO 22857:2013, which provides guidelines on data protection during trans-border flows of personal health data[1874];
- ISO 22600–1:2014 on privilege management and access control[1875];
- ISO/HL7 10781:2015 on EHR functional model, which provides the set of functional requirements, but is under review[1876];
- ISO 27799:2016 on information security of HITs, which is based on ISO/IEC 27002[1877];
- ISO 25237:2017 on pseudonymisation, that provides a basic methodology for techniques in the health care sector[1878];
- ISO 13606–1:2019, ISO 13606–2:2019, ISO 13606–3:2019, ISO 13606–4:2019, and ISO 13606–5:2019 on EHR communication architecture, its security, the privileges necessary to access the EHR data, and the

1873 ISO. *ISO 17090–1:2013 Health informatics — Public key infrastructure — Part 1: Overview of digital certificate services*. Tech. rep. ISO/TC 215, 2013.

1874 ISO. *ISO 22857:2013 Health informatics — Guidelines on data protection to facilitate trans-border flows of personal health data*. Tech. rep. ISO/TC 215, 2013.

1875 ISO. *ISO 22600–1:2014 Health informatics — Privilege management and access control — Part 1: Overview and policy management*. Tech. rep. ISO/TC 215, 2014; ISO. *ISO 22600–2:2014 Health informatics — Privilege management and access control — Part 2: Formal models*. Tech. rep. ISO/TC 215, 2014; ISO. *ISO 22600–3:2014 Health informatics — Privilege management and access control — Part 3: Implementations*. Tech. rep. ISO/TC 215, 2014.

1876 ISO. *ISO/HL7 10781:2015 Health Informatics — HL7 Electronic Health Records-System Functional Model, Release 2 (EHR FM)*. Tech. rep. ISO/TC 215, 2015.

1877 ISO. *ISO 27799:2016 Health informatics — Information security management in health using ISO/IEC 27002*. Tech. rep. ISO/TC 215, 2016.

1878 ISO. *ISO 25237:2017 Health informatics — Pseudonymization*. Tech. rep. ISO/TC 215, 2017.

1879 ISO. *ISO 13606–1:2019 Health informatics — Electronic health record communication — Part 1: Reference model*. Tech. rep. ISO/TC 215, 2019; ISO. *ISO 13606–2:2019 Health informatics — Electronic health record communication — Part 2: Archetype interchange specification*. Tech. rep. ISO/TC 215, 2019; ISO. *ISO 13606–3:2019 Health informatics — Electronic health record communication — Part 3: Reference archetypes and term lists*. Tech. rep. ISO/TC 215, 2019; ISO. *ISO 13606–4:2019 Health informatics — Electronic health record communication — Part 4: Security*. Tech. rep. ISO/TC 215, 2019; ISO. *ISO 13606–5:2019 Health informatics — Electronic health record communication — Part 5: Interface specification*. Tech. rep. ISO/TC 215, 2019.

interface specifications[1879]. ISO 13606 was originally designed by the European Committee for Standardization (CEN)[1880];

The standards on privacy management of personal health information in general, for privacy requirements of EHR systems, and audit trail of EHRs are currently under development in the ISO/TC 215 Technical Committee[1881].

Data format standards, vocabulary standards, and laboratory test and code standards are examples of categories of standards used for the EHR system and its source system[1882]. As an example, the Digital Imaging and Communications in Medicine (DICOM) standard provides the framework for communication and management of medical imaging information and related data[1883]. SNOMED CT standardised health terms that are globally used for EHRs, EMRs, PHRs systems and e-health technologies in general[1884].

Several different standards have been developed to achieve semantic interoperability[1885]. Among them, Health Level 7 (HL7) Group created

---

1880 European Union Agency for Network & Information Security, *ICT security certification opportunities in the healthcare sector*, p. 22, explains that the work of CEN aimed to create European standards that are harmonised with existing international standards.

1881 *See* ISO/AWI 22697 at <www.iso.org/standard/73697.html>. *See* ISO/AWI TS 14441 at <www.iso.org/ standard/80018.html>. *See* ISO/DIS 27789 at <www.iso .org/standard/75313.html>. Last accessed 06/10/2021.

1882 *See* the classification in Schulz, Stegwee, and Chronaki, "Standards in healthcare data"; Magnuson, Merrick, and Case, "Public Health Information Standards"; Sinha et al., *Electronic health record: standards, coding systems, frameworks, and infrastructures*; MITRE, *Electronic Health Records Overview*.

1883 *See* the official website at <www.dicomstandard.org/>. Last accessed 06/10/2021.

1884 SNOMED CT also has an ontological layer. *See* the official website at <www.snomed.org/>. Last accessed 06/10/2021.

1885 *See* Julien, "Electronic Health Records"; and Pulkit Mehndiratta, Shelly Sachdeva, and Sudhanshu Kulshrestha. "A model of privacy and security for electronic health records". In: *International Workshop on Databases in Networked Information Systems*. Springer. 2014, pp. 202–213, p. 204, which repors: "Health Level 7 (HL7), Clinical Document Architecture (CDA), CEN EN 13606 EHRcom, openEHR, Digital Imaging and Communications in Medicine Structured Reporting (DICOM SR), Web Access to DICOM Persistent Objects (ISO WADO), integrating the Healthcare Enterprise (IHE), Retrieve Information for Display (RID) and IHE Cross-Enterprise Document Sharing (XDS)".

the most widely implemented international standards for clinical-data interchange[1886].

HL7 defined standards and protocols for the structure of the data exchange both as messages and as documents[1887]. In particular, ISO/HL7 27931:2009 applies to the electronic data exchange in healthcare environments[1888], and ISO/HL7 21731:2014 provides the reference information model for the exchange[1889]. In the HL7 FHIR v. 4 protocols[1890], there are three privacy-related specifications: FHIR Security, FHIR Resource Consent and FHIR AuditEvent[1891]. These HL7 protocols have been included in the HIPAA's requirements[1892]. In addition, the HL7 FHIR framework released ontologies on health data that use the Web Ontology Language (OWL)[1893].

It is worth mentioning the openEHR project, which provides principles for creating an interoperable EHR systems software architecture that is based on a multilevel and single-source modelling framework[1894]. In

---

1886 *See* the information on this standard at the official website <www.hl7.org/>. Last accessed 06/10/2021. The history of the group was reported by Hammond, "Standards for Global health information systems"; and Cimino and Shortliffe, *Biomedical Informatics: Computer Applications in Health Care and Biomedicine*, pp. 300–302.

1887 ISO/HL7 27951:2009 Health informatics – Common terminology services, release 1 and ISO/HL7 27932:2009 Data Exchange Standards — HL7 Clinical Document Architecture, Release 2 are under review.

1888 ISO. *ISO/HL7 27931:2009 Data Exchange Standards — Health Level Seven Version 2.5 — An application protocol for electronic data exchange in healthcare environments*. Tech. rep. ISO/TC 215, 2009.

1889 ISO. *ISO/HL7 21731:2014 Health informatics — HL7 version 3 — Reference information model — Release* Tech. rep. ISO/TC 215, 2014.

1890 *See* <hl7.org/fhir/>. Last accessed 06/10/2021.

1891 A description of FHIR is provided by Hammond, "Standards for Global health information systems", pp. 103–104.

1892 *See* 45 C.F.R. § 170.215, § 170.299, § 170.315(d).

1893 *See* Athanasios Kiourtis et al. "Aggregating the syntactic and semantic similarity of healthcare data towards their transformation to HL7 FHIR through ontology matching". In: *International Journal of Medical Informatics* 132 (2019), p. 104002; Athanasios Kiourtis et al. "Structurally Mapping Healthcare Data to HL7 FHIR through Ontology Alignment". In: *Journal of Medical Systems* 43.3 (2019), pp. 62–75, which describes the knowledge base.

1894 Duarte Gonçalves-Ferreira et al. "OpenEHR and general data protection regulation: evaluation of principles and requirements". In: *JMIR medical informatics* 7.1 (2019), e9845. *See* also Kalra, Beale, and Heard, "The openEHR foundation"; Sinha et al., *Electronic health record: standards, coding systems, frameworks, and infrastructures*, pp. 163–174.

2003 the openEHR Foundation was established to openly publish EHR technical specifications, clinical models, open-source software, and several educational resources[1895]. The research created an information model that is separated from the content model, meaning that the logic structure of the EHR is defined in the first model while datasets are external. In 2019, this framework was tested for compliance with the GDPR. In particular, openEHR features have been matched with GDPR requirements. As an example, the legal requirement "period of storage limitation" is associated with the sentence "the system must allow the definition of deadlines for the processing of specific personal data, in order with the purpose of processing", and openEHR is scrutinised to assess whether it meets this requirement. The storage limitation principle, integrity, confidentiality, availability principles, interoperability, access rights and accountability are all matched in the openEHR project. Other requirements, however, have not yet been satisfied.

Cross-Enterprise Document Sharing (XDS) provides a standards-based specification for managing the sharing of documents, i.e. HIE, between different healthcare entities, ensuring interoperability[1896]. XDS can be used for national, regional or local EHR environments. This standard was developed by the US initiative called Integrating the Healthcare Enterprise (IHE), which has been active in promoting standards and solutions for healthcare communication service.

IHE also created a centralised access control system for the XDS environment: the Secure Retrieve (SeR) supplement[1897]. SeR functions with one authorisation decision manager. Therefore, it is not applicable where multiple data controllers use the EHR system. However, other IHE solutions may be useful in a complex EHR environment. The technical framework of IHE is even promoted by the European Commission[1898].

The IHE Basic Patient Privacy Consent (BPPC) provides a widely recognised mechanism to record patient's consent in a machine-readable

---

1895 *See* the mission of the Foundation at <www.openehr.org/about/vision_and_mission>. Last accessed 06/10/2021.

1896 *See* the information on XDS at <wiki.ihe.net/index.php/Cross-Enterprise_Document_Sharing>. Last accessed 06/10/2021.

1897 *See* the information on SeR at <wiki.ihe.net/index.php/Secure_Retrieve>. Last accessed 06/10/2021.

1898 *See* Commission Decision (EU) 2015/1302 of 28 July 2015 on the identification of 'Integrating the Healthcare Enterprise' profiles to reference in public procurement. O.J. L. 199, 29.7.2015.

form[1899]. Patient's consent is identified by a document with Extensible Markup Language (XML) that contains machine-readable indications. Despite the fact that IHE is a US-based developer, several policies available in the BPPC are applicable in the EU context. In fact, supportable policies are: "opt-in to clinical use" (which applies where consent is required by law), "specific document is marked as available in emergency situations" (which allows processing in a vital interest scenario), "additionally allow specific research project" (which applies to secondary use of personal data), "limit access to functional roles providers" and "limit access to structural roles" (which is fundamental in the EHR context). The BPPC is limited to a fixed list of policies. On the other hand, the Advanced Patient Privacy Consents (APPC) defines the structural representation necessary to capture, manage, and communicate patient's consent between systems and entities, independently of a set of policies. So, this solution seems more useful than BPPC for managing consent and access to EHR documentation.

As the EHR system involves several source systems, identity and access management are aspects where PETs are really useful. Several users may access the record with different duties, so techniques on secure accessibility are crucial. Access control is a typical security measure, which limits the risk that unauthorised entities might access the system[1900]. It has been pointed out that the most EHR systems incorporate access control mechanisms, but several different models may be adopted[1901].

---

1899 IHE International: Basic Patient Privacy Consent. IHE ITI TF Vol. 3 Section 5.0. This document was revised in June 2020 and is available at <www.ihe.net/uploadedFiles/Documents/ITI/IHE_ITI_TF_Vol3. pdf>. *See* also the document of the European Commission on BPPC at <progressivestandards.org/standard/basic-patient-privacy-consents-ihe-bppc/>. Last accessed 06/10/2021.

1900 *See* e.g. in European Union Agency for Network & Information Security, *Handbook on Security of Personal Data Processing*; Commission Nationale de l'Informatique et des Libertés, *Privacy Impact Assessment (PIA). Knowledge basis*, pp. 24–27. *See* also security concepts in Agenzia per l'Italia Digitale, *Linee Guida per l'adozione di un ciclo di sviluppo di software sicuro*; Agenzia per l'Italia Digitale, *Linee Guida per la modellazione delle minacce e individuazione delle azioni di mitigazione conformi ai principi del Secure/Privacy by Design*; Perri, *Privacy, diritto e sicurezza informatica*, pp. 111–123.

1901 *See* Jorge Calvillo-Arbizu, Isabel Román-Martínez, and Laura M. Roa-Romero. "Standardized access control mechanisms for protecting ISO 13606-based electronic health record systems". In: *IEEE-EMBS International Conference on Biomedical and Health Informatics (BHI)*. IEEE. 2014, pp. 539–542, which proposes a mechanism based on the eXtensible Access Control Markup Language (XACML).

The first solution for access control is following ISO 13606:2019 standard, which describes the identity management system. This is a high-level framework. Each entity should have specific attributes to be an identity and follow the identification and authentication process. The privacy-related capabilities of an identity management system are to[1902]:

- "implement mechanisms, including policies, processes; and technology, for minimal disclosure;
- authenticate entities that use identity information;
- minimize the ability to link identities;
- record and audit the use of identity information;
- protect against inadvertently generating risks to privacy, e.g. those posed by inadequately protecting identity information in logs and audit trails;
- implement policies for selective disclosure;
- implement policies to engage a human entity for explicit direction or consent, for activities related to their sensitive identity information".

So, within the implementation of an identity system, organisational policies and procedures should be set, and an audit control and record system should monitor the entity's activities.

Role-Based Access Control (RBAC) or Attribute-Based Access Control (ABAC) are two different privacy and security techniques that may be used in the EHR system. Within RBAC access to a system is granted on the basis of a defined user's role (e.g. professional category). The model implements several security principles, such as the separation of duties principle and is suited to an EHR context where the roles are limited and previously defined. In fact, a role has fixed privileges. ABAC, on the other hand, gives specific series of attributes and combines them with access policies. This model seems more suited to an EHR context where access rights are more granular and complex[1903]. However, the concrete solution to be implemented should be evaluated on a case-by-case basis.

Finally, the EHR system uses a network for information sharing and stores data in a repository. On the one hand several technologies and PETs can be used to secure the content of the communications, such as

---

1902 *See* ISO, *ISO 13606–1:2019 Health informatics — Electronic health record communication — Part 1: Reference model.*

1903 *See* on RBAC and ABAC Guasconi et al., *Reinforcing trust and security in the area of electronic communications and online services. Sketching the notion of "state-of-the-art" for SMEs in security of personal data processing*, pp. 18–19. *See* Danezis et al., *Privacy and Data Protection by design – from policy to engineering*, pp. 24–26.

encrypted channels or VPN[1904]; on the other hand, full disk encryption (FDE) techniques at the software or hardware level or file system-level encryption (FSE) are tools for protecting EHR data storage[1905].

This Chapter has described several tools for designing privacy and data protection in general and in the e-health context in particular. The next Chapter uses the theoretical and applied perspectives examined in these five chapters to provide a set of DPbD guidelines for the EHR system.

1904 *See* the description of several secure communication techniques in Danezis et al., *op. cit.*, pp. 27–31; Diffie and Landau, *Privacy on the line: The politics of wiretapping and encryption*, pp. 11–56. *See* also Commission Nationale de l'Informatique et des Libertés, *The CNIL's Guide on Security of personal data*, p. 13, which indicates both basic precautions and advanced techniques.

1905 *See* the analysis of encryption in Danezis et al., *Privacy and Data Protection by design – from policy to engineering*, pp. 40–42; Perri, *Privacy, diritto e sicurezza informatica*, pp. 125–142.

# Chapter 6 Guidelines for implementing DPbD in the EHR system

## 6.1 *Introductory remarks*

This Chapter provides a set of guidelines for DPbD management with technical and organisational measures to be implemented in EHRs in the European Union legal framework. The GDPR and the current data protection law for data concerning health in the EU are the foundations of the comprehensive set of guidelines. The aim of this Chapter is to provide further guidance for data controllers and developers on how to comply with DPbD obligations in the EHR environment. In fact, the book, examines how an e-health system should be designed, and the data processing be carried out in a way that supports and implements data protection principles and legal requirements in order to protect personal health data.

First of all, the Chapter explains the methodology employed to formulate the guidelines. It draws upon both the theoretical analysis and the insights discussed in Chapter 2, 3 and 4 and the applied perspective on privacy engineering, standards and tools presented in Chapter 5. This Chapter then provides and discusses the guidelines for an EHR system[1906]. The set of guidelines is classified according to the different timeframes of the processing (i.e. "before the processing" and "during the processing"), and to technical and organisational requirements or goals, which take into account the criteria of Article 25 GDPR, the data protection principles, and the different data states (i.e. data at rest, data in transit, data in use). After that, the Chapter investigates some possible scenarios at the liability level in the event of inappropriate or ineffective DPbD implementation.

1906 The set of guidelines is an evolution of and improvement on the DPbD model of privacy management that was published in: Bincoletto, G. (2019). A Data Protection by Design Model for Privacy Management in Electronic Health Records. In: M. Naldi, G. F. Italiano, K. Rannenberg, M. Medina, & A. Bourka (Eds.), Privacy Technologies and Policy, Springer International Publishing, pp. 161–181. This paper was submitted and accepted at the Annual Privacy Forum of 2019, which has been organised by ENISA and by the European Commission at the LUISS University in Rome. *See* the programme of the Conference at <2019.privacyforum.eu/programme>. Last accessed 06/10/2021.

### 6.2 The methodology of the set of guidelines

According to the ENISA's Report "Privacy and Data Protection by Design – from policy to engineering", a privacy by design process is the output of several steps: the identification of risks, the identification of solutions and the formulation of recommendations, and the implementation of those recommendations[1907]. The approach is characterised by an iterative and continuous process.

Even DPbD is an ongoing procedure. It is a never-ending approach. A DPbD implementation has been theoretically divided into "four steps": "gap analysis with the specific legal framework", "risk analysis", "project steering and budget planning", and "implementation"[1908]. This research tries to create a set of guidelines for DPbD implementation in EHR systems and in the EU legal framework. In particular, the legal rules are the GDPR and the data protection framework for data concerning health described above. The comparison with the US legal framework will be taken into account since it provides useful examples of organisational and technical safeguards for medical records.

The set of DPbD guidelines defines requirements and comprehensive data protection measures that may aid data controllers (and system developers) when they opt for the architectural choices and the appropriate organisational and technical measures to be implemented, including PETs and standards. So, the set identifies requirements and formulates recommendations as comprehensive guidelines for the implementation, that may be used in the "requirement phase" of a DPbD engineering approach. The main goal is to achieve compliance with the law since data protection becomes a core component of a system.

The proposed requirements and measures take into account the legal analysis of Article 25 of the GDPR and of the data protection principles and rights, the legal investigation of the data protection framework that applies to data concerning health, including the comparative insights, and the methodologies, tools and solutions described in the technical part of this book.

---

1907 *See* Danezis et al., *Privacy and Data Protection by design – from policy to engineering*, p. 12.

1908 Voigt and Von dem Bussche, *The EU General Data Protection Regulation (GDPR). A Practical Guide.*

As Article 25 GDPR applies to the full life cycle of the data processing and at the time of determination of its means, the guidelines will be divided in:

- Before the processing, i.e. at the time of the determination of the means of the processing, which includes “before collection” of personal data;
- During the processing, i.e. at the time of the processing activities, which includes “collection”, “use” and “deletion” of personal data;
- (After the processing, that refers to the moment where personal data are anonymised after an anonymisation process, or are deleted).

Actually, when data are anonymised, they fall out of the scope of the GDPR, including Article 25. So, the guidelines focus on the first two time periods, but some brief considerations on the third period may still be provided at the end of the discussion.

These guidelines may specify the precise timing of “collection”, “use” and “deletion” where the requirement is strictly connected with these activities. When it is not, it will be indicated before or during the processing. However, all the measures should always be implemented and often reviewed to comply with the ongoing DPbD approach.

Within this categorisation, the separate dimension of technical and organisational measures of Article 25 of the GDPR will be taken into account. This distinction follows the recommendation of the Norwegian Data Protection authority to identify both “data-oriented design requirements” and “process-oriented design requirements”[1909]. In addition, the technical measures are divided among the three states of data: data at rest (recording, structuring, storage), data in use (collection, use, consultation), data in transit (transmission, making available).

As explained above, DPbD measures are aimed at demonstrating compliance with GDPR requirements[1910]. Thus, to demonstrate compliance with Article 25, each subset of guidelines assigns the related data protection principles to the various guidelines and indicates the articles of the GDPR in brackets. It has been pointed out that from an individual viewpoint “the data subject should have control over the collections, the uses, the storage and the disclosures” of his or her personal data in the EHR[1911]. So, the set of guidelines takes into account the exercise of the data subject's rights, too.

1909 *See* Chapter 5, Section 5.2.

1910 *See* Chapter 2, Section 2.4.2.

1911 Bincoletto, “A Data Protection by Design Model for Privacy Management in Electronic Health Records”, p. 172.

The model presented during the Annual Privacy Forum of 2019 divided the guidelines into four groups according to the actors mainly involved[1912]. One part was explicitly dedicated to the developer of the EHR system ("the technical measures") and three parts to the data controller and data processor ("the creation of the EHR", "the use of the EHR" and "the organisational and administrative measures")[1913]. The content of the first version of the model is used here as part of the set of guidelines, but the classification has changed, and the guidelines have been enhanced. The benefit of that approach was to highlight the specific and different duties of the subjects involved and the two important dimensions of the creation of the patient's profile in the EHR and the use of the collected data. However, as demonstrated in Chapter 2 in Section 2.4.1, the developer is not directly bound to Article 25[1914].

For this second version of the guidelines a different comprehensive classification is provided. Even so, it should be specified that the developer remains a pivotal player in the DPbD implementation. The data controllers, e.g. the hospital and the pharmacy, frequently outsource the development of the EHR system and its environment to a processor. In addition, under Article 32 of the GDPR the processor shall implement security measures. Therefore, the developers should participate in the technical solutions that require a technical intervention in the EHR system. The organisational and administrative measures remain tasks of the data controllers, who will be liable under Article 83 of the GDPR[1915].

It should now be specified that the measures for the EHR system are presented within several security and data protection measures applicable to data processing where data concerning health are processed on a large scale. The guidelines may be applied to the EHR system and its source systems, e.g. HIS and CIS. The aim is to provide a comprehensive set of guidelines that may be useful for a "typical EHR environment".

This category refers to the EHR system that has been described in Table 3.1, after the description of the state of the art of this technology[1916]. The EHR of patient Jane Doe can be accessed and used by multiple entities that are involved in her care: laboratory and radiology clinics, the general practitioner, the hospital, and pharmacies of the national, regional or local

1912 Bincoletto, *op. cit.*
1913 *See* Bincoletto, *op. cit.*, p. 173.
1914 The liability issues are investigated *infra*, Section 6.5.
1915 The last section of this Chapter examines the liability issue.
1916 *See* Chapter 3, Section 3.4.1.

health service. The organisation of the health service is usually established by law. There are several source systems of healthcare providers (e.g. CIS and administrative system of the laboratory) that are connected for the HIE. So, the "typical EHR system" follows the definition of ISO/TR 20514:2005(en), which includes both the technical and the organisational levels.

The next section connects the theoretical perspective on DPbD and the legal framework with the applied perspective on the EHR system and the technical tools for designing data protection, and describes the guidelines.

## *6.3 Applying DPbD to an EHR system*

Before providing a detailed classification in the next section, a description of the DPbD approach for the EHR and the guidelines will be provided here in order to better explain the technical and organisational measures.

### 6.3.1 DPbD and the EHR system

The data controllers in the EHR environment should have knowledge of the flow of personal data in the system, of the characteristics of their data processing activities and the applicable legal requirements under EU and Member State law. It is necessary to collect the complete set of legal requirements and guidelines of authorities (DPA, governments), and of stakeholders that are relevant to the project development. It has been suggested to order these rules in terms of hierarchy and applicability[1917].

Generally, a map of the data flows is highly recommended since DPbD safeguards should be applied in the whole data management life cycle. Data controllers should also map the technical infrastructure of the envisaged or existing systems. The data controller should evaluate all the criteria of Article 25 of the GDPR: the state of the art, the costs, the contextual factors of the processing activities, and the risks to rights and freedoms posed by these activities. DPbD and security compliance budget planning should be defined proactively.

The concrete characteristics of the data processing should be evaluated according to Article 25 of the GDPR[1918]. Applying the criterion of "nature,

---

1917 Stevovic et al., "Enabling privacy by design in medical records sharing", p. 390.
1918 *See* Chapter 2, Section 2.4.4.

scope, context and purposes of the data processing", the preliminary questions, and resulting answers, for a "typical" EHR system are:

- *What is the personal data processing operation?* In the EHR context, there are typically several data controllers, which may or may not be joint controllers. If they are not, then each controller has its own purpose and determines the means of the processing. In a centralised context, one controller, e.g. a local health authority, delegates the processing to hospitals, clinics, or laboratories, but officially remains the only data controller[1919]. The "typical EHR environment" assumes that there are multiple data controllers. Each controller shall apply the DPbD requirement. The processing in the EHR system is typically on a large scale[1920]. Healthcare providers collect personal data about an individual, store them in their CDR or another internal repository that is connected to the EHR storage system (i.e. registry component), and use them through HIS, CIS or other internal systems. The integrated view of patient's data, the order entry and access to multiple knowledge resources are the functions of the EHR that allow the processing activities. This system has an interface that allows entry and query of patient's data. The source systems should be interoperable[1921]. Healthcare providers transmit data through the HIE in the local or national EHR environment. If the EHR is interoperable across Member States, personal data can be exchanged in the eHDSI between a country of origin and a country of treatment. Personal data in the EHR may be disclosed to other specified recipients under Member State law (e.g. to public authorities).
- *What are the types of personal data processed?* Both common personal data, namely contact details, administrative data, billing data, and data concerning health, including medical history, diagnoses, clinical notes, parameters and vital signs, prescriptions, radiology images and laboratory results. EHR and its source systems should be comprehensive enough to provide a useful overview of patient's health.
- *What is the purpose of the processing?* The purpose is primarily providing medical treatment or healthcare and healthcare-related services, and payment services. However, Member State law may allow other

1919 On the roles in the processing *see* Chapter 3, Section 3.4.2.

1920 However, in the case of PHR the processing may not be on a large scale.

1921 As mentioned in Chapter 5, Section 5.5, the XDS Cross Enterprise Document Sharing is a standard for managing the sharing of documents between healthcare providers.

purposes, including scientific research in the medical field, statistical research, public interest in public health, and governance purposes of the organisations.

- *What are the means used for the processing of personal data?* The means are clinical and medical ICT systems. In the EHR environment automated means are not commonly used for healthcare purposes, unless other e-health technologies are connected to the EHR. Automated means are used during scientific research activities (e.g. for mapping health threats in the population, or for genetic research). When automated means are used, Article 22 of the GDPR applies and explicit consent is required for that purpose.
- *Where does the processing of personal data take place?* The EHR environment is defined under national, regional or local law. In general, processing activities operate at the local level in a Member State. In a cross-border interoperability scenario, processing operates across two Member States.
- *What are the categories of data subjects?* Both children and adults who are patients.
- *Who are the recipients of the data?* In the EHR environment, treating physicians, nurses, professionals, and their staff use personal data. The collected data may be also used by the workforce and staff, and the administrative and accounting services. Outside the EHR environment, personal data may be shared with other specific recipients under Member State law for defined and limited purposes (e.g. public health).

As regards the evaluation of the risks, the assessment should identify threats, and estimate the likelihood and severity of possible hazards[1922]. According to the fairness principle of Article 5(a) of the GDPR, data controllers should evaluate whether the processing activities have an impact on rights and freedoms, whether it may discriminate individuals, whether the processing involves vulnerable natural persons, or creates power imbalances. Data controllers should also identify other risks posed by processing operations. In the context of ICTs and HITs common security threats are unauthorised access and disclosure of personal data, unauthorised alteration of personal data, unauthorised deletion or loss of personal data, malicious intent (e.g. hackers), interception of communications, man in the middle, malware, ransomware, identity theft, or social engineering.

1922 *See* Chapter 5, Section 5.4. The LIDDUN threat trees or the CNIL tools may be used.

For the processing operations of the use case, the impact to rights and freedoms from loss of confidentiality, integrity and availability of the EHR system or its source systems may be considered high, since the data subject may encounter significant inconveniences by the unauthorised disclosure or modification of data concerning health[1923]. The system is interconnected to several systems, the processing is performed by a large number of staff members and on a large scale, and the e-health sector is frequently prone to attacks. So, the likelihood should be considered as high-level. Accidental loss, destruction or damage and unlawful use of data concerning health in the EHR impinge on the right to respect for private and family life, the right to data protection, and potentially other rights and freedoms of the Charter of Fundamental Rights. Actually, wrong or incomplete data concerning health may put the data subject's health and life in danger. As argued above, significant economic, psychological and social harm may be caused by the hazards mentioned[1924]. Even the severity should be considered at high-level. Hence, high-level likelihood combined with high-level severity results in a high risk level[1925].

Following the evaluation of the risk level in light of the concrete data processing operations, the DPbD solutions should balance and take into account the state of the art of the technologies and of the organisational practices, and the costs of implementing the measures[1926]. Thus, the controllers should choose the measures that are available in the market and that are the most effective among them in achieving the legal protection[1927]. According to ENISA, "the most recent stage of technological development" or "the stage that incorporates the newest possible features and functionalities" satisfies the concept of state of the art[1928]. Among the

---

1923 In a specific use case on health service provision, ENISA evaluated the risk of a small clinic that provided health services within an electronic medical record. The authority considered the impact from loss of confidentiality, integrity and availability as high. *See* European Union Agency for Network & Information Security, *Handbook on Security of Personal Data Processing*, pp. 39–41. In the same handbook other use cases on e-health technologies (e.g. remote monitoring) ended with high risk levels.

1924 On the concerns of e-health technologies *see* Chapter 3, Section 3.2.

1925 *See* Chapter 5, Section 5.4.

1926 Bincoletto, "A Data Protection by Design Model for Privacy Management in Electronic Health Records", p. 172.

1927 *See* Chapter 2, Section 2.4.3.

1928 Guasconi et al., *Reinforcing trust and security in the area of electronic communications and online services. Sketching the notion of "state-of-the-art" for SMEs in security of personal data processing.*

technologies, the controller could choose PETs, privacy design patterns, and a specific privacy engineering methodology (e.g. PRIPARE).

At the same time, the data controller can estimate the costs and choose the measures that are feasible and affordable for their organisation. In sum, a cost-benefit analysis (i.e. subjective analysis) goes in parallel with the study of the existing solutions provided by the market (i.e. objective analysis).

In addition to taking into account the criteria of Article 25, it is worth remembering that two adjectives are used in the provision. The appropriate technical and organisational measures shall implement data protection principles in an effective manner. The discretion with regard to the "appropriate" and "effective" criteria remains a subjective evaluation of the data controllers, who can proactively define metrics and key performance indicators[1929]. This evaluation may be later subject to scrutiny by a DPA or a court[1930].

1929 *See* European Data Protection Board, *Guidelines 4/2019 on Article 25 Data Protection by Design and by Default*, 7, point 16.

1930 For all these considerations *see* Chapter 2, Section 2.4.6 and *infra* Section 6.5.

So, the abstract ongoing procedure of DPbD implementation may be visualised as in the following Figure 6.1.

*Fig. 6.1 DPbD cycle overview*

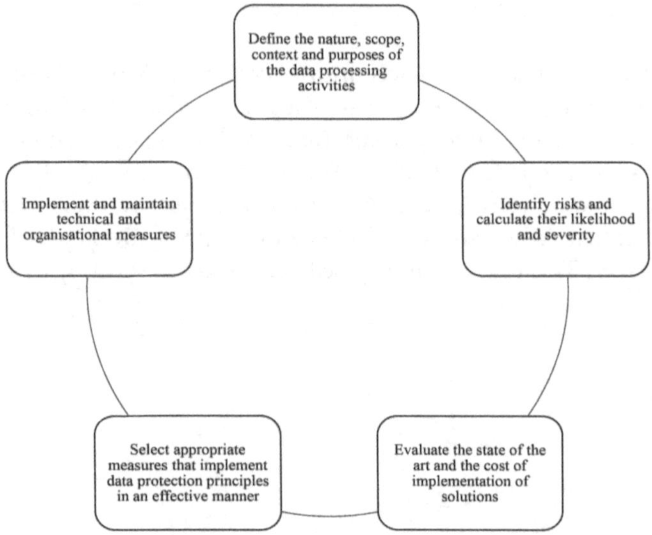


### 6.3.2 Technical guidelines and measures

The implementation of effective technical measures for the EHR is the first sub-set of guidelines to be dealt with. The key data protection principles are integrity and confidentiality (i.e. security) and accountability (Article 5(f), Article 32 GDPR). Nonetheless, even other data protection principles should be taken into account in the technical design stage before and during the processing activities.

As discussed in the previous Chapter, international standards and privacy engineering methodologies may play an important role in developing a secure system, and adopting these solutions may even help data controllers prove and certify legal compliance[1931]. In particular, HL7 and ISO standards on EHR may be used to ensure interoperability and a systematic

1931 The standards are indicated in Chapter 5, Section 5.5.

architecture[1932]. In addition, the EHR system should ensure the interoperability between the source systems, the vocabulary, and data formats even if they are developed by different providers.

As regards the data at rest, limits should be set on data storage before processing[1933]. Some strategies should apply to the database management system[1934]. In the EHR data controllers store both administrative/billing data and data concerning health. It has been pointed out that when administrative data reveal information on the health status of the data subject (e.g. the type of medical visit or scheduled tests) they should be considered sensitive. Removing the correlation between purely administrative data and sensitive data (e.g. during payment and administrative services) protects the confidentiality of data concerning health. So, administrative personal data could be separated from sensitive data through the separation of databases during the EHR development and in the source systems[1935]. The separation may be even operated at repository level. In addition, some data concerning health have been defined as particularly sensitive[1936]. Therefore, these data – whose types have been identified in an organisational policy – could be stored in separate modules with strict conditions for access.

---

1932 Above all, *see* ISO 18308:2011, ISO/HL7 21731:2014, ISO 27799:2016, ISO 13606:2019.

1933 For the following considerations *see* also Bincoletto, "A Data Protection by Design Model for Privacy Management in Electronic Health Records", pp. 173–175.

1934 The following guideline also applies the "separate" strategy of Hoepman. *See* Hoepman, "Privacy Design Strategies (The Little Blue Book)".

1935 In Article 29 Working Party, Police, and Justice, *The Future of Privacy: Joint Contribution to the Consultation of the European Commission on the Legal Framework for the Fundamental Right to Protection of Personal Data*, p. 14, Article 29 Working Party argues that "patient names and other personal identifiers maintained in hospitals' information systems should be separated from data on the health status and medical treatments. They should be combined only in so far as it is necessary for medical or other reasonable purposes in a secure environment". The separation of data concerning health and demographic data is also a feature of the openEHR framework. *See* Gonçalves-Ferreira et al., "OpenEHR and general data protection regulation: evaluation of principles and requirements". *See* also Carro, Masato, and Parla, *La privacy nella sanità*, p. 69; Mehndiratta, Sachdeva, and Kulshrestha, "A model of privacy and security for electronic health records", p. 210.

1936 *See* Chapter 3, Section 3.3.1 and 3.4.2.

Encryption could be used for EHR storage to enhance the protection of data concerning health[1937]. This measure should be carefully evaluated by the controller since encryption may be used on specific files or on the full storage through software or hardware, and it affects the internal accessibility and availability of the systems. However, a robust encryption algorithm should protect the EHR server to ensure data integrity and confidentiality.

Implementing back-up and recovery mechanisms is necessary to secure the integrity of the content of the EHR and the source systems. In light of the importance of data concerning health for an individual's care, personal data should be backed up at least daily, and a complete back up of the system should be performed at least monthly[1938]. These backups should be encrypted and protected with physical security measures.

Moreover, the EHR system and its data at rest should be protected with intrusion controls and prevention systems against external attacks. Details of incidents and data breaches should be recorded. Firewalls and antivirus protection are common software security measures[1939].

The implementation of audit and log systems is a key strategy since they can track user activity in the system. This is relevant for the EHR system and the source systems because at a later stage it tracks misuse and unlawful use in a complex environment[1940]. Collecting ID number, date

---

1937 According to HIPAA encryption is an addressable measure in software and hardware for data at rest and in transit. *See* 45 C.F.R. § 170.315(d)(7) and Herold and Beaver, *The practical guide to HIPAA privacy and security compliance*, p. 223. The CNIL recommended encryption for the storage of the French medical record. *See* Commission Nationale de l'Informatique et des Libertés, *Référentiel relatif aux traitement de données personnelles pour les cabinets médicaux et paramédicaux*, p. 12.

1938 *See* Herold and Beaver, *The practical guide to HIPAA privacy and security compliance*, p. 338. The CNIL recommended regular back-ups in Commission Nationale de l'Informatique et des Libertés, *Référentiel relatif aux traitement de données personnelles pour les cabinets médicaux et paramédicaux*, p. 12.

1939 It should be specified that security measures should be implemented even beyond the EHR system. As an example, the workstation should be secured. Antivirus and malware protection are typical security measures. Typical physical security is equally important. Personal data should not be transferable from the workstation to external storage devices. *See* European Union Agency for Network & Information Security, *Handbook on Security of Personal Data Processing*, p. 66; Commission Nationale de l'Informatique et des Libertés, *Référentiel relatif aux traitement de données personnelles pour les cabinets médicaux et paramédicaux*, pp. 9- 10.

1940 This measure is also recommended in the HIPAA's requirements at 45 C.F.R. § 170.315(d)(10).

and hour, type of operation and reason for access of an event in the EHR allows the precise identification of the user and the potential source of an internal unlawful processing activity of data in use. Thus, any activity on record, including consultation, transmission, and modification, should be tracked and any discrepancies must be reported and signalled by alerts through an anomaly detection tool and an automated monitoring system. The log files should refer both to accesses to the EHR databases and accesses to the software or application. A logging level should be set before processing to include specific events and exclude useless ones since log files should be limited in size to be successfully archived and monitored[1941]. During the data use, log files should be backed up and retained securely for a certain period of time to protect their integrity[1942]. It has been pointed out that logging, reporting and auditing are evidence and tactics for demonstrating compliance and accountability[1943]. The patient may even ask to have access to the log files to learn who accessed their personal data.

During processing, all these measures should be checked and, if needed, updated frequently (Art. 24 GDPR) according to the state of the art and the cost of implementation. Both hardware and software resources should be reviewed and updated. Back-ups should be performed, and penetration tests should be carried out periodically.

Data in use should be secured[1944]. The implementation of appropriate measures for the identification, authentication and authorisation of users of the EHR systems and source systems (the workforce, staff and healthcare professionals) are fundamental for the principles of fairness, integrity, confidentiality and transparency. Identification refers to the process "to determine who the user is", authentication "to prove who a user is" and authorisation relates "to what a user can do in the system"[1945].

---

1941 *See* Guasconi et al., *Reinforcing trust and security in the area of electronic communications and online services. Sketching the notion of "state-of-the-art" for SMEs in security of personal data processing*, pp. 34–35.

1942 *See* Guasconi et al., *op. cit.*, p. 35, which suggests hashing and digitally signing the log files.

1943 *See* Colesky, Hoepman, and Hillen, "A critical analysis of privacy design strategies".

1944 *See* also Bincoletto, "A Data Protection by Design Model for Privacy Management in Electronic Health Records", p. 176.

1945 On access control *see* Chapter 22 of Herold and Beaver, *The practical guide to HIPAA privacy and security compliance*. It applies to HIPAA, but as argued above the measures are useful for the DPbD implementation in electronic medical records such as the EHR and its source systems.

Thus, to ensure security of the EHR system and source systems, a system and application access and identity control should be implemented[1946]. The data controller should also implement multiple modules of presentation for the personal data at the interface level in order to differentiate between common personal data, data concerning health, and particularly sensitive data, access to which will be subject to additional authorisation.

The subjects who have concrete access to the EHR system and source systems are healthcare professionals providing treatment, administration officers and other staff. Access to personal data should be restricted to authorised subjects only, and this authorisation should be given temporarily to the subjects involved in the patient's care[1947]. Among these subjects access should be limited to specific categories of healthcare professionals[1948]. Access should be based on the role in the patient's care (nurse vs. physician) by creating different access privileges and query privileges, and a reason for the access should be contextually specified in the record. User role management should be automated, and access should be set as modular or granular. Automatic log-off should be defined[1949]. An emergency access privilege should also be implemented to protect the vital interest of the patient. Level and access rights and privileges should be reviewed regularly. Remote access (e.g. from home) should be granted sparingly. Data controllers should define specific access control strategies, such as Role-Based Access Control (RBAC) or Attribute-Based Access Control (ABAC)[1950].

The identity verification and authentication of users accessing the EHR system and source systems should be robust. It may be advisable to use digital signature, ID badges, or smart cards that should be added to usernames and passwords. Something that is possessed by the user, such as a token, should be added to something known by the user, such as their password.

---

1946 Even in the US according to the HIPAA security Rule, an access control should be implemented. *See* 45 C.F.R § 170.315(d), and Thompson, *Building a HIPAA-Compliant Cybersecurity Program*, p. 155. Identity and access management is recommended for HITs by European Union Agency for Network & Information Security, *ICT security certification opportunities in the healthcare sector*, p. 18.

1947 This guideline also applies the "hide" strategy of Hoepman. *See* Hoepman, "Privacy Design Strategies (The Little Blue Book)".

1948 On these aspects it is useful to remember the case held by the Portuguese Data Protection Authority (CNPD) against a public hospital in 2018 reported in Chapter 3, Section 3.4.2.

1949 This measure is also recommended by the HIPAA's requirements at 45 C.F.R. § 170.315(d).

1950 *See* Chapter 5, Section 5.5.

Actually, multi-factor authentication is highly recommended by ENISA and by the HIPAA as an authentication method to confirm identity[1951]. For example, to access the system the user should use both username and password, and a token or a biometric mechanism[1952]. The user ID should be unique (not common authentication), and the password should be complex and have at least eight characters and it should be changed every six months[1953]. As an example, even for trainee professionals there should be a temporary and distinct authentication.

Data in use could also be pseudonymised[1954]. According to data minimisation, personal data are processed only insofar as they are adequate, relevant, and limited to the amount necessary for the purposes for which they are processed. So, state of the art pseudonymisation techniques could be applied to data concerning health[1955].

The interface of the EHR system and the source systems should automatically prompt the user to obtain patient consent or define a legal ground to prove the lawfulness of the processing[1956]. Data controllers

---

1951 *See* Guasconi et al., *Reinforcing trust and security in the area of electronic communications and online services. Sketching the notion of "state-of-the-art" for SMEs in security of personal data processing*, p. 19. *See* 45 C.F.R. § 170.315(d)(13).

1952 In order to minimise the processing of sensitive data of the workforce, a token may be preferable to biometric techniques.

1953 Obviously, passwords should not be written on a post-it note on the desk, but they should be stored in a secure way (e.g. in hashed form). They should be created with lower-case and upper-case and a combination of alphanumeric and special characters. The workstation should be automatically logged off after a certain period of time. *See* e.g. Guasconi et al., *Reinforcing trust and security in the area of electronic communications and online services. Sketching the notion of "state-of-the-art" for SMEs in security of personal data processing*, pp. 21–23; Commission Nationale de l'Informatique et des Libertés, *The CNIL's Guide on Security of personal data*, pp. 7, 11.

1954 This guideline also applies the "minimise" strategy of Hoepman. *See* Hoepman, "Privacy Design Strategies (The Little Blue Book)".

1955 On pseudonymisation techniques for health data *see* e.g. the PEP project, which provides polymorphic encryption and pseudonymisation for personalised healthcare in a research environment, in Eric R. Verheul et al. "Polymorphic Encryption and Pseudonymisation for Personalised Healthcare." In: *IACR Cryptol. ePrint Arch.* (2016), pp. 1–60. The project was referenced by ENISA as an advanced cryptography-based pseudonymisation solution in European Union Agency for Network & Information Security, *Recommendations on shaping technology according to GDPR provision. An overview on data pseudonymisation*, pp. 27–28.

1956 As an example, the legal ground could be indicated with an icon in the interface.

should also implement an automatic alert system that notifies when the legal basis ceases to apply[1957]. However, this function is not necessary when the "healthcare exception" applies, but when the legal ground is the consent of the data subject and when this consent is necessary to control the access rights of the categories of healthcare professionals[1958]. The Member State may provide more guidance on this aspect by defining the legal grounds for the EHR by law. As previously mentioned, the standard ISO/TS 17975:2015(en) provides an informational consent framework for healthcare organisations that have to obtain consent[1959]. Alternatively, a consent and choice mechanism should be implemented to facilitate obtaining consent. Data controllers should record patient's consent in a machine-readable form[1960].

During the processing, the EHR system should provide the processes to exercise the rights of the data subjects. In fact, the patient should be able control the processing in accordance with the right to self-determination. The requests of the data subject may be processed in the EHR system and source system directly. The data subject should be able to access personal data collected in the EHR by electronic means and obtain a copy. So, either the data subject should receive credentials for accessing the data or the data should be sent to the data subject. In this last scenario, the e-mail message service should be secured with encryption. It is important to remember that a medical explanation might be required for access[1961].

Where applicable, other requests to be processed are: request for concealment, request to update inaccurate data, and request for data portabili-

---

1957 If the legal basis is the vital interest, after the first medical treatment to save the patient's life, the controller shall obtain consent when required by law or use the "healthcare exception". If the legal basis is consent, when the data subject withdraws their consent, the system should alert the data controller and another legal ground should be indicated, or the system should be stopped for that individual. When the data subject is a child, and consent is given by the holder of parental responsibility over him or her at the moment the child becomes an adult, it is mandatory to collect a new consent. Meanwhile, the system should be stopped for that patient. *See* Bincoletto, "A Data Protection by Design Model for Privacy Management in Electronic Health Records", p. 176.

1958 *See* Chapter 3, Section 3.4.2.

1959 ISO/TS. *ISO/TS 17975:2015(en) Health informatics – Principles and data requirements for consent in the Collection, Use or Disclosure of personal health information*. Tech. rep. ISO/TS, 2015.

1960 *See* Chapter 5, Section 5.5.

1961 *See* Chapter 3, Section 3.4.2.

ty and automated decision making. In particular, the right to concealment is granted at the Member State level to conceal particularly sensitive data that concerns health (e.g. HIV disease). Technical mechanisms for concealment should be established. The right to rectification mainly concerns common personal data. The versioning of the patient's EHR should always be retained for proofing purposes[1962]. The right to data portability does not apply to public entities (e.g. hospitals) and it applies only to personal data provided by the data subject. However, the portability of data concerning health in a structured, common and automatic format empowers the data subject and so the patient may easily seek healthcare services elsewhere. The right to not be subject to a decision based solely on automated means is applicable in the e-health context, but in a typical EHR environment automated processing is not used for the main purpose of providing healthcare. It may be used for secondary research purposes. When this happens, the right may apply[1963].

As regards data in transit, the implementation of a firewall in the infrastructure can better protect the EHR network and the network of the source systems[1964]. A secure communication channel, a web application firewall, VPN, and HL7 standards are recommended. It has also been suggested to encrypt the communication channel of the EHR through cryptographic protocols[1965].

Finally, the system should ensure interoperability to allow the transfer and portability of data concerning health[1966]. To ensure interoperability

---

1962 As an example, the openEHR framework provides versioning of the data repository with digital signatures. Data is not deleted, but a new version is created. *See* Gonçalves-Ferreira et al., "OpenEHR and general data protection regulation: evaluation of principles and requirements".

1963 *See* further in Chapter 3, Section 3.4.2.

1964 *See* Herold and Beaver, *The practical guide to HIPAA privacy and security compliance*, pp. 340–342.

1965 *See* Fatemeh Rezaeibagha, Khin Than Win, and Willy Susilo. "A systematic literature review on security and privacy of electronic health record systems: technical perspectives". In: *Health Information Management Journal* 44.3 (2015), pp. 23–38, p. 29; Thompson, *Building a HIPAA-Compliant Cybersecurity Program*, p. 156; Carro, Masato, and Parla, *La privacy nella sanità*, p. 69. It is also recommended by the HIPAA. *See* 45 C.F.R. § 170.315(d)(9). *See* the guidelines on protecting the internal network of a system in Commission Nationale de l'Informatique et des Libertés, *The CNIL's Guide on Security of personal data*, pp. 13–15.

1966 In this sense, the openEHR project seems to be a good model. *See* Gonçalves-Ferreira et al., "OpenEHR and general data protection regulation: evaluation of principles and requirements".

across Member States, when provided by national law, data controllers should implement the existing tools provided by the eHDSI and the EC's exchange format tools on the patient summary, laboratory results, medical imaging and reports, and hospital discharge reports, which are usually collected in the EHR system[1967].

### 6.3.3 Organisational guidelines and measures

The data controller should implement appropriate and effective organisational measures[1968]. They refer to policies and procedures to be created at the management level of the data processing. As stated above, a gap analysis on the rules on data protection and health law at the Member State and local level is always recommended since the policies and procedures should be consistent with them (Art. 9(4) GDPR)[1969]. The data controller should monitor any progress and changes in the rules and update the organisational measures accordingly. At the administrative level, the risk analysis and risk management assessment are fundamental. Lawfulness, transparency, purpose limitation, data minimisation, storage limitation, and accuracy principles play a crucial role in this part (Art. 5(a) – (f) GDPR).

As regards the organisational requirements and goals before processing, the first strategy should be determining whether subjects fall under the scope of the GDPR, and under which status (Artt. 2 and 3 GDPR)[1970]. As previously mentioned, in the EHR environment there might be different controllers and processors. In the presence of joint controllers, a specific agreement should define the respective responsibilities and roles (Art. 26 GDPR). The controller should authorise the processor for the delegated ac-

---

1967 *See* Chapter 3, Section 3.4.3.

1968 For the following considerations *see* also Bincoletto, "A Data Protection by Design Model for Privacy Management in Electronic Health Records", pp. 175–178.

1969 As an example, in the PRIPARE methodology the legal assessment should be performed through "the identification of the relevant privacy principles according to the legal framework" and "the identification of legal requirements that the system will have to comply with in order to be legally compliant, taking into account the information flows and potential risks", including soft laws such as opinions of the DPAs. *See* Notario et al., *PRIPARE. Privacy-and Security-by design Methodology Handbook. 2016*, pp. 29–30.

1970 *See* Chapter 2, Section 2.4.1.

tivities in written form (Art. 28 GDPR). To define the concrete role of the delegated processing activities, the controller and processor should stipulate a contract or another legal act. At the same time, the controller and processor could delegate processing activities to third parties as defined by the GDPR[1971]. All the delegated activities should be regularly audited to check for compliance[1972].

A DPIA should be carried out as an organisational measure and preliminary step of the DPbD approach (Art. 35 GDPR)[1973]. The identification of risks and evaluation of solutions to be adopted should be documented since the data controller may be asked to explain why a particular measure should have mitigated a specific risk[1974]. Where required by Member State law, a prior consultation with the DPA should also be performed (Art. 36 GDPR).

The data controllers should identify a DPO, who may or may not be the same person for several data controllers in the EHR environment (Art. 37 GDPR). The DPO should be involved from the initial stages of the DPbD implementation to evaluate all aspects of compliance. This officer should monitor compliance with the GDPR and be in a position of authority within the internal management of the controller. The DPO should remain independent and objective (Art. 38 GDPR). In light of the officer's tasks, this officer could map all possible disclosure of personal data required by law (e.g. law enforcement, governance purposes of the healthcare service, public health purposes)[1975]. Policy and procedures may be set to organise possible disclosures and to limit shared personal data[1976]. In fact, when specific data concerning health shall be shared outside the

1971 *See* Chapter 2, Section 2.4.1.

1972 As an example, Carro, Masato, and Parla, *La privacy nella sanità*, p. 70 suggested the following steps: planning the audit; analysing all the documentation; interviewing the subjects involved (e.g. processor and DPO); collecting the evidence from the system and from the people; analysing the results, reporting them and finding solutions and procedures to improve compliance.

1973 *See* Chapter 5, Section 5.4. *See* also Chapter 2, Section 2.5.2.

1974 In this sense the CNIL's templates or visualisation of the measures that address specific risks are useful tools.

1975 In the PRIPARE project, the sentence "describe any disclosure, access to or transference of personal data that may be allowed" is included in the guidelines of openness, transparency and notice principles. *See* Notario et al., *PRIPARE. Privacy-and Security-by design Methodology Handbook. 2016*, p. 125.

1976 By comparison, the identification of all possible uses and disclosures is typical in the HIPAA context. *See* Herold and Beaver, *The practical guide to HIPAA privacy and security compliance*, p. 133.

EHR environment due to legal obligations, this disclosure does not mean that the entire data of the EHR shall be transmitted to the public recipient, but only the limited data necessary for that purpose[1977].

Creating and maintaining data protection materials and documents and conducting data protection training for the workforce and staff are other important guidelines for the accountability principle[1978]. The documentation is important since the data controller should provide evidence that the processing is data protection-compliant. The recommended policies are: privacy policy (Artt. 13 and 14 GDPR), policy on accuracy, data retention policy, policy on communication, notification and cooperation with the DPA (Artt. 31, 33 and 34 GDPR), and the policies for handling data subject requests and rights.

In more detail, the information in the privacy policy should be provided in a transparent and easily accessible form, using clear and plain language (Art. 12 GDPR). Since the data subject as a patient receives several other forms of documentation, including information on treatment and the consent form for treatment purposes, a clear and engaging privacy policy text should be drafted. In this respect, privacy icons and multiple modules could be very useful[1979]. As regards the information on the data subjects' rights, the privacy policy should be precise on the limits in the healthcare context with regard to the right to erasure and the right to data portability[1980]. At the same time, the method for exercising the right to access data

1977 The PRIPARE guidelines on data minimisation specify that the data controller should: "limit the purpose of personal data shared with third parties: when personal data is externally shared with third parties, share it only for those purposes identified in the privacy notice (or the legal framework authorizing the sharing) and consented by the user, or for purposes which are compatible with them; when any new personal data is proposed to be shared with third parties, evaluate whether the sharing is authorized and whether the privacy notice needs to be expanded". *See* Notario et al., *PRIPARE. Privacy-and Security-by design Methodology Handbook. 2016*, p. 124.

1978 In this sense, HIPAA rules are good examples of establishing binding periodical training and even sanctions where covered entities are not compliant. *See* Chapter 4, Section 4.4.3.

1979 This guideline also applies the "inform" strategy of Hoepman and its architectural tactic of "explain". *See* Colesky, Hoepman, and Hillen, "A critical analysis of privacy design strategies", p. 37. On the icons *see* Rossi and Palmirani, "What's in an Icon?".

1980 *See* Chapter 3, Section 3.4.2. Taking into account when the exercise of rights is not admitted is also an insight of the HIPAA Privacy Rule that defines the limits of the rights and how the covered entity can handle the request and deny it. *See* Chapter 4, Section 4.4.2.

concerning health could be indicated in the privacy policy to facilitate the exercise of this pivotal right. Considering that the EHR could be interoperable across Member States, and that the right to receive healthcare treatment is granted in every Member State, translations of the privacy policy in at least English, French and German should be provided[1981].

The policy on accuracy ensures the quality of the personal data collected[1982]. The accuracy of data concerning health should be reviewed regularly, also to protect the health of the patient and ensure an efficient healthcare service. Since data concerning health usually are retained for a long period, an internal data retention policy could define the types of information and the respective storage timeline (provided by law frequently[1983]). The policies on communication, notification and cooperation with the DPA should identify the procedures for these activities (Art. 31 GDPR). Templates and forms could be arranged before the start of processing.

A record of the processing activities should be created and maintained (Art. 30 GDPR). Examples of records are frequently provided by the national DPAs[1984].

The workforce and internal staff, both medical and non-medical professionals, should participate in a course on data protection and security and administrative staff should be specifically bound by confidentiality clauses in their contracts[1985]. As part of the training, the controller could allocate data protection responsibilities to specific officers (e.g. chief infor-

---

1981 Actually, according to a Report requested by the European Commission, the most widely spoken mother tongues in 2012 were: German (16 %); Italian and English (13 % each), French (12 %), Spanish and Polish (8 % each). *See* this report by Special Eurobarometer 386 "Europeans and their languages" at <ec.europa.eu/ commfrontoffice/publicopinion/archives/ebs/ebs_386_en.pdf>. Last accessed 06/10/2021.

1982 The recommendation of the PRIPARE guidelines on accuracy and quality is to "ensure the quality of personal data collected, created, used, maintained and shared: when personal data is collected or created, confirm to the greatest extent practicable that it is accurate, useful, objective, relevant, timely and complete". *See* Notario et al., *PRIPARE. Privacy-and Security-by design Methodology Handbook. 2016*, p. 124.

1983 *See* Chapter 3, Section 3.4.2.

1984 *See* e.g. the simplified model provided by the Italian DPA and the *modèle de registre simplifié* of the CNIL respectively at <www.garanteprivacy.it/home/docweb/-/docweb-display/docweb/9048342> and <www.cnil.fr/fr/ RGDP-le-registre-des-activites-de-traitement>. Last accessed 06/10/2021.

1985 An example of confidentiality agreement for French companies is provided by Commission Nationale de l'Informatique et des Libertés, *The CNIL's Guide on Security of personal data*, p. 6.

mation officer, data processing manager) by giving clear and documented instructions and by providing internal guidelines on data protection and security[1986]. It is highly advisable to define roles and responsibilities for managing data protection documentation and procedures[1987].

Before processing, the data controllers should prearrange the organisational chart to identify the subjects and categories of subjects and roles that can access the source systems and the EHR, and this register should be updated frequently. For example, in the hospital the persons involved in the patient's care, and then the users of the systems, change constantly. Entitlement creep should be avoided. Specific policies and procedures should be established for the creation, maintenance, and revocation of access[1988]. The data controller should also define a policy on authentication and passwords[1989]. The authorised roles should correspond to scalable levels of access, from mere access to administrative data to access to all the content of the EHR and source systems.

---

1986 Once again, the HIPAA rules are particularly valuable. *See* for a practical point of view chapter 25 of Herold and Beaver, *The practical guide to HIPAA privacy and security compliance*.

1987 The PRIPARE guidelines on the accountability principle state that it is necessary to "establish an organization-wide privacy governance program: develop an organization-wide privacy plan which defines the strategies to implement privacy policies, controls and procedures. Develop operational privacy policies and procedures that govern the use of privacy controls. Disseminate privacy governance policies. Enforce the use of privacy controls as established by the privacy governance policies". *See* Notario et al., *PRIPARE. Privacy-and Security-by design Methodology Handbook. 2016*, p. 129. The idea of the creation of privacy programmes is common in the US and in the FTC's actions. *See* e.g. Pardau and Edwards, "The FTC, the Unfairness Doctrine, and Privacy by Design: New Legal Frontiers in Cybersecurity".

1988 *See* Herold and Beaver, *The practical guide to HIPAA privacy and security compliance*, p. 335. *See* also Stevovic et al., "Enabling privacy by design in medical records sharing", p. 391, who propose this requirement for their project.

1989 As an example, the CNIL recommended adopting a user password policy that complies with its security recommendations provided in the *Délibération n. 2017–012 du 19 janvier 2017 portant adoption d'une recommandation relative aux mots de passe*, and it requires a strong authentication mechanism with health professional cards or any alternative two-factor authentication tool. *See* Commission Nationale de l'Informatique et des Libertés, *Référentiel relatif aux traitement de données personnelles pour les cabinets médicaux et paramédicaux*, p. 9 and the *Délibération* at <www.cnil.fr/fr/authentification-par-mot-de-passe-les-mesures-de-securite-elementaires>. Last accessed 06/10/2021. *See* also the security framework on authentication in Commission Nationale de l'Informatique et des Libertés, *The CNIL's Guide on Security of personal data*, pp. 7–9.

In addition, access rights and privileges should be adjusted in the access control policy according to data types (laboratory results, medications, prescription, medical history). Each role (e.g. nurse, surgeon) can have access to a limited set of data or to all data (e.g. general practitioner). It may be advisable that for booking and paying medical services sensitive data should be obscured from the administrative staff in light of data minimisation or they should be pseudonymised[1990]. So, the type of medical treatment or the related information of the scheduled test could be obscured or pseudonymised in the receipt. Anyway, health-related inferences might be made by the administrative staff. The duty of confidentiality upon employees and staff applies even beyond data protection issues in the contractual clauses on non-disclosure, and in the ethical professional codes[1991].

A complete security policy, a breach response plan and disaster recovery plan should be implemented and later reviewed periodically and at least once a year (Art. 32 GDPR)[1992]. The data controller should assign security responsibility to designated staff members (e.g. chief security officer). So, security and data breach management should not be limited to planning the policies applicable when a data breach occurs, but should be proac-

---

1990 *See* Bincoletto, "A Data Protection by Design Model for Privacy Management in Electronic Health Records", pp. 176–177.

1991 It may be specified that an ethics committee is frequently appointed in healthcare facilities to evaluate biomedical research and ethical issues. *See* e.g. the Operational Guidelines for Ethics Committees that review biomedical research of the World Health Organization, which were released in 2020 at <www.who.int/tdr/ publications/documents/ethics.pdf>. Last accessed 06/10/2021. The ethics committees should also evaluate the protection of research participant's confidentiality.

1992 According to Rezaeibagha, Win, and Susilo, "A systematic literature review on security and privacy of electronic health record systems: technical perspectives", p. 29, the application of security operations for the EHR system should include documented operating procedures, tests against malware, technical vulnerability management, testing of operational software, and checks and updates. Processes, procedures and tests should be established to ensure the availability of the system under adverse conditions. According to ENISA, in a high-risk processing the security policy should even be revised every six months. *See* European Union Agency for Network & Information Security, *Handbook on Security of Personal Data Processing*, p. 55; and European Union Agency for Network & Information Security, *ICT security certification opportunities in the healthcare sector*, p. 18, which includes an effective security policy, a disaster recovery plan and procedures for incident handling in the organisational measures for an HIT.

tive by defining procedures that can prevent a breach from occurring. Audits and check-lists should be used periodically to verify policies and procedures. Any breach should be documented thoroughly[1993].

Moreover, a certification mechanism may be a good voluntary means for ensuring trust in the systems (Artt. 25(3) and 42 GDPR)[1994]. The data controller could apply from a certification to the national accreditation body (Art. 43 GDPR)[1995]. Adopting a code of conduct may be another possible strategy (Artt. 24(3) and 40 GDPR).

During processing, in particular at the time of data collection, data controllers should find the applicable legal ground for the data processing (Art. 9 GDPR)[1996]. They should provide binding information to the data subject in the privacy policy[1997]. The privacy policy could be accessible in the EHR system and source systems. The privacy policy should be provided to data subjects either when their personal data are collected directly from them during a treatment or when they are obtained without their direct intervention. As an example, when a physician of the hospital accesses to the data collected in the EHR by the general practitioner, the privacy policy of the hospital under Article 14 of the GDPR should be provided to the patient. Other information may be provided later on request on the basis of the data subject's right to access.

According to data minimisation, purpose limitation, and accuracy principles, at the time of the collection and afterwards, the data controller should ensure that personal data are processed only as long as they are accurate, relevant, necessary and not excessive in relation to the purposes

---

1993 On security management *see* ISO/IEC 27001:2013, ISO/IEC 27035:2016, ISO 27799:2016, ISO 13606:2019, ISO/IEC 27007:2020.

1994 Some concrete examples of certifications are provided in European Union Agency for Network & Information Security, *Recommendations on European Data Protection Certification*, pp. 32–43.

1995 *See* Chapter 2, Section 2.5.3.

1996 In the PRIPARE project, a guideline of the purpose legitimacy and specification principle was "ensure legitimacy to collect and process personal data: collect, create, use, maintain, and share personal data, only if and to the extent authorized by a clearly defined legal basis (including user consent or any other legal basis). Collect, create, use, maintain, and share sensitive personal data only if and to the extent strictly authorized by a clearly defined legal basis that provides a relevant case for the collection of that sensitive personal data". *See* Notario et al., *PRIPARE. Privacy-and Security-by design Methodology Handbook. 2016*, p. 122.

1997 This guideline also applies the "inform" strategy of Hoepman. *See* Hoepman, "Privacy Design Strategies (The Little Blue Book)".

for which they are collected and processed[1998]. This concept may be formalised in internal guidelines. At the same time, it should be noted that the EHR and its source systems should equally pursue the completeness of data concerning health to provide an efficient healthcare service to the patient on the "healthcare exception" ground.

Furthermore, during data processing activities data controllers should keep all documentation updated, including processing records. In particular, the privacy policy should be revised when practices or activities change. The data subject should have the opportunity to access or search the updated version of the privacy policy of the EHR and its source systems. Workforce training should be updated, too. It may be advisable that new training modules should be added once a year to take into account the new DPA's opinions or guidelines, soft law and rules established at the Member State and local level.

Performing a periodical gap analysis with the applicable legal requirements helps identify any changes that require new technical and organisational measures. Internal audits can periodically check compliance of the processing activities. If a data breach occurs, the response plan should be implemented to mitigate the effects and, where applicable, the breach should be communicated to the data subjects or to the DPA. All other subjects (e.g. processor, third parties) could be informed in order to assist the controller during the activities that mitigate the event. Moreover, when the data subject lodges a complaint or presents a request, the controller should respond to the subject in a reasonable timeframe and by commonly used means[1999].

Finally, after processing, meaning if the data controllers stops using the EHR and personal data are deleted or anonymised, Article 25 does not apply. However, it should be noted that this condition happens only if data are appropriately de-identified by removing all the identifiers and all

---

1998 In the PRIPARE project, the guideline of collection limitation was: "limit the personal data collected to the strict minimum consented and necessary. When personal data is collected or retained, require only those personal data that are relevant and necessary for the purpose that has been previously identified, authorized and consented by the data subject. Suitably specify the purpose for which the personal data can be used and the rationale for that. When personal data is processed, only process it for the purpose for which it was originally obtained, or for purposes compatible with it". *See* Notario et al., *PRIPARE. Privacy-and Security-by design Methodology Handbook. 2016*, p. 122.

1999 Recital 59 GDPR states that the request should be answered in one month.

details[2000]. So, appropriate technical solutions should be implemented to avoid any abuse to ineffective anonymisation of data concerning health. Moreover, this category of data is frequently associated with an unlimited or very long data retention period. Actually, the data subject may not have the right to erasure of data concerning health in the EHR context[2001]. Therefore, the measures should be implemented even beyond the lifetime of the data subject and beyond the period of the healthcare treatment or service.

This section has explained how to apply Article 25 in the EHR context and presented several guidelines. The following section classifies the set of guidelines to be implemented before and during data processing activities and assigns data protection principles.

## 6.4 *The set of guidelines*

Technical requirements and goals are defined in the following Tables 6.1 – 6.6. The organisational requirements follow in Tables 6.7 – 6.11. Descriptions and data protection principles (and rights) juxtapose the set of guidelines[2002].

---

2000 *See* e.g. the list of identifiers of the HIPAA in Chapter 4, Section 4.4.1.

2001 The data should be retained under Member State law at least in paper form. *See* Chapter 3, Section 3.4.2.

2002 The manner in which the classification of the measures is provided can be compared with the typical ENISA annex where the authority presents proposed measures in a large table with "measure category, measure identifier, measure description, relevant standards" as columns. *See* European Union Agency for Network & Information Security, *Handbook on Security of Personal Data Processing.*

*Table 6.1 DPbD technical guidelines of data at rest before processing*

| MEASURE | DESCRIPTION | PRINCIPLE |
|---|---|---|
| Map data flows in the projected EHR | Data controllers should have clear data flows in the EHR environment and source systems | Accountability and security, data minimisation |
| Separate administrative personal data from sensitive data at the database level | Data controllers should implement this separation of databases during EHR development | Confidentiality and integrity, data minimisation |
| Separate sensitive data from particularly sensitive data at the database level | Data controllers should implement this separation of databases during EHR development | Confidentiality and integrity |
| Encrypt the EHR database | Data controllers could encrypt the EHR system (full disk) or their databases at the file system level | Confidentiality and integrity |
| Implement back-up and recovery mechanism | Data controllers should implement back-up and recovery mechanisms | Integrity |
| Implement intrusion control system | Data controllers should implement an efficient intrusion control system | Confidentiality and integrity |
| Implement audit and log systems | Data controller should implement efficient audit and log system for collecting ID number, date and hour, type of operation and reason for access of an event in the EHR | Accountability, integrity and confidentiality, transparency |

*Table 6.2 DPbD technical guidelines of data at rest during processing*

| MEASURE | DESCRIPTION | PRINCIPLE |
|---|---|---|
| Review the solutions adopted before processing | Data controllers should technically review the implemented solutions frequently | Integrity, confidentiality, accountability |
| Back up personal data on a daily basis and the entire system on a monthly basis | Data controllers should back up personal data at least daily and the systems monthly | Integrity and availability |
| Carry out periodic penetration tests | Data controller should carry out penetration tests periodically | Integrity |

*Table 6.3 DPbD technical guidelines of data in use before processing*

| MEASURE | DESCRIPTION | PRINCIPLE |
|---|---|---|
| Implement an access control system | Data controllers should choose an efficient and appropriate access control mechanism for the authorisation of the users in the systems | Integrity and confidentiality |
| Define identity management system | Data controllers should choose an efficient and appropriate mechanism to identify users in the systems | Integrity and confidentiality |
| Use appropriate authentication mechanism | Data controllers should choose an efficient and appropriate mechanism for the authentication of users in the systems | Confidentiality and data minimisation |

| MEASURE | DESCRIPTION | PRINCIPLE |
|---|---|---|
| Implement multiple modules of presentation of data in the interface | Data controllers should differentiate between different types of data at the interface level | Confidentiality |

*Table 6.4 DPbD technical guidelines of data in use during processing*

| MEASURE | DESCRIPTION | PRINCIPLE |
|---|---|---|
| Pseudonymise data concerning health | Data controller should pseudonymise data concerning health to minimise use by unauthorised users | Data minimisation |
| Create a prompt on the legal ground in the interface | The EHR system and the source systems should prompt the user to obtain patient consent or define a legal ground | Lawfulness |
| Use a consent mechanism | Where applicable, data controllers should use a consent mechanism to obtain consent in a machine-readable form | Lawfulness |
| Use the anomaly detection tool and the automated monitoring system | Data controller should monitor the log files | Confidentiality and integrity |
| Use the automatic alert system on legal ground | When the legal basis ceases to apply, the event should be flagged in the system and stopped until a new legal ground applies | Lawfulness |

| MEASURE | DESCRIPTION | PRINCIPLE |
|---|---|---|
| Create an electronic access mechanism for the data subject or secure message service | Data controllers should implement a secure mechanism for granting access and a copy of data to the data subjects | Accountability, right to access |
| Create a mechanism to conceal specific data | Where applicable, data controllers should conceal specific data concerning health whose access is limited | Accountability, right of concealment |
| Ensure data portability | Where applicable, data controllers should transmit data to other controllers | Accountability, right to data portability |

*Table 6.5 DPbD technical guidelines of data in transit before processing*

| MEASURE | DESCRIPTION | PRINCIPLE |
|---|---|---|
| Implement a secure transmission network | Data controllers should implement mechanisms to secure the EHR network | Confidentiality and integrity |
| Implement the existing tools provided by the eHDSI | Data controllers should implement the EC's exchange format tools to ensure interoperability across Member States of patient summary, laboratory results, medical imaging and reports, and hospital discharge reports | Accountability |

*Table 6.6 DPbD technical guidelines of data in transit during processing*

| MEASURE | DESCRIPTION | PRINCIPLE |
|---|---|---|
| Monitor the secure transmission network | Data controllers should monitor the mechanisms to secure the EHR network | Confidentiality and integrity |

*Table 6.7 DPbD organisational guidelines before processing 1*

| MEASURE | DESCRIPTION | PRINCIPLE |
|---|---|---|
| Determine the status | The subjects should determine whether they fall under the scope of the GDPR, and under which status (controller or processor) | Applicability |
| Perform a gap analysis on the rules | Data controllers should analyse the applicable legal requirements | Applicability |
| Evaluate the state of the art | Data controllers should understand what corresponds to the state of the art of technologies and organisational practices | Taking into account the state of the art |
| Identify the nature, scope, context and purposes of the processing | Data controllers should analyse the concrete characteristics of their data processing activities | Taking into account the nature, scope, context and purposes |
| Identify the risks posed by the processing | Data controllers should identify the risks for rights and freedoms of individuals beyond the DPIA | Taking into account the risks of varying likelihood and severity, fairness |

| MEASURE | DESCRIPTION | PRINCIPLE |
|---|---|---|
| Establish a DPbD compliance budget | Data controllers should estimate the costs and allocate resources to implement the measures | Taking into account the cost of implementation |
| Use a certification mechanism | Data controllers could apply for a certification from national accreditation bodies | Accountability and transparency |
| Authorise the processor's activities | The controllers should authorise the processor on the delegated activities in written form | Accountability |
| Stipulate the contract with the processor | Data controllers should stipulate contracts or other legal acts with the processors | Accountability |
| Where applicable, stipulate the agreement with joint data controllers | Joint controllers should stipulate an agreement to determine the respective responsibilities | Accountability |

*Table 6.8 DPbD organisational guidelines before processing 2*

| MEASURE | DESCRIPTION | PRINCIPLE |
|---|---|---|
| Perform the DPIA | Data controllers should perform a DPIA, except in the case of individual healthcare professionals | Accountability |
| Identify the DPO | Data controllers should designate a DPO, which may be a unique subject for the EHR environment | Accountability |
| Assign data protection tasks and allocate responsibilities to specific staff and third parties | Data controllers should assign duties on data protection management to specific internal staff or third parties | Accountability |
| Create a record of the processing activities | Data controllers should create a record of processing activities | Accountability |
| Conduct appropriate levels of training for staff | Data controllers should train their workforce and staff members on data protection and security | Accountability |
| Define the categories of particularly sensitive data | Where still not provided by law, data controllers could identify particularly sensitive data | Confidentiality and accountability |

| MEASURE | DESCRIPTION | PRINCIPLE |
|---|---|---|
| Create an access control policy | Data controllers should establish the identity, roles and categories of users having access to the source systems and to the EHR and adjust access rights and privileges | Confidentiality, data minimisation |
| Create a specific policy on monitoring access | Data controllers should define policies and procedures related to maintaining and revoking access rights and privileges | Confidentiality |
| Create a specific policy on authentication | The data controller should also define a policy on authentication and passwords | Confidentiality |

*Table 6.9 DPbD organisational guidelines before processing 3*

| MEASURE | DESCRIPTION | PRINCIPLE |
|---|---|---|
| Document compliance activities | Data controllers should document the compliance activity at the organisational level | Accountability |
| Create the privacy policy | Data controllers should create the privacy policies | Transparency |
| Define the policy on data accuracy | Data controllers should define procedures and policies applicable to ensuring the accuracy of personal data | Accuracy |

| MEASURE | DESCRIPTION | PRINCIPLE |
|---|---|---|
| Define the applicable data retention policy | Data controllers should define procedures and policy applicable to defining the data retention period | Storage limitation |
| Create the policy for the exercise of data subject's rights | Data controllers should define procedures and policy applicable to handling data subject's requests | Accountability |
| Create the policy on the communication of data protection events | Data controllers should define procedures and policies for communicating a data breach to the data subjects | Accountability and transparency |
| Create the policy on notification of data protection events | Data controllers should define procedures and policies for communicating a data breach to the DPA | Accountability |
| Create the policy for replying to the DPA or public requests | Data controllers should define procedures and policies applicable for requests from the DPA or other authorities | Accountability |
| Create the policy on security, the data breach response plan and the disaster recovery plan | Data controllers should define procedures and policies on security | Integrity, confidentiality, and availability |
| Create the policy on disclosures | Data controllers should define procedures and policy applicable to disclosures required by law | Accountability and confidentiality, data minimisation |

*Table 6.10 DPbD organisational guidelines data collection*

| MEASURE | DESCRIPTION | PRINCIPLE |
|---|---|---|
| Identify the legal ground | Data controllers should define a legal ground for every processing activity and related purpose | Lawfulness |
| Where applicable, obtain explicit consent | If Member State law requires consent, the data controller should obtain explicit consent, which is separate from consent to the treatment or to secondary uses of the EHR | Lawfulness |
| Inform data subject | Data controllers should provide the privacy policies to data subjects | Transparency |
| Apply limits to the collection | Data controllers should collect only accurate data that are necessary for limited and defined purposes. Internal guidelines should be established in this regard | Purpose limitation, data minimisation, accuracy |

*Table 6.11 DPbD organisational guidelines during processing*

| MEASURE | DESCRIPTION | PRINCIPLE |
|---|---|---|
| Document compliance activities | Data controllers should document compliance activity at the organisational level | Accountability |
| Maintain a record of processing activities | Data controllers should maintain a record of processing activities | Accountability |
| Update the levels of training for staff | Data controllers should train their workforce on the data protection framework | Accountability |
| Audit the processors and third parties | Data controllers should audit the compliance of processors and third parties | Accountability |
| Update privacy policies and any other data protection documents | All documents should be revised periodically | Transparency |
| Update inaccurate data and delete data after the retention period | Data controllers should keep data up-to-date and delete them when the retention period is finished | Accuracy, storage limitation |
| Perform periodic gap analysis with the rules | Data controllers should monitor the applicable legal requirements | Applicability |
| Perform regular internal audits for each aspect of compliance | Data controllers should monitor compliance at the organisational level, including periodically reviewing policies and procedures on security | Accountability |

| MEASURE | DESCRIPTION | PRINCIPLE |
|---|---|---|
| Perform periodic risk assessment that addresses new risks | Data controllers should assess new risks | Taking into account the risk |
| Where applicable, communicate and notify a data breach | Data controllers should communicate and notify a data breach in the presence of high risks | Accountability |
| Respond to requests and complaints from individuals | Data controllers should define procedures and policies applicable to handling the data subject's requests and complaints | Accountability |

### 6.5 Notes on liability issues: possible scenarios

The obligation to implement DPbD measures is on data controllers. However, other subjects are involved in the concrete implementation: the processor, the developer, the DPO, third parties, internal officers and the workforce in general (medical or administrative staff). This section provides some brief notes on liability in the event of inappropriate or ineffective DPbD implementation.

The GDPR establishes administrative fines for violations of the legal requirements that cause material or immaterial harm to data subjects, including the DPbD obligation[2003]. Article 82(1) – (2) GDPR introduces the right to compensation and liability as follows:

2003 *See* Chapter 2, Section 2.4. On the GDPR framework on sanctions *see* Gabriela Zanfir-Fortuna. "Chapter VIII Remedies, Liability and Penalties (Articles 77–84). Article 82. Right to compensation and liability". In: *The EU General Data Protection Regulation (GDPR): A Commentary.* Oxford University Press, 2020, pp. 1160–1179. ISBN: 9780198826491; Waltraut Kotschy. "Chapter VIII Remedies, Liability and Penalties (Articles 77–84). Article 83. General conditions for imposing administrative fines". In: *The EU General Data Protection Regulation (GDPR): A Commentary.* Oxford University Press, 2020, pp. 1180–1193. ISBN: 9780198826491; Orla Lynskey. "Chapter VIII Remedies, Liability and Penalties (Articles 77–84). Article 84. Penalties". In: *The EU General Data Protection Regu-*

> "1. Any person who has suffered material or non-material damage as a result of an infringement of this Regulation shall have the right to receive compensation from the controller or processor for the damage suffered.
> 2. Any controller involved in processing shall be liable for the damage caused by processing which infringes this Regulation. A processor shall be liable for the damage caused by processing only where it has not complied with obligations of this Regulation specifically directed to processors or where it has acted outside or contrary to lawful instructions of the controller".

As regards DPbD, the data controller is liable under Article 83(2)(d) and (4)(a) of the GDPR, when it causes a damage by its processing[2004]. Pur-

---

*lation (GDPR): A Commentary*. Oxford University Press, 2020, pp. 1194–1201. ISBN: 9780198826491; Emilio Tosi. "Illecito trattamento dei dati personali, responsabilizzazione, responsabilità oggettiva e danno nel GDPR: funzione deterrente-sanzionatoria e rinascita del danno morale soggettivo". In: *Contratto e Impresa* 3 (2020), pp. 1115- 1151; Emilio Tosi. *Responsabilità civile per illecito trattamento dei dati personali e danno non patrimoniale*. Giuffrè Francis Lefebvre, 2019. ISBN: 9788828817192; Emilio Tosi. "La responsabilità civile per trattamento illecito dei dati personali". In: *Privacy Digitale. Riservatezza e protezione dei dati personali tra GDPR e nuovo Codice Privacy*. Giuffrè Francis Lefebvre, 2019, pp. 619–675. ISBN: 9788828811381; Giovanni Mulazzani. "Le sanzioni amministrative in materia di protezione dei dati personali nell'ordinamento europeo ed in quello nazionale". In: *La protezione dei dati personali in Italia. Regolamento UE n. 2016/679 e d.lgs. 10 agosto 2018, n. 101*. Zanichelli, Torino, 2019, pp. 768–795. ISBN: 9788808820433; Panetta, *Circolazione e protezione dei dati personali, tra libertà e regole del mercato. Commentario al Regolamento UE n. 2016/679 (GDPR) e al novellato D.lgs. n. 196/2003 (Codice Privacy)*, pp. 435–444; Fabio Bravo. "Riflessioni critiche sulla natura della responsabilità da trattamento illecito di dati personali". In: *Persona e mercato dei dati. Riflessioni sul GDPR*. Wolters Kluwer, 2019, pp. 384–418. ISBN: 9788813370510; Voigt and Von dem Bussche, *The EU General Data Protection Regulation (GDPR). A Practical Guide*, pp. 201–217. On sanctions in the healthcare field *see* Giovanni Comandé and Denise Amram. "La violazione della privacy in sanità, tra diritto civile e diritto penale". In: *Itinerari di medicina legale e delle responsabilità in campo sanitario*. G. Giappichelli Editore, 2021. ISBN: 9788892132634.

2004 Article 83(2) establishes that "administrative fines shall, depending on the circumstances of each individual case, be imposed in addition to, or instead of, measures referred to in points (a) to (h) and (j) of Article 58(2). When deciding whether to impose an administrative fine and deciding on the amount of the administrative fine in each individual case due regard shall be given to the following (...)", including (d) which introduces Article 25: "the degree of responsibility of the controller or processor taking into account technical and

suant to Article 82(3) GDPR, the controller can be exempted from liability if it proves that it is not in any way responsible for the event giving rise to the damage[2005]. According to Tosi, GDPR liability is a particular form of strict liability since the rules consider processing inherently dangerous and create a reversal of the burden of proof[2006]. At the same time, it might be argued that if the measures had been adequate, the damage would not have occurred[2007].

First of all, it may be highlighted that the broad discretion for data controllers on DPbD implementation leaves enough space for courts to rule and on DPAs to sanction. On the one hand, the adequacy of the measures is related to an objective case-by-case evaluation of the court or the DPA. On the other hand, DPbD implementation is performed on a case-by-case

organisational measures implemented by them pursuant to Articles 25 and 32".

2005 *See* also Recital 146 GDPR: "The controller or processor should compensate any damage which a person may suffer as a result of processing that infringes this Regulation. The controller or processor should be exempt from liability if it proves that it is not in any way responsible for the damage. The concept of damage should be broadly interpreted in the light of the case-law of the Court of Justice in a manner which fully reflects the objectives of this Regulation. This is without prejudice to any claims for damage deriving from the violation of other rules in Union or Member State law. Processing that infringes this Regulation also includes processing that infringes delegated and implementing acts adopted in accordance with this Regulation and Member State law specifying rules of this Regulation. Data subjects should receive full and effective compensation for the damage they have suffered. Where controllers or processors are involved in the same processing, each controller or processor should be held liable for the entire damage. However, where they are joined to the same judicial proceedings, in accordance with Member State law, compensation may be apportioned according to the responsibility of each controller or processor for the damage caused by the processing, provided that full and effective compensation of the data subject who suffered the damage is ensured. Any controller or processor which has paid full compensation may subsequently institute recourse proceedings against other controllers or processors involved in the same processing".

2006 *See* Tosi, "Illecito trattamento dei dati personali, responsabilizzazione, responsabilità oggettiva e danno nel GDPR: funzione deterrente-sanzionatoria e rinascita del danno morale soggettivo", p. 1131; Tosi, *Responsabilità civile per illecito trattamento dei dati personali e danno non patrimoniale*; Tosi, "La responsabilità civile per trattamento illecito dei dati personali", pp. 657–659. The author argues that proof is a so-called *probatio diabolica*, i.e. a proof that is very hard to prove.

2007 Tosi, *op. cit.*, p. 658, where the author highlights that this is a statement coming from reasoning that pre-empts a legal interpretation.

basis, and the criteria to be taken into account are mainly subjective. Thus, finding arguments for contesting compliance with Article 25 seems neither easy nor immediate[2008].

The state of the art of PETs and measures changes over time. The cost of implementation is a complex criterion to evaluate. The risk assessment and the concrete characteristics of processing are highly subjective. Therefore, compliance checking has been defined as a "moving target"[2009]. All the criteria of Article 25 will be taken into account during the judgement to ascertain the interruption of the causal link between the data controller's processing operations and adopted measures and the occurred damage[2010]. The controller will be liable when the data processing is not compliant with the obligation and the damage is caused by this processing[2011].

In 2019 and 2020 some DPAs started to sanction data controllers for non-compliance with the requirements of Article 25. A few interesting investigations and proceedings can be reported and briefly analysed here.

In 2019, the Romanian DPA sanctioned Unicredit Bank S.p.A. on the basis of Article 25(1) GDPR for failing to implement appropriate technical and organisational measures. In particular, the data controller disclosed data concerning personal identification numbers and payers' addresses during external and internal transactions of 337,042 data subjects without appropriate and adequate measures to control the data processing opera-

2008 Bygrave claimed that heavy sanctions related to Article 25 are difficult to handle since the language of the provision is vague and relatively abstract. *See* Bygrave, "Chapter IV Controller and Processor (Articles 24–43). Article 25. Data protection by design and by default", p. 579. At that time, the author quoted the decision of the Romanian DPA of 27 June 2019 to support the belief that controllers cannot escape compliance with DPbD. On this deliberation *see* the next paragraphs.

2009 *See* Schiffner et al., "Towards a roadmap for privacy technologies and the General Data Protection Regulation: A transatlantic initiative", p. 28.

2010 *See* Tosi, *Responsabilità civile per illecito trattamento dei dati personali e danno non patrimoniale*, pp. 75–76.

2011 As an example, according to Bravo who uses Italian civil law categories, this obligation is an "*ex lege* obligation", since it is generated from a fact or an act acknowledged by law as generating the legal obligation established by a provision. In particular, it is an "obligation to act" that protects personal data ("obblighi protettivi"). This category is derived from the German doctrine and is also used in the Italian legal system. *See* Bravo, "Riflessioni critiche sulla natura della responsabilità da trattamento illecito di dati personali", pp. 404–414.

tions[2012]. The data controller failed to appropriately implement the data minimisation principle with effective measures at the time of the data processing activities.

In the same year, the Berlin Commissioner for Data Protection investigated the data processing carried out by the real estate company Deutsche Wohnen SE. The configuration of the archive systems used by this data controller did not ensure that personal data were kept for no longer than was necessary for the specified purposes[2013]. The Commissioner sanctioned the company for over 14 million Euro on the basis of Article 25 GDPR. The data retention system was ruled to be as inappropriate as such, even before the occurrence of a data breach. In this particular case, the controller failed to implement the storage limitation principle with appropriate measures.

High fines have been imposed in the telecommunication sector[2014]. In 2019 the Hellenic DPA sanctioned the Hellenic Telecommunications Organization on the basis of Articles 5(1)(c) and 25(1) GDPR for failing to implement appropriate organisational measures to control processing activities related to advertisement purposes and to the recipients of consumer contact lists[2015]. Personal data of former consumers were included in the registers for telemarketing purposes, used for unsolicited promotional calls, and not deleted after requests. In 2020, the Italian DPA found Vodafone Italia S.p.A. to have violated Article 5(1) – (2) and Article 25(1) GDPR due to its failure to implement appropriate technical and organisational measures to test and ensure compliance of the collection of personal data from the first phase of data processing, despite the signifi-

2012 On the decision of this DPA *see* the official website at <www.dataprotection .ro/index.jsp?page=Comunicat_ Amenda_Unicredit&lang=en>, and the press release of the EDPB at <edpb.europa.eu/news/national-news/ 2019/first-fine-romanian-supervisory-authority_en>. Last accessed 06/10/2021.

2013 *See* the official press release at <www.datenschutz-berlin.de/filead min/user_upload/pdf/pressemitteilungen/2019/20191105-PM-B ussgeld_DW.pdf>; and the press release of the EDPB at <edpb.europa.eu/news/ national-news/2019/berlin-commissioner-data-protection-imposes-fine-real-estate-company_it>. Last accessed 06/10/2021.

2014 *See* the statistics by CMS and available at <www. enforcementtracker.com/?insights>. Last accessed 06/10/2021.

2015 *See* decision no. 31/2019 at <www.dpa.gr/el/enimerwtiko/prakseisArxi s/ epiboli-prostimoy-se-etaireia-parohis-ypiresion-tilefonias-gia-parabiasi>; and the press release of the EDPB at <edpb.europa.eu/news/national-news/2019/ administrative-fines-imposed-telephone-service-provider_en>. Last accessed 06/10/2021.

cant number of complaints and alerts[2016]. Actually, the company violated many requirements of the GDPR[2017]. As regards the DPbD obligation, the Italian DPA held that the telemarketing activities and the first contacts with several potential customers (data subjects) that were carried out by operators of the sales network and by tele-marketers were not continuously performed in compliance with the GDPR[2018]. In particular, the control systems did not exclude the existence of subscriptions to contracts and service activation from unlawful and unsolicited telemarketing calls[2019]. The processing operations resulted in aggressive telemarketing practices towards data subjects. Interestingly, the authority explained that key elements of the data protection by design obligation include attention to prevention, functionality, security, transparency and centrality of the data subjects' interests. The Italian DPA held that the data controller did not adopt appropriate measures to exclude and mitigate risks by explaining how systems should have been designed to effectively monitor the data processing operations. On top of a 12 million Euro administrative fine, Vodafone received the order to adjust measures and access systems to secure its databases. In the same year and industry, the Italian DPA sanctioned other telecommunications companies (TIM S.p.A.[2020], Iliad Italia S.p.A.[2021] and Wind Tre S.p.A.[2022]) on the basis of several articles of the GDPR, including Article 25, for failing to integrate appropriate technical and organisational measures in their data processing activities.

---

2016 Garante per la protezione dei dati personali, Provvedimento del 12 novembre 2020, published in Registro dei provvedimenti n. 224 del 12 novembre 2020, available at <www.ItalianDPAprivacy.it/web/guest/home/ docweb/-/docweb-display/docweb/9485681>. Last accessed 06/10/2021.

2017 *See* for more details Bincoletto, "Italy – Italian DPA Against Vodafone: History of a €12 million Fine".

2018 *See* Bincoletto, *op. cit.*, p. 556.

2019 *See ibid.*

2020 Garante per la protezione dei dati personali, Provvedimento del 15 gennaio 2020, published in Registro dei provvedimenti n. 7 del 15 gennaio 2020, available at <www.garanteprivacy.it/web/guest/home/docweb/-/ docweb-display/docweb/9256486>. Last accessed 06/10/2021.

2021 Garante per la protezione dei dati personali, Provvedimento del 9 luglio 2020, published in Registro dei provvedimenti n. 138 del 9 luglio 2020, available at <www.garanteprivacy.it/home/docweb/-/docweb-display/ docweb/9435807>. Last accessed 06/10/2021.

2022 Garante per la protezione dei dati personali, Provvedimento del 9 luglio 2020, published in Registro dei provvedimenti n. 143 del 9 luglio 2020, available at <www.garanteprivacy.it/home/docweb/-/docweb-display/ docweb/9435753>. Last accessed 06/10/2021.

In the e-health care sector, in 2020 the Swedish DPA sanctioned seven healthcare providers for failing to conduct assessments and risk analysis on processing with electronic health records systems, limit the access level of users, and implement appropriate security measures[2023]. The DPA did not apply Article 25, but Articles 5, 24 and 31 GDPR. However, it is interesting to report these decisions since, on the one hand, they show that the DPIA, the access control system, and the identity management system are pivotal in the context of EHRs; on the other hand, the measures for limiting authorisation to access the EHR should be implemented from the design stage of the systems and should actually result from the application of DPbD. In fact, on December 2020 the Norwegian DPA sanctioned the Østfold HF Hospital on the basis of Articles 25 and 32 for unappropriated access control and management system of patients' lists in the years 2013–2019[2024].

As pointed out by Hielke Hijmans, President of the Litigation Chamber of the Belgian DPA, the GDPR does not apply only to companies, but also to citizens[2025]. The implementation of Article 25 concerns all data processing under the GDPR. The Belgian DPA sanctioned a couple of private individuals who had installed a video surveillance system on their property consisting of five cameras on the basis of improper placement of two of these cameras[2026]. The proceeding started with the complaint by two neighbours who noticed that surveillance cameras were filming part of the public highway and their private property and that the couple had

2023 *See* <www.imy.se/nyheter/brister-i-hur-vardgivare-styr-personalens-atkomst-till-journaluppgifter/>; and the press release of the EDPB at <edpb.europa.eu/news/national-news/2020/ deficiencies-how-healthcare-providers-control-staff-access-patient-journal_en>. Last accessed 06/10/2021.

2024 *See* the decision at <www.datatilsynet.no/contentassets/580ab399d02d4d369de8c5905757d4b2/~20_02291-4-vedtak-om-overtredelsesgebyr-og-palegg-208484_13_1.pdf>; and the press release of the EDPB at <https://edpb.europa.eu/news/national-news/2020/ norwegian-dpa-imposes-administrative-fine-ostfold-hf-hospital_en>. Last accessed 06/10/2021.

2025 *See* the press release of 25 November 2020 at <https://www.autoriteprotectiondonnees.be/citoyen/ lapd-impose-une-amende-pour-traitement-illegitime-dimages-de-cameras-de-surveillance>. Last accessed 06/10/2021.

2026 *See* the official press release at <https://www.autoriteprotectiondonnees.be/citoyen/ lapd-impose-une-amende-pour-traitement-illegitime-dimages-de-cameras-de-surveillance>. The decision is available in Dutch at <https://www.autoriteprotectiondonnees.be/publications/ decision-quant-au-fond-n-74–2020.pdf>. *See* also the press release of the EDPB at <https://edpb.europa.eu/news/national-news/2020/belgian-dpa-fine-unlawful-processing-video-images_en>. Last accessed 06/10/2021.

use some captured pictures during an administrative dispute procedure regarding environmental planning by transferring data to an external expert. The Belgian DPA found that images (i.e. personal data) were collected and disclosed by transmission without a lawful legal ground for processing. The legitimate interest of the couple in protecting their property and domestic context did not justify filming the public highway or the property of others and using the images in a dispute procedure. The couple, as data controller, should have properly placed the cameras. According to this authority, the controller infringed Article 25(1) GDPR due to this improper placement.

The brief analysis of the above mentioned investigations and proceedings shows once again that compliance with Article 25 is strictly related to the appropriate implementation of data protection principles. Authorities may contest compliance in every aspect of data processing and evaluate the adopted measures item by item. In the future, DPAs might release specific guidelines or opinions on DPbD obligations at the enforcement level to explain their approaches to evaluating the measures of Article 25.

Secondly, some considerations should be provided for each category of subjects.

When in the EHR environment there are joint controllers, their agreement should specify the respective duties and responsibilities (Art. 26 GDPR). It is important to allocate responsibilities for the implementation of DPbD technical and organisational measures. The data subjects have the possibility to exercise their rights against each controller. In fact, each controller remains responsible for any damage caused by the processing, and each subject is liable for the entire damage[2027]. This is a case of joint and several liability[2028].

As regards the processor, this subject is typically a contractor or the outsourcing company that manages the ICT systems (e.g. external service provider). The data controller should carefully choose a processor that is able to provide guarantees of compliance[2029]. In fact, the controller may

2027 *See* Article 82(4) GDPR.

2028 *See* Tosi, *Responsabilità civile per illecito trattamento dei dati personali e danno non patrimoniale*, p. 43. Internally, it will be necessary to investigate the different causal contribution of each controller. Then, the compensation for damages will be divided between the joint controllers according to the different levels of liability. *See* also Tosi, "La responsabilità civile per trattamento illecito dei dati personali", p. 650.

2029 *See* Dimitri De Rada. "La responsabilità civile in caso di mancato rispetto del GDPR. Privacy by default, privacy by design e accountability nell'ottica del

be liable for *culpa in eligendo et in vigilando* when the subject chooses a processor that does not provide the appropriate guarantees[2030]. The processor's duties are defined in the contract or legal act adopted pursuant to Article 28 GDPR between this subject and the data controller.

According to Article 82(2) GDPR, the processor can be liable for any damage caused by processing when specific obligations that the GDPR places on its role are not fulfilled, e.g. the implementation of security measures[2031]. When the processor engages a sub-processor, this subject remains fully liable to the data controller for the performance of the processor's duties pursuant to Article 28(4) GDPR[2032]. Moreover, the processor is liable when this subject acts in a manner that is inconsistent with or contrary to the instructions given by the data controller in their contract. This last scenario may actually establish a joint liability between the controller and the processor. Where all these scenarios do not apply, and the data controller has been fined for violation of Article 25 GDPR, this subject may still sue the processor in a recourse action on the basis of the contract and under civil or private law. The processor should demonstrate that they followed the instructions and adopted the appropriate measures.

Beyond the elements listed in Article 28(3)(c) and (e) GDPR, it may be argued that the contract between the processor and the controller should specifically stipulate that the processor should assist the controller for the fulfilment of the obligations of Article 25 GDPR by appropriate

---

Diritto Privato". In: *Federalismi.it* 23 (2019), pp. 1–16, p. 10, which considers this contract a DPbD measure in itself. In the Guidelines on Article 25 the EDPB recommends on the one hand that controllers "should not choose producers or processors who do not offer systems enabling or supporting the controller to comply with Article 25, because controllers will be held accountable for the lack of implementation thereof"; on the other hand, the authority recommends "controllers to require that producers and processors demonstrate how their hardware, software, services or systems enable the controller to comply with the requirements to accountability in accordance with DPbDD, for example by using key performance indicators to demonstrate the effectiveness of the measures and safeguards at implementing the principles and rights". *See* European Data Protection Board, *Guidelines 4/2019 on Article 25 Data Protection by Design and by Default*, p. 30. So, the controller should seek guarantees and be very careful in their choice.

2030 *See* Tosi, *Responsabilità civile per illecito trattamento dei dati personali e danno non patrimoniale*, pp. 60–61.

2031 *See* once again Article 28 GDPR.

2032 According to Tosi, *Responsabilità civile per illecito trattamento dei dati personali e danno non patrimoniale*, p. 63, the designation is *tamquam non esset* for the controller from a liability point of view.

and effective technical and organisational measures. The controller that processes data concerning health may choose a processor that has received a certification or uses a code of conduct[2033].

The developer is a role that the GDPR takes into account only in Recital 78 to encourage an application of DPbD and DPbDf beyond the duty of the data controllers[2034]. A contract usually regulates the relation between the developer and the customer, which may be either the processor or the data controller. This contract is regulated under Member State law, private law and commercial law especially.

In that contract, the parties may include a specific declaration on the application of the GDPR requirements and of the principle of DPbD[2035]. In particular, the controller may ask the developer to write a statement to prove that its product (e.g. the source system and/or the EHR system) has been analysed on the basis of GDPR requirements and that the adequacy analysis demonstrates that it complies with these regulatory requirements. The contract could otherwise make reference to specific standards to be adopted during development. As a result, the standards or the DPbD implementation will be part of the contractual agreement and will bind the developer from a private or civil law perspective. A controller who has been fined under the GDPR could enforce the DPbD requirement on contractors and service providers when this requirement was documented in the contract[2036]. However, under the GDPR and against the data subjects, the data controller remains the only subject liable for the violation.

Another subject that inevitably and actively participates in the DPbD implementation is the DPO, who advises the controller and processor on the obligations to carry out, including DPbD[2037]. Since the DPO shall

---

2033 Article 28(5) GDPR establishes that a certification or a code of conduct could be used for demonstrating the provision of guarantees by the processor. The use of codes of conducts, standards and certification is highly recommended by the EDPB in European Data Protection Board, *Guidelines 4/2019 on Article 25 Data Protection by Design and by Default*, p. 30.

2034 *See* Chapter 2, Section 2.4.1.

2035 The CNIL recommended including specific clauses in sub-contractors' contracts in Commission Nationale de l'Informatique et des Libertés, *Référentiel relatif aux traitement de données personnelles pour les cabinets médicaux et paramédicaux*, p. 10.

2036 In the PRIPARE's guidelines on accountability, it is recommended to "include privacy requirements in documents related to contracts, procurement and acquisition". *See* Notario et al., *PRIPARE. Privacy-and Security-by design Methodology Handbook. 2016*, p. 130.

2037 *See* Article 39 GDPR.

monitor compliance with the GDPR requirements and with the internal policies and procedures, the officer shall control the implementation of the DPbD measures. The DPO shall especially monitor the DPbD implementation at the organisational level, including the risk assessment level. The EDPB encourages the active involvement of the office on DPbD and DPbDf activities in the whole processing life-cycle[2038]. When the DPO does not perform these tasks, this officer may be liable to the data controller and the processor under contract law for lack of professional diligence[2039].

Finally, during processing third parties and internal workforce may process personal data on behalf of the controller and they may not implement the required measures. Since the controller will remain liable under the GDPR, it is necessary to stipulate specific confidentiality clauses in the contracts and other clauses that establish the duty to follow internal procedures and guidelines to guarantee the fulfilment of technical and organisational DPbD measures.

Despite the complexity of Article 25 and of the enforcement level, the data controller should carefully apply this requirement and be protected at a contractual level since the administrative fines set by the GDPR could have a great impact on their business, especially if they are SMEs[2040].

2038 *See* European Data Protection Board, *Guidelines 4/2019 on Article 25 Data Protection by Design and by Default*, p. 29.

2039 *See* Tosi, *Responsabilità civile per illecito trattamento dei dati personali e danno non patrimoniale*, pp. 89–91.

2040 The EDPB suggests the following steps for SMEs: “do early risk assessments; start with small processing – then scale its scope and sophistication later; look for producer and processor guarantee of DPbDD, such as certification and adherence to code of conducts; use partners with a good track record; talk with DPAs; read guidance from DPAs and the EDPB; adhere to codes of conduct where available; get professional help and advice”. *See* European Data Protection Board, *Guidelines 4/2019 on Article 25 Data Protection by Design and by Default*, p. 30.

# Chapter 7 Conclusions

## *7.1 Concluding remarks*

The digital revolution has deeply transformed the provision of healthcare. The e-health context is one of the most data-intensive sectors and it is constantly evolving. Private and public healthcare providers are using electronic health data to ensure more effective and efficient services.

Several EU policies allocate resources to transform and enhance the protection of the right to health. E-health technologies represent both great opportunities and significant challenges. The protection of personal health data is one of the important challenges to be faced. The digital revolution has also changed the way law regulates phenomena. Law and technology should cooperate to create or apply rules in cyberspace. Since multiple processing activities occur in everyday life and in different contexts, the data protection field has become crucial in safeguarding rights and freedoms.

This research started with the concepts of *regulation by design* and *privacy by design*. *Code* creates an embedded set of rules in the technological design of ICTs and absorbs values. The design of ICTs is thus never neutral.

Technical regulation goes hand-in-hand with regulation of the market, social norms and the law. Law may interfere with the architectural constraints that are decided by developers by mandating the incorporation of legal rules in the design of technologies and related practices. It has been highlighted that law regulates *ex post*, while architecture *ex ante*. The interaction between law and design could address some legal issues in the privacy and data protection domain.

The approach of privacy by design aims to build privacy principles and requirements into the design and architecture of ICTs and organisational practices to improve legal compliance. The investigation focused on the history and philosophy that have created this principle. Starting from the research by Cavoukian, PbD proposes to minimise privacy risks and increase users' protection by following certain principles. In recent years, PbD has been promoted by authorities internationally and in some legal systems, including in the US by the FTC and in the EU framework.

An extensive critical analysis of the concept of PbD has been provided. When adopting a legal rule on PbD, or endorsing its concrete implementation, several advantages and disadvantages collide. It has been demonstrated that a provision on PbD should be framed in a detailed form with some criteria for implementation, it should be well drafted and clearly worded, and it should be neutral in order to be effective. A thorough legal analysis of all the applicable legal rules should be performed when applying PbD, but incorporating principles and requirements is a significant challenge since hard-coding law involves representing rules in a machine-readable way, interpreting legal rules, and identifying and balancing rights and interests. These complex activities are usually carried out by legal experts. As a result, these experts must be involved in the PbD implementation, which must be the result of interdisciplinary work.

PbD is a proactive, dynamic and global approach that requires concrete organisational measures, and involves investments and allocated resources, but companies sometimes lack a knowledgeable organisation and are reluctant to pay high costs. At the same time, PbD may be considered a business opportunity, a competitive advantage and a positive paradigm for increasing trust and confidence in products and services.

In the digital environment there is an information asymmetry between users and companies. This operates in knowledge and power. In the age of "surveillance capitalism", given the current economic and business models, a more effective approach to protecting personal data and privacy is necessary to challenge these dynamics and better protect rights.

PbD may be considered an innovative approach but shaping technology at the service of the law is not a trivial problem. Strategies for PbD implementation should be developed on a case-by-case basis since one solution does not fit all situations and contexts. Balancing the benefits and criticisms, PbD is an opportunity to govern new phenomena and implement privacy principles and rights. In fact, the EU chose to establish a specific "by design" provision in the GDPR.

Article 25 of the GDPR and the DPbD obligation have been investigated in detail through a legal analysis since this provision requires taking into account various criteria while implementing appropriate technical and organisational measures before and during data processing operations to safeguard principles and data subjects' rights in an effective manner. This provision is not the only requirement in the EU framework that mandates data protection by design. Other Regulations establish similar obligations to create consistency within the EU legal system and modernise all the sectors where personal data are processed.

DPbD is an enforceable obligation with which data controllers subject to the material and territorial scopes of the GDPR must comply. Even though the provision explicitly refers to the controller only, the processor shall assist this subject in fulfilling the DPbD obligation. As regards developers of ICTs, they are not included in Article 25. However, it may be argued that they are encouraged to implement DPbD measures since controllers may select products and services on the basis of the adopted design choices.

Once again, there is no "one-size-fits-all" solution for complying with such a requirement in the whole project and during the data management life-cycle. Appropriate and effective measures must be selected according to objective (i.e. state of the art) and subjective criteria (i.e. cost of implementation, contextual factors of the data processing operations, risk assessment) for implementing data protection principles and safeguarding data subjects' rights. Several examples of measures that achieve these principles and rights have been provided, but the selection should be sector- and case-specific.

Data protection by default is another obligation mandated by Article 25. DPbDf requires the controller to implement appropriate technical and organisational measures as default settings for ensuring that the processing does not include personal data that are not necessary for the specific purpose. This provision directly entails the design of the technologies and how they automatically process personal data. The measures for implementing DPbD and DPbDf may eventually overlap, but it has been argued that the controller should have in mind both distinct principles and fulfil them by adopting a holistic "data protection first" approach. The implementation of Article 25 should also be coordinated with other rules that the GDPR sets out: security requirements, risk assessment rules and certification mechanisms upfront.

The comparison between PbD and DPbD has shown that these concepts are different, and their wording is frequently misleading. It has been pointed out that they represent broad proactive approaches. PbD is an international concept perceived as a principle and advocated by scholars and policymakers for the protection of privacy and personal data. It also includes the protection of default settings. DPbD and DPbDf are instead separately defined in Article 25 GDPR and are established for the protection of persona data. DPbD is a fully enforceable and flexible obligation, while PbD entails a visionary and ethical dimension. It is arguable that Article 25 has a broad formulation that means that it is difficult to implement, but this provision is technologically neutral, dynamic and leaves room for specific customised solutions. It is also relevant to stress that when advocating respect for DPbD, possible conditions may limit the right to data protection, and some balancing may be necessary against other rights and freedoms.

The legal analysis moved to the healthcare context to contextualise the DPbD approach. The investigation of the data protection concerns of e-health technologies demonstrated that data concerning health deserve high protection and higher guarantees are established by the law. Data on health status can render the individual vulnerable in multiple ways. The right to respect for private life, the duties of medical and professional confidentiality, and data protection laws set a variety of rules for protecting personal health data.

The current legal framework in the EU is primarily the GDPR, but other legal sources are applicable at EU and Member States' levels. The investigation focused on this framework by providing the definition of personal health data, by discussing the legal grounds for their processing and other relevant legal requirements that apply in the context of e-health and are useful for a DPbD implementation. In particular, it has been highlighted that personal health data are included in the list of special categories of data by the GDPR because they reveal information on the health status of the data subject and merit heightened protection. The definition of this data type is broad and open to interpretation. Processing is allowed in exceptional situations where a legal ground applies. The GDPR enhanced the protection of personal health data by increasing data subjects' rights to be protected and the obligations to comply with. Special considerations have been made on the exercise of these rights and on the extent of the obligations.

The protection of personal data may be balanced against public health interests in particular scenarios, such as the recent pandemic, with additional safeguards in place. In fact, the health sector is frequently subject to national rules that derogate or further specify processing activities with legislative measures that are necessary and proportionate insofar as they respect the rights and freedoms of individuals in a democratic society.

Then a case study in the e-health domain was introduced: the EHR system. This technology is widely used for processing data concerning health at the EU level, in Member States and even across them in an interoperability scenario. The state of the art and the applicable legal framework were analysed as the EHR environment entails complex data processing operations. The description of the state of the art employed internationally recognised concepts and standards.

The EHR is a widely used technology that is considered a priority by EU policies and strategies. This system collects and processes all the personal health data of the patient and shares them among all authorised operators that are involved in the medical treatment. From a technical point of view, several entities as source systems (i.e. healthcare providers) aggregate data in repositories in a given period of time (e.g. patient's life period), and use the whole resulting system in different ways of interaction according to multiple functions. In particular, it has been reported that the EHR is primarily used for patient care delivery and patient care management, but it is useful for patient care support processes and financial and other administrative processes since it collects both common personal data and personal health data. Three functions of the EHR were grouped: the storage with the data at rest; the network where the data are transferred; and the computation area where the data are used.

Then, the book discussed the EU legal framework applicable to the processing of data in the EHR systems. The legal analysis focused on the roles in the processing, the legitimate grounds, the necessary data protection safeguards for the national legal frameworks, and the rights and duties in the EHR environment. It also investigated the interoperability issues of the cross-border processing (and exchange) of personal health data with EHRs where data protection and security risks increase since systems are more interconnected and the amount of personal health data rises as well as the number of actors involved. It has been demonstrated that the GDPR lays down the main requirements with which healthcare providers must comply during data processing in the EHRs and that DPbD obligation must play a major role in the development of EHR systems.

Furthermore, PbD has been recognised as an international principle for the proactive protection of personal data, and is based on FIPs which were first developed in the US. In US federal law there is a specific rule for the implementation of technical and organisational measures in the e-health care context and for EHRs. Given these premises, a comparison with the US legal framework was provided by analysing the applicable principles and provisions. It may be pointed out that the protection of personal health data is actually a global issue.

The research provided an overview of information privacy law in the US and of privacy principles in US federal law. The goal was to examine the similarities and differences with the data protection principles of the GDPR in light of a PbD or DPbD implementation. In the US, informational privacy law sets the rules that protect personal information, but the framework is sectorial and fragmented. Reading the FIPs and the OECD's Guidelines it may be argued that the GDPR provides broader principles and more guarantees. Thus, the application of a PbD or a DPbD approach might differ between the US and the EU since the implementation may follow partially different principles. Nonetheless, the core data protection or informational privacy principles are similar. It has been reported that some US scholars and the American Law Institute are proposing new formulations of the FIPs that go beyond the OECD's principles. In particular, the ALI's project is a prominent effort to reform the FIPs by including both the OECD's and GDPR's concepts in light of a modern path forward of informational privacy. However, FIPs alone are not sufficient to affect the design of technologies and business practices.

Moreover, the US legal framework for health informational privacy and for EHRs, and HIPAA Privacy and Security Rules, were analysed. These Rules establish federal standards for protecting personal health information processed by covered entities. HIPAA requires appropriate administrative, physical and technical safeguards and sets limits and conditions on use and disclosure of information.

The research compared HIPAA Privacy and Security Rules with the DPbD requirement in the e-health context. The elements of this comparative analysis were the scope of application and the rationale of the norms, the object and the recommended measures, and the underlying principles and rights. The analysis showed that, despite some interesting similarities, an EHR may not be used in both EU and US legal frameworks since the DPbD principle goes beyond a set of measures to be implemented. At the same time, HIPAA requirements can be considered useful examples of measures for developing some guidelines for the EHRs. HIPAA gives an important role to technical means for protecting privacy, but DPbD is a more global approach that guarantees further protection. An explicit legal recognition of PbD in US law may bring these frameworks together.

The research was then dedicated to a more applied perspective in the technological domain that investigates existing technical tools, approaches and methods for designing data protection. This part employed an interdisciplinary methodology.

It was pointed out that the EHR system is complex since it has a set of components that includes both hardware and software: database management systems and their hardware, EHR software with its architecture and interface, and the network. Given some general notions on systems and software engineering, it was shown that privacy or data protection needs should be formulated as requirements for system development. Despite interpretation and translation concerns, legal rules should be analysed, specific requirements or use cases should be identified and developed into functional or non-functional system requirements by following a methodology. Different methodologies may be adopted for software development. The choice should take into account the challenges that the selected methodology presents in connection with the DPbD implementation. In addition, the methods should consider the personal data life-cycle, which can be classified as data collection, data use and data erasure, where personal data may be at rest, in use, or in transit.

An overview of privacy engineering approaches was provided by looking at some significant contributions related to PbD and DPbD. Privacy engineering is used to design systems with privacy or data protection built into the technical design. Several approaches were defined and analysed. In general, engineering methodologies may combine the use of patterns, tactics, goals, strategies, and PETs with the definition of requirements and use cases. A methodology for DPbD implementation should take into account the GDPR's principles and requirements. In fact, engineering approaches are fundamental for a concrete implementation, but they should be combined with the applicable data protection principles and with a preventive risk analysis.

Since the risk assessment framework is crucial for Article 25 of the GDPR, the research examined the relevant concepts that are applicable to this assessment, including likelihood and severity and how they can be evaluated before the start of data processing. Moreover, this part discussed some applicable methodologies for the data protection impact assessment, which have been developed by scholars and DPAs.

After that, the research focused on the e-health care sector and the case study on EHRs, by presenting some suitable PETs and recognised international standards that are useful for EHR system implementation. All these technical insights represent tools for defining the measures to be applied in the EHR environment.

Hence, theoretical and applied perspectives of the research were combined in applying DPbD in the case study. This research tried to create a set of guidelines for DPbD implementation in EHR systems and in the EU legal framework. To provide more concrete guidance on the integration of data protection rules in the concept development phase of the EHR system and its data processing management, the comprehensive guidelines were developed by classifying both technical and organisational measures and by assigning the related data protection principles and data subjects' rights. So, the GDPR's requirements and the current data protection law for data concerning health in the EU are the foundation of this set of guidelines. The comparison with the US legal framework was also taken into account since it provides useful examples of organisational and technical safeguards for medical records.

The set of DPbD guidelines defined requirements and comprehensive data protection measures that may aid data controllers and system developers when they make architectural choices in the requirement phase of a DPbD engineering approach, and for the appropriate organisational and technical measures to be implemented in the data processing activities. In fact, the guidelines apply to the full life cycle of data processing, i.e. before processing and during processing activities.

In the end, since the obligation to implement DPbD measures is upon data controllers, but other subjects are involved in the concrete implementation, the research provided some brief notes on liability in the event of inappropriate or ineffective DPbD implementation. It was argued that the broad discretion upon data controllers on the DPbD implementation leaves enough space for courts on ruling and on DPAs on sanctioning. In fact, the adequacy of the measures is related to an objective case-by-case evaluation of the court or the DPA, but the implementation is performed on a case-by-case basis under subjective criteria. Future DPAs' opinions or case law might provide specific guidance on the enforcement of DPbD obligation.

## 7.2 *Open questions*

Some brief open concerns may be summarised here.

First of all, it should be highlighted once again that balancing interests and rules while applying DPbD is a non-trivial problem. The tools and methodologies for integrating privacy or data protection in functional and non-functional system requirements are frequently developed without interdisciplinary approaches. So, it should be stressed that the legal and technical sides should always cooperate in defining problems and finding solutions.

Moreover, since DPbD is a global approach that requires a technical implementation by design, it may even be difficult to modify existing systems from an engineering perspective. The GDPR sets high administrative fines. So, data controllers should choose products and services in the market that indicate the DPbD implementation. This situation creates competitive concerns. Developers are out of the scope of the Regulation. Despite this, it may be argued that producers and technology developers are forced to adopt DPbD solutions to be still competitive in the market.

DPbD could set a global standard on data protection, but it should be adopted and implemented in several frameworks. Nowadays the big tech players in the "black box society" are outside the EU borders. The EU should find a way to be in the market and simultaneously lead by example in the protection of principles and rights.

In the healthcare sectors data controllers are frequently public entities. Since many technical solutions and technologies for adopting DPbD are expensive (e.g. standards), the cost of implementation criterion of Article 25 GDPR may create obstacles, or discourage implementation. However, the public sector should lead by example in effectively protecting rights and freedoms. Allocating appropriate resources for public entities and healthcare providers may enhance DPbD implementation in the e-health care sector.

Finally, specific EU certification on DPbD, codes of conduct for different sectors, including e-health, and more guidelines and opinions are needed in the future. It should be clear how courts and DPAs will rule on DPbD compliance.

## 7.3 *Future research*

In the future this research may be applied to a specific Member State or to more Member States at a comparative level to investigate how concrete EHR environments apply DPbD by following the GDPR requirements and Article 25. This will be an empirical study that uses a bottom-up approach based on existing projects of hospitals or clinics.

Alternatively, a new theoretical study may classify all the applicable rules for EHR systems or e-health technologies in general at the Member States' level to identify the residual limits for the legal and organisational interoperability in a cross-border context and to compare the rules adopted under Article 9(4) GDPR after the entry into force of the Regulation. Actually, the cross-border context remains an interesting point of research since the European Commission and eHealth Network are still working on the "Transformation of Health and Care in the Digital Single Market" and "Interoperability & standardisation: connecting eHealth services" policies.

The comparative analysis between the EU and the US may be extended to other legal frameworks. For example, Canada is an interesting legal framework to investigate since it is the country where the PbD concept was first developed, it has an active data protection authority, and the rules are established both at national and provincial levels. China is another intriguing legal system. Advanced e-health technologies are produced there. This country is a big tech player in the market.

Moreover, the insights of this work may also be applied to develop other sets of DPbD guidelines for different case studies and emerging trends in the e-health sector, such as telemedicine and telecare or e-referrals and m-apps. Every e-health technology has its own specific processing characteristics, but the GDPR remains the applicable legal framework and the main source of rules at the EU level.

Future research may include the use of AI and Big Data in the e-health context. AI algorithms are used for clinical care and medical research, for predictions and targeted healthcare provision. The aim is to provide personalised treatment and potentially prevent diseases. However, privacy and data protection concerns of this automated processing, including how to apply DPbD and protect data subjects' rights, should be addressed with an interdisciplinary approach by legal and technical scholars.

Finally, it might be worth investigating how to apply DPbD obligation to ensure secondary uses of data concerning health in medical research projects. These types of processing should still protect the rights and freedoms of data subjects when data are pseudonymised. At the same time the research could benefit public health and innovation. The secondary use of health data for research purposes is becoming increasingly important: the rights of the individual need to be balanced with the public interest in public health, following the necessity and proportionality principles.

This book attempted to show that the interaction between law and design could address some problems in the existing EU legal framework and in the particular e-health context. Data protection by design is and remains an intriguing legal concept that requires a technical implementation. This research is a piece of the puzzle, but there is still a lot of work to be done.

# Bibliography


Abedjan, Ziawasch *et al.* “Data science in healthcare: Benefits, challenges and opportunities”. In: *Data Science for Healthcare*. Springer, 2019, pp. 3–38. ISBN: 9783030052492.

Abril, Patricia Sanchez and Anita Cava. “Health privacy in a techno-social world: a cyber-patient’s bill of rights”. In: *Nw. J. Tech. & Intell. Prop.* 6 (2007), pp. 244–277.

Aceto, Giuseppe, Valerio Persico, and Antonio Pescapé. “The role of Information and Communication Technologies in healthcare: taxonomies, perspectives, and challenges”. In: *Journal of Network and Computer Applications* 107 (2018), pp. 125–154.

Acquisti, Alessandro, Curtis Taylor, and Liad Wagman. “The economics of privacy”. In: *Journal of economic Literature* 54.2 (2016), pp. 442–492.

Acquisti, Alessandro et al. “Nudges for privacy and security: Understanding and assisting users’ choices online”. In: *ACM Computing Surveys (CSUR)* 50.3 (2017), pp. 1–41. Adams, Maurice and Jacco Bomhoff. *Practice and Theory in Comparative Law*. Cambridge University Press, 2012. ISBN: 9780511863301.

Adams, Samantha, Nadezhda Purtova, and Ronald Leenes. *Under observation: The interplay between eHealth and surveillance*. Springer, 2017. ISBN: 9783319483429.

Agencia Espanõla de Protección de Datos, AEPD. *A Guide to Privacy by Design*. AEPD, 2019.

Agenzia per l’Italia Digitale, AGID. *Linee Guida per l’adozione di un ciclo di sviluppo di software sicuro*. Linee guida per lo sviluppo del software sicuro. Allegato 1, 2020.

— Linee Guida per la modellazione delle minacce e individuazione delle azioni di mitigazione conformi ai principi del Secure/Privacy by Design. Linee guida per lo sviluppo del software sicuro. Allegato 4, 2020.

Agre, Philip E. and Marc Rotenberg. *Technology and privacy: The new landscape*. Mit Press, 1998. ISBN: 9780262011624.

AI High-Level Expert Group. Ethics Guidelines for Trustworthy Artificial Intelligence, AI HLEG. European Commission, 2019.

Alexy, Robert. *A theory of constitutional rights*. Oxford University Press, 2010. ISBN: 9780199584239.

— “Constitutional rights, balancing, and rationality”. In: *Ratio Juris* 16.2 (2003), pp. 131- 140.

Alexy, Robert and Aleksander Peczenik. “The concept of coherence and its significance for discursive rationality”. In: *Ratio Juris* 3 (1990), pp. 130–147.

Allen, Anita L. “Coercing privacy”. In: *Wm. & Mary L. Rev.* 40 (1998), pp. 723–757.

Alpa, Guido. “La “proprietà” dei dati personali”. In: *Persona e mercato dei dati. Riflessioni sul GDPR*. Wolters Kluver, 2019, pp. 11–33. ISBN: 9788813370510.

Alpa, Guido, Francesco Pulitini, Stefano Rodotà, and Franco Romani. *Interpretazione giuridica e analisi economica*. Giuffrè Editore, 1982.

Alpa, Guido and Giorgio Resta. *Le persone e la famiglia. Vol. 1: Le persone fisiche e i diritti della personalità*. Wolters Kluwer Italia s.r.l., 2019. ISBN: 9788859820871.

Alshammari, Majed and Andrew Simpson. “Towards a principled approach for engineering privacy by design”. In: *Privacy Technologies and Policy. 5th Annual Privacy Forum, 2017*. Springer, 2017, pp. 161–177.

Amram, Denise. “Building up the “Accountable Ulysses” model. The impact of GDPR and national implementations, ethics, and health-data research: Comparative remarks”. In: *Computer Law & Security Review* 37 (2020), p. 105413.

Andersen, Kristian G., Andrew Rambaut, W. Ian Lipkin, Edward C. Holmes, and Robert F. Garry. “The proximal origin of SARS-CoV-2”. In: *Nature medicine* 26.4 (2020), pp. 450- 452.

Andoulsi, Isabelle and Petra Wilson. “Understanding liability in eHealth: Towards greater clarity at European Union level”. In: *eHealth: Legal, ethical and governance challenges*. Springer, 2013, pp. 165–180. ISBN: 9783642224744.

Angiolini, Chiara. Lo statuto dei dati personali. Uno studio a partire dalla nozione di bene. G. Giappichelli Editore, 2020. ISBN: 9788892134362.

Anglim, Christopher, Jane E. Kirtley, and Gretchen Nobahar. *Privacy Rights in the Digital Age*. Grey House Publishing, 2016. ISBN: 9781642650778.

Anjum, Adeel *et al.* “An efficient privacy mechanism for electronic health records”. In: *Computers & Security* 72 (2018), pp. 196–211.

Arak, P. and A. Wójcik. Transforming eHealth into a political and economic advantage. Polityka Insight, 2017.

Areheart, Bradley A. and Jessica L. Roberts. “GINA, Big Data, and the Future of Employee Privacy”. In: *Yale L.J.* 128 (2018), pp. 710–790.

Arisi, Marta and Paolo Guarda. “Blockchain and eHealth: seeking compliance with the General Data Protection Regulation”. In: *BioLaw Journal-Rivista di BioDiritto* 2 (2020), pp. 477–496.

Armstrong, Timothy K. “Digital rights management and the process of fair use”. In: *Harv. JL & Tech.* 20 (2006), pp. 49–121.

Article 29 Working Party, WP29. *Advice paper on special categories of data (“sensitive data”)*. Ref. Ares (2011) 444105, 20.04.2011, 2011.

— *ANNEX – health data in apps and devices*. Annex to the letter of 5.2.2015, 2015.

— *Guidelines on Automated individual decision-making and Profiling for the purposes of Regulation 2016/679*. WP251 17/en, 2017.

— *Guidelines on consent under Regulation 2016/679*. WP259 17/en, 2017.

— *Guidelines on Data Protection Impact Assessment (DPIA) and determining whether processing is “likely to result in a high risk” for the purposes of Regulation 2016/679*. WP248 17/en, 2017.

— *Guidelines on Data Protection Officers (‘DPOs’)*. WP243 17/en, 2017.

— *Guidelines on Personal data breach notification under Regulation 2016/679*. WP250 18/en, 2018.

— *Guidelines on the right to data portability*. WP242 16/en, 2017.

— *Guidelines on transparency under Regulation 2016/679*. WP260 17/en, 2018.

— *Opinion 05/2014 on Anonymisation Techniques*. WP216 14/en, 2014.

— *Working Document on the processing of personal data relating to health in electronic health records (EHR)*. WP131 2007/en. 2007.

Article 29 Working Party, Working Party on Police, and Justice. *The Future of Privacy: Joint Contribution to the Consultation of the European Commission on the Legal Framework for the Fundamental Right to Protection of Personal Data*. 02356/09/EN, WP 168, 2009.

Ashley, Kevin D. "Reasoning with cases and hypotheticals in HYPO". In: *International journal of man-machine studies* 34.6 (1991), pp. 753–796.

Athan, Tara, Guido Governatori, Monica Palmirani, Adrian Paschke, and Adam Wyner. "LegalRuleML: Design principles and foundations". In: *Reasoning Web International Summer School*. Springer. 2015, pp. 151–188.

Azencott, Chloé-Agathe. "Machine learning and genomics: precision medicine versus patient privacy". In: *Philosophical Transactions of the Royal Society A: Mathematical, Physical and Engineering Sciences* 376.2128 (2018), p. 20170350.

Bamberger, Kenneth A., Serge Egelman, Catherine Han, Amit Elazari Bar On, and Irwin Reyes. "Can you pay for privacy? consumer expectations and the behaviour of free and paid apps". In: *Berkeley Tech. LJ* 35 (2020), pp. 328–365.

Bamberger, Kenneth A. and Deirdre K. Mulligan. "Privacy on the Books and on the Ground". In: *Stan. L. Rev.* 63 (2010), pp. 247–315.

— Privacy on the ground: driving corporate behavior in the United States and Europe. MIT Press, 2015. ISBN: 9780262029988.

Barbas, Samantha. "Saving privacy from history". In: *DePaul L. Rev.* 61 (2011), pp. 973- 1048.

Bartolini, Cesare, Robert Muthuri, and Cristiana Santos. "Using ontologies to model data protection requirements in workflows". In: *JSAI International Symposium on Artificial Intelligence*. Springer, 2015, pp. 233–248.

Bechtold, Stefan. "Digital rights management in the United States and Europe". In: *The American Journal of Comparative Law* 52.2 (2004), pp. 323–382.

Beck, Kent *et al. Manifesto for agile software development*. <agilemanifesto.org/>. 2001.

Beckers, Kristian. "Comparing privacy requirements engineering approaches". In: *2012 Seventh International Conference on Availability, Reliability and Security*. IEEE. 2012, pp. 574–581.

Becla, Lidia *et al.* "Health technology assessment in the era of personalized health care". In: *International journal of technology assessment in health care* 27.2 (2011), pp. 118–126.

Bellotti, Victoria and Abigail Sellen. "Design for privacy in ubiquitous computing environments". In: *Proceedings of the Third European Conference on Computer-Supported Cooperative Work 13–17 September 1993, Milan, Italy ECSCW'93*. Springer. 1993, pp. 77–92.

Bennett Moses, Lyria. "Regulating in the face of sociotechnical change". In: *The Oxford handbook of law, regulation and technology*. Oxford University Press, 2017, pp. 573–596.

Benoît-Rohmer, Florence, Heinrich Klebes, et al. *Council of Europe law: towards a pan-European legal area*. Council of Europe Publishing, 2005. ISBN: 9789287155948.

Bernstein, Gaia. "When new technologies are still new: windows of opportunity for privacy protection". In: *Vill. L. Rev.* 51 (2006), pp. 921–950.

Betti, Emilio. Interpretazione della legge e degli atti giuridici. Giuffrè Editore, 1949.

Biasiotti, Mariangela, Enrico Francesconi, Monica Palmirani, Giovanni Sartor, and Fabio Vitali. "Legal informatics and management of legislative documents". In: *Global Center for ICT in Parliament Working Paper* 2 (2008).

Bieber, Eric J., Frank M. Richards, and James M. Walker. *Implementing an electronic health record system*. Springer, 2005. ISBN: 9781846281150.

Bignami, Francesca. "Formal versus Functional Method in Comparative Constitutional Law". In: *Osgoode Hall Law Journal* 53 (2 2016), pp. 442–471.

Bincoletto, Giorgia. "A Data Protection by Design Model for Privacy Management in Electronic Health Records". In: *Privacy Technologies and Policy, 7th Annual Privacy Forum, APF 2019, Rome, Italy, June 13–14, 2019*. Ed. by Maurizio Naldi, Giuseppe F. Italiano, Kai Rannenberg, Manel Medina, and Athena Bourka. Lecture Notes in Computer Science. Springer International Publishing, 2019, pp. 161–181. ISBN: 9783030217525.

— "Data protection issues in cross-border interoperability of Electronic Health Record systems within the European Union". In: *Data & Policy* 2 (2020), pp. 1–11. DOI: 10. 1017/dap.2020.2.

— "European Union – EDPB Guidelines 4/2019 on Data Protection by Design and by Default". In: *Eur. Data Prot. L. Rev.* 6 (4 2020), pp. 574–579.

— "Italy – Italian DPA Against Vodafone: History of a C12 million Fine". In: *Eur. Data Prot. L. Rev.* 6 (4 2020), pp. 554–559.

— "Italy – Supreme Court of Cassation on Automated Decision Making: Invalid Consent if an Algorithm is Not Trasparent". In *Eur. Data Prot. L. Rev.* 7 (2 2021), pp. 248–253.

— "Italy – Italian DPA Balancing Data Protection and Freedom of Expression: Essentiality and Fairness as key principles". In *Eur. Data Prot. L. Rev.* 7 (1 2021), pp. 115–119.

— La privacy by design. Un'analisi comparata nell'era digitale. Privacy e innovazione. Aracne editrice, 2019. ISBN: 9788825524000.

Bioethics (DH-BIO) Committee. DH-BIO Statement on human rights considerations relevant to the COVID-19 pandemic. DH-BIO/INF (2020) 2. 14 April 2020, 2020.

Blackstone, William. *Commentaries on the laws of England. Book 1: Of the rights of persons. 1765–1769*. Chicago, Ill.: University of Chicago Press, 1979. ISBN: 0226055361.

Blobel, Bernd. "Interoperable EHR Systems–Challenges, Standards and Solutions". In: *European Journal for Biomedical Informatics* 14.2 (2018), pp. 10–19.

Blobel, Bernd, DM. Lopez, and C. Gonzalez. "Patient privacy and security concerns on big data for personalized medicine". In: *Health and Technology* 6.1 (2016), pp. 75–81.

Bobbio, Norberto. *Studi per una teoria generale del diritto*. G. Giappichelli Editore, 1970.

— Teoria dell'ordinamento giuridico. G. Giappichelli Editore, 1960.

Bogdandy, Armin von and Bast Jürgen. *Principles of European Constitutional Law*. Hart Publishing, 2020. ISBN: 9781841138220.

Bolognini, Luca, Enrico Pelino, and Camilla Bistolfi. Il regolamento privacy europeo: commentario alla nuova disciplina europea sulla protezione dei dati, in vigore da maggio 2016. Giuffrè Editore, 2016. ISBN: 9788814166594.

Bongiovanni, Giorgio et al. *Handbook of legal reasoning and argumentation*. Springer, 2018. ISBN: 9789048194513.

Bonnici, Jeanne Pia Mifsud. "Exploring the non-absolute nature of the right to data protection". In: *International Review of Law, Computers & Technology* 28.2 (2014), pp. 131- 143.

Borgesius, Frederik Zuiderveen, Jonathan Gray, and Mireille van Eechoud. "Open data, privacy, and fair information principles: Towards a balancing framework". In: *Berkeley Technology Law Journal* 30.3 (2015), pp. 2073–2131.

Botrugno, Carlo. "Telemedicine in daily practice: Addressing legal challenges while waiting for an EU regulatory framework". In: *Health Policy and Technology* 7.2 (2018), pp. 131- 136.

Bradford, Anu. *The Brussels effect: How the European Union rules the world*. Oxford University Press, 2020. ISBN: 9780190088583.

Brasher, Elizabeth A. "Addressing the Failure of Anonymization: Guidance from the European Union's General Data Protection Regulation". In: *Colum. Bus. L. Rev.* (2018), pp. 209–253.

Bravo, Fabio. "Il consenso e le altre condizioni di liceità". In: *Il nuovo Regolamento europeo sulla privacy e sulla protezione dei dati personali*. Zanichelli, Torino, 2017, pp. 101–177. ISBN: 9788808521057.

— "Riflessioni critiche sulla natura della responsabilità da trattamento illecito di dati personali". In: *Persona e mercato dei dati. Riflessioni sul GDPR*. Wolters Kluwer, 2019, pp. 384–418. ISBN: 9788813370510.

Brighi, Raffaella and Maria Gabriella Virone. "Una tutela 'by design' del diritto alla salute. Prospettive di armonizzazione giuridica e tecnologica". In: *A Matter Of Design. Making Society Through Science And Technology* (2014), pp. 1211–1222.

Brownsword, Roger. “Law, liberty and technology”. In: *The Oxford handbook of law, regulation and technology*. Oxford University Press, 2017, pp. 41–68.

— Law, Technology and Society: Reimagining the Regulatory Environment. Routledge, 2019. ISBN: 9780815356462.

Burdon, Mark. *Digital Data Collection and Information Privacy Law*. Cambridge Intellectual Property and Information Law. Cambridge University Press, 2020. ISBN: 9781108283717.

Burk, Dan L. “Legal and technical standards in digital rights management technology”. In: *Fordham L. Rev.* 74 (2005), pp. 537–573.

Burk, Dan L. and Julie E. Cohen. “Fair use infrastructure for rights management systems”. In: *Harv. JL Tech* 15 (2001), pp. 41–83.

Burton, Cédric. “Chapter IV Controller and Processor (Articles 24–43). Article 32. Security of processing”. In: *The EU General Data Protection Regulation (GDPR): A Commentary*. Oxford University Press, 2020, pp. 630–639. ISBN: 9780198826491.

Büschel, Isabell, Rostane Mehdi, Anne Cammilleri, Yousri Marzouki, and Bernice Elger. “Protecting human health and security in digital Europe: how to deal with the “privacy paradox”?” In: *Science and engineering ethics* 20.3 (2014), pp. 639–658.

Bygrave, Lee A. “Data protection by design and by default: deciphering the EU’s legislative requirements”. In: *Oslo Law Review* 4.2 (2017), pp. 105–120.

Bygrave, Lee A. “Hardwiring privacy”. In: *The Oxford Handbook of the Law and Regulation of Technology*. Ed. by Eloise Scotford and Karen Yeung. Oxford: Oxford University Press, 2017. Chap. 31, pp. 754–775. ISBN: 9780199680832.

— “Chapter III Rights of the Data Subject (Articles 12–23). Article 22. Right to automated individual decision-making, including profiling”. In: *The EU General Data Protection Regulation (GDPR): A Commentary*. Oxford University Press, 2020, pp. 522–542. ISBN: 9780198826491.

— “Chapter IV Controller and Processor (Articles 24–43). Article 25. Data protection by design and by default”. In: *The EU General Data Protection Regulation (GDPR): A Commentary*. Oxford University Press, 2020, pp. 571–581. ISBN: 9780198826491.

— Data privacy law: an international perspective. Vol. 63. Oxford University Press, 2014. ISBN: 9780199675555.

— “Privacy and data protection in an international perspective”. In: *Scandinavian studies in law* 56.8 (2010), pp. 165–200.

— “The ‘Strasbourg Effect’ in Data Protection: Its Logic, Mechanics and Prospects in Light of the ‘Brussels Effect’”. In: *University of Oslo Faculty of Law Research Paper No. 2020–14* (2020).

Bygrave, Lee A. and Luca Tosoni. “Chapter I General principles (Articles 1–4). Article 4(1). Personal Data”. In: *The EU General Data Protection Regulation (GDPR): A Commentary*. Oxford University Press, 2020, pp. 103–114. ISBN: 9780198826491.

— "Chapter I General principles (Articles 1–4). Article 4(15). Data concerning health". In: *The EU General Data Protection Regulation (GDPR): A Commentary*. Oxford University Press, 2020, pp. 215–224. ISBN: 9780198826491.

Cadwalladr, Carole and Emma Graham-Harrison. "Revealed: 50 million Facebook profiles harvested for Cambridge Analytica in major data breach". In: *The Guardian* 17 (2018), p. 22.

Caggia, Fausto. "Il trattamento dei dati sulla salute, con particolare riferimento all'ambito sanitario". In: *Il codice del trattamento dei dati personali. Giappichelli, Torino* 8 (2007), p. 405.

Califano, Licia. "Fascicolo sanitario elettronico (Fse) e dossier sanitario. Il contributo del Garante privacy al bilanciamento tra diritto alla salute e diritto alla protezione dei dati personali". In: *Sanità Pubblica e Privata* (3 2015), pp. 141–159.

— "The Electronic Health Record (EHR): Legal framework and issues about personal data protection". In: *Pharmaceuticals Policy and Law* 19.3 - 4 (2017), pp. 141–159.

Callahan, Daniel. "The WHO definition of 'health'". In: *Hastings Center Studies* (1973), pp. 77–87.

Calo, Ryan and Alex Rosenblat. "The taking economy: Uber, information, and power". In: *Colum. L. Rev.* 117 (2017), pp. 1623–1690.

Calvillo-Arbizu, Jorge, Isabel Román-Martínez, and Laura M. Roa-Romero. "Standardized access control mechanisms for protecting ISO 13606-based electronic health record systems". In: *IEEE-EMBS International Conference on Biomedical and Health Informatics (BHI)*. IEEE. 2014, pp. 539–542.

Calzolaio, Simone. "*Privacy by design*. Principi, dinamiche, ambizioni del nuovo Reg. Ue 2016/679". In: *Federalismi.it* 24 (2017), pp. 1–21.

— "*Privacy by design*. Principi, dinamiche, ambizioni del nuovo Reg. Ue 2016/679". In: *Federalismi.it* 24 (2017), pp. 1–21.

Cannataci, Joseph A. *Preliminary evaluation of the privacy dimensions of the coronavirus disease (COVID-19) pandemic*. A/75/147. Special Rapporteur of the Human Rights Council on the right to privacy, 2020.

Carey, Peter. *Data protection: a practical guide to UK and EU law*. Oxford University Press, 2018. ISBN: 9780198815419.

Carro, Giuseppe, Sarah Masato, and Massimiliano Domenico Parla. *La privacy nella sanità*. Giuffrè, Torino, 2018. ISBN: 9788814225215.

Caso, Roberto. *Digital Rights Management. Il commercio delle informazioni digitali tra contratto e diritto d'autore*. Cedam, 2004. ISBN: 8813252536.

— *Digital Rights Management. Il commercio delle informazioni digitali tra contratto e diritto d'autore*. Trento: Digital Reprint. <eprints.biblio.unitn.it/4375/>, 2006.

Caso, Roberto (ed.) *Digital Rights Management. Problemi teorici e prospettive applicative. Atti del convegno tenuto presso la Facoltà di Giurisprudenza di Trento il 21 e 22 marzo 2007*. Quaderni del Dipartimento di Scienze Giuridiche, n. 70 dell'Università di Trento, 2008. ISBN: 9788884432193.

Casonato, Carlo. "Health at the time of covid-19: tyrannical, denied, unequal health". In: paper presented at the conference Biolaw, Globalization and Pandemic. Challenges in the context of COVID-19 (2020), pp. 1–7.

Cate, Fred. "Protecting privacy in health research: the limits of individual choice". In: *Calif. L. Rev.* 98 (2010), pp. 1765–1804.

— "The Failure of Fair Information Practice Principles". In: *Consumer Protection in the Age of the Information Economy*. 2006, pp. 343–379. ISBN: 9780754680468.

Cavallaro, Maria Cristina and Guido Smorto. "Decisione pubblica e responsabilità dell'amministrazione nella società dell'algoritmo". In: *Federalismi.it* 16 (2019), pp. 2–22.

Cavoukian, Ann. "Evolving FIPPs: proactive approaches to privacy, not privacy paternalism". In: *Reforming European Data Protection Law*. Springer, 2015, pp. 293–309. ISBN: 9789401793858.

— Global privacy and security, by design: Turning the "privacy vs. security" paradigm on its head. 2017.

— "Operationalizing privacy by design: A guide to implementing strong privacy practices". In: *Information and privacy commissioner of Ontario, Canada* (2012).

— "Privacy by design". In: Information and privacy commissioner of Ontario, Canada (2009).

— *Privacy by design: From rhetoric to reality*. Information and privacy commissioner of Ontario, Canada, 2014.

— "Privacy by design: leadership, methods, and results". In: *European Data Protection: Coming of Age*. Springer, 2013, pp. 175–202. ISBN: 9789400751705.

Cavoukian, Ann et al. "Privacy by design: The 7 foundational principles". In: *Information and privacy commissioner of Ontario, Canada* 5 (2009).

Cavoukian, Ann. "Privacy by design: the definitive workshop. A foreword by Ann Cavoukian, Ph. D". In: *Identity in the Information Society* 3.2 (2010), pp. 247–251.

— "Understanding How to Implement Privacy by Design, One Step at a Time". In: *IEEE Consumer Electronics Magazine* 9.2 (2020), pp. 78–82.

Cavoukian, Ann and Michelle Chibba. "Privacy seals in the USA, Europe, Japan, Canada, India and Australia". In: *Privacy and data protection seals*. Springer, 2018, pp. 59–82. ISBN: 9789462652286.

Cavoukian, Ann and Marilyn Prosch. The roadmap for privacy by design in mobile communications: A practical tool for developers, service providers, and users. Information and Privacy Commissioner of Ontario, 2011.

Cavoukian, Ann, Stuart Shapiro, and R. Jason Cronk. "Privacy engineering: Proactively embedding privacy, by design". In: *Office of the Information and Privacy Commissioner* (2014).

Cavoukian, Ann et al. "Biometric encryption: creating a privacy-preserving 'Watch-List' facial recognition system". In: *Security and privacy in biometrics*. Springer, 2013, pp. 215- 238. ISBN: 9781447152309.

Chaum, David. "Showing credentials without identification". In: *Workshop on the Theory and Application of Cryptographic Techniques*. Springer. 1985, pp. 241–244.

— "Untraceable electronic mail, return addresses, and digital pseudonyms". In: *Communications of the ACM* 24.2 (1981), pp. 84–90.

Cimino, James J. and Edward H. Shortliffe. *Biomedical Informatics: Computer Applications in Health Care and Biomedicine*. Springer-Verlag, 2006. ISBN: 9780387289861.

Cohen, I. Glenn and Harry S. Graver. "Cops, docs, and code: a dialogue between big data in health care and predictive policing". In: *UCDL Rev.* 51 (2017), p. 437.

Cohen, Julie E. "Examined lives: Informational privacy and the subject as object". In: *Stan. L. Rev.* 52 (1999), pp. 1373–1437.

— "DRM and Privacy". In: *Berkeley Tech. LJ* 18 (2003), pp. 575–617.

Colesky, Michael, Jaap-Henk Hoepman, and Christiaan Hillen. "A critical analysis of privacy design strategies". In: *2016 IEEE Security and Privacy Workshops (SPW)*. IEEE. 2016, pp. 33–40.

Comandé, Giovanni. "Ricerca in sanità e data protection un puzzle... risolvibile". In: *Rivista Italiana di Medicina Legale (e del Diritto in campo sanitario)* 1 (2019), pp. 189–207.

— "Unfolding the legal component of trustworthy AI: a must to avoid ethics washing". In: *Annuario di Diritto Comparato e di Studi Legislativi* XI (2020), pp. 39–62.

Comandé, Giovanni and Denise Amram. "La violazione della privacy in sanità, tra diritto civile e diritto penale". In: *Itinerari di medicina legale e delle responsabilità in campo sanitario*. G. Giappichelli Editore, 2021. ISBN: 9788892132634.

Comandé, Giovanni, Denise Amram, and Gianclaudio Malgieri. "The democracy of emergency at the time of the coronavirus: the virtues of privacy". In: *Opinio Juris in comparatione, preprint* 1 (2020), pp. 106–121.

Comandé, Giovanni, Luca Nocco, and Violette Peigné. "An empirical study of healthcare providers and patients' perceptions of electronic health records". In: *Computers in Biology and Medicine* 59 (2015), pp. 194–201.

— "Il fascicolo sanitario elettronico: uno studio interdisciplinare". In: *Rivista Italiana di Medicina Legale (e del Diritto in campo sanitario)* 1 (2012), pp. 106–121.

Comandé, Giovanni and Giulia Schneider. "Regulatory Challenges of Data Mining Practices: The Case of the Never-ending Lifecycles of 'Health Data'". In: *European Journal of Health Law* 25.3 (2018), pp. 284–307.

Commission Nationale de l'Informatique et des Libertés, CNIL. *Deliberation N°. 2020- 046 of 24 April 2020 delivering an opinion on a proposed mobile application called 'StopCovid'*. CNIL, 2020.

— *La forme des choix. Données personnelles, design et frictions désirables*. Cahier n. 6. 2019.

— *Privacy Impact Assessment (PIA). Knowledge basis*. 2018.

— *Privacy Impact Assessment (PIA). Methodology*. 2018.

— *Privacy Impact Assessment (PIA). Templates*. 2018.

— *Référentiel des durées de conservation dans le domaine de la santé hors recherche*. 2020.

— *Référentiel relatif aux traitement de données personnelles pour les cabinets médicaux et paramédicaux*. 2020.

— *The CNIL's Guide on Security of personal data*. 2018.

Conley, Ed and Matthias Pocs. "GDPR Compliance Challenges for Interoperable Health Information Exchanges (HIEs) and Trustworthy Research Environments (TREs)". In: *European Journal of Biomedical Informatics* 14.3 (2018), pp. 48–61.

Cooley, Thomas M. *Law of Torts*. Callaghan & Company, 1888.

Costa, Luiz and Yves Poullet. "Privacy and the regulation of 2012". In: *Computer Law & Security Review* 28.3 (2012), pp. 254–262.

Council of Europe, CoE. *Digital solutions to fight COVID-19. 2020 Data Protection Report*. Council of Europe. October 2020, 2020.

— Guidelines on artificial intelligence and data protection. Council of Europe, 2019.

Council of the European Union, EU Council. Council Conclusions on Safe and efficient healthcare through eHealth. 2980th Employment, Social Policy, Health and Consumer Affairs Council meeting. Council of the European Union. Brussels: 1.12.2009, 2009.

Council of the European Union, EU Council. *Council conclusions on Health in the Digital Society — making progress in data-driven innovation in the field of health*. Council conclusions 52017XG1221(01). Brussels, Belgium: Council of the European Union, Dec. 21, 2017.

Cowie, Martin R. et al. "e-Health: a position statement of the European Society of Cardiology". In: *European heart journal* 37.1 (2016), pp. 63–66.

Cuffaro, Vincenzo, Roberto D'Orazio, and Vincenzo Ricciuto. *I dati personali nel diritto europeo*. G. Giappichelli Editore, Torino, 2019. ISBN: 9788892112742.

Custers, Bart, Francien Dechesne, Alan M. Sears, Tommaso Tani, and Simone Van der Hof. "A comparison of data protection legislation and policies across the EU". In: *Computer Law & Security Review* 34.2 (2018), pp. 234–243.

D'Acquisto, Giuseppe and Maurizio Naldi. *Big data e privacy by design. Anonimizzazione Pseudonimizzazione Sicurezza*. Torino: G. Giappichelli Editore, 2017. ISBN: 9788892106291.

D'Acquisto, Giuseppe, Maurizio Naldi, Raffaele Bifulco, Oreste Pollicino, and Bassani Marco. *Intelligenza artificiale, protezione dei dati personali e regolazione*. Torino: G. Giappichelli Editore, 2018. ISBN: 9788892112575.

D'Acquisto, Giuseppe and Georgia Panagopoulou. *Guidelines for SMEs on the security of personal data processing*. European Union Agency for Network and Information Security, 2016.

D'Acquisto, Giuseppe *et al.* Privacy by design in big data: an overview of privacy enhancing technologies in the era of big data analytics. European Union Agency for Network and Information Security, 2015.

Da̧browska-Kłosin´ska, Patrycja. "Tracing individuals under the EU regime on serious, crossborder health threats: An appraisal of the system of personal data protection". In: *European Journal of Risk Regulation* 8.4 (2017), pp. 700–722.

Danezis, George and Seda Gürses. "A critical review of 10 years of privacy technology". In: *Proceedings of surveillance cultures: a global surveillance society* (2010), pp. 1–16.

Danezis, George *et al. Privacy and Data Protection by design – from policy to engineering*. European Union Agency for Network and Information Security, 2014.

Danzon, Patricia and Michael Furukawa. "e-Health: effects of the Internet on competition and productivity in health care". In: *The economic payoff from the internet revolution*. Brookings Institution Press, 2001, pp. 209–244. ISBN: 9780815700654.

Data MIT Critical and M. Komorowski. *Secondary analysis of electronic health records*. Springer, 2016. ISBN: 9783319437422.

Davies, Simon G. "Re-engineering the right to privacy: how privacy has been transformed from a right to a commodity". In: *Technology and privacy: The new landscape* 143 (1997), pp. 143–166.

Davis, Janet and Lisa P. Nathan. "Value sensitive design: Applications, adaptations, and critiques". In: *Handbook of Ethics, Values, and Technological Design: Sources, Theory, Values and Application Domains*. Springer, 2015, pp. 11–40. ISBN: 9789400769700.

De Hert, Paul. "Data protection as bundles of principles, general rights, concrete subjective rights and rules: piercing the veil of stability surrounding the principles of data protection". In: *Eur. Data Prot. L. Rev.* 3 (2017), pp. 160–179.

— "The EU data protection reform and the (forgotten) use of criminal sanctions". In: *International Data Privacy Law* 4.4 (2014), pp. 262–268.

De Hert, Paul and Vagelis Papakonstantinou. "The new General Data Protection Regulation: Still a sound system for the protection of individuals?" In: *Computer law & security review* 32.2 (2016), pp. 179–194.

De Hert, Paul, Vagelis Papakonstantinou, Gianclaudio Malgieri, Laurent Beslay, and Ignacio Sanchez. "The right to data portability in the GDPR: Towards user-centric interoperability of digital services". In: *Computer Law & Security Review* 34.2 (2018), pp. 193–203.

De Rada, Dimitri. "La responsabilità civile in caso di mancato rispetto del GDPR. Privacy by default, privacy by design e accountability nell'ottica del Diritto Privato". In: *Federalismi.it* 23 (2019), pp. 1–16.

De Terwangne, Cécile. "Chapter II Principles (Articles 5–11). Article 5. Principles relating to processing of personal data". In: *The EU General Data Protection Regulation (GDPR): A Commentary*. Oxford University Press, 2020, pp. 309–397. ISBN: 9780198826491.

— "Chapter III Rights of the Data Subject (Articles 12–23). Article 16. Right to rectification". In: *The EU General Data Protection Regulation (GDPR): A Commentary*. Oxford University Press, 2020, pp. 469–474. ISBN: 9780198826491.

De Vanna, Francesco. "The Construction of a Normative Framework for Technology-Driven Innovations: A Legal Theory Perspective". In: *Use and Misuse of New Technologies*. Springer, 2019, pp. 185–208. ISBN: 9783030056483.

DeBellis, Michael and Christine Haapala. “User-centric software engineering”. In: *IEEE Expert* 10.1 (1995), pp. 34–41.

Degoulet, P., D. Luna, and F.G.B. de Quiros. “Clinical information systems”. In: *Global Health Informatics*. Elsevier, 2017, pp. 129–151. ISBN: 9780128045916.

Del Federico, Caterina and Anna Rita Popoli. “Le definizioni”. In: *La protezione dei dati personali in Italia. Regolamento UE n. 2016/679 e d.lgs. 10 agosto 2018, n. 101*. Zanichelli, Torino, 2019, pp. 63–88. ISBN: 9788808820433.

Demetzou, Katerina. “Data Protection Impact Assessment: A tool for accountability and the unclarified concept of ‘high risk’ in the General Data Protection Regulation”. In: *Computer Law & Security Review* 35.6 (2019), p. 105342.

Demotes-Mainard, Jacques et al. “How the new European data protection regulation affects clinical research and recommendations?” In: *Therapie* 74.1 (2019), pp. 31–42.

Demuynck, Liesje and Bart De Decker. “Privacy-preserving electronic health records”. In: *IFIP International Conference on Communications and Multimedia Security*. Springer. 2005, pp. 150–159.

Deng, Mina, Kim Wuyts, Riccardo Scandariato, Bart Preneel, and Wouter Joosen. “A privacy threat analysis framework: supporting the elicitation and fulfilment of privacy requirements”. In: *Requirements Engineering* 16.1 (2011), pp. 3–32.

Denise, Amram. “Ricerca e protezione dei dati personali concernenti la salute: il tentativo di armonizzazione al livello europeo post GDPR e le interpretazioni offerte dai sistemi irlandese, belga, spagnolo e italiano”. In: *Rivista Italiana di Medicina Legale (e del Diritto in campo sanitario)* 1 (2019), pp. 211–223.

DeNoncour, Matthew. *Healthcare technology regulation in the US*. In: *Healthtech, Law and Regulation.* Elgar Commercial Law and Practice, 2020 pp. 80–113. ISBN: 9781839104893.

Dennedy, Michelle, Jonathan Fox, and Tom Finneran. *The privacy engineer's manifesto: getting from policy to code to QA to value*. Apress, 2014. ISBN: 9781430263562.

Devillier, Nathalie. “Les dispositions de la loi de modernisation de notre système de santé relatives aux données de santé”. In: *Journal International de Bioéthique et d'Éthique des Sciences* 28.3 (2017), pp. 57–123.

DeVries, Will Thomas. “Protecting privacy in the digital age”. In: *Berkeley Tech. LJ* 18 (2003), pp. 283–311.

DG Health and Food Security, *Assessment of the EU Member States' rules on health data in the light of the GDPR*. European Commission. Luxembourg: Publications Office of the European Union, 2021.

Di Federico, Giacomo. “Access to Healthcare in the European Union: Are EU Patients (Effectively) Protected Against Discriminatory Practices?” In: *The Principle of Equality in EU Law*. Springer, 2017, pp. 229–253. ISBN: 9783319661377.

Di Federico, Giacomo and Stefania Negri. *Unione Europea e Salute. Principi, azioni, diritti e sicurezza*. Cedam Wolters Kluwer, 2020. ISBN: 9788813370886.

Di Iorio, Concetta Tania and Fabrizio Carinci. "Privacy and health care information systems: where is the balance?" In: *eHealth: Legal, Ethical and Governance Challenges*. Springer, 2013, pp. 77–105. ISBN: 9783642224744.

Diamantopoulou, Vasiliki, Christos Kalloniatis, Stefanos Gritzalis, and Haralambos Mouratidis. "Supporting privacy by design using privacy process patterns". In: *IFIP International Conference on ICT Systems Security and Privacy Protection*. Springer. 2017, pp. 491–505.

Diciotti, Enrico. *Interpretazione della legge e discorso razionale*. G. Giappichelli Editore, 1999.

Diffie, Whitfield and Susan Landau. *Privacy on the line: The politics of wiretapping and encryption*. Updated and expanded edition. The MIT Press, 2007. ISBN: 9780262042406.

Diver, Laurence and Burkhard Schafer. "Opening the black box: Petri nets and Privacy by Design". In: *International Review of Law, Computers & Technology* 31.1 (2017), pp. 68–90.

Docksey, Christopher. "Chapter IV Controller and Processor (Articles 24–43). Article 24. Responsibility of the controller". In: *The EU General Data Protection Regulation (GDPR): A Commentary*. Oxford University Press, 2020, pp. 555–570. ISBN: 9780198826491.

— "Four fundamental rights: finding the balance". In: *International Data Privacy Law* 6.3 (2016), pp. 195–209.

Domingo-Ferrer, Josep and Alberto Blanco-Justicia. "Privacy-Preserving Technologies". In: *The Ethics of Cybersecurity*. Springer, Cham, 2020, pp. 279–297.

Douglass, Bruce Powel. *Agile Systems Engineering*. Online version. Morgan Kaufmann, 2016. ISBN: 9780128023495.

Douville, Thibault. "Les variations du droit au déréférencement, note sous CJUE 24 sept. 2019 [2 arrêt]". In: *Recueil Dalloz* 7854 (9 2020), pp. 515–522.

Ducato, Rossana. "Data protection, scientific research, and the role of information". In: *Computer Law & Security Review* 37 (2020), p. 105412.

— "*Database* genetici, biobanche e "Health Information Technologies"". In: *Il diritto dell'era digitale*. Il Mulino, Bologna, 2016, pp. 305–320. ISBN: 9788815266170.

Dumortier, Jos and Griet Verhenneman. "Legal regulation of electronic health records: a comparative analysis of Europe and the US". In: *eHealth: Legal, Ethical and Governance Challenges*. Springer, 2013, pp. 25–56. ISBN: 9783642224744.

— "Legal regulations on electronic health records: a prerequisite or an unavoidable by-product? – The legal aspects of electronic health records in Europe and the US analysed". In: *ICRI Research Paper, Interdisciplinary Centre for Law and ICT, K.U. Leuven* 5 (2011).

Duquenoy, Penny, Nermeen Magdi Mekawie, and Mark Springett. "Patients, trust and ethics in information privacy in eHealth". In: *eHealth: Legal, Ethical and Governance Challenges*. Springer, 2013, pp. 275–295. ISBN: 9783642224744.

Durante, Massimo. *Potere computazionale. L'impatto delle ICT su diritto, società, sapere*. Meltemi Press, 2019. ISBN: 9788855190558.

Durante, Massimo and Ugo Pagallo. *Manuale di informatica giuridica e diritto delle nuove tecnologie*. Utet Giuridica, 2012. ISBN: 9788859807773.

Durst, Ludovica. "Il trattamento di categorie particolari di dati in ambito sanitario". In: Circolazione e protezione dei dati personali, tra libertà e regole del mercato. Commentario al Regolamento UE n. 2016/679 (GDPR) e al novellato D.lgs. n. 196/2003 (Codice Privacy). Giuffrè Francis Lefebvre, 2019, pp. 65–79. ISBN: 9788828809692.

Edmunds, Margo. "Governmental and legislative context of informatics". In: *Public health informatics and information systems*. Springer, 2014, pp. 47–66. ISBN: 9780387227450.

Edwards, Lilian, Michael Veale, Orla Lynskey, Carly Kind, and Rachel Coldicutt. "The Coronavirus (Safeguards) Bill 2020: Proposed protections for digital interventions and in relation to immunity certificates". In: *LawArXiv, pre-print* (2020).

eHealth Network. *eHealth Network Guidelines to EU Member States and the European Commission on an interoperable eco-system for digital health and investment programmes for a new/updated generation of digital infrastructure in Europe*. eHealth Network, 2019.

— *Guidelines on minimum/non-exhaustive patient summary dataset for electronic exchange in accordance with the cross-border Directive 2011/24/EU*. eHealth Network, 2013.

— *Interoperability guidelines for approved contact tracing mobile applications in the EU*. eHealth Network. Brussels, Belgium, 13 May 2020, 2020.

Elvy, Stacy-Ann. "Paying for privacy and the personal data economy". In: *Colum. L. Rev.* 117 (2017), pp. 1369–1460.

Epstein, Richard A. "Privacy and the Third Hand: Lessons from the Common Law of Reasonable Expectations". In: *Berkeley Tech. LJ* 24 (2009), pp. 1199–1227.

Estler, Hans-Christian, Martin Nordio, Carlo A. Furia, Bertrand Meyer, and Johannes Schneider. "Agile vs. structured distributed software development: A case study". In: *Empirical Software Engineering* 19.5 (2014), pp. 1197–1224.

ETSI. *ETSI TR 103 456 V1.1.1 (2017–10) Implementation of the Network and Information Security (NIS) Directive*. Tech. rep. ETSI/CYBER, 2017.

European Commission, EC. *Annex to the Commission Recommendation on a European Electronic Health Record exchange format*. European Commission. Brussels: COM (2019) 800 final, 2019.

— *Commission Implementing Decision 2019/1765 of 22 October 2019 providing the rules for the establishment, the management and the functioning of the network of national authorities responsible for eHealth, and repealing Implementing Decision 2011/890/EU (notified under document C (2019) 7460)*. European Commission. Brussels: COM (2019), 7460 O.J. L. 270, 24.10.2019. 2019.

— *Commission Recommendation (EU) 2019/243 of 6 February 2019 on a European Electronic Health Record exchange format*. European Commission. Brussels: COM (2019) 800 final, 2019.

— *Commission Recommendation (EU) 2020/518 of 8 April 2020 on a common Union toolbox for the use of technology and data to combat and exit from the COVID-19 crisis, in particular concerning mobile applications and the use of anonymised mobility data*. L 114/7. 14 April 2020, 2020.

— *Commission Staff Working document accompanying the document Communication from the Commission to the European Parliament, the Council, the European Economic and Social Committee and the Committee of the Regions on enabling the digital transformation of health and care in the Digital Single Market*. Brussels: SWD (2018) 126 final. 2018.

— *Communication for the Commission Guidance on Apps supporting the fight against COVID 19 pandemic in relation to data protection*. 2020/C 124 I/01), 2020.

— *Communication from the Commission to the European Parliament and the Council on Promoting Data Protection by Privacy Enhancing Technologies (PETs)*. European Commission. COM(2007) 228 final, 2007.

— *Communication from the Commission to the European Parliament, the Council, the European Economic and Social Committee and the Committee of the Regions on enabling the digital transformation of health and care in the Digital Single Market; empowering citizens and building a healthier society*. European Commission. Brussels: COM (2018), 233 final. 2018.

— *Communication from the Commission to the European Parliament, the European Council, the Council, the European Economic and Social Committee and the Committee of the Regions A European strategy for data*. European Commission. Brussels, 19.2.2020 COM (2020) 66 final, 2020.

— *Communication from the Commission to the European Parliament, the European Council, the Council, the European Economic and Social Committee and the Committee of the Regions on enabling the digital transformation of health and care in the Digital Single Market; empowering citizens and building a healthier society*. European Commission. Brussels, 25.4.2018 COM (2018) 233 final, 2018.

— *Communication from the Commission to the Council, the European Parliament, the European Economic and Social Committee and the Committee of the Regions on e- Health – making healthcare better for European citizens: An action Plan for a European e-Health Area*. European Commission. Brussels: COM (2004), 356 final. 2004.

— "eHealth Action Plan 2012–2020. Innovative healthcare for the 21st century". In: Communication from the commission to the European parliament, the council, the European economic and social committee and the committee of the regions. Brussels, 6.12. 2012 (2012).

— *Green paper on mobile Health*. European Commission. COM(2014) 219 final, 2014.

— *New European Interoperability Framework, Promoting seamless services and data flows for European public administrations*. European Commission. Luxembourg: Publications Office of the European Union, 2017.

— *Proposal for a Council Decision authorising Member States to sign, in the interest of the European Union, the Protocol amending the Council of Europe Convention for the Protection of Individuals with regard to Automatic Processing of Personal Data (ETS No. 108)*. European Commission. Brussels: COM (2018), 449 final. 2018.

— *Recommendation of 2 July 2008 on cross-border interoperability of electronic health record systems*. European Commission. Brussels: COM (2008) 3282 final, 2008.

— *Report from the Commission to the European Parliament and the Council on the operation of Directive 2011/24/EU on the application of patients' rights in cross-border healthcare*. European Commission. COM/2018/651 final, 2018.

— *Road-map*. European Commission. Ref. Ares (2018) 5986687, 22.11.2018, 2018.

European Commission, EC and College of Europe. *Synopsis Report. Consultation: Transformation Health and Care in the Digital Single Market*. Publications Office of the European Union. 2018.

European Data Protection Board, EDPB. *Guidelines 03/2020 on the processing of data concerning health for the purpose of scientific research in the context of the COVID-19 outbreak*. European Data Protection Board, 2020.

— *Guidelines 04/2020 on the use of location data and contact tracing tools in the context of the COVID-19 outbreak*. EDPB. 21 April 2020, 2020.

— *Guidelines 1/2018 on certification and identifying certification criteria in accordance with Articles 42 and 43 of the Regulation*. European Data Protection Board. Version 3.0, 2019.

— *Guidelines 1/2019 on Codes of Conduct and Monitoring Bodies under Regulation 2016/679*. European Data Protection Board, 2019.

— *Guidelines 1/2021 on Examples regarding Data Breach Notification.* 14 January 2021. Version for public consultation. European Data Protection Board, 2021.

— *Guidelines 3/2018 on the territorial scope of the GDPR (Article 3)*. European Data Protection Board, 2019.

— *Guidelines 4/2019 on Article 25 Data Protection by Design and by Default.* 13 November 2019. Version for public consultation. European Data Protection Board, 2019.

— *Guidelines 4/2019 on Article 25 Data Protection by Design and by Default.* 20 October 2020. Version 2.0. European Data Protection Board, 2020.

European Data Protection Board, EDPB and EDPS European Data Protection Supervisor. *EDPB-EDPS Joint Opinion 1/2019 on the processing of patients' data and the role of the European Commission within the eHealth Digital Service Infrastructure (eHDSI)*. EDPB and EDPS Joint Opinion 1/2019, 2019.

European Data Protection Supervisor, EDPS. *Annual Report 2019*. 2019.

— *Assessing the necessity of measures that limit the fundamental right to the protection of personal data: a Toolkit*. European Data Protection Supervisor, 2017.

— *EDPS Guidelines on assessing the proportionality of measures that limit the fundamental rights to privacy and to the protection of personal data*. European Data Protection Supervisor, 2019.

— *Opinion 3/2018, EDPS Opinion on online manipulation and personal data*. 2018.

— *Opinion 3/2020 on the European strategy for data*. European Data Protection Supervisor, 2020.

— *Opinion 5/2018, Preliminary Opinion on privacy by design*. 2018.

— *Opinion of the European Data Protection Supervisor on Promoting Trust in the Information Society by Fostering Data Protection and Privacy*. 2010.

— *Preliminary Opinion 8/2020 on the European Health Data Space*. 2020.

European Union Council. *Council conclusions on Health in the Digital Society; making progress in data-driven innovation in the field of health*. Council of the European Union. 2017/C 440/05, 2017.

European Union Agency for Network & Information Security, ENISA. *Handbook on Security of Personal Data Processing*. European Union Agency for Network and Information Security, 2017.

European Union Agency for Network & Information Security, ENISA. *ICT security certification opportunities in the healthcare sector*. European Union Agency for Network and Information Security, 2018.

— *Recommendations on European Data Protection Certification*. European Union Agency for Network and Information Security, 2017.

— *Recommendations on shaping technology according to GDPR provision. An overview on data pseudonymisation*. European Union Agency for Network and Information Security, 2018.

— *Recommendations on shaping technology according to GDPR provision. Pseudonymisation techniques and best practices*. European Union Agency for Network and Information Security, 2019.

Everson, Eric. "Privacy by design: Taking ctrl of big data". In: *Clev. St. L. Rev. 65* (2016), pp. 27–43.

Expert Panel on effective ways of investing in Health, EXPH. *Assessing the impact of digital transformation of health services*. Luxembourg: Publications Office of the European Union. 2019.

Faccioli, Elisa and Marco Cassaro. "Il "GDPR" e la normativa di armonizzazione nazionale alla luce dei principi: "accountability" e "privacy by design"". In: *Il Diritto industriale* 6 (2018), pp. 561–566.

Faini, Fernanda. *Data society. Governo dei dati e tutela dei diritti nell'era digitale*. Giuffrè Francis Lefebvre, 2019. ISBN: 9788828811947.

Faralli, Carla, Raffaella Brighi, Michele Martoni, et al. *Strumenti, diritti, regole e nuove relazioni di cura: Il Paziente europeo protagonista nell'e-Health*. G. Giappichelli Editore, 2015. ISBN: 9788892100671.

Farina, Massimo. *Il cloud computing in ambito sanitario tra security e privacy*. Giuffrè Francis Lefebvre, 2019. ISBN: 9788828817550.

Fátima Marin, H. de and Connie Delaney. "Patient Engagement and Digital Health Communities". In: *Global Health Informatics*. Elsevier, 2017, pp. 218–231. ISBN: 9780128045916.

Federal Trade Commission, FTC. *Privacy Online: A Report to Congress*. FTC Report, 1998.

— *Protecting Consumer Privacy in an Era of Rapid Change, Recommendations for Businesses and Policymakers*. FTC Report, 2012.

Feldman, Dan and Eldar Haber. "Measuring and protecting privacy in the always-on era". In: *Berkeley Tech. LJ* 35 (2020), pp. 197–250.

Ferretti, Agata, Manuel Schneider, and Alessandro Blasimme. "Machine Learning in Medicine: Opening the New Data Protection Black Box". In: *Eur. Data Prot. L. Rev.* 4 (2018), pp. 320–332.

Feteris, Eveline T. *Fundamentals of legal argumentation*. Vol. 1. Springer, 2017. ISBN: 9789402411270.

Filipova, Olga and Rui Vilão. *Software Development From A to Z*. Springer, 2018. ISBN: 9781484239445.

Filippi, Claudio and Silvia Melchionna. "I trattamenti di dati in ambito sanitario". In: *Le nuove frontiere della privacy nelle tecnologie digitali*. Aracne Editrice, 2016, pp. 469-533. ISBN: 9788825507942.

Finocchiaro, Giusella. Il nuovo Regolamento europeo sulla privacy e sulla protezione dei dati personali. Zanichelli, Torino, 2017. ISBN: 9788808521057.

— "Il principio di *accountability*". In: *Giurisprudenza Italiana* 171.12 (2019), pp. 2778-2782.

— "Riflessioni su diritto e tecnica". In: *Dir. dell'informazione e dell'informatica* (4–5 2012), pp. 831–840.

Flanagan, Mary, Daniel C. Howe, and Helen Nissenbaum. "Embodying values in technology: Theory and practice". In: *Information technology and moral philosophy*. Cambridge University Press, 2008, pp. 322–353. ISBN: 9780511498725.

Flaumenhaft, Yakov and Ofir Ben-Assuli. "Personal health records, global policy and regulation review". In: *Health policy* 122.8 (2018), pp. 815–826.

Flear, Mark. *Governing Public Health: EU Law, Regulation and Biopolitics*. Bloomsbury Publishing, 2015. ISBN: 9781849462204.

Floridi, Luciano. *The fourth revolution: How the infosphere is reshaping human reality*. Oxford: Oxford University Press, 2014. ISBN: 9780199606726.

Foglia, Massimo. "Patients and Privacy: GDPR Compliance for Healthcare Organizations". In: *European Journal of Privacy Law & Technologies* (Special issue 2020), pp. 43–50.

Formiche, rivista n. 158. *Orwell 2020. Il virus della sorveglianza*. Rubettino, 2020. ISBN: 9788849863314.

Francis, Leslie P. "When patients interact with EHRs: problems of privacy and confidentiality". In: *Hous. J. Health L. & Pol'y* 12 (2011), pp. 171–199.

Friedman, Batya, Peter H. Kahn, and Alan Borning. "Value sensitive design and information systems". In: *The handbook of information and computer ethics* (2008), pp. 69–101.

Frosini, Tommaso Edoardo, Oreste Pollicino, Ernesto Apa, and Marco Bassini. *Diritti e libertà in Internet*. Le Monnier università, 2017. ISBN: 9788800746502.

Frosini, Vittorio. *Informatica diritto e società*. Giuffrè Editore, 1992. ISBN: 9788814039294.

Frosini, Vittorio and Donato Antonio Limone. *L'insegnamento dell'informatica giuridica*. Liguori, 1990. ISBN: 8820719169.

Galgano Zorzi, Nadia. "Le due anime del GDPR e la tutela del diritto alla *privacy*". In: *Persona e mercato dei dati. Riflessioni sul GDPR*. Wolters Kluwer, 2019, pp. 35–94. ISBN: 9788813370510.

Gellert, Raphaël. "Understanding data protection as risk regulation". In: *J. Int. Law* 18.11 (2015), pp. 3–16.

George, Carlisle, Diane Whitehouse, and Penny Duquenoy. *eHealth: legal, ethical and governance challenges*. Springer Science & Business Media, 2012. ISBN: 9783642224744.

Georgieva, Ludmila and Christopher Kuner. "Chapter II Principles (Articles 5–11). Article 9 Processing of special categories of personal data". In: *The EU General Data Protection Regulation (GDPR): A Commentary*. Oxford University Press, 2020, pp. 365–384. ISBN: 9780198826491.

Giakoumopoulos, Christos, G. Buttarelli, and M. O'Flamerty. *Handbook on European data protection law*. European Union Agency for Fundamental Rights and Council of Europe, Luxembourg, 2018. ISBN: 9789294919014.

Gilbert, Francoise. "Privacy of Medical Records – The Health Insurance Portability and Accountability Act of 1996 Creates a Framework for the Establishment of Security Standards and the Protection of Individually Identifiable Health Information". In: *N.D.L. Rev.* 73 (1997), pp. 93–108.

Giovanella, Federica. *Copyright and Information Privacy: Conflicting Rights in Balance*. Edward Elgar Publishing, 2017. ISBN: 9781785369353.

Giovannangeli, Selvaggia F. "L'informativa agli interessati e il consenso al trattamento". In: Circolazione e protezione dei dati personali, tra libertà e regole del mercato. Commentario al Regolamento UE n. 2016/679 (GDPR) e al novellato D.lgs. n. 196/2003 (Codice Privacy). Giuffrè Francis Lefebvre, 2019, pp. 100–141. ISBN: 9788828809692.

Girardi, Francesco, Gaetano De Gennaro, Lucio Colizzi, and Nicola Convertini. "Improving the Healthcare Effectiveness: The Possible Role of EHR, IoMT and Blockchain". In: *Electronics* 9.6 (2020), pp. 884–900.

Goldman, Eric. "An Introduction to the California Consumer Privacy Act (CCPA)". In: *Santa Clara Univ. Legal Studies Research Paper* (2020). SSRN: <papers.ssrn.com/sol3/papers. cfm?abstract_id=3211013&download=yes>.

Gonçalves-Ferreira, Duarte *et al.* "OpenEHR and general data protection regulation: evaluation of principles and requirements". In: *JMIR medical informatics* 7.1 (2019), e9845.

Gonzalez, Elena Gil, Paul De Hert, and Vagelis Papakonstantinou. "The proposed ePrivacy Regulation: the Commission's drafts and the Parliament's drafts at a crossroads?" In: *Data Protection and Privacy. Data Protection and Democracy*. Hart Publishers, 2020, pp. 267- 298. ISBN: 9781509932740.

González, Elena Gil and Paul de Hert. "Understanding the legal provisions that allow processing and profiling of personal data — an analysis of GDPR provisions and principles". In: *Era Forum*. Vol. 19. 4. Springer. 2019, pp. 597–621.

González Fuster, Gloria. “Chapter III Rights of the Data Subject (Articles 12–23). Article 18. Right to restriction of processing”. In: *The EU General Data Protection Regulation (GDPR): A Commentary*. Oxford University Press, 2020, pp. 485–491. ISBN: 9780198826491.

Gostin, Lawrence O., James G. Hodge Jr., and Lauren Marks. “The Nationalization of Health Information Privacy Protections”. In: *Tort & Insurance Law Journal* (2002), pp. 1113- 1138.

Graeme, Laurie. *Genetic privacy: a challenge to medico-legal norms*. Cambridge University Press, 2002. ISBN: 0521660270.

Granger, Marie-Pierre, Kristina Irion *et al.* “The Court of Justice and the Data Retention Directive in Digital Rights Ireland: telling off the EU legislator and teaching a lesson in privacy and data protection”. In: *European Law Review* 39.4 (2014), pp. 835–850.

Granieri, Massimiliano. “Il trattamento di categorie particolari di dati personali nel Reg. UE 2016/679”. In: *Le Nuove leggi civili commentate* 1 (2017), pp. 165–190.

Graziadei, Michele. “The functionalist heritage”. In: *Comparative Legal Studies: Traditions & Transitions*. Oxford University Press, 2019, pp. 100–127. ISBN: 9780511522260.

Greco, Laura. “Il trattamento dei dati sanitari”. In: *La protezione dei dati personali in Italia. Regolamento UE n. 2016/679 e d.lgs. 10 agosto 2018, n. 101*. Zanichelli, 2019, pp. 220–250. ISBN: 9788808820433.

Greco, Laura and Alessandro Mantelero. “Industria 4.0, robotica e privacy-by-design”. In: *Dir. informazione e informatica* 6 (2018), pp. 875–900.

Greenawalt, Kent. “Constitutional and statutory interpretation”. In: *The Oxford Handbook of Jurisprudence and Philosophy of Law*. 2002. ISBN: 9780199270972.

Greer, Scott L. “Resistance in European Union health care policy”. In: *The Routledge Handbook of European Public Policy*. Taylor & Francis Group, 2017, pp. 357–363. ISBN: 9781317404026.

Greer, Scott L. et al. *Everything you always wanted to know about European Union health policies but were afraid to ask*. World Health Organization. Regional Office for Europe, 2014. ISBN: 9789289050272.

Griffiths, Devin. “The comparative method and the history of the modern humanities”. In: *History of Humanities* 2.2 (2017), pp. 473–505.

Grimmelmann, James. “Regulation by software”. In: *Yale LJ* 114 (2004), pp. 1719–1758. Group, ISS Bioethics COVID-19 Working. *Data protection in COVID-19 emergency*. Rapporto ISS COVID-19 n. 42/2020, 2020.

Gstrein, Oskar Josef. “Right to be Forgotten: European Data Imperialism, National Privilege, or Universal Human Right?” In: *Review of European Administrative Law* (1 2020), pp. 125–152.

Guadarrama, Alexis. “Mind the Gap: Addressing Gaps in HIPAA Coverage in the Mobile Health Apps Industry”. In: *Hous. L. Rev.* 55 (2018), pp. 999–1025.

Guarda, Paolo. “"Ok Google, am I sick?": artificial intelligence, e-health, and data protection regulation”. In: *BioLaw Journal-Rivista di BioDiritto* 15.1 (2019), pp. 359–375.

— "Biobanks and electronic health records: open issues". In: *Comparative Issues in the Governance of Research Biobanks*. Springer, 2013, pp. 131–141. ISBN: 9783642331169.

— *Fascicolo sanitario elettronico e protezione dei dati personali*. Vol. 94. Università degli Studi di Trento, Quaderni del Dipartimento di Scienze Giuridiche, 2011. ISBN: 9788884433671.

— "I dati sanitari". In: *I dati personali nel diritto europeo*. G. Giappichelli Editore, Torino, 2019, pp. 591–626. ISBN: 9788892112742.

— "Telemedicine and Application Scenarios: Common Privacy and Security Requirements in the European Union Context". In: *Trento Law and Technology Research Group Research Paper n. 23* (2015).

Guarda, Paolo and Rossana Ducato. "From electronic health records to personal health records: emerging legal issues in the Italian regulation of e-health". In: *International Review of Law, Computers & Technology* 30.3 (2016), pp. 271–285.

Guarda, Paolo and Livia Petrucci. "Quando l'intelligenza artificiale parla: assistenti vocali e sanità digitale alla luce del nuovo regolamento generale in materia di protezione dei dati". In: *BioLaw Journal-Rivista di BioDiritto* 2 (2020), pp. 425–446.

Guarda, Paolo, Silvio Ranise, and Hari Siswantoro. "Security analysis and legal compliance checking for the design of privacy-friendly information systems". In: *Proceedings of the 22nd ACM on Symposium on Access Control Models and Technologies*. 2017, pp. 247- 254.

Guarda, Paolo and Nicola Zannone. "Towards the development of privacy-aware systems". In: *Information and Software Technology* 51.2 (2009), pp. 337–350.

Guasconi, Fabio, Georgia Panagopoulou, Giuseppe D'Acquisto, Athena Bourka, and Prokopios Drogkaris. *Reinforcing trust and security in the area of electronic communications and online services. Sketching the notion of "state-of-the-art" for SMEs in security of personal data processing*. European Union Agency for Network and Information Security, 2018.

Guastini, Riccardo. *Interpretare e argomentare*. Giuffrè Editore, 2011. ISBN: 9788814192951.

— "Principi costituzionali: identificazione, interpretazione, ponderazione, concretizzazione". In: *Dialoghi con Guido Alpa. Un volume offerto in occasione del suo LXXI compleanno*. 2018, pp. 313–324. ISBN: 9788832136050.

— *Problemi di teoria del diritto*. Il Mulino, 1980.

— *Saggi scettici sull'interpretazione*. G. Giappichelli Editore, 2017. ISBN: 9788892109629.

Gürses, Seda and Jose M. Del Alamo. "Privacy engineering: Shaping an emerging field of research and practice". In: *IEEE Security & Privacy* 14.2 (2016), pp. 40–46.

Gürses, Seda, Carmela Troncoso, and Claudia Diaz. "Engineering privacy by design". In: *Computers, Privacy & Data Protection. International Conference on Privacy and Data Protection* 14.3 (2011), pp. 1–25.

Gürses, Seda and Joris Van Hoboken. "Privacy after the agile turn". In: *The Cambridge Handbook of Consumer Privacy*. Cambridge University Press, 2018, pp. 579–601. ISBN: 9781316831960.

Gutwirth, Serge, Paul De Hert, and Laurent De Sutter. "The trouble with technology regulation: why Lessig's 'Optimal Mix' will not work". In: *Regulating technologies: Legal futures, regulatory frames and technological fixes*. Oxford University Press, 2008, pp. 193–218. ISBN: 9781841137889.

Hafiz, Munawar. "A collection of privacy design patterns". In: *Proceedings of the 2006 conference on Pattern languages of programs*. 2006, pp. 1–13.

— "A pattern language for developing privacy enhancing technologies". In: *Software: Practice and Experience* 43.7 (2013), pp. 769–787.

Hagan, Margaret. "Design Comes to the Law School". In: *Modernising Legal Education*. Cambridge University Press, 2020, pp. 109–125. ISBN: 9781108663311.

— "Legal Design as a Thing: A Theory of Change and a Set of Methods to Craft a Human- Centered Legal System". In: *Design Issues* 36.3 (2020), pp. 3–15.

Hall, Mark A. "Fiduciary Principles in Health Care". In: *The Oxford Handbook of Fiduciary Law*. Oxford University Press, 2019. ISBN: 9780190634100.

Hammond, W. Ed. "Standards for Global health information systems". In: *Global Health Informatics*. Elsevier, 2017, pp. 94–108.

Hansen, Marit, Meiko Jensen, and Martin Rost. "Protection goals for privacy engineering". In: *2015 IEEE Security and Privacy Workshops*. IEEE. 2015, pp. 159–166.

Hansen, Marit, Konstantinos Limniotis, Athena Bourka, and Prokopios Drogkaris. *Recommendations on shaping technology according to GDPR provision. Exploring the notion of data protection by default*. European Union Agency for Network and Information Security, 2018.

Hart, Herbert Lionel Adolphus. *The concept of law*. Oxford University Press, 1997.

Hart, Herbert Lionel Adolphus and Joseph Raz. *The concept of law*. Oxford University Press, 2012. ISBN: 9780199644704.

Hartley, Carolyn P. and Edward Douglass Jones. *EHR implementation: A step-by-step guide for the medical practice*. American Medical Association, 2012. ISBN: 9781603596305.

Hartzog, Woodrow. *Privacy's blueprint: the battle to control the design of new technologies*. Harvard University Press, 2018. ISBN: 9780674976009.

— "The Inadequate, Invaluable Fair Information Practices". In: *Md. L. Rev.* 76 (2016), pp. 952–982.

Hartzog, Woodrow and Frederic Stutzman. "Obscurity by design". In: *Wash. L. Rev.* 88 (2013), pp. 385–418.

Hayes, G. "The requirements of an electronic medical record to suit all clinical disciplines". In: *Yearbook of medical informatics* 6.01 (1997), pp. 75–82.

Herold, Rebecca and Kevin Beaver. *The practical guide to HIPAA privacy and security compliance*. CRC Press, 2015. ISBN: 9781439855591.

Herring, Jonathan. *Medical law and ethics*. Oxford University Press, 2016. ISBN: 9780198846956.

Herrnfeld, Hans-Holger. "Article 67 Data protection by design and by default". In: *European Public Prosecutor's Office*. Nomos, 2021, pp. 513–514. ISBN: 9783848748846.

Hert, Paul de and Vagelis Papakonstantinou. "The Council of Europe Data Protection Convention reform: Analysis of the new text and critical comment on its global ambition". In: *Computer Law & Security Review* 30.6 (2014), pp. 633–642.

Hervey, Tamara K. and Jean V. McHale. *European Union health law*. Cambridge University Press, 2015. ISBN: 9781107010499.

— *Health law and the European Union*. Cambridge University Press, 2004. ISBN: 9780511617553.

Hijmans, Hielke et al. *The European Union as guardian of internet privacy*. Springer, 2016. ISBN: 9783319340906.

Hildebrandt, Mireille. "Legal protection by design: objections and refutations". In: *Legisprudence* 5.2 (2011), pp. 223–248.

Hildebrandt, Mireille and Laura Tielemans. "Data protection by design and technology neutral law". In: *Computer Law & Security Review* 29.5 (2013), pp. 509–521.

Hiller, Janine, Matthew S. McMullen, Wade M. Chumney, and David L. Baumer. "Privacy and security in the implementation of health information technology (electronic health records): US and EU compared". In: *BUJ Sci. & Tech. L.* 17 (2011), pp. 1–39.

Hoda, Rashina, Norsaremah Salleh, and John Grundy. "The rise and evolution of agile software development". In: *IEEE software* 35.5 (2018), pp. 58–63.

Hoepman, Jaap-Henk. "Privacy design strategies". In: *IFIP International Information Security Conference*. Springer, 2014, pp. 446–459.

Hoepman, Jaap-Henk. "Privacy Design Strategies (The Little Blue Book)". In: *Radboud University Repository* (2018).

Hoffman, Robert R. and Gary Klein. "Explaining explanation, part 1: theoretical foundations". In: *IEEE Intelligent Systems* 32.3 (2017), pp. 68–73.

Hoffman, Sharona. "Employing e-health: the impact of electronic health records on the workplace". In: *Kan. JL & Pub. Pol'y* 19 (2009), pp. 409–432.

— "Medical Privacy and Security". In: *The Oxford Handbook of U.S. Health Law*. 2017, pp. 267–288. ISBN: 9780199366521.

Hoffman, Sharona and Andy Podgurski. "Balancing privacy, autonomy, and scientific needs in electronic health records research". In: *SMUL Rev.* 65 (2012), pp. 85–144.

— "E-Health hazards: provider liability and electronic health record systems". In: *Berkeley Tech. LJ* 24 (2009), pp. 1523–1582.

— "In sickness, health, and cyberspace: protecting the security of electronic private health information". In: *BCL. Rev.* 48 (2007), pp. 331–386.

Hooghiemstra, Theo. "Informational Self-Determination, Digital Health and New Features of Data Protection". In: *Eur. Data Prot. L. Rev.* 5 (2019), pp. 160–174.

Hsieh, Roger. “Improving HIPAA Enforcement and Protecting Patient Privacy in a Digital Healthcare Environment”. In: *Loy. U. Chi. LJ* 46 (2014), pp. 175–223.

Hulstijn, Joris and Brigitte Burgemeestre. “Design for the Values of Accountability and Transparency”. In: *Handbook of Ethics, Values, and Technological Design: Sources, Theory, Values and Application Domains*. Springer, 2015, pp. 303–333. ISBN: 9789400769700.

Husa, Jaakko. “Farewell to functionalism or methodological tolerance?” In: Rabels Zeitschrift für ausländisches und internationales Privatrecht/The Rabel Journal of Comparative and International Private Law H. 3 (2003), pp. 419–447.

— “Functional Method in Comparative Law–Much Ado About Nothing?” In: *European Property Law Journal* 2.1 (2013), pp. 4–21.

Hustinx, Peter. “Privacy by design: delivering the promises”. In: *Identity in the Information Society* 3.2 (2010), pp. 253–255.

Iakovidis, Ilias. “Towards personal health record: current situation, obstacles and trends in implementation of electronic healthcare record in Europe”. In: *International journal of medical informatics* 52.1 – 3 (1998), pp. 105–115.

IBM. “The 5 Vs of big data”. In: *IBM Watson Health Perspectives* (2016). IEEE, Standards University. *Standards Glossary*. IEEE, 2016.

Ionescu-Dima, Catalina. “Legal challenges regarding telemedicine services in the European Union”. In: *eHealth: Legal, Ethical and Governance Challenges*. Springer, 2013, pp. 107- 133. ISBN: 9783642224744.

Irti, Natalino and Emanuele Severino. “Le domande del giurista e le risposte del filosofo (un dialogo su diritto e tecnica)”. In: *Contratto e impresa* 16.2 (2000), pp. 665–679.

Isaak, Jim and Mina J. Hanna. “User data privacy: Facebook, Cambridge Analytica, and privacy protection”. In: *Computer* 51.8 (2018), pp. 56–59.

ISO. Health informatics — Electronic health record — Definition, scope and context. 20514:2005(en). Tech. rep. ISO/TR, 2005.

ISO/IEC 31010:2019 Risk management — Risk assessment techniques. Tech. rep. ISO/TC 262, 2019.

ISO 13606–1:2019 Health informatics — Electronic health record communication — Part 1: Reference model. Tech. rep. ISO/TC 215, 2019.

ISO 13606–2:2019 Health informatics — Electronic health record communication — Part 2: Archetype interchange specification. Tech. rep. ISO/TC 215, 2019.

ISO 13606–3:2019 Health informatics — Electronic health record communication — Part 3: Reference archetypes and term lists. Tech. rep. ISO/TC 215, 2019.

ISO 13606–4:2019 Health informatics — Electronic health record communication — Part 4: Security. Tech. rep. ISO/TC 215, 2019.

ISO 13606–5:2019 Health informatics — Electronic health record communication — Part 5: Interface specification. Tech. rep. ISO/TC 215, 2019.

ISO 17090–1:2013 Health informatics — Public key infrastructure — Part 1: Overview of digital certificate services. Tech. rep. ISO/TC 215, 2013.

ISO 18308:2011 Health informatics — Requirements for an electronic health record architecture. Tech. rep. ISO/TC 215, 2011.

ISO 22600–1:2014 Health informatics — Privilege management and access control — Part 1: Overview and policy management. Tech. rep. ISO/TC 215, 2014.

ISO 22600–2:2014 Health informatics — Privilege management and access control — Part 2: Formal models. Tech. rep. ISO/TC 215, 2014.

ISO 22600–3:2014 Health informatics — Privilege management and access control — Part 3: Implementations. Tech. rep. ISO/TC 215, 2014.

ISO 22857:2013 Health informatics — Guidelines on data protection to facilitate transborder flows of personal health data. Tech. rep. ISO/TC 215, 2013.

ISO 25237:2017 Health informatics — Pseudonymization. Tech. rep. ISO/TC 215, 2017.

ISO 27799:2016 Health informatics — Information security management in health using ISO/IEC 27002. Tech. rep. ISO/TC 215, 2016.

ISO 31000:2018 Risk management — Guidelines. Tech. rep. ISO/TC 262, 2018.

ISO/Guide 73:2009(en) Risk management — Vocabulary. Tech. rep. ISO/TMBG, 2009.

ISO/HL7 10781:2015 Health Informatics — HL7 Electronic Health Records-System Functional Model, Release 2 (EHR FM). Tech. rep. ISO/TC 215, 2015.

ISO/HL7 21731:2014 Health informatics — HL7 version 3 — Reference information model — Release 4. Tech. rep. ISO/TC 215, 2014.

ISO/HL7 27931:2009 Data Exchange Standards — Health Level Seven Version 2.5 — An application protocol for electronic data exchange in healthcare environments. Tech. rep. ISO/TC 215, 2009.

ISO/IEC 15408–1:2009 Information technology — Security techniques — Evaluation criteria for IT security — Part 1: Introduction and general model. Tech. rep. ISO/IEC, 2009.

ISO/IEC 24760–1:2019 IT Security and Privacy — A framework for identity management — Part 1: Terminology and concepts. Tech. rep. ISO/IEC, 2019.

ISO/IEC 27001:2013(en) Information technology — Security techniques — Information security management systems — Requirements. Tech. rep. ISO/IEC, 2013.

ISO. ISO/IEC 27002:2013 Information technology — Security techniques — Code of practice for information security controls. Tech. rep. ISO/IEC, 2013.

ISO/IEC 27005:2018(en) Information technology — Security techniques — Information security risk management. Tech. rep. ISO/IEC, 2018.

ISO/IEC 27035–1:2016 Information technology — Security techniques — Information security incident management — Part 1: Principles of incident management. Tech. rep. ISO/IEC, 2016.

ISO/IEC 27035–2:2016 Information technology — Security techniques — Information security incident management — Part 2: Guidelines to plan and prepare for incident response. Tech. rep. ISO/IEC, 2016.

ISO/IEC 27701:2019 Security techniques — Extension to ISO/IEC 27001 and ISO/IEC 27002 for privacy information management — Requirements and guidelines. Tech. rep. ISO/IEC, 2019.

ISO/IEC 29100:2011 Information technology — Security techniques — Privacy frame- work. Tech. rep. ISO/IEC, 2011.

ISO/IEC 29101:2018 Information technology — Security techniques — Privacy architecture framework. Tech. rep. ISO/IEC, 2018.

ISO/IEC 29134:2017 Information technology — Security techniques — Guidelines for privacy impact assessment. Tech. rep. ISO/IEC, 2017.

ISO/IEC TR 27550:2019 Information technology — Security techniques — Privacy engineering for system life cycle processes. Tech. rep. ISO/IEC, 2019.

ISO/IEC TS 19608:2018 Guidance for developing security and privacy functional requirements based on ISO/IEC 15408. Tech. rep. ISO/IEC, 2018.

ISO/IEC/IEEE International Standard-Systems and software engineering - System life cycle processes. Tech. rep. ISO/IEC/IEEE 15288 First edition 2015-05-15, 2015.

ISO/IEC/IEEE. ISO/IEC/IEEE 26515:2018 Systems and software engineering — Developing information for users in an agile environment. Tech. rep. ISO/IEC/ IEEE Second edition 2018-12, 2018.

ISO/TS. ISO/TS 17975:2015(en) Health informatics - Principles and data requirements for consent in the Collection, Use or Disclosure of personal health information. Tech. rep. ISO/TS, 2015.

Istepanian, Robert, Swamy Laxminarayan, and Constantinos S Pattichis. *M-health*. Springer, 2006. ISBN: 9780387265599.

IT Security Association Germany, TeleTrusT. *Guidelines "State of the Art"*. TeleTrusT and ENISA, 2020.

Jacobson, Peter D. "Medical records and HIPAA: is it too late to protect privacy". In: *Minn. L. Rev.* 86 (2001), pp. 1497–1514.

Jacques, Lauren Bair. "Electronic health records and respect for patient privacy: A prescription for compatibility". In: *Vand. J. Ent. & Tech. L.* 13 (2011), pp. 441–462.

Jasmontaite, Lina, Irene Kamara, Gabriela Zanfir-Fortuna, and Stefano Leucci. "Data protection by design and by default: Framing guiding principles into legal obligations in the GDPR". In: *Eur. Data Prot. L. Rev.* 4 (2018), pp. 168–189.

Jerker B. Svantesson, Dan. "Chapter I General Provisions (Articles 1–4). Article 3. Territorial scope". In: *The EU General Data Protection Regulation (GDPR): A Commentary*. Oxford University Press, 2020, pp. 74–99. ISBN: 9780198826491.

Joly, Yann and Bartha Maria Knoppers. *Routledge handbook of medical law and ethics*. Routledge, 2016. ISBN: 9781138204126.

Julien, Stephen P. "Electronic Health Records". In: *Public Health Informatics and Information Systems*. Springer, 2014, pp. 174–190. ISBN: 9780387227450.

Kalloniatis, Christos, Petros Belsis, and Stefanos Gritzalis. "A soft computing approach for privacy requirements engineering: The PriS framework". In: *Applied Soft Computing* 11.7 (2011), pp. 4341–4348.

Kalloniatis, Christos, Evangelia Kavakli, and Stefanos Gritzalis. "Addressing privacy requirements in system design: the PriS method". In: *Requirements Engineering* 13.3 (2008), pp. 241–255.

Kalra, Dipak, Thomas Beale, and Sam Heard. "The openEHR foundation". In: *Studies in health technology and informatics* 115 (2005), pp. 153–173.

Kamara, Irene. "Co-regulation in EU personal data protection: the case of technical standards and the privacy by design standardisation 'mandate'". In: *European journal of law and technology* 8.1 (2017), pp. 1–24.

Kamara, Irene and Paul De Hert. "Data protection certification in the EU: Possibilities, actors and building blocks in a reformed landscape". In: *Privacy and data protection seals*. Springer, 2018, pp. 7–34. ISBN: 9789462652286.

— "Understanding the balancing act behind the legitimate interest of the controller ground: A pragmatic approach". In: *Brussels Privacy Hub* 4.12 (2018), pp. 1–35.

Kamarinou, Dimitra, Christopher Millard, and Jatinder Singh. "Machine Learning with Personal Data: Profiling, Decisions and the EU General Data Protection Regulation". In: *Journal of Machine Learning Research* (2017).

Kaminski, Margot E. "The right to explanation, explained". In: *Berkeley Tech. LJ* 34 (2019), p. 189.

Katsh, Ethan and Orna Rabinovich-Einy. "The Internet of On-Demand Healthcare". In: *Digital Justice: Technology and the Internet of Disputes*. Oxford University Press, 2017, pp. 82–107. ISBN: 9780190464585.

Kelsen, Hans. *General Theory of Law and State, the 20th Century Legal Philosophy*. Oxford University Press, 1949.

— *General Theory of Norms*. Oxford University Press, 1991. ISBN: 9780198252177.

Kierkegaard, Patrick. "E-prescription across Europe". In: *Health and Technology* 3.3 (2013), pp. 205–219.

Kindt, Els J. *Privacy and Data Protection Issues of Biometric Applications. A Comparative Legal Analysis*. Springer Netherlands, 2013. ISBN: 9789400775220.

Kiourtis, Athanasios, Argyro Mavrogiorgou, Andreas Menychtas, Ilias Maglogiannis, and Dimosthenis Kyriazis. "Structurally Mapping Healthcare Data to HL7 FHIR through Ontology Alignment". In: *Journal of Medical Systems* 43.3 (2019), pp. 62–75.

Kiourtis, Athanasios, Sokratis Nifakos, Argyro Mavrogiorgou, and Dimosthenis Kyriazis. "Aggregating the syntactic and semantic similarity of healthcare data towards their transformation to HL7 FHIR through ontology matching". In: *International Journal of Medical Informatics* 132 (2019), p. 104002.

Kischel, Uwe. *Comparative Law*. Oxford University Press, 2019. ISBN: 9780198791355.

Klitou, Demetrius. *Privacy-invading technologies and privacy by design. Safeguarding Privacy, Liberty and Security in the 21st Century*. Vol. 25. Information Technology and Law Series. Springer, 2014. ISBN: 9789462650251.

Koelewijn, Wouter. "Privacy from a Medical Perspective". In: *The Handbook of Privacy Studies: an Interdisciplinary Introduction*. Amsterdam University Press, 2019, p. 333. ISBN: 9789462988095.

Kokott, Juliane and Christoph Sobotta. "The distinction between privacy and data protection in the jurisprudence of the CJEU and the ECtHR". In: *International Data Privacy Law* 3.4 (2013), pp. 222–228.

Kolfschooten, Hannah van. "EU Coordination of Serious Cross-Border Threats to Health: The Implications for Protection of Informed Consent in National Pandemic Policies". In: *European Journal of Risk Regulation* 10.4 (2019), pp. 635–651.

Kolfschooten, Hannah van and Anniek de Ruijter. "COVID-19 and privacy in the European Union: A legal perspective on contact tracing". In: *Contemporary Security Policy* (2020), pp. 1–14.

Koops, Bert-Jaap and Ronald Leenes. "Privacy regulation cannot be hardcoded. A critical comment on the 'privacy by design' provision in data-protection law". In: *International Review of Law, Computers & Technology* 28.2 (2014), pp. 159–171.

Koot, Matthijs and Cees de Laat. "Privacy from an Informatics Perspective". In: *The Handbook of Privacy Studies: an Interdisciplinary Introduction*. Amsterdam University Press, 2019, pp. 213–255. ISBN: 9789462988095.

Kosta, Eleni. "Chapter IV Controller and Processor (Articles 24–43). Article 35. Data protection impact assessment". In: *The EU General Data Protection Regulation (GDPR): A Commentary*. Oxford University Press, 2020, pp. 665–679. ISBN: 9780198826491.

Kotschy, Waltraut. "Chapter VIII Remedies, Liability and Penalties (Articles 77–84). Article 83. General conditions for imposing administrative fines". In: *The EU General Data Protection Regulation (GDPR): A Commentary*. Oxford University Press, 2020, pp. 1180–1193. ISBN: 9780198826491.

Kouroubalia, A. and D. G. Katehakis. "The new European interoperability framework as a facilitator of digital transformation for citizen empowerment". In: *Journal of Biomedical Informatics* 94 (2019), p. 103166.

Kranenborg, Herke. "Chapter III Rights of the Data Subject (Articles 12–23). Article 17. Right to erasure ('right to be forgotten')". In: *The EU General Data Protection Regulation (GDPR): A Commentary*. Oxford University Press, 2020, pp. 475–484. ISBN: 9780198826491.

Krebs, David. "Privacy by design: Nice-to-have or a necessary principle of data protection law". In: *J. Intell. Prop. Info. Tech. & Elec. Com. L.* 4 (2013), pp. 2–20.

Krisby, Ryan M. "Health care held ransom: modifications to data breach security & the future of health care privacy protection". In: *Health Matrix* 28 (2018), pp. 365–401.

Kroener, Inga and David Wright. "A strategy for operationalizing privacy by design". In: *The Information Society* 30.5 (2014), pp. 355–365.

Kulk, Stefan and Frederik Zuiderveen Borgesius. "Privacy, Freedom of Expression, and the Right to Be Forgotten in Europe". In: *The Cambridge Handbook of Consumer Privacy*. Cambridge University Press, 2018, pp. 301–320. ISBN: 9781316831960.

Kuner, Christopher, Lee A. Bygrave, Christopher Docksey, and Laura Drechsler. *The EU General Data Protection Regulation (GDPR): A Commentary*. Oxford University Press, 2020. ISBN: 9780198826491.

Kuner, Christopher. "Chapter V Transfers of Personal Data to Third Countries or International Organisations (Articles 44–50)". In: *The EU General Data Protection Regulation (GDPR): A Commentary*. Oxford University Press, 2020, pp. 755–862. ISBN: 9780198826491.

Kuner, Christopher. *Territorial Scope and Data Transfer Rules in the GDPR: Realising the EU's Ambition of Borderless Data Protection*. University of Cambridge Faculty of Law Research Paper No. 20/2021.

Kung, Antonio. "PEARs: privacy enhancing architectures". In: *Proceedings of the Annual Privacy Forum of 2014*. Springer. 2014, pp. 18–29.

La Fors-Owczynik, Karolina. "Profiling 'Anomalies' and the Anomalies of Profiling: Digitalized Risk Assessments of Dutch Youth and the New European Data Protection Regime". In: *Under Observation: The Interplay Between eHealth and Surveillance*. Springer, 2017, pp. 107–138. ISBN: 9783319483429.

Laanti, Maarit, Jouni Similä, and Pekka Abrahamsson. "Definitions of agile software development and agility". In: *European Conference on Software Process Improvement*. Springer. 2013, pp. 247–258.

Lachaud, Eric. "ISO/IEC 27701 Standard: Threats and Opportunities for GDPR Certification". In: *Eur. Data Prot. L. Rev.* 6 (2 2020), pp. 194–210.

Lautenbach, Geranne. *The concept of the rule of law and the European Court of Human Rights*. Oxford University Press, 2013. ISBN: 9780199671199.

Le Métayer, Daniel. "Whom to Trust? Using Technology to Enforce Privacy". In: *Enforcing Privacy*. Springer, 2016, pp. 395–437. ISBN: 9783319250472.

Le Métayer, Daniel and Sourya Joyee De. *PRIAM: a Privacy Risk Analysis Methodology*. Research Report RR-8876, Inria, Research Centre Grenoble, 2016.

Leenes, Ronald. "Chapter IV Controller and Processor (Articles 24–43). Article 42. Certification". In: *The EU General Data Protection Regulation (GDPR): A Commentary*. Oxford University Press, 2020, pp. 732–743. ISBN: 9780198826491.

— "Chapter IV Controller and Processor (Articles 24–43). Article 43. Certification bodies". In: *The EU General Data Protection Regulation (GDPR): A Commentary*. Oxford University Press, 2020, pp. 744–754. ISBN: 9780198826491.

Leenes, Ronald and Bert-Jaap Koops. "'Code' and privacy-or how technology is slowly eroding privacy". In: *SSRN: <ssrn.com/abstract=661141>* (2005).

Leenes, Ronald, Rosamunde Van Brakel, Serge Gutwirth, and Paul De Hert. *Data protection and privacy: the age of intelligent machines*. Hart Publishing, 2017. ISBN: 9781509919345.

Legrand, Pierre. *Le droit comparé*. Presses universitaires de France, 2011. ISBN: 9782130590767.

Lenhard, Jörg, Lothar Fritsch, and Sebastian Herold. "A literature study on privacy patterns research". In: *2017 43rd Euromicro Conference on Software Engineering and Advanced Applications (SEAA)*. IEEE. 2017, pp. 194–201.

Lentzsch, Christopher, Kai-Uwe Loser, Martin Degeling, and Alexander Nolte. "Integrating a Practice Perspective to Privacy by Design". In: *International Conference on Human Aspects of Information Security, Privacy, and Trust*. Springer. 2017, pp. 691–702.

Leone, Valentina, Luigi Di Caro, and Serena Villata. "Taking stock of legal ontologies: a feature-based comparative analysis". In: *Artificial Intelligence and Law* (2019), pp. 1–29.

Lessig, Lawrence. *Code*. 2.0. New York: Basic Books, 2006. ISBN: 0465039146.

— *Code and other Laws of Cyberspace*. 1999. ISBN: 9780465039128.

— "What things regulate speech: CDA 2.0 vs. filtering". In: *Jurimetrics* 38.4 (1998), pp. 629- 670.

Levin, Avner. "Privacy by Design by Regulation: The Case Study of Ontario". In: *Can. J. Comp. & Contemp. L.* 4 (2018), pp. 115–159.

Lloyd, Ian. *Information technology law*. Oxford University Press, 2020. ISBN: 9780198830559.

Lodder, Arno R. "European Union E-Commerce Directive-Article by Article Comments". In: *Guide to European Union Law on E-Commerce*. Vol. 4. Elgar Commentaries series, 2017, pp. 15–58. ISBN: 9781785369339.

Lowrance, William W. *Privacy, confidentiality, and health research*. Vol. 20. Cambridge University Press, 2012. ISBN: 9781139107969.

Lucas, Jacques. "Le partage des données personnelles de santé dans les usages du numérique en santé l'épreuve du consentement exprès de la personne". In: *Ethics, Medicine and Public Health* 3.1 (2017), pp. 10–18.

Lupiáñez-Villanueva, Francisco et al. *Benchmarking Deployment of Ehealth Among General Practitioners*. Luxembourg: Publications Office of the European Union, 2018.

Lynskey, Orla. "Chapter III Rights of the Data Subject (Articles 12–23). Article 20. Right to data portability". In: *The EU General Data Protection Regulation (GDPR): A Commentary*. Oxford University Press, 2020, pp. 497–507. ISBN: 9780198826491.

— "Chapter VIII Remedies, Liability and Penalties (Articles 77–84). Article 84. Penalties". In: *The EU General Data Protection Regulation (GDPR): A Commentary*. Oxford University Press, 2020, pp. 1194–1201. ISBN: 9780198826491.

— "The Data Retention Directive is incompatible with the rights to privacy and data protection and is invalid in its entirety: Digital Rights Ireland". In: *Common Market Law Review* 51.6 (2014), pp. 1789–1811.

— *The foundations of EU data protection law*. Oxford University Press, 2015. ISBN: 9780198718239.

Macagno, Fabrizio, Maurizio Manzin, Federico Puppo, and Serena Tomasi. "Arguments of interpretation and argumentation schemes". In: *Studies on argumentation and legal philosophy. Further steps towards a pluralistic approach* (2015), pp. 51–80.

MacCormick, Neil. "Argumentation and interpretation in law". In: *Argumentation* 9.3 (1995), pp. 467–480.

Madir, Jelena. *Healthtech, Law and Regulation.* Elgar Commercial Law and Practice, 2020. ISBN: 9781839104893.

Magnuson, J.A. and Brian E. Dixon. *Public health informatics and information systems*. Springer, 2020. ISBN: 9783030412159.

Magnuson, J.A., Riki Merrick, and James T. Case. "Public Health Information Standards". In: *Public health informatics and information systems*. Springer, 2014, pp. 133–155. ISBN: 9780387227450.

Magnuson, J.A. and Patrick W. O'Carroll. "Introduction to public health informatics". In: *Public health informatics and information systems*. Springer, 2014, pp. 3–18. ISBN: 9780387227450.

Malgieri, Gianclaudio. "Data Protection and Research: A vital challenge in the era of Covid-19 Pandemic". In: *Computer Law & Security Review* (2020).

Malgieri, Gianclaudio and Giovanni Comandé. "Sensitive-by-distance: quasi-health data in the algorithmic era". In: *Information & Communications Technology Law* 26.3 (2017), pp. 229–249.

— "Why a right to legibility of automated decision-making exists in the general data protection regulation". In: *International Data Privacy Law* (2017).

Mantelero, Alessandro. "AI and Big Data: A blueprint for a human rights, social and ethical impact assessment". In: *Computer Law & Security Review* 34.4 (2018), pp. 754–772.

— "Gli autori del trattamento dati: titolare e responsabile". In: *Giurisprudenza Italiana* 171.12 (2019), pp. 2799–2805.

— *Il costo della privacy tra valore della persona e ragione d'impresa*. Vol. 24. Giuffrè Editore, 2007. ISBN: 9788814135682.

— "Il nuovo approccio della valutazione del rischio nella sicurezza dei dati. Valutazione d'impatto e consultazione preventiva (Artt. 32–39)". In: *Il nuovo Regolamento europeo sulla privacy e protezione dei dati personali.* Zanichelli, 2017, pp. 287–330. ISBN: 9788808521057.

— "La gestione del rischio". In: *La protezione dei dati personali in Italia. Regolamento UE n. 2016/679 e d.lgs. 10 agosto 2018, n. 101*. Zanichelli, 2019, pp. 449–502. ISBN: 9788808820433.

— "La privacy all'epoca dei Big Data". In: *I dati personali nel diritto europeo*. G. Giappichelli Editore, Torino, 2019, pp. 1181–1212. ISBN: 9788892112742.

— "Regole tecniche e regole giuridiche: iterazioni e sinergie nella disciplina di *internet*". In: *Contratto e impresa* (2 2005), pp. 658–686.

— "Regulating AI within the Human Rights Framework: A Roadmapping Methodology". In: *European Yearbook on Human Rights*. Intersentia Ltd., 2020, pp. 477–502. ISBN: 9781780689722.

Mantovani, Eugenio *et al.* "Towards a Code of Conduct on Privacy for mHealth to Foster Trust Amongst Users of Mobile Health Applications". In: *Data Protection and Privacy: (In)visibilities and Infrastructures*. Springer, 2017, pp. 81–106. ISBN: 9783319507965.

Markopoulou, Dimitra, Vagelis Papakonstantinou, and Paul de Hert. "The new EU cybersecurity framework: The NIS Directive, ENISA's role and the General Data Protection Regulation". In: *Computer Law & Security Review* 35.6 (2019), p. 105336.

Marques, Isabel CP. and João JM. Ferreira. "Digital transformation in the area of health: systematic review of 45 years of evolution". In: *Health and Technology* (2019), pp. 1–12.

Martinelli, Silvia. *Diritto all'oblio e motori di ricerca. Memoria e privacy nell'era digitale*. Vol. 5. Giuffrè Editore, 2017. ISBN: 9788814220661.

Martínez-Pérez, Borja, Isabel De La Torre-Díez, and Miguel López-Coronado. "Mobile health applications for the most prevalent conditions by the World Health Organization: review and analysis". In: *Journal of medical Internet research* 15.6 (2013), e120.

— "Privacy and security in mobile health apps: a review and recommendations". In: *Journal of medical systems* 39.1 (2015), pp. 181–189.

McLennan, Stuart, Leo Anthony Celi, and Alena Buyx. "COVID-19: Putting the General Data Protection Regulation to the Test". In: *JMIR Public Health and Surveillance* 6.2 (2020), e19279.

Mehndiratta, Pulkit, Shelly Sachdeva, and Sudhanshu Kulshrestha. "A model of privacy and security for electronic health records". In: *International Workshop on Databases in Networked Information Systems*. Springer. 2014, pp. 202–213.

Melchionna, Silvia and Francesca Cecamore. "Le nuove frontiere della sanità e della ricerca scientifica". In: *Circolazione e protezione dei dati personali, tra libertà e regole del mercato. Commentario al Regolamento UE n. 2016/679 (GDPR) e al novellato D.lgs. n. 196/2003 (Codice Privacy)*. Giuffrè Francis Lefebvre, 2019, pp. 579–620. ISBN: 9788828809692.

Mendoza, Isak and Lee A. Bygrave. "The right not to be subject to automated decisions based on profiling". In: *EU Internet Law*. Springer, 2017, pp. 77–98. ISBN: 9783319649559.

Mengoni, Luigi. "Diritto e tecnica". In: *Riv. trim. dir. proc. civ.* 2 (2001), pp. 1–10.

Michaels, Ralf. "The Functional Method of Comparative Law". In: *The Oxford Handbook of Comparative Law*. Oxford University Press, 2019, pp. 340–382. ISBN: 9780198810230.

Milieu, Ltd. and Time.lex. *Overview of the national laws on electronic health records in the EU Member States and their interaction with the provision of cross-border eHealth services Report*. Brussels: 201/65. 2014.

MITRE, Corporation. *Electronic Health Records Overview*. National Institutes of Health National, Center for Research Resources. 2006.

Monateri, Pier Giuseppe. "Il diritto comparato tra disciplina critica, scienza normale e ingegneria politica". In: *Comparare. Una riflessione tra le discipline*. Mimesis Edizioni, 2020, pp. 205–224. ISBN: 9788857567310.

— *Methods of Comparative Law*. Edward Elgar, 2014. ISBN: 9781781006535.

Moore, Dominique. "Chapter III Rights of the Data Subject (Articles 12–23). Article 23. Restrictions". In: *The EU General Data Protection Regulation (GDPR): A Commentary*. Oxford University Press, 2020, pp. 543–554. ISBN: 9780198826491.

Mossialos, Elias, Rita Baeten, Govin Permanand, and Tamara K. Hervey. *Health systems governance in Europe: the role of European Union law and policy*. Cambridge University Press, 2010. ISBN: 9780511750496.

Mostert, Menno, Annelien L. Bredenoord, Bart Van Der Sloot, and Johannes J.M. Van Delden. "From privacy to data protection in the EU: implications for big data health research". In: *European Journal of Health Law* 25.1 (2017), pp. 43–55.

Mulazzani, Giovanni. "Le sanzioni amministrative in materia di protezione dei dati personali nell'ordinamento europeo ed in quello nazionale". In: *La protezione dei dati personali in Italia. Regolamento UE n. 2016/679 e d.lgs. 10 agosto 2018, n. 101*. Zanichelli, Torino, 2019, pp. 768–795. ISBN: 9788808820433.

Mulder, Trix. "Health apps, their privacy policies and the GDPR". In: *European Journal of Law and Technology* 10 (1 2019).

— "The Protection of Data Concerning Health in Europe". In: *Eur. Data Prot. L. Rev.* 5 (2019), p. 209.

Mulligan, Deirdre K. and Kenneth A Bamberger. "Saving governance-by-design". In: *Calif. L. Rev.* 106 (2018), p. 697.

Mulligan, Deirdre K. and Jennifer King. "Bridging the gap between privacy and design". In: *U. Pa. J. Const. L.* 14 (2011), pp. 989–1034.

Mulligan, Stephen P., Wilson C. Freeman, and Linebaugh Chris D. *Data Protection Law: An Overview*. Congressional Research Service R45631, 2019.

Munns, Christina and Subhajit Basu. *Privacy and healthcare data: 'choice of control' to 'choice' and 'control'*. Taylor & Francis, 2016. ISBN: 9781472426864.

Newman, Lauren. "Keep Your Friends Close and Your Medical Records Closer: Defining the Extent to Which a Constitutional Right to Informational Privacy Protects Medical Records". In: *J.L. & Health* 32 (2019), pp. 1–26.

Nicholson Price II, William. "Risk and Resilience in Health Data Infrastructure". In: *Colo. Tech. L.J.* 16 (2017), pp. 65–86.

Nicola, Fernanda G. and Oreste Pollicino, "The Balkanization of Data Privacy Regulation". In: *W. Va. L. Rev.* 61 (2020), pp. 60–105.

Niezen, Maartje GH. "Unobtrusiveness in mHealth design and use: A systematic literature study". In: *Under Observation: The Interplay Between eHealth and Surveillance*. Springer, 2017, pp. 9–29. ISBN: 9783319483429.

Nissenbaum, Helen. "From preemption to circumvention: if technology regulates, why do we need regulation (and vice versa)". In: *Berkeley Tech. LJ* 26 (2011), pp. 1367–1386.

— "Privacy as contextual integrity". In: *Wash. L. Rev.* 79 (2004), pp. 119–158.

Norwegian Data Protection Authority, Datatilsynet. *Guidelines on software development with Data protection by Design and by Default*. 2017.

Notario, Nicolás et al. "PRIPARE: a new vision on engineering privacy and security by design". In: *Cyber Security and Privacy Forum*. Springer. 2014, pp. 65–76.

Notario, Nicolás et al. "PRIPARE: integrating privacy best practices into a privacy engineering methodology". In: *2015 IEEE Security and Privacy Workshops*. IEEE. 2015, pp. 151- 158.

Notario, Nicolás et al. *PRIPARE. Privacy-and Security-by design Methodology Handbook*. 2017.

Noto La Diega, Guido. "Against the Dehumanisation of Decision-Making". In: *J. Intell. Prop. Info. Tech. & Elec. Com. L.* 9 (2018), pp. 3–33.

Nys, Herman. *IEL Medical Law*. Kluwer Law International, 2020. ISBN: 9789065449436.

O'Connor, Yvonne, Wendy Rowan, Laura Lynch, and Ciara Heavin. "Privacy by design: informed consent and internet of things for smart health". In: *Procedia computer science* 113 (2017), pp. 653–658.

Oderkerk, Marieke. "The Need for a Methodological Framework for Comparative Legal Research: Sense and Nonsense of "Methodological Pluralism" in Comparative Law". In: *Rabels Zeitschrift für ausländisches und internationales Privatrecht/The Rabel Journal of Comparative and International Private Law* (2015), pp. 589–623.

OECD. *Guidelines on the Protection of Privacy and Transborder Flows of Personal Data, in the form of a Recommendation by the Council of the OECD*. 1980.

— *Guidelines on the Protection of Privacy and Transborder Flows of Personal Data, the OECD Privacy Framework*. 2013.

— *How's Life in the Digital Age? Opportunities and Risks of the Digital Transformation for People's Well-being*. 2019.

— *OECD Recommendation on Health Data Governance*. 2017.

Office of the National Coordinator for Health Information Technology, ONC. *Nationwide Privacy and Security Framework for Electronic Exchange of Individually Identifiable Health Information*.Office of the National Coordinator for Health Information Technology, U.S. Department of Health and Human Services, 2008.

— *Office-based Physician Electronic Health Record Adoption*. 2019.

Oliveira Rodrigues, Cleyton Mário de *et al.*. "Legal ontologies over time: a systematic mapping study". In: *Expert Systems with Applications* 130 (2019), pp. 12–30.

Omaggio, Vincenzo and Gaetano Carlizzi. *Ermeneutica e interpretazione giuridica*. G. Giappichelli Editore, 2010. ISBN: 9788834814239.

Pagallo, Ugo. *La tutela della privacy negli Stati Uniti d'America e in Europa: modelli giuridici a confronto*. Giuffrè Editore, 2008. ISBN: 8814142696.

— "On the principle of privacy by design and its limits: Technology, ethics and the rule of law". In: *European Data Protection: In Good Health?* Springer, 2012, pp. 331–346. ISBN: 9789400729032.

— "Privacy e design". In: *Informatica e diritto* 18.1 (2009), pp. 123–134.

Palmieri, Alessandro. "DRM e disciplina europea della protezione dei dati personali". In: *Digital Rights Management. Problemi teorici e prospettive applicative. Atti del convegno tenuto presso la Facoltà di Giurisprudenza di Trento il 21 e 22 marzo 2007*. Quaderni del Dipartimento di Scienze Giuridiche, n. 70 dell'Università di Trento, 2008, pp. 197–212. ISBN: 9788884432193.

Palmieri, Alessandro and Roberto Pardolesi. "Dal diritto all'oblio all'occultamento in rete: traversie dell'informazione ai tempi di Google". In: *Nuovi Quaderni del Foro italiano* 1 (2014), pp. 16–33.

— "Polarità estreme: oblio e archivi digitali. Nota a Corte di Cassazione, sez. I civile, ordinanza 27–03–2020, n. 7559". In: *Foro it.* 1570 (parte I 2020).

Palmieri, L. "Dai segreti alla riservatezza e poi al segreto". In: *Medicina Legale Quaderni Camerti* (XV 1993).

Palmieri III, Nicholas F. "Who Should Regulate Data: An Analysis of the California Consumer Privacy Act and Its Effects on Nationwide Data Protection Laws". In: *Hastings Sci. & Tech. LJ* 11 (2020), pp. 37–60.

Palmirani, Monica. "Legislative change management with Akoma-Ntoso". In: *Legislative XML for the semantic Web*. Springer, 2011, pp. 101–130.

Palmirani, Monica, Giorgia Bincoletto, Valentina Leone, Salvatore Sapienza, and Francesco Sovrano. "Hybrid Refining Approach of PrOnto Ontology". In: *Electronic Government and the Information Systems Perspective. EGOVIS 20*. Springer, 2020, pp. 3–17.

— "PrOnto Ontology Refinement Through Open Knowledge Extraction". In: *Legal Knowledge and Information Systems. JURIX 2019*. 2019, pp. 205–210.

Palmirani, Monica, Michele Martoni, Arianna Rossi, Cesare Bartolini, and Livio Robaldo. "Legal Ontology for Modelling GDPR Concepts and Norms". In: *Legal Knowledge and Information Systems. JURIX 2018*. 2018, pp. 91–100.

— "PrOnto: Privacy ontology for legal reasoning". In: International Conference on Electronic Government and the Information Systems Perspective. Springer. 2018, pp. 139- 152.

Palmirani, Monica and Fabio Vitali. "Akoma-Ntoso for legal documents". In: *Legislative XML for the semantic Web*. Springer, 2011, pp. 75–100.

Palmirani, Monica et al. "LegalRuleML: XML-based rules and norms". In: *International Workshop on Rules and Rule Markup Languages for the Semantic Web*. Springer. 2011, pp. 298–312.

Panetta, *Rocco. Circolazione e protezione dei dati personali, tra libertà e regole del mercato. Commentario al Regolamento UE n. 2016/679 (GDPR) e al novellato D.lgs. n. 196/2003 (Codice Privacy)*. Giuffrè Francis Lefebvre, 2019. ISBN: 9788828809692.

Papageorgiou, Achilleas et al. "Security and privacy analysis of mobile health applications: the alarming state of practice". In: *IEEE Access* 6 (2018), pp. 9390–9403.

Pardau, Stuart L. and Blake Edwards. "The FTC, the Unfairness Doctrine, and Privacy by Design: New Legal Frontiers in Cybersecurity". In: *J. Bus. & Tech. L.* 12 (2016), pp. 227–276.

Pardolesi, Roberto and Giorgio Pino. "Post-diritto e giudice legislatore. Sulla creatività della giurisprudenza". In: *Foro it.* col. 113 (parte V 2017).

Parker, David M., Steven G. Pine, and Zachary W. Ernst. “Privacy and Informed Consent for Research in the Age of Big Data”. In: *Penn St. L. Rev.* 123.3 (2019), pp. 703–733.

Parsons, David. “Agile software development methodology, an ontological analysis”. In: <www.researchgate.net/> (2011).

Pascuzzi, Giovanni. *Il diritto dell’era digitale*. Il Mulino, Bologna, 2020. ISBN: 9788815290328.

— *Il problem solving nelle professioni legali*. Il Mulino, Bologna, 2017. ISBN: 9788815272997.

— *La creatività del giurista. Tecniche e strategie dell’innovazione giuridica*. Zanichelli, 2013. ISBN: 9788808164162.

Pasquale, Frank. “Health Information Law”. In: *The Oxford Handbook of U.S. Health Law*. 2017, pp. 193–212. ISBN: 9780199366521.

Pasquale, Frank and Tara Adams Ragone. “Protecting health privacy in an era of big data processing and cloud computing”. In: *Stan. Tech. L. Rev.* 17 (2013), pp. 595–654.

Pedrazzi, Giorgio. “Il ruolo del Responsabile della protezione dei dati (DPO) nel settore sanitario”. In: *Rivista Italiana di Medicina Legale (e del Diritto in campo sanitario)* 1 (2019), pp. 181–186.

Peeters, Miek. “Free movement of patients: Directive 2011/24 on the application of patients’ rights in cross-border healthcare”. In: *European Journal of Health Law* 19.1 (2012), pp. 29–60.

Perri, Pierluigi. *Privacy, diritto e sicurezza informatica*. Giuffrè Editore, 2007. ISBN: 8814137021.

Petkova, Bilyana and Franziska Boehm. “Profiling and the Essence of the Right to Data Protection”. In: *The Cambridge Handbook of Consumer Privacy*. Cambridge University Press, 2018, pp. 285–300. ISBN: 9781316831960.

Pfaffenberger, Bryan. “Technological dramas”. In: *Science, Technology, & Human Values* 17.3 (1992), pp. 282–312.

Pierce, Robin. “Machine learning for diagnosis and treatment: Gymnastics for the GDPR”. In: *Eur. Data Prot. L. Rev.* 4 (2018), pp. 333–343.

— “Medical Privacy: Where Deontology and Consequentialism Meet”. In: *The Handbook of Privacy Studies: an Interdisciplinary Introduction*. Amsterdam University Press, 2019, pp. 327–331. ISBN: 9789462988095.

Pierucci, Alessandra and Jean-Philippe Walter. *Joint Statement on Digital Contact Tracing*. Chair of the Committee of Convention 108 and Data Protection Commissioner of the Council of Europe. Strasbourg, 28 April 2020, 2020.

Pino, Giorgio. “Conflitto e bilanciamento tra diritti fondamentali. Una mappa dei problemi”. In: *Ragion Pratica* 28 (2007), pp. 219–276.

— *Diritti e interpretazione. Il ragionamento giuridico nello Stato costituzionale*. Il Mulino, 2010. ISBN: 9788815134271.

Pitruzzella, Giovanni, Oreste Pollicino, and Stefano Quintarelli. *Parole e potere: libertà d’espressione, hate speech e fake news*. EGEA, 2017. ISBN: 9788823836419.

Pizzetti, Franco. *Il caso del diritto all'oblio*. Vol. 2. G. Giappichelli Editore, 2013. ISBN: 9788834828168.

— *Privacy e il diritto europeo alla protezione dei dati personali: Dalla Direttiva 95/46 al nuovo Regolamento europeo*. G. Giappichelli Editore, 2016. ISBN: 9788892104501.

Platsas, Antonios E. "The functional and the dysfunctional in the comparative method of law: some critical remarks". In: *Electronic Journal of Comparative Law* 12.3 (2008).

Plutino, Marco. "'Immuni'. Un'*exposure notification* app alla prova del bilanciamento tra tutela dei diritti e degli interessi pubblici". In: *MediaLaws Rivista di Diritto dei Media* 2 (2020), pp. 172–193.

Poba-Nzaou, Placide and Sylvestre Uwizeyemungu. "Variation in electronic health record adoption in European public hospitals: a configurational analysis of key functionalities". In: *Health and Technology* 9.4 (2019), pp. 439–448.

Polcˇák, Radim. "Chapter III Rights of the Data Subject (Articles 12–23). Article 12. Transparent information, communication and modalities for the exercise of the rights of the data subject". In: *The EU General Data Protection Regulation (GDPR): A Commentary*. Oxford University Press, 2020, pp. 398–412. ISBN: 9780198826491.

Poletti, Dianora. "Il trattamento dei dati inerenti alla salute nell'epoca della pandemia: cronaca dell'emergenza". In: *Persona e Mercato* (2 2020), pp. 66–76.

Politi, Fabrizio. *Studi sull'interpretazione giuridica*. G. Giappichelli Editore, 2019. ISBN: 9788892120648.

Pollicino, Oreste. "Fighting Covid-19 and Protecting Privacy Under EU Law – A Proposal Looking at the Roots of European Constitutionalism". In: *blog-iacl-aidc.org* (2020).

— "L''autunno caldo' della Corte di giustizia in tema di tutela dei diritti fondamentali in rete e le sfide del costituzionalismo alle prese con i nuovi poteri privati in ambito digitale". In: *Federalismi.it* 19 (2019), pp. 2–15.

Polonetsky, Jules, Omer Tene, and Evan Selinger. "Consumer Privacy and the Future of Society". In: *The Cambridge Handbook of Consumer Privacy*. Cambridge University Press, 2018, pp. 1–21. ISBN: 9781316831960.

Porcedda, Maria Grazia. "'Privacy by Design' in EU Law". In: *Privacy Technologies and Policy. 6th Annual Privacy Forum, APF 2018*. Springer. 2018, pp. 183–204.

Pormeister, Kärt. "The GDPR and Big Data: Leading the Way for Big Genetic Data?" In: *Annual Privacy Forum*. Springer. 2017, pp. 3–18.

Posner, Richard A. "The right of privacy". In: *Ga. L. Rev.* 12 (1977), pp. 393–422.

— "The uncertain protection of privacy by the Supreme Court". In: *The Supreme Court Review* 1979 (1979), pp. 173–216.

Post, David G. "What Larry Doesn't Get: Code, Law and Liberty in Cyberspace". In: *Stanford Law Review* 52 (2000), pp. 1439–1459.

Pougnet, Richard and L. Pougnet. "Le dossier médical partagé: pour un usage centré sur la personne?" In: *Éthique & Santé* 16.2 (2019), pp. 64–70.

Pritts, Joy. *The state of health privacy: an uneven terrain (a comprehensive survey of state health privacy statutes)*. Health Privacy Project, Institute for Health Care Research and Policy, 1999.

Pritts, Joy L. "Altered states: state health privacy laws and the impact of the Federal Health Privacy Rule". In: *Yale J. Health Pol'y L. & Ethics* 2 (2001), pp. 327–364.

Prosser, William. "Privacy". In: *Cal. L. Rev.* (48 1960), p. 383.

Purnhagen, Kai P., Anniek De Ruijter, Mark L. Flear, Tamara K. Hervey, and Alexia Herwig. "More Competences than You Knew? The Web of Health Competence for European Union Action in Response to the COVID-19 Outbreak". In: *European Journal of Risk Regulation* (2020), pp. 1–10.

Quarta, Alessandra and Guido Smorto. *Diritto privato dei mercati digitali*. Le Monnier università, 2020. ISBN: 9788800749756.

Quinn, Paul and Paul De Hert. "The Patients' Rights Directive (2011/24/EU) – Providing (some) rights to EU residents seeking healthcare in other Member States". In: *Computer Law & Security Review* 27.5 (2011), pp. 497–502.

Quintana, Y. and C. Safran. "Global health informatics — an overview". In: *Global Health Informatics*. Elsevier, 2017, pp. 1–13. ISBN: 9780128045916.

Raz, Joseph. *Between authority and interpretation: On the theory of law and practical reason*. Oxford University Press, 2009. ISBN: 9780199562688.

Reed, Chris. *Making laws for cyberspace*. Oxford University Press, 2012. ISBN: 9780199657605.

Reidenberg, Joel R. "Lex informatica: The formulation of information policy rules through technology". In: *Tex. L. Rev.* 76 (1997), pp. 553–593.

Resta, Giorgio. *Dignità, persone, mercati*. G. Giappichelli Editore, 2014. ISBN: 9788834849323.

— "La protezione dei dati personali nel diritto dell'emergenza Covid-19". In: *Giustiziacivile.com* (2020).

— "Personnalité, Persönlichkeit, Personality: Comparative Perspectives on the Protection of Identity in Private Law". In: *European Journal of Comparative Law and Governance* 1.3 (2014), pp. 215–243.

Resta, Giorgio, Alessandro Somma, and Vincenzo Zeno Zencovich. *Comparare. Una riflessione tra le discipline*. Mimesis Edizioni, 2020. ISBN: 9788857567310.

Rezaeibagha, Fatemeh, Khin Than Win, and Willy Susilo. "A systematic literature review on security and privacy of electronic health record systems: technical perspectives". In: *Health Information Management Journal* 44.3 (2015), pp. 23–38.

Ricciardi, Walter. "Assessing the impact of digital transformation of health services: Opinion by the Expert Panel on Effective Ways of Investing in Health (EXPH)". In: *European Journal of Public Health* 29.Supplement_4 (2019), ckz185–769.

Richards, Neil and Woodrow Hartzog. "Taking trust seriously in privacy law". In: *Stan. Tech. L. Rev.* 19 (2015), pp. 431–472.

Richards, Neil M. and Woodrow Hartzog. "Privacy's Constitutional Moment". In: *SSRN: <ssrn.com/ abstract=3441502>* (2019).

Rimmelzwaan, Job. "Use of a Wearable Device to Promote Healthy Behaviors Among Employees of a Small-to-Medium Enterprise in the Netherlands". In: *Under Observation: The Interplay Between eHealth and Surveillance*. Springer, 2017, pp. 59–69. ISBN: 9783319483429.

Robaldo, Livio et al. "Formalizing GDPR provisions in Reified I/O logic: the DAPRECO knowledge base". In: *Journal of Logic, Language and Information* (2019), pp. 1–49.

Rodotà, Stefano. "Diritto, scienza, tecnologia: modelli e scelte di regolamentazione". In: *Rivista critica del diritto privato* 3 (2004), pp. 357–376.

— *Il diritto di avere diritti*. Gius. Laterza & Figli Spa, 2012. ISBN: 9788842096085.

Rodotà, Stefano and Paolo Conti. *Intervista su privacy e libertà*. GLF Editori Laterza, 2005. ISBN: 9788842076414.

Romanou, Anna. "The necessity of the implementation of Privacy by Design in sectors where data protection concerns arise". In: *Computer law & security review* 34.1 (2018), pp. 99–110.

Romeo, Francesco. "Dalla Giuritecnica di Vittorio Frosini alla *Privacy by Design*". In: *Informatica e diritto* 2 (2016), pp. 9–23.

Rossi, Arianna, Rossana Ducato, Helena Haapio, Stefania Passera, and Monica Palmirani. "Legal Design Patterns: Towards A New Language for Legal Information Design". In: *Internet of Things. Proceedings of the 22nd International Legal Informatics Symposium IRIS*. 2019, pp. 517–526.

Rossi, Arianna and Helena Haapio. "Proactive Legal Design: Embedding Values in the Design of Legal Artefacts". In: *Internet of Things. Proceedings of the 22nd International Legal Informatics Symposium IRIS*. 2019, pp. 537–544.

Rossi, Arianna and Monica Palmirani. "What's in an Icon?" In: *Data Protection and Privacy: Data Protection and Democracy*. Hart Publishing, 2020, pp. 59–92. ISBN: 9781509932740.

Rotenberg, Marc. "Fair information practices and the architecture of privacy (What Larry doesn't get)". In: *Stan. Tech. L. Rev.* (2001), pp. 1–35.

Rubinstein, Ira S. "Big data: the end of privacy or a new beginning?" In: *International Data Privacy Law* 3.2 (2013), pp. 74–87.

— "Regulating privacy by design". In: *Berkeley Tech. LJ* 26 (2011), pp. 1409–1456.

Rubinstein, Ira S. and Nathaniel Good. "Privacy by Design: a Counterfactual Analysis of Google and Facebook Privacy Incidents'". In: *Berkeley Technology Law Journal* 28 (2013), pp. 1333–1409.

— "The trouble with Article 25 (and how to fix it): the future of data protection by design and default". In: *International Data Privacy Law* (2019), pp. 1–20.

Ruffo, Giancarlo Francesco, Francesco Bergadano, Alessandro Mantelero, and Giovanni Sartor. *Privacy digitale. Giuristi e informatici a confronto*. G. Giappichelli Editore, 2005. ISBN: 9788834858059.

Rustad, Michael L. and Thomas H. Koenig. "Towards a global data privacy standard". In: *Fla. L. Rev.* 71 (2019), pp. 365–453.

Sacco, Rodolfo. “Legal formants: a dynamic approach to comparative law (Installment I of II)”. In: *The American Journal of Comparative Law* 39.1 (1991), pp. 1–34.

— “Legal formants: a dynamic approach to comparative law (installment II of II)”. In: *The American Journal of Comparative Law* 39.2 (1991), pp. 343–401.

Sacco, Rodolfo and Piercarlo Rossi. *Introduzione al diritto comparato*. Utet Giuridica, 2019. ISBN: 9788859820826.

Samuel, Geoffrey. *An Introduction to Comparative Law Theory and Method*. Hart Publishing, 2014. ISBN: 9781849466431.

Samuelson, Pamela. “DRM {and, or, vs.} the law”. In: *Communications of the ACM* 46.4 (2003), pp. 41–45.

Santosuosso, Amedeo. *Intelligenza artificiale e diritto. Perché le tecnologie di IA sono una grande opportunità per il diritto*. Mondadori Università, 2020. ISBN: 9788861848283.

Saripalle, Rishi, Christopher Runyan, and Mitchell Russell. “Using HL7 FHIR to achieve interoperability in patient health record”. In: *Journal of biomedical informatics* 94 (2019), p. 103188.

Sarrat, Jules and Raphael Brun. “DPIA: how to carry out one of the key principles of accountability”. In: *Privacy Technologies and Policy. 6th Annual Privacy Forum, APF 2018*. Springer. 2018, pp. 172–182.

Sartor, Giovanni. “A formal model of legal argumentation”. In: *Ratio Juris* 7.2 (1994), pp.177–211.

— “Human rights and information technologies”. In: *The Oxford handbook of law, regulation and technology*. Oxford University Press, 2017, pp. 424–450.

— “Il diritto della rete globale”. In: *Ciberspazio e diritto* 4 (2003), pp. 67–94.

— “Il diritto nell’informatica giuridica”. In: *Rivista di filosofia del diritto* 4.Speciale (2015), pp. 71–92.

— *L’informatica giuridica e le tecnologie dell’informazione: Corso di informatica giuridica*. Vol. 2. G. Giappichelli Editore, 2016. ISBN: 9788892105935.

— “Legislative information and the web”. In: *Legislative XML for the Semantic Web*. Springer, 2011, pp. 11–20.

Sartor, Giovanni, Maria Angela Biasiotti, and Fabrizio Turchi. *Tecnologie e abilità informatiche per il diritto*. G. Giappichelli Editore, 2018. ISBN: 9788834839409.

Sartore, Federico. “Privacy-by-design, l’introduzione del principio nel corpus del GDPR”. In: *Circolazione e protezione dei dati personali, tra libertà e regole del mercato. Commentario al Regolamento UE n. 2016/679 (GDPR) e al novellato D.lgs. n. 196/2003 (Codice Privacy)*. Giuffrè Francis Lefebvre, 2019, pp. 295–307. ISBN: 9788828809692.

Schachter, Madeleine. *Informational and decisional privacy*. Carolina Academic Press, 2003.

Schiffner, Stefan et al. “Towards a roadmap for privacy technologies and the General Data Protection Regulation: A transatlantic initiative”. In: *Privacy Technologies and Policy. 6th Annual Privacy Forum, APF 2018*. Springer. 2018, pp. 24–42.

Schmahl, Stefanie and Marten Breuer. *The Council of Europe: its law and policies.* Oxford University Press, 2017. ISBN: 9780199672523.

Schneider, Giulia. "Disentangling health data networks: a critical analysis of Articles 9 (2) and 89 GDPR". In: *International Data Privacy Law* (2019), pp. 253–271.

Schulz, Stefan, Robert Stegwee, and Catherine Chronaki. "Standards in healthcare data". In: *Fundamentals of Clinical Data Science.* Springer, Cham, 2019, pp. 19–36.

Schwartz, Paul M. "Privacy and democracy in cyberspace". In: *Vand. L. Rev.* 52 (1999), pp. 1607–1701.

— "Privacy and the economics of personal health care information". In: *Tex. L. Rev.* 76 (1997), p. 1.

— "Beyond Lessig's code for internet privacy: cyberspace filters, privacy control, and fair information practices". In: *Wis. L. Rev.* 2000.4 (2000), pp. 743–788.

— Schwartz, Paul M. and Daniel J. Solove. "Reconciling personal information in the United States and European Union". In: *Calif. L. Rev.* 102 (2014), pp. 877–916.

Searle, John R. *Expression and meaning: Studies in the theory of speech acts.* Cambridge University Press, 1985. ISBN: 9780511609213.

Selinger, Evan, Jules Polonetsky, and Omer Tene. *The Cambridge Handbook of Consumer Privacy.* Cambridge University Press, 2018. ISBN: 9781316831960.

Shabani, Mahsa and Pascal Borry. "Rules for processing genetic data for research purposes in view of the new EU General Data Protection Regulation". In: *European Journal of Human Genetics* 26.2 (2018), pp. 149–156.

Shabo, Amnon. "Electronic Health Record". In: *Encyclopedia of Database Systems.* Springer, 2017, pp. 101–177. ISBN: 9781489979933.

Shenoy, Akhil and Jacob M. Appel. "Safeguarding confidentiality in electronic health records". In: *Cambridge Quarterly of Healthcare Ethics* 26.2 (2017), pp. 337–341.

Sigulem, D., M.P. Ramos, and R. de Holanda Albuquerque. "The New Medicine: From the Paper Medical Record to the Digitized Human Being". In: *Global Health Informatics.* Elsevier, 2017, pp. 152–167. ISBN: 9780128045916.

Sinha, Pradeep K., Gaur Sunder, Prashant Bendale, Manisha Mantri, and Atreya Dande. *Electronic health record: standards, coding systems, frameworks, and infrastructures.* Wiley – IEEE Press, 2013. ISBN: 9781118281345.

Sion, Laurens, Kim Wuyts, Koen Yskout, Dimitri Van Landuyt, and Wouter Joosen. "Interactionbased privacy threat elicitation". In: *2018 IEEE European Symposium on Security and Privacy Workshops (EuroS&PW).* IEEE. 2018, pp. 79–86.

Sion, Laurens et al. "An architectural view for data protection by design". In: *2019 IEEE International Conference on Software Architecture (ICSA).* IEEE. 2019, pp. 11–20.

Siranyan, Valérie. "La protection des données personnelles des patients face à la modernisation de notre système de santé". In: *Médecine & Droit* 158 (2019), pp. 112–117.

Slomovic, Anna. "eHealth and privacy in US employer wellness programs". In: *Under Observation: The Interplay Between eHealth and Surveillance*. Springer, 2017, pp. 31-58. ISBN: 9783319483429.

Soceanu, A. "Managing the Interoperability and Privacy of e-Health Systems as an Interdisciplinary Challenge". In: *Systemics, Cybernetics and Informatics* 14.5 (2016), pp. 42- 47.

Solove, Daniel J. "A taxonomy of privacy". In: *U. Pa. L. Rev.* 154 (2005), pp. 477–560.

— "Conceptualizing privacy". In: *Calif. L. Rev.* 90 (2002), pp. 1087–1156.

— "Fourth amendment pragmatism". In: *BCL Rev.* 51 (2010), pp. 1511–1538.

— "The Myth of the Privacy Paradox". In: *Geo. Wash. L. Rev.* 89 (2021), pp. 1–51.

Solove, Daniel J. and Woodrow Hartzog. "The FTC and the new common law of privacy". In: *Colum. L. Rev.* 114 (2014), pp. 583–676.

Solove, Daniel J. and Paul M. Schwartz. "ALI Data Privacy: Overview and Black Letter Text". In: *UCLA Law Review* 68 (2020).

— "Health privacy". In: *Information privacy law*. Wolters Kluwer Law & Business, 2018, pp. 475–602. ISBN: 9781454892755.

— *Information privacy law*. Wolters Kluwer Law & Business, 2011. ISBN: 9780735510401.

— *Information privacy law*. Wolters Kluwer Law & Business, 2018. ISBN: 9781454892755.

— *Privacy Law Fundamentals*. International Association of Privacy Professionals, 2019. ISBN: 9781948771252.

— *Privacy, information, and technology*. Wolters Kluwer Law & Business, 2009. ISBN: 9780735579101.

Somma, Alessandro. *Introduzione al diritto comparato*. Giappichelli, 2019. ISBN: 9788892130197.

Soro, Antonello. *Persone in rete*. Fazi Editore, 2018. ISBN: 9788893254359.

Spedicato, Giorgio. "Law as Code? *Divertissment* sulla *lex informatica*". In: *Ciberspazio e diritto* 2 (2009), pp. 233–259.

Spiecker gen. Döhmann, Indra, Vagelis Papakonstantinou, Gerrit Hornung, and Paul de Hert. *The EU General Data Protection Regulation (GDPR): A Commentary*. Oxford University Press, 2020. ISBN: 9780198826491.

Spiekermann, Sarah and Lorrie Faith Cranor. "Engineering privacy". In: *IEEE Transactions on software engineering* 35.1 (2008), pp. 67–82.

Stalla-Bourdillon, Sophie, Gefion Thuermer, Johanna Walker, Laura Carmichael, and Elena Simperl. "Data protection by design: building the foundations of trustworthy data sharing". In: *Data & Policy* 2 (2020), e4, 1–10.

Stallman, Richard. *The GNU project*. <www.gnu.org/gnu/initial-announcement.htm l>. 1998.

Standards, National Institute of and NIST Technology. *NIST Privacy Framework: A Tool for Improving Privacy Through Enterprise Risk Management, Version 1.0*. National Institute of Standards and Technology, 2020.

Steinz, Thomas. “The Evolution of European Data Law”. In: *The Evolution of EU Law*. Oxford University Press, 2021. ISBN: 9780199592968.

Stevens, Leslie, Christine Dobbs, Kerina Jones, and Graeme Laurie. “Dangers from within? Looking inwards at the role of maladministration as the leading cause of health data breaches in the UK”. In: *Data Protection and Privacy: (In)visibilities and Infrastructures*. Springer, 2017, pp. 205–239. ISBN: 9783319507965.

Stevovic, Jovan, Eleonora Bassi, Alessio Giori, Fabio Casati, and Giampaolo Armellin. “Enabling privacy by design in medical records sharing”. In: *Reforming European Data Protection Law*. Springer, 2015, pp. 385–406. ISBN: 9789401793858.

Stylianou, Andreas and Michael A. Talias. “Big data in healthcare: a discussion on the big challenges”. In: *Health and Technology* 7.1 (2017), pp. 97–107.

Sutton, Reed T et al. “An overview of clinical decision support systems: benefits, risks, and strategies for success”. In: *NPJ Digital Medicine* 3.1 (2020), pp. 1–10.

Sweileh, Waleed M et al. “Bibliometric analysis of worldwide scientific literature in mobile-health: 2006–2016”. In: *BMC medical informatics and decision making* 17.1 (2017), pp. 72–84.

Tamó-Larrieux, Aurelia. *Designing for privacy and its legal framework: data protection by design and default for the internet of things*. Law, Governance and Technology Series. Springer, 2018. ISBN: 9783319986241.

Tarello, Giovanni. “Argomenti interpretativi”. In: *Digesto civ.* (1987), pp. 3–11.

Tavani, Mario, Mario Picozzi, and Gabriella Salvati. *Manuale di deontologia medica*. Giuffrè Editore, 2007. ISBN: 9788814137297.

Taylor, Mark. *Genetic data and the law: a critical perspective on privacy protection*. Vol. 16. Cambridge University Press, 2012. ISBN: 9780511910128.

Terry, Nicholas P. and Leslie P. Francis. “Ensuring the privacy and confidentiality of electronic health records”. In: *U. Ill. L. Rev.* (2007), pp. 681–736.

Terry, Nicolas P. “Electronic health records: international, structural and legal perspectives”. In: *Journal of Legal Medicine* 12.1 (2004), pp. 26–39.

— “Meaningful adoption: What we know or think we know about the financing, effectiveness, quality, and safety of electronic medical records”. In: *Journal of Legal Medicine* 34.1 (2013), pp. 7–42.

— “Privacy and the health information domain: properties, models and unintended results”. In: *European Journal of Health Law* 10.3 (2003), pp. 223–237.

— “Protecting patient privacy in the age of big data”. In: *UMKC L. Rev.* 81 (2012), pp. 385- 415.

— “Regulatory disruption and arbitrage in health-care data protection”. In: *Yale J. Health Pol'y L. & Ethics* 17 (2017), pp. 143–208.

Thompson, Eric C. *Building a HIPAA-Compliant Cybersecurity Program*. Apress, 2017. ISBN: 9781484230602.

Tien, Lee. “Architectural regulation and the evolution of social norms”. In: *Yale JL & Tech.* 7 (2004), pp. 1–22.

TIPIK, Legal. *Report on the implementation of specific provisions of Regulation (EU) 2016/679*. European Commission. Directorate General for Justice and Consumers, Unit C.3 Data Protection, 2021.

Tomes, Jonathan P. "20 Plus Years of HIPAA and What Have We Got". In: *Quinnipiac Health L.J.* 22 (2018), pp. 39–106.

Torregiani, Stefano. "Il dato non personale alla luce del Regolamento (UE) 2018/1807: tra anonimizzazione, *ownership* e *Data by Design*". In: *Federalismi.it* 18 (2020), pp. 317- 341.

Tosi, Emilio. "Illecito trattamento dei dati personali, responsabilizzazione, responsabilità oggettiva e danno nel GDPR: funzione deterrente-sanzionatoria e rinascita del danno morale soggettivo". In: *Contratto e Impresa* 3 (2020), pp. 1115–1151.

— "La responsabilità civile per trattamento illecito dei dati personali". In: *Privacy Digitale. Riservatezza e protezione dei dati personali tra GDPR e nuovo Codice Privacy*. Giuffrè Francis Lefebvre, 2019, pp. 619–675. ISBN: 9788828811381.

— *Responsabilità civile per illecito trattamento dei dati personali e danno non patrimoniale*. Giuffrè Francis Lefebvre, 2019. ISBN: 9788828817192.

Tosoni, Luca. "Chapter I General principles (Articles 1–4). Article 4(5). Pseudonymisation". In: *The EU General Data Protection Regulation (GDPR): A Commentary*. Oxford University Press, 2020, pp. 132–137. ISBN: 9780198826491.

Tovino, Stacey A. "The HIPAA Privacy Rule and the EU GDPR: illustrative comparisons". In: *Seton Hall L. Rev.* 47 (2017), pp. 973–994.

Tranberg, Charlotte Bagger. "Proportionality and data protection in the case law of the European Court of Justice". In: *International Data Privacy Law* 1.4 (2011), pp. 239–248.

Tsormpatzoudi, Pagona, Bettina Berendt, and Fanny Coudert. "Privacy by design: from research and policy to practice–the challenge of multi-disciplinarity". In: *Privacy Technologies and Policy, Third Annual Privacy Forum, APF 2015, Luxembourg, Luxembourg, October 7–8, 2015*. Lecture Notes in Computer Science. Springer, 2015, pp. 199–212.

Turkington, Richard C. and Anita L. Allen. *Privacy Law: cases and materials*. West Group, 2002.

Ukrow, Jorg. "Data Protection without Frontiers: On the Relationship between EU GDPR and Amended CoE Convention 108". In: *Eur. Data Prot. L. Rev.* 4 (2018), pp. 239–247.

US Department of Health, Education & Welfare. *Report of the Secretary's Advisory Committee on Automated Personal Data Systems, Records Computers and the Rights of citizens*. United States, DHEW Publication NO. (OS)73–94. 1973.

Valcke, Catherine. *Comparing law: comparative law as reconstruction of collective commitments*. Cambridge University Press, 2018. ISBN: 9781108555852.

Van den Hoven, Jeroen, Pieter E Vermaas, and Ibo Van de Poel. *Handbook of ethics, values, and technological design: Sources, theory, values and application domains*. Springer, 2015. ISBN: 9789400769700.

Van der Sloot, Bart. "Legal Fundamentalism: Is Data Protection Really a Fundamental Right?" In: *Data protection and privacy: (In)visibilities and infrastructures*. Springer, 2017, pp. 3–30. ISBN: 9783319507965.

— *The General Data Protection Regulation in Plain Language*. Amsterdam University Press, 2020. ISBN: 9789048553594.

Van der Velden, Maja. "Design as regulation". In: *International Conference on Culture, Technology, and Communication*. Springer. 2016, pp. 32–54.

Van Dijk, N., A. Tanas, K. Rommetveit, and C. Raab. "Right engineering? The redesign of privacy and personal data protection". In: *International Review of Law, Computers & Technology* 32.2 – 3 (2018), pp. 230–256.

Van Langenhove, P. et al. "eHealth European Interoperability Framework". In: Vision on eHealth EIF, a study prepared for the European Commission by the Deloitte team 1 (2013).

Van Lieshout, Marc. "Privacy and Innovation: From Disruption to Opportunities". In: *Data protection on the move*. Springer, 2016, pp. 195–212. ISBN: 9789401773768.

Van Rossum, H., H. Gardeniers, et al. *Privacy-enhancing technologies: The path to anonymity*. Registratiekamer, Information, and Privacy Commissioner of Ontario, 1995.

Veale, Michael, Reuben Binns, and Jef Ausloos. "When data protection by design and data subject rights clash". In: *International Data Privacy Law* 8.2 (2018), pp. 105–123.

Véliz, Carissa. "Medical Privacy and Big Data". In: *Philosophical Foundations of Medical Law* (2019), p. 306.

Vergottini, Giuseppe de and Carlo Bottari. *La sanità elettronica*. Bononia University Press, 2018. ISBN: 9788869233234.

Verheul, Eric R., Bart Jacobs, Carlo Meijer, Mireille Hildebrandt, and Joeri de Ruiter. "Polymorphic Encryption and Pseudonymisation for Personalised Healthcare." In: *IACR Cryptol. ePrint Arch.* (2016), pp. 1–60.

Villa, Vittorio. *Una teoria pragmaticamente orientata dell'interpretazione giuridica*. G. Giappichelli Editore, 2012.

Virone, Maria Gabriella. *Il Fascicolo Sanitario Elettronico. Sfide e bilanciamenti tra Semantic Web e diritto alla protezione dei dati personali*. Aracne Editrice, 2015. ISBN: 9788854883840.

Voigt, Paul and Axel Von dem Bussche. *The EU General Data Protection Regulation (GDPR). A Practical Guide*. Springer International Publishing, 2017. ISBN: 9783319579580.

Vokinger, Kerstin N., Daniel J. Stekhoven, and Michael Krauthammer. "Lost in Anonymization – A Data Anonymization Reference Classification Merging Legal and Technical Considerations". In: *The Journal of Law, Medicine & Ethics* 48.1 (2020), pp. 142–148.

Wachter, Sandra, Brent Mittelstadt, and Luciano Floridi. "Why a right to explanation of automated decision-making does not exist in the general data protection regulation". In: *International Data Privacy Law* 7.2 (2017), pp. 76–99.

Wachter, Sandra, Brent Mittelstadt, and Chris Russell. "Counterfactual Explanations without Opening the Black Box: Automated Decisions and the GPDR". In: *Harv. JL & Tech.* 31 (2017), p. 841.

Waldman, Ari Ezra. "Data Protection by Design? A Critique of Article 25 of the GDPR". In: *Cornell Int'l L.J.* 53 (2020), pp. 147–167.

— "Privacy's Law of Design". In: *UC Irvine L. Rev.* 9 (2018), pp. 1239–1288.

Walton, Douglas, Giovanni Sartor, and Fabrizio Macagno. "An argumentation framework for contested cases of statutory interpretation". In: *Artificial Intelligence and Law* 24.1 (2016), pp. 51–91.

Warnier, Martijn, Francien Dechesne, and Frances Brazier. "Design for the Value of Privacy". In: *Handbook of ethics, values, and technological design: Sources, theory, values and application domains*. Springer, 2015, pp. 432–445. ISBN: 9789400769700.

Warren, Samuel D. and Louis D. Brandeis. "Right to privacy". In: *Harv. L. Rev.* 4 (1890), pp. 193–220.

Webb, Andrew G. "Mobile Health, Wearable Health Technology and Wireless Implanted Devices". In: *Principles of Biomedical Instrumentation*. Cambridge Texts in Biomedical Engineering. Cambridge University Press, 2018, pp. 235–270. ISBN: 9781316286210.

Webster, Frank. *Theories of the information society*. Routledge, 2006. ISBN: 9780415406338.

Wen, CL. "Telemedicine, eHealth and Remote Care Systems". In: *Global Health Informatics*. Elsevier, 2017, pp. 168–194. ISBN: 9780128045916.

Westin, Alan F. *Privacy and Freedom*. Atheneum, New York, 1967.

White, Tamela J. and Charlotte A. Hoffman. "The Privacy Standards Under the Health Insurance Portability and Accountability Act: A Practical Guide to Promote Order and Avoid Potential Chaos". In: *W. Va. L. Rev.* 106 (2004), pp. 709–780.

Wicks, Elizabeth. "Electronic health records and privacy interests: The English experience". In: *eHealth: Legal, ethical and governance challenges*. Springer, 2013, pp. 57–76. ISBN: 9783642224744.

Wiese Schartum, Dag. "Making privacy by design operative". In: *International Journal of Law and Information Technology* 24.2 (2016), pp. 151–175.

Wilensky, Sara E. and Joel B. Teitelbaum. *Essentials of Health Policy and Law*. Jones & Bartlett Learning, 2019. ISBN: 9781284151619.

Wills, Nathan J. "A tripartite threat to medical records privacy: Technology, HIPAA's privacy rule and the USA Patriot Act". In: *JL & Health* 17 (2002), pp. 271–296.

Winn, Peter. "Katz and the origins of the reasonable expectation of privacy test". In: *McGeorge L. Rev.* 40 (2009), pp. 1–12.

Woodrow, Barfield and Ugo Pagallo. *Law and artificial intelligence.* Edward Elgar Publishing. 2020. ISBN: 9781789905144.

Wong, Janis and Tristan Henderson. “The right to data portability in practice: exploring the implications of the technologically neutral GDPR”. In: *International Data Privacy Law* 9.3 (2019), pp. 173–191.

Wuyts, *Kim*, Riccardo Scandariato, and Wouter Joosen. “Empirical evaluation of a privacy- focused threat modeling methodology”. In: *Journal of Systems and Software* 96 (2014), pp. 122–138.

— “LIND(D)UN *privacy* threat tree catalog”. In: *CW Reports 675* (2014).

Wuyts, Kim, Griet Verhenneman, Riccardo Scandariato, Wouter Joosen, and Jos Dumortier. “What electronic health records don’t know just yet. A privacy analysis for patient communities and health records interaction”. In: *Health and Technology* 2.3 (2012), pp. 159–183.

Yasnoff, William A. “Privacy, Confidentiality, and Security of Public Health Information”. In: *Public Health Informatics and Information Systems*. Springer, 2014, pp. 155–172. ISBN: 9780387227450.

Yordanov, Atanas. “Nature and Ideal Steps of the Data Protection Impact Assessment under the General Data Protection Regulation”. In: *Eur. Data Prot. L. Rev.* 3 (2017), pp. 486- 495.

Zanfir-Fortuna, Gabriela. “Chapter III Rights of the Data Subject (Articles 12–23). Article 13. Information to be provided where personal data are collected from the data subject”. In: *The EU General Data Protection Regulation (GDPR): A Commentary*. Oxford University Press, 2020, pp. 413–433. ISBN: 9780198826491.

— “Chapter III Rights of the Data Subject (Articles 12–23). Article 14. Information to be provided where personal data have not been obtained from the data subject”. In: *The EU General Data Protection Regulation (GDPR): A Commentary*. Oxford University Press, 2020, pp. 434–448. ISBN: 9780198826491.

— “Chapter III Rights of the Data Subject (Articles 12–23). Article 15. Right of access by the data subject”. In: *The EU General Data Protection Regulation (GDPR): A Commentary*. Oxford University Press, 2020, pp. 449–468. ISBN: 9780198826491.

— “Chapter III Rights of the Data Subject (Articles 12–23). Article 21. Right to object and automated individual decision-making”. In: *The EU General Data Protection Regulation (GDPR): A Commentary*. Oxford University Press, 2020, pp. 508–521. ISBN: 9780198826491.

— “Chapter VIII Remedies, Liability and Penalties (Articles 77–84). Article 82. Right to compensation and liability”. In: *The EU General Data Protection Regulation (GDPR): A Commentary*. Oxford University Press, 2020, pp. 1160–1179. ISBN: 9780198826491.

Zeno Zencovich, Vincenzo. “Comparing comparative law”. In: *Comparare. Una riflessione tra le discipline*. Mimesis Edizioni, 2020, pp. 227–240. ISBN: 9788857567310.

Zeno Zencovich, Vincenzo and Giorgio Resta. *Il diritto all’oblio su Internet dopo la sentenza Google Spain*. Roma TrEpress, 2015. ISBN: 9788897524274.

Zuboff, Shoshana. *The age of surveillance capitalism: The fight for a human future at the new frontier of power*. Profile Books, 2019. ISBN: 9781610395694.

Zweigert, Konrad and Hein Kötz. *Introduction to comparative law*. Vol. 3. Clarendon Press Oxford, 1998.
— *Introduzione al diritto comparato*. Vol. 1. Giuffrè Editore, 2011. ISBN: 9788814155857.

# Table of Legislation and Cases

*EU legislation*

Directive 95/46/EC of the European Parliament and of the Council of 24 October 1995 on the protection of individuals with regard to the processing of personal data and on the free movement of such data. OJ L281, 23.11.1995.

Directive 2000/31/EC of the European Parliament and of the Council of 8 June 2000 on certain legal aspects of information society services, in particular electronic commerce, in the Internal Market ('Directive on electronic commerce'). OJ L178, 17.7.2000.

Directive 2002/58/EC of the European Parliament and of the Council of 12 July 2002 concerning the processing of personal data and the protection of privacy in the electronic communications sector (Directive on privacy and electronic communications), OJ L201, 31.7.2002.

Regulation (EC) No 1338/2008 of the European Parliament and of the Council of 16 December 2008 on Community statistics on public health and health and safety at work. OJ L354, 31.12.2008.

Directive 2011/24/EU of the European Parliament and of the Council of 9 March 2011 on the application of patients' rights in cross-border healthcare. OJ L88, 4.4.2011.

Proposal for a Regulation of the European Parliament and of the Council on the protection of individuals with regard to the processing of personal data and on the free movement of such data (General Data Protection Regulation). COM/2012/011 final – 2012/0011 (COD).

Charter of Fundamental Rights of the European Union. OJ C.326, 26.10.2012.

Regulation (EU) No 1024/2012 of the European Parliament and of the Council of 25 October 2012 on administrative cooperation through the Internal Market Information System and repealing Commission Decision 2008/49/EC ('the IMI Regulation') Text with EEA relevance. OJ L316, 14.11.2012.

Regulation (EU) No 1025/2012 of the European Parliament and of the Council of 25 October 2012 on European standardisation, amending Council Directives 89/686/EEC and 93/15/EEC and Directives 94/9/EC, 94/25/EC, 95/16/EC, 97/23/EC, 98/34/EC, 2004/22/EC, 2007/23/EC, 2009/23/EC and 2009/105/EC of the European Parliament and of the Council and repealing Council Decision 87/95/EEC and Decision No 1673/2006/EC of the European Parliament and of the Council, OJ L316, 14.11.2012.

Regulation (EU) No 524/2013 of the European Parliament and of the Council of 21 May 2013 on online dispute resolution for consumer disputes and amending Regulation (EC) No 2006/2004 and Directive 2009/22/EC (Regulation on consumer ODR). OJ L165, 18.6.2013.

Decision No 1082/2013/EU of the European Parliament and of the Council of 22 October 2013 on serious cross-border threats to health and repealing Decision No 2119/98/EC. OJ L293, 5.11.2013.

Regulation (EU) No 536/2014 of the European Parliament and of the Council of 16 April 2014 on clinical trials on medicinal products for human use, and repealing Directive 2001/20/EC. OJ L158, 27.5.2014.

Regulation (EU) No 910/2014 of the European Parliament and of the Council of 23 July 2014 on electronic identification and trust services for electronic transactions in the internal market and repealing Directive 1999/93/EC. OJ L257, 28.8.2014.

Commission Decision (EU) 2015/1302 of 28 July 2015 on the identification of 'Integrating the Healthcare Enterprise' profiles for referencing in public procurement. OJ L199, 29.7.2015.

Regulation (EU) 2016/679 of the European Parliament and of the Council of 27 April 2016 on the protection of natural persons with regard to the processing of personal data and on the free movement of such data, and repealing Directive 95/46/EC (General Data Protection Regulation). OJ L119, 4.5.2016.

Directive (EU) 2016/680 of the European Parliament and of the Council of 27 April 2016 on the protection of natural persons with regard to the processing of personal data by competent authorities for the purposes of the prevention, investigation, detection or prosecution of criminal offences or the execution of criminal penalties, and on the free movement of such data, and repealing Council Framework Decision 2008/977/JHA, OJ L119, 4.5.2016.

Directive (EU) 2016/1148 of the European Parliament and of the Council of 6 July 2016 concerning measures for a high common level of security of network and information systems across the Union. OJ L194, 19.7.2016.

Regulation (EU) 2017/745 of the European Parliament and of the Council of 5 April 2017 on medical devices, amending Directive 2001/83/EC, Regulation (EC) No 178/2002 and Regulation (EC) No 1223/2009 and repealing Council Directives 90/385/EEC and 93/42/EEC. OJ L117, 5.5.2017.

Regulation (EU) 2017/746 of the European Parliament and of the Council of 5 April 2017 on *in vitro* diagnostic medical devices and repealing Directive 98/79/EC and Commission Decision 2010/227/EU. OJ L117, 5.5.2017.

Council Regulation (EU) 2017/1939 of 12 October 2017 implementing enhanced cooperation on the establishment of the European Public Prosecutor's Office ('the EPPO'). OJ L283, 31.10.2017.

Proposal for a Regulation of the European Parliament and of the Council concerning the respect for private life and the protection of personal data in electronic communications and repealing Directive 2002/58/EC (Regulation on Privacy and Electronic Communications), COM/2017/010 final – 2017/03 (COD).

Regulation (EU) 2018/1725 of the European Parliament and of the Council of 23 October 2018 on the protection of natural persons with regard to the processing of personal data by the Union institutions, bodies, offices and agencies and on the free movement of such data, and repealing Regulation (EC) No 45/2001 and Decision No 1247/2002/EC. PE/31/2018/REV/1. OJ L295, 21.11.2018.

Regulation (EU) 2018/1240 of the European Parliament and of the Council of 12 September 2018 establishing a European Travel Information and Authorisation System (ETIAS) and amending Regulations (EU) No 1077/2011, (EU) No 515/2014, (EU) 2016/399, (EU) 2016/1624 and (EU) 2017/2226. PE/21/2018/REV/1, OJ L236, 19.9.2018.

Council Decision (EU) 2019/682 of 9 April 2019 authorising Member States to ratify, in the interest of the European Union, the Protocol amending the Council of Europe Convention for the Protection of Individuals with regard to Automatic Processing of Personal Data. OJ L115, 2.5.2019.

Regulation (EU) 2019/881 of the European Parliament and of the Council of 17 April 2019 on ENISA (the European Union Agency for Cybersecurity) and on information and communications technology cybersecurity certification and repealing Regulation (EU) No 526/2013 (Cybersecurity Act) PE/86/2018/REV/1. OJ L151, 7.6.2019.

Regulation (EU) 2020/561 of the European Parliament and of the Council of 23 April 2020 amending Regulation (EU) 2017/745 on medical devices, as regards the dates of application of certain of its provisions. OJ L130, 24.4.2020.

Commission Implementing Decision (EU) 2020/1023 of 15 July 2020 amending Implementing Decision (EU) 2019/1765 as regards the cross-border exchange of data between national contact tracing and warning mobile applications with regard to combatting the COVID-19 pandemic. C/2020/4934. OJ L227I, 16.7.2020.

*Case law of the Court of Justice of the European Union*

Case C-101/01 *Criminal proceedings v. Bodil Lindqvist* [2003].

C-131/12 *Google Spain SL and Google Inc. v. Agencia Espanõla de Protección de Datos and Mario Costeja González* [2014].

Joined Cases C-293/12 and C-594/12. *Digital Rights Ireland Ltd v. Minister for Communications, Marine and Natural Resources and Others and Kärntner Landesregierung and Others* [2014].

C-201/14 *Smaranda Bara and Others v. Casa Na ̦tionala ̆ de Asigura ̆ri de Sa ̆na ̆tate and Others* [2015].

C-230/14 *Weltimmo s.r.o. v Nemzeti Adatvéédelmi és Információszabadság Hatóság* [2015].

C-13/16 *Valsts policijas Rīgas regiona pārvaldes Kārtības policijas pārvalde contro Rīgas pašvaldības SIA "Rīgas satiksme"* [2017].

Case C-190/16 *Werner Fries v. Lufthansa CityLine GmbH* [2017].

Case C-121/17 *Teva UK Ltd. and Others v. Gilead Sciences Inc.* [2018].

C-311/18 *Data Protection Commissioner v. Facebook Ireland Limited and Maximillian Schrems* [2020].

*National legislation*

*Canada*

Personal Information Protection and Electronic Documents Act. SC 2000, c 5 "PIPEDA".

*EU Member States*

France: Code de la santé publique, version consolidée au 1 septembre 2020; Décret n° 2016–914 du 4 Juillet 2016.

Italy: Decreto-legge 18 ottobre 2012, n. 179 e legge di conversione 17 dicembre 2012, n. 221 recante "Ulteriori misure urgenti per la crescita del Paese". G.U. Serie Generale n. 294 del 18–12–2012 – Suppl. Ordinario n. 208.

D.Lgs. 18 maggio 2018, n. 51 Attuazione della direttiva (UE) 2016/680 del Parlamento europeo e del Consiglio, del 27 aprile 2016, relativa alla protezione delle persone fisiche con riguardo al trattamento dei dati personali da parte delle autorità competenti a fini di prevenzione, indagine, accertamento e perseguimento di reati o esecuzione di sanzioni penali, nonché alla libera circolazione di tali dati e che abroga la decisione quadro 2008/977/GAI del Consiglio. 18G00080. GU Serie Generale n. 119 del 24–05–2018.

Luxembourg: Loi du 24 juillet 2014 "relative aux droits et obligations du patient, portant création d'un service national d'information et de médiation dans le domaine de la santé".

*US*

Privacy Act of 1974, 88 Stat. 1896, as amended 5 U.S.C. § 552a. Americans with Disabilities Act of 1990 or ADA 42 U.S.C. § 12101.

Health Insurance Portability and Accountability Act of 1996 (HIPAA), 110 Stat. 1936 (1996); 45 USC § 1320d-2(b).

45 Code of Federal Regulations (C.F.R.), parts § 160 through § 164 and § 170 as amended in 2020.

Children's Online Privacy Act of 1998, 15 U.S.C. 6501–6505. Federal Trade Commission Act (FTC Act), 15 USC. § 45.

Genetic Information Nondiscrimination Act of 2008, Public Law 110–233, 122 STAT. 881.

Health Information Technology (HITECH) Provisions of American Recovery and Reinvestment Act of 2009, Title XIII, Subtitle D (Pub. L. 111–5, 123 Stat. 115, codified in relevant part at 42 U.S.C. §§ 17937 and 17954).

Commercial Privacy Bill of Rights Act of 2011, S. 799, 112th Congress (2011).

California Consumer Privacy Act of 2018, California Civil Code Civ. Division 3, sections 1798.100.

*US Case law*

*Olmstead v. United States* 277 U.S. 438 (1928).

*Barber v. Time, Inc.*, 159 S.W.2d 291 (Mo. 1942)

*Hamberger v. Eastman* 206 A. 2d 239 (1964)

*Grisworls v. Connecticut* 381 U.S. 479 (1965).

*Katz v. United States* 389 u.S. 347 (1967).

*Whalen v. Roe* 429 U.S. 589 (1977).

*Doe v. Roe* 93 Misc. 2d 201 (1977)

*Union Pacific Railway Co. v. Botsford*, 141 U.S. 250 (1891)

*Carson v. Here's Johnny Portable Toilets, Inc.*, 698 F.2d 831 (6th Cir. 1983)

*Wood v. Hustler Magazine, Inc.*, 736 F.2d 1084 (1984)

*Peninsula Counseling Center v. Rahm* 105 Wn.2d 929 (1986)

*California v. Greenwood* 486 U.S. 35 (1988).

*Moore v. Regents of the University of California* 793 P.2d 479 (Cal. 1990).

*Estate of Behringer v. Medical Center at Princeton* 249 N.J. Super. 597 (1991)

*Planned Parenthood v. Casey*, 505 U.S. 833 (1992)

*Doe v. Southeastern Pennsylvania Transp. Authority* 886 F. Supp. 1186 (E.D. Pa. 1994)

*Doe v. Mills*, 536 N.W.2d 824 (Mic. App. 1995). *Susan S. v. Israels*, 55 Cal.App.4th 1290 (1997)

*Creely v. Genesis Health Ventures, Inc.*, 2004 U.S. Dist. LEXIS 25489 (ED Pa Dec. 17, 2004).

*United States Ex Rel. Pogue v. Diabetes Treatment Ctrs. of Am.*, 2004 U.S. Dist. LEXIS 21830 (DDC May 17, 2004).

*Rigaud v. Garofalo*, 2005 U.S. Dist. LEXIS 7791 (ED Pa May 2, 2005).

*Arons v. Jutkowitz*, 9 N.Y.3d 393, 850 N.Y.S. 2d 345, 880 N.E.2d 831, 2007 N.Y. LEXIS 3355 (NY Nov. 27, 2007).

*Holman v. Rasak*, 486 Mich. 429, 785 N.W.2d 98, 2010 Mich. LEXIS 1446 (Mich July 13, 2010).

*Bereston v. Uhs of Del.*, Inc., 2018 D.C. App. LEXIS 83 (DC Mar. 8, 2018).

*Montgomery v. Cuomo*, 291 F. Supp. 3d 303, 317 n.42 (W.D.N.Y. 2018)

*Martin v. Rolling Hills Hosp., Llc*, 2020 Tenn. LEXIS 154 (Tenn Apr. 29, 2020).

*International Conventions*

Convention for the Protection of Human Rights and Fundamental Freedoms, 1950.

OECD, Guidelines on the Protection of Privacy and Transborder Flows of Personal Data, in the form of a Recommendation by the Council of the OECD, 1980.

Convention for the protection of Human Rights and Dignity of the Human Being with regard to the Application of Biology and Medicine (ETS No.164). Oviedo, 04.04.1997.

Council of Europe Recommendation No. R(97) 5 on the protection of medical data of 13 February 1997.

OECD, Guidelines on the Protection of Privacy and Transborder Flows of Personal Data, the OECD Privacy Framework, 2013.

Recommendation CM/Rec (2016) 8 of the Committee of Ministers to the member States on the processing of personal health-related data for insurance purposes, including data resulting from genetic tests, of 26 October 2016.

Council of Europe Convention for the Protection of Individuals with Regard to Automatic Processing of Personal Data ("Convention 108"), as amended in 2018.

Recommendation CM/Rec (2019) 2 of the Committee of Ministers to member States on the protection of health-related data of 27 March 2019.

*Case law of the European Court of Human Rights*

*I v. Finland* (Application no. 20511/03, 2008).